Here is Release #2 (March 1984)

to

Employee and Union Member Guide to Labor Law

By The National Lawyers Guild

Enclosed is Release #2 for your copy of **Employee and Union Member Guide to Labor Law.** This release contains extensive case annotations and text revisions to reflect the latest legislative and case law developments and ensures your volume of being completely up to date.

Noted below are several items of particular interest in this release:

§ 2.02[2][c]. Dual Motive Discharges. The Supreme Court has ruled on the test ennunciated in the **Wright Line** decision allocating the burden of proof in a dual motive discharge. This section has been rewritten to reflect the even more liberal interpretation of the NLRA.

§ 3.10. Secondary Boycotts. This section has been substantially revised in light of several recent Supreme Court and Board decisions affecting in particular common situs picketing, application of the GE related-work test, access to reserve gates, handbilling and union protection under the publicity proviso.

§ 3.11. Lockouts. This new section has been added to address the increased use of lockouts. Included is an analysis of the general types of lockouts the NLRB will hold to be illegal, burdens of proof, supportive lockouts in multi-employer contracts, integrity of a no-strike clause and replacement of locked out employees.

Clark Boardman Company, Ltd.
435 Hudson Street
New York, New York 10014

(over)

FILING INSTRUCTIONS

Special Note: Before filing Release #2, make sure your volume is up to date. If the title page of your volume contains the code "(Release #1, 4/83)," your volume is up to date. Follow instructions below. If you do not see this code, contact the publisher for updating assistance before filing this release.

Remove and Discard Old Pages Numbered:	*Insert New Pages Numbered:*
Title page to xlii	Title page to xl
1-43 and 1-44	1-43 and 1-44
2-13 to 2-16.2	2-13 to 2-16.2
2-25 to 2-40	2-25 to 2-40.1
2-59 to 2-66	2-59 to 2-66
3-4.1	3-4.1
3-101 to 3-106	3-101 to 3-106.3
3-109 and 3-110	3-109 to 3-110.1
3-113 to 3-117	3-113 to 3-125
6-3 and 6-4	6-3 and 6-4
6-9 to 6-16	6-9 to 6-16
6-18.1 to 6-22	6-18.1 to 6-22.1
6-25 to 6-28.2	6-25 to 6-28.2
6-31 to 6-38	6-31 to 6-38.2
6-43 and 6-44	6-43 to 6-44.1
6-49 to 6-52	6-49 to 6-52.1
8-7 to 8-10	8-7 to 8-10.1
8-17 to 8-22	8-17 to 8-22.1
8-25 to 8-32	8-25 to 8-32.1
8-35 and 8-36	8-35 and 8-36
8-39 to 8-48	8-39 to 8-48.1
8-57 to 8-70	8-57 to 8-70.1
8-77 to 8-82	8-77 to 8-82.1
8-93 to 8-98	8-93 to 8-98
10-1 to 10-4	10-1 to 10-4.1
10-13 to 10-28	10-13 to 10-28.1
10-31 to 10-66	10-31 to 10-65

Employee and Union Member Guide to Labor Law

A Manual for Attorneys Representing the Labor Movement

Employee and Union Member Guide to Labor Law

A Manual for Attorneys Representing the Labor Movement

(Release #2, 3/84)

Employee and Union Member Guide to Labor Law

A Manual for Attorneys Representing the Labor Movement

by the National Labor Committee
of the National Lawyers Guild

Robert H. Gibbs and Dan Siegel
Editors

Clark Boardman Company, Ltd.
New York, New York
1984

(Release #2, 3/84)

Library of Congress Cataloging in Publication Data

Main entry under title:

Employee and union member guide to labor law.

Includes index.
1. Labor laws and legislation—United States. 2.
Trade-unions—United States. I. National Lawyers Guild.
KF3369.E46 344.73'01 81-10090
ISBN 0-87632-113-9 347.3041 AACR2

Preface

Few areas of the law are both as complex and as volatile as labor law. Constructed of a bewildering maze of often conflicting statutes, common-law doctrines, contract-established rules, and administrative agency edicts, labor law can be extraordinarily frustrating for attorneys who seek symmetry and clearly discernible patterns in the law. Even within a narrow area, the applicable law can vary tremendously, depending on whether one is litigating before the National Labor Relations Board (NLRB) or seeking enforcement of an NLRB decision in one of the Circuit Courts of Appeal. In short, there is no simple way to learn the law in this area or to avoid the necessity of constantly keeping abreast of developments in the field to update one's knowledge.

This is not surprising, since few areas of the law encompass issues of such central importance to the society as a whole. The conflict between labor and management is at the heart of our economic system, which, in turn, is at the heart of the entire social structure. For that reason, labor law can be fairly said to be among the most political of legal areas. Laws and court decisions in this area historically have reflected the shifting balance of forces in the economic arena.

The original National Labor Relations Act, the Wagner Act, was passed in 1935—a time when the workers' movement was organizing and developing its influence as never before. As the society sought to contain the organizing upsurge within acceptable legal channels, the Act that was passed was relatively pro-labor: It legalized union organization and gave union organizers certain rights; it contained provisions outlawing certain employer "unfair labor practices"; and it contained no similar sanctions against union activity.

In 1947, however, with the union movement on the defensive

and the Cold War and McCarthy eras on the horizon, the Taft-Hartley Act was passed, drastically revising the National Labor Relations Act. Provisions of the Taft-Hartley Act defined certain conduct by unions as unlawful for the first time, and its Section 14(b), the anti-union "right to work" provision, allowed states to enact legislation outlawing union contracts that require employees to join the union within a designated time period.

Similarly, the powerful civil rights movement in the fifties and sixties was able to win passage of the Civil Rights Act of 1964, with its Title VII prohibitions against hiring and job discrimination based on race, religion, national origin, or sex. However, as the activity of the civil rights movement diminished in the seventies, a period of government retrenchment and retreat began. This has been accompanied by court decisions chipping away at the law's teeth, raising ever more difficult standards of proof for the antidiscrimination advocate.

It is the political essence of labor law, then, that explains its vast, sprawling jumble of rules. And it is this character that helps to explain why it is such an important, exciting, challenging field to many of the attorneys who practice it.

We would not suggest here that labor law has ever been the solid ally of the worker. Far from it. At best it has established procedures and channels through which the labor movement can obtain redress as part of its overall political battle. Unfortunately, even these procedures often fail to provide meaningful remedies, and employers often find it economically profitable to violate the law. At its worst, labor law has shackled the workers' struggle, placing financially and organizationally draining obstacles in the way of organizing and legitimizing the intervention of the courts and government on the management side of the conflict.

It has been suggested that the United States is virtually unique among industralized nations in the extent to which the labor struggle is channeled into legal procedures. It is thus a fact of life that almost any serious effort of workers directed against their employers, be they unionized or not, will require them to deal with the legal system. Often, workers and their unions find themselves facing batteries of corporate lawyers, who have virtually unlimited resources with which to pursue the anti-union struggle.

This problem has been exacerbated in recent years by the explosive growth of professional "union-busting" concerns. Often integrated into large corporate law firms, this multimillion-dollar industry has developed through its ability to help employers stay at the very edge of the law in their conflicts with their workers. These concerns aim to use every possible legal and quasi-legal tactic to frustrate organizing, drain precious resources into interminable legal battles, and make a mockery of the "legal rights" of workers.

Such a situation places unions at a great disadvantage. With resources far more limited than those of employers, unions must constantly assess how much they can allocate to the legal struggle, aware that every penny they divert cannot be used for the important work of organizing and serving their members.

The problem is even worse for individual or unorganized workers. Their concerns might be varied: fighting the employer around an individual discharge or grievance, organizing in opposition to discrimination or unsafe conditions on the job, or fighting for reform within their union. In any case, their resources are the most limited, and the legal battle can be the most draining. They often seek assistance from general practitioners or legal services attorneys, some of whom might be inexperienced in the field or limited in the resources they can devote to the case.

In such a situation, we know that *Guide to Labor Law* cannot be a panacea. It would be impossible totally to encompass the field of labor law in one volume. Nevertheless, we do hope to make a contribution to the legal component of the labor struggle.

This volume was written by dozens of members and friends of the National Lawyers Guild whom we consider to have special expertise in their field. We have aimed at providing advice that gives the important parameters of the law in a practical context. The topics covered were chosen for both the frequency with which they arise and the context in which they arise. Because we recognize that the law is, at best, a tool for the labor movement to use in its development, we have chosen areas that we think are related to that development.

It is our hope that this volume can be useful to the experienced and inexperienced practitioner alike. For the inexperienced practitioner, our aim is to provide a practical volume that will help start serious research, answer basic questions, and help avoid some common pitfalls. For the more experienced attorney, we hope to provide a useful desk reference for quick answers to important questions.

While our goals may be lofty, we recognize that this first edition is only a start at producing the best manual possible. We will be updating, revising, and expanding it on a regular basis. For this reason, we welcome suggestions on how it can be improved in order better to fulfill its goals. We would be delighted to receive suggestions for new topics to include, or better ways to present those we have included. The editors can be reached through the National Labor Committee, NLG, 853 Broadway, 17th Floor, New York, N.Y. 10003.

Guide to Labor Law is a publication of the National Labor Committee. Nationwide, there are more than twenty local labor committees affiliated with the National Lawyers Guild and hundreds of affiliated attorneys, legal workers, and law students.

Acknowledgments

This book was in the planning stages for approximately six years. During that time, many of the chapters have been redrafted, and the names of some authors have been forgotten. We apologize to them for our bad memories and thank both them and those whose names follow for their contributions to what we trust will be a useful work for rank-and-file workers and their legal assistants.

Those initially involved in the organization of the manual included Neil Herring, Martin Eichner, Ken Cloke, and Warren Adler, all from California. Subsequently Dan Siegel and Robert Gibbs took over the overall responsibility for bringing the manual to completion, which included finishing a number of chapters and making final editorial decisions about chapters that had been revised.

Chapter 1, "Organizing the Unorganized," was written by members of the District of Columbia chapter and the Chicago chapter labor committees, including Carolyn Cairns, now of Seattle, Robert Hodge, Roberta Brown, and Jim Fennerty. These drafts were reviewed and revised by Robert Gibbs and Chris Mrak of Seattle and John McTernan of Los Angeles. The 1983 updates were prepared by Lance Compa and Robert Gibbs. The materials on fair representation were prepared by Burt Boltuch of Oakland with help from Art Read of New Jersey.

Chapter 2, "Opposing Discriminatory Discharges," was written by Jonathan Siegel of the National Labor Law Center. Neil Herring of Los Angeles and Amy Gladstein of New York worked on an earlier draft. The 1983 updates were prepared by Amy Gladstein, Robert Gibbs, and Scott Dutton. The 1984 release was prepared by Amy Gladstein.

Chapter 3, "Protecting the Right to Strike," was written principally by Mike Healey of Pittsburgh with the assistance of Grant Crandall of West Virginia and Alan Vomacka of Houston on earlier drafts and Dan Siegel of Oakland on the final editing. The 1983 updates were prepared by Robert Gibbs with the help of Grant Crandall of West Virginia. Laura Rassett and Chris Mrak of Seattle wrote the materials on secondary boycotts. John McTernan of Los Angeles prepared the 1983 materials on political strikes. Chris Mrak and Laura Rassett prepared the 1984 release on secondary activity and lockouts.

Chapter 4, "Stopping Runaway Shops," was originally prepared by Matthew Robbins and Leonard Page of Detroit. Subsequent revisions were by Jay Roth of Los Angeles and Barbara Zack Quindel of Milwaukee with the assistance of Mary Radcliffe and Robert Gibbs of Seattle. The 1983 updates were prepared by Marianne Goldstein-Robbins, Barbara Zack-Quindell, Art Heitzer, Jeff Myers, and John Williamson, Jr., all of Milwaukee.

Chapter 5, "Fighting for a Safe and Healthy Workplace," was initially prepared by Emily Novick and others in the Boston chapter. By the time of publication, substantial revisions were needed, and a major rewrite was done by Peter Van Schaick of New York. Carol Oppenheimer of Washington, D.C., and Emily Speiler of West Virginia reviewed the final draft. The 1983 update was prepared by San Francisco attorneys Nina Gagnon Fendel, Abby Ginzberg, and Marci Seville. Felix Munoz Velarde from the Employment Law Center and Judy Kurtz of Equal Rights Advocates, assisted in the update of Section 5.07.

Chapter 6, "Obtaining Benefits for the Disabled Worker," was initially prepared by Boston chapter members. The final draft of the section on Social Security disability was prepared by Sandra Horwich of Richmond, California, and was reviewed by James A. Douglas and Croil Anderson of Seattle. The 1984 release was prepared by James A. Douglas of Seattle, with the assistance of Joyce Schwensen. The workers' compensation section was reviewed by Gordon Gaines of San Francisco. Overall editing for this chapter was done by Robert Gibbs. The 1983 revisions dealing with Social Security disability were prepared by Mark Bronstein. Victoria Heldman prepared the 1983 update to the third party section. The 1983 updates on the subject of welfare were prepared by Mark Coven and Barbara Sard. Emily Novick did the 1983 updates to the workers' compensation section and provided overall coordination to the updates for 1983 for this chapter.

Chapter 7, "Rank and File Rights in the Shop," was prepared by Chicago chapter members Robert Hodge, Carolyn Cairns, Jim Fennerty, and Roberta Brown, with review by John McTernan. Final review of this chapter was by Robert Gibbs. The 1983 updates were prepared by Robert Gibbs.

Chapter 8, "Rights of Union Members within Their Unions," was written by Golden Gate law students Roy Otis and Suzanne Sherbell and Dan Siegel from Oakland with the help of authors of earlier drafts. The 1983 and 1984 revisions of this chapter were done by Paul Levy of Public Citizen Litigation in Washington, D.C., now of New York City.

Chapter 9, "Internal Union Elections," was written by Dan Siegel and Golden Gate student Larry Norton, with earlier drafts prepared by Robert Gibbs, Bruce Bentley of Seattle, and Diane Dickstein of Oakland. The 1983 update was prepared by Robert Gibbs.

Chapter 10, "Protecting the Right to a Pension," was written by Jim Klimaski, Bill Anspach, and Katharyn Marks of Washington, D.C., and reviewed by Robert Gibbs. The 1984 release was prepared by Katharyn Marks, James Klimaski and Janet Bartelmay of Washington, D.C.

Chapter 11, "The Duty to Bargain Collectively," was prepared by Nola Hitchcock-Cross of Milwaukee and Robert Gibbs. Chris Linder assisted with this chapter.

Final editing was done by Lyn Grossman, Associate Editor, and Rodney Eubanks, Group Managing Editor, of Clark Boardman Company, Ltd., publisher.

Robert H. Gibbs
Dan Siegel

Table of Chapters

Table of Contents

CHAPTER 2

Opposing Discriminatory Discharges 2-1

CHAPTER 6
Obtaining Benefits for the Disabled Worker 6-1

CHAPTER 8

CHAPTER 9

Internal Union Elections 9-1

CHAPTER 10
Protecting the Right to a Pension

CHAPTER 1

Organizing the Unorganized

§ 1.01. The Role of the Lawyer in Organizing

This chapter makes the following assumptions about the proper method of union organizing and how a lawyer relates to it. First, workers should organize with national unions in their industry, not in independent or unrelated unions that isolate them from other workers in their industry or from the trade union movement as a whole. Second, the major guidance for the organizing effort must come from union organizers and union members who are assisting the unorganized workers. Third, and most important, the goal of organizing is to build a functioning union that will be able not only to win an election but to negotiate and administer a contract or conduct a successful strike.

Building the organization is the primary task. It can only be accomplished by the workers themselves, through their own understanding, communication, and activity. The modicum of class consciousness and solidarity needed for effective unionism is based on relations among the workers and their own faith in one another. An exaggerated reliance on the union organizer, or on the union as a strong outside force, or on a lawyer or group of lawyers at their disposal, will end in a lost election, failure to get a contract, or an empty shell of a union.

The idea that *the workers organize themselves* is central to the proper conduct of an organizing campaign. The job of an organizer, or a lawyer involved in organizing, is to assist the process. There is a terrible tendency for unorganized workers (and many organized workers, unfortunately) to ask "What's the legality?" or "Why don't we go to the Labor Board?" on issues that are really organizational. For organizers it is hard enough, but upon lawyers it is even more incumbent (because their response will carry more weight), to fight this trend and insist that the workers address the problem themselves. Advancing under their own power, even if progress is slow, builds a sounder union in the long run. Before making a move, therefore, a lawyer involved in organizing must ask, Will this action help the workers organize themselves, or will it take the struggle out of their hands?

The lawyer should resist anything more than a background role in the actual organizing process. Direct involvement is for union organizers and already-organized union members who are helping the unorganized workers. These are the people who will continue to have a relationship with them through the organizing, contract negotiations, and strikes in the future. It is from the organizers and other workers that new union members learn the principles and policies of the union and develop a long-term understanding of unionism.

The objection will be made that some union organizers, or a particular union's principles and policies, are too conservative to be effective. Be that as it may, it is not the job of a lawyer to inject his or her version of "correct" politics into an organizing effort. Remedying internal union problems is for the membership to accomplish. And organizing unorganized workers is such a fragile process, so vulnerable to frustration by employer resistance, that political disruption virtually guarantees that no union will be organized and those workers will never have the chance to affect their union's policies. In summary, the lawyer involved in organizing, as either a union lawyer or an independent lawyer aiding a campaign, must remember that organizing is the workers' job and guiding the organizing is the organizer's job. If a lawyer is directly involved, there is a fundamental flaw in the organizing process, which must be corrected.

A final assumption of this chapter is that the lawyer has access to the standard reporting services and other sources for help in handling cases and writing briefs.[1] This chapter will touch on the

---

[1] These sources include the BNA and CCH reporting services; the annual reports of the NLRB; Scholossberg & Sherman, Organizing and the Law; Kenneth McGuiness, How to Take a Case before the NLRB (BNA, 1976); Feerick, Baer, & Arfa, NLRB Representation Elections—Law, Practice and

basics, but will concentrate on broader questions of organizing strategy and tactics, with key cases footnoted but not elaborated.

§ 1.02. Source of Labor Law

[1] Historical Development

Union organization has moved from a criminal conspiracy in the 19th century to a legally accepted form of association today. In the conventional view, the National Labor Relations Act (NLRA), or the Wagner Act, of 1935 was labor's "Magna Carta," putting the stamp of government approval on union organization and collective bargaining. Looked at critically, however, the Wagner Act is better described as a defensive measure passed by a Congress and upheld by a Supreme Court fearful of growing industrial disorder and a potentially uncontrolled working class or, even worse from their point of view, a working class led by communists and socialists.

Passage of the NLRA followed a great wave of strikes in 1933 and 1934, among them the San Francisco and Minneapolis general strikes. The Supreme Court decisions upholding the Act in *Jones & Laughlin*[2] did not come until 1937, *after* more mass organizing and strikes, including the formation of the CIO and the Akron rubber and Flint auto sit-downs. It was clearly the desire of Congress and the courts to contain this outburst of worker militance and channel it into predictable paths. However, one should not jump to the conclusion that the law and the role of government are negative. Much of the impetus for the pre-NLRA orga-

---

Procedure (Harcourt Brace Jovanovich, 1979-80); Developing Labor Law (a BNA publication); the monthly Labor Law Journal (a CCH publication); and the following publications of the Board itself (most are available from the Superintendent of Documents, Gov't Printing Office, Washington, D.C., and some are in the reporters): NLRB Weekly Rep.; NLRB Rules and Regs. and Statements of Procedure; NLRB Casehandling Manual; An Outline of Law and Procedure in Representation Cases; Guide for Hearing Officers in Representation Cases; Division of Trial Examiners Public Manual; Classified Index of NLRB Decisions and Related Court Decisions; and Classified Index of Decisions of the Regional Directors of the NLRB in Representation Proceedings.

[2] NLRB v. Jones & Laughlin Steel Corp., 301 U.S. 1 (1937).

nizing came from Section 7 of the National Industrial Recovery Act of 1932, which protected the right to organize, even though that Act was found unconstitutional in *Schechter.*[3] (The NLRA was passed six weeks later.) The workers' perception of Roosevelt and the Democrats as sympathetic to organizing should not be underestimated either. Furthermore, the post-*Jones & Laughlin* organizing breakthroughs in less concentrated industries were heavily influenced by the NLRA and the relatively pro-labor National Labor Relations Board (NLRB). And the NLRA prohibition of open anti-union campaigning by employers (now allowed under the Taft-Hartley Act revisions) assisted organizing efforts.

Organizing law today contains the same contradictory elements of restraint and encouragement, but the balance has swung to the employers' advantage. It began with the replacement of the pro-labor NLRB chairman Edwin S. Smith with a "neutral" chairman by Roosevelt under employer pressure in 1941. Later came court decisions on free speech, such legislation as Taft-Hartley and Landrum-Griffin, and such modern employer tactics as the J.P. Stevens resistance (hardly limited to that company) and the rise of anti-union consultants.

Given this unfavorable context, the labor lawyer's first job is to convince workers that the law cannot be relied on for protection or for solutions to organizing problems. It can only be used as a tool, usually one of last resort, to keep the organizing process alive. It will more often be used by employers to try to destroy an organizing effort. Delays in NLRB proceedings, unreliability of Board and court decisions, and employer influence in the political and judicial structure must all be explained to workers preparing to organize. They must understand they have to rely on themselves in the end. Once this is understood, proper use of charges and objections can help sustain an organizing movement.

[2] Present Scope

The NLRA later was amended by the Taft-Hartley Act and now is formally the Labor Management Relations Act (LMRA). The Act covers private employers engaged in interstate commerce

[3] Schechter Poultry Corp. v. U.S., 295 U.S. 495 (1935).

involving $50,000 a year or more and their employees.[4] Expansion of the Commerce Clause and the addition of nonprofit hospitals have brought virtually all private and semiprivate enterprises under the jurisdiction of the Act and the NLRB. There are, however, some major exceptions: railway and airline employees covered by the Railway Labor Act, agricultural and domestic workers, and independent contractors and supervisors.

These exceptions should not be minimized. Railway and airplane employees are a basic sector of the work force. While in some respects the Railway Labor Act makes organizing easier—certification is available on a card check in some circumstances—it enmeshes the workers in a web of arbitration and conciliation procedures that makes it difficult for the transport unions to give the kind of leadership to the overall union movement that they gave in the 19th century. The problems of farm workers outside NLRA coverage are well known from the experience of the United Farm Workers and other farm unions in California, Arizona, Texas, Ohio, Connecticut, and other scenes of recent organizing efforts. Organizing drives among domestic workers, chiefly in New York, have also run up against this problem.[5] Grossly exploited woodcutters in the South have run afoul of the independent contractors exception, which led to problems for the Gulf Coast Pulpwood Association in the early 1970s.[6] The question of who is a supervisor for purposes of the Act is a constant issue in NLRB proceedings.[7]

Public employees are covered under a myriad of state laws governing state, county, and municipal labor relations. There is a single federal law, the Federal Labor Relations Act, covering federal workers. Generally, these laws parallel the NLRA in that they permit workers to organize, protect themselves against unfair labor practices, and set up election mechanisms to determine representation questions. In contrast to the Act, most public em-

---

[4] *See Appendix A: Jurisdictional standards,* in NLRB Guide for Hearing Offices in Representation Cases.

[5] *See* Nat'l Law. Guild Lab. Newsletter, No. 13 (1975) for an article on this topic.

[6] *See* Nat'l Law. Guild Lab. Newsletter, No. 7 (1973); Nat'l Law. Guild Lab. Newsletter, No. 10 (1974).

[7] *See* Section 1.03[6], *infra.*

ployee laws prohibit strikes and provide some form of arbitration for unsettled disputes. Until recently these no-strike laws were more honored in the breach than the observance, but the recent Proposition 13-style attacks on public workers have driven their unions to embrace the arbitration requirements in many instances.

Several of the states, especially "right-to-work" states, have no laws protecting the right of public employees to organize. What little organization has taken place among these workers has been marked by bitter recognition strikes reminiscent of the pre-NLRA period in industry, as in the Charleston, S.C., hospital strike in 1967 and the Memphis sanitation strike in 1968.

While most of this chapter focuses on organizing in the private sector, the principles, strategies, and tactics discussed are equally valid in public sector organizing.

§ 1.03. Early Stages of the Organizing Process

[1] Beginning to Organize

The lawyer has no role in getting an organizing movement under way, but it helps to know how the process begins. Usually it starts in one of two ways. If a nonunion worker has a friend or relative in a union shop, they talk about work and unions, and the union member puts the unorganized workers in touch with the union. Alternatively, a union targets a key location in its industry or area and purposely develops contacts with workers there in an effort to begin organizing.

An organizer begins with individual or small group meetings at workers' homes or in coffee shops near the workplace. If the potential is there, such meetings will build on themselves, and more workers will become interested in organizing. The objective in these early stages is to put together an organizing committee representative of the work force composition and capable of carrying the organizing effort into the workplace. This requires careful efforts to draw key workers—workers respected by others in their departments—into the organizing movement.

Cards can be obtained from committed in-plant organizers as

these initial meetings progress, but a well-conducted campaign does not dwell on cards. A good organizer will downplay cards to emphasize the need to build a union, not sign cards. Only when the organizing committee is fully assembled and a solid base in the rank and file has been built, should cards be put into the shop, so that a majority can be quickly signed up. Dragging out a campaign to get cards detracts from the effort to build the union, and usually means the organizing is in trouble.

One question faced by lawyers and organizers in a campaign's early stages is how secret the activities and identities of employee organizers will be. While the initial steps can often be kept confidential, inevitably word gets around. At this point, the last thing the union wants is for its key organizers to get picked off by the employer under a pretext for discharge.

Employer knowledge of the campaign and the identity of organizers is a key element in winning a discriminatory discharge case. Some unions make it a practice to send the employer a letter stating that a campaign is under way and naming members of the organizing committee. In some cases, this gives added confidence to worker-organizers.

Others believe this creates an illusion that organizers are somehow protected and that such legalisms will determine the outcome of the campaign. These unions prefer to explain the risks involved and secure a commitment from the key leaders to continue organizing in the face of the risks. This will allow the organizing process to develop naturally out of the workers' own problems and concerns. The workplace organizers conduct themselves with discretion, but not conspiratorially. They know employer resistance will be forthcoming. Outright firing will probably chill the organizing and require charges, letter or no letter. Just as likely nowadays, though, are the more sophisticated anti-union campaigns being peddled by consultants around the country.

The question of whether to send a letter to the employer should not be handled by rote. It should be an issue for the organizing committee to discuss with the organizer and lawyer involved in the campaign. It should be treated as a tactical option that might knock the employer off balance, give confidence to organizing committee members, or boost the campaign in the shop as a whole. These possible advantages must be weighed against the dangers discussed above.

[2] Demand for Recognition and Bargaining

The objective of organizing is to secure recognition and a contract from the employer, not just to get NLRB certification. Accordingly, once a solid majority is obtained, the workers and their union should demand that the employer recognize the union voluntarily and begin bargaining, without petitioning the NLRB for an election. This demand should be made personally, with the largest possible number of workers confronting the boss. Break time or lunchtime provides a good opportunity for the demand en masse.

A letter stating that the union represents a majority and demands recognition and bargaining should be handed to the employer. Depending on how the authorization cards were handled (confidentially or openly), they can be presented to the employer as proof of a majority or the workers can insist on a card check by a neutral party (a local minister, a local ballot association, a panel of outsiders, etc.). All kinds of possibilities should be pushed, in order to force the employer either to accede or to discredit itself by refusing.

The workers should be advised to note carefully all statements made by the employer at the encounter. As a practical matter, most employers know how to keep quiet when a demand for recognition is made. A petition to the NLRB is necessary in almost all cases. Still, the face-to-face demand for recognition with maximum employee participation is a good way to reinforce the workers' belief that they have a union, and it can also be important in future refusal-to-bargain charges if subsequent unfair labor practices destroy the union's majority. See Section 1.07[2].

[3] The NLRB Petition

After recognition is refused, the union should petition for an

NLRB election. The employer may petition also, but the union should file its own petition in order to keep an offensive posture.

The NLRB will begin processing a petition for election[8] supported by signed and dated authorization cards showing support from 30 percent of the employees seeking representation.[9] Experience has shown that employer tactics in an organizing campaign usually frighten off some union support, so most unions will file a petition only with a two-thirds or three-fourths majority. (A majority was already needed to demand recognition.)

Four copies of the petition and the supporting cards must be filed with the Board (the cards can be sent or presented separately within forty-eight hours of filing the petition). In line with the organizational objective, a delegation of workers should present the petition and cards to the Board if the regional office is near enough. A Board agent will contact the employer to determine whether it meets the jurisdictional requirement and to obtain a list of employees and their jobs to compare with the authorization cards.

Close attention must be paid to filling out the petition form correctly. The status of borderline occupations (e.g., clericals, group leaders, technicians, drivers) should be determined in advance and specified for inclusion or exclusion in the unit sought (see the fuller discussion in Section 1.03[6], *infra*). The accurate full name of the employer is important, too. Petitions have been held up for the lack of an "Inc.," which could be critical, since the date of the petition begins the period when employer actions can be the basis of objections to an election.

[4] The Prehearing Conference

The Board will try to set up the election without going through a formal hearing by an informal process in which the parties agree on the bargaining unit, the payroll period for voter eligibility, the date for delivery of the Excelsior list (list of names and addresses

---

[8] *See* Appendix B, Petition for Election.

[9] § 101.18, Rules & Regulations and Statements of Procedure, NLRB; Felton Oil Co., 78 NLRB 1033, 22 LRRM 1332; U.S. Gypsum Co., 157 NLRB 652, 61 LRRM 1384; 161 NLRB No. 61, 63 LRRM 1308.

of bargaining unit workers who are eligible to vote in the election), the date, time, and place of the election, and other administrative matters. There are two types of informal arrangements: a consent election, in which objections to the election and challenged ballots will be decided by the regional director without appeal to the NLRB in Washington, and a stipulated election, in which objections and challenges go to the Board with the regional director's findings and recommendations. Which one is preferred depends on which region is involved and the makeup of the Board.

These informal proceedings are often handled by lawyers for the parties alone with a Board agent. For organizational purposes, it is much better to involve a representative group of workers in the process. The position of the workers is that they already have a union. The election is necessary to prove it because the employer did not recognize their union. Since they have a union, they should act like it and workers at these informal prehearing conferences should be encouraged to argue strenuously on all the points to be resolved. This has the added benefit, if a lawyer is assisting them, of establishing the proper relationship between the workers and their attorney. The attorney brings his or her background knowledge of the law to the process, but the workers bring their material knowledge of the workplace, the work force, the work schedule, etc., which are the primary factors in setting up the election. The lawyer's role is to back up the workers while they take the lead in confronting the employer.

The informality of this prehearing conference should be taken advantage of to accentuate the class differences involved. Workers should be encouraged to wear work clothes if possible, or casuals. Seating should be arranged so that the workers confront the employer. The delegation should be prepared beforehand on the issues, and each person should be ready to talk about one of them. For example, if payday is a Thursday, Tuesday or Wednesday may be preferable for the election. One worker should be ready then to argue that he or she doesn't want the paychecks to be used as leverage in the election. Another should be ready to argue about where the election should take place—a cafeteria, an unused warehouse space, etc., preferably away from office or management areas. The prehearing conference should become as much as possible a prototypical grievance meeting between the workers and the boss. If the employer's attorney takes a leading role, or if he or she is there alone representing the employer, his/her lack of knowledge of the plant or office or shop should be attacked by the employees to emphasize that the issues are joined by the workers and the boss, not the lawyers.

[5] The Formal Hearing

Arranging a consent or stipulation election through a prehearing conference is happening less frequently as employers recognize the importance of stalling to crush union organization. Contesting the makeup of the bargaining unit has become standard operating procedure. This issue, or others raised by the employer, is handled at a formal hearing presided over by an NLRB hearing officer—not an Administrative Law Judge (ALJ)—who is usually an experienced Board attorney or field examiner.[10] Strictly speaking, the hearing is nonadversarial; the purpose is to develop as complete a record as possible. Nonetheless, the hearing is conducted by examination and cross-examination, motions, objections, argument, etc. The hearing is another opportunity to develop the struggle between the workers and the boss. It should not be approached solely as a technical legal battle. As many workers as possible should attend and be involved—again, dressed as workers and prepared to take an active role.

The question of workers attending the hearings can become an important test of organizational resolve. The Board will issue subpoenas to necessary witnesses. As a last resort, the union can press for the broadest number of employees to be subpoenaed to the hearing. A much better approach for organizing purposes, however, is for the workers themselves to raise this issue in the workplace. A meeting with the boss should be demanded, and organizing committee members should argue strenuously for the release of the greatest number of workers—the entire shop if feasible—to attend the hearing. Instead of being passive recipients of subpoenas, with the overtone of coercion that they carry,

[10] Guide for Hearing Officers (*supra* note 1) is especially useful in preparing for a hearing.

the workers will be actively fighting for their rights. They thus will demonstrate that they have organized a union, and the NLRB procedure will be an opportunity to prove it, not a test of whether they have it. This approach should be handled with caution, however. A forceful demand and agitation to attend the hearing should not cross the line to insubordination or refusal to work.[11] The issue should be taken up aggressively but with discipline. If the employer takes a hard line in limiting attendance, that should be turned into an example of why the union is needed and why the workers have to prove the union's majority.

At the hearing, the lawyer or organizer, even with a full grasp of the matter, should go frequently off the record to consult with the workers and to elicit the key questions from the workers for cross-examination of company witnesses. The workers should have strategy meetings before and after each session of the hearing, just as if they were caucusing in negotiations. The idea is to use any tactic that assures the workers it is they who are taking on the employer, not just their lawyer or organizer.

[6] Appropriate Bargaining Unit

Some employers are in a position to raise broadly the issue of the appropriate bargaining unit. Where a company has two plants fairly close to each other, for example, with common operations and common management, it can argue with some prospect of success that the appropriate bargaining unit is the workers from both plants, even if the organizing has taken place only in one plant. It can also argue the opposite if the union is organizing both plants and there are substantial differences.

Before demanding recognition or petitioning, workers seeking to organize should pool their knowledge of the employer, along with whatever information can be obtained through research, to make sure they will not run into any bargaining unit problems in relation to the employer's overall operations. When this is resolved, they are still left with the question of which individuals will be included in or excluded from the bargaining unit. Even in

[11] *See* the recent decision in Service Employees Local 250 v. NLRB, 101 LRRM 2004 (D.C. Cir. 1979).

industry, where job categories are fairly clear-cut, an employer can always raise difficult questions about group leaders, for example, who work in production but may or may not have a role in disciplining employees, or plant clericals, who are paid on a salaried basis but spend their entire time in production areas, have lunch with production workers, work overtime with production workers, or otherwise have a mutuality of interest with them. This problem is even more troublesome in service industries and public employment, where traditional categories are less clearly defined. In any case, the workers and their organizer should determine, before demanding recognition or petitioning, whom they want included or excluded.

The presumption should favor the widest possible bargaining unit. More classifications in the union mean a stronger union with broad representation in the workplace. This presumption has to be balanced, though, by an assessment of the likelihood of building and holding a majority. The decision should follow meetings and discussions with all the workers, both to arrive at a sound decision and to develop the understanding that, in recommending inclusions or exclusions, they are the ones who are building and shaping their union.

It must be remembered, too, that the employer is approaching the unit question with an eye to preventing or destroying the union's majority. It may seek to load the unit with clericals or quasi-forepeople group leaders, who it assumes will be anti-union. Since the employer usually knows of organizing activity well before a petition is filed, it might also try to shuffle duties and responsibilities to stack the unit when the petition emerges—reducing a working foreperson to group leader and relieving him/her of disciplinary responsibility, for example, to get him/her into the unit; or, conversely, promoting key union supporters to "backup forepeople" to get them out of the unit. The established classifications and practices have to be defined so that such last-minute changes can be exposed. All these considerations make full discussion even more necessary.[12]

[12] An Outline of Law and Procedure in Representation Cases (*supra* note 1) contains a full discussion of considerations in determining bargaining unit issues.

[7] Organizing during the Stall

One of the most difficult problems facing unorganized workers who have run into employer stalling tactics after petitioning for an election is to hold and continue to build their union while the process drags on. A full discussion of what's going on and why the employer is stalling can help.

Meetings and discussions should include all the workers, not just the key in-plant organizers. Workers must have the feeling that they, the membership, are helping to determine the union's position and contributing to the union's arguments—just as they will later do in proposing contract demands or deciding policy issues. At the same time, attention should not be focused primarily on the NLRB proceedings. Committee building, signing up new members, and developing shop issues and activity should continue getting top priority. If a lawyer is involved in the Board proceedings, he or she must be self-effacing in relation to the overall campaign.

§ 1.04. The Election Campaign—Campaign Tactics

Once the hearing procedure is concluded and the election is scheduled, the period of intense campaigning will be under way. Although the ideal, as stated earlier, is to make the election a natural by-product of the workers' organizing themselves, the election inevitably tends to dominate the organizational effort. Resisting this tendency and keeping the organizing on course takes careful work. This is the task of the organizer and the organizing committee; they should develop issues and activities that solidify the presence of the union in the workplace (leaflets, buttons, T-shirts, plant gate meetings, lunchroom meetings, grievance handling, etc.) and in the community (rallies, bumper stickers, car caravans, letters to the editor, advertisements, etc.).

[1] Roles of Organizer and Lawyer

Lawyers should not be directly involved in the election campaign handling do's and don'ts or other such technicalities because this feeds the impulse to rely on lawyers and legal answers to organizational problems. It is the organizer's job to run through the do's and don'ts and to advise workers to keep records and notes of events that can be used in future proceedings. Where a lawyer can be useful is in developing documentation, affidavits, testimony, and other tools for use in unfair labor practice charges or objections to election proceedings if they become necessary. This is a backup job, which must be done discreetly. The lawyer should not inject himself or herself into the campaign and turn it into a course on unlawful employer conduct. The problem is not to ferret out the unlawful conduct; the problem is for the workers to fight it and overcome it by their own organizational efforts.

[2] Union Conduct in Organizing

A well-conducted campaign will reflect an understanding by rank-and-file organizers of what is involved in building their union. Technical matters, such as when and where to distribute leaflets, the use of buttons and stickers, the content of union propaganda, etc., are explained and guided by the union organizers. If the in-plant organizers maintain the discipline required for effective unionism, there will not be a problem.

One of the biggest dangers for the union is a breakdown of organizational discipline by secondary union supporters. In the heat of a campaign, especially when the employer has fomented a "Vote No" movement, workers who are pro-union but not part of a trained organizing committee often make statements threatening dire consequences for anti-union activity. The union must take positive steps to prevent such statements or disavow them in order to avoid future charges or objections. It is not a bad idea to issue written instructions to in-plant organizers on this point.

[3] Written Propaganda

[a] Law Governing Content of Campaign Propaganda

After opening up campaign propaganda in 1977 to practically any falsehood or distortion, the NLRB recently returned to a "truth-in-advertising" standard.[13] The former, lax standard, based on the work of some professors who surveyed workers during and after an election campaign, inherently favored employers. A union campaign based on lies and distortions, even if for tactical reasons it ends in an election victory, will in the long run undermine the union objectives—a solid organization and a secure contract. Such an employer campaign, however, could result in both an election loss and the employer's overall objective —union-free status. Under the restored standard, a substantial misrepresentation without the opportunity for an effective reply can be a ground for setting aside an election. Thorough knowledge of this standard and related cases is critical for lawyers and organizers in the field.

In general, distribution of written campaign propaganda is protected under Section 7 of the LMRA, which establishes the right of employees to distribute literature "for mutual aid or protection." However, literature inflammatory enough to "threaten" disorder or other interruption of business functioning is not so protected.[14] This matter is more fully discussed in Section 1.08 [12], *infra.*

---

[13] Shopping Kart Food Mkt., Inc., 228 NLRB 1311 (1977); Gen. Knit of Cal., Inc., 239 NLRB 191 (1978). *See also* Truesdale, *From General Shoe to General Knit,* Lab. L.J. 67, 1979.

[14] Eastex, Inc., v. NLRB, 437 U.S. 556, 98 LRRM 2717 at 2723 n.22 (1978). *See also* discussion by the General Counsel of the NLRB of the Board's refusal to issue a complaint in the discharge of a worker for refusal to remove literature of a "workers organization" from the plant. The literature sought financial aid for the criminal defense of a worker at another plant who was charged with assaulting a Nazi employee at the other worker's plant. The leaflet attacked the Nazi and employer collaboration and called on workers to unite against the capitalists. 101 LRR 361.

[b] Need to Avoid Overdependence on "Paper Organizing"

The detailed legalities of propaganda content and distribution are available from many sources. More important here for the radical lawyer involved in organizing the unorganized is the whole question of written materials in an organizing campaign. Most lawyers and even many union organizers, who are comfortable with printed matter, love to spell out the arguments for the union or instructions to in-plant organizers in writing in the belief that a well-written leaflet will convince fence-sitting workers and well-written instructions will motivate in-plant organizers. While well-written materials are an essential element of a campaign, it must be remembered that workers are convinced primarily by other workers to support the union. The ideal campaign would take place without a single leaflet, carried instead by the meetings, discussions, and other activities of the workers themselves. Building the union does not depend on the quantity or quality of written materials. Organization is doomed if a campaign breaks down into a battle of leaflets or other gimmicks even if the union wins the election. In this light, the mode of leaflet distribution is as important as the content. In-plant organizers must have specific assignments for leaflet distribution to their workmates at the workplace so that they are, in effect, doing a union steward's job of keeping the members informed. Leaflets should be put into the workers' hands by the in-plant organizer, not left to be picked up from a pile. The point is to create the union's presence inside the plant, shop, or office, in the form of workers actively building their union. If a campaign has heated up but leaflets are still being passed out at the parking lot entrance, that campaign is in trouble.

[4] Other Campaign Tactics

Buttons, stickers, T-shirts, blazers, and other campaign paraphernalia are effective devices for further highlighting the union's presence at the workplace. Generally, as long as they are not obscene and do not interfere with the work, there is a wide range of possible use. Tighter standards are applied to hospitals and stores and other service establishments that deal with the public.[15]

Mass activities, such as demonstrations and plant gate meetings, are also important for creating union presence at the workplace. These require a high level of organization and, if accomplished, portend an eventually successful campaign. In anti-union areas, creating a union presence in the community is also important. Here, community rallies, car caravans, and the aggressive use of local media come into play. All such tactics must be worked out by the union organizers, the organizing committee, and the rank and file, but the lawyer's familiarity with these subjects can be an important backup if complications set in. Local ordinances, First Amendment forum law, preemption, and FCC community service requirements are all areas the radical labor lawyer should be able to work in.

§ 1.05. The Election Campaign—In-Plant Representation as a Union-Building Tool

However advanced the level of organizing activities discussed above, the key to building a union (and winning an election campaign in the process) is shop floor representation. It was pointed out, for example, that Board proceedings should be turned into "grievance meetings" and leaflet distribution should reflect the activity of union stewards toward their members. Even more effective is the handling of shop problems by in-plant union organizers. Section 7 LMRA rights protect any concerted activity by workers in connection with wages, hours, and working conditions. A union does not even have to be on the scene, let alone organizing or certified, for concerted activity to be protected. When typical shop problems arise, therefore—an improper bump, an unfair transfer, a violation of seniority, excessive disci-

[15] *See, e.g.*, Gulf & W. Indus., Inc., 166 NLRB No. 15; R.H. Macy & Co. (Davison-Paxon Co. Div.), 191 NLRB No. 10; Fabri-Tek, Inc. v. NLRB, 352 F.2d 577 (8th Cir. 1965); Devilbiss Co., 102 NLRB 1317; NLRB v. Power Equip. Co., 319 F.2d 861 (6th Cir. 1963); NLRB v. Baptist Hospital, Inc., 101 LRRM 2556 (1979). *See also* Section 1.08 [16], *infra.*

pline, an unfair time study, etc.—the rank-and-file organizers should be prepared to confront the foreperson or other superior responsible and to argue just as determinedly as if a contract had been violated.

Legal considerations enter when aggressive in-plant representation can be used by the employer as grounds for insubordination. In-plant organizers must be careful to use whatever internal procedures the employer has set up. Most companies have so-called grievance procedures. They are an opportunity for union building if properly used by in-plant organizers. Aggressive representation gives the union a no-lose situation: If the problem is solved, it legitimates and builds up the union in the eyes of the workers; if the employer doesn't budge, only further organization and a union contract with a genuine grievance procedure can solve the problem.

Especially useful here is application of the *Weingarten/Quality Manufacturing* rule in a nonunion context, which was decided in *Glomac Plastics.*[16] The right to have a co-worker present at any meeting with a boss where the employee has a reasonable expectation of disciplinary action being taken can be a real tool in an organizing campaign. Organizing committee members should be thoroughly grounded in this area and carry the message back to the workers in their departments. Here, again, is a potential squeeze on the employer: If the boss refuses to permit the co-worker to accompany the potential disciplinee, the union has an unfair labor practice charge in reserve; if he or she permits it and the discipline is avoided, the union takes the credit; if he or she permits it and the discipline is imposed, the union can redouble its arguments for the protection of a contract and a real grievance procedure.

§ 1.06. The Election Campaign—Employers' Anti-Union Tactics

A technical approach to organizing emphasizes the do's and don'ts of employer conduct, and seeks to discover violations to

[16] *See* NLRB v. J. Weingarten, Inc., 420 U.S. 251 (1975); ILGWU v. Quality Mfg. Co., 420 U.S. 276 (1975); Glomac Plastics, Inc., 234 NLRB No. 199 (1978).

be remedied through Board proceedings. A realistic approach recognizes that every employer anti-union campaign violates Section 7 rights. The employer's campaign is inherently coercive by virtue of the control it exercises over the workers. In this context, the organizing position is not "If the employer breaks the law, we'll file a charge," but "The employer will break the law, and we have to overcome it by organizing." The goal is not to discover unfair labor practices but to organize in spite of them. Charges and objections only come in when the organizing has faltered.

Even when those involved in organizing—lawyers, organizers, organizing committee members—fully understand that every employer campaign breaks the law and they have to organize in the teeth of the violations, the time still often comes when the violations are too much to withstand. A shift into legal proceedings, without abandoning the real organizing effort, then becomes necessary.[17]

The broad categories of employer anti-union tactics are well-known: surveillance and interrogation, threats of strikes and shutdowns, threats or promises of changes in wages, benefits, or conditions, discriminatory firings, transfers, layoffs, shift assignments, etc. The point has already been made that these are not illegal aberrations that the employer falls into by mistake, but conscious policy to bust union organization. The trick is to do it without getting caught. Most employers now turn to consultants who specialize in this business.

These are three major areas of anti-union campaigning: (1) the

---

[17] For a discussion of the tactics used by the "new" union busters and possible legal recourses available, *see* Bernstein, Union Busting and the Law: From Benign Neglect to Malignant Growth (1980; Center to Protect Workers Rights, 1899 L St., N.W. Suite 800, Washington, D.C. 20036).

A regular report on the different union-busting firms and their operations is published by the Nat'l Organizing Coordinating Committee of the AFL-CIO. Report on Union Busters (RUB Sheet) is available from AFL-CIO, 815 16th St., N.W. 20006. Issue No. 21 reports on an NLRB settlement against W. Coast Indus. Ass'n, which requires that it cease and desist from interfering in any manner with the Section 7 rights of employees of *any* employer. This suggests the device of naming union-busting firms in unfair labor practice charges filed against an employer so as to gain relief against them for the employees in question and for workers at other employers who may be the victims of such union-busting tactics.

manipulation of business operation and practice totally under the employer's control, (2) the use of carrot-and-stick psychology techniques by anti-union communications specialists, and (3) the one-on-one and small group campaign by supervisors and salaried employees.

[1] Control of the Business

The foundation of the employer campaign is the creation of fear and confusion among workers who have freely decided they want a union. It is around the employer's control of the workers, the plant, and the paychecks that the secret, illegal campaign is constructed. Under the camouflage of "business need" and "continuation of normal practices," the following are just a few of the tactics used:

(1) Overtime is deliberately scheduled to interfere with union meetings. Overtime is also consciously used to increase paychecks beyond their normal size during the crucial pre-election days.

(2) New employees are screened and hired to pack voting lists. Supervisors suddenly become workers, and workers suddenly become supervisors. Workers are "permanently" laid off to spread fear and remove them from the voting.

(3) Raises are handed out, jobs promised, promotions instituted, all carefully targeted for votes, all "laundered" for legality.

(4) Work schedules are changed, lunch hours shifted or staggered, and starting and quitting times altered or varied, all to prevent employees from communicating with one another about the union organizing efforts.

(5) Active union supporters are put on isolated jobs, transferred to other shifts, sent on work assignments outside the plant.

(6) Active union supporters are grouped together for workplace meetings so that they will not influence other workers when the employer makes an anti-union pitch,

while the employer is free to threaten or fire workers who decide to talk back.

(7) The enforcement of rules and regulations is juggled, either taking the pressure off to give the air of an industrial paradise, or rigidly applying the rules to sow fear among the workers (the most artful employers go both ways, depending on the level and nature of union support in a particular department, building, shift, or other subdivision).

In addition to tactics like these, the employer's control of the business is the basis for much of the anti-union propaganda in written materials and meetings. "The union can only demand, the company doesn't have to agree," "We pay you a check to work, who will pay you a check to strike?", "The union cannot guarantee they will get you what the company already gives you," and other such statements can be tailored to meet the legal requirements, but there is no doubt about their coercive effect.

[2] Psychological Techniques

The anti-union campaigners have learned how to abuse communication techniques to violate rights without coming within the technical reach of the Act. For example, they pound away with messages of "union violence" and "union strikes" to identify the union with strikes and violence in the minds of the workers. This tactic is familiar to psychologists as a "saturation technique" or "buzz effect" designed to make employees believe something they know is contrary to the reality of their own situation and the character of their fellow workers.

These specialists arrange for so-called impartial outside groups to come into the plant during the campaign, allegedly to give the workers a chance privately to express their feelings about wages, working conditions, and management. In fact, the answers provide the groundwork for the anti-union campaign. In many cases, these "surveys" are not confidential at all. Supervisors can spot certain individuals who will then be special targets during the employer campaign.

Another example of the "carrot" side of the carrot-and-stick approach perfected by these specialists is their use of "heart-to-heart" talks, encounter groups, and "group awareness" sessions smoothly to alter the employees' union support. In some workplaces, for example, employers arrange for "role-playing" sessions, complete with free meals and drinks, at a local resort. "You play boss and I'll play worker" is one technique. This can be followed up by a "backup supervisor" training program, in which scores of workers are given anti-union training and the impression they will someday become supervisors. Total interference, yet legal under the Act as it is now enforced.

[3] Use of Supervisory Pressure

Perhaps the most effective aspect of the illegal "hidden campaigns" of the modern anti-union employer is the use of forepeople and supervisors against workers who desire a union. Direct threats of discharge and/or other retaliation made by supervisors are discussed in Section 1.10[1], *infra.* Another, more sophisticated method involves information gathering and subtler forms of coercion. In this sort of anti-union campaign, the employer trains and utilizes the large number of supervisory and salaried employees in a workplace to produce a psychological, social, and economic profile of each individual worker and his or her attitude toward the union. On the basis of this information, the employer designs a program to bring overwhelming individual pressure on each worker to abandon or weaken his or her support for the union.

By its very nature, this part of the hidden campaign is illegal. However, because it is usually conducted orally, it is nearly impossible to expose. The anti-union specialists, either in-house or outside consultants, hold regular classes for forepeople, supervisors, and salaried employees to train them in its tactics. These employees fan out on the floor under cover of job responsibilities, but they are really doing a job on the workers. They report back to the specialists as to where each worker stands, and plans are developed to apply maximum pressure tailored to the vulnerable spot of each worker. This process is repeated with increasing frequency as election time nears, reaching a fever pitch in the final days, especially the last twenty-four hours before the election, when the surface campaign has ended.

The following items appear on a "vulnerability questionnaire" typical of those used by companies in fashioning their one-on-one campaigns:

> #2. If the employees in this unit were given the chance to vote by secret ballot in a union election, indicate the results:
> ____% would vote for a union
> ____% would vote against a union
>
> #12. How many have close relatives who belong to a union? ____
>
> #13. How many have unstable family situations (illness in the family, divorce, separation, etc.)? ____
>
> #14. How many have above average debt and credit problems? ____
>
> #16. How many employees in this unit would you classify as "job hoppers"? ____
>
> #18. How many employees in this unit are opinion leaders? ____
>
> #63. Do any employees in this unit wear long hair . . . or sharp clothes to work? / / Yes / / No
>
> #64. Do your female employees wear miniskirts . . . or pantsuits to work? / / Yes / / No

To take one example of how this kind of information is used, suppose a foreperson or office manager has an employee with a sick spouse who requires regular treatments and medication. To that employee, the supervisor will be instructed to emphasize that "if the union gets in, the medical benefit plan will be up for negotiation and there's no telling how it will turn out." This statement is technically legal, but in the context of the employee's individual worry, as revealed by the vulnerability questionnaire, it amounts to a devastating threat of a loss or cutback of medical benefits for his or her spouse. Note that this threat is not made in a piece of campaign literature or in a captive audience meeting (although it may well be, in generalized form). It is made in a one-on-one, no-witness, conversational context that the employee is likely never to mention, let alone challenge as an unfair labor practice.

The following list of instructions to supervisors is typical of the kind of advice they get from the consultants.

Supervisory Tips

1. Spend as much time as possible on the floor moving around your area. Observe any unusual activity going on. Immediately check on people from other areas and other shifts in your area.
2. Watch activity at shift change in your area. Which employees group together?
3. Watch when your people go on breaks and whom they go with.
4. Segregate the new men from the KNOWN men. Don't assign them to work together. If need be, put all your KNOWN men working together.
5. At least one supervisor should be in the recreation room at each lunch period. Move around but don't be obvious.
6. Supervisors should stop in the recreation room before each shift. Sit around and have a coke or a coffee. Make the KNOWN uncomfortable. If necessary, sit with them. Supervisors should also stop directly after each shift. Also note activity on parking lot and in tunnel.
7. At least one supervisor should eat lunch in the cafeteria at each period to observe the activity.
8. *Write down* any bits of information you hear or see. You do not know how pertinent they might be. Turn them in to your unit manager daily.
9. Check bathrooms occasionally for loitering and graffiti on the walls.
10. Don't talk union at your workplace meetings unless it is from a script or it is brought up by someone else. Be very careful of your answers and don't leave yourself open. If you are not sure of your answer, tell the individual you will get back to him as soon as possible with the answer.

11. Keep a diary of unusual events (people, dates, times) for reference in event it may be necessary at some future date to recall exactly what happened.

This list clearly constitutes orders to engage in surveillance, discrimination, coercion, etc. But it is standard operating procedure and the law is ineffective to stop it.

[4] Spying and "Vote No" Committees

In addition to their use inside the plant, forepeople and supervisors are regularly sent on spying missions in the community at large. There is supposed to be no surveillance of workers' union activity. In fact, there is seldom a meeting of half a dozen or more workers where the employer has not arranged coverage. For example, forepeople will be "just shopping" in the area where the meeting takes place, noting whose cars are there and who is entering and leaving the meeting. Or forepeople covertly recruit employees to attend and report on the meetings. For each one of these violations exposed, ninety-nine stay undetected and unchallenged.

White-collar workers, especially salaried or technical workers, are also utilized in one of the most effective anti-union devices cooked up by the employers: the "Vote No" committees that surface as a union campaign heats up. The employer insulates itself from liability—much like a Mafia don—while guiding anti-union salaried employees in setting up these "Vote No" committees. Without such interference, the reality of the situation would not give rise to this type of activity. It is planned, sponsored, and carried out secretly by the employer—total interference, yet practically impossible to detect and prevent.

[5] Captive Audience Meetings

The captive audience meeting is the most glaring example of the inherent coerciveness in an employer's anti-union campaign. The herding of employees into a room where they sit in rows before representatives of management at a head table or podium reflects every experience of facing a higher authority they have ever had—as students before a teacher, believers before a clergyperson, etc. Until a few years ago, in-plant organizers could take such meetings as an opportunity to take on the company. Then a disturbing Board decision removed the chance for organized opposition at a captive audience meeting—at least such opposition as could be called disruptive, which was the best kind.[18] Now organizers must handle such meetings by demanding to ask questions in order to discredit the employer afterwards if the demand is refused. If the employer does permit questions (which is unlikely), the union supporters should be prepared to dig into the key issues. In handling a captive audience meeting, much depends on the employer's anti-union advisors and the approach they counsel. Unions usually know these consultants' tactics from earlier campaigns and can work out an approach for minimizing the damage from a captive audience meeting. The AFL-CIO is also undertaking a compilation of anti-union consultants and their practices.

[6] Blocking Charges

The NLRB has adopted a general policy of holding in abeyance any representation or deauthorization case whenever one of the parties in the case files unfair labor practice charges that allege conduct that tends to interfere with the exercise of free choice in a Board election. A nonparty to a representation or deauthorization case may also halt the processing of an election petition by filing Section 8(a)(2), 8(a)(5), 8(b)(3), or 8(b)(7) charges on the ground that the nature of these alleged violations may condition or preclude a question concerning representation. This general policy has been popularly characterized as the "blocking charge" rule.

Of course there are exceptions to the blocking charge rule. A charging party can avoid the rule by signing a request to proceed with the election despite the filing of charges. Even in the absence of a request to proceed, the regional director may proceed with

---

[18] J.P. Stevens Co., 219 NLRB 156. *See also* Prescott Indus. Prods., 205 NLRB 51.

an election if he/she is of the opinion that the employees could exercise free choice in an election notwithstanding the unfair labor practice charges or if the charges are so related to a question concerning representation that holding the election will resolve common issues. Another exception is where the charges are filed too late to permit any investigation before a scheduled election. In this situation, the regional director has the discretion to proceed with the election and then impound the ballots until the investigation of the unfair labor practice charge has been completed. If the charge has merit, the ballots will not be tallied. Where such an unfair labor practice charge is filed after the filing of an election petition, the processing of the petition will be suspended pending investigation of the charge.

If the charges are found to lack merit, upon their dismissal or withdrawal, the Board will proceed with the representation case even if there is an appeal unless the regional director exercises his or her discretion to halt further processing of the case until the conclusion of the appeal. In certain appeal cases, those involving Section 8(a)(2), 8(a)(5), 8(b)(3), 8(b)(7), or 8(a)(1) (alleging employer assistance in filing a concurrent decertification petition), the regional director must obtain clearance from the Board before proceeding to an election.

If the charges are found to have merit and a complaint is to issue, the regional director will determine whether further processing of the representation case should be blocked. The standard used in reaching this conclusion is whether the charges, accepting the allegations to be true, would have an impact on the holding of a free election. Where the charges involve violations of Section 8(a)(2), 8(a)(5), or 8(b)(3) and the petitioner is the alleged company union, the petition will be dismissed subject to reinstatement upon final disposition of the charges.

Although the blocking charge rule has been promulgated to ensure that elections are conducted in an atmosphere free of any taint of unfair labor practices, in fact, the operation of this rule can often serve as a tool in the overall company strategy to delay elections and frustrate organization.

The blocking charge rule becomes a most effective employer tool in situations involving company unions or anti-union committees. Here, the blocking charge rule is an anti-union weapon because of the particular rules developed and applied by the Board in Section 8(a)(2) cases. For example, in a campaign where the workers are very well organized and are not succumbing to the company's anti-union campaign, if a company union or anti-union committee in collusion with the company files unfair labor practice charges *against the company* alleging conduct that if proved would affect the election, it can effectively stall an election for a considerable period of time. First, the anti-union committee can refuse to request to proceed. Then a regional director, may decide not to proceed with the election on the ground that a free election cannot be held. Thus, the result may be the cancellation or delay of an election that the union would probably have won. Moreover, the company profits from its illegality in this kind of a situation. Even more frustrating, the union is then caught in a situation over which it has no control because it is neither the charging party nor the respondent. A further dilemma is presented to the union when it tries to extricate itself from this predicament. If the union attempts to establish that it is not in collusion with the company by filing Section 8(a)(2) charges against the company union or anti-union committee, it further aggravates the situation because the Board will then consider these charges blocking charges. Moreover, if Section 8(a)(2) charges have been filed, the Board will not honor a request to proceed until after a Board order has issued on the unfair labor practice charges—some six to nine months or more down the road.[19] This scenario is also applicable in a rival union situation, with even worse consequences.

Of course, beyond these specific problems with the blocking charge rule, a general problem of inconsistent or unfair application of the rule by regional directors is also a serious problem. Very often, a regional director will, after finding that charges have merit, cancel a scheduled election and refuse to reschedule it until the investigation has been completed on the basis of the abstract proposition that the charges will adversely affect the election regardless of the real situation in the shop. Regional directors have also adopted a procedure of going forward with an election but impounding the ballots, leaving the workers in limbo for months as to whether or not the union won while the unfair

[19] *See* Carlson Furniture Indus. Inc., 157 NLRB 851.

labor practice charges are litigated. Another very serious problem is that a regional director may cancel a scheduled election in order to complete the investigation of charges filed shortly before the election date. Although the Board rules specifically state that late-filed charges constitute an exception to the blocking charge rule, a closer look at the exception reveals that the regional director has discretion to postpone the election, hold the election and impound the ballots, or conduct the election and issue the tally of ballots. Since the exercise of regional directors' discretion is practically irreversible it is obvious that gross abuses in the application of the blocking charge rule can occur. Thus, the blocking charge rule is another possible anti-union tool in the hands of the company, one that can be aggravated by unfair or ignorant application by the Board.

Of course, where a progressive union is the incumbent, the blocking charge rule may be used to defeat or slow a decertification or deauthorization petition by a company union or some other union that would not effectively represent the membership. If a legitimate, progressive union is seeking certification and the employer has engaged in a major unfair labor practice that has destroyed the union's chances of winning the election,[20] it may be desirable to delay or avoid the election through a blocking charge and a bargaining order.

§ 1.07. The Legal Response to Employer Destruction of an Election Campaign

[1] Unfair Labor Practice Charges

If employer tactics succeed in pushing the organizing drive off course, charges and objections may be needed to keep it alive. To develop the strongest case requires full discussion among the organizer, the lawyer, the organizing committee, and the rank and file. While the campaign is under way, the problem is to learn what the employer is up to and to prepare documentation and statements *without* shifting the workers' attention from their own positive campaign. Investigating potential charges and objections

[20] *See* Section 1.08[10], *infra.*

at this stage, therefore, should be done with discretion in side meetings and discussions, rather than in general organizing meetings.

After a campaign has broken down and Board proceedings are under way, the legal case can be moved to center stage. Here, again, though, it should be approached as an organizing tool. The widest number of witnesses should be prepared, preferably from among key workers to whom others look for leadership. As many workers as possible, even if they will not testify, should be involved in meetings and discussions to prepare the legal case. Even after a case is thoroughly prepared, such meetings should continue so that time delays do not erode interest and support. All the while, the emphasis should remain on shop issues, not legal technicalities, so that the workers have the sense of actively contributing to the union's case, instead of being passively lectured on the law. After the unfair labor practice hearing or hearing on objections takes place, further meetings should evaluate how the hearing went and prepare employees for further delays during appeals. At the same time, there should be renewed emphasis on shop issues and positive organizing to prepare for a new campaign (or for bargaining, if Board-ordered bargaining is a prospect).

[2] Bargaining Orders

It is possible for the union to be certified as the bargaining agent and the employer to be ordered to bargain by the NLRB without an election, or after an election is lost by the union. Normally the following conditions are required for this to happen:

(1) The union represents a majority of workers in an appropriate bargaining unit. Representation must be reflected by authorization cards from a majority, and the cards must be unimpeachable—signed; dated; clearly expressing authorization to represent the workers in collective bargaining; not obtained under duress, by pretense, "to get an election," or for any other diversionary reason.

(2) A demand for recognition and bargaining has been made,

and the employer has refused it. In extreme cases, however, this condition is not necessary (see item (3)).

(3) The employer commits such extensive unfair labor practices (other than the refusal to bargain) that the union majority is destroyed or holding a fair election is impossible. Where the election was held, objection to the election must accompany a refusal to bargain charge. In extreme cases where this occurs before the union demands recognition, the Board can issue a bargaining order to remedy just a Section 8(a)(1) violation[21] (this is the so-called *Gissel* doctrine, based on the 1969 Supreme Court decision in that case).[22]

In a recent case,[23] the Board asserted its authority to issue a bargaining order even where the union has not shown a majority status, though it declined to issue the order in that case. Still, the extraordinary remedies fashioned by the Board—access to the workplace, equal time in captive audience meetings, and others—might give the union a better opportunity for real organizing than a flat bargaining order would.

On appeal, the Third Circuit remanded the case to the Board for consideration of whether the extreme character of the employer's unfair labor practices warranted the issuance of a bargaining order even in the absence of evidence of a majority.[24]

Many employers complain that the *Gissel* doctrine gives the union "two bites at the apple" because the company can win the election but still be ordered to bargain. In practice, however, it is the union that is put at a disadvantage. First of all, the *Gissel* doctrine applies only to "massive" unfair labor practices, which an employer with competent advice can easily avoid and still obtain the desired effect of undermining the union's majority. Second, while the bargaining order is designed to remedy the destruction of the union's majority, it does not restore the majority itself. The massive violations have taken their toll. The union

---

[21] *See* NLRB v. Gissel Packing Co., Inc., 395 U.S. 575 (1969); Bernel Foam Prods. Co., 146 NLRB 1277 (1964); N.W. Eng'r Co., 148 NLRB 1136 (1964).

[22] NLRB v. Gissel, *supra* note 21.

[23] United Dairy Farmers Co-op, 101 LRRM 1278.

[24] United Dairy Farmers Co-op Ass'n v. NLRB, 633 F.2d 1054, 105 LRRM 3034 (3d Cir. 1980). The Board issued a bargaining order. United Dairy Farmers Co-op, 257 NLRB No. 129, 107 LRRM 1577 (1981).

is usually bargaining from a weak position and faces the prospect of a disastrous strike or inferior contract.

Coming up with a functioning union and a decent contract from this situation is perhaps the ultimate test of organizing principles. The card majority must have been solid to begin with. In the unfair labor practice hearing, individual workers will have to testify that they signed cards because they wanted to join the union and have the union represent them. Company lawyers will cross-examine them sharply: "Didn't you just want an election?"; "Didn't you just want to get the organizer off your back?"; etc. The majority of good faith union adherents must be unshaken. A lawyer can be invaluable in this kind of proceeding, preparing witnesses for their testimony and cross-examination.

Even more important to emerging with a good contract or conducting a successful strike, the union cadres in the workplace must be intact and ready to rebuild. The organizing committee must organize support for the union in contract negotiations just as they organized for recognition. The employer will sit at the table, but inside the workplace will try to freeze the union into a minority position, unelected and illegitimate in the eyes of the workers. Only a redoubled organizing effort with all the tactics discussed earlier can overcome this.

[3] Striking for Recognition

The great strikes of the years prior to passage and enforcement of the Wagner Act were usually recognition strikes to force the employer to sit down and bargain with the workers. Conditions for returning to work were usually laid out so that a contract emerged from the strike settlement. Still, recognition was the basic issue.

The emphasis on NLRB proceedings has made recognition strikes rare, but not extinct. Restaurant workers often strike for recognition where their picket lines will have enough impact to force the employer to the table. If this is done without filing a petition, however, the petition must be filed within thirty days of the beginning of such picketing, and the Board will expedite the election procedure. The same can be done in any workplace that has been organized, but it will succeed only under ideal conditions—where the union has been solidly organized and can pull off a successful strike. In newly organized shops where the workers have not had much union experience, this is a risky proposition at best.

The same can be said for a post-election strike for recognition where the union has won the election but certification is held up by employer objections. The Steelworkers faced such a predicament at the Newport News Shipbuilding and Drydock Company in early 1979. After ousting a company union by a 9000 to 7500 vote, the union was put on the horns of a dilemma by the prospect of drawn-out Board and court proceedings on objections to the election. The enthusiasm and militance of the most active in-plant organizers would be diluted by the delay. On the other hand the substantial anti-Steelworkers vote indicated that a solid strike would be hard to accomplish, and the company could make hay out of contrasting its "legal" appeals to the union's "strong-arm" tactics. Adopting the views of their key in-plant cadres, the union called the strike. Though it ended in three months without recognition, concessions by the company on return-to-work details permitted the strikers to go back in with their heads high. With pride and motivation, they can possibly rebuild the union inside the shop, which will mean more in the long run for the health of the union than if it had not called the strike and seen its key cadres' support deteriorate. One can only conclude that striking for recognition is extremely risky and requires the highest level of organization and analysis.

[4] Dealing with the Board

Whether the facts and precedents a lawyer is working with are favorable or not, his or her relationship with the Board is critical to effective representation. Petitions, charges, and objections begin with the individual Board agent who is assigned the investigation of the relevant facts. Usually these are younger people, recently out of law school. Although they are less experienced than more senior Board personnel, their influence in producing charges or hearings on objections should not be underestimated.

While they don't make the decision, if they are convinced they are right they will press hard for a complaint or hearing order to issue.

There are two key elements in working with the Board agents. First, get them involved with the workers, with the shop, and with the union organizers or lawyers. Just as workers are moved to organize by contacts with co-workers more than by leaflets or copies of contracts, Board agents are moved more by personal contacts with organizers and workers than by field manuals or Board opinions. It is not that a bias is induced or that they are susceptible to improper influence. Rather, this kind of personal contact helps them understand the lawbreaking that takes place in *every* anti-union campaign.

To develop such involvement, the organizer or lawyer should personally assist the Board agent in meeting workers. It is better to drive around to the workers' homes, letting the Board agent see how the workers live, than to meet in a motel room or a federal office. Driving around together also gives the organizer or lawyer a chance to show the Board agent the shop and to talk about the shop and the campaign. You should not try to make a personal friend of the Board agent—you have to be aggressively pushing your case all the time—but you should humanize the situation so that he or she sees it in terms of the individuals involved.

The second key element in dealing with Board agents is, to the extent possible, to *do their work for them.* Board agents have the same energy quotient as most people. If they find that the fact situation has been laid out in detail in a supplement to the charge or objections, that the issues have been clarified, that witnesses are prepared to give clear statements, that appointments have been made and kept, and so on, they will have that much more energy to grasp the case and argue for it themselves.

Another level of dealing with the Board is on hearings and appeals. Briefs, extensions, appeals, deadlines, and other procedural matters are spelled out in the Statement of Procedures and Rules and Regulations, but a lawyer finds himself or herself constantly needing to check out details in person or by telephone. You need to know the status of a case or who is handling it. You want to expedite a decision. You need an emergency extension of time. For these and like matters, a personal relationship with the regional director's office and with the executive secretary's office in Washington, even if by telephone, is invaluable. A lawyer with a continuing practice in organizing law should be personally acquainted with key regional personnel and have at least a telephone acquaintance with some of the executive secretary's staff. While it must remain professional and businesslike, such a relationship allows one to make calls and appointments that yield prompt responses to questions and problems. One final note of caution: To avoid giving the impression of deliberately bypassing the region, a lawyer should inform the regional office when he or she is dealing with the executive secretary's office.

§ 1.08. Solicitation and Distribution—Rights of Employee Organizers

Among the most important organizing rights are solicitation (approaching employees to seek their support) and distribution (handing out literature). The law in this area is said to be a balance between the statutory right of employees to organize themselves for collective bargaining purposes and employers' Fifth Amendment and common-law rights to control their private property and to maintain production and discipline.

The most appropriate and efficient location for effective organization is the workplace. It is therefore not surprising that most employers have rules designed to keep solicitation and distribution from interfering with profit making. The use of such rules to interfere with organizing activities has created a large body of law outlining how the balance will be struck.

No restrictions may be placed on workers' organizing rights absent a showing that such restrictions are necessary to maintain production or discipline.[25] This principle applies both to organizing for a union and to leafleting about employment or union matters whether by the union, individuals, or a caucus.[26] The NLRB uses two basic presumptions in deciding upon the validity

---

[25] NLRB v. Babcock & Wilcox Co., 351 U.S. 105, 113 (1956); Republic Aviation v. NLRB, 324 U.S. 793 (1945).

[26] Eastex v. NLRB, 98 LRRM 2717 (1978).

of no-solicitation and no-distribution rules.[27]

(1) Rules barring union solicitation during employees' nonworking time are presumptively invalid even if limited to working areas, while rules forbidding such solicitation during working time are presumptively valid.[28]

(2) Rules prohibiting distribution of literature in nonwork areas during nonworking time are presumptively invalid, while rules forbidding such distribution in work areas are presumptively valid even if they cover both working and nonworking time.[29]

The professed reason for allowing more stringent controls on distribution of literature is its potential for littering and crowding work areas and passageways. Beyond these considerations, distribution cannot be barred in nonwork areas during nonwork time any more than can solicitation.[30]

In *Essex International,*[31] the Board found a difference between the terms "work time" and "working hours"—a distinction so fine that it had been declared nonexistent two years earlier.[32] The Board decided that a rule using the term "working hours" was overbroad and invalid, unless clarified, since the term might suggest to employees that they were precluded from engaging in solicitation or distribution during their entire work shift. The Board further decided, however, that the term "work time" clear-

---

[27] Solicitation refers to solicitation of membership and may include the distribution of membership cards. Distribution refers to the distribution of union or other protected literature, i.e., literature dealing with working conditions, employment laws, internal union matters, etc. The principles that determine the lawfulness of no-solicitation rules also apply to no-distribution rules, except that no-distribution rules have some unique characteristics, as noted below.

[28] Walton Mfg. Co., 126 NLRB 697 (1960)(contains a review of Republic Aviation v. NLRB, *supra*); NLRB v. Babcock & Wilcox, *supra;* and NLRB v. United Steelworkers (Nutone), 357 U.S. 357 (1958).

[29] Stoddard-Quirk Mfg. Co., 138 NLRB 615 (1962).

[30] Minneapolis-Honeywell Regulator Co., 139 NLRB 849 (1962).

[31] 211 NLRB 749 (1974). The holding in Essex International was reversed in part in T.R.W., Inc., 257 NLRB No. 47, 107 LRRM 1481 (1981), where the Board held that there was no meaningful distinction between "working time" and "working hours," and that prohibitions against solicitation during either were presumptively invalid.

[32] Avon Convalescent Center, Inc., 200 NLRB 702 (1972)(prohibitions against solicitation during work time or working hours held to be invalid).

ly illustrated to workers that they must refrain from solicitation or distribution only during performance of actual job duties and were free to engage in organizing efforts during lunch and break periods, even if these times were paid for by the company.

It is important to note that these are rebuttable presumptions. For example, an employer may extend a no-distribution rule beyond the work area or extend a no-solicitation rule to include nonwork time if it can show that such an extension is necessary to maintain production or discipline.[33] Conversely, in representing workers, an attempt should be made to show that "littering" or "maintenance of production and discipline" are merely pretexts for anti-union rules[34] or that the employer allows solicitation during work time for charity or other purposes[35] or that the incumbent union is allowed to distribute during work time.[36] Generally, however, except under extraordinary circumstances, a no-solicitation/no-distribution rule during nonwork time and in nonwork areas will be invalid. Similarly, a rule against solicitation "on company time on company property" is invalid.[37]

[1] Equal Rights to Communicate

An employer may enforce a no-solicitation/no-distribution rule even though the employer itself is engaging in anti-union solicitation.[38] The lower court in *Nutone* held that if the justification for a broad no-solicitation/no-distribution rule was a clean plant and the need to maintain discipline, that object was vitiated by the employer's engaging in solicitation and distribution.[39] The Supreme Court reversed, holding that if, by virtue of the location of the plant and of the facilities and resources available to the

---

[33] *See, e.g.,* Republic Aviation v. NLRB, 324 U.S. 793 (1945); Minneapolis-Honeywell Regulator Co., *supra.*

[34] *See, e.g.,* Wm. H. Block Co., 150 NLRB 341 (1964); *see also* Section 1.08[8], *infra.*

[35] *See* Section 1.08[9], *infra.*

[36] *See* Section 1.08[10], *infra.*

[37] WIPO, Inc., 199 NLRB 649 (1972).

[38] NLRB v. Steelworkers (Nutone), 357 U.S. 357, 78 S. Ct. 1268, 2 L. Ed. 2d 1383 (1958).

[39] United Steelworkers v. NLRB, 243 F.2d 593 (D.C. Cir. 1956).

union, the opportunities for reaching employees with a pro-union message, in spite of a no-solicitation rule, are at least as great as the employer's ability to promote its anti-union message, an otherwise valid rule will not be invalidated.[40] In short, evidence must be presented that the employer's solicitation has created an imbalance in opportunity for communication. If, however, solicitation is forbidden during both work and nonwork time, an employer who makes anti-union speeches on company time and premises must give the union an equal chance.[41]

[2] Lunch and Rest Periods

Lunch and rest periods, even if paid for by the employer, are the workers' own time and solicitation cannot be prohibited.[42] An employer may not restrict employees' use of the restrooms to prevent them from discussing the union.[43] If employees are being paid but are not working because their machines are being repaired, they cannot be prevented from soliciting.[44]

[3] No Solicitation/No Distribution "Except as Provided by Law"

A rule that prohibits solicitation or distribution "except as provided by law" (or similar language) is invalid, since it places the burden of knowing the law on the worker.[45]

[4] No Solicitation/No Distribution "without Approval"

Rules barring solicitation or distribution without management

---

40 357 U.S. 357, *supra.*

41 Montgomery Ward & Co. v. NLRB, 339 F.2d 889 (6th Cir. 1965).

42 *See, e.g.,* Republic Aviation Corp. v. NLRB, *supra* note 25; Hanna Bldg. Corp. 223 NLRB No. 94 (1976); Mitsubishi Aircraft Int'l Inc., 212 NLRB 856 (1974).

43 Roselyn Bakeries, Inc., 192 NLRB 1165 (1971).

44 KDI Precision Prods., Inc., 185 NLRB 335 (1970).

45 Fasco Indus. v. NLRB, 412 F.2d 589 (4th Cir. 1969); Chrysler Corp., 227 NLRB No. 186 (1976); Trailmobile Div. of Pullman, Inc., 221 NLRB 178 (1976).

approval are invalid restrictions on employee organizing rights absent a showing of special circumstances.[46] This invalidity cannot be rebutted by extrinsic evidence that the employees did in fact discuss organizing during breaks.[47] This holding is based on familiar concepts: that the right to approve expression asserts a power to censor, which is *per se* a burden, and that nonuse or benevolent use of the right to approve is immaterial.

[5] Nonenforcement of Rules

The cases are divided on whether an overbroad rule is remedied by nonenforcement as to union organizing. A few cases have held that if no evidence is introduced to show that the rule is enforced, the rule does not unlawfully interfere with protected rights.[48] However, the majority of reported cases hold that nonenforcement is irrelevant to the rule's invalidity.[49]

[6] Clarification of Overbroad Rules

The Board has several times held that any ambiguity in a no-solicitation/no-distribution rule must work against the employer who promulgates it.[50] A rule that prohibits solicitation

---

[46] Joseph Horne Co., 186 NLRB No. 754 (1970)(solicitation); M.C. Ricciardi Co., 180 NLRB 195 (1969)(solicitation); Mid States Sportswear, Inc., 168 NLRB 559 (1968), *enforced without discussion,* 412 F.2d 537 (5th Cir. 1969)(distribution); M & S Steel Co., 148 NLRB 789, *enforced,* 353 F.2d 80 (5th Cir. 1964)(distribution). *But see* NLRB v. Shawnee Indus., Inc., 333 F.2d 221 (10th Cir. 1964)("without approval" rule is not an unfair labor practice in the absence of evidence that any employee requested and was denied approval).

[47] James H. Matthews & Co. v. NLRB, 354 F.2d 432 (8th Cir. 1965), *cert. denied,* 384 U.S. 1002 (1966); Allied Chalmers Corp., 224 NLRB No. 158 (1976). *But see* Gooch Packing, Inc., 187 NLRB 351 (1971).

[48] Sinko Mfg. & Tool Co., 149 NLRB 201 (1964), *enforced in part and enforcement denied in part on other issues sub nom.* Toy Workers, Local 18 v. NLRB, 369 F.2d 226 (7th Cir. 1966).

[49] *See, e.g.,* Valley Die Cast Corp., 176 NLRB 498 (1969); Marinette Marine Corp., 179 NLRB 627 (1969).

[50] NLRB v. Miller, 341 F.2d 870, 874 (2d Cir. 1965), *enforcing* 148 NLRB 1577 (1964); Farah Mfg. Co., 187 NLRB 601 (1970); St. Peter's Medical Center, 223 NLRB No. 140 (1976).

during nonwork time is invalid even if it is not applied to nonwork time if such interpretation has never been clearly explained to employees.[51] Discharge or discipline of an employee for solicitation during what is clearly work time cannot be sustained if the rule is too broad and has never been clarified as to nonwork time.[52] If, however, the employer has clarified an otherwise overbroad rule, it may be validated by the Board, although the Board will not consider subjective evidence that the employees understood.[53] An employer may correct an unlawfully broad rule by publication of the correction in a rule book for new employees and an announcement over the public address system;[54] a mere statement to employees that they may engage in union activities on company time and property provided there is no interference with production will not dissipate an unlawfully broad rule that is posted in the plant and printed in the employees' handbook.[55] An employer cannot correct an overbroad rule by posting a correction for a short period of time[56] or correcting the rule a few days before an election.[57]

[7] Existence of Rule

Even if no rule is posted or published, if an employer tells employees not to organize on company time or on company property, an unlawful rule has been promulgated.[58] In the absence of a valid rule, an employer cannot discipline an employee who has engaged in union activities, even if the solicitation or

---

[51] NLRB v. Southwire Co., 352 F.2d 346 (5th Cir. 1965), *enforcing as modified* 145 NLRB 1329 (1964); M.C. Ricciardi Co., *supra* note 46.

[52] Marriott Corp. (Children's Inn), 223 NLRB No. 141 (1975); Groendyke Transps., Inc., 211 NLRB 921 (1974).

[53] Essex Int'l, *supra* note 31; Ragu Foods, Inc., 217 NLRB 1109 (1975).

[54] Furnas Elec. Co., 183 NLRB 1 (1970).

[55] Cribben & Sexton Co., dba Waste King-Universal Prods., 148 NLRB 1462 (1964).

[56] J.R. Simplot Co. (Food Processing Div.), 137 NLRB 1552 (1962).

[57] Olympic Prods., Inc. (Subsidiary of Eddie Bauer, Inc.), 201 NLRB 442 (1973).

[58] Fostex Mfg. Co., Inc., 184 NLRB 22 (1970); Fashion Fair, Inc., 163 NLRB 88 (1967).

distribution took place during work time in work areas. Under these circumstances, the discipline may arise only from "abdication of working duties," rather than from the activity itself.[59]

[8] Valid Rule for Illegal Purpose

A rule that is otherwise valid is unlawful if its purpose is not maintenance of production or an unlittered work area but rather hindrance of organizing efforts.[60] Timing is important here for purposes of showing the true intent of the rule. A few cases have held that a rule may be promulgated after the beginning of union activity if the employer can show disruption of production.[61]

[9] Discrimination in Rule Enforcement

An employer acts unlawfully if a reasonable rule is administered in an arbitrary or discriminatory manner.[62] An employee may not be discharged or disciplined for solicitation or distribution if such action is motivated by anti-union sentiment.[63] An employer may not permit solicitation for charitable or social purposes but prohibit solicitation for union activity.[64] However, if solicitation for other purposes is sufficiently restricted, the Board may find that application of the rule has not been discriminatory

---

[59] J.L. Hudson Co., 198 NLRB 172 (1972); Story Oldsmobile, Inc., 140 NLRB 1049, *enforced,* 355 F.2d 28 (6th Cir. 1966).

[60] United Steelworkers v. NLRB, 393 F.2d 661 (D.C. Cir. 1968); NLRB v. Denver Tent & Awning Co., 138 F.2d 410 (10th Cir. 1943); Marion Mfg. Co., 161 NLRB 55, *enforced per curiam,* 338 F.2d 306 (4th Cir. 1968); Ward Mfg., Inc., 152 NLRB 1270 (1965); Alberts, Inc., 213 NLRB 686 (1974).

[61] NLRB v. Roney Plaza Apts., 597 F.2d 1046 (5th Cir. 1979); NLRB v. Mangurians's, Inc., 566 F.2d 463, 465 (5th Cir. 1978); NLRB v. Montgomery Ward., 544 F.2d 996 (10th Cir. 1977).

[62] NLRB v. Peyton Packing Co., 142 F.2d 1009 (5th Cir. 1944); Werthan Bag Corp. of Nashville, 167 NLRB 11 (1967); Logan Mfg. Co., 162 NLRB 1586 (1967); Standard Mfg. Co., 147 NLRB 1608 (1964).

[63] Story Oldsmobile, Inc., *supra* note 59. For more complete discussion, see Section 1.10, *infra.*

[64] Seng Co., 210 NLRB 936 (1974); G.C. Murphy Co., 171 NLRB 370 (1968); Time-O-Matic, Inc., v. NLRB, 264 F.2d 96 (7th Cir. 1959).

and is thus not invalid as motivated by anti-union objectives.[65] The pattern of enforcement must be sufficiently arbitrary to show anti-union sentiment as its underlying cause. Thus, it is an unfair labor practice for an employer to deny a union the use of a company-owned meeting hall that is the only available hall in a company-owned town[66] or for an employer to allow some groups but not the union to use its facilities.[67]

An employer may not curb pro-union solicitation or distribution while allowing anti-union activity,[68] nor may an employer discipline pro-union adherents for conduct permitted to anti-union employees.[69] The decision in *Nutone,*[70] which allows an employer to deny union access to company property even though the employer engages in anti-union activity, must be borne in mind in arguing a discrimination case of this type. It is unlikely that the holding of *Nutone* would be applied if the anti-union activity is engaged in by the employees themselves.

[10] Discrimination against Rival Unions

Similarly, an employer may not adopt or disparately enforce a no-solicitation/no-distribution rule that has the effect of protecting a company-dominated or incumbent union from rival union activity.[71] An employer has a responsibility to see that the rights

---

65 Hosiery Corp. of America v. NLRB, 422 F.2d 784 (4th Cir. 1970)("flower fund" for sick employees and discount purchase of product); Serv-Air, Inc., 395 F.2d 557 (10th Cir. 1968)(flowers for widows of deceased employees and one discussion with employees concerning payroll deductions for particular charity).

66 NLRB v. Stowe Spinning Co., 336 U.S. 226 (1949).

67 Trustees of Columbia Univ. in City of N.Y., 225 NLRB No. 9 (1976).

68 Rockwell Int'l Corp., 226 NLRB 130 (1976); ITT Semi-Conductor, Inc., 165 NLRB 716, *enforced without discussion,* 395 F.2d 257 (5th Cir. 1968); NLRB v. Electro Plastics Fabrics, Inc., 381 F.2d 374 (4th Cir. 1967); Murray Ohio Mfg. Co., 156 NLRB 840 (1966).

69 Standard Prods. Co., 159 NLRB 159 (1966); ATI Warehouse, Inc., 169 NLRB 580 (1968).

70 *See* discussion accompanying note 38, *supra.*

71 NLRB v. Link-Belt Co., 311 U.S. 584 (1941); Bonnell Co., Inc. v. NLRB, 405 F.2d 593 (5th Cir. 1969); NLRB v. Clark Bros., 163 F.2d 373 (2d Cir. 1947); Carter Carburetor Corp. v. NLRB, 140 F.2d 714 (8th Cir. 1944); Citizen News Co., 88 NLRB 1413 (1950).

of rival union adherents are protected against attacks by other employees.[72] However, an employer need not provide access for organizers, even if a rival group is soliciting, if the employer can show that it had no knowledge of the rival group's activities, and, hence, that there was no intent to discriminate.[73]

[11] Waiver of Organizational Rights by Union

The Supreme Court has held that employees have a right to distribute in support of their bargaining representatives on company property during nonwork time regardless of a collective bargaining agreement provision in which the union has agreed that no distribution will be made on its behalf.[74] The Court found that such a ban would interfere with employees' Section 7 rights, which cannot be waived by the union, and that the plant bulletin board does not provide an adequate alternative to distribution, since it does not give the union's adversaries equal access to communication.[75] The overriding consideration was that a contractual waiver would permit unions to stifle opposition to the union itself.[76]

In post-*Magnavox* decisions, the Board has held that unions are also precluded from bargaining away the right of employees to distribute any "organizational literature" that pertains to matters encompassed by Section 7 (as distinguished from literature concerning only the selection or rejection of the bargaining repre-

---

[72] Brewton Fashions, Inc. v. NLRB, 361 F.2d 8 (5th Cir. 1966), *cert. denied,* 385 U.S. 842 (1966).

[73] Holyoke Cinema Shops, Inc., 139 NLRB 1321, *remanded for further evidence sub nom.* Retail Clerks, Local 1441 v. NLRB, 326 F.2d 663 (D.C. Cir. 1963), *cert. denied, sub nom.* Clothing Workers v. Retail Clerks, Local 1441, 377 U.S. 981 (1964), *reaff'd on remand,* 155 NLRB 769 (1966).

[74] NLRB v. Magnavox, 415 U.S. 322 (1974).

[75] *See also* Section 1.08[14], *infra.*

[76] In a pre-*Magnavox* decision, the Board found that employees had engaged in protected, concerted activity when they distributed a newsletter protesting wages, working conditions, and inadequate representation by the union. The Board found the distribution to be a concerted effort for the purpose of seeking improvements in wages and working conditions and did not undermine the union, but rather sought to spur it to more effective representation. Samsonite Corp., 206 NLRB 343 (1973).

sentative). These decisions have been the most important for dissident workers. In *Yellow Cab, Inc.*,[77] leaflets urging other employees to attend a demonstration in support of workers striking against another employer were protected by Section 7 because they attempted to promote labor solidarity against union busting, even though the leaflet campaign was not supported by the union. In *Ford Motor Co.*,[78] the Board upheld the right of employees to distribute leaflets discussing, among other things, forced overtime and held that the union could not waive this right. It is significant to note that the leaflets in question discussed general economic and political conditions as well. The Board found that the presence of "social comment" does not detract from the leaflets' protection under Section 7, provided that *some portion of the material pertains to the particular employment.*[79] The Board broadened the rule in *Massey-Ferguson, Inc.*,[80] when it held that the union cannot waive the right of dissident members to distribute a leaflet criticizing the policies of the national union and explaining the impact of such policies on local membership; the Board found the distribution to be protected, concerted activity even though there was no reference made to the company or working conditions. The union and the employer cannot decide, in a collective bargaining agreement, that distribution rights will be limited to specified types of union-approved notices posted on the plant bulletin board.[81]

[12] Content of Literature

For both union literature and literature distributed by rank-

[77] 210 NLRB 568 (1974).

[78] 221 NLRB 99 (1975).

[79] *Id.*, slip opinion at 4, 7. While upholding distribution rights for a newsletter that discussed both working conditions and political propaganda, the Board did not support distribution rights for another newsletter devoted entirely to a discussion of the U.S. presidential election.

[80] 211 NLRB 487 (1974); *see also* McDonnell Douglas Corp., 210 NLRB 280 (1974) (leaflets dealing with internal union affairs fall within the protection of Section 7 and are therefore covered by *Magnavox*).

[81] Gen. Motors Corp. (Chevrolet Eng'r Center), 212 NLRB 133 (1974); Gen. Motors Corp., 211 NLRB 986 (1974).

and-file groups of other caucuses, committees, or individuals at the workplace, the content of the literature distributed determines whether it is protected under Section 7 of the Act. This requires a determination of whether the literature is for "mutual aid or protection" of employees. In a recent case, the Supreme Court upheld the NLRB's finding that distribution of a union newsletter urging employees to oppose incorporation of a state right-to-work law into a revised state constitution and criticizing a presidential veto of an increase in the federal minimum wage was protected.[82] The Court specifically rejected the employer's argument that "mutual aid or protection" applied only to the employment relationship at the work site. Mutual aid encompasses concerted activities in support of employees of employers other than those working for the employer in question.[83] The Court also held that the mutual aid clause protects employees from retaliation by their employers when they seek to improve working conditions by resort to administrative and judicial forums or by appeals to legislators to protect their interests as employees.

But not all literature is protected. For example, political campaign literature by candidates for public office has been held to be unprotected.[84] It is questionable whether communist political groups would have the right to distribute their newspapers or literature on employer premises.[85] Moreover, literature so inflammatory that it "threatens" disorder or other interruption of the functioning of the business would probably fall within the exception noted in *Republic Aviation* with respect to interference with discipline or production.[86] However, literature dealing with racial

---

[82] Eastex, Inc., v. NLRB, 437 U.S. 556, 98 LRRM 2717, U.S. Supreme Court (1978).

[83] *Id.,* at 227 n. B.

[84] Ford Motor Co., 221 NLRB 663 (1975), *enforced,* 546 F.2d 418 (3d Cir. 1976).

[85] Ford Motor Co. (Roughe Complex), 233 NLRB No. 102 (1977), decision of Administrative Law Judge, at VIII, (concession of General Counsel that distribution on employer's premises of literature urging participation in Revolutionary Communist Party celebration, and Party's newspaper, were unprotected).

[86] Eastex, *supra* note 14, at 2723 n.22. *See also* discussion by the General Counsel of the NLRB of the Board's refusal to issue a complaint in the discharge of a worker for refusal to remove literature of a "workers organization" from

discrimination in South Africa that refers to the effect of such discrimination on prices and employment is protected.[87]

[13] Other Union Activity

[a] Signs, Buttons, Union Cards

Asking, suggesting to, or ordering an employee not to wear a union button is unlawful.[88] A few cases have suggested that expression of displeasure over the wearing of buttons is insufficient without a threat of reprisal,[89] but these are not a majority. The cases are divided on whether an employer can bar the wearing of buttons where tension exists in the plant. In one case, in which the incumbent union threatened a walkout and violence, the Sixth Circuit nonetheless upheld the Board's finding that no exceptional circumstances justify a ban on buttons.[90] Another case found it lawful to ban "scab" buttons in order to maintain discipline.[91]

An employer may also ban buttons or signs that will tend to distract employees from work that requires precision or is dangerous;[92] it must be shown, however, that the ban is necessary.[93] It would be useful, therefore, if safety is asserted as the reason

---

the plant. The literature sought financial aid for the criminal defense of a worker at another plant who was charged with assaulting a Nazi employee at the other worker's plant. The leaflet attacked the Nazis and employer collaboration and called on workers to unite against the capitalists, 101 LRR 361.

87 W. Pac. Indus., 99 LRRM 1478.

88 NLRB v. Mayrath Co., 317 F.2d 424 (7th Cir. 1963); NLRB v. Essex Wire Corp., 245 F.2d 589 (9th Cir. 1957); Shelby Mfg. Co., 155 NLRB 464 (1965), *enforced on this issue,* 390 F.2d 595 (6th Cir. 1968); Crane Packing Co, 165 NLRB 1003 (1967).

89 NLRB v. Mallory & Co., Mallory Plastics Co. Div., 355 F.2d 509 (7th Cir. 1966).

90 Kimble Glass Co. v. NLRB, 230 F.2d 484 (6th Cir. 1956).

91 Caterpillar Tractor Co. v. NLRB, 230 F.2d 357 (7th Cir. 1956).

92 Fabri-Tek, Inc. v. NLRB., 352 F.2d 577 (8th Cir. 1965) (oversized, flashing buttons banned; more conventional buttons allowed); Clover Indus., Div. of GTI Corp., 188 NLRB 252 (1971) (large buttons banned for safety reasons).

93 Gray-Syracuse, Inc., 170 NLRB 1684 (1968)(employer failed to meet this burden).

for a ban on union buttons, to ascertain whether other types of jewelry or ornaments may be worn by employees who operate machinery.[94]

Employees may not be denied the right to carry union cards on company premises[95] or to wear union T-shirts.[96]

[b] No-Talk Rules

An employer may ban all talking about nonwork subjects during work time,[97] but it may not discriminatorily apply the rule against organizing discussions[98] and may not institute such a rule solely for the purpose of preventing such discussions.[99] Free discussion of union matters during nonwork time may not be banned.[100] Management may not promulgate rules banning criticism of company rules or policies.[101]

[c] Reading of Literature

It is unlawful to prohibit employees from reading organizational literature during nonwork time[102] or to threaten to pick up

94 *See, e.g.,* Portage Plastics Co., 163 NLRB 753 (1967).

95 Colonial Shirt Corp., 96 NLRB 711 (1951).

96 Devilbiss Co., 102 NLRB 1317 (1953).

97 Mylan-Sparta Co., Inc., 78 NLRB 1144 (1948).

98 Brennans, Inc., 147 NLRB 1545, *enforced on this issue,* 366 F.2d 560 (5th Cir. 1966); Witbeck dba Witbeck's IGA Supermarket, 155 NLRB 40, *enforced,* 382 F.2d 574 (6th Cir. 1967); Delta Finishing Co. (Div. of Stevens & Co.), 111 NLRB 659 (1955).

99 Am. Commercial Bank, 226 NLRB No. 182 (1976); NLRB v. Bendix Corp. (Research Laboratories Div.), 299 F.2d 308 (6th Cir. 1962); Nat'l Food Stores, Inc., t/a Big Bear Super Markets, 169 NLRB 94 (1968); Motorola, Inc., 163 NLRB 335 (1967).

100 W.J. Ruscoe Co., 166 NLRB 618, *enforced,* 406 F.2d 725 (6th Cir. 1969)(cannot ban union discussions because other workers object to them).

101 NLRB v. Lexington Chair Co., 361 F.2d 283 (4th Cir. 1968).

102 Plasticold Co., 168 NLRB 135 (1968)(ban on reading several minutes before lunch was unlawful because early start of break was customary and had been permitted in past by management).

or actually pick up literature left on tables.[103] In the absence of a posted rule against distribution, the employer may not seize literature left at unattended work stations.[104] While an employer may prohibit distribution in work areas, once the literature has come into the workers' hands, it may not be seized from them.[105]

[14] Organizers' Access to Plant Bulletin Boards

Section 7 of the LMRA has not been interpreted to provide employees with an absolute right to use employer bulletin boards to post union organizing information.[106] However, in court and NLRB decisions alike, discriminatory practices with respect to posting union notices on company bulletin boards used by employees have been found to violate Section 8(a)(1).[107] A company that generally allows the posting of noncompany matters cannot preclude the use of its bulletin boards for union information[108] or information relating to campaigns for union office.[109] Likewise, the company cannot allow anti-union materials to be posted while disallowing pro-union materials,[110] or suddenly enforce a written policy requiring permission for posting information if the policy has never before been followed.[111]

Employers also violate Section 8(a)(1), and possibly 8(A)(2), if they extend use of company bulletin boards to one union engaged in organizing efforts and deny this privilege to another union similarly engaged. Such favoritism is said to interfere with the employees' statutory right to organize freely.[112]

---

103 Hemco Corp., 194 NLRB 789 (1972).

104 Woolworth, Inc., 530 F.2d 1245 (5th Cir. 1976).

105 NLRB v. Elias Bros. Big Boy, Inc., 325 F.2d 360 (6th Cir. 1963).

106 Group One Broadcasting Co., 222 NLRB 160 (1975).

107 NLRB v. Challenge-Cook Bros., 374 F.2d 147 (6th Cir. 1967); Green Giant Co., 223 NLRB 371 (1976); Container Corp. of America, NLRB, 1979, 102 LRRM 1162, 244 NLRB 53.

108 NLRB v. Challenge-Cook Bros., *supra;* Group One Broadcasting Co., *supra.*

109 Timpte, Inc., 233 NLRB 162 (1977).

110 Green Giant Co., *supra.*

111 Vincent's Steak House, Inc., 216 NLRB 100 (1975).

112 NLRB v. Clark Phonograph Record Co., 176 F.2d 341 (3d Cir. 1949); Leboe Tire & Rubber Co., 208 NLRB 84 (1974); Hi-Temp., Inc., 204 NLRB 1098 (1973).

An employee who posts dissident literature and is consequently the subject of threats or retaliation by the employer may have an unfair labor practice charge against the employer.[113]

A union that removes from its bulletin board in the plant material posted by a dissident member criticizing the union's actions may be guilty of an unfair labor practice as well, the D.C. Circuit held,[114] reversing the Board's finding that there was no unfair labor practice.[115]

[15] Restrictions on Access by Off-Duty Employees

In the case of *Lenkurt,* the Board held that an employer's rule restricting access by off-duty employees may be valid in certain circumstances.[116] The no-access rule must be nondiscriminatory in applying to all off-duty employees for any purpose whatsoever and it must not be disparately applied against union or concerted activities. The rule of *Lenkurt* must be narrowly construed to prevent undue interference with the rights of employees. The no-access rule is valid only if it is limited to the "interior of plant and other work areas," is clearly disseminated to all employees, and restricts access by off-duty employees for any reason. A rule denying off-duty employees access to outside nonworking areas is not valid unless justified by business reasons.[117]

The case law establishing these strictures is as follows:

In *Lenkurt,*[118] the NLRB held that off-duty workers were more akin to nonemployees and therefore their off-duty organizing rights could be restricted in the same way as those of outside organizers are. Thus, an employer may promulgate a no-access rule if it is "non-discriminatory," i.e., if it denies off-duty em-

[113] Nugent Service (NLRB, 1973), 84 LRRM 1510. In this case, the Board found no violation in the discharge of an employee for posting "reform slate" literature after the employer had previously removed such literature. The Board stated that the prospect of "continual strife" limited the rights of employees to use bulletin boards in this situation.

[114] Helton v. NLRB, — F.2d — , 107 LRRM 2819 (D.C. Cir 1981).

[115] Teamsters Local 505 (Roadway Express)(NLRB, 1980), 103 LRRM 1318.

[116] GTE Lenkurt, 204 NLRB 921 (1974).

[117] Tri-County Medical Center, 222 NLRB 1089 (1976).

[118] *Supra* note 116.

ployees access for any purpose and is not disparately enforced against union organizers. If, however, there are no alternative means of communication available, under *Babcock & Wilcox,* access must be allowed.[119]

Subsequent cases have interpreted *Lenkurt* as establishing only the validity of a rule that prohibits access by off-duty employees to the plant itself and adjacent work areas, unless further restrictions are necessary to maintain production and discipline.[120] A no-access rule cannot be applied to employees who have completed their shift but are still on company property pursuant to the work relationship.[121] NLRB has also ruled that, unless it is justified by business reasons, a rule that denies off-duty employees entry to lots, gates, and other outdoor nonwork areas is invalid.[122]

The NLRB has distinguished these cases from *Lenkurt* on the grounds that the rule in that case was aimed at employees who enter or remain on the premises when not on duty or scheduled for work, while the rules held invalid in subsequent cases were aimed directly at solicitation by employees whose presence was work related or whose use of nonwork areas did not collide with any business interest of the employer. In the latter instances, the employer's rule infringed upon normal employee organizing rights during nonwork time. It may be argued that employees on layoff status have the same rights as do off-shift employees under *Tri-County Medical.*[123]

[16] Industry Exceptions

Certain exceptions to the general rules on solicitation and distribution have been carved out for retail stores and hospitals

[119] *Supra* note 25.

[120] Presbyterian Medical Center, 227 NLRB No. 135 (1977); Clear Lake Hospital, 223 NLRB 1 (1976); Tri-County Medical Center, 222 NLRB No. 174 (1976).

[121] East Bay Newspapers, Inc., d.b.a. Contra Costa Times, 225 NLRB No. 128 (1976); Bulova Watch Co., Inc., 200 NLRB 798 (1974).

[122] Tri-County Medical Center, *supra* note 120.

[123] This argument was adopted by an ALJ in Bethlehem Steel Corp., 19-CA-8087 and 8627.

because of the presence of the public on work areas in stores and special needs for a quiet, tranquil work area in hospitals.

[a] Retail Stores

A retail store may ban solicitation or distribution on its selling floor, even by employees on free time;[124] organizing rights during free time in nonselling and nonworking areas cannot be curtailed.[125]

[b] Health Care Institutions

An employer may limit solicitation and distribution, even during nonwork time, but only in patient care areas.[126] The distinction between patient care areas and patient access areas is all-important. Patient care areas definitely include operating rooms, patient rooms, and places where patients receive treatment, (e.g., X-ray and therapy).

A hospital may lawfully ban solicitation in corridors and sitting rooms on patient floors or on floors where operating or therapy rooms are located, but it may not ban solicitation in such places as the cafeteria, gift shop, and first floor lobbies.[127] Nor may the hospital ban solicitation and distribution in a cafeteria patronized by employees.[128]

While hospitals have requested that the Board broaden its "special circumstances" rule to encompass all public areas within the hospital, the Board has consistently refused to do so.[129]

---

124 Marshall Field & Co. v. NLRB, 200 F.2d 375 (7th Cir. 1952).

125 Montgomery Ward & Co. v. NLRB, 339 F.2d 889 (6th Cir. 1965); Montgomery Ward & Co. (Rome, N.Y.), 162 NLRB 369 (1967); Marshall Field & Co., *supra.*

126 St. John's Hosp. & School of Nursing, Inc., 222 NLRB No. 182 (1975); Baylor University Medical Center, 225 NLRB No. 102 (1976).

127 NLRB v. Baptist Hosp. 1979, 101 LRRM 2556.

128 Beth Israel Hosp. v. NLRB, 1978, 98 LRRM 2727.

129 Nat'l Jewish Hosp. & Research Center, 226 NLRB 195 (1976) (specialized nature of care given to ambulatory and asthmatic patients did not require a solicitation/distribution ban on all public areas); Lutheran Hosp. of Milwaukee,

A hospital may not ban the wearing of union buttons if the rule is adopted only after union activity begins or if the ban does not extend to other types of buttons.[130]

§ 1.09. Solicitation and Distribution—Rights of Outside Organizers

The key case in the law relating to nonemployee organizers is *NLRB v. Babcock & Wilcox,*[131] in which it was unanimously held that, although employee organizers must be allowed to solicit or distribute on plant premises, an employer may forbid outside organizers to enter its property for the purpose of solicitation and distribution unless the employees are otherwise inaccessible by reasonable means of communication. If they are, the employer's property rights must yield.

[1] Access to Parking Lots

The problems that *Babcock* presents for organizing efforts have been sharpened by subsequent interpretations as to what constitutes "reasonable attempts" by nonemployees to use alternative means of communication. In *Monogram Models, Inc.,*[132] the court rejected a proposed "big city rule" and held that the size of the city (Chicago) was not, in and of itself, determinative of the accessibility of the employees. The court denied access to company premises even though the union was able to show that organizing efforts were hampered by metropolitan traffic conditions once employees left the parking lot and that the union had been denied its request for a name and address list. In a subsequent case, the NLRB suggested that organizers stand outside the gate

---

Inc., 224 NLRB 36 (1976). *See also* General Counsel's Memorandum 79-76 (Oct. 5, 1979), *Guidelines for Handling No-Solicitation No-Distribution Rules in Health Care Facilities,* 102 LRRM 164.

130 Baptist Memorial Hospital, 225 NLRB 69 (1976)(United Fund buttons had been permitted in past); Ohio Masonic Home, 205 NLRB 357 (1973)(rule adopted after union activity began, discriminatory enforcement).

131 351 U.S. 105 (1956).

132 192 NLRB 705 (1971).

and try to catch license numbers as the workers drove past.[133] In *Scholle Chemical Corporation,*[134] outside organizers were allowed to contact employees in plant lots where employees could not otherwise be reached without trespassing on the private property of another factory.

The rule of *Babcock,* barring outside organizers from company premises, was extended to customer parking lots of retail stores, even though this area was open to the public.[135] On remand, the NLRB and the Eighth Circuit upheld the ban on solicitation by nonemployees, finding that reasonable alternative means of communication existed.[136]

The key to any challenge to an employer's ban on outside organizing is meeting the "reasonable alternatives" hurdle. As the cases indicate, the showing must be a strong one. The NLRB itself is divided on how great a showing must be made, although the conservative forces at this time comprise a majority.

[2] Entrances

Whether nonemployee organizers have a right to stand outside plant entrances depends initially on whether the entrance area is on the employer's property, e.g., walkways, driveways, etc. If the area is not privately owned, organizers may solicit or distribute literature. The general rule for property owned by the employer is controlled by *Babcock & Wilcox,*[137] i.e., nonemployee organizers will be barred from entrance areas unless there is no reasonable alternative for communicating with employees. The burden is upon the employer to establish that the area is, in fact, its property.[138] Entrance areas on the employer's property may also be used by outside organizers if it can be shown that such areas are open

[133] Falk Corp., 192 NLRB 716 (1971). *See also* Dexter Thread Mills, Inc., 199 NLRB 543 (1972).

[134] 192 NLRB 724 (1971).

[135] Cent. Hardware Co. v. NLRB, 407 U.S. 539, 92 S. Ct. 2238 (1972).

[136] Cent. Hardware Co. v. NLRB, 468 F.2d 252 (8th Cir. 1972).

[137] *Supra* note 131.

[138] Winett, Inc., 135 NLRB 1205, 1810 (1962).

to or generally accessible to the public.[139]

[3] Department Stores

Department stores can ban nonemployee organizers from all areas of the store; organizers must confine their activities to store entrances when employees are entering or leaving. This exclusion can cover not only public selling areas, elevators, escalators, and stairways, but also public nonselling areas (e.g., restrooms) and employee areas (e.g., employee restaurants).[140]

[4] Shopping Center Cases

In 1968, the Supreme Court held, on First Amendment grounds, that outside organizers could not be barred from picketing a store in a shopping center.[141] The basis of the decision was that the center served as the functional equivalent of a municipal business district, thus creating the requisite state action to impose First Amendment protection. However, in 1976, the Supreme Court overturned this decision and held that the First Amendment rights of picketing workers (employee and nonemployee) were superseded by the property rights of the owners of shopping center stores.[142] The case was remanded to the NLRB for consideration of whether the Wagner Act gave workers the right

---

139 Monogram Models, 170 NLRB No. 84 (1968) (organizers were standing on the shoulder of a road that intersected the entrance to the employer's private property and was subject to an easement for purposes of a public highway. *See* the discussion of First Amendment protection in relation to company towns in Section 1.09[6], *infra.*

140 May Dep't Store, 198 NLRB 491 (1972); Marshall Field & Co. v. NLRB, 200 F.2d 375 (7th Cir. 1952); Associated Dry Goods Corp., 103 NLRB 271 (1953); Goldblatt Bros., Inc., 77 NLRB 1262 (1953).

141 Food Employees Local 599 v. Logan Valley Plaza, Inc., 391 U.S. 308, 85 S. Ct. 1601, 20 L. Ed.2d 603 (1963).

142 Hudgens v. NLRB, 424 U.S. 507 (1976). *But see* Pruneyard Shopping Center v. Robins, — U.S. — (1980), No. 79-289, decided June 9, 1980, upholding the California Supreme Court's finding that the First Amendment to the California State Constitution is broader than the First Amendment to the U.S. Constitution and therefore protects leafletting in shopping centers.

to picket on shopping center premises even though the First Amendment did not. On remand, the NLRB so held.[143]

[5] Vacation Resort Cases

While it is thought by many that the law is more flexible concerning organizing of resort area employees, the cases actually indicate that only in extreme situations will the courts allow organizing rights precedence over property rights. Thus, in *S & H Grossinger,*[144] in which nearly two-thirds of the workers lived on the premises and left only irregularly and unpredictably, the court allowed access because employees were virtually insulated from efforts to reach them. One of the reasons for this holding was that the employer had been found guilty of other unfair labor practices. In a later case, the NLRB granted access, but the court reversed because most of the employees had to cross a public road to get to their living quarters and, the court reasoned, organizers could wait on this road to talk to workers.[145]

[6] Company Towns

While the right of outside organizers to distribute literature on an employer's private property is controlled by *Babcock & Wilcox,*[146] the question changes if that private property is used by the public in general. There then arises a First Amendment argument to the effect that company towns that are freely accessible to the public and are in fact used by the public may not be declared off limits to certain groups at the whim of the employer. The balance is struck between an employer's private property rights and the public's right to free speech; the more an owner

---

[143] 230 NLRB No. 113, 97 LRRM 1376. *See also* Giant Food Markets (NLRB 1979), 100 LRRM 1598.

[144] 156 NLRB 233 (1965), *enforced as modified,* 392 F.2d 26 (2d Cir. 1967).

[145] Kutsher's Hotel and Country Club, Inc., 427 F.2d 200 (2d Cir. 1970), *setting aside* 175 NLRB 1114 (1969). *See also* New Pines, Inc., 191 NLRB 144, *enforcement denied,* 468 F.2d 427 (2d Cir. 1972); Tamiment, Inc., 180 NLRB 1074, *enforcement denied,* 451 F.2d 794 (3d Cir. 1971).

[146] *Supra,* 351 U.S. 105 (1956).

opens up its property for use by the public in general, the more its property rights become circumscribed by the First Amendment.[147]

The debate generally centers on the question of whether the place in question is open to the public. For example, it has been held to be a violation of the LMRA for an employer to bar union organizers from distributing literature at the plant entrance if that entrance is subject to an easement for purposes of a public highway.[148] On the other hand, an industrial park on which an employer's plant was located was held to be private property not open to the public; thus, the employer could bar the distribution of literature by outside organizers in front of the entrance to the plant itself.[149]

In *Petersen v. Talisman Sugar Corp.*,[150] the Fifth Circuit held that a sugar company must grant union officials and religious workers access to Jamaican migrants in its labor camp. The court looked at a number of factors, including the fact that the camp handled municipal functions, such as fire protection and garbage collection. The camp had no public telephones, but it had its own post office. The workers could receive only emergency calls. The 38,000-acre labor camp was surrounded by canals and fences. Although employees were taken to the nearest town every other Saturday, the court held this to be insufficient access. The court found that the labor camp was more analogous to the traditional company town than was the shopping center in *Amalgamated Food Employees v. Logan Valley Plaza.*[151] While *Petersen* was decided under the Sugar Act and the Wagner-Peyser Act, the court noted that the same decision would have resulted under the NLRA. The court found that under the NLRA *NLRB v. Lake Superior Lumber Corp.*[152] would have been controlling. In the latter case, the court held that union organizers must be permitted on that employer's

[147] Marsh v. Alabama, 326 U.S. 501, 66 S. Ct. 276 (1946)(state may not impose criminal sanctions against a person who distributes religious literature on the sidewalk of a company-owned town, where the town was accessible to the public in general).

[148] Monogram Models, 170 NLRB 636.

[149] NLRB v. Solo Cup Co., 422 F.2d 1149 (7th Cir. 1970).

[150] 478 F.2d 73 (5th Cir. 1973).

[151] *Supra.*

[152] 167 F.2d 147 (6th Cir. 1946).

premises since the circumstances were such that without such access organizing efforts would be seriously handicapped. The court in *Petersen* nevertheless found that the constitutional questions in both cases were identical.

In *NLRB v. Stow Spinning*,[153] the Supreme Court held that an employer could not deny a union request to use the only available meeting hall in a company town if the employer's motive was to discourage organizing. The NLRB subsequently set a stricter standard, deciding that such denial was an unfair labor practice regardless of motive.[154]

[7] Use of Force against Outside Organizers

Physical assault against union organizers or union leaders by the employer, its supervisors, or any person acting as the employer's agent is a per se violation of the Act, since it constitutes direct interference with employee organizing rights.[155] In addition, an employer may not forcibly eject organizers from company property,[156] incite employees to attack them,[157] or otherwise intimidate them.[158] Responsibility will attach to the employer if it directs, authorizes, ratifies, or fails to intercede against such force when it is within its power to do so.[159]

[8] Creation of Right of Access to Company Property by Employer's Refusal of Right of Access to Bargaining Unit Names and Addresses

The "*Excelsior* Rule"[160] provides that within seven days after the

---

[153] 336 U.S. 266 (1949).

[154] Phillips Petroleum Co., 92 NLRB 1344 (1951).

[155] Spectator Sportswear, Inc., 1962 CCH NLRB 11,004, 49 LRRM 1684 (trial examiner's findings adopted in the absence of exceptions).

[156] Harlan Fuel Co., 8 NLRB 25 (1938).

[157] Drexel Furniture Co., 48 NLRB 683 (1943); E.A. Laboratories, Inc., 80 NLRB 625 (1948).

[158] NLRB v. Boswell Co., 136 F.2d 585 (9th Cir. 1943).

[159] NLRB v. Dorsey Trailers, Inc., 179 F.2d 589 (5th Cir. 1950); J.D. Jewell, 99 NLRB 61 (1952).

[160] Excelsior Underwear, Inc., 156 NLRB 1236 (1966); *see also* NLRB v. Wyman-Gordon Co., 394 U.S. 759 (1969).

Board has approved a consent-election agreement or directed an election, the employer must file an election eligibility list, which the Board then makes available to all parties. The problem is that this rule is of no help to organizers in getting authorization cards signed. However, refusal by management to provide a list is some evidence that the union has exhausted all means of communication other than allowing the union access to company property.[161] It is therefore essential that a request be made for such a list, even though it is not likely that it will be granted. In *Monogram Models, Inc.,*[162] one Board member dissented from the majority decision to deny the union access to parking lots, in part because of the employer's refusal to provide a name and address list. In *Tamiment, Inc.,*[163] the court denied access to company property on the ground that the union had not made sufficient effort to contact employees through alternative means. The majority seemed to be persuaded by the employer's assertion that if the union had asked for a name and address list the company would have provided one. While this is unlikely, the case illustrates how critical the request itself can be.

§ 1.10. Employer Retaliation

One of the major reasons the original NLRA was enacted was to prohibit employers from retaliating against workers for union or other concerted activity. Although Section 8(a)(1),(3) of the Act is specifically designed to provide protection against retaliation, enforcement of these subsections has had little noticeable impact on employers' practices. One of the reasons, of course, is the general problem of the length of time it takes for an aggrieved employee to obtain relief if the company decides to resist.[164]

161 *See* Babcock & Wilcox, *supra.*

162 192 NLRB 705 (1971).

163 180 NLRB 1074, *enforcement denied,* 451 F.2d 794 (3d Cir. 1971).

164 The labor relations policies of J.P. Stevens are a classic illustration of the ineffectiveness of Board enforcement. However, the Board is increasingly willing to seek Section 10(j) injunctions where there is a pattern of anti-union activity. *See* G.C. Irving's remarks at 102 LRR 205 and 253.

Another is that Section 8(a)(3) has been construed by the NLRB to require proof of three elements by the General Counsel: (1) union activity or employer suspicion thereof, (2) knowledge or suspicion by the employer of union organizing activity, and (3) an anti-union animus on the part of the employer. This is a heavy burden and thus effectively bars the common discharge involving union or dissident activity from NLRB relief.

The most common forms of employer retaliation are (1) threats by supervisors, (2) interrogation, (3) discharge, (4) demotions, transfers, and discipline, (5) retaliation for filing charges, and (6) discipline or discharge for alleged communist activities or Communist Party membership. In addition to retaliation, employers also use bribery, rewards, and promises.

[1] Threats by Supervisors

Supervisors are the employer's first line of defense against a unionization drive.[165] They are used to gather information and to discourage the average employee from signing the union authorization card. Despite various efforts by union-busting "professionals" to add some sophistication to supervisors' anti-union conduct, the common Section 8(a)(1) case involves anti-union threats of discharge or other retaliation by supervisors.

An employer is responsible for threats made to employees by supervisors even if it told the supervisors not to make such threats if employees are not made aware of this policy.[166] An employer may also be liable for threats made by rank-and-file employees to other employees if the threatened employees rea-

[165] *See, e.g.*, Hughes, The Supervisor's Handbook on Maintaining Non-Union Status (Executive Enterprises, Inc., 10 Columbus Circle, N.Y., N.Y. 10019). An advertisement for this book includes the following highly descriptive comment: "No one plays a more important part in maintaining the company's non-union status than first-line supervisors. They represent the company to their subordinates. They are the people employees look to for advice and guidance in their day-to-day work. And they are the people who can do the most to convince employees to vote "no" in a union representation election—or nip an organizing drive in the bud and make elections unnecessary."

[166] Neco Elec. Prods. Corp., 124 NLRB 481, 44 LRRM 1418 (1959); *aff'd on other grounds*, 289 F.2d 757, 46 LRRM 2534 (D.C. Cir. 1960).

sonably believe that the other employees are acting on behalf of the employer.[167] On the other hand, the NLRB has held that if coercive statements are made in letters sent to employees by another employee and there are no circumstances that would reasonably identify the employer with the statements, there is no unfair labor practice.[168] In other words, if a supervisor threatens an activist employee in the presence of other employees or makes other employees aware of the threat, then there may be a Section 8(a)(1) unfair labor practice. Employers also commonly make statements that can be construed as threats during union election campaigns. That question is treated elsewhere in this section.[169]

[2] Interrogation of Employees

Aside from threats, an employer may also resort to interrogating employees in order to gather intelligence about union organizing drives or union activity. Most commonly, these interrogations take place in the office or in some other situation where the employee is alone with the interrogator.

In *Blue Flash Express, Inc.*,[170] the NLRB held that interrogation is not per se unlawful if (1) its purpose is legitimate, (2) it is accompanied by assurances that no reprisals will be taken, and (3) it is not accompanied by other unfair labor practices. However, in response to a directive from the Court of Appeals for the District of Columbia Circuit, the NLRB revised the *Blue Flash* doctrine, holding that, absent unusual circumstances, interrogation or polling of employees is a violation of Section 8(a)(1) unless the following safeguards are observed: (1) The purpose of the poll is to determine the truth of a union's claim of majority; (2) this purpose is communicated to the employees; (3) assurances that no reprisals will be taken are given; (4) employees are polled by secret ballot; and (5) the employer has not committed unfair labor

[167] Int'l Ass'n of Machinists v. NLRB, 311 U.S. 72, 7 LRRM 282 (1940).

[168] Morganton Full Fashioned Hosiery Co., 107 NLRB 1534, 33 LRRM 1421 (1954).

[169] *See* Section 1.10[5].

[170] 109 NLRB 591 (1954).

practices or otherwise created a coercive atmosphere.[171]

Another circuit has suggested that the following questions should be asked to determine if the interrogation is illegal:

(1) Is there a history of employer hostility and discrimination?

(2) Did the interrogator appear to be seeking information on which to base taking action against an individual employee?

(3) Was the interrogation conducted by officials high in the company hierarchy?

(4) Was the employee called from work to the boss's office or otherwise questioned in an atmosphere of "unnatural formality"?

(5) Were the employees' replies evasive or untruthful, indicating that the interrogation actually inspired fear?[172]

[3] Discharge for Organizing Activities

It is a violation of Section 8(a)(3) for an employer to discipline or discharge an employee[173] for his or her organizing activities.[174] However, in order to establish a Section 8(a)(3) discharge case, the employee must show protected activity and knowledge and

[171] Operating Eng'rs, Local 49 v. NLRB (Struksnes Constr. Co.), 353 F.2d 852 (D.C. Cir. 1965). *But see* Gen. Mercantile & Hardware Co. v. NLRB, 461 F.2d 952 (8th Cir. 1972)(in the absence of anti-union animus, questioning of employees about their signing of authorization cards does not violate Section 8(a)(1) where no suggestion was made of reprisals or hostility toward the union). This decision represents a retreat back to *Blue Flash, supra* note 170.

[172] Bourne v. NLRB, 332 F.2d 47, 56 LRRM 2241 (2d Cir. 1964) (the court denied enforcement on the facts of the case). *See also* Sinclair Glass Co., 465 F.2d 209, 80 LRRM 3082 (7th Cir. 1972) (woman interrogated and threatened).

[173] Even a supervisor may in some circumstances be protected from discharge if the discharge is motivated by a desire to stifle employees' exercise of their rights. DRW Corp., 248 NLRB 95, and discussion at 103 LRR Analysis 61.

[174] Section 8(a)(3) reads: "It shall be an unfair labor practice for an employer by discrimination in regard to hire or tenure of employment or any term or condition of employment to encourage or discourage membership in any labor organization . . ." This general prohibition is, however, qualified by an exception for closed-shop agreements.

animus on the part of the employer. These requirements place an extremely heavy burden on the charging party.

If the employer's conduct has an inherent tendency to discourage (or encourage) such activities, the question of whether such an effect actually occurs is irrelevant. It is unnecessary to prove intent by independent evidence; the employer is presumed to have intended the reasonably forseeable consequences of its acts.[175] One must, however, prove that the employer had knowledge of the employee's activities, although such knowledge will be implied in a proper case.[176] Knowledge may be inferred in a small plant situation where everyone knows everyone else's business.

It is rare, of course, that an employer will admit that a worker was discharged because of union activities. It is generally easy to find some pretext for firing someone, since few people have perfect work records. Whether a discharge is lawful or is retaliatory, with the alleged lawful reason a pretext, is a question of fact, and the NLRB will look at such things as timing, differences in treatment of other workers for similar offenses, the nature of the alleged employee infraction, and the totality of the circumstances.[177]

Questions about the discharge that may yield answers supporting the argument that the alleged reasons were pretexts include the following:

(1) Did the employer refuse to give the discharged employee a reason for the discharge?

---

[175] Radio Officers' Union v. NLRB, 347 U.S. 17 (1953); NLRB v. G & J Co., 346 F.2d 960 (3d Cir. 1965).

[176] The practitioner can be most useful, in some cases, where he or she can advise the activist or dissident before the discipline occurs. For instance, it is sometimes good practice to send management copies of leaflets containing the name of the caucus or union trying to organize, plus the names of some of the employee activists who are most vulnerable to discipline or discharge. If a clear record of this communication is kept (e.g., certified mail), it will be difficult for the employer to deny knowledge of the activity.

[177] Penn Traffic Co., Riverside Div., 218 NLRB No. 54 (1975); Classic Prods. Corp., 226 NLRB No. 14 (1976); St. Anne's Home, Div. of DePaul Community Health Center, 221 NLRB No. 131 (1975); Fort Lock Corp., Inc., 216 NLRB No. 31 (1975).

(2) Did the employer's explanation of the discharge vary?
(3) Do facts support the employer's stated reason for the discharge?
(4) Are employees still on the payroll whose job performance is deficient in much the same manner as was that of the discharged employee?
(5) Did the employer tolerate the shortcomings reportedly underlying the discharge before the union activity began?
(6) Was the discharged employee forewarned that his or her job was in jeopardy?
(7) Did the discharged employee have a previously satisfactory work record?
(8) Was the discharge effected in accordance with established procedures?
(9) Did the discharged employee's misconduct warrant the drastic action of discharge?
(10) Did the discharged employee's immediate supervisor participate in the decision to discharge?
(11) Was turnover of employees before organizational activity began relatively small, as compared with the turnover after such activities began?

Other discharges may reflect dual motivations for discharge, i.e., both anti-union animus and a valid reason for discipline. The Board has recently adopted a new test for "dual motive" cases. Using an analysis similar to that of the U.S. Supreme Court in *Mt. Health City School District v. Doyle* (429 U.S. 274), the Board states the test as follows: (1) The General Counsel must make a prima facie showing sufficient to support the inference that protected activity was a "motivating factor" in the employer's decision. (2) The employer then has the burden of demonstrating that the same action would have taken place even in the absence of the protected conduct.[178] The Board previously followed an "in part" test.[179] Several circuits have followed the *Wright Line* test, although the circuits were divided before the adoption of *Wright Line* by the

[178] Wright Line, 251 NLRB No. 150, 105 LRRM 1169 (1980). *See also* NLRB General Counsel Memorandum 80-58, 11/4/80.

[179] The Youngstown Osteopathic Hospital Ass'n, 224 NLRB 574 (1976).

Board.[180]

It may be desirable to avoid the application of the *Wright Line* test. This may be possible by arguing that the case in question is a pretext case and not a dual motive case, although the General Counsel of the NLRB does not recognize this distinction. There is no Supreme Court case on dual motivation, although similar issues have arisen in other contexts.[181]

[4] Demotions, Transfers, and Discipline

Section 8(a)(3) forbids discrimination in any "*term or condition* of employment in order to encourage or discourage membership in a labor organization." It thus covers all aspects of the work relation and requires similarity in treatment among all employees or applicants[182] affected by the "term or condition" involved. Retaliatory action held to fall without the proscription includes demotions, transfers, exclusion from bonus or insurance programs, denial of credit from company sources, assignment to more arduous work, denial of overtime work, and imposition of overtime.[183] It is also an unfair labor practice to discipline or discharge a steward for soliciting grievances from other employees or to transfer or otherwise discriminate against a worker for complaining about working conditions.[184]

These forms of discrimination merely illustrate the scope of

---

[180] Statler Industries v. NLRB, 644 F.2d 902 (1st Cir. 1981); Peavey Co. v. NLRB, 648 F.2d 460 (7th Cir. 1981); NLRB v. Charles Batchelder Co., 106 LRRM 3050 (2d Cir. 1981); NLRB v. Lloyd Fry Roofing Co., No. 78-1537 (6th Cir. June 10, 1981); NLRB v. Nevis Industries, No. 80-7131 (9th Cir. June 8, 1981).

[181] Mount Healthy City School Bd. of Educ. v. Doyle, 429 U.S. 274 (1977)(First Amendment violation alleged in discharge of school employee); Village of Arlington Heights v. Metropolitan Dev. Corp., 429 U.S. 252 (1977)(Fair Housing Act of 1968 and Equal Protection clause); Board of Trustees at Keen State College v. Sweeney, 439 U.S. 24, 18 FEP cases 520 (1978).

[182] Phelps Dodge Corp. v. NLRB, 313 U.S. 127 (1941).

[183] Ross Sand Co., Inc., 219 NLRB No. 110 (1975); Fla. Drum Co., Inc., 213 NLRB No. 95 (1974); Fox & Jacobs, Inc., 221 NLRB No. 187 (1975); U.S. Plastics Corp., 213 NLRB No. 42 (1974); Davidson-Kennedy Co., 221 NLRB No. 41 (1975); Ford Motor Co., 221 NLRB No. 99 (1975).

[184] Ford Motor Co., *supra* note 183.

the protection available. There is no definitive catalogue; the protection of Section 8(a)(3) extends to all terms and conditions.

It should also be noted that the Act forbids discrimination in regard to "hire."[185] Students of labor history will know that this section was intended to do away with the notorious "yellow dog contract," which required a promise not to join a union as a term and condition of employment.[186] While this section is not as relevant today, it still can be used if activists are blacklisted or otherwise discriminated against.[187]

[5] Retaliation for Filing Charges

It is violative of Section 8(a)(4) for an employer or its agent to discharge or otherwise discriminate against an employee for filing charges with the NLRB or for giving testimony before the NLRB.[188] An employee who makes informal statements to NLRB investigators is also protected.[189] The truth or falsity of the statement does not affect the protection.[190] One must, however, prove that the employer's motives were discriminatory.[191] Again, the NLRB will look at all the surrounding circumstances, including timing of the discharge or discipline, the employee's work record, and other unfair labor practice charges against the employer. It might be noted in passing that the statements given to the NLRB by employees are not subject to prehearing discovery by the employer by means of the federal Freedom of Information Act.[192]

---

185 Section 8(a)(3), *supra* note 174.

186 *See generally,* Boyer & Morais, Labor's Untold Story (1955).

187 *See, e.g.,* NLRB v. J.P. Stevens, 96 LRRM 2150.

188 NLRB v. Lester Bros., Inc., 337 F.2d 706 (4th Cir. 1964); NLRB v. Gibbs Corp., 308 F.2d 247 (5th Cir. 1962); M & S Steel Co., 148 NLRB 789 (1964); Royal Norton Mfg. Co., 189 NLRB 489, 77 LRRM 1022 (1971).

189 NLRB v. Scrivener d.b.a. A.A. Elec. Co., 67 L.C. 12 (U.S. Sup. Ct. 1972).

190 Kramer Co., 29 NLRB 921 (1941).

191 Bilton Insulation, Inc. v. NLRB, 303 F.2d 98 (4th Cir. 1962); Fitzgerald Mills Corp., 139 NLRB 802 (1962).

192 Wellman Indus., Inc. v. NLRB, 490 F.2d 427 (4th Cir. 1974). It is also an unfair labor practice for an employer to request a copy of the employee's statement to the NLRB; *see* NLRB v. Maxwell, 106 LRRM 2387 (9th Cir. 1981). *See also* NLRB General Counsel, *FOIA Guidelines in Closed Cases,* Memorandum 79-6, 100 LRR 122.

[6] Conclusion

As with most questions that involve the NLRB, the major lesson of this section is that, although protection against employer retaliation for union activity exists, that protection can be too little and too late. The discharged activist can expect a two- to three-year wait before prevailing. Many employers know this and are willing to risk substantial back pay awards and legal fees in order to preserve their nonunion status. It is left to the ingenuity of the people reading this text to protect the activist in spite of these obstacles.

§ 1.11. Protecting Undocumented Workers' Right to Organize[193]

With the increasing number of undocumented workers entering the United States in search of jobs, the legal system has had to confront the question of the union rights of the undocumented. The legal response, while positive in some regards, is limited in its ability to provide full relief to the victims of unfair labor practices, because of the continuing deportability of the workers here without authorization. This continuing jeopardy of the undocumented flows from the restrictive immigration laws, especially as they apply to immigrants from Mexico and other Latin American countries.

Until recently, most unions either took a hostile attitude toward the undocumented, viewing them as difficult to organize or as a class of potential strikebreakers, or ignored the problems of the undocumented workers. The masses of undocumented workers who have been driven to this country to seek work have forced many unions to reevaluate their positions. A number have actively taken on the organizing of the undocumented. Among these are locals of the International Ladies Garment Workers Union (ILGWU), United Auto Workers (UAW), United Electrical Workers Union (UE), International Longshoremen and Warehousemen's Union (ILWU), United Steel Workers of America (USWA), and Teamsters (IBT). This positive development re-

193 Reprinted in full from 9(6) Immigration Newsletter 1 (1980).

flects an understanding of the need for unity among all workers, documented or not, in order to improve working conditions. As unions strive to organize the undocumented, the NLRB has had to confront the special legal status of the undocumented.

In one of the first cases involving the labor law rights of undocumented workers, the Board rejected the employer's claim that the union had lost its majority as a result of the deportation of several undocumented workers. Following a union election, the standard NLRB procedure is to certify the successful union as the collective bargaining representative. Absent unusual circumstances, this certification is valid for one year before the Board will consider a decertification petition. In this case, the Board held that the one-year certification bar still applied and refused to find the deportation of several workers to be such an unusual circumstance as to negate the bar.[194]

The NLRB's order was enforced by the Seventh Circuit, which held that there was no conflict between the Board's decision and the Immigration and Naturalization Act (INA), since the INA does not prohibit employers from hiring undocumented workers, nor does it prohibit workers from voting in union elections under the LMRA. Further, declining to certify the unit would encourage violations of the INA, since employers would be encouraged to hire undocumented workers in order to avoid unionization.[195]

In a subsequent case, the same employer objected to the certification of the bargaining unit that contained undocumented workers. The day following the dismissal of the employer's objections, the employer called the INS to investigate the employees whom the employer knew to be undocumented. Five employees were subsequently deported as a result of this investigation. The NLRB found violations of Section 8(a)(1) in the employer's asking the employees about their immigration status after they had selected the union as their representative and of Section 8(a)(1) and (3) in its calling the INS to report the workers, since its motive was to discourage union activities. The Board noted that it would not be a violation to call the INS about undocumented workers where the employer was not shown to be motivated by

---

[194] Sure-Tan, Inc., 231 NLRB 138 (1977).

[195] NLRB v. Sure-Tan, Inc., 583 F.2d 355 (7th Cir. 1978), *case notes in* 10 Rutgers Camden L.J. 747 (1979) and 14 Tex. Int'l L.J. 317 (1979).

anti-union animus. This caveat is an important one, since motive is always difficult to prove in unfair labor practice cases.[196]

Sure-Tan II arose on the motion of the NLRB General Counsel for clarification of the Board's ruling in *Sure-Tan I.* The General Counsel suggested that the remedy for the discharged workers be considerably more limited than the usual remedy for discharged workers. He suggested that the reinstatement offer extend *only* to those discriminatees who were able to reenter the United States *lawfully* and that back pay accrue only from the time the *lawfully* returned discriminatee was denied employment after his or her return. Thus, the only remedy in cases such as these would be a virtually meaningless "cease and desist" order. Fortunately, the Board rejected this limited view of the remedy and ordered reinstatement and full back pay. The effectiveness of this remedy obviously turns on the ability of the workers to get themselves back into the country somehow and make themselves available for work.

Practically, the General Counsel's limited view of the scope of the Board's remedy suggests the need for undocumented workers who are charging parties to be represented by independent or union counsel at the NLRB proceedings in order to seek the broadest remedies. The NLRB attorney may otherwise follow the narrow approach of the General Counsel in his/her arguments to the Administrative Law Judge.

The status of undocumented workers as "employees" within the meaning of the LMRA was also the subject of a Ninth Circuit case, in which the court agreed with the majority in *Sure-Tan* that the Board's interpretation of "employee" best furthers the policies of the immigration laws. The court also considered the possible conflict of the Board's remedies with state laws prohibiting the employment of undocumented workers.[197]

This employer raised the argument, against the reinstatement order, that it was prohibited from employing undocumented workers by Section 2805(a) of the California Labor Code, which had been found not to be preempted by the INA in *Decanas v.*

---

[196] Sure-Tan Inc., 246 NLRB No. 134 (1979) (hereinafter Sure-Tan II).

[197] NLRB v. Apollo Tire Co., 604 F.2d 1180 (9th Cir. 1979), *for a critical case note, see* Illegal Aliens as Employees under the NLRA, 68 Geo. L.J. 851 (1980).

Bica.[198]

The Ninth Circuit rejected this argument, saying that there had not yet been definitive decisions by the California courts on whether administrative regulations would allow Section 2805(a) to be construed so as not to conflict with the INA.

Approximately a dozen states have laws similar to the California one. The relationship of these laws to the INA and NLRB remedies remains to be seen. Of note is that many unions supported laws prohibiting the hiring of the undocumented. It is, however, generally agreed that the laws have proved ineffective because of the difficulty of proving employer intent. It would be ironic for the unions if these same ineffective laws were most effective in denying adequate relief to undocumented workers discharged by employers for engaging in union activities.

In addition to the limitation inherent in the Board's inability to order the INS to admit the undocumented workers into the country with permission to work, the Board's computation and orders of payment of back pay are limited by the restrictive immigration laws. In *Sure-Tan II,* the NLRB described how back pay should be computed in cases of undocumented workers. The back pay period is to run from the discriminatory loss of employment to the bona fide reinstatement offer. Discriminatees located but found to be unavailable for work (e.g., those unable to reenter the country) will have their back pay tolled accordingly. If the worker cannot be found, the back pay is returned to the employer after two years.

Obviously this remedy benefits the employer guilty of misconduct if its workers cannot get back into the country or cannot be located. It may be anticipated that many undocumented workers would choose not to return to their former employer, where they would be under the constant threat of deportation. The employer would only need to wait for some time after reinstatement and then make an anonymous tip to the INS about this worker effectively to avoid an NLRB finding of an unfair labor practice.

Besides the cases described above, which dealt with whether undocumented workers are "employees" and what kinds of remedies should apply where they are unfairly discharged, the Board has recently considered the question of whether undocu-

---

198 424 U.S. 351 (1976).

mented workers may appropriately be considered outside of an appropriate bargaining unit. Once a representation petition has been filed with the NLRB, the Board must decide what "an appropriate bargaining unit" is, assuming that the parties cannot agree. In *Duke City Lumber Co.,*[199] the Board held that a unit that excluded undocumented workers was not "an appropriate unit."

The issue of the impact on union elections of threats to report undocumented workers to INS has been considered in a number of cases. These cases turn on the totality of the circumstances in a determination of whether there was an influence on the "laboratory conditions" desired by the Board, whether the threats were made by someone who was an agent for one of the parties, and whether the threats were repudiated.[200]

While these cases begin to spell out the right of undocumented workers to participate in unions, other laws may be used to blunt employer efforts to destroy union organizing campaigns. A good example is the case of the Sbicca Shoe Workers in Los Angeles.[201] The Retail Clerks Union Local 1428 lost a union election by 10 votes out of 700 and filed unfair labor practice charges. The next day the INS attempted to deport 120 of the voters. The union was able to obtain a temporary restraining order to stall the deportations, asserting violations of the U.S. Constitution and the INA. Not only was the litigation able temporarily to prevent deportations, but, according to attorney Peter Schey, "the results indicate that when required to follow congressionally mandated procedures, INS cannot establish the deportability of approximately 50% of the persons they take into detention."[202] The action filed in that case was predicated on coerced confessions and violation of the right to remain silent.

A recently certified national class action involving similar is-

---

199 251 NLRB 12, 104 LRRM 1515 (1980).

200 *See* NLRB v. Miramar of Cal., Inc., 102 LRRM 2241 (9th Cir. 1979); Teamsters Local 748, 246 NLRB 121, 103 LRRM (1979); Information Magnetics Corp., 227 NLRB 1493 (1977); Mike Yurosek & Son, 225 NLRB 148 (1976), *enforced,* 597 F.2d 661 (9th Cir. 1979); Professional Research, Inc., 218 NLRB 96 (1975).

201 *See also* Vallejo v. Sureck (U.S.D.C. Cal. 1978).

202 *See* Bowman, *Sbicca Workers Winning,* 7 NLG Immigration Newsletter No. 4 at 5.

sues may provide protection to workers facing deportation. The class includes

> all persons arrested by the INS subsequent to May 16, 1978 who following arrest have been or may be subject to custodial interrogation by INS agents (i) without first being notified of their right to legal representation, or (ii) without first being advised that statements they make can be used against them in administrative and criminal proceedings, or (iii) without being provided access to available counsel of their choice.[203]

If injunctive relief is obtained in this case, undocumented workers around the country may be able to make use of the order to prevent their deportation until the case is resolved. Counsel for the class is the National Center for Immigrant Rights.[204]

Denial of the right to counsel before interrogation, or persuading the undocumented workers to accept voluntary departure, is a persistent practice of the INS. The lack of authority for a valid search of a workplace for undocumented workers is another abuse.[205] Legal and constitutional violations inherent in the INS workplace raids, or "area control operations," have been thoroughly described.[206] These violations may provide the basis for litigation stalling the deportation of members of a bargaining unit. It may also be possible to obtain an injunction preventing deportation until after a union representation election if a petition for representation has been filed.

Fear of employer retaliation or report to the INS leads many undocumented workers to accept minimum wage or occupational health and safety violations or employment discrimination. The magnitude of the exploitation is suggested by a 1980 Department of Labor study reporting $15 million in underpayments to 94,000 undocumented workers in the first half of fiscal 1980. In New York City alone, 35 percent of the 500 shops surveyed were violating the minimum wage laws.

The agencies enforcing those laws have yet to develop effective

---

203 Vallejo et al. v. INS, No. CV 78-1912 WMB, U.S.D.C., C.D. Cal.

204 1550 West 8th Street, Los Angeles, Cal. 90017; (213) 487-2531.

205 *See* Blackie's House of Beef, Inc. v. Castillo, 467 F. Supp. 170 (D.D.C. 1978).

206 U.S. Commission on Civil Rights, The Tarnished Golden Door, 79-95.

means of enforcing them where the victims of the violations are undocumented. Some have made some efforts. The Department of Labor Wage and Hour Division has set up strike forces in a number of major cities to target industries known to employ undocumented workers, but without strong protection for undocumented workers who assist the agencies, they will generally be unwilling to testify.

In the long run, the most effective protection that the undocumented will have in this society is to build strong and militant unions that can stop employment discrimination, stop safety violations, and obtain decent wages.

A union can also negotiate special clauses in collective bargaining agreements to meet the needs of the undocumented. The ILGWU in Los Angeles has negotiated clauses requiring the employer to deny the INS access to its shop unless the INS has a valid search warrant and notifies the union immediately. Another clause gives a worker one week to deal with problems arising from his or her immigration status. This might include time spent at hearings or in getting back into the United States after "voluntary departure." See Appendix 1A below.

In order to minimize the enforcement problems of labor and protective legislation, as well as to eliminate a major division within the working class, a broad amnesty for the undocumented would be in the interest of trade unions. The limited amnesty proposed by some would be inadequate, since many undocumented workers would be outside its scope and would continue to have limited protections in law. Many would continue to be fearful of concerted activity for fear of deportation. Anything short of a broad amnesty will see undocumented workers continuing to be exploited with poor wages and bad working conditions.

Appendix 1A. Sample Clauses from ILGWU Union and Hollander, Inc., Contract

ARTICLE XIX: IMMIGRATION AND NATURALIZATION SERVICE

The Union recognizes its obligation as the representative of the employees, irrespective of their National Origin or Resident Status.

As representative of the employees, the International Ladies' Garment Worker's Union will take all necessary action to protect these employees against:

a. Invasion of their rights;

b. Unreasonable search and seizure;

c. Harassment and annoyances that result when Immigration agents are permitted on company premises without a legal and constitutional right.

Pursuant to the collective bargaining agreement the employer shall:

a. Notify the Union immediately, or as soon as practical, in the event any I.N.S. agent is seen at or near the company premises.

b. Refuse admittance to any agents of I.N.S. who do not possess a valid warrant, exigent circumstances the exception.

c. Notify the Union and the shop steward as soon as possible, to enable an authorized representative or attorney for the Union to take steps to protect the rights of its members.

d. If the Immigration and Naturalization Service produces a valid search and/or arrest warrant, then as soon as possible the Employer agrees to give telephone notice to the I.L.G.W.U. and oral notice to the authorized shop steward of the search and/or arrests.

e. The Employer agrees not to reveal any names, addresses or immigration status of any employees unless required to do so by law.

f. The Employer agrees to reinstate any employee who has been absent due to I.N.S. proceedings and who has returned to work within seven (7) days of the start of that absence, or has requested an extension of time to report within that same seven (7) day period. Such extension shall be at the sole discretion of the Employer.

ARTICLE XX: EMPLOYEE RECORD CHANGE

The Employer shall recognize any worker for the purpose of continous service who during his or her employment has legally undergone a change of name, sex, social security number or identity, who to the satisfaction of the Employer is the same person as prior to the change.

ARTICLE XXI: HOLD HARMLESS

It is understood that neither Article XIX or XX shall require the Employer to violate the law, abridge his legal responsibilities, or circumvent any ordinances or laws.

CHAPTER 2

Opposing Discriminatory Discharges

It is important to understand that in our society a working person may be discharged by his/her employer for "good reason, bad reason, or no reason at all" (to cite an oft-quoted phrase), unless there is some affirmative bar to the discharge. Such obstacles to the unfettered will of the employer occur primarily in two forms: (1) statutes and other legal prohibitions (federal and state) that cover the employer in question and state specific grounds upon which an employee may not be discharged and (2) contracts (labor union or individual).

The single most important statutory protection for those involved in workplace organizing is the National Labor Relations Act (NLRA), which, at least on its face, bars discrimination, including discharge, against workers involved in organizing and other activity. There are also, of course, a variety of other federal statutes that prohibit discrimination (including discharge) against employees on the basis of race, sex, national origin, religion, age, and, to a limited extent, handicapped status, veteran status, etc. In addition, many states have state labor relations acts covering employees not within the jurisdiction of the NLRA, public employee relations acts covering state and municipal employees, and state antidiscrimination laws paralleling, to some extent, the federal laws described above.

Of equal, if not greater, import is the job security provided by a contract. Occasionally, one will be confronted with an ex-employee who has an individual employment contract, oral or written. This chapter will not be concentrating on such a situation, which can often be pursued through a normal state court breach of contract action. Much more frequent is the case of the organized worker who is working under a union contract. Most of these contracts specify both the disciplinary procedure through and the grounds upon which an employee may be discharged and usually contain a general ground for discharge as well, such as allowing discharge for "good cause" or "just cause" only. This can be the most important protection afforded to the discharged employee and the most important remedy to pursue.

For that employee totally without any statutory or contractual protection, there is a growing (though still not very significant in scope) body of state court decisions creating what has been called the new tort of abusive discharge. Put simply, the thread running through these cases is that the law will not permit the discharge of an otherwise unprotected employee if the grounds for such discharge offend public policy.

This chapter cannot provide an in-depth treatment of the remedies described above. The intention herein, then, will be to provide a tactical overview of the factors to be considered by the practitioner in shaping the discharge remedy, in-depth treatment of the two most important remedies (the protections of the NLRA and the union contract), and a brief survey of other federal statutory remedies. Finally, this chapter will take a brief excursion into the world of abusive discharge, a world in which the unbridled power of the boss to fire an employee at will is vanquished by the power of public policy.

§ 2.01. Shaping the Discharge Case

In order to shape the most effective legal strategy for combating the discharge, the practitioner must know what factors to consider and what questions to ask from the moment that contact with the client is established. Some factors should be clarified the moment the call comes in; others, during the interview and investigation. The intent of this section is to provide an overview and checklist of items to be considered in shaping the ultimate strategy. It is probably best to pursue these factors in a chronological fashion.

[1] Initial Client Contact

There are a few things to clarify with your client during the initial phone call:

[a] Date of Discharge

Every remedy herein has a statute of limitations. Some of these, particularly union contract requirements, can be extremely short (with only two or three days from the date of the discharge in which the initial grievance must be filed), so it may be necessary to move very quickly in order to prevent the loss of a possible remedy.

[b] Union Relationship

As mentioned above, it is imperative to find out immediately if there is a union contract, which remedies exist under it, and what is necessary to protect them. Generally, union contracts will specify both specific and general grounds for discharge, as well as the workings of the grievance/arbitration machinery to be utilized in pursuing the discharge complaint. Often, the union must file a grievance very quickly in order to protect the client's rights. While many unions are quite conscientious about such matters, it is wise to be scrupulous in seeing that your client's rights are protected, particularly if he/she is either a union reformer or someone controversial with the responsible officials. Thus, the client should be advised to demand immediately that the union file the grievance and get the process in motion. A certified, return-receipt letter to the union is a good idea, if time allows.

[c] Arranging the Interview

Finally, of course, set up a serious interview time. The client should be encouraged to bring every scrap of material possibly relevant to the employment and discharge. This would include the discharge letter, work evaluations, work rules, leaflets for workplace activities in which the employee participated, union publications, lists of the names and addresses of potential witnesses, and, if one exists, the union contract. Each employee has the right to be furnished a copy of the contract by the union pursuant to the Landrum-Griffin Act.[1]

[1] 29 U.S.C. § 414.

[2] During the Interview and Investigation

Now that there is a little more time, the following things need to be known in order to develop the strategy for fighting the discharge:

[a] Employer's Litigation History and Disciplinary Patterns

It is very important to "know the beast," as it were. While most employers will vigorously contest opposition to a discharge, there are significant differences in the strategies of different employers. Prior litigation may have made the employer vulnerable or hard-line against various strategies. Further, the disciplinary pattern can be very helpful in evaluating whether the client has been the victim of differential treatment.

[b] Employee's Job Description and Duties

Understanding the client's particular job function and what has been traditionally expected of him/her is helpful in evaluating the circumstances of the discharge.

[c] Employee's Work History and Length of Service

Employees with long, solid work histories are more likely to be given the benefit of the doubt by an arbitrator or judge. Know about any prior discipline. If you do not, the employer will be sure to introduce it at the appropriate time.

[d] Events Leading Up to the Discharge

What happened? How did it happen? Who did what? Who witnessed it?

[e] Employer's Stated Reason for the Discharge

What is the employer's explanation of what happened? What is its proof?

[f] Employee's Perceived Reason for the Discharge

Depending on the sophistication of the worker, the client can be the best source of information as to why the discharge really occurred.

[g] Events after the Discharge

Sometimes, after the actual discharge, forepeople or other employer representatives may make statements to other employees or take actions that evidence their satisfaction in the discharge of your client. Do not stop the investigation at the point when they walk your client out the door.

[h] Employee's In-Plant Activities

Know your client. Is he/she a strong union advocate? A shop steward? A union reformer? A fighter against racism or sexism on the floor? Obviously, what you are looking for is a motive for the firing—something that causes your client to be discriminated against and that also is protected by law or contract.

[i] Employee's Personal Characteristics

Even if your client did not engage in protected activity, his/her race, sex, religion, national origin, or age may place him/her in a class protected against discriminatory treatment.

[j] The Contract

Determine with certainty whether a contract exists, how to enforce it, etc.

[k] Proof

Obviously, as in any litigation, the kind of proof available to establish your version of events must be constantly considered. One particularly advantageous method of developing proof, as well as of forcing the employer to commit itself to its version of the discharge, is the unemployment insurance case. The client should be advised to file immediately for unemployment. Besides the obvious benefit of producing some immediate income for the client, the hearing that occurs if the employer contests the award can be an excellent place to examine company witnesses under oath, test your theory of the case (to the extent it is tactically wise to do so), etc.

[3] Juggling the Remedies

At this point in the investigation, it is important to keep in mind a broad overview of the potential remedies. Thus, you will be honing in and developing your proof with one or more of the following possible remedies in mind.

[a] If There Is a Union Contract

Use the grievance/arbitration procedure. If the union fails properly to represent your client's case in part, or refuses to do so at all, consider a duty of fair representation suit.

Bring a charge before the National Labor Relations Board (NLRB) that the discharge was taken with the purpose of encouraging or discouraging membership in any labor organization in violation of Section 8(a)(3) of the NLRA.

[b] Whether or Not There Is a Union Contract

Bring a charge before the NLRB that the discharge was taken (1) in retaliation for the exercise of rights guaranteed in Section 7 of the NLRA, i.e., activities for the purpose of mutual aid or protection (a violation of Section 8(a)(1) of the NLRA), (2) to discourage or encourage membership in any labor organization (a violation of Section 8(a)(3) of the NLRA), or (3) in retaliation for filing charges with or giving evidence to the NLRB (a violation of Section 8(a)(4) of the NLRA).

File a suit if the employee is a member of a class protected under state or federal law (or, in some situations, has advocated or fought for the rights of members of the protected class) *and* the federal or state law covers the employer. Among the federally protected classes against whom discrimination is forbidden are race, national origin, sex, religion, age, being handicapped (limited), and being an Occupational Safety and Health Act (OSHA) complainant.

As a last resort, if you still are having a problem finding a remedy, consider the tort of abusive discharge (discharge for reasons that "offend the public policy").

Some nonunion employers have in-house grievance procedures. These usually are toothless, but you might consider utilizing them as a showing of good faith.

Also consider a state court contract action, various state torts, etc.

[4] Selecting the Remedy

Now that you have an awareness of the potential remedies you might try, it is time to select the strategy for handling the case. At least the following factors have to be considered:

[a] Strength of the Case

Obviously, some of the potential remedies are not more than

possible theories. How good is the proof for each theory? How good is the forum? How good are the employer's defenses?

[b] Availability of Witnesses

To be considered with the strength of the case is the extent to which co-workers and others will really back up the client. The forum may be important here. Some people find it easier to be completely truthful and open when talking to an investigator for a governmental agency in private than when testifying in open court. Sometimes the opposite is true.

[c] The Union

Consideration must be given to how well the union will represent the client in the grievance/arbitration machinery. Consider both the particular relationship between the client and the pertinent union officials, as well as the union's general ability and history of representing its members.

[d] The Arbitrator

In considering whether to use contractual procedures, the particular arbitrator who will be hearing the case can be a pivotal factor in the decision. Some contracts specify the particular arbitrator or panel of arbitrators who will hear all arbitrations; in other cases, panels are requested and received from state and national arbitration boards. In any case, much information can be gathered about arbitrators' prior experience and written decisions (copies of which can be obtained).

[e] Time

Depending on the contract and area, there can be significant time differences among arbitration proceedings, NLRB trials (especially if appeals are invoked by the employer), and federal and state court litigation. Thus, the client's ability to support him/herself during the litigation can be crucial. Also, if the client has come to you late, certain remedies may be precluded.

[f] Money

It costs the employee nothing to be represented by the union through the contractual procedures. The NLRB can cost nothing if the employee files the charge. Once the NLRB issues a complaint, an attorney is appointed. Of course, your client may have private counsel at all stages of the proceedings if s/he wants it. This is often recommended in politically controversial cases or if complex issues are present, since the NLRB cannot be relied on to supply effective representation. Of course, it is well known what federal litigation costs.

[g] The Employer

Knowledge of the employer allows you to know its weak points and the most effective avenues (if any) of approach.

[h] Interrelationship of Remedies Chosen

Some remedies are mutually exclusive—the most important being in the area of NLRB deferral to arbitration. Others, like most federal antidiscrimination laws, are independent, neither precluding nor automatically including anything else. Even in such situations, however, one can encounter credibility problems if too many alternative theories of the employer's motive for the discriminatory discharge are offered.

[i] Political Goals

The client may be a known fighter for union rights or against racial discrimination. He/she and his/her forces may want to file a federal court case in order to call a press conference. They may want to make a show at the NLRB. Valid, credible legal tactics may be selected on the basis of the organizing going on. Listen to the client(s) in this respect.

[j] Relationship to the Client

Someone who has been fired can be very anxious about his/her future; it is important to establish a realistic relationship early on. Most discharge remedies provide only back pay as damages; no one is going to get rich from the indignity s/he has suffered. Procedures can be time consuming. Most important, there is no such thing as a guaranteed remedy for a discharge. Given the current political and social climate, some areas of discrimination law in particular are becoming very difficult to prevail in. The law is not the servant of working people. In short, a sober and realistic outlook can be very useful in weathering the storms ahead.

§ 2.02. Discharges under the NLRA

Three separate sections of the NLRA forbid discrimination, including discharge, by an employer. Section 8(a)(1) guarantees that workers cannot be discharged for the exercise of rights guaranteed under Section 7 of the NLRA, i.e., concerted activities for the purpose of mutual aid and protection. Section 8(a)(3) forbids employers to take action that encourages or discourages membership in any labor organization. Section 8(a)(4) forbids employer to discriminate against workers for filing charges or giving testimony before the NLRB.

The bulk of the following discussion herein will be on Section 8(a)(1) because this section is most often applicable to cases involving rank-and-file workers and because there is less available material on it. Section 8(a)(3) is relatively straightforward and will be covered in less detail. Section 8(a)(4) will not be discussed because it is used relatively rarely and is straightforward.

Before plunging into the law, however, it is appropriate to give

damages for mental anguish may be recoverable under theories of abusive discharge or state discrimination laws, but not under the National Labor Relations Act or, in most situations, as a result of a grievance or arbitration procedure. Additionally, the NLRB interest rates on back pay have been increased to 16 percent. This figure is based on the "adjusted prime rate" used by the Internal Revenue Service.[1.1]

§ 2.02. Discharges under the NLRA

Three separate sections of the NLRA forbid discrimination, including discharge, by an employer. Section 8(a)(1) guarantees that workers cannot be discharged for the exercise of rights guaranteed under Section 7 of the NLRA, i.e., concerted activities for the purpose of mutual aid and protection. Section 8(a)(3) forbids employers to take action that encourages or discourages membership in any labor organization. Section 8(a)(4) forbids employers to discriminate against workers for filing charges or giving testimony before the NLRB. These sections of the NLRA generally apply only to "employees" within the meaning of Section 2(3) of the Act. In certain limited instances, the discharge of a *supervisor* may be a violation of the Act.[1.2]

The bulk of the following discussion herein will be on Section 8(a)(1) because this section is most often applicable to cases involving rank-and-file workers and because there is less available material on it. Section 8(a)(3) is relatively straightforward and

---

[1.1] NLRB General Counsel Memorandum 82-5, January 26, 1982.

[1.2] Parker-Robb Chevrolet, 262 NLRB No. 58, 110 LRRM 1289 (1982), *enforced,* — F.2d —, 113 LRRM 3175 (D.C. Civ. 1983). In this case, the NLRB seriously restricted the circumstances under which a supervisor's discharge is remediable under the Act. Prior to *Parker-Robb Chevrolet,* the Board held that the discharge was remediable whenever it was part of a pattern of conduct aimed at coercing employees in the exercise of their Section 7 rights. In *Parker-Robb Chevrolet* the Board explicitly rejected this precedent and held that a supervisor's discharge is only violative of the Act if (1) the supervisor is discharged for refusing to commit an unfair labor practice, e.g., *Gerry's Cash Markets,* 238 NLRB No. 161, *enforced,* 602 F.2d 1021, 101 LRRM 3116 (1st Cir. 1979) or (2) if a supervisor is discharged or disciplined for testifying before the Board or during the processing of an employee's grievance.

will be covered in less detail. Section 8(a)(4) will not be discussed because it is used relatively rarely and is straightforward.

Before plunging into the law, however, it is appropriate to give a brief overview of the procedures and problems involved in bringing a case before the NLRB.

[1] Bringing a Case before the NLRB[2]

Your case is initiated by filing a charge of an Unfair Labor Practice (ULP) with the NLRB, at one of the regional offices.[3] While there is no requirement that a NLRB charge form be used, all the information sought thereon must be provided. The charge may be set forth in very general terms. In fact this is desirable, as it is the only piece of material provided to the NLRB that is also provided to the employer, unless a complaint is issued and a hearing held thereon. The NLRB will serve the employer a copy of the charge. However, if there is a statute of limitations problems, the employer and NLRB should be served at the same time to preserve the case. The charge must be filed and served within six months of the ULP.

Within a week or so, the NLRB will contact the charging party, telling him/her the name of the NLRB agent who will be conducting the investigation and seeking all evidence immediately. At this point, it is advisable to make contact with the agent, by letter or phone, to outline the general theory of the case and set up an investigation schedule. The agent will want to take affidavits from the charging party and relevant witnesses. While there

---

[2] For more detailed information, *see* K.C. McGuiness, How to Take a Case before the National Labor Relations Board, (4th ed., BNA). This is an excellent book on NLRB procedure; it does not cover substantive law.

[3] The NLRA grants the NLRB jurisdiction over all businesses "affecting commerce." The NLRB has voluntary jurisdictional standards for the size of the employer over which it will assert jurisdiction, with $50,000 in yearly "inflow" or "outflow" required as a general nonretail business standard and $500,000 yearly gross volume of business required for retail establishments. While there are special rules pertaining to combined enterprises, charitable institutions, defense contractors, etc., as a practical matter, most private, profit-making concerns will fall under NLRB jurisdiction. See Appendix A for jurisdictional standards.

is nothing unlawful about preparing an affidavit in advance and merely submitting it to the agent, s/he generally prefers to take his/her own affidavits and to interview the witnesses.

While the styles of agents differ, the most important advice to remember is simply to stay on top of the case—talk to the agent frequently; accompany the charging party to give the affidavit (and make sure that everything important is in it); see to it that the agent gets the addresses of witnesses, copies of contracts, etc. If the agent is expressing doubt about the case, give him/her legal citations of similar circumstances. Do not be afraid to fight, to speak to the agent's supervisor, or even to set up an appointment with the regional director. If any of your witnesses do not read English, be sure to insist that the Board provide a translator who can take the affidavit in the witness's first language and certify the English translation as official.[3.1]

The investigation is the most important part of the case. As a general rule, NLRB agents seek to take no more than thirty days on an investigation. At the agenda meeting, the case is discussed with the NLRB agent, regional director, assistant to the regional director, regional attorney, and supervisor. After this meeting, the NLRB agent will advise you whether or not the NLRB will issue a complaint. If not, it will give you an opportunity to withdraw the charge before it is dismissed. Of course, if the NLRB agrees to issue a complaint, it will attempt a settlement with the employer, which is often impossible.

If the NLRB indicates that it intends to dismiss the complaint, it can be preferable to withdraw your complaint unless there are statute of limitations problems. You can learn from the NLRB's analysis of the weaknesses in your case, develop new information, look for other witnesses, and refile if you want to within the six-month period. If there would not be time to refile or if you are confident that there is absolutely no additional information that you could give to the NLRB, then you may wish to have them dismiss the complaint, at which time you can take an appeal to the NLRB in Washington. Your chances of success on this appeal are minimal, absent novel legal issues or gross procedural irregularities. If the NLRB issues a complaint, there will be a six-

[3.1] *See* NLRB v. Doral Building Services, 666 F.2d 432, 109 LRRM 2342 (9th Cir. 1982).

to twelve-month wait until a hearing before an Administrative Law Judge (ALJ).

There is minimal discovery in a NLRB case. The answer of the charged party must be filed within ten days of the date of service of the complaint; summary judgment would be appropriate if the answer is late or defective. Otherwise, you can expect little in the way of discovery unless a deposition is necessary to preserve the testimony of a witness. The affidavits given to the NLRB agent will be made available only if the affiant is called as a witness and will be made available for the purpose of cross-examination. (Note, however, that once the case is finally closed, they will be available pursuant to the Freedom of Information Act.[4])

The burden of proof is on the general counsel, who will proceed first with the presentation of witnesses. You will function as co-counsel, having the right to participate in the direct examination before cross-examination by the opposing party and the opportunity to present your additional witnesses or other testimony prior to the close of the case in chief. The co-counsel also, of course, has the right to cross-examine the witnesses of the opposing party. In general, then, the co-counsel has full rights at the hearing to present alternative theories of the case and substantiating evidence. An important exception to bear in mind, however, is that the Board may, as the technical complainant in the matter, execute settlement agreements with the opposing party without the charging party's approval. Fortunately, the Board usually prefers to get such approval.

The hearing is conducted before an ALJ, whose identity is usually unknown until the time of the hearing. The parties will generally file briefs in the matter. Many practitioners complain that it has been taking ALJs longer and longer to render their decisions, with some cases taking six to twelve months. An appeal from the decision of the ALJ can be taken directly to the NLRB in Washington, which generally assigns the case to a three-member panel. There is no cost involved; exceptions are filed and counsels submit briefs as in any appellate proceeding.

---

[4] *See* NLRB v. Robbins Tire & Rubber Co., 437 U.S. 214, 98 LRRM 2617 (1978); and NLRB General Counsel, *FOIA Guidelines in Closed Cases,* Memorandum 79-6, 100 LRR 122 (1979).

NLRB decisions generally take anywhere from six months to a year to render.

The NLRB's decision can be appealed directly to the appropriate circuit court of appeals. It used to be possible to "forum-shop" by taking appeals to the D.C. Circuit, but this is no longer possible, as the D.C. Circuit now routinely allows the transfer of cases back to the "home" circuit. There has been an increasing tendency of the circuit courts to refuse to enforce NLRB interpretations of the NLRA; attention should be paid to the case law of the particular circuit. Circuit courts have seized upon procedural and due process requirements to void NLRB decisions; thus, such areas should be closely monitored.

Because the process of simply obtaining an order requiring reinstatement can take more than 4 years and the question of back pay is only litigated thereafter, it is very important to have every discharged worker keep a detailed, *contemporaneous* record of his/her search for work. This record will be needed in any subsequent NLRB back pay hearing.

[2] Substantive Law under the NLRA[5]

[a] Section 8(a)(1)—Concerted Activities for Mutual Aid and Protection

[i] Scope

Section 8(a)(1) provides that it shall be an ULP for an employer "to interfere with, restrain or coerce employees in the exercises of the rights guaranteed in Section 7." Section 7 of the NLRA gives employees the right to engage in "concerted activities for the purpose of collective bargaining or other mutual aid or protection." Thus, the protection theoretically afforded under this

[5] For more detailed information, *see* The Developing Labor Law: The Board, the Courts and the National Labor Relations Act (BNA)(the best concise summary of developments in substantive NLRB law); Labor Relations Reporter, Labor Relations Expediter (BNA) (a good, quick reference, which can be cross-referenced to the Labor Relations Reporter). *See also* NLRB decisions in either the NLRB Official Reporter or the LRRM Reporter series.

section is not limited to union activity. It can include activity in a plant where there is no union, activity directed at union reform, and activity that deals with the concerns a union is supposed to have, but may not enforce, in a plant where there is a union.

Under this section, it is not necessary to prove an illegal motive with respect to the discharge, as it is in Section 8(a)(3) cases. What must be shown is a discriminatory effect upon activities protected under Section 7.[6] For an activity to be held protected under Section 7, a twofold test must be met:

(1) It must be for the mutual aid and protection of the workers; this test addresses the content of the demands raised by the activity.

(*Text continued on page 2-17*)

---

[6] *See* Salt River Valley Water Users Ass'n v. NLRB, 206 F.2d 325, 32 LRRM 2598 (9th Cir. 1953).

(2) It must be done in a concerted fashion.

Each of these requirements will be discussed separately below:

[ii] Mutual Aid and Protection

Many demands that activists put forward in a plant will deal not only with strictly economic issues, such as wages, hours, and working conditions, but also with more general issues, such as race or sex discrimination, the role of union officials, practices of the employer at other plants, etc. The question that arises is whether these activities can be presented in such a way as to fall within the legal definition of "mutual aid and protection" that has evolved in NLRB and court decisions.

Economic issues: Economic issues, such as wages, hours, and working conditions, are clearly included. The leading case in this area is a Supreme Court ruling that a strike over lack of heat in a plant was a dispute over the conditions of employment within the meaning of the statute:

> The activities of these seven employees cannot be classified as indefensible by any recognized standard of conduct. Indeed, concerted activities by employees for the purpose of trying to protect themselves from working conditions as uncomfortable as these are unquestionably activities to correct conditions which modern labor management treats as too bad to have to be tolerated in a humane and civilized society like ours.[7]

This case is the classic example of an activity that will be considered protected. The action taken dealt directly with a condition of employment. The condition protested was within the control of the employer. The employees engaged in a concerted

[7] NLRB v. Wash. Aluminum Co., 370 U.S. 9, 50 LRRM 2235 (1962). One question left open in this case is whether the working conditions protested need meet any standard of "badness" before the protest is protected. In Rowen & Blair Elec. Co., 200 NLRB 639, 82 L.R.R.M. 1235, the NLRB held that "protests against the routine discomforts of life as a building trades craftsmen were protected" though not necessarily meritorious. Thus, it appears that any protest concerning conditions should be protected.

form of action to protest the condition—a strike. In cases such as this, the NLRB does not usually question whether the activity engaged in is protected.

Listed below are some cases dealing with working conditions; these are just a starting point for research. In *Detroit Forming, Inc.,*[8] the employer was held to have violated Section 8(a)(1) in discharging an employee for organizing other workers to complain to the health department about inadequate ventilation, heat, and noise. In *Oklahoma Allied Telephone Co.,*[9] the employer was held to have violated Section 8(a)(1) in discharging an employee for protesting working conditions that required employees to work in a closed room filled with paint fumes without adequate circulation or air conditioning. In *Valley Mold Co.,*[10] the employer was held to have violated Section 8(a)(1) in discharging employees who left their work after floor fans were removed from their work area. There was a union in the plant, but the stoppage was spontaneous and not called by the union. The NLRB held, nevertheless, that the activity was protected. In *Morris-Knudsen Co. v. NLRB,*[11] complaints of employees working under unsafe conditions and other employees concerned about such conditions were held to be protected.[12]

Protests against layoffs, speedups, overtime work not required by contract, and safety conditions are all considered protests against working conditions and are protected.

In *Evangelical Lutheran Good Samaritan Society,*[13] employees discharged for agitating against proposed layoffs were held to have been discharged in violation of Section 8(a)(1). In *NLRB v. Okla-Inn,*[14] employees who walked out to protest increased job assign-

---

[8] 204 NLRB 205, 83 LRRM 1564.

[9] 210 NLRB 916, 86 LRRM 1393.

[10] 191 NLRB 498, 77 LRRM 1490.

[11] 358 F.2d 411, 61 LRRM 2625 (9th Cir. 1966).

[12] Strikes over "abnormally dangerous conditions" are covered by Section 502 of the NLRA, which provides that the quitting of work by employees over an abnormally dangerous condition shall not be deemed a strike. See Chapter 5, *infra,* for a further discussion of this issue.

[13] 191 NLRB 35, 77 LRRM 1412, *enforced,* 477 F.2d 297, 82 L.R.R.M. 3213 (9th Cir. 1973).

[14] 488 F.2d 498, 84 LRRM 2585 (10th Cir. 1973).

ments were held to have been discharged in violation of Section 8(a)(1).

If there is a contractual agreement concerning overtime, or regularly scheduled overtime, refusal to abide by it is not protected activity. However, if the employer schedules extra overtime, or previously unscheduled overtime, refusal to perform such work is protected activity.[15]

Issues outside the direct control of the employer: The more difficult questions concern demands that either (1) affect working conditions but are not directly under the control of the employer, e.g., changes in minimum wage laws or removal of international union representatives, or (2) are not, in the eyes of the NLRB, directly related to the demanders' own working conditions, e.g., support of the striking employees of another employer.

While the original definition of activities for "mutual aid and protection" centered around the question of whether the change demanded was a change that the employer had the authority to make, the NLRB and several circuits have developed a broader definition of protected activity. The NLRB has found efforts to influence legislation, complaints to statutory agencies concerning wages, health, and job discrimination, and activities concerning the leadership of the union to be protected activity. Circuits that have reviewed these cases have evolved tests based on whether the demand relates to the working situation, rather than whether the employer has the ability to meet the demands being put forward.

Two especially significant cases are *Kaiser Engineers v. NLRB*[16] and *Eastex, Inc. v. NLRB.*[17] In *Kaiser,* an employee was discharged for sending a letter to legislators stating opposition to a competitor's application to immigration authorities for authorization to import foreign engineers. While the company argued that it had the right to discharge the employee because protected activity was limited to an activity taking place within the employer-

---

[15] *See* Schultz, Snyder & Steele Lumber Co., 198 NLRB 431, 81 LRRM 1079; First Nat'l Bank of Omaha v. NLRB, 413 F.2d 921, 71 LRRM 3019 (8th Cir. 1969).

[16] 538 F.2d 1397, 92 LRRM 3153 (9th Cir. 1976).

[17] 437 U.S. 556, 98 LRRM 2717 (1978), *aff'g* 550 F.2d 198, 94 LRRM 3201 (5th Cir. 1977).

employee relationship and relating to the terms and conditions of employment, the court rejected this narrow interpretation of Section 7, reasoning:

> It is true . . . that the activity involved no request for action on the part of the company, did not concern a matter over which the company had direct control, and was outside the strict confines of the employment relationship. It is also true, however, that the members of the Civil Engineering Society had a legitimate concern in national immigration policy insofar as it might affect their job security.
>
> Concerted activity of employees, lobbying legislators regarding changes in national policy which affect their job security, can be action taken for mutual aid or protection within the meaning of § 7.

In *Eastex,* a leaflet urging employees to lobby Congress against right-to-work laws and for a higher minimum wage was found to be within the meaning of Section 7 of the NLRA. In a thorough and detailed decision, the Supreme Court affirmed the reasoning of *Kaiser* and found that it would unduly limit the "mutual aid or protection" clause of the NLRA and "frustrate the purposes of the Act" were it to leave unprotected activity of this kind. Central to the Court's reasoning is the finding that the issues dealt with are so clearly linked to the employees' jobs and work lives.

Similarly, complaints to various federal, state, and municipal agencies have been held to be protected activity under Section 8(a)(1) of the Act.[18]

Internal union activities as cause of discharge: Increasingly, employers are seeking to prevent rank-and-file activists from struggling to improve the trade unions by discharging them for activity direct-

[18] *See* Walls Mfg. Co., 137 NLRB 1317, 50 LRRM 1376, *enforced,* 321 F.2d 753, 53 LRRM 2428 (D.C. Cir. 1963)(letter to state health department); King Soopers, Inc., 22 NLRB 80, 91 LRRM 1292 (filing of charges with state civil rights agency and with EEOC is concerted protected activity because worker was acting in interests of all employees covered by the collective bargaining agreement); Detroit Forming, *supra;* Alleluia Cushion Co., Inc., 221 NLRB 162, 91 LRRM 1131 (complaint under state occupational safety and health act); G.U.R., Inc., 201 NLRB 147, 82 LRRM 1139, (participation in compliance investigation under federal statute).

ed against the incumbent trade union leadership on such grounds as "disloyalty" or "sowing disunity among workers." (See discussion of these defenses, *infra.*) There are several helpful NLRB and court decisions dealing with this question. The NLRB has held discharges for internal union activity to be violations of Section 8(a)(1) in the following situations:

In *Tracy Towing Line, Inc.,*[19] an employee discharged for making a "slanderous statement," the statement that the union president worked for the employer, was held to have been discharged in violation of Section 8(a)(1).

In *Jacobs Transfer, Inc.,*[20] the employer discharged a worker who was leader of a rank-and-file "reform committee" that published a newsletter accusing the union of negligence in contract enforcement. The employer claimed that the justification for the discharge was disloyalty, but the NLRB found that the real reason was his protected concerted activity of publishing a newsletter containing charges of union misconduct and also alleging employer and union collusion against employee interests. The NLRB noted that the assertions in the newsletter were made in good faith and with the belief they were true.

In *Leviton Manufacturing Co.,*[21] employees who had been union officials were discharged illegally for filing a civil suit against both the company and new union officials alleging that, because of their, the complainants, success as union officials in improving working conditions, the company and the newly elected union officials engaged in a campaign to defeat them in the union election. Again, the NLRB raised the question of good faith, stating that such activity was protected under the Act unless it was done with malice or in bad faith.

In *Samsonite Corp.,*[22] a group of union stewards and members who believed that the union was not representing them properly published a newsletter. The employer fired them and subsequently defended the discharges on the ground that the demands made in the newsletter were not demands that the employer

---

[19] 166 NLRB 81, 65 LRRM 1575, *enforced,* 417 F.2d 865, 65 LRRM 1575 (2d Cir. 1969).

[20] 201 NLRB 210, 82 LRRM 1360.

[21] 203 NLRB 309, 83 LRRM 1265.

[22] 206 NLRB 343, 84 LRRM 1369.

could satisfy, using the employer control test. The NLRB quoted *NLRB v. Nu-Car Carriers, Inc.,*[23] which held that "attempts by some members of a union to bring about a change in the union's attitude about particular collective bargaining contracts is certainly concerted activity protected by Section 8(a)(1) of the Act." The employer cannot defend its interference by saying that the concerted activity was directed against the position taken by the union, not directly against the employer. The NLRB noted that the fact that some of the articles in the newsletter contained "gratuitous remarks" or "social comment" matters did not detract from the conclusion that its distribution was concerted protected activity.

There are also several court of appeals cases concerning this issue:

NLRB v. Nu-Car Carriers,[24] is helpful mainly for its language, quoted in *Samsonite.*[25]

In *NLRB v. R.C. Can Co.,*[26] the court held that a walkout by a minority of workers to force the company to negotiate was protected activity. However, this decision contains the following language, which may prove troublesome in the future:

> If action of individuals or a small group is in criticism of, or opposition to, the policies and actions theretofore taken by the labor organization then such divisive dissident action is not "protected activity." *(citations omitted)* If, on the other hand, it seeks to generate support for and an acceptance of the demands put forth by the union, it is protected. . . . *(citations omitted)*

In *NLRB v. Buschman Co.,*[27] the employer discharged a worker for "creating disunity among employees." The workers had circulated a petition demanding that the international representative not be present at contract negotiations because he had refused to call a strike vote in the local. The Sixth Circuit upheld the NLRB's ruling that such activity was protected. A similar case is *NLRB v.*

[23] 189 F.2d 756, 28 LRRM 2160 (3d Cir. 1951).

[24] *Id.*

[25] *Supra,* note 22.

[26] 328 F.2d 974, 55 LRRM 2462 (5th Cir. 1964).

[27] 380 F.2d 255, 65 LRRM 2937 (6th Cir. 1967).

Glenn Berry Manufacturers,[28] in which the Tenth Circuit upheld the NLRB's ruling that a petition seeking removal of the workers' international representative was concerted protected activity.

Employer defenses: As already discussed, employers often claim that the activity engaged in constitutes disloyalty. This is especially true if the workers have sought to bring their struggle to other workers through the distribution of leaflets at other factories or to the public. Most courts, in examining this defense, look at two factors: (1) whether the material publicized related directly to the labor dispute[29] and (2) whether the material was truthful.[30] The distribution of inaccurate information that is not deliberately or maliciously false does not render the activity unprotected.[31] Concerted protected activity does not lose its status because it is prejudicial to the employer.[32]

Employers have also begun to defend these cases by arguing that, whatever protected activity the discharged employee may have engaged in, the reason for the discharge was the fact that the worker was a Communist. For discussion of this, see Section 7.04, *infra.*

In *Whittaker Knitting Mills, Inc.,*[33] the NLRB held that the employer was not aware of certain discharged workers' activities on behalf of a union and that the discharges were lawfully based on an investigation that revealed omissions in the employees' applications, an investigation that had been triggered by the fact that the employer had learned that the workers were Communists. In *Picker Corp.,*[34] an ALJ found that the reason a worker who had initiated discussions with a union and admittedly had been labeled "disruptive" by the employer was discharged was the

---

[28] 422 F.2d 748, 73 LRRM 2301 (10th Cir. 1970).

[29] *See* NLRB v. Local No. 1229, IBEW, 346 U.S. 464, 33 LRRM 2183 (1953). *Cf.* Roanoke Hospital. v. NLRB, 538 F.2d 607, 92 LRRM 3158, NLRB v. Nat'l Furniture Mfg. Co., 315 F.2d 280, 52 LRRM 2451 (7th Cir. 1963). *See also* Montefiore Hosp., 243 NLRB No. 106, *enforcement denied,* 621 F.2d 510 (2d Cir. 1980); Allied Aviation, 248 NLRB 229.

[30] *See* Roanoke Hosp., *supra* note 29.

[31] Walls Mfg. Co., Inc., *supra;* Owens-Corning Fiberglass Corp., 407 F.2d 1357, 70 LRRM 3070 (4th Cir. 1969); Jacobs Transfer, *supra.*

[32] Circle Bindery, *supra.*

[33] 207 NLRB 1019, 85 LRRM 1159.

[34] 222 NLRB 296, 91 LRRM 1315.

supervisor's hatred of communism. Significantly, the ALJ found that the word "disruptive" did not connote a dim view of the worker's protected activity but rather the supervisor's view that anyone linked to communism would be disruptive. In defeating this line of defense, one point to raise is that motive is supposed to be irrelevant in a Section 8(a)(1) case. Any action which deters workers from engaging in concerted protected activity should be considered illegal.

[iii] Concerted Activities

Politically, it often makes sense for rank-and-file workers to mobilize as much support as possible for their demands before presenting them openly to the employer. Often, however, the activity is discovered during its formative stages, e.g., an individual worker speaks out in the heat of the struggle or is unsuccessful in initially gathering support. In such situations, the employer will often discharge the worker and defend the discharge on the ground that the individual did not act in concert with other employees or did not speak for other employees but as an individual. However, a discharge under such conditions can still fall within the definition of concerted activity.

Basic rules: Listed below are some basic rules that may be helpful in handling such cases:

(1) One employee engaging in the organizing of another employee around a protected demand is engaging in concerted activity:

> Manifestly, the guarantees of Section 7 of the Act extend to concerted activity which in its inception involves only a speaker and a listener, for such activity is an indispensable preliminary step to employee self organization.[35]

Further, "concerted activity may take place where one person is seeking to induce action from a group."[36]

[35] Root-Carlin, Inc., 92 NLRB 1313, 27 LRRM 1235.

[36] Salt River Valley Ass'n v. NLRB, *supra.*

(2) Lack of success in enlisting other employees to engage in the activity is not a defense:

> Nor would the protection have been lost because the effort failed to obtain the support of the employees solicited. Given "the object of initiating or inducing or preparing for group action . . . preliminary discussions are not disqualified as concerted activities merely because they have not resulted in organized action" for "inasmuch as almost any concerted activity for mutual aid and protection has to start with some kind of communication between individuals, it would come very near to nullifying the rights of organization and collective bargaining guaranteed by Section 7 of the Act if such communications are denied protection because of lack of fruition." *Mushroom Transportation Inc. v. NLRB,* 330 F.2d 683, 685 (C.A. 3 1964). *(other citations omitted)* And this principle obtains even where the employees refusing their support do so because they feel "disturbed" by the solicitor or deem him a "troublemaker".[37] *(citations omitted)*

(3) Failure to obtain explicit authorization from the employees on whose behalf the discharged worker spoke is also not a defense, so long as the worker undertook to speak not for him/herself but for all workers.[38]

In *Oklahoma Allied Telephone Co.,*[39] one employee unilaterally went to see the employer about repairing the air conditioning in the workplace. The NLRB held:

> The Board has held that even individual protests are protected as concerted activity if the matter at issue is of moment to the group of employees complaining and if the matter is brought to the attention of management by a spokesman, voluntary or appointed for that purpose, so long as such person is speaking for the benefit of the interest group: *Carbet Corporation,* 191 NLRB 892. *(other citations omitted)*

But see *Continental Manufacturing Corp.,*[40] in which activity was held not concerted because it concerned only individual action, and

---

[37] Detroit Forming Co., *supra.*

[38] *See* Ohio Oil Co., 92 NLRB 1597, 27 LRRM 1288.

[39] *Supra.*

[40] 155 NLRB 255, 60 LRRM 1290.

National Wax Co.,[41] in which the NLRB held that actions manifesting pure self-interest are not protected.

When complaints are made to agencies enforcing specific statutes designed for the protection of workers, the actions of one individual are usually found to be concerted.[42] For example, the NLRB has held that

> since minimum safe and healthful employment conditions for the protection and well-being of employees have been legislatively declared to be in the overall public interest, the consent and concert of action emanates from the mere assertion of such statutory rights. Accordingly, where an employee speaks up and seeks to enforce statutory provisions relating to occupational safety designed for the benefit of all employees, in the absence of any evidence that fellow employees disavow such representation, we will find an implied consent thereto and deem such activity to be concerted.[43]

The lines drawn by the NLRB and the respective circuit courts can differ, however, on the question of the distinctions between pure self-interest and invocation of statutory rights for the benefit of the workers in general.

While the NLRB has adopted the theory of constructive concerted activity, i.e., activity taken by a single employee who is seeking to enforce a right accorded to all employees by statute or by contract, the courts of appeals have in general limited the applicability of this doctrine. While the rule that individual enforcement of the collective bargaining agreement is concerted activity has been adopted by four circuits,[44] it has also been

---

41 251 NLRB 147, 105 LRRM 1371; *see also* City Disposal Systems v. NLRB, — F.2d —, 110 LRRM 3225 (6th Cir. 1982). See also Comet Fast Freight, 262 NLRB No. 40, 110 LRRM 1321 (1982) which is indicative of a general trend to cut back the definition of concerted protected activity.

42 *See* Alleluia Cushion, *supra;* Triangle Tool, 226 NLRB No. 205, 94 LRRM 1108.

43 King Soopers, Inc., *supra.*

44 Interboro Contractors, 157 NLRB 1295, 61 LRRM 153 (1966), *enforced,* 388 F.2d 495, 67 LRRM 2083 (2d Cir. 1967); NLRB v. Selwyn Shoe Mfg. Co., 428 F.2d 217, 74 LRRM 2474 (8th Cir. 1970); NLRB v. Ben Pekin Corp., 452 F.2d 205, 78 LRRM 2429 (7th Cir. 1971); Randolph Division, Ethan Allen, Inc. v. NLRB, 513 F.2d 706, 89 LRRM 2013 (1st Cir. 1975).

rejected by several others.[44.1] The Supreme Court has granted certiorari on this issue, *City Disposal Systems* v. *NLRB,* 683 F.2d 1005, 110 LRRM 3225 (6th Cir. 1982). In this case, the Sixth Circuit refused to enforce an NLRB order finding the discharge of a single employee who refused to operate an unsafe truck a violation. Certiorari was granted to consider whether the assertion of a right grounded in a collective bargaining agreement constitutes concerted protected activity. The rule that individual enforcement of statutes concerning working conditions is concerted has met with even less approval.[44.2] Certain courts have, however, found such activity protected if the individual employee has raised certain statutory claims that affect other employees.[44.3]

The best tactic in these cases, if they are brought before the NLRB, is to present proof that other employees ratified the activity that precipitated the discharge. If the employer is litigious and will force the NLRB to seek an enforcement order in the court of appeals, it might be advisable either to arbitrate the discharge (if it was for enforcing a contractual right) or to bring a civil suit. A civil suit may be brought under the no-retaliation provision of the statute or, if no such specific provision exists, under the common law doctrine of abusive discharge. *See* Section 2.05, *infra.*

Specific forms of protest that are considered concerted: In the absence of a collective bargaining contract limiting the right of workers to strike, employees should be protected from discharge for threat-

---

44.1 Aro, Inc. v. NLRB, 596 F.2d 713, 101 LRRM 2153 (6th Cir. 1979); NLRB v. Buddies Supermarket, 481 F.2d 714, 83 LRRM 2625 (5th Cir. 1973); NLRB v. Northern Metal Company, 440 F.2d 881, 76 LRRM 2958 (3d Cir. 1971). Royal Development Co. v. NLRB, — F.2d —, 112 LRRM 2932 (9th Cir. 1983).

44.2 *See, e.g.,* Krispy Kreme Donut Co. v. NLRB, 245 NLRB 135, *enforcement denied,* 635 F.2d 304 (4th Cir. 1980) (individual discharged for filing workers' compensation claim not engaged in concerted activity); NLRB v. Bighorn Beverages, 614 F.2d 1238 (9th Cir. 1980); Roadway Express, 532 F.2d 751 (4th Cir. 1976); C & I Air Conditioning, 486 F.2d 977, 84 LRRM 2625 (9th Cir. 1973); Pelton Castel, Inc. v. NLRB, — F.2d —, 105 LRRM 2125 (7th Cir. 1980); Bay-Wood Industries, Inc. v. NLRB, — F.2d —, 108 LRRM 3175 (8th Cir. 1981).

44.3 *See* Lloyd A. Fry Roofing Co. v. NLRB, 651 F.2d 442, 107 LRRM 2927 (6th Cir. 1981) (attempting to enforce employee's compliance with governmental safety regulations); NLRB v. Charles H. Hauley Associates, — F.2d —, 108 LRRM 2613 (5th Cir. 1981) (complaints advanced on behalf of all employees without their expressed support concerted); Frank Briscoe, Inc. v. NLRB, — F.2d —, 103 LRRM 1110 (individual EEOC complaints concerted).

ening to strike or for striking to effect certain changes in their working conditions.[45] Petitions, letters and other signed writings to the employer or state agencies are protected concerted activity.[46]

Workers who engaged in safety protests concerning workplace conditions have been held protected.[47]

Employees discharged for their role in the formation of grievance committees are also protected. In *Columbia University,*[48] the discharge of a worker for attempting to form a grievance committee was held illegal; and, in *AMP, Inc.,*[49] the discharge of a worker who demanded a group meeting with the employer to discuss worker grievances and the subsequent discharge of employees who protested the first employee's discharge were held illegal.[50]

Individual action to enforce a collective bargaining agreement is protected, as the agreement is considered the product of concerted activity. In *H.C. Smith Construction Co.,* the employer discharged an employee for attempting to implement what he believed to be the correct interpretation of the contract: the NLRB held that in such a situation it was "immaterial that the employee did not purport to act as a spokesman of his fellow workers."[51] This rule applies only if there is a contract; an individual's resort

---

[45] *See* Washington Aluminum, *supra;* Bob's Casing Crews, Inc., v. NLRB, 458 F.2d 1301, 78 LRRM 1060 (5th Cir. 1972); Molders Union v. NLRB, 410 F.2d 1061, 70 LRRM 3435 (D.C. Cir. 1969); Hijos de Ricardo Vela, Inc., 194 NLRB 377, 78 LRRM 1632, *enforced,* 475 F.2d 58, 82 LRRM 2967; United M & M, Inc. v. NLRB, 95 LRRM 2369, 554 F.2d 1276 (4th Cir. 1977).

[46] *See* Isaac & Vinson Security System, 193 NLRB 29, 78 LRRM 1525 (workers were unlawfully discharged for signing a letter protesting working conditions). *See also* S.W. Latex Corp., 175 NLRB 58, 70 LRRM 1592; Owens-Corning Fiberglass Corp. v. NLRB, *supra;* NLRB v. Austin Co., 165 F.2d 592, 21 LRRM 2132.

[47] Modern Carpet Indus., 236 NLRB 132, *enforced,* 611 F.2d 811 (10th Cir. 1979); Zurn Indus., 255 NLRB 88; Anheuser-Busch, 239 NLRB 207.

[48] 217 NLRB 1080, 89 LRRM 1218, *supplemented by the Board on remand,* 236 NLRB 793, 98 LRRM 1353.

[49] 218 NLRB 33, 89 LRRM 1272.

[50] *See also* NLRB v. Sequovah Mills, Inc., 409 F.2d 606 (10th Cir. 1969); NLRB v. Kearney & Trecker Corp., 237 F.2d 416, 38 LRRM 2747 (7th Cir. 1956).

[51] 174 NLRB 1173, 70 LRRM 1462 (1969). *See also* Interboro Contractors, 157 NLRB 1295, 61 LRRM 153, *enforced,* 388 F.2d 495, 67 LRRM 2083 (2d Cir. 1967); B & M Excavating, Inc., 155 NLRB 1152, 60 LRRM 1466, *enforced,* 368 F.2d 624, 63 LRRM 2479 (9th Cir. 1966); Bunney Bros. Constr. Co., 139 NLRB 1519, 51 LRRM 1532; NLRB v. Ben Pekin, 425 F.2d 205 (7th Cir. 1971); NLRB v. Selwyn

to company-initiated grievance procedures is not concerted protected activity.[52]

An individual employee may be protected for engaging in concerted activity aimed at evaluating the adequacy of the union's representation and seeking improvement of that representation.[52.1]

[b] Section 8(a)(3)—Discharges Intended to Discourage Union Membership

[i] Scope

Section 8(a)(3) provides that it is an ULP for an employer "by discrimination in regard to hiring or tenure of employment . . . to encourage or discourage membership in any labor organization."

[ii] Burden of Proof

To prove a discharge unlawful under this section, it is necessary to prove that it was motivated by an intent to discourage or encourage union membership and that it actually did so. Thus, in these cases, unlike Section 8(a)(1) cases, the anti-union *motive* of the employer in discharging the worker becomes a necessary element of the case.[53] (See discussion, *infra,* on the *Wright Line*

Shoe Mfg. Corp., 428 F.2d 217 (8th Cir. 1970). *But,* for a split in the circuits, *see* NLRB v. N. Metal Co., 440 F.2d 881 (3d Cir. 1971); NLRB v. Buddies Supermarkets, 481 F.2d 174 (5th Cir. 1973); ARO, Inc. v. NLRB, 596 F.2d 713 (6th Cir. 1979).

52 *See* G.C. Advice Memo, Carson Pirie Scott & Co., 93 LRRM 1253.

52.1 NLRB v. Lummus Industries, Inc., — F.2d —, 110 LRRM 3052 (11th Cir. 1982). Comments regarding sellouts and possible bribery were not sufficient to deny protection to the employee's actions, since they were not made with knowledge of their falsity or with reckless disregard for their truth or falsity. The employee was not actually making accusations, but was trying to determine whether other employees had heard rumors of sellouts.

53 Because of the need to prove motive to discourage union membership, in presenting a section 8(a)(3) discharge case to the NLRB, always include an allegation that the discharge is also a violation of Section 8(a)(1). It is possible

case). As one court stated,

> An employee can be discharged for a good reason, a bad reason, or no reason at all where anti-union motivation has not been established by substantial evidence. . . .[54]

However, a specific anti-union motive need not be proved in certain cases. If the "natural forseeable consequences" of the action are discouragement of union membership[55] or if the actions taken are "inherently discriminatory or destructive,"[56] no proof of motive need be supplied as the motive may be inferred from the actions themselves. In discharge cases, it is presumed that if the discharge is based on knowledge of union activities, it serves to discourage membership in the union.[57]

In these cases, then, the difficult aspect of proof is not that the action taken serves to discourage union activities, but that it was taken with knowledge of the discharged employee's union activities. The employer's defense is usually a claim that there could be no discrimination because there was no knowledge of the union activities of the discharged worker.

The charging party bears the burden of proving knowledge of union activities. The difficulty in proving knowledge is obvious—employers do not give an admission of knowledge with a pink slip. The heart of a Section 8(a)(3) case is determining how to prove knowledge. Each case must be developed individually. Listed below, though, are some general principles.

---

that the NLRB will find that, while Section 8(a)(3) was not violated, Section 8(a)(1) was. *See* NLRB v. Corning Glass Works, 293 F.2d 784, 48 LRRM 2759 (1st Cir. 1961). Moreover, any violation of Section 8(a)(3) is automatically a violation of Section 8(a)(1), so you are not in any way posing inconsistent theories.

[54] Bob White Target Co. v. NLRB, 466 F.2d 583, 80 LRRM 347 (10th Cir. 1972).

[55] Radio Officers' Union v. NLRB, 347 U.S. 17, 33 LRRM 2417 (1954).

[56] Erie Resistor Corp., 373 U.S. 221, 53 LRRM 2121 (1963).

[57] *See* Labor Board v. Jones & Laughlin Steel Corp., 301 U.S. 1, 46, 1 LRRM 703, Associated Press v. Labor Board, 301 U.S. 103, 132, 1 LRRM 732.

[iii] Elements in Establishing Employer Intent or Knowledge

(1) Small plant rule: If a plant has a small number of workers, it has been held that the employer may be assumed to know about union activities occurring within it.[58]

(2) Acceptability of circumstantial evidence: "In an 8(a)(3) case the crucial inquiry is not how, but whether—no matter how—the employer knew of or suspected union activity when he acted."[59] Thus, circumstantial evidence can be adduced to show knowledge.[60] This is an important point because many regional offices will demand during the initial investigation that the charging party produce direct proof of knowledge.

Indirect proof of knowledge can be established through the following factors:

Timing of and circumstances surrounding the discharge: When was the worker discharged—at the end of a pay period or in the middle? immediately after a significant organizing activity in the shop? The answers to these questions aid in proving that the timing and circumstances surrounding the discharge were not usual but unusual. In *Ri-Del Tool Manufacturing,* the NLRB found that the abruptness of the discharge indicated that union activity was known to the employer and held that the discharge of the worker contemporaneously with the commencement of the union campaign

> makes operative the principle that abruptness, manner, and timing of the discharge case [*sic*] light upon the issue of whether an employee was terminated for cause or whether the reasons asserted therefore [*sic*] are advanced as a pretext to hide anti-union hostility.[61]

---

58 Wiese Plow Welding Co., Inc., 123 NLRB 616, 43 LRRM 1495; Columbia University, *supra.*

59 Grismac Corp., 205 NLRB 1108, 84 LRRM 1256.

60 *See* Ri-Del Tool Mfg., 199 NLRB 96, 81 LRRM 1469; Corrie Corp., 375 F.2d 149, 64 LRRM 2731 (4th Cir. 1967); Health Int'l, Inc., 196 NLRB 318, 80 LRRM 1004.

61 Ri-Del Tool Mfg., *supra. See also* Arlington Ridge Dev. Co., 203 NLRB 787, 83 LRRM 1517.

Adequacy of employer's explanation of the discharge: In almost every case, the employer will advance an excuse for the discharge; the adequacy of the explanation must be scrutinized. If it is a business reason, is business up or down? Was the discharged worker replaced? Were other workers laid off? Have business records been introduced to support the defense?[62]

Prior anti-union animus: Has the employer expressed an opinion about unions? Have threats been made to the employees concerning the effect of unionization? Any such conversations or interrogation can be used to indicate animus on the part of the employer.

Differential treatment of this employee: If the employee is charged with violating a plant rule, when was the rule promulgated? Was it ever announced? Have other employees in the plant been discharged for similar conduct?[63]

As can be seen, many different factors can be used to construct a circumstantial case.

[c] Dual Motive Discharges: The *Wright Line* Decision

Some complaints of unlawful discharge under Section 8(a)(1) and all complaints under Section 8(a)(3) require proof of the employer's *motivation* in taking action against the employee. A particular problem of proof has traditionally occurred in so-called dual motive cases, i.e., cases in which more than one motive for the action is proven where one of the motives is prohibited by the Act and the other is not. Preliminarily, dual motive cases are to be distinguished from pretext cases. In the former, there are two (or more) reasons for the action taken, at least one of which is illegal. In the latter, the articulated lawful reason for the action is shown to be a sham. Admittedly, the distinction can be quite hazy.

The NLRB, noting the confusion of its own ALJs and the splits in the circuit courts of appeals, endeavored to clarify the issue in

[62] *See* Grismac Corp., *supra;* Syracuse Tank & Mfg. Co., 133 NLRB 513, 48 LRRM 1723.

[63] *See* Shell Oil Co., 95 NLRB 102, 28 LRRM 1298, *enforced,* 196 F.2d 637, 30 LRRM 2101 (5th Cir. 1952).

Wright Line.[64] The NLRB notes that it had previously employed the "in part" test in dual motive situations. Thus, if the adverse action were caused in part by an unlawful motive, illegality would be presumed.[66]

In an effort to remedy this confused situation, the NLRB, in its *Wright Line*[70] decision, gives a lengthy exposition of the *Mount Healthy*[71] case and concludes that in all cases alleging violations of Section 8(a)(3) and in Section 8(a)(1) cases turning on employer motivation,

> [W]e shall require that the General Counsel make a prima facie showing sufficient to support the inference that protected conduct was a "motivating factor" in the employer's decision. Once this is established, the burden will shift to the employer to demonstrate that the same action would have taken place even in the absence of the protected conduct.[72]

The NLRB takes great pains to distinguish this test from the "dominant motive" test on the ground that under the "dominant motive" test, the general counsel has the burden of proving that the unlawful motive was dominant, whereas under the "shifting burden" test, essentially, the employer has the burden of proving that it was not. This, the NLRB states, is its original concept and it is now just adding a bit more ability for the employer to show a legitimate business justification for its conduct.

The Supreme Court affirmed the test ennunciated in *Wright Line* during the 1982–83 term in *NLRB* v. *Transportation Management Corp.*[73] Justice White, writing for the full Court, found that the

---

64 251 NLRB 150, 105 LRRM 1169 (1980).

65 [Reserved.]

66 Youngstown Osteopathic Hosp. Ass'n, 224 NLRB 574, 575, 92 LRRM 1328 (1976).

67 [Reserved.]

68 [Reserved.]

69 [Reserved.]

70 *Supra* note 64.

71 *Supra* note 65.

72 Wright Line, *supra* note 64, at 1175.

73 NLRB v. Transportation Management Corp., — U.S. —, 113 LRRM 2857 (1983).

74 [Reserved.]

NLRB's allocation of the burden of proof in a dual-motive discharge case was a permissible interpretation of the NLRA. Specifically, the Court held that it was permissible to allocate to the employer the burden of proving, as an affirmative defense, that the discharge "would have occurred in any event and for valid reasons." In so finding, the Court rejected the reasoning of several circuit courts that the NLRB was required to prove not only that anti-union animus was a motivating factor but also that the discharge would not have taken place independently of the protected conduct of the employee. The Court reasoned that it was fair to impose this burden on the employer because the employer is the wrongdoer and thus: "It is fair that he bear the risk that the influence of legal and illegal motive cannot be separated."

One other helpful aspect of this decision is that the Court reaffirmed its support for the NLRB's long standing rule that it need not be shown that anti-union animus was the sole reason for the discharge, stating the test to be "to establish an unfair labor practice the General Counsel need show by a preponderance of the evidence *only* that a discharge is *in any way* motivated by a desire to frustrate union activity." [Emphasis added.] This statement appears to be even more liberal than the Board's requirement that the General Counsel prove that anti-union animus was a "motivating" factor.

[d] *Weingarten* Rights to Have a Representative Present at Disciplinary Interview

[i] Scope

In regard to the immediate circumstances of the discharge, the so-called *Weingarten* rights become a relevant concern. In *NLRB v. Weingarten, Inc.,*[74.3] the United States Supreme Court established an employee's right to a union representative's presence at an interview with management that the employee reasonably believes may result in disciplinary action. The employee must affir-

[74.1] [Reserved.]
[74.2] [Reserved.]
[74.3] 420 U.S. 251 (1975).

matively assert this right to avoid its waiver. Routine shop floor discussions correcting work technique do not constitute a situation in which the right adheres because such discussions do not raise reasonable fears of disciplinary action. The exercise of this right may not interfere with legitimate employer prerogatives. Thus, the employer may decline to interview the employee and yet continue its investigatory and disciplinary procedure without triggering the right. The union representative functions to assist the employee in clarifying the facts or in presenting extenuating circumstances; the employer, however, has no duty to bargain with this representative.

Weingarten rights are based on the employee's Section 7 right to engage in concerted activities for mutual aid or protection. A recent Board case holds that *Weingarten* rights, because derived from Section 7, apply to an employee's request for the presence of a co-worker at a disciplinary interview in an unorganized workplace.[74.4] The Supreme Court reasoned that the right to representation allows the union to protect both the individual employee and the bargaining unit from an employer who attempts unjustified discipline. The right should also facilitate the fair resolution of investigations on the basis of a full factual presentation. Finally, the *Weingarten* representation right serves to help redress the imbalance in bargaining power between employees and employers.

[ii] The Request

Weingarten rights arise only if the employee requests representation. It has been held that an employee invoked this right when she asked, "Should I have someone in here with me, someone from the union?" This employer continued the interview without informing the employee of her right to terminate it. Doing so was an unfair labor practice.[74.5] A signed interview consent form is ineffective to waive a prior assertion of *Weingarten* rights if that consent is coercively obtained, for example, by a threat to turn

---

[74.4] Materials Research Corp., 262 NLRB No. 122, 110 LRRM 1401 (1982).

[74.5] NLRB v. Illinois Bell Telephone Co., 674 F.2d 618, *enforcement denied in part,* 109 LRRM 3244 (7th Cir. 1982).

the matter over to management and police.[74.6] A request for the presence of a co-worker or a "witness" likewise invokes this right.[74.7] However, an employee's failure to assert the right acts to waive it, as the right adheres only on the employee's request.[74.8] Finally, it should be noted that the union representative cannot assert the employee's right. The employee himself/herself must make the request.[74.9]

[iii] "Disciplinary" Interview

Weingarten rights adhere only if the employee reasonably believes an interview will result in disciplinary action. An objective test is employed, taking into account the circumstances in each case: The employee must have some reason for apprehension. This apprehension may be grounded upon prior arguments,[74.10] incidents,[74.11] comments,[74.12] etc. It is recognized that in any interview in which an employee is questioned or instructed concerning his/her work, disciplinary questions are latently present. Such circumstances do not, without more, invoke the representation right. That right arises if the employee reasonably believes that a significant purpose of the interview is to gather facts in support of disciplinary action that management is seriously considering.[74.13] Such a reasonable belief is not present if the employee is assured that s/he will not be disciplined as a result of the meeting.[74.14]

Weingarten rights do not apply to interviews held solely to in-

---

74.6 Montgomery Ward & Co. v. NLRB, 664 F.2d 1095, 109 LRRM 2005 (8th Cir. 1982).

74.7 Dupont, 262 NLRB No. 135, 110 LRRM 1419 (1982).

74.8 Prudential Insurance Co. v. NLRB, 108 LRRM 3041 (5th Cir., 1982).

74.9 Appalachian Power Co., 253 NLRB No. 135, 106 LRRM 1041 (1981).

74.10 Brown & Connolly Inc., 237 NLRB 271, *enforced,* 593 F.2d 1373, 98 LRRM 1572 (1st Cir. 1979).

74.11 AAA Equipment Service Co., 238 NLRB 390, *enforcement denied,* 598 F.2d 1142, 99 LRRM 1262, (8th Cir. 1979).

74.12 Lennox Industries Inc., 244 NLRB No. 88, *enforced,* 637 F.2d 340, 102 LRRM 1298 (5th Cir. 1981), *cert. denied,* 119 DLR A-12 (June 22, 1981).

74.13 AAA Equipment Service Co., *supra* note 74.11.

74.14 Spartan Stores, Inc., 235 NLRB 5222, *enforcement denied,* 628 F.2d 953 (6th Cir. 1980).

form an employee of predetermined disciplinary action.[74.15] A key question is whether the employee is summoned solely to receive discipline or whether the employer seeks additional facts and/or evidence at the interview.[74.16] Though the employer and employee converse concerning the reasons for the predetermined discipline this will not, standing alone, transform the interview into one in which *Weingarten* rights apply.[74.17] Nor does such a transformation occur if an employer solicits the employee's views or questions concerning predetermined and preannounced disciplinary action.[74.18]

According to the Supreme Court, the exercise of *Weingarten* rights may not interfere with legitimate employer prerogatives. This has been interpreted to mean that an employer faced with a request for representation that effectively invokes *Weingarten* rights may grant the request, discontinue the interview, or non-coercively offer the employee a choice of no interview or waiver of his/her representation right. If the interview is terminated by either the employee or the employer, the employer remains free to conduct an investigation of the employee's conduct and to take disciplinary action. This is a legitimate employer prerogative. The employee is thus presented with a difficult dilemma. He or she may forego the opportunity to speak on his/her own behalf or forego his/her representation right. The employer's disciplinary options are not limited whichever course the employee chooses, except that without the interview the employer may lack sufficient information to defend a discharge.

[iv] The Representative

If the employee invokes his/her representation right but specifically requests a particular representative who the employee knows is at the time of the interview unavailable through no fault of the employer's, then the employer may proceed to interview

---

[74.15] Baton Rouge Water Works Co., 246 NLRB No. 161, 103 LRRM 1056 (1979).

[74.16] Texaco, Inc., 246 NLRB No. 164, 103 LRRM 1091 (1979).

[74.17] Baton Rouge Water Works Co., *supra* note 74.15.

[74.18] Texaco Inc., *supra* note 74.16.

the employee and has no duty to inform him/her of alternatives.[74.19] It is the union's duty, and not the employer's, to inform bargaining unit members of alternative representation, and it is a legitimate employer prerogative to hold disciplinary interviews without delay. If there is no union, the employee may have a co-worker present.[74.20]

The discharge of an employee who refused to leave the shop floor to attend a disciplinary interview without the presence of a shop steward has been upheld on the ground that such refusal undermined the employer's legitimate right to maintain discipline. The employee should have gone to the interview and refused to answer questions. *Weingarten* rights mature only at the onset of the interview.[74.21] A more recent Board decision suggests that the employee's rights in this situation are ineffective even when s/he is unlawfully interviewed if s/he refuses to respond.[74.22] In this case, the employee's rights only became effective once the employer took disciplinary action explicitly based upon the employee's refusal to answer.

The union representative at a *Weingarten* interview functions to assist an inarticulate and often intimidated employee in telling his/her story and fully developing the facts and circumstances. The employer has, however, no duty to bargain with the union representative. The employee's *Weingarten* rights are violated if the employer bars his/her representative from speaking[74.23] but are not violated if the employee's representative is barred from speaking until after the employee has finished.[74.24] The employee has a right to a preinterview consultation with his/her union representative and they have the right to be informed of the subject matter being investigated. However, a general statement as to subject matter will suffice if it serves to identify the misconduct in question. The employer need not reveal its case, information it has obtained, or even the specifics of the misconduct being

---

74.19 Coca Cola Bottling Co. of Los Angeles, 227 NLRB 1276, 94 LRRM 1200 (1977).

74.20 Materials Research Corp., *supra* note 74.4.

74.21 Roadway Express Inc., 246 NLRB No. 180, 103 LRRM 1050 (1979).

74.22 Salt River Ass'n, 262 NLRB No. 129, 110 LRRM 1396 (1982).

74.23 NLRB v. Texaco, Inc., 659 F.2d 124, 1108 LRRM 2850 (9th Cir. 1981).

74.24 Southwestern Bell Telephone Co. v. NLRB, 667 F.2d 470, 109 LRRM 2602 (5th Cir. 1982).

investigated.[74.25]

[v] Remedy

A test similar to the *Wright Line* dual motive test has been articulated for determining the appropriate remedy for *Weingarten* violations. The general counsel must show that an interview was held in violation of *Weingarten* and that the employee was subsequently disciplined for conduct that was the subject of that interview. If this is shown, a prima facie case has been made, and the burden shifts to the employer to show that its decision to discipline the employee was not based on information obtained at the unlawful interview.[74.26] If the employer meets its burden, the appropriate remedy is usually a cease and desist order, sometimes accompanied by an order to post a notice informing other employees of that order. If after the general counsel makes a prima facie case, the employer fails to carry its burden, that is, fails to show that facts obtained in the unlawful interview played no part in the disciplinary decision, then a make-whole order (back pay, reinstatement, and the expungement of all disciplinary records) is appropriate. It should be noted that the inference that disciplinary action following a *Weingarten* violation is a result of that violation has been specifically rejected for the purpose of determining the appropriate remedy.[74.27] The Eleventh Circuit has held that back pay and reinstatement are precluded if the employee was discharged for cause. This holding was grounded in Section 10(c) of the LMRA. On its face, this case applied only to an employee's theft of company property but the potential extensions of this doctrine are unlimited.[74.28] If the employer concededly relied on an employee's conduct at an unlawful interview,

---

74.25 Pacific Telephone & Telegraph Co., 262 NLRB No. 127, 110 LRRM 1411 (1982) *enforced in part,* 113 LRRM 3529 (9th Cir. 1983).

74.26 Kraft Foods, Inc., 251 NLRB No. 6, 105 LRRM 1233 (1980).

74.27 NLRB v. Southern Bell Telephone & Telegraph Co., — F.2d —, 110 LRRM 2880 (11th Cir. 1982).

74.28 Montgomery Ward & Co. v. NLRB, *supra* note 74.6. Several other circuit courts have refused to order reinstatement as a remedy for a *Weingarten* violation. See NLRB v. Illinois Bell Telephone Co., 674 F.2d 618, 109 LRRM 3244 (7th Cir. 1982); NLRB v. Fixtures Mfg. Co., 669 F.2d 547, 109 LRRM 2581 (8th Cir. 1982).

the make-whole remedy is generally applied.[74.29] The Board has stated that, under certain circumstances, the make-whole remedy is appropriate if the employer bases its disciplinary decision on the employee's failure to provide a satisfactory explanation at an unlawful disciplinary interview. However, which circumstances make this remedy appropriate and which do not are still unclear.[75]

In cases involving *Weingarten* violations, practitioners may under some circumstances find it useful to argue that, by analogy to Fifth Amendment cases, not only may the employer not discipline on the basis of information obtained at an illegal interview, but also an employer may not legally discipline on the basis of evidence gathered as a result of information obtained at such an interview. From this perspective, if an employer gathers incriminating evidence as a result of leads obtained at an illegal interview, then such evidence is "tainted fruit of the poisonous tree" and cannot be lawfully used to justify disciplinary action. A practitioner making this argument should be prepared to rebut the claim that this line of reasoning violates the Supreme Court's intent by transforming the disciplinary interview into a full-blown adversary proceeding. The counterargument is that acceptance of this legal theory does not affect the disciplinary interview at all; it only implements the Supreme Court's *Weingarten* decision by helping to ensure that an employer may not profit from a violation of an employee's rights.

[vi] Exercise of the Right

The interpretation outlined here poses substantial problems for an employee attempting to assert this right. The Supreme Court postulated this rule to protect an inarticulate employee and to redress the perceived power imbalance between the employer and employee in a disciplinary situation. However, the rule is so

---

[74.29] Salt River Ass'n, *supra* note 74.22; Chromalloy America Corp., 263 NLRB No. 22, 110 LRRM 1506 (1982); Interstate Security Services, Inc., 263 NLRB No. 2, 110 LRRM 1535 (1982).

[75] *See* Pacific Telephone & Telegraph Co., *supra* note 74.25; *but see* Ohio Masonic Home, 251 NLRB 606, 105 LRRM 1281 (1980).

hedged with qualifications that it is unlikely that an employee in such a situation will be able properly to assert the right. Beyond this, problems of proof are inevitable when an employer refuses the employee's request for representation; by definition, at that point no nonmanagement observer is present to corroborate the employee's version of ensuing events. An employee's insistence upon this right may deprive him/her of any potential benefit to be gained from an interview while not limiting the employer's discretion to discipline. Unless the employer explicitly (or tacitly but clearly) relies either on the employee's failure to explain his/her conduct or on information obtained at the illegal interview, the remedy will be a cease and desist order, possibly accompanied by the posting of notice. Such a remedy is, of course, of no use to the particular employee who has been disciplined and is likely to have little deterrent effect on the employer.

Faced with a *Weingarten* interview, an employee should assert the right to representation; the employer may acquiesce. If the employer does not acquiesce, the employee should participate in the interview without representation to take advantage of the opportunity (however limited it may be) to defend himself/herself. Such an employee should make every effort to ascertain the information the employer possessed prior to the interview's onset in order to build a case for a possible make-whole remedy in subsequent proceedings. At the same time, an employee faced with an illegal interview should strive to make a record of his/her request for *Weingarten* representation and of the employer's refusal thereof. Any independent record of the proceedings that can be obtained either during or immediately following the illegal

(*Text continued on page 2-41*)

the relevant deferral time.[92]

[d] Administrative Proceedings

Pursuant to Section 706 of Title VII, the complainant is required to file a sworn charge of discrimination with the EEOC within 180 days of the alleged unlawful practice. Timely filing with the EEOC is a legal prerequisite for Title VII litigation.[93] In "deferral states," the complainant has 300 days from the date of the alleged unlawful practice to file with the EEOC. Since the charge cannot be deemed filed with the EEOC until after the appropriate deferral period has run (see above), this means that the charge must be filed with the EEOC within 240 days (to take advantage of its automatic referral procedures) or 180 days in states with agencies a year or less old. This will allow the running of the appropriate deferral period and still allow the charge to be filed with the EEOC within the 300-day requirement. The Supreme Court has held that the EEOC cannot deem a charge filed until after the deferral period has run.[94]

After a charge is filed, the EEOC has ten days to serve a notice of the charge on the respondent. It is directed then to investigate the charge as expeditiously as possible or practicable within 120 days. If it finds no cause for the charge, it will dismiss the complaint. If it finds just cause for the charge, it is directed to attempt to conciliate.

The EEOC has the authority to instigate litigation in federal court to enforce its finding of discrimination.[95] Should it fail to do so within 180 days (or sooner if it has dismissed the action), it will issue a "right to sue" letter to the complainant advising him/her of the termination of its actions and of his/her right to sue in federal court within 90 days of the receipt of such letter.

---

92 *See* Love v. Pullman Co., 404 U.S. 522, 4 FEP Cases 150 (1972).

93 Smith v. Office of Economic Opportunity, State of Ark., 538 F.2d 226, 13 FEP Cases 131 (8th Cir. 1976).

94 Mohasco Corp. v. Silver, 100 S. Ct. 2486, 23 FEP Cases 1 (1980).

95 As a practical matter, the EEOC is unlikely to instigate litigation except in large class matters or in matters of particular legal significance.

Charging parties may request such a letter after 180 days, whether or not the EEOC has taken any action.

[e] Federal Litigation

No attempt will be made here to discuss the difficult problems of proof in such litigation. Procedurally, it is like any other federal litigation. The ninety-day filing requirement from the date of the "right to sue" is strictly enforced.

Of particular interest to practitioners in such litigation is the availability of attorney's fees to the prevailing plaintiff or, under much stricter standards, the prevailing defendant.[96] The Title VII action has been deemed primarily equitable in nature because it allows for injunctive relief to end discriminatory employment practices and reinstate the discharged employee (along with providing money damages for back pay). Because of this, jury trials are not permitted, although appeals courts have allowed the impaneling of an advisory jury in Title VII cases.[97]

[2] Civil Rights Act of 1866[98]

[a] Covered Employers

This federal statute covers all private employers, regardless of size. Only the federal government is exempt from the coverage of this law, as the Supreme Court has explicitly ruled that Title VII is the exclusive remedy for such employees.[99]

---

[96] Section 706(k) of the Act.

[97] *See* Cox v. Babcock & Wilcox Co., 471 F.2d 13, 5 FEP Cases 374 (4th Cir. 1972); Moss v. Lane Co., 471 F.2d 853, 5 FEP Cases 376 (4th Cir. 1972).

[98] 42 U.S.C. § 1981.

[99] Brown v. Gen. Servs. Administration, 425 U.S. 820, 12 FEP Cases 1361 (1976).

[b] Prohibited Discrimination

This Act provides:

> All persons within the jurisdiction of the United States shall have the same right in every State and Territory to make and enforce contracts, to sue, be parties, give evidence, and to the full and equal benefit of all laws and proceedings for the security of persons and property as is enjoyed by white citizens, and shall be subject to like punishment, pains, penalties, taxes, licenses, and exactions of every kind, and to no other.[100]

As employment is a contractual relationship, the Supreme Court has held that this section provides a remedy for racial discrimination in employment. It is separate and distinct from the Title VII remedy, with no interrelationship between its time deadlines (which are subject to state contract statutes of limitations) and Title VII enforcement rules.[101]

White employees are protected by the law along with all others who are subject to discriminatory treatment based on race.[102] While there is some authority indicating that national origin discrimination is subject to protection under the Act on the theory that the word "race" in the statute is not subject to narrow or technical definitions,[103] Section 1981 clearly does not extend as far as Title VII: Neither sex[104] nor religious[105] discrimination is prohibited by it.

[c] Administrative Agency and Proceedings

None.

---

[100] 42 U.S.C. § 1981.

[101] *See* Johnson v. Ry. Express Agency, 421 U.S. 454, 10 FEP Cases 817 (1975).

[102] McDonald v. Santa Fe Trail Transp. Co., 427 U.S. 273, 12 FEP Cases 1577 (1976).

[103] Manzanares v. Safeway Stores, 593 F.2d 968, 19 FEP Cases 191 (10th Cir. 1979).

[104] *See, e.g.,* Krieger v. Republic Van Lines, 435 F. Supp. 335, 15 FEP Cases 392 (D.C. Tex. 1977); Beamon v. W.B. Saunders Co., 413 F. Supp. 1167, 15 FEP Cases 103 (E.D. Pa. 1976).

[105] *See* Shanks v. Harrington, 21 FEP Cases 590. (N.D. Iowa 1979).

[d] Federal Litigation

Once more, we will not delve into the general standards of proof required under the law. It is important to note, however, that the trend in the circuits has been to require proof of discriminatory intent in 1981 actions.[106] The main tactical advantages available under this statute compared to Title VII are the ability to bypass the EEOC and file a court action immediately, the broader damages allowed under it, and its wider coverage of employers. Finally, there is some authority holding that jury trials are allowed under this law.[107] Thus, many practitioners use this law in conjunction with Title VII when they litigate employment discrimination matters to which it applies.

[3] Age Discrimination in Employment Act[108]

[a] Covered Employers

The Age Discrimination in Employment Act (ADEA) applies to the private employer "in an industry affecting commerce who has twenty or more employees for each working day in each of twenty or more calendar weeks in the current or preceeding [*sic*] calendar year"[109] and to states and any agency or political subdivision thereof.[110] Further, it protects federal employees. Any employment agency that regularly seeks to procure employees for an employer is also covered. Finally, most labor

---

106 *See* Chicano Police Officers Ass'n v. Stover, 522 F.2d 918 (10th Cir. 1977); Guardians Ass'n of N.Y.C. Police Dept., Inc., v. Civil Serv. Comm'n, 633 F.2d 232 (2d Cir. 1980); Crawford v. W. Elec. Co., 614 F.2d 1300 (5th Cir. 1980); Golden v. Local 55 of the Int'l Ass'n of Firefighters, 633 F.2d 817 (9th Cir. 1980); Metrocare v. Washington Metropolitan Area Transit Auth., 25 FEP Cases 76, (D.C. D.C. 1981).

107 Setser v. Novack Inv. Co., 638 F.2d 1137, 24 FEP Cases 1793 (8th Cir. 1981).

108 29 U.S.C. § 621.

109 Section 11(b).

110 Section 11(b).

unions, with some exceptions based on size,[111] are subject to the Act's prohibitions as well.

[b] Prohibited Discrimination

Among the various discriminatory practices outlawed by the ADEA are the following:

> Sec. 4(a) It shall be unlawful for an employer—(1) to fail or refuse to hire or to discharge any individual or otherwise to discriminate against any individual with respect to his compensation, terms, conditions, or privileges of employment, because of such individual's age. . . .

Bear in mind, however, that Section 12(a) of the ADEA specifically limits the coverage of the Act to "individuals who are at least 40 years of age but less than 70 years of age."

[c] Administrative Agency

The Secretary of Labor's authority to investigate and attempt to conciliate complaints arising under the ADEA has been delegated to the EEOC.[112] Section 14(b) of the ADEA contains language similar to Section 706 of Title VII requiring federal deferral to state agency proceedings for 60 days (or less when the state dismisses the complaint) or 120 days in the first year of operation of such a state agency.

[d] Administrative Proceedings

As with Title VII, the aggrieved individual must file a charge with the EEOC within 180 days of the alleged discrimination, or 300 days in states with their own Fair Employment Practices

---

111 *See* Section 11(e), (f) of the ADEA.

112 See the general comments in Section 2.04[1][b], *supra*.

(FEP) agencies, or 30 days after receiving notice of termination or state proceedings, whichever comes first.

As with charges under Title VII, the EEOC has automatic referral procedures for charges under the ADEA. Thus, there is a practical deadline of 240 days for filing with the EEOC in deferral states (or 180 days with agencies a year or less old) in order for the charge to be referred to the state agency and still deemed filed with the EEOC within the 300-day limit.[113] Suit in federal court may not be commenced until sixty days after the filing of such a charge with the EEOC[114] or with the appropriate state FEP agency.[115]

A further important note: while the circuit courts are split in their interpretation of this provision, the ADEA terminates the individual's right to sue upon the EEOC's commencement of an action.[116]

[e] Federal Litigation

The statute of limitations for filing suit in federal court pursuant to the ADEA is two years from the date of the injury. Said statute is tolled for a period of one year while the Secretary of Labor attempts conciliation.[117] The 1978 Amendments to the ADEA specifically authorized a jury trial for any action under it if one item of damages sought is an "amount owing"[118] whether or not equitable relief is sought.[119] Money damages and injunctive relief are available under the Act.

---

113 *See* Mohasco Corp. v. Silver, *supra.*

114 Section 7(d) of the ADEA.

115 *See* Oscar Mayer & Co. v. Evans, 441 U.S. 750, 19 FEP Cases 1167 (1979). *See* Section 2.04[1][d], *supra,* for further comments on EEOC proceedings.

116 Section 7(c)(1) of the ADEA.

117 Section 7(e)(2) of the ADEA.

118 Section 7(c)(2) of the ADEA.

119 *See also* the Supreme Court's discussion in Lorillard v. Pons, 434 U.S. 575, 16 FEP Cases 885 (1978).

[4] Other Federal Remedies

For the protections available to discharged workers under the Occupational Safety and Health Act and related safety and health law, see Chapter 5, *infra.*

Practitioners litigating a discharge concerning sexual discrimination should consider additional counts under the Equal Pay Act.[120] While not a discharge remedy per se, it prohibits pay disparities on sexual lines for work requiring equal skills, effort, and responsibility performed under equal or similar working conditions. Complaints pursuant to it can be brought to the EEOC, but this is not a prerequisite to instigation of an action (although as a practical matter a Title VII charge alleging unequal pay would bring the same allegations before the Commission). The statute of limitations is two years, but is extended to three in cases of willful violations. The main advantage of the Equal Pay Act is that, in addition to back pay damages, liquidated damages up to the amount of the back pay are available.

Finally, Sections 503 and 504 of the Rehabilitation Act of 1973[121] provide some protection for people with physical or mental impairments (or histories thereof) discriminated against by employers who have federal contracts worth $2500 or more or who receive federal assistance.

§ 2.05. Abusive Discharges

In appropriate circumstances, and if no other discharge remedy seems to hold great promise, the rapidly expanding tort of abusive discharge should be considered. While still recognized by only a limited number of state courts and in only limited circumstances, it nevertheless holds some potential as a remedy for the at-will employee.

For the nonunion employee hired without contract (at will), the traditional common-law rule is that he/she may be discharged at any time, for any reason, or as one court put it "for good cause, for no cause, or even for cause morally wrong.

---

[120] 29 U.S.C. § 206(d).

[121] 29 U.S.C. §§ 793, 794.

. . ."[122] Therefore, unless such employees have been dismissed on the basis of race, sex, age, union activity, or some other legally protected basis, they have traditionally been without legal recourse.

However, in recent years, state courts have begun to recognize the tort remedy of abusive discharge if employees are discharged for engaging in activity which the public policy encourages or seeks to protect. One of the clearest analyses of this new remedy can be found in the California State Supreme Court decision in *Tameny v. Atlantic Richfield Co.*[123]

In *Tameny,* the plaintiff sued ARCO for his discharge after fifteen years of apparently satisfactory service. He alleged that the sole basis for the discharge was his refusal to participate in an illegal scheme to fix retail gasoline prices. He filed his action in both tort and contract. Both the trial and appeals courts held his only remedy to be an implied contract and dismissed the tort action. The California Supreme Court reversed, with Justice Matthew Tobriner writing for a 6-1 majority:

> [R]elevant authorities both in California and throughout the country establish that when an employer's discharge of an employee violates fundamental principles of public policy, the discharged employee may maintain a tort action and recover damages traditionally available in such actions.[124]

The court went on to assert that such "traditional damages" could include punitive damages in appropriate circumstances.

While Justice Tobriner may be overreaching somewhat in his broad assertion that this tort is recognized "throughout the country," it is nonetheless true that a significant number of state courts have recognized it to some extent in cases in which discharged employees have engaged in some conduct that the society clearly encourages.[125] Still other courts have favorably noted

---

[122] Payne v. W. & Atl. Ry., 81 Tenn. Rep. 507, 519-520 (1884).

[123] Tameny v. Atl. Richfield Co., 610 P.2d 1330 (Cal. 1980).

[124] *Tameny, supra* at 1331.

[125] *See, e.g.,* Nees v. Hocks, 536 P.2d 512 (Ore. 1975) (serving on a jury); Frampton v. Cent. Ind. Gas Co., 297 N.E.2d 425 (Ind. 1973)(filing workers' compensation claim); Leach v. Lauhoff Grain Co., 366 N.E.2d 1145 (Ill. 1977)(same); Sventko v. Kreger Co., 245 N.W.2d 15 (Mich. 1976)(for reasons

these developments but found it unnecessary to express definite approval.[126]

These and other courts have specifically noted the need to protect workers who are neither high-level employees nor members of unions, while at the same time being careful not greatly to endanger the fundamental prerogative of the capitalist employer to run its business efficiently and profitably. Indeed, a few courts have emphasized that the discharge must be on account of "an activity in which there was a public community interest."[127] Thus, it may be said that there may be a tort worth pursuing or developing in an otherwise hopeless discharge situation, and that the practitioner should, at the very least, give some consideration to the notion.[128]

---

otherwise offensive to public policy); Monge v. Beebe Rubber Co., 316 A.2d 549 (N.H. 1974)(refusal of female employee to "date" her supervisor); Harless v. First Nat'l Bank in Fairmont, 246 S.E.2d 270 (W. Va. 1978)(reporting violation of state and federal consumer credit laws); Jackson v. Minidoka Irrigation Dist., 98 Idaho 330, 563 P.2d 54 (1977); Scroghan v. Kraftco Corp., 551 S.W.2d 811 (Ky. 1977); Walsh v. Consol. Freightways, Inc., 563 P.2d 1205 (Ore. 1977); Petermann v. Int'l Bhd. of Teamsters, 344 P.2d 25 (Cal. 1959); Geary v. U.S. Steel Corp., 319 A.2d 174, 180 (1974)(including intruding into areas of the employer's life that are private and of no legitimate business concern).

126 Roberts v. Atl. Richfield Co., 568 P.2d 764, 770 (Wash. 1977); Fortune v. Nat'l Cash Register Co., 364 N.E.2d 1251, 1257 (Mass. 1977). For an expansion of the *Fortune* doctrine, *see* McKinney v. Nat'l Dairy Council, 491 F. Supp. 1108 (D. Mass. 1980).

127 Scroghan v. Kraftco Corp., *supra,* at 812 (going to law school held primarily a "private concern"). *See also* Campbell v. Ford Indus., Inc., 546 P.2d 141 (Ore. 1976)(wanting to examine the books of a corporation is primarily a "private" interest of shareholder).

128 *See, e.g.,* Blades, Employment at Will v. Individual Freedom: On Limiting the Abusive Exercise of Employer Power, 67 Colum. L. Rev. 1404 (1967); note, Protecting At Will Employees against Wrongful Discharge: The Duty to Terminate Only in Good Faith, 93 Harv. L. Rev. 1816 (1980); Ewing, Sunlight in the Salt Mines 29 Harv. L. Bull. 18 (1977); Ewing, Freedom inside the Organization (E.P. Dutton, 1977)(full-length book by the editor of the Harvard Business Review).

[b] Duty of Fair Representation Cases in Federal Court

[i] Jurisdiction

Under Section 9 of the National Labor Relations Act, as amended, the union is the exclusive bargaining representative of the employees. It is because of this right granted to unions that

---

Locomotive Engineers, 510 F.2d 853, 858-859 (1975).

2. Arbitrary conduct.

Postal Workers, 618 F.2d at 1255; Smith v. Hussmann Refrigerator Co., 619 F.2d 1229, 1253-54 (1980) (en banc).

a. Decision. Smith, 619 F.2d at 1237-40; Buchholtz v. Swift & Co., 609 F.2d 317, 327-28 (1979). *But see* King v. Space Carriers, Inc., 608 F.2d 283, 288 (1979).

b. Procedure. Compare Smith, 619 F.2d at 1241 and 1253-54 *with* King, 608 F.2d at 288.

3. Perfunctory handling. Tatum v. Frisco Transportation Co., 626 F.2d 55 (1980).

NINTH CIRCUIT:

1. Bad motive.

Beriault v. Local 40, ILWU, 501 F.2d 258, 263-264 (1974); Retana v. Elevator Operators, Local 14, 453 F.2d 1018, 1023 (1972).

2. Arbitrary conduct.

Robesky v. Qantas Empire Airways, Ltd., 573 F.2d 1082, 1089 (1978); *see* Castaneda v. Dura-Vent Corp., 648 F.2d 612 (1981); Hughes v. Teamsters Local 683, 554 F.2d 365, 368 (1977).

3. Perfunctory handling.

Robesky, 573 F.2d 1090-91.

a. Negligence. Stephens v. Postmaster General, 623 F.2d 594, 595 (1980); Franklin v. Southern Pacific Transportation Co., 593 F.2d 899, 901 (1979); Price v. Southern Pacific Transportation Co., 586 F.2d 750, 754 (1978); Tenonio v. NLRB, 110 LRRM 2941.

4. General principles.

a. Discretion—whether to process grievance. Fristoe v. Reynolds Metals Co., 615 F.2d 1209, 1215 (1980); *accord,* Singer v. Flying Tiger Line Inc., 652 F.2d 1349, 1355 (1981); Fountain v. Safeway Stores, Inc., 555 F.2d 753, 756-57 (1977); *see* Atwood v. Pacific Maritime Ass'n, 657 F.2d 1055 (1981).

b. Discretion—how to process grievance. Ness v. Safeway Stores, Inc., 598 F.2d 558, 560 (1979); *see* Kaylor v. Crown Zellerbach, Inc., 643 F.2d 1362 (1981).

TENTH CIRCUIT:

Eason v. Frontier Air Lines, 636 F.2d 293 (1981); Denver Stereotypers v. NLRB, 623 F.2d 134 (1980); Foust v. Electrical Workers, 572 F.2d 710 (1978), *rev'd in part,* 442 U.S. 42 (1979).

ELEVENTH CIRCUIT:

The Eleventh Circuit follows precedent from the old Fifth Circuit. Bonner v. City of Prichard, 661 F.2d 1206, 1207 (11th Cir. 1981).

the courts have imposed the duty upon unions who are the exclusive bargaining representative. Thus, as shown above, the duty arises from Section 9 of the Act.

Since *Steele v. Louisville & NRR,*[89.23] the federal courts have found that they have jurisdiction over unions in duty of fair representation cases on the basis of 28 U.S.C. § 1337, which grants courts jurisdiction of any action arising under any act of Congress regulating commerce. The National Labor Relations Act is such a congressional action.[89.24] They have also claimed jurisdiction through Section 301 of the NLRA. The primary issue involving court jurisdiction has been whether the Board preempted court jurisdiction. *Vaca* finally settled that issue by declaring that the federal courts had such jurisdiction.

Although both the courts and the Board have jurisdiction to hear fair representation cases, most of such cases are filed with the courts, not the Board. There are three reasons for this: (1) The Board has a 6-month statute of limitations under Section 10(b). (2) The charging party is left with no recourse if the general counsel decides not to issue a complaint. (3) The Board has substantially less remedial authority than the courts have.

[ii] Statute of Limitations

The Supreme Court recently resolved the confusion following its decision in *UPS v. Mitchell.*[89.25] In *Del Costello v. International Brotherhood of Teamsters,*[89.26] the Court held that the six month statute of limitations of § 10 of the National Labor Relations Act would

---

DISTRICT OF COLUMBIA CIRCUIT:

Local 6885 v. Postal Workers, 665 F.2d 1096 (1981); Teamsters Local 860 v. NLRB, 652 F.2d 1022 (1981); Lewis v. Greyhound Lines-East, 555 F.2d 1053 (1977).

89.23 *Supra* note 89.1

89.24 Beriault v. Warehousemen's Union, 501 F.2d 258 (9th Cir. 1974).

89.25 451 U.S. 56, 101 S. Ct. 1559, 67 L. Ed. 732, 107 LRRM 2001 (1981).

89.26 — U.S. —, 76 L. Ed. 2d 476 (1983).

govern both in suits against the employer and the union. It failed to reach the question of the retroactive application of this statute of limitations, but at least one circuit has found that the six month statute should apply retroactively.[89.27]

Beyond the issue of which statute of limitations applies, there are several others. For example, when does the statute begin to run? Generally, when the last timely grievance has been heard by the arbitrator or committee.[89.34] The statute of limitations may be tolled by false assertions made by the union[89.35] or by filing a timely Title VII action.[89.36] The same statute of limitations does not necessarily apply to both parties if contract and tort statutes differ.[89.37]

[iii] Plaintiff Must Prove Two Elements to Prevail

The plaintiff must prove not only that the union breached its duty of fair representation but also that the employer breached the collective bargaining agreement.[89.38]

89.27 Perez v. Dana, — F.2d —, 114 LRRM 2814 (3d Cir, 1983).

89.28 [Reserved.]

89.29 [Reserved.]

89.30 [Reserved.]

89.31 [Reserved.]

89.32 [Reserved.]

89.33 [Reserved.]

89.34 Butler v. Yellow Freight, 514 F.2d 442, 88 LRRM 3169 (8th Cir.), *cert. denied,* 423 U.S. 924 (1975); Warren v. Teamsters, 544 F.2d 334 (8th Cir. 1976).

89.35 DeVries v. Interstate, 91 LRRM 2764.

89.36 Beasley v. Motor Freight Express, 401 F. Supp. 662 (E.D. Va. 1975).

89.37 Cowan v. Local 728, *supra;* and Price, *supra.*

89.38 Gratien v. Bethlehem Steel, 68 CCH 12,628; Mumford v. Glover, 503 F.2d 878, 87 LRRM 2945 (5th Cir.). If no breach of duty is proved, the case against employer must also be dismissed. Powell v. Globe, 81 CCH 13,186; Warren v. Teamsters, 544 F.2d 334, 93 LRRM 2734 (8th Cir. 1976). If no contract violation exists, can a breach of duty be found? Patrick v. IUOE, 456 F.2d 672 (8th Cir. 1972).

[iv] Allegations, Conclusions: Sufficiency

Various cases have considered the sufficiency of the plaintiff's allegation.[89.39]

[v] Effect Given Dismissal of Charge Filed with NLRB Alleging Breach of Duty

Several cases have considered whether dismissal of a NLRB charge alleging the union's breach of its duty is res judicata.[89.40]

[vi] Exhaustion of Remedies

The employee is required to exhaust his/her contractual remedy, that is, to use the grievance and arbitration procedures of the collective bargaining agreement. Failure to do so will result in dismissal of the charges against both the union and the employer.[89.41] However, the same cannot be said for the necessity of exhausting the member's internal union remedies to address the union's breach.

If internal union procedures are inadequate to effect the relief sought by the member, failure to exhaust internal union remedies will generally be excused and he or she will be permitted to pursue the claim for breach of the duty of fair representation and

---

[89.39] Bazarte v. UTU, 429 F.2d 868 (3d Cir. 1970); Balowski v. GM, 372 F.2d 829, 64 LRRM 2397 (6th Cir. 1967); Rapp v. M & G, 83 LRRM 2531; Sedlark v. G.M., 66 CCH 11,994, 54 FRD 230; Dill v. Greyhound, 435 F.2d 231 (6th Cir. 1976), *cert. denied,* 402 U.S. 952 (1971); Powell v. Globe Industries, 81 CCH 13,186; Pawlowski v. Local Union No. 337, 71 CCH 13,810; Lusk v. Eastern Products, 427 F.2d 705 (4th Cir. 1970).

[89.40] Not res judicata: Brady v. C. Freightways, 82 LRRM 2245 (S.D. Ohio 1972); Ruzicka v. G.M., 336 F. Supp. 842 (E.D. Mich. 1972); Thomas v. Ford Motor Co. (E.D. Mich. 1973).

Is res judicata: Rudolph v. Wagner Elec., 80 LRRM 2937 (E.D. Mo. 1972).

Not res judicata but entitled to great evidential weight: Arnold v. Plumbers, 388 F. Supp. 1105, *aff'd.,* 529 F.2d 511 (3d Cir. 1975).

[89.41] Priest v. Wolverine Express, 75 CCH 10,516; Quinn v. Dixie Highway Express, 67 CCH 12,503; Czosek v. O'Mara, 397 U.S. 25 (1970).

breach of the collective bargaining agreement.[89.42] This policy must be distinguished from the standard that requires exhaustion of the contractual grievance mechanism. Because of the policy encouraging private resolution of grievances arising out of the collective bargaining process, the courts will require the employee to have exhausted his or her remedies under the grievance procedure.[89.43] The employee will therefore be expected to have filed a grievance and to have made reasonable efforts to encourage the union to prosecute it as far as possible. The union may decide at any step of the procedure that upon investigation the grievance does not merit further processing. The general rule is that the employee does not have an individual right to process his/her grievance through additional steps of the procedure without the union's representation.

[vii] Jury Trial Right in Claim Against Union

The right to a jury trial, well established for contract claims against employers, is unsettled where the claim is against the union. Some courts have found that there is no right to a jury trial,[89.44] while others have allowed a jury trial limited to the question of damages.[89.45] Some courts have allowed an advisory jury, pursuant to the Federal Rules of Civil Procedure.

89.42 Clayton v. UAW, 451 U.S. 679 (1981).

89.43 Republic Steel Corporation v. Maddox, 379 U.S. 650 (1965).

89.44 Davidson v. Teamsters Local 135, 96 LRRM 2808 (S.D. Ind. 1977); Atwood v. Pacific Maritime Ass'n., 432 F. Supp. 491 D.C. Ore. 1977); Coleman v. Kroger Co., 399 F. Supp. 24 (W.D. Va. 1975); Acheson v. Bottlers' Union Local 896, 83 LRRM 2845 (N.D. Cal. 1973); Harrison v. Chrysler Corp., 60 FRD 9 (S.D. Ind. 1973), *rev'd and remanded on other grounds,* 558 F.2d 1273 (7th Cir. 1977); Brady v. TWA, 196 F. Supp. 504 (D. Del. 1961), *aff'd.,* 401 F.2d 87 (3d Cir. 1968), *cert. denied,* 393 U.S. 1048 (1969).

89.45 Smith v. Hussman Refrigerator, 100 LRRM 2238 (8th Cir. 1979), *rehearing en banc granted,* 101 LRRM 2822 (June 19, 1979); Minnis v. UAW, 531 F.2d 850 (8th Cir. 1975); Rojo v. Aeronaves de Mexico, 432 F. Supp. 491 (C.D. Cal. 1978); Steele v. Local 1162, 432 F. Supp. 369 (N.D. Iowa 1977); Lucas v. Philco-Ford Corp., 380 F. Supp. 139 (E.D. Pa. 1974); Rowan v. Howard Sober, Inc., 384 F. Supp. 1121 (E.D. Mich. 1974).

[viii] Damages and Other Remedies

In *Bowen v. United States Postal Service,*[89.46] the Supreme Court reversed the generally accepted principal that the union is not responsible for back pay, but usually only is responsible for attorneys' fees. The Court held that compensatory damages should be apportioned between the defendants based on their fault. The trial court had assessed as the union's share of the back wages, that amount that would have accrued after a hypothetical arbitration award. The Supreme Court did not explicitly approve this apportionment, noting that the union had not objected to the formula, but rather to the payment of any portion of the back pay. Punitive damages are not recoverable against the union.[89.47]

If a plaintiff is successful in federal court, a broad range of remedies is possible. A court may enjoin the union from discriminating; or it may issue a mandatory injunction requiring the union to grant the discriminatees the same benefits enjoyed by all other employees,[89.48] compelling arbitration,[89.49] or requiring reinstatement if presentation of the grievance to the union would be useless since the union itself discriminates.[89.50]

The court may also charge the union with past and prospective damages suffered by the employee. These damages, however, are limited to the amount attributable to the union's breach of duty. In other words, the employer is responsible for the damages caused by its breach of the contract. The union is liable only for additional damages resulting from its breach of the duty of fair representation. Damages for mental distress or punitive damages can be awarded only if the union's conduct is outrageous and extraordinary. Specifically, the union must subject the employee to violence, harassment, physical abuse, scorn or ridicule of coworkers, or specific malice.[89.51]

The courts are split on whether unions can be charged with the

---

[89.46] — U.S. —, 74 L.Ed. 2d 402 (1983).

[89.47] IBEW v. Foust, — US —, 101 LRRM 2365 (1979).

[89.48] Central of Georgia Ry v. Jones, 229 F.2d 648 (5th Cir.) *cert denied,* 352 U.S. 848 (1956).

[89.49] Vaca v. Sipes, *supra.*

[89.50] *Id.*

[89.51] Harrison v. United Transportation Union, 530 F.2d 558 (4th Cir. 1975), *cert. denied,* 425 U.S. 958 (1976).

attorneys' fees of prevailing plaintiffs.[89.52] However, under *Alyeska Pipeline Service Co. v. Wilderness Society,*[89.53] attorneys' fees are recoverable if a common benefit is conferred or if the losing party "acted in bad faith, vexatiously, wantonly or for oppressive reasons."[89.54] The *Alyeska* decision applies to DFR cases.[89.55]

[ix] The Relationship between Union and Employer Responsibility

A finding of unfair representation has become a prerequisite to a holding of employer violation of Section 301 of the Labor Management Relations Act. As discussed above, failure to exhaust contractual remedies is a defense to a Section 301 and unfair representation suit. An employee, however, can continue his/her action against the employer if s/he shows that the union refused to process his/her grievance or did so in an arbitrary or perfunctory manner.[89.56] This holding in *Vaca* essentially means that an employee can sue his/her employer for breach of contract only if s/he also shows that the union breached its duty.

Although the holding may appear to favor the employer, it

89.52 *Compare* Sanabria v. ILA Local 1575, 101 LRRM 2282 (1st Cir. 1979) (no recovery in DFR case under Puerto Rican law); and Cronin v. Sears Roebuck & Co., 445 F. Supp. 277 (E.D. Mo. 1978), *aff'd.,* 100 LRRM 2023 (8th Cir. 1978) *with* Figuerora de Arroyo v. Sindicato de Trabajadores Packinghouse, 425 F.2d 281 (1st Cir. 1970) (attorneys' fees recoverable; no standard enunciated) (the recent *Sanabria* case did not mention *de Arroyo*); Scott v. Teamsters Local 377, 96 LRRM 2902 (N.D. Ohio 1977), *on remand from* 548 F.2d 1244 (6th Cir. 1977); Pierce v. Fox Mfg. Co., 97 LRRM 2321 (N.D. Ga. 1977); and Ransdell v. Machinists, 443 F. Supp. 936 (E.D. Wisc. 1978) (attorneys' fees are part of plaintiff's compensatory damages).

89.53 421 U.S. 240 (1975).

89.54 *Id.,* at 258-59.

89.55 Negri v. Service Employees Local 87, 98 LRRM 2508 (N.D. Cal. 1978). *See, e.g.,* Richardson v. CWA, 530 F.2d 126, 132 (8th Cir. 1976), *cert. denied,* 429 U.S. 824 (1977) (bad faith); Harrison v. UTU, 530 F.2d 558 (4th Cir. 1975), *cert. denied,* 425 U.S. 958 (1976); Negri v. Service Employees Local 87, 98 LRRM 2508 (N.D. Cal. 1978) (recoverable if *demonstrable* bad faith); Farmer v. Local 1064, 99 LRRM 2166 (E.D. Mich. 1978) (union acted discriminatorily and in bad faith); Scott v. Teamsters Local 377, 548 F.2d 1244 (6th Cir. 1977) (bad faith).

89.56 Vaca v. Sipes, *supra.*

protects and preserves the arbitration process and the goal of labor relations—private settlement of labor problems between labor and management. Without such a rule, an employee could sue each time s/he lost an arbitration decision or the union decided not to process his/her grievance. Since *Vaca,* the courts have continued to require an unfair representation decision as a prerequisite to finding the employer liable. Conversely, the courts do not require a breach of contract as necessary for union liability

CHAPTER 3

Protecting the Right to Strike

The power of workers and their unions to strike, i.e., to withhold their labor power from production, is a fundamental political right of workers. It is the ultimate and most powerful weapon workers have to force concessions from the owners of industry to their legitimate demands concerning wages, hours, working conditions, and issues of a political nature. It is not a tactic that workers will undertake lightly because, in spite of the sometimes romantic view of strikes, a strike is a serious undertaking, and one that usually entails sacrifices for a period of time. It is a tactic used when company and/or governmental policies or demands make using the strike weapon a necessity.

Historically, state and federal courts have been quick to place severe legal restrictions upon the use of the strike and the tactics used during the strike. In the 1800s, employers initially sought to impose criminal liability on strikers under the doctrine of criminal conspiracy. This first occurred in the case of the Philadelphia cornwainers.[1] Later, business began to attack union efforts by

[1] Commonwealth v. Pullis, Philadelphia Mayor's Court (1806).

The power of workers and their unions to strike, i.e., to withhold their labor power from production, is a fundamental political right of workers. It is the ultimate and most powerful weapon workers have to force concessions from the owners of industry to their legitimate demands concerning wages, hours, working conditions, and issues of a political nature. It is not a tactic that workers will undertake lightly because, in spite of the sometimes romantic view of strikes, a strike is a serious undertaking, and one that usually entails sacrifices for a period of time. It is a tactic used when company and/or governmental policies or demands make using the strike weapon a necessity.

Historically, state and federal courts have been quick to place severe legal restrictions upon the use of the strike and the tactics used during the strike. In the 1800s, employers initially sought to impose criminal liability on strikers under the doctrine of criminal conspiracy. This first occurred in the case of the Philadelphia cornwainers.[1] Later, business began to attack union efforts by

(*Text continued on page 3-5*)

[1] Commonwealth v. Pullis, Philadelphia Mayor's Court (1806).

seeking civil remedies for damages and injunctions for the regulation of union activities.[2] A favorite tort theory of these companies was that organized labor's pressure for higher wages and better working conditions constituted a tort against the right of businesspeople to run their businesses as they saw fit.[3]

In 1894, the American Railway Union launched a major strike under the leadership of Eugene Debs. An injunction was issued under the Sherman Anti-Trust Act for unlawful restraint of trade,[4] and the strike was broken. Similarly, the employers in the case of the Danbury hatters[5] used the Sherman Anti-Trust Act to obtain injunctive relief and claim treble damages. During this same period, in *Vegalahn v. Gunter,*[6] it was held that intentional infliction of economic harm even by legal means could be actionable in tort unless justified by legitimate purposes creating a defense or a privilege. In 1914 the Clayton Anti-Trust Act was passed, theoretically exempting unions from restrictions fostered by the antitrust laws. The Supreme Court gutted the exception in *Duplex Printing Press v. Deering,*[7] and unions continued to bear the weight of injunction and damage actions brought under the federal antitrust acts.

The excessive interference of the courts in the day-to-day conflict between management and labor was eased somewhat with the passage of the Railway Labor Act[8] in 1926, the Norris-LaGuardia Act in 1932,[9] and the Wagner Act in 1935.[10] The popular mythology is that these acts represent reforms freely given by the government. The reality is that the mass struggles of the late 1920s and 1930s, in which millions of workers marched and demonstrated, forced the government to grant these concessions.[11] As a result of this legislation, labor was given the legal

---

[2] *See* Commonwealth v. Hunt, 38 Am. Dec. 346 (1842).

[3] Walker v. Cronin, 107 Mass. 555 (1871).

[4] In re Debs, 158 U.S. 564 (1895).

[5] Loewe v. Lawler, 208 U.S. 274 (1908).

[6] 167 Mass. 92 (1896).

[7] 254 U.S. 443 (1921).

[8] 45 U.S.C. § 151 et seq.

[9] 29 U.S.C. § 101 et seq.

[10] 29 U.S.C. §§ 51-169.

[11] *See* Boyer & Morais, Labor's Untold Story (United Electrical Workers, 1976).

right to organize and protection against abusive court injunctions in the hope that the trade union movement could be channeled so as to lessen industrial conflict between labor and management. The legislation restricted employers in one main respect—it gave unions the right to organize. However, the existence of management rights clauses in virtually every major collective bargaining agreement since that time has continued to protect management's unrestricted right to control the organization and pace of work in industry.

Since the 1930s, particularly since World War II, employers have followed a policy of seeking to separate union officials from the rank and file by convincing them that the interests of the companies and those of the workers are not antagonistic. From this has come the acceptance by most union officials of no-strike clauses in virtually every major collective bargaining agreement, often stringent legal restraints on union activities, and the lengthening of collective bargaining agreements from one to three years. The ultimate point has come in the steel industry with the Experimental Negotiating Agreement, which forbids strikes even at the end of the contract term and replaces the strike with a system for compulsory arbitration of disputed contract terms.

The legal restrictions have come in the form of the Taft-Hartley Act (which John L. Lewis called a slave labor law), which banned secondary boycotts and authorized injunctions against strikes (contract strikes) in situations where the national health or safety is endangered. *Boys Markets*[12] and its progeny (those decisions interpreting union contracts, particularly the arbitration and no-strike obligations in the contract) have virtually banned so-called wildcat strikes because of the almost universal use of no-strike and/or mandatory arbitration clauses in union contracts. The Department of Labor has reported that of 1717 contracts examined in 1966, 94 percent designated arbitration as the terminal point for the resolution of disputes;[13] the figure is probably even higher today.

This chapter will focus on legal tactics that can be used in strike situations and on how protection for the right to strike can best be provided. The chapter assumes some basic knowledge of the

[12] Boys Markets, Inc. v. Retail Clerk's Union Local 770, 398 U.S. 235 (1970).

[13] U.S. Dept. of Labor Bull. No. 1425-26 (1966).

law; while the case law will be discussed in some detail, the focus is on tactics. The chapter is based upon a number of premises:

(1) The fundamental interests of the workers and those of the companies are antagonistic;
(2) The judicial system and the history and pattern of collective bargaining, with the accompanying common law of arbitration, have placed severe restraints on the ability of workers to protect themselves;
(3) Leaders of trade unions and the workers' movement must recognize these constraints and, if they are to serve the interests of the majority of rank-and-file workers, must be willing, *when necessary,* to ignore and defy such restraints.

Why are these premises important? Because economic problems are worsening, and the Right has launched an offensive against unions and workers' rights. In this climate, strikes will become increasingly common; many will be entirely spontaneous, regardless of any legal restrictions. The task is fully to defend unions and rank-and-file workers who face possible legal sanctions for strike activities.

§ 3.01. No-Strike Obligations of Unions under Collective Bargaining Agreements

[1] The Norris-LaGuardia Act and *Boys Markets*

Congress, in recognition of the abusive use of court injunctions against working people and their unions,[14] passed the Norris-LaGuardia Act.[15] This Act severely limited the power of the federal courts to issue injunctions in conflicts between labor and

[14] *See* F. Frankfurter & N. Greene, The Labor Injunction, which discusses the historical abuses of the use of injunctive relief in labor disputes. A number of specific examples are given.

[15] Anti-Injunction Act, 29 U.S.C. § 101 et seq.

management.[16] Five decades later, the Norris-LaGuardia Act is a hollow shell as a result of the U.S. Supreme Court decision in the landmark *Boys Markets*[17] case and later decisions expanding upon and interpreting *Boys Markets.* Before discussing *Boys Markets* and the cases following it is necessary to trace the developments leading up to it; the reader should take careful note of the stranglehold that no-strike clauses and the courts have placed on the labor movement.

The Norris-LaGuardia Act embodies, or once embodied, a federal policy against the intervention of the federal courts in labor disputes.[18] It was passed in direct response to the growing power of the workers' movement in the 1930s, and it recognized the abusive use of federal court injunctions in disputes between labor and management. The open use of and support by the federal court in employer's efforts to suppress union organizing was creating a volatile situation,[19] and the Act was in large measure needed to diffuse the situation.

By 1947, the pendulum was swinging the other way, and Congress passed the Taft-Hartley Act.[20] This Act was part of a growing wave of anti-Communist hysteria and was a frontal assault on the labor movement in this country.[21] Section 301[22] of the Taft-Hartley Act was, at that time, neither very controversial nor well understood. Section 301 gave federal courts jurisdiction over suits for breach of collective bargaining agreements. Section 301(b) indicates that a union is to be bound by the acts of its agents, and Section 301(d) states that "in determining whether any person is acting as an agent of another person so as to make any such person responsible for his acts, *the question of whether the specific acts performed were actually or subsequently ratified shall not be control-*

---

16 Several states also passed anti-injunction acts, sometimes called little Norris-LaGuardia Acts. If your state has such an act, you are in a much better position to restrict the use of injunctions during strikes.

17 Boys Markets, *supra* note 12.

18 The Supreme Court explained this policy in Milk Wagon Drivers Union v. Lake Valley Farm Prods., Inc., 311 U.S. 91 (1940).

19 *See* The Labor Injunction, *supra* note 14; Labor's Untold Story, *supra* note 11.

20 29 U.S.C. § 141 et seq.

21 *See* Labor's Untold Story, *supra,* note 11

22 29 U.S.C. § 185.

ling " (emphasis added). This is quite different from the standard of proof established in the Norris-LaGuardia Act, which required *clear proof* of actual participation, ratification, or authorization before a union could be held liable or responsible for the unlawful acts of individual officers, members, or agents.[23] The Supreme Court soon faced the task of accommodating the differing provisions and policies of the Norris-LaGuardia and Taft-Hartley Acts.

[2] Pre-*Boys Markets* Decisions: The Process of Accommodation Begins

In *Textile Workers of America v. Lincoln Mills,*[24] the union sued under Section 301, seeking specific performance of the contractual duty to arbitrate. The court held that Section 301 gives federal courts the power to order specific enforcement of a contractual duty to arbitrate pursuant to the collective bargaining agreement, in spite of the provisions of the Norris-LaGuardia Act. The court also held that Section 301 permitted the courts to fashion federal common law for the enforcement of collective bargaining agreements.

The Steelworkers Trilogy[25] established arbitration as the primary vehicle to "maintain" industrial peace. Through these cases, the U.S. Supreme Court established a federal labor policy that created a strong presumption in favor of arbitration. The Supreme Court heralded this policy as follows:

> The present federal policy is to promote industrial stabilization through the collective bargaining agreement. A major factor in achieving industrial peace is the inclusion of a provision for the arbitration of grievances in the collective bargaining agreement.
>
> An order to arbitrate the particular grievance should not be denied unless it can be said with positive assurances that the arbitration

[23] 29 U.S.C. § 106.

[24] 353 U.S. 448, 40 LRRM 2113 (1957).

[25] USWA v. Enterprise Wheel and Car Corp., 363 U.S. 593 (1960); USWA v. Warrior Gulf and Navigation Co., 363 U.S. 574, 46 LRRM 2416 (1960); USWA v. American Mfg. Co., 363 U.S. 564 (1960).

clause is not susceptible of an interpretation that covers the asserted dispute. *Doubts should be resolved in favor of arbitration.* [26] (emphasis added)

It should be noted that the Supreme Court had by this time approved the use of injunctive relief under the Railway Labor Act, ruling in 1957 that the Norris-LaGuardia Act did not preclude issuance of injunctive relief if a union struck over a dispute subject to arbitration under the Railway Labor Act.[27]

A further link in the chain leading to *Boys Markets* was forged in *Teamsters v. Lucas Flour,*[28] in which the court held that a grievance procedure leading to binding arbitration implied an agreement not to strike over grievances subject to arbitration. Thus, the courts were free to imply a no-strike obligation despite the lack of a specific no-strike clause in the contract.

A brief respite in the march towards *Boys Markets* occurred in *Sinclair Refining v. Atkinson.*[29] In this case, the court held that the Norris-LaGuardia Act did prohibit issuance of an injunction against strikes over arbitrable grievances. It was only eight short years before the court reversed itself. In fact, the Supreme Court seems to have contradicted itself when one considers *Teamsters v. Lucas Flour,* decided a short while before *Sinclair.*

[3] The *Boys Markets* Decision: Prerequisites for Issuance of a *Boys Markets* Injunction

Boys Markets[30] reversed *Sinclair,* the court holding that federal district courts can issue injunctive relief to stop a strike over a

---

[26] Nolde Bros., Inc. v. Local No. 358, Bakery and Confectionary Workers Union, 97 S. Ct. 1067 (1977) extends the scope of the *Trilogy* doctrine to cover a severance pay dispute that arose after the expiration of the contract. The presumption in favor of arbitration must be negated expressly, or by clear implication according to the Court. *See also* USW v. USS, 82 Lab. Cas. Par. 10,134 (D. Minn. 1977); and Union v. Helia San Jeronimo Corp., 96 LRRM 2279 (D.P.R. 1977) dealing with specific waivers of arbitration by agreement.

[27] Bhd. of R.R. Trainmen v. Chicago River & Ind. R.R., 353 U.S. 301 (1957).

[28] Local 174, Int'l Bhd. of Teamsters v. Lucas Flour, 369 U.S. 95 (1962).

[29] Sinclair Refining v. Atkinson, 370 U.S. 195 (1962).

[30] Boys Markets, *supra* note 12.

dispute subject to a mandatory grievance and arbitration procedure. This decision was a serious blow to one of the most important weapons labor has but there is specific language in *Boys Markets* stating that federal courts are not to issue an injunction simply because management requests one. The Supreme Court outlines specific guidelines for the federal courts to follow in ruling on requests for injunctive relief.[31] Subsequent decisions have confirmed that there are a number of prerequisites for the issuance of a *Boys Markets* injunction:

[a] Contractual Obligation to Arbitrate

The strike must be over an issue that the parties are contractually bound to arbitrate. One of the chief rationales of *Boys Markets* and its progeny is that the employer's agreement to arbitrate is the quid pro quo for a no-strike agreement, whether the agreement is express or implied. The federal labor law policy embodied in these decisions is the encouragement of collective bargaining and administrative techniques for the peaceful resolution of industrial disputes.[32] Therefore, if the arbitration obligation has been terminated or if the dispute is not subject to arbitration under the contract, an injunction should not issue.[33] If the union has reserved the right to strike over certain issues, or over any issue, the court should not award injunctive relief.[34] Furthermore, if the contract contains a grievance procedure and makes arbitration optional, an injunction should not issue.[35]

---

[31] 370 U.S. at 228.

[32] Boys Markets, *supra* note 12. Also note that the Supreme Court had already approved the utilization of such injunctive powers under the Railway Labor Act in Bhd. of Trainmen v. Chicago River & Ind. R.R., 353 U.S. 30 (1957), where the court held that the Norris-LaGuardia Act did not preclude the issuance of injunctive relief where a union struck over a dispute subject to arbitration under the Railway Labor Act.

[33] Teledyne Wisc. Motor v. UAW, Local 283, 91 LRRM 2313 (7th Cir. 1976) (dispute not subject to arbitration); A.S. Abell Co. v. Typographical Union, 85 LRRM 2368 (D. Md. 1974) (where the contract had expired).

[34] Associated Gen. Contractors v. Teamsters, 454 F.2d 1324 (7th Cir. 1972); Martin Highland, Inc. v. U.S. District Court, 460 F.2d 789 (9th Cir. 1972).

[35] Emery Air Freight Corp. v. Local Union 295, 449 F.2d 586 78 LRRM 2766 (2d Cir. 1971), *cert. denied,* 405 U.S. 1066, 79 LRRM 3092 (1972).

[b] Management Willingness to Arbitrate

Management must be willing to arbitrate the underlying dispute and the court must order arbitration as a condition of injunctive relief. The *Boys Markets* decision made this an explicit condition for management to obtain injunctive relief.[36] If the employer seeks to avoid arbitration while seeking injunctive relief, the injunction should not issue.[37] Rarely will an employer decline to arbitrate an issue that is at the heart of a strike shutting down the workplace.

[c] Injunction Warranted in Equity

The court must consider whether an injunction would be warranted under the ordinary principles of equity. The *Boys Markets* court summarized this succinctly when it stated—

> Beyond this, the District Court must, of course, consider whether issuance of an injunction would be warranted under ordinary principles of equity—whether breaches are occurring and will continue, or have been threatened and will be committed; whether they have caused or will cause irreparable injury to the employer; and whether the employer will suffer more from the denial of an injunction than the union will from its issuance.[38]

It is extremely important to force the company to meet its burden of proving that the equities are in its favor. The reality is that courts will generally rule that the equities in a *Boys Markets* strike are in favor of the company.[39] One notable exception is the situation in which the company overreacts to minor employee misconduct in such a manner as to provoke a shutdown that then

---

36 370 U.S. at 228. *Also see* Emery Air Freight Corp., *supra* note 35.

37 *See* Chief Freight Lines Co. v. Teamsters Local 886, 514 F.2d 572, 89 LRRM 2044 (10th Cir. 1975).

38 370 U.S. at 228, 82 S. Ct. at 1346.

39 *See, e.g.*, Gen. Bldg. Contractors Ass'n v. IUOE, 371 F. Supp. 1130, 86 LRRM 1130 (E.D. Pa. 1974). Also check the opinions in your local federal district court—such requests for injunctive relief are rarely denied.

causes the company serious injury.[40] The courts also tended to accept without much question the proposition that an illegal strike causes serious injury.[41] One defense the union must raise is that if the company has suffered injury and if, in fact, it has a cause of action against the union for this injury, then it has an adequate remedy at law in a damage action. While this issue must be raised strongly, the courts tend to reject it.[42]

[4] Jurisdiction of State Courts and Removal to Federal Court

While Section 301 gives jurisdiction to the U.S. district courts, the Supreme Court has held that Congress did not intend to dislodge the preexisting jurisdiction of state courts to rule on matters involving alleged violations of collective bargaining agreements.[43] In fact, in another case, it sustained a state court's award of damages for breach by the union of no-strike provisions of a contract (the Norris-LaGuardia Act was not considered because no injunctive relief was sought).[44]

A Section 301 suit filed in a state court is removable to the federal courts under the federal removal statute.[45] At the time of any removal there will generally be a state court temporary restraining order in effect. In a 1974 case, the court resolved the possible procedural problems, stating:

> An ex-parte restraining order issued by a state court prior to removal remains in force after removal no longer than it would have remained in effect under state law, but in no event does the order

---

[40] In Anheuser-Busch, Inc. v. Teamsters Local, 633, 511 F.2d 1097, 88 LRRM 2785 (1st Cir. 1975), *cert denied* 90 LRRM 2744 (1975), the company responded to minor infractions (wearing of tank-top shirts on the job and imposition of discipline for doing so) in such a way as to cause a shutdown. The First Circuit held that injunctive relief was inappropriate.

[41] Gen. Bldg. Contractors Ass'n, *supra* note 39.

[42] Boys Markets, *supra* note 12; William E. Arnold Co. v. Carpenters Dist. Council, 417 U.S. 12, 86 LRRM 2212 (1974).

[43] Charles Dowd Box Co. v. Courtney, 368 U.S. 502 (1962).

[44] Local 174, Int'l Bhd. of Teamsters v. Lucas Flour, *supra* note 28.

[45] 28 U.S.C. § 1441; Avco Corp. v. Aero Lodge No. 735, 390 U.S. 557, 67 LRRM 2881 (1968).

> remain in force longer than the time limitations imposed by Rule 65(b). . . . [46]

Rule 65(b) of the Federal Rules of Civil Procedure provides that temporary restraining orders expire within ten days unless extended.

The Norris-LaGuardia Act imposes stringent procedural requirements upon federal courts, which must be met before the issuance of an injunction.[47] While the Supreme Court has not yet addressed this question, the courts of appeals agree that the procedural requirements of the Norris-LaGuardia Act are to be applied by the federal courts in these cases.[48]

Besides the legal consideration mentioned above, there are tactical questions that must be considered in determining whether to seek removal. Knowledge of the relative sympathies of the judges who will hear the case in the respective courts is, of course, important. Likewise, an attorney should consider whether removal will speed or slow the judicial process. It is also important, when one is seeking removal, to pay strict attention to timing and other requirements. These are included in the removal statute, the Federal Rules of Civil Procedure, and the local rules of many district courts. Failure to follow these requirements may render a removal attempt ineffective and even result in a default.

[5] Presumption of Arbitrability in *Boys Markets* Cases

This issue was resolved long before *Boys Markets* in the Steelworkers Trilogy.[49] In the *Warrior and Gulf Navigation* case, the court stated:

> An order to arbitrate the particular grievance should not be denied

---

[46] Granny Goose Foods, Inc. v. Teamsters Local 70, 415 U.S. 423, 85 LRRM 2481 (1974).

[47] *See generally* 29 U.S.C. § 101 et seq.

[48] United States Steel Corp. v. UMWA, 456 F.2d 483, 79 LRRM 2518 (3d Cir. 1972); Celotex Corp. v. OCAW, 516 F.2d 242, 89 LRRM 2372 (7th Cir. 1975); Detroit Newspaper Publishers Ass'n v. Detroit Typographical Union, 471 F.2d 872, 82 LRRM 2332 (1972), *cert. denied,* 411 U.S. 967.

[49] Steelworkers Trilogy, *supra* note 25.

> unless it may be said with positive assurance that the arbitration clause is not susceptible of an interpretation that covers the asserted dispute. *Doubts should be resolved in favor of coverage.*[50] (emphasis added)

In *Gateway Coal v. UMW,*[51] the court held that the presumption of arbitrability set forth in the Steelworkers Trilogy was applicable to cases involving the grant of injunctive relief under *Boys Markets.* That case involved a safety issue not clearly covered by the grievance and arbitration clause of the contract, but the court held that ambiguities regarding what is or is not arbitrable do not constitute "express exceptions" or "forceful evidence" of an intent to exclude an issue from arbitration.[52] Under this decision, most courts will hold that the presumption of arbitrability is applicable if the issue before the court is the right of the company to obtain injunctive relief in a strike over an issue arguably subject to the grievance and arbitration machinery.

[6] Tactical Considerations in Opposing Company Requests for a *Boys Markets* Injunction

The first line of inquiry is to determine whether the strike falls within one of the exceptions to *Boys Markets.* (The exceptions are discussed more fully in Section 3.02. If it falls within one of the exceptions, no injunction should issue. However, most often the union will not be in a position to argue persuasively that the strike falls within one of the *Boys Markets* exceptions. Force the company and the court to adhere to the strict procedural requirements contained in the Norris-LaGuardia Act and push the equitable arguments aggressively.

Frequently a company will obtain a temporary restraining order (TRO) against a strike. Often such an order is obtained ex parte with no notice to the union or its counsel. It is important to try to block the issuance of a TRO, or at least to stall its

[50] Warrior Gulf Navigation, 363 U.S. at 582-83.

[51] Gateway Coal Co. v. United Mine Workers of America, 414 U.S. 368, 85 LRRM 2049 (1974).

[52] 414 U.S. at 380 n. 10.

issuance. Once granted, TROs tend to be routinely coverted into preliminary or permanent injunctions after further hearings. If a TRO is in existence before the union gets into court, the burden of proof has effectively been shifted to the union. An additional consideration is that violations of a TRO are punishable through the sanction of contempt of court, even though the union may later block the issuance of a preliminary or permanent injunction.

If a dispute occurs over which the company may seek a *Boys Markets* injunction, contact the company attorney and the judge likely to preside over requests for injunctive relief by telegram (or certified mail) and by phone; inform them that you are the union's attorney for all purposes and that you would like immediate notification if the company files for injunctive relief. Inform them also that you would like prior notification of any meeting/hearing regarding the company's request for injunctive relief. This may prevent the issuance of an ex parte TRO.

Section 7 of the Norris-LaGuardia Act allows for the issuance of a TRO without notice to the union under certain limited circumstances.[53] The company must allege that there will be substantial and irreparable injury to its property without the issuance of a TRO. The court could issue a TRO on the basis of sworn testimony that would be sufficient, if sustained, to justify issuing a TRO upon a hearing after notice. TROs issued without notice become void after the expiration of five days.

Note also that the local rules of many U.S. district courts and some state courts require that counsel seeking a TRO first attempt to notify the party sought to be enjoined.

If a TRO is issued without notice and the union attorney has previously requested to be notified of any hearing on such matter, there are two courses of action to follow: (1) As part of the equitable arguments use this as an example of the unfairness of the company's actions; and (2) use it to help mobilize workers in the current efforts.

Before the court may issue a *Boys Markets* injunction, it must take testimony and make specific findings of fact as to (1) what the strike issues are and (2) the arbitrability of those issues.[54] If

---

[53] Section 7 of the Norris-LaGuardia Act, 29 U.S.C. § 107.

[54] Boys Markets, 398 U.S. at 254; Shore Line R.R. v. Locomotive Firemen, 61 LRRM 2388 (6th Cir. 1966).

the strike issues are not subject to the grievance and arbitration machinery, then no injunction should issue.[55] The plaintiff (the company) has the burden of proving that the strike comes within the *Boys Markets* exceptions to the Norris-LaGuardia Act and, that the dispute is over an arbitrable grievance.[56] In a 1972 case, the court stated:

> The employer must provide the court with an evidentiary basis for making the findings required by *Boys Markets* as a prerequisite to the issuance of an injunction. Parade in this case *did not affirmatively allege that the strike was over an arbitrable issue.* . . . When asked at the hearing whether Parade conceded that the situation in dispute presented an arbitrable issue under the collective bargaining agreement, Parade's counsel refused to commit himself and *suggested that an arbitrator might properly determine that question in the future.* We think that is not enough.[57] (emphasis added)

Further, the courts are still required to apply the traditional equity standards, including

> whether breaches are occurring and will continue; or have been threatened and will be committed; whether they have caused or will cause irreparable injury to the employer; and whether the employer will suffer more from the denial of an injunction than will the union from its issuance.[58]

General equitable principles and the Norris-LaGuardia Act,[59] consider the injunction an extraordinary remedy; consequently, before one is issued, irreparable injury must be shown by the party seeking it.

---

[55] Buffalo Forge Co. v. USWA, 428 U.S. 397 (1976); *see also* Section 3.02, *infra.*

[56] N. Am. Coal Corp. v. Local 2262, UMWA, 497 F.2d 459, 465 (6th Cir. 1974); Boys Markets, 398 U.S. at 253-54; Plain Dealer Publishing Co. v. Cleveland Typographical Union No. 53, 520 F.2d 1220 (6th Cir. 1975), *cert. denied,* 96 S. Ct. 3221 (1976).

[57] Parade Publications, Inc. v. Phila. Mailers Union No. 14, 459 F.2d 369 (3d Cir. 1972).

[58] Dissenting opinion in Sinclair, 370 U.S. at 228, cited in Boys Markets, 398 U.S. 235 at 254.

[59] Norris-LaGuardia Act (Section 7, 29 U.S.C. Sec. 107).

In a 1975 case,[60] a work stoppage occurred when the company disciplined some workers for wearing tank tops. Both the union and the company agreed that the underlying dispute was arbitrable, and the district court issued an injunction. The appellate court reversed, holding that no injunction should issue because no irreparable injury was shown. The court stated:

> [W]e conclude that the limited incursion upon the Norris-La-Guardia Act which was authorized by Boys Markets is insufficient to support the injunction issued below. Although the district court's findings on injury make reference to the fact that the plant was effectively shut down, *an employer cannot be permitted to qualify for injunctive relief simply by responding to minor employee infractions in a way that brings serious and irreparable damage upon himself by causing a shutdown.* This is what happened here. As the district court noted, the real controversy is whether the employees shall be allowed to wear tank top shirts pending submission of the agreement to arbitration.
>
> Viewed from this perspective, the appellee's expected injury cannot be said to be either irreparable or one which outweighs the loss which the union is likely to suffer from the issuance of an injunction.[61] (emphasis added)

Such holdings must be expanded, particularly in an era of economic crises and increasing attacks on unions and workers' rights. It appears that, because of ever-tightening profit margins, management harassment and discipline of workers for minor infractions are increasing and will inevitably lead to strikes.

NRI v. Steelworkers,[62] involved similar issues, but with one key distinguishing feature. The company instituted new work rules, which the workers refused to follow. The company suspended a large number of workers, and the union struck. The company stated it was willing to suspend enforcement of the work rules and to proceed directly to arbitration. The union wanted to process the cases through normal channels, with a discharged union

---

60 Anheuser-Busch, Inc. v. Int'l Bhd. of Teamsters, 511 F.2d 1097 (1st Cir. 1975), *cert. denied,* 423 U.S. 875 (1975).

61 511 F.2d at 1099-1100.

62 NRI v. United Steelworkers of America, 562 F.2d 1069 (8th Cir. 1977), *cert. denied,* 98 S. Ct. 1486 (1978).

representative present at each step. The company refused. The court distinguished *Anheuser-Bush* by stating:

> Here NRI did not bring about the disruption itself by insisting upon enforcement of minor work rules. The company was willing to and *did in fact suspend enforcement of its rules pending resolution of the underlying dispute through arbitration.* In addition, the injury to NRI threatened by the continued disruption of employees at the Hot Springs plant, even in the absence of work rules is clearly greater than the potential harm of having one's employees present an unsightly appearance to visitors.[63]

However, the court made a false distinction. The stoppages occurred not because of the new work rules, but because the company suspended workers who refused to follow the rules and refused to permit a discharged union representative to participate in the grievance/arbitration procedure.

[7] Tactical Considerations: Procedural Requirements of the Norris-LaGuardia Act

As noted previously, the strict procedural requirements of the Norris-LaGuardia Act apply to suits for injunctions brought under Section 301.[64] Section 6 of the Norris-LaGuardia Act provides that no officer, no member, and no union may be held liable for the unlawful acts of individuals, members, or agents, "*except upon clear proof of actual participation in, or actual authorization of, such acts, or of ratification of such acts after actual knowledge thereof.*"[65] (emphasis added)

In *UMW v. Gibbs,*[66] the court explained the burden of proof requirement as follows:

> [T]he plaintiff in a civil case need not satisfy the criminal standard

[63] 96 LRRM at 2126.

[64] *See* cases cited in note 48, *supra. See also* United States Steel Corp. v. UMWA, 519 F.2d 1236 (5th Cir. 1975), *cert denied,* 428 U.S. 910 (1976); N.Y. Tel. Co. v. Communications Workers, 445 F.2d 39 (2d Cir. 1971).

[65] 29 U.S.C. § 106.

[66] United Mine Workers of America v. Gibbs, 383 U.S. 715 (1966).

> of reasonable doubt on the issue of participation, authorization, or ratification; neither may he prevail by meeting the ordinary civil burden of persuasion, but he is required to persuade by a substantial margin, to come forward with "more than a mere preponderance of the evidence to prevail."[67]

It is extremely important continually to emphasize the "clear proof" standard to the court. Courts continually decide civil cases on the traditional preponderance of the evidence standard and if its inadequacy is not emphasized, courts may allow the companies to slide by on that standard. This is important for a number of reasons. A finding at this stage that a union or an individual is liable for a strike in breach of a collective bargaining agreement may subject both the individual and the union to contempt of court proceedings for alleged violations of a district court injunction. It may also increase the risk to the union of financial liability in a suit for damages under Section 301.

Section 7 of the Norris-LaGuardia Act lists several findings of fact that a court must make before it has jurisdiction to issue an injunction. Frequently, courts do not clearly make such findings before issuing a *Boys Markets* injunction; this is particularly true at the stage where the TRO is issued. Force the proof as to each finding of fact required by Section 7.

Section 7(a) requires the finding that "unlawful acts have been threatened and will be committed unless restrained or have been committed and will be continued unless restrained." If the company seeks injunctive relief based upon threats or past activity, argue that the alleged threats and past activity are too vague to support the extraordinary use of injunctive power, since threats are common in labor-management relations. If a work stoppage has recently ended, state that there is nothing to enjoin and that the possibilities of future *Boys Markets* strikes are too vague and remote to support the company's request for injunctive relief. (Prospective issuance of *Boys Markets* injunctions is discussed in Section 3.03.)

Section 7(a) also states that an injunction may issue only against organizations or persons participating in or ratifying the

---

[67] *Id. See also* United Bhd. of Carpenters & Joiners of America v. United States, 330 U.S. 395 (1947).

unlawful act. There may be occasions to consent to an injunction against an illegal strike, but do not consent to a broad, sweeping injunction. The company's complaint usually lists several union officers, individuals, and various branches of the union. Move to dismiss those individuals, officers, and branches of the union for which there exists no factual support for the company's allegations.

Section 7(b) of the Act requires a finding that "substantial and irreparable injury to complainant's property will follow." Refer to *Anheuser-Busch,*[68] in which the court denied injunctive relief because no irreparable injury was shown and because the employer responded to a minor employee violation in such a manner as to bring on a strike (see Section 3.01[6]). A large number of work stoppages result from oppressive management policies in which workers are disciplined for minor work infractions.

Section 7(c) invokes a traditional equitable balancing test and requires, as a condition to the grant of injunctive relief, that "as to each item of relief granted greater injury will be inflicted upon complainant by the denial of relief than will be inflicted upon the defendants by the granting of relief."[69]

The final requirement for our purposes is a finding that the company has no adequate remedy at law. Again the courts tend to find that the company does not have an adequate remedy at law.

Section 8 of the Norris-LaGuardia Act prohibits issuance of an injunction if the company has "failed to make every reasonable effort to settle the dispute either by negotiation or with the aid of any available governmental machinery of mediation or voluntary arbitration." The court will condition the grant of the injunction upon company participation in arbitrating the underlying dispute.[70] In an earlier case, the court gave its view on the use of injunctive relief when it stated:

> [The] prime purpose [of the Norris-LaGuardia Act] was to restrict the federal equity power in such matters within greatly narrower limits than it had come to occupy (footnote omitted). It sought

---

[68] Anheuser-Busch, *supra* note 60.

[69] 29 U.S.C. § 107(c).

[70] Boys Markets, 398 U.S. at 254.

> to make injuction a last line of defense, available not only after other legally required methods, but after all reasonable methods as well, had been tried and found wanting.[71]

That decision recognizes that the injunction is an extraordinary remedy to be used in very narrow circumstances when needed.

If the union has been enjoined from certain strike activity, an immediate appeal to the circuit court of appeals should be considered. Section 10 of the Norris-LaGuardia Act gives precedence to an appeal from the issuance of a temporary injunction and requires that a bond be posted by the party appealing. The decision to appeal will vary from case to case. Two considerations are the potential union financial liability absent an appeal and the necessity to restrain constant court interference in labor disputes.

Failure to comply with the procedural requirements of the Norris-LaGuardia Act and meet the prerequisites for granting of injunctive relief under *Boys Markets* provides the basis for dissolution of the injunction, either on appeal to the circuit court or on a petition to reconsider in the district court. It can also lead to the recovery of attorney's fees against the bond the company posted with the court. Section 7 requires that the party seeking the injunction file a bond with sufficient security to reimburse the party enjoined for any loss or expense suffered from an erroneously issued injunction.

In *Detroit Newspaper Publishers v. Detroit Typographical Union,*[72] the union had obtained an injunction against the employer. The court of appeals reversed the district court's grant of injunctive relief, stating that the lower court had failed to make findings of fact showing irreparable harm and that the evidence did not show irreparable harm.

The Third Circuit reversed a district court award to the union of attorney's fees, costs, and expenses in *Celotex v. O.C.A.W.*[73] The court stated that, although the Section 7 requirements of the Norris-LaGuardia Act had not been met (no oral testimony was

---

[71] Bhd. of R.R. Trainmen, Enterprise Lodge No. 27 v. Toledo P. & W. R.R., 321 U.S. 50, 58-59 (1944).

[72] Detroit Newspaper Publishers Ass'n v. Detroit Typographical Union No. 18, 471 F.2d 872 (8th Cir. 1972), *cert. denied,* 411 U.S. 967 (1973).

[73] Celotex v. O.C.A.W., 516 F.2d 242 (3d Cir. 1975).

taken), there was no prejudice to the union.[74]

[8] NLRB Jurisdiction in Issues Also Litigated under Section 301 of the Taft-Hartley Act

The National Labor Relations Board (NLRB) retains jurisdiction to deal with an unfair labor practice that violates a collective bargaining agreement. Section 301, giving the federal district courts jurisdiction over suits for violation of contracts between employers and unions, is not an exclusive remedy.[75] Likewise, when an action is arguably an unfair labor practice prohibited by Section 8 of the Act and is at the same time a breach of the collective bargaining agreement, the NLRB's jurisdiction is not exclusive, and the federal district courts retain jurisdiction under Section 301.

What happens when both the federal courts and the NLRB become involved in the same dispute? In *Edward D. Sultan Co. v. Local 427,*[76] the federal court presided over a company suit for damages under Section 301, alleging breach of the no-strike provisions of the contract. The NLRB had already ruled that the union had violated the Act by striking and picketing in an effort to force the company to rescind the agreement in violation of the no-strike clause. The district court granted the company's motion for summary judgment under the doctrines of collateral estoppel and res judicata because all relevant facts had already been litigated before the NLRB and decided against the union.

If there is a difference between the ruling of the NLRB in an unfair labor practice proceeding and that of the federal district court in an action for enforcement of a contract under Section 301, the Board's position is that its decision takes precedence.[77] However, not all the circuit courts would agree with this conclu-

---

[74] *Id. See also* Emery Air Freight Corp. v. Local 295 Int'l Bhd. of Teamsters, 449 F.2d 586 (2d Cir. 1971), *cert. denied,* 405 U.S. 1066 (1972).

[75] Smith v. Evening News, 371 U.S. 195 (1962); *see also* NLRB v. C. & C. Plywood Corp., 385 U.S. 421 (1967).

[76] 559 F. Supp. 1204, 95 LRRM 3081 (D. Hawaii 1977).

[77] Jacob's Transfer, 227 NLRB 181, 95 LRRM 1589 (1977).

sion. In *NLRB v. Heyman,*[78] the employer filed a Section 301 suit in the district court, seeking rescission of a labor contract the Teamsters alleged was binding. The district court agreed with the company and rescinded the agreement. The company then terminated the contract and refused to make welfare and pension fund payments required by the contract. The union filed a charge with the Board, which held that the company had violated Section 8(a)(5) of the Act. The circuit court refused to enforce the Board's order, holding that (1) the Board's jurisdiction over unfair labor practices does not replace federal district court jurisdiction under Section 301 and (2) the Board erred when it refused to give any weight to the district court decision under Section 301.

It is the general rule in *Boys Markets* strikes that companies will pursue their claims under Section 301 for both damages and injunctive relief. The primary reason is the quickness with which they can obtain injunctive relief blocking wildcat strikes, as opposed to the relatively slow procedures of the NLRB.

§ 3.02. Exceptions to the No-Strike Provisions of *Boys Markets* and Its Progeny

The exceptions to the no-strike decisions of *Boys Markets* and its progeny are relatively limited and are frequently the source of conflicting interpretations by various courts. This is ironic, since *Boys Markets* itself was initially understood as a relatively narrow exception to the anti-injunction restrictions of the Norris-LaGuardia Act.

Whenever one is faced with defending a union in court against a company request for a *Boys Markets* injunction, the first consideration should be whether the particular strike involves an exception to *Boys Markets.* Meet with union officials and with strikers to discover (1) the issue at the heart of the dispute and (2) the extent of union officials' involvement, if any. This meeting should occur, if possible, before the first appearance in court. If the company is trying to get a quick TRO without hearings, make it clear to the court that the case falls within one of the exceptions to *Boys Markets.*

[78] NLRB v. Walter E. Heyman, 92 LRRM 3603 (9th Cir. 1976).

It is generally crucial that an injunction, even a TRO, be staved off. An injunction can cripple a legitimate strike effort, and efforts should focus on delaying issuance of an injunction or fitting it under one of the exceptions to *Boys Markets.*

[1] Sympathy Strikes

Injunctive relief is not available against a sympathy strike despite the presence in the labor contract of a no-strike clause and/or mandatory grievance and arbitration procedures. Such strikes (1) are not over an arbitrable grievance, (2) do not violate a union's no-strike obligation, and (3) thus do not fall within the *Boys Markets* exception to the Norris-LaGuardia Act. In *Buffalo Forge v. Steelworkers,*[79] one company had two separate collective bargaining agreements with two separate locals of the same union (production and maintenance workers). During the contract terms of those agreements, a different union was certified to represent the company's office, technical, and maintenance employees. Those employees struck for a contract, and the production and maintenance workers honored the picket lines. The court held that the strike was not over a grievance the union had agreed to arbitrate and thus could not be enjoined. The key cases interpreting the *Buffalo Forge* decision arose out of the massive wildcat strikes that occurred in the coalfields from 1975 through 1977. Some differences among the various circuit courts exist.

Southern Ohio Coal v. UMW,[80] involved a situation in which the company had obtained injunctions against three UMW locals prior to the Supreme Court decision in *Buffalo Forge.* Shortly after *Buffalo Forge* was decided, a wave of wildcat strikes spread throughout the coalfields and included the three locals already subject to the injunctions. The company sought contempt adjudications against the locals, but the district court denied the company's request in light of *Buffalo Forge.* The company raised three contentions that tested the limits of *Buffalo Forge:* (1) This case

[79] Buffalo Forge Co. v. United Steelworkers of America, 428 U.S. 397 (1976).

[80] S. Ohio Coal Co. v. United Mine Workers of America, 551 F.2d 695 (6th Cir. 1977).

involved one bargaining unit and one national contract, whereas in *Buffalo Forge* different bargaining units and different contracts were involved; (2) the underlying strike and the picketing in *Southern Ohio Coal* were illegal, whereas the underlying strike in *Buffalo Forge* was legal; and (3) the *Buffalo Forge* decision was wrong. The Sixth Circuit rejected all these contentions.

However, in *Cedar Coal v. UMW,*[81] a case involving the same series of wildcat strikes noted above, the Fourth Circuit reached a slightly different conclusion. A strike occurred at one mine of the Cedar Coal Company over a job classification dispute, a dispute subject to the grievance and arbitration machinery. A second local of Cedar Coal engaged in a sympathy strike in favor of the first local. At a third local, the Matrinka mines of the Southern Ohio Coal Company, the miners also engaged in a sympathy strike. The court ruled as follows on each of the three locals of the UMW: (1) It enjoined the underlying strike at the first Cedar Coal local, concluding that the dispute was subject to binding arbitration. (2) It enjoined the sympathy strike by the second Cedar Coal local because the same company was involved, the same collective bargaining agreement was involved, and the purpose of the sympathy strike was to compel the company to concede to an arbitrable issue at a sister local (this conflicts with the Sixth Circuit and arguably also conflicts with *Buffalo Forge*). (3) It refused to enjoin the sympathy strike at the Southern Ohio mines, concluding that *Buffalo Forge* barred injunctive relief if a different employer was involved. The court noted that the *Buffalo Forge* bar against injunctive relief precludes issuance of an injunction if the only dispute between the company and the union is over the meaning or application of implied or express no-strike provisions contained in the labor contract (i.e., no arbitrable dispute) and if such a dispute has been brought about by another dispute that is not arbitrable.

In *Ziegler Coal v. UMW,*[82] the underlying strike was once again at Cedar Coal. Employees of Ziegler Coal refused to cross picket lines set up by stranger pickets. The company raised the contention that its employees were in fact engaged in an extension of

---

[81] Cedar Coal Co. v. United Mine Workers of America, 560 F.2d 1153 (4th Cir. 1977).

[82] Ziegler Coal Co. v. Local 1870 UMWA, 566 F.2d 582 (7th Cir. 1977).

the illegal primary strike begun by another UMW local at Cedar Coal and not in a sympathy strike. The Seventh Circuit held that *Buffalo Forge* controlled and rejected the company's contentions, stating that neither the illegality of the underlying strike nor the fact of a possible benefit accruing to its employees from a concession by the employer at the mine with the underlying dispute allowed for an injunction. Despite the conflict between the circuits, the Supreme Court denied *certiorari* in all three cases noted above.

The Third Circuit muddied the waters a little more in *Bituminous Coal Operators' Association v. UMW.*[83] The coal operators sought declaratory and injunctive relief for a declaration that the UMW had breached the national collective bargaining agreement by failing to take effective steps to ensure compliance by its members and end an alleged pattern and practice of illegal strikes and picketing. The coal operators sought, in essence, a prospective injunction. The district court granted the union's motion to dismiss, but the Third Circuit reversed and remanded for a reconsideration of the request for declaratory relief. The court also held that individual mines might be entitled to prospective injunctive relief, holding that the Norris-LaGuardia Act does not bar an injunction to prevent future but identical walkouts at identical locations over issues similar to those already adjudicated. The court held that the coal operators were not entitled to injunctive relief, reasoning that the issue of the *UMW's obligation to discipline members who engage in wildcat strikes was not subject to the grievance and arbitration procedure.* It also noted that the request for prospective injunctive relief was phrased much too broadly.

[2] *Buffalo Forge:* Injunctive Relief after the Arbitration Decision

It is important to remember that the *Buffalo Forge* restrictions against the grant of injunctive relief in sympathy strikes apply prior to arbitration. If an arbitrator specifically holds that a sympathy strike violates the labor agreement, the strike may be en-

---

[83] Bituminous Coal Operators' Ass'n v. United Mine Workers of America, 585 F.2d 586 (3d Cir. 1978).

joined. In *Alyeska Pipe Line v. Teamsters,*[84] the court enforced an arbitration award ordering the union to stop picketing, even though the underlying dispute was not arbitrable. The arbitrator had concluded that the no-strike clause had been violated.

Whether an arbitrator will hold that a sympathy strike violates the contract will hinge upon specific language in the no-strike clause. Generally, a waiver of the right to engage in sympathy strikes must be clear and unmistakable. Such a waiver will not be simply presumed from a broad no-strike clause. (This matter is discussed more fully in Section 3.02[3]).

[3] Position of the NLRB On Sympathy Strikes

The NLRB considers sympathy strikes protected activity. The Board will not find a waiver of the right to engage in a sympathy strike unless the intention to waive the right is clearly shown.[85] The NLRB generally holds that the discharge of workers for engaging in a sympathy strike is an unfair labor practice under the Act, but the circuits are split on enforcing the Board orders.[86]

[4] Political Strikes

Political strikes, such as strikes against particular governmental policies, are not subject to the grievance and arbitration procedures in contracts and thus are not enjoinable under *Boys Markets.* These strikes are extremely common in Europe and Latin American but rarely occur here. Two recent cases of such strikes are the UMW strikes for black lung legislation (late 1960s) and the UMW strikes in Alabama against the importation of South African coal (1970s).

---

[84] Alyeska Pipe Line v. Teamsters, 557 F.2d 1263 (9th Cir. 1977).

[85] NLRB v. Rockaway News Supply, 345 U.S. 71, 31 LRRM 2432 (1952); NLRB v. S. Greyhound Lines, 426 F.2d 1299, 74 LRRM 2080 (5th Cir. 1970).

[86] Gary-Hobart Co. v. NLRB. 511 F.2d 284, 88 LRRM 2830 (7th Cir. 1975); Hoffman Beverage Co., 163 NLRB 981, 65 LRRM 1011 (1967); AMCAR Division, ACF Industries v. NLRB, 106 LRRM 2518 (8th Cir. 1981); Delaware Coca-Cola Bottling Co. v. Teamsters, Local 326, 104 LRRM 2776 (3d Cir. 1980); NLRB v. Gould, Inc., 105 IRRM 2588 (10th Cir. 1980); Montana-Dakotas Utilities Co. v. NLRB, 79 LRRM 2854 (8th Cir. 1972); NLRB v. Keller-Crescent Co, 92 LRRM

In *U.S. Steel v. UMW,*[87] UMW miners in Alabama struck to protest importation of South African coal mined under slave labor conditions. The court declared that injunctive relief was not available because the strike was not over an arbitrable issue. U.S. Steel sought to have the strike enjoined on the basis of a contract clause requiring submission to the grievance and arbitration machinery of local trouble of any kind. The court rejected this attempt, explaining,

> [T]he trouble must be related to a grievance arising from the employment relationship between the company affected by the work stoppage and the striking employees,

and went on to add

> Under *Boys Markets* guidelines, however, we must focus on the union's grievance, for the evil remedied in *Boys Markets* was substitution by the union of economic weapons for arbitration to force the employer to respond to its demands.[88]

However, a company can still take this issue to arbitration under the contract as a possible violation of a no-strike clause, and the courts will enforce an arbitrator's back-to-work order.[89]

With the deepening of the economic crisis and the increasing involvement of unions in nonworkplace issues, strikes of a political nature will increase. Some recent examples are (1) as noted above, coalfield strikes for black lung legislation, (2) coalfield strikes protesting federal court intervention in labor disputes, and (3) various refusals by longshoremen to load ships bound for certain countries (Chile, Iran, Soviet Union).

These strikes probably will not be subject to *Boys Markets* injunctions unless there is an explicit waiver of the right to engage in such strikes.[90] The rationale controlling such decisions will

3591 (7th Cir. 1976); Iowa Beef Processors v. Meatcutters, 101 LRRM 2235 (8th Cir. 1979).

[87] United States Steel Corp. v. United Mine Workers of America, 519 F.2d 1236 (5th Cir. 1975), *cert. denied,* 428 U.S. 910 (1976).

[88] 519 F.2d at 1248.

[89] United States Steel Corp. v. UMWA, *supra. See also* Parade Publications v. Phila. Mailers Union No. 14, 459 F.2d 369 (3d Cir. 1972); Emery Air Freight Corp., *supra* note 74.

[90] While not exactly on point, the following cases give us a good idea as to how the courts will deal with such strikes: Parade Publications, *supra;* Napa

probably be the *Buffalo Forge* one, which presently controls the courts and the NLRB in sympathy strikes.

[5] Strikes Directed against the Union Leadership

Within the labor movement, there is a growing contradiction between some union officials and the rank-and-file members. Rank-and-file members sometimes feel that union officials have more in common with the companies and at times see union officials as doing the company's dirty work. This view is reinforced by (1) high salaries for union officials, (2) frequent statements by some union officials as to how labor and management must find more ways to cooperate, (3) lack of democratic procedures in some unions, including denial of the right to ratify contracts through membership vote, (4) the neglect by some unions of the day-to-day problems workers face on the shop floor, (5) the increasing agreement of many union officials to the necessity of no-strike clauses, and (6) the influence of organized crime in some major unions. As a result, an increasing number of strikes are directed against the union leadership itself.

These strikes do not arise from disputes concerning the employment relationship, so no arbitrable issue is presented. Consequently, they are not subject to *Boys Markets* injunctions. The employer suing for injunctive relief has the burden of proving that the strike falls within the *Boys Markets* exception to the Norris-LaGuardia Act and specifically has the burden of showing that the dispute is over an arbitrable grievance.[91] The Third Cir-

---

Pittsburgh, Inc., v. Automotive Employees Local 926, 502 F.2d 321 (3d Cir. 1974); Amstar Corp. v. Amalgamated Meatcutters, 468 F.2d 1372 (5th Cir. 1972); Inland Steel Co. v. UMWA Local 1545, 505 F.2d 293 (8th Cir. 1974). Decisions concerning the boycott of Soviet trade by the International Longshoremen's Association over the Soviet invasion of Afghanistan have split on whether this amounted to an illegal secondary boycott. The First Circuit found it to be so. Allied Int'l v. ILA, 106 LRRM 2659 (1981). The Fifth Circuit disagreed. Baldovin v. Longshoremen, 105 LRRM 2539 (1980). The ILA has petitioned the D.C. Circuit for review of the NLRB's decision in ILA, Local 799, 108 LRRM 1033 (1981).

[91] N. Am. Coal Co. v. Local Union 2262, UMWA, 497 F.2d 459, 465 (6th Cir. 1974).

cuit summarized the company's burden of proof as follows:

> The employer must provide the court with an evidentiary basis for making the findings required by *Boys Markets* as a prerequisite to the issuance of an injunction. Parade in the case did not affirmatively allege that the strike was over an arbitrable issue. When asked at the hearing whether the situation (in dispute) presented an arbitrable issue under the collective bargaining agreements, Parade's counsel refused to commit himself and suggested that the arbitrator might properly determine that question in the future. We think that this is not enough.[92]

In *Barnes and Tucker v. UMW,*[93] a new contract was negotiated between the company and union leaders. Ratification by the membership was not required, and the contract went into effect. Members of UMW Local 1269 opposed the contract and refused to work. The strike was specifically directed by the local union membership against the union leadership. The federal district court dissolved a previously issued injunction, in spite of an arbitration clause covering "any local trouble of any kind." It should be strongly noted, however, that despite the denial of an injunction in a strike of this kind, the employer is very likely to resort to severe disciplinary measures against participating workers.

[6] Strikes over Abnormally Dangerous Working Conditions

Section 502 of the Taft-Hartley Act provides an exception to *Boys Markets* and its progeny. This section states in part:

> [N]or shall the quitting of labor by an employee or employees in good faith because of abnormally dangerous conditions for work at the place of employment . . . be deemed a strike under the Act.

It would seem that Section 502 clearly states a public policy

---

[92] Parade Publications, Inc. v. Phila. Mailers Union No. 14, 459 F.2d 369, 373 (3d Cir. 1972).

[93] Barnes & Tucker Co. v. UMWA, 338 F. Supp. 924 (W.D. Pa. 1972).

against the compulsory arbitration of safety disputes. It is crucial to extend workers' health and safety rights under this section—it is in many cases literally a matter of life and death.

Gateway Coal v. UMW [94] involved a safety dispute in a Southwestern Pennsylvania coal mine. A union miner had found that the airflow into the mine was one-half the normal flow because there was a block in the intake airway. The miners were evacuated. It was discovered that company foremen had deliberately falsified the airflow reports, a practice that could have caused many deaths. In fact, the foremen pleaded nolo contendere to criminal charges for falsifying safety records. After a brief suspension, two of the foremen were returned to work. The miners struck to protest the presence of the foremen in the mine. The company offered to arbitrate, and the union refused.

The company filed a Section 301 suit alleging that the strike violated the contract clause compelling arbitration to settle all local and district disputes and that the immediate dispute should be taken to arbitration. The district court enjoined the strike, but the Third Circuit reversed. The Supreme Court held that the strike was enjoinable.

The Supreme Court held that it takes more than a good faith belief in imminent danger to support a Section 502 walkout; there must be objective evidence to support the existence of an abnormally dangerous condition. The Supreme Court specifically extended the "presumption of arbitrability" first enunciated in the Steelworkers Trilogy[95] to *Boys Markets* cases, stating that Section 502 is irrelevant in determining whether a dispute is arbitrable. In light of *Gateway,* if a contract has a no-strike clause and an arbitration clause, courts have generally held that safety issues must be submitted to arbitration unless specifically excluded.[96] To qualify a strike as an exception to an explicit or implied no-strike obligation, the union must present objective evidence that an abnormally dangerous working condition exists. The pivotal question becomes, What is an abnormally dangerous working condition?

---

[94] Gateway Coal v. United Mine Workers of America, 414 U.S. 368, 85 LRRM 2049 (1974).

[95] *Supra* note 25.

[96] Transway Corp. v. Hawaii Teamsters, 411 F. Supp. 299 (D. Hawaii 1976).

In *U.S. Steel v. UMW,*[97] the company sought damages for a strike involving a dispute over safety conditions. The jury, answering interrogatories, found that the union had presented sufficient proof of a dangerous working condition in the mine to fall within Section 502.

The court sidestepped the issue of defining "abnormally dangerous working condition" in *U.S. Steel v. UMW,*[98] in which the company failed to provide an overhead safety shield in a mine shaft in violation of federal safety laws. The miners refused to work until a safety committee was in existence, but the union refused to nominate a committee unless five suspended workers were reinstated. The court found that the union was using Section 502 protections to resolve issues other than safety.

In *Peabody Coal v. UMW,*[99] a miner was injured at work, and the union demanded that he be represented by the safety committee in negotiations; the union walked out when the company refused. The NLRB found that the issue should have been submitted to arbitration and that the walkout violated the contract.

If the NLRB finds that a walkout because of abnormally dangerous conditions was supported by objective evidence and that the company fired workers for this protected concerted activity, it may order reinstatement with back pay.[100]

[a] Violence as "Abnormally Dangerous Conditions for Work"

In *Plain Dealer Publishing Company v. Cleveland Typographical Union No. 53,*[101] one of five craft unions at the plant was involved in contract negotiations. It decided to strike and to set up a picket line. The other four unions voted not to observe the picket line,

---

[97] United States Steel v. United Mine Workers, 381 F. Supp. 990 (W.D. Pa. 1974).

[98] United States Steel v. United Mine Workers, 393 F. Supp 942 (W.D. Pa. 1975).

[99] Peabody Coal Co. v. United Mine Workers of America, 93 LRRM 2532 (D.C. Ill. 1978).

[100] Union Boiler Co. v. NLRB, 90 LRRM 3057 (4th Cir. 1975), *aff'g* 87 LRRM 1268.

[101] 520 F.2d 1220 (10th Cir. 1974).

and two of them attempted to cross the next day. Those unions were met with threats of violence if they attempted to cross the picket line. The company sought a *Boys Markets* injunction against those four unions, which the court rejected, holding that the situation was an exception to the *Boys Markets* injunction under Section 502.

Although threats of violence at the place of employment are not specifically dealt with in the Act, the Board agrees that they are within the reach of Section 502. In *Combustion Engineering Power Systems v. Hudson,*[102] two workers were threatened with physical harm by ex-employees if they continued certain dangerous work. They stopped working, and the company fired them despite their foreman's promise to the contrary. The NLRB held that the company violated the Act by discharging the employees because of their protected work activity of engaging in a temporary work stoppage to protect themselves and to seek relief from hazardous work conditions.[103]

The Board also applies the objective test ("ascertainable, objective evidence") in determining that abnormally dangerous conditions exist.[104] The Board also notes that when objective evidence exists, the contrary belief of others will not diminish its reasonableness, even if the belief or evidence may later prove to have been in error.[105] Not every threat or act of violence will give rise to an abnormally dangerous condition. In *Redwing Carriers,*[106] drivers refused to cross a picket line because they had been threatened with violence and shoved. However, in that same strike, fifty other drivers crossed the picket line 3600 times without incident; the NLRB found evidence insufficient to warrant a finding of abnormally dangerous working conditions. (Note that the issue of refusing to cross another union's picket line because of fear of violence is also mingled with sympathy strike issues.)

---

[102] 224 NLRB 542, 93 LRRM 1049 (1976).

[103] *See also* Interlake v. Jensen, 89 LRRM 1794 (NLRB, 1975); Okla. Tel. Co. Inc. v. C.W.A., 86 LRRM 1393 (NLRB 1974).

[104] Redwing Carriers, Inc., 130 NLRB 1208, *modified,* 137 NLRB 1545.

[105] Roadway Express, Inc., 217 NLRB 278, *enforced,* 527 F.2d 766 (4th Cir. 1976).

[106] Redwing Carriers, *supra* note 104.

[b] Tactics in a Safety Strike

Where possible, the union's evidence in support of the Section 502 exception should include—

(1) detailed eyewitness testimony from workers with a good knowledge of safety issues;
(2) reports from the union safety committee concerning the issue in dispute, and, particularly, indicating if it is a recurring pattern;
(3) reports or citations from any official government agency (OSHA, MSHA), although these usually will not be available until after the strike; and
(4) some indication as to whether there were injuries in the instant circumstances, or in previous, virtually identical circumstances.

These should be combined not only with the arguments under the case law but also with the public policy arguments under the existing safety legislation. Justice Douglas's dissent in *Gateway* emphasized that under federal mine safety legislation the first priority and concern was the health and safety of the miner and that the federal acts recognized the urgent need to provide more effective means and measures for improving working conditions and practices of the nation's coal mines to prevent death and serious harm. Justice Douglas concluded that the public policy of the federal mine safety acts combined with Section 502 of the Taft-Hartley Act precluded deferral of safety issues to arbitration.

[7] Unfair Labor Practice Strikes: Still an Exception to *Boys Markets?*

The main dicisions involving this issue were decided before the string of decisions that includes *Boys Markets, Gateway Coal,* etc., and before the constant judicial emphasis regarding the "strong national labor policy" favoring arbitration. The decisions came at a time when the Norris-LaGuardia Act still had some backbone to it.

In *Mastro Plastics,*[107] the Supreme Court affirmed the NLRB ruling that the contractual no-strike clause did not bar a strike against serious unfair labor practices and that discharged workers had to be reinstated if the strike had been caused by the employer's serious and flagrant unfair labor practices. The Supreme Court reasoned that the application of the no-strike clause in that dispute would have eliminated the employees' right to strike even if the company ousted the employees' lawful bargaining representative and, by threats of discharge, forced the employees to sign membership cards in a different union. This decision applies only if the strike is in protest against serious unfair labor practices.[108]

Generally, a union's failure to follow the grievance and arbitration procedures will lead to unfair labor practice strikes being considered unprotected.[109] This is particularly true where the unfair labor practice is not flagrant or serious.[110]

There are several situations in which unfair labor practice strikes or strikers may receive protection:

(1) If the dispute is not arbitrable, the strike is protected.
(2) If the employer terminates the contract and claims not to be bound by it, the strike is protected.[111]
(3) In a nonunion shop, if there is no labor agreement restricting the workers' right to strike, the protection flows from the Norris-LaGuardia Act and Section 13[112] of the Wagner Act.
(4) An employee who is discriminatorily discharged and subsequently participates in an unfair labor practice strike cannot be denied reinstatement for violating the no-strike clause; the company may not with one hand

---

[107] Mastro Plastics Corp. v. NLRB, 350 U.S. 270, 37 LRRM 2587 (1956).

[108] Arlan's Dept. Store, 133 NLRB 802, 48 LRRM 1731 (1961); Dow. Chem. Co. v. NLRB, 636 F.2d 1352 (3d Cir. 1980); NLRB v. Laborers' Local 721, 107 LRRM 2407 (1st Cir. 1981).

[109] Banner Press, Inc., v. NLRB, 347 F.2d 230, 64 LRRM 2623 (6th Cir. 1967).

[110] Arlan's Dep't Store, *supra* note 108.

[111] Mrs. Fay's Pies, 145 NLRB 1416 (1963).

[112] 29 U.S.C. § 163.

fire the employee, denying him or her employee status, and then with the other hand bind him or her with contractual restrictions on the right to strike.[113]

(5) If an employer agrees to condone a strike in violation of a no-strike clause on condition that it end by a specified date and the strike ends by the deadline but the employer discharges the strikers anyway, a strike in protest against the discharges is a protected unfair labor practice strike.[114]

§ 3.03 Prospective Injunctions under Section 301: A Novel Expansion of the Narrow *Boys Markets* Exception to the Norris-LaGuardia Act

In geographical areas and times in which wildcat strikes are common, employers often seek injunctive relief against future wildcat strikes. This was particularly true in the coalfields in the mid-1970s, when wildcat strikes involving tens of thousands of miners were commonplace. Company arguments often state that prospective injunctive relief is only requiring the union and its membership to comply with the law and with the no-strike clauses in the contract. The reply should be threefold:

(1) Prospective injunctive relief not only implies wrongdoing in the past but also assumes future wrongdoing by the union.

(2) While it is unlikely that your clients will disobey a prospective injunction, it is unfair to subject them to possible contempt sanctions in the future based upon the occurrence of contingent and unpredictable events.

(3) If the court accepts the company's arguments that the union is simply being made to live up to the law and the contract in the future, argue that in such a case the company should have no objection to an injunction requiring it to live up to the labor agreement and the law in the future. This argument should be used particularly if the wildcat strike was provoked by outrageous conduct and/

[113] Stergiou Painting & Sheeting Co., 213 NLRB 59, 7 LRRM 1620 (1974).

[114] Jones & McKnight, Inc., 183 NLRB 10, 76 LRRM 1474 (1970).

or actions in violation of the contract on the part of the employer.

Section 9 of the Norris-LaGuardia Act states that every injunction growing out of a labor dispute

> shall include only a *prohibition of such specific act or acts as may be expressly complained of in the bill of complaint* or petition filed in such case and *as shall be expressly included in said findings of fact made and filed by the court.* (emphasis added)

Section 9 of the Norris-LaGuardia Act and Rule 65 of the Federal Rules of Civil Procedure require that an injunction be specific so that a party has warning of what conduct may subject one to contempt proceedings.[115]

Once again, the decisions of the different circuit courts vary. When litigating this issue, focus on the cases in your circuit. In *Southern Ohio Coal v. UMW,*[116] the Sixth Circuit listed several conditions that must be met before future strikes may be enjoined:

(1) The current strike must be enjoinable under *Boys Markets.*
(2) The union must have engaged in a pattern of strikes involving arbitrable grievances, and that pattern must be likely to continue.
(3) The strikes must constitute a pattern that would warrant relief under *Boys Markets.*
(4) The decree must be limited to specifically identified areas of dispute that have already been adjudicated and that satisfy *Boys Markets* guidelines.

In another case, the Seventh Circuit affirmed a district court grant of prospective injunctive relief.[117] The court, citing the Norris-LaGuardia Act, had previously reversed a grant of pro-

---

[115] United States Steel Corp. v. UMWA, 519 F.2d 1236, 1245 (5th Cir. 1975), *cert. denied,* 428 U.S. 910 (1976); Donovan Constr. Co. of Minn. v. Constr. Prod. & Maintenance Laborers Union Local 383, 533 F.2d 481 (9th Cir. 1976); BCOA v. UMWA, 431 F. Supp. 774 (W.D. Pa. 1977).

[116] S. Ohio Coal Co. v. UMWA, 551 F.2d 695, 94 LRRM 2609 (6th Cir. 1977), *cert. denied,* 98 S. Ct. 227 (1977).

[117] Old Ben Coal Corp. v. Local 1487, UMWA, 500 F.2d 950 (7th Cir. 1974).

spective injunctive relief involving the same parties,[118] but the union engaged in more strikes after that decision. The injunction specifically incorporated language of the collective bargaining agreement and the court rejected the union's challenge that the injunction was vague.[119]

The Third Circuit adopted another approach in *U.S. Steel v. UMW,*[120] *holding* that board injunctions could issue if—

(1) the court finds from the evidence that past violations are likely to recur, or
(2) the pattern of past violations indicates that different violations will occur.

Differing from the Seventh Circuit, the Third Circuit rejected the view that the court could simply frame an injunction from the language contained in the grievance and arbitration clauses of the collective bargaining agreement. It also noted that prospective injunctive decrees must inform the local union what specific steps it must take to prevent illegal work stoppages.

When considering various courses to take in these situations, particularly when considering settling the issues arising out of a wildcat strike, never consent to a permanent injunction. In *Air Transport Association v. PATCO,*[121] the court held that a permanent injunction entered into through a settlement agreement between the parties in 1970 was applicable to slowdowns that occurred in 1978. One aggravating factor was that federal government employees are prohibited by statute from striking.

§ 3.04. Damage Suits for Breaches of No-Strike Clauses

The employer's second weapon against labor in *Boys Markets* strikes is a suit for damages for breach of the no-strike obligation

---

118 Old Ben v. Local 1487, UMWA, 457 F.2d 162 (7th Cir. 1972).

119 *Id. See also* C.F. & I. Steel Corp. v. UMWA, 507 F.2d 170 (10th Cir. 1974).

120 United States Steel Corp. v. UMWA, 534 F.2d 1063 (3d Cir. 1976), *rehearing denied,* 534 F.2d 1084.

121 98 LRRM 2985 (D.C. N.Y. 1978).

contained in the collective baraining agreement. Section 301[122] gives the federal district court jurisdiction over suits for breach of contract between an employer and a labor organization. There are two questions to resolve: (1) What is the liability of individual union members? (2) What is the potential liability of the union or its various subdivisions?

[1] Individual Liability of Union Members

Section 301(b) states in part:

> Any money *judgment against a labor organization* in the district court of the United States shall be enforceable only against the organization as an entity and its assets, and *shall not be enforceable against an individual member or his assets.* (emphasis added)

While the individual union members are bound by the no-strike clauses of the contract, they may not be held liable for a breach of the no-strike clause if the union itself is not liable.[123] Cases decided under Section 303 holding unions liable for illegal secondary boycotts are to the same effect, even if the company's complaint purportedly is based upon state law.[124]

Liability of individual members for participation in an unauthorized strike in violation of the collective bargaining agreement is prohibited by Section 301(b) of the LMRA.[125] The court in *Atkinson*[126] left open the question of individual liability. While individual union members may not be held liable for damages if the union as an entity is held liable for breaches of no-strike clauses, the company still retains the power to impose other

---

[122] 29 U.S.C. 185.

[123] Atkinson v. Sinclair Ref. Co., 320 U.S. 238 (1962); Republic Steel v. UMWA, 570 F.2d 467 (3d Cir. 1978); Sinclair Oil Corp. v. Oil, Chem. & Atomic Workers, 152 F.2d 49 (7th Cir. 1971); Jessop Steel Co. v. United Steelworkers, 428 F. Supp. 172, 94 LRRM 3089 (W.D. Pa. 1977); Lodice v. Calabrese, 291 F. Supp. 592, 80 LRRM 2680 (D.C. N.Y. 1972).

[124] Universal Communications Corp. v. Burns, 449 F.2d 691 (5th Cir. 1971).

[125] Complete Auto Transit, Inc. v. Reis, — U.S. —, 101 S. Ct. 1836, 107 LRRM 2145 (1981).

[126] *Supra* note 123.

appropriate disciplinary action against workers, including discharge.[127]

[2] Tactical Considerations

It is quite common for the company to sue individual union officials and members, as well as the union as an entity. It is sometimes an effective scare tactic, intimidating strikers into submission. Picture the concern of a worker who, with little knowledge of federal labor law, is served with court papers by a U.S. marshall and in those court papers sees that she or he is being sued for $100,000. It is crucial that a meeting be held as soon as possible with the local union and with all individuals being sued to explain exactly what the court papers mean, what their potential legal rights and liabilities are, and what will be done by their lawyer. One of the priorities will be to file a motion to dismiss, including a motion to dismiss the named individuals.

[3] Union Financial Liability under Section 301

Section 301 clearly allows employers to seek damages against the union for breach of its no-strike obligation; in some cases, it has been used to attempt to break unions financially. Section 301(b) states that a union shall be bound by the acts of its agents, and Section 301(e) further states:

> [I]n determining whether any person is acting as an agent of another person so as to make such other person responsible for his acts, *the question of whether the specific acts performed were actually authorized or subsequently ratified shall not be controlling.* (emphasis added)

When representing local, district, and international unions, make it clear that if they publicly advocate, participate in, encourage, ratify, or condone wildcat strikes they are potentially

---

[127] NLRB v. Rockaway News Supply, *supra* note 85; Atkinson v. Sinclair Ref. Co., *supra* note 123; Sinclair Oil Corp. v. Oil, Chem. & Atomic Workers, *supra* note 123.

incurring financial liability for the union. In doing this, it is crucial to understand that one of the main thrusts of the employer's drive to establish "labor peace" is to force the union leadership to control and block militant actions by rank-and-file workers. In Section 301 suits (and other suits) for damages, management's intent is to create union liability for the acts of any of its members and, more important, to force unions to police and tightly control their membership. The result is that most union officials will oppose wildcat strikes regardless of their legitimacy and necessity in certain situations.

For a court to hold the union liable for the acts of individuals (or to hold the international liable for the strike of one of its locals) it must find some form of ratification or authorization by the union.[128] The attempts by companies to impose liability upon international unions for wildcat strikes involving individual members or locals of the same union generated a great deal of confusion among the different federal courts for some time and was only recently resolved by the Supreme Court in *Carbon Fuel v. UMW.*[129]

The Third Circuit had reached the conclusion that an express no-strike obligation imposed an affirmative obligation upon district and international unions to use their best efforts to end unauthorized strikes and that the failure to do so could lead to financial liability.[130] In *U.S. Steel v. UMW,*[131] the court extended this obligation to a no-strike obligation implied by binding arbitration provisions in the contract.[132]

There is a line of older cases directly contrary to the Third Circuit's views on this issue. In *UMW v. Coronado Coal,*[133] the court held that the affiliation of local unions with an international union was not a sufficient basis to make the local unions agents of the international union or vice versa. A local union is a legal

---

[128] Carbon Fuel v. UMWA, 100 S. Ct. 412 (1979); Republic Steel Corp. v. UMWA, *supra* note 123; United States Steel v. UMWA, *supra* note 115.

[129] Carbon Fuel Co. v. United Mine Workers of America, 102 LRRM 3017 (1979).

[130] Eazor Express V. Int'l Bhd. of Teamsters, 520 F.2d 951 (1975).

[131] United States Steel v. UMWA, 534 F.2d 1063, 91 LRRM 3031 (3d Cir. 1976).

[132] *See* Carbon Fuel, *supra* note 129, at n. 4.

[133] UMWA v. Coronado Coal, 259 U.S. 344 (1922).

entity apart from its parent organization, and the international union should not be held responsible for illegal conduct of its local unions that it has not specifically authorized or ratified.[134]

The Fourth, Sixth, and Seventh Circuits have adhered to this view, rejecting the Third Circuit's reasoning in *Eazor Express.* Those courts clearly reject the proposition that a union may be held liable for its failure to use its best efforts to curtail unauthorized strikes and have stated that a union in such circumstances may only be held liable for unauthorized strikes based upon some form of authorization, participation, encouragement, or subsequent ratification.[135]

The Supreme Court appears to have fully resolved the question in *Carbon Fuel v. UMW.*[136] Forty-eight unauthorized wildcat strikes had been engaged in by local unions of the UMW at the Carbon Fuel Company's mines from 1969 to 1973. The efforts by District 17 of the UMW to persuade strikers to return to work consistently failed. Carbon Fuel sought injunctive relief and damages under Section 301 of the Labor-Management Relations Act (LMRA). The Fourth Circuit vacated the district court's judgments against the international union and District 17 of the UMW. (At the same time, judgments against the locals were affirmed in part.) Rejecting the contention that the union had an obligation to use all reasonable means to prevent and halt wildcat strikes, the Supreme Court affirmed on the following grounds:

(1) "The legislative history of Section 301 is clear that Congress limited the responsibility of unions for strikes in breach of contract to cases where the union may be found responsible according to the common law rule of agency." The court noted in footnote 5 that a union would definitely be found liable for an *authorized* strike in breach of contract.

---

134 Reisings Sunrise Bakery, 94 LRRM 2263 (E.D. La. 1976); United Constr. Workers v. Haislip Bakery Co., 223 F.2d 872, 36 LRRM 2315 (4th Cir. 1955); UMWA, 143 NLRB 795, 53 LRRM 1414.

135 S. Ohio Coal Co. v. UMWA, 551 F.2d 695, 94 LRRM 2609 (6th Cir. 1977); Old Ben Coal Co. v. Local 1487, UMWA, 457 F.2d 162 (7th Cir. 1972); Carbon Fuel, *supra,* 583 F.2d 1346 (4th Cir. 1978).

136 Carbon Fuel Co. v. United Mine Workers, 102 LRRM 3017, 100 S. Ct. 412 (1979).

(2) Section 301(b) provides that a union shall be bound by the acts of its agents, and Section 301(e) provides that the common law of agency determines whether one person is acting as an agent of another.

(3) Congressional policy in favor of arbitration *does not extend to imposing an obligation on the union* (which had agreed to arbitrate grievances) to use reasonable means to control the actions of local unions that violate the agreement.

The Court also noted the history of the parties' relationship, the history of collective bargaining, and the relationship of the International Union to the local unions. It noted that locals lacked the authority to strike without authorization from the UMW and that the UMW had "repeatedly expressed its opposition to wildcat strikes." A potential problem would exist if there were a specific contractual clause imposing upon the union an obligation to take disciplinary or other actions to get unauthorized strikers back to work.

[4] Local Union Financial Liability

While the international or district union might avoid liability because it did not authorize or ratify an illegal walkout by a local union, the local union itself might be liable not only for injunctive relief but also for damages. In fact, judgments against the locals in *Carbon Fuel* were affirmed by the Fourth Circuit, which applied the "mass action" theory, noting that it was a pragmatic approach to a difficult problem and further noting that all members of the locals, including officers, participated in the strikes involved in that case.[137]

The mass action theory originated in *United States v. UMW,*[138] in which the court stated, "as long as a union is functioning as a union it must be held responsible for the mass action of its members." The court in *Eazor Express* noted:

[137] Carbon Fuel, 582 F.2d at 1350 (4th Cir. 1978).

[138] United States v. United Mine Workers of America, 77 F. Supp. 563 (D.D.C. 1948).

> [M]any courts hold the union responsible on the theory that mass action by union members must realistically be regarded as union action. The premise is that large groups of men do not act collectively without leadership and that a functioning union must be held responsible for the mass action of its members.[139]

The court recognized the limitations of this theory in *U.S. Steel v. UMW,* stating:

> Consistent with this theory, however, the liability must be limited to the entity whose membership acts in concert. In most cases, as here, the entity will be the local union. *Thus absent a showing of complicity on the part of a larger union entity*—the District or International Union, for example—*only the local may be held liable under the mass action theory.*[140] (emphasis added)

In *Turnkey Constructors v. Cement Masons,*[141] the local union was held liable for a boycott despite the fact that the only union official authorized to direct any such action (the business agent) did not authorize it or participate in it. The court held that liability did not depend on advance authorization by the union, particularly where virtually the entire membership of the local participated. The court noted that the illegal boycott was conducted by the union as a functional entity, which distinguished the case from those in which a national union is charged with "liability for the unauthorized acts of only a segment of its membership and without participation by authorized leadership."[142]

[5] Bankruptcy Considerations

A very real threat to some local unions is the total depletion of union funds after the union is held liable under Section 301 for damages. Courts will sometimes award unrealistic and outra-

---

139 Eazor Express, 520 F.2d at 963 (3d Cir. 1975).

140 United States Steel Corp., United Mine Workers of America, 534 F.2d 1063, 1074 (3d Cir. 1976).

141 Turnkey Constructors v. Cement Masons, etc., 580 F.2d 798 (5th Cir. 1978).

142 *Id.* at 800. *See also* Vulcan Materials Co. v. United Steelworkers of America, 430 F.2d 446 (5th Cir. 1970), *cert. denied,* 401 U.S. 963.

geous awards to companies. In one such case, a truck drivers' union struck in breach of a no-strike clause and was found financially liable to several motor carriers under Section 301.[143] The union filed for bankruptcy and was adjudged bankrupt under Section 18(f) of the Bankruptcy Act. The court went on to hold that a bankrupt union's separate liability to each of several motor carriers under the Act was not dischargeable under Section 17(a)(8) of the Bankruptcy Act. The rationale was that the union's liability was for willful injury to the carrier's property within the meaning of the Bankruptcy Act.

[6] Union Financial Liability under *Buffalo Forge* in Sympathy Strikes

Buffalo Forge clearly established that a U.S. district court could not enjoin a sympathy strike pending an arbitrator's determination of whether or not the strike was forbidden under the no-strike provisions of the contract. In *U.S. Steel v. UMW,*[144] the court held that, because the work stoppage was a sympathy strike and was not over an arbitrable issue, the sympathy strike neither breached the collective bargaining agreement nor entitled the company to an award of monetary damages.

As noted before, there have been some differences in the various circuits' interpretations of *Buffalo Forge,* particularly in cases where all locals involved (whether on sympathy strike or involved in the underlying arbitrable dispute) represent workers at the same company and are bound by the same collective bargaining agreement. If a court of appeals finds that *Buffalo Forge* does not apply in such a sympathy strike situation, then it will hold the union liable for monetary damages.

In *U.S. Steel v. UMW,*[145] the court held that three UMW local representing workers at three U.S. Steel mines were liable under the Taft-Hartley Act for breach of an implied no-strike obliga-

[143] In re Freight Drivers, 100 LRRM 3087.

[144] United States Steel v. United Mine Workers of America, 548 F.2d 67, 94 LRRM 2049 (3d Cir. 1976).

[145] United States Steel Corp. v. United Mine Workers of America, 100 LRRM 2654 (3d Cir. 1979).

tion when their members refused to cross picket lines set up by a fourth UMW local to further its dispute at that mine. The court's rationale was that the fourth local's dispute was subject to compulsory arbitration under the same collective bargaining agreement.

The key determination of an award of damages in these cases will be whether or not the strike falls within the *Buffalo Forge* exception to *Boys Markets,* something that will vary slightly in the different courts of appeals.

[7] Tactical Considerations in Negotiating the Collective Bargaining Agreement to Avoid Financial Liability of International, District, and Local Unions Stemming from Wildcat Strikes

The *Boys Markets* cases rely in large part on the federal policy of allowing free collective bargaining and of presuming arbitrability. In negotiating the contract, the union must aggressively push for the following provisions:

(1) The grievance and arbitration machinery should have a provision giving the union the option, by membership referendum, of taking a dispute to arbitration or of striking over it. It is unlikely that many unions would push for such a provision at the present time, since no-strike clauses seem to be almost universally accepted. This optional clause would not lead to frivolous strikes, as the provision for membership ratification ensures that only major disputes would lead to strikes. The union should avoid broad no-strike clauses or mandatory arbitration provisions.

(2) There should be a clause specifically exempting disputes not subject to the contract from the grievance and arbitration procedure (political strikes, strikes over union disputes, etc.).

(3) A clause permitting union members to honor picket lines established at their workplace by another union or by a different local of the same union should be included. Such a clause barred the company from obtaining damages in one case.[146]

(4) If the union membership consists of workers who generally

[146] Reisings Sunrise Bakery v. Local 35, 94 LRRM 2263 (E.D. La. 1976).

are not at one work site (e.g., truck drivers), it is advisable to seek the inclusion of a clause allowing workers to refuse to cross picket lines set up at another company.[147] However, clauses that would permit workers to refuse to cross an illegal secondary picket line are illegal.[148]

(5) The union should protect membership safety rights by insisting upon a clause allowing the union safety committee to close all or part of a workplace because of abnormally dangerous conditions creating an imminent risk of death or injury.[149] A corollary to this should be a clause protecting an individual worker's individual safety right to refuse work s/he believes to be abnormally dangerous (the UMWA-BCOA contract contains such a clause).

§ 3.05. Rights and Liabilities of Individual Strikers: Discipline, Discharge, and Reinstatement

[1] Basic Law

The legal protections for the right of workers to strike are contained in various federal labor laws,[150] including the Norris-LaGuardia Act and the LMRA.[151] Section 13 of the LMRA states that the Act shall not be construed to interfere with or impede or diminish in any way the right to strike except as expressly stated therein. Protection afforded to striking workers varies according to the type of strike involved.

Section 2(3) states that workers who strike in connection with any current labor dispute or any unfair practice continue to be regarded as employees and are accorded rights to reinstatement under certain conditions. Section 7 of the LMRA gives employees the right to engage in protected concerted activities (this includes

[147] *See* Truck Drivers Local 413 v. NLRB, 334 F.2d 539, 55 LRRM 2878 (D.C. Cir. 1964) (specifically upholds the legality of such clauses).

[148] *See* Drivers Local 695 v. NLRB, 361 F.2d 547, 62 LRRM 2135 (D.C. Cir. 1960); Bricklayers v. NLRB, 562 F.2d 775, 95 LRRM 3316 (1977).

[149] *See* Section 502 of the Taft-Hartley Act.

[150] 29 U.S.C. § 101 et seq.

[151] 29 U.S.C. § 151 et seq.

strikes), and Section 8 protects the right to engage in concerted activities from both company (Section 8(a)) and union (Section 8(b)) infringement.

However, there have been many political and legal developments restricting the rights of workers to engage in strikes. Section 301 of the LMRA (Taft-Hartley Act) allows suits by both unions and employers for breach of a collective bargaining agreement. This law, coupled with the inclusion of mandatory grievance/arbitration machinery and/or no-strike clauses in almost every major collective bargaining agreement since World War II, has virtually banned strikes during the term of a collective bargaining agreement. Furthermore, Section 8(b)(4) of the Act forbids secondary boycotts, and Section 303 allows suits for damages caused by secondary boycotts. Section 301 and Section 303 have cost unions millions of dollars.

[2] Other Notable Restrictions on the Right of Workers to Strike

Particular restrictions on the right to strike are also contained in the following:

(1) Section 8(d) of the LMRA requires that a party seeking to modify or terminate a collective bargaining agreement give sixty days' notice to the other party and continue to work during that period without resort to a strike or lockout.

(2) Section 8(g) of the Act requires that a union intending to strike or picket a health care institution give ten days' notice.

(3) Title III of the Taft-Hartley Act allows the government to obtain an eighty-day injunction if a federal district court determines that a strike imperils the national health and safety.[152]

(4) In addition to the voluntary inclusion of no-strike clauses in labor agreements, workers in some industries find themselves shackled by agreements forbidding

[152] 29 U.S.C. § 171 et seq.

strikes even at the expiration of the collective bargaining agreement.[153]

(5) Federal and state laws contain numerous restrictions barring public employees from striking (state and federal government workers, postal workers, police, firemen, teachers, etc.).

Strikes in violation of a collective bargaining agreement (running afoul of explicit or implied no-strike obligations) or of state or federal law will give employers the basis for discipline and/or discharge of strikers. The ability of the employer to do this is often, in essence, a political question determined by the relative strength of labor and management. To understand the existing law and the tactics to be employed, each type of strike will be dealt with separately.[154] In determining whether a strike is legal, the courts consider both its purpose and the means employed. This is the first consideration in determining if strikers are subject to discipline for engaging in the strike or for their conduct during the strike.

[3] Economic Strikes

A key legal consideration to remember is that, under Section 2(3) of the Act, strikers retain employee status while on strike. Generally, an economic strike is over wages, hours, and working conditions,[155] and it commonly occurs at the expiration of the term of a collective bargaining agreement or in a situation in which workers seek a union contract for the first time. An economic strike is not caused, nor is it prolonged, by unfair labor practices on the part of the employer (this will be discussed further in Section 3.05[4]).

---

[153] In the Basic Steel Industry, the rank and file finds itself shackled by the Experimental Negotiating Agreement (ENA), which forbids strikes even when the contract term expires. Disputes arising in the negotiation of contract terms are submitted to binding arbitration, and the rank and file has no vote on the ratification of the contract.

[154] Dorchy v. Kansas, 272 U.S. 306, 311 (1926).

[155] NLRB v. Thayer Co., 213 F.2d 148, 34 LRRM 2250 (1st Cir. 1954), *cert. denied,* 348 U.S. 883 (1954).

Economic strikers retain their employee status while on strike; however, the employer may hire permanent replacements for the strikers and may legally refuse to reinstate a striker who has been permanently replaced when the strike is over.[156] Since economic strikers are engaged in protected concerted activity under Section 7 of the LMRA, the employer violates Section 8(a)(1) and Section 8(a)(3) of the Act when it discharges a striker for engaging in an economic strike.[157] Reality dictates that employers find a pretext for the discharge of economic strikers.

Once a strike ends, economic strikers have reinstatement rights under the *Laidla/Fleetwood* doctrine as follows:

(1) Economic strikers remain employees.
(2) Economic strikers can unconditionally apply for reinstatement.
(3) If the striker's job has not been filled with a permanent replacement, the employer must generally reinstate the striker if the vacancy exists.
(4) If the employer has abolished jobs during a strike, it must reinstate strikers when the jobs are reestablished unless it can show a legitimate and substantial reason for failing to do so.
(5) If there are permanent replacements, economic strikers are entitled to full reinstatement upon the departure of the replacements unless (a) they have acquired regular and substantially equivalent employment or (b) the employer can sustain the burden of proving that the failure to offer full reinstatement was for legitimate and substantial business reasons.[158]

While economic strikers are entitled to reinstatement, in many instances, they are not entitled to immediate reinstatement if

[156] NLRB v. Mackey Radio and Tel., 304 U.S. 333, 2 LRRM 360 (1939).

[157] NLRB v. United States Cold Storage Corp., 203 F.2d 924, 32 LRRM 2024 (5th Cir. 1953), *cert. denied,* 346 U.S. 819 (1953).

[158] NLRB v. Fleetwood Trailer Co., Inc., 389 U.S. 375, 66 LRRM 2737 (1967); NLRB v. Great Dane Trailers, 388 U.S. 26, 65 LRRM 2465 (1967); Laidlaw Corp., 171 NLRB 175, 68 LRRM 1252 (1968), *enforced,* 414 F.2d 99, 71 LRRM 3054 (1969), *cert. denied,* 397 U.S. 920.

they have been permanently replaced. The burden of proof is on the employer to show that the replacements are permanent. The employer has failed to meet its burden of proof if the alleged decision to make the replacements permanent was not communicated to the union, the strikers, or the replacements.[159] The most common practice is for the company to send a certified letter to each individual striker and to the union, informing them of the decision to hire permanent replacements (often an effective scare tactic). If notice is inadequate, argue that the "replacements" are temporary. The company does not have a duty to reinstate economic strikers to other plants, unless the other plant is an accretion to the existing one.[160] Look for signs that work is being transferred from the struck plant to another plant of the company.

Companies often are reluctant to recall employees after a few years. However, the employer generally has the names, addresses, and phone number of the strikers, and the union should keep the company provided with an updated list. It is a Section 8(a)(3) discrimination violation to fail to inform economic strikers of job openings, even if it has been some time since the beginning of the strike.[161] This is particularly true in rural areas (mining and textile industries) in which one employer dominates a community, since strikers will generally not be able to find other regular and substantially equivalent employment. Working full time at minimum wage is not the equivalent of working full time at most union wages.

[a] Particular Issues

[i] Collective Bargaining: The Strike for a New Contract

Economic strikers may lose their reinstatement rights in some instances, but they still retain their eligibility to vote in a repre-

[159] NLRB v. Murray Prods., 584 F.2d 934, 99 LRRM 3269 (9th Cir. 1978) (in this case, the replacements were originally told they were temporary).

[160] Bryan Infants Wear Co., 235 NLRB 180, 98 LRRM 1140 (1978).

[161] Am. Mach. Corp. v. NLRB, 424 F.2d 1321, 73 LRRM 2977, 2981 (5th Cir. 1970), *enforcing* 70 LRRM 1173 (1969).

sentation election held within twelve months of the start of a strike.[162] The NLRA requires that the company continue to bargain in good faith during the strike.[163] The refusal of an employer to bargain in good faith during an economic strike converts the strike to an unfair labor practice strike[164] with broader reinstatement rights attached.

Some companies will resist any serious bargaining for twelve months because at that point the union's strength in a representation election is sapped. The unfortunate reality is that companies can avoid NLRB sanctions for bad faith bargaining by going through the motions of bargaining. Blue Diamond Coal Company's tactics during the Stearns miners' strike from 1976 to 1979 are an example of this.

[ii] Striker Misconduct

Strikers guilty of misconduct during a strike lose any reinstatement rights.[165] Striker misconduct typically involves picket line misconduct, violence, and serious threats of violence. It should not encompass exuberant picket line conduct, but do not be surprised if the companies take an expansive view of misconduct.

---

[162] *See* Section 9(c)(3) of the National Labor Relations Act (hereinafter cited as NLRA), 29 U.S.C. § 159e(c)(3).

[163] NLRB v. Remington Rand, 130 F.2d 919, 927, 11 LRRM 575 (2d Cir. 1942).

[164] NLRB v. Pecheur Lozenge Co., 209 F.2d 393, 33 LRRM 2324 (2d Cir. 1953), *cert. denied,* 347 U.S. 953.

[165] NLRB v. Fansteel Metallurgical Corp., 306 U.S. 249 (1939); U.A.W. v. NLRB (Kohler Co.), 300 F.2d 699 (D.C. Cir. 1962), *cert. denied,* 370 U.S. 911; Kayser Roth v. NLRB, 447 F.2d 396. In *Kayser Roth,* the court noted that the general standard for determining whether a striker may be discharged is whether the acts participated in are "beyond the ordinary incidence which are to be expected in the maintenance of a picket line." The exception is where the employer's acts in the instigation of the strike are so provocative and such flagrant violations of the law that the acts of the strikers were the natural consequence of provocative acts. Oneita Knitting Mills v. NLRB, 375 U.S. 385 (allowing reinstatement).

[iii] Discrimination in Hiring Replacements

The company may hire replacements in ways discussed above, but it may not discriminate between union and nonunion applicants. Such discrimination violates Section 8(a)(3). (But note that a strike is in serious trouble if union applicants cross a picket line to take jobs from strikers.)

[iv] Benefits

The company may not offer greater benefits to nonstrikers or the replacements, such as the *Erie Resistor* grant of superseniority,[166] nor may the company cut off benefits of qualified strikers while giving them to nonstrikers or replacements.[167]

[b] Tactical Considerations

[i] Converting an Economic Strike to an Unfair Labor Practice Strike

Unfair labor practice strikers have greater reinstatement rights than economic strikers do. Once the strike begins, the union should carefully document employer conduct that concretely or arguably constitutes unfair labor practices, such as bad faith bargaining, violence, threats of violence, coercion, surveillance, etc. Union witnesses should be interviewed in detail and charges filed with the NLRB. Picket line signs should not only mention wages and working conditions but also stress unfair labor practices of the employer.

[ii] Employer Discrimination: Section 8(a)(3) Violations

The company refusal to reinstate a striker must not be based

166 373 U.S. 221 (1963).

167 NLRB v. Great Dane Trailers, 388 U.S. 26 (1967) (vacation benefits).

upon anti-union animus (hostility).[168] Of course, the company will never admit to anti-union animus in denying strikers reinstatement; a pretext will always be used. As noted previously, the company has the burden of proof for showing (1) that the replacements are permanent, not temporary, and (2) that there is a legitimate and substantial business necessity for abolishing jobs or changing operations so as to cost strikers their jobs. The company's intent need not be shown by direct proof (indeed, it rarely will be); the intent may be presumed from conduct inherently destructive of employee rights under the LMRA.[169]

[iii] Strike Settlement Agreements

Concurrent with the signing of a collective bargaining agreement, the union and company must reach an agreement that protects the rights of strikers; such an agreement should be a precondition to the signing of the contract. The terms of the agreement will vary according to the history of the parties' relationship, the relative degrees of misconduct on each side, and the relative strength of each of the parties.

Unfortunately, some strike settlement agreements are weak and limit the rights of economic strikers. The NLRB will accept such agreements as determinative of the reinstatement rights of economic strikers if—

(a) the preferential recall period is not unreasonably short;
(b) the agreement results from good faith bargaining;
(c) the employer does not seek to undermine the union's status through the agreement; and
(d) the agreement does not have a discriminatory intent or objective.[170]

The key feature of any strike settlement agreement must be job protection for all strikers. The strike settlement agreement must

168 NLRB v. Brown, 380 U.S. 278 (1965).

169 *Id.;* NLRB v. Erie Resistor Corp., *supra.*

170 United Aircraft Corp., 192 NLRB 382, 77 LRRM 1785 (1971).

be challenged when it leads to a drastic weakening of the union. Here are some key factors for a solid legal basis to stand on:

(a) an increase in the number of overtime hours being worked while strikers are still out of work,
(b) failure of the employer to fill vacancies during the preferential hiring period for economic strikers, and
(c) dramatic increase in new hirings *after* the expiration of the preferential hiring period.[171]

[4] Unfair Labor Practice Strikes

These are strikes begun in whole or in part in response to unfair labor practices committed by the employer.[172] An economic strike may be converted to an unfair labor practice strike if the employer's unfair labor practices were a contributing factor, even if the strike was promoted in whole or in part by economic reasons.[173] There must be a causal link. Unfair labor practice strikers have the following reinstatement rights (much more substantial than those of economic strikers);

(1) They are entitled to reinstatement even if the employer has hired permanent replacements.[174]
(2) The company may not avoid its duty to reinstate strikers by subcontracting work during the course of the strike.[175]
(3) They may vote in representation elections, and their temporary replacements may not.[176]
(4) Strikers guilty of strike misconduct or discharged for cause under Section 10(c) of the Act lose their reinstate-

[171] Laher Spring & Elec. Co., 192 NLRB 464, 77 LRRM 1800 (1971).

[172] NLRB v. Mackey Radio & Tel., *supra;* NLRB v. Moore Business Forms, Inc., 98 LRRM 2773 (5th Cir. 1978).

[173] F.W. Corp., 239 NLRB 65, 99 LRRM 1669 (1978).

[174] NLRB v. Mackey Radio and Tel., *supra;* Phillip Cary Mfg. Co. v. NLRB, 331 F.2d 720 (6th Cir. 1964), *cert. denied,* 379 U.S. 888 (1964).

[175] Hawaii Meat Co., Ltd., 139 NLRB 966, 51 LRRM 1430 (1962).

[176] *See* Section 9(c)(3) of the NLRA, 29 U.S.C. § 159(c)(3); Tampa Sand and Material Co., 50 LRRM 1438 (1962).

ment rights.[177] The NLRB will decide whether, under the circumstances, there was cause for the company's refusal to reinstate strikers engaged in Section 7 activities and whether reinstatement effectuates the purposes of the Act (*Thayer* doctrine).[178]

(5) The unfair labor practice strikers must make an unconditional application to return to work or demonstrate that such application would be futile.[179]

It is important to note that a sympathy strike takes on the unfair labor practice characteristics of the primary strike.[180]

If an employer violates Section 8(a)(3) in violating the reinstatement rights of unfair labor practice strikers, the back pay obligation is triggered by the discharge itself. The striker need not request reinstatement to trigger the obligation.[181] Letters from the company to the strikers stating that they will be permanently replaced on a certain date written before permanent replacements are hired have the effect of discharging the strikers[182] and may convert an economic strike into an unfair labor practice strike.

[5] Prohibited Strikes

[a] Sit-Down Strikes

On the ground that they "show disregard for the property rights of owners," sit-down strikes are not protected concerted activity under Section 7 of the LMRA and such strikers are subject to discharge under the law.[183] The only effective protection is a strong union's ability to negotiate a settlement protecting the

[177] NLRB v. Wash. Aluminum Co., 370 U.S. 9 (1962).

[178] Blades Mfg. Co., 144 NLRB 561 (1963), *enforcement denied*, 344 F.2d 998 (8th Cir. 1965).

[179] Swearingen Aviation Corp. v. NLRB, 568 F.2d 458, 97 LRRM 2972 (5th Cir. 1978).

[180] C.K. Smith & Co., 227 NLRB 147, 95 LRRM 1617 (1977).

[181] Abilities & Goodwill, Inc., 100 LRRM 1470 (NLRB 1979).

[182] NLRB v. Int'l Van Lines, 409 U.S. 48 (1972).

[183] NLRB v. Fansteel Metallurgical Corp., *supra*.

rights of such strikers.[184]

A rare instance in which a sit-down strike was held protected involved the following circumstances: (1) The workers were protesting an immediate situation; (2) the stoppage was prompted by unfair labor practices on the part of the employer; and (3) no grievance procedure was available.[185] The key point seemed to be that no grievance procedure was available. In other cases in which short in-plant stoppages were held to be protected activity, the facts involved both immediate response to company unfair labor practices and no available grievance procedure.[186] This is most likely to be the case if there is no union in the plant.

[b] Minority Strikes

If a minority of the bargaining unit strikes without union authorization it is generally not protected under the LMRA.[187] If the object of the strike is to protect a union's demands and policies the strikers might be protected.[188]

[c] Partial Strikes

The following actions, considered partial strikes, all subject workers to potential discharge:

(1) Refusing overtime.[189] However, in the *Teledyne* case,[190]

---

[184] The best historical example of this is the massive sit-ins during the organizing drives in the auto industry in the 1930s.

[185] Meilman Food Indus., Inc., 97 LRRM 372 (NLRB 1978).

[186] *See generally* United Merchants & Mfrs., Inc. v. NLRB, 554 F.2d 1276, 95 LRRM 2369 (4th Cir. 1977) (short in-plant stoppage held to be protected activity); Cone Mills v. NLRB, 413 F.2d 445, 71 LRRM 2916 (4th Cir. 1960) (short in-plant stoppage held to be unprotected activity because there was a grievance procedure available).

[187] Emporium Capwell Co. v. W. Add. Comm. Org., 420 U.S. 50 (1975), NLRB v. Draper Corp., 15 LRRM 580 (4th Cir. 1944).

[188] NLRB v. R.C. Can Co., 328 F.2d 974, 55 LRRM 2642 (5th Cir. 1964).

[189] Scott Paper Box Co., 23 LRRM 1380 (NLRB 1949).

[190] Teledyne Wis. Motor v. Local 283, UAW, 530 F.2d 727 (1976).

the refusal to work overtime was held protected because of contractual provisions authorizing the membership to refuse overtime if members of the local were unemployed. A company injunction request was denied because the contract had neither a mandatory arbitration provision nor a no-strike clause.

(2) Refusing to perform certain tasks while accepting others.[191]

(3) Slowdowns.[192]

(4) Intermittent work stoppages.[193]

Once again, the best protection for workers is a strong union that has carefully negotiated protective clauses into the contract.

[d] Strikes in Breach of Contract (*Boys Markets* Strikes)

Workers are subject to potential discharge if they strike in breach of contractual no-strike clauses in the absence of serious unfair labor practices by the employer.[194] However, because companies need to keep their businesses operating, they are generally unable to discharge everyone who engages in such a strike. Furthermore, companies might violate Section 8(a)(3) of the LMRA if they discriminatorily discharge union officials for their participation in an illegal strike.[195] The chief protection for workers is the inclusion in the contract of an optional no-strike clause, as described in Section 3.04[7], *supra*. When workers strike over an unfair labor practice, even with a no-strike clause, they have certain rights as unfair labor practice strikers unless the union has

[191] Montgomery Ward & Co., 17 LRRM 111 (NLRB 1945), *enforcement denied,* 19 LRRM 2908, (8th Cir. 1965).

[192] Elk Lumber Co., 26 LRRM 1493 (NLRB 1950); NLRB v. Blades Mfg., *supra;* Pac. Tel. & Tel. Co., 33 LRRM 1433 (1954).

[193] Pac. Tel. & Tel. Co., 33 LRRM 1433 (1954).

[194] Goya Foods, Inc., 99 LRRM 1282 (1978); Food Fair Stores, Inc., v. NLRB, 491 F.2d 388, 395 (3d Cir. 1974).

[195] Precision Castings, 96 LRRM 1540, 233 NLRB 183 (1977); Chrysler Corp., 232 NLRB 466 (1977); Gould Corp., 237 NLRB 124, 99 LRRM 1059 (1978), *enforcement denied,* 612 F.2d 729 (1978).

expressly waived the right to engage in such strikes.[196]

[6] Sympathy Strikes: Refusal to Cross Picket Lines

The NLRB has consistently held that a sympathy strike—the refusal to cross another union's picket lines—is a form of protected concerted activity.[197] This is the NLRB's position whether the picket line is at one's own place of work or at another employer's premises. However, there is a division among the courts of appeals as to whether or not Section 7 of the LMRA protects the refusal to cross a picket line at another employer's premises. Furthermore, the law allows varying responses by the employer to a sympathy strike, depending upon the situs of the strike.

[a] Picket Line at Employer's Premises

Workers may lawfully refuse to cross a picket line at their own place of work, and the company cannot discharge them; however, the company can treat them as economic strikers subject to temporary or permanent replacement.[198] If the pickets are unfair labor practice strikers, workers who refuse to cross acquire the status of unfair labor practice strikers.[199]

One major warning is that the picket line must have protected status (i.e., not a *Boys Markets* strike); ignorance of its unprotected status is irrelevant if a worker is discharged.[200] This rule is ludicrous in the concrete realities of strikes and picket line activity; it assumes that workers on the spot will understand the facts surrounding the particular picket line and will be able to evaluate the legal criteria for determining if a strike is protected, criteria

---

[196] Mastro Plastics v. NLRB, 350 U.S. 270 (1956), 137 NLRB 1545.

[197] Redwing Carriers, Inc., 50 LRRM 1440 (NLRB 1962), *enforced,* 54 LRRM 2707 (D.C. Cir. 1963), *cert. denied,* 377 U.S. 905; Newberry Eng'r Corp., 94 LRRM 1307 (1970).

[198] Newberry Eng'r Corp., 94 LRRM 1307 (1970); Gould, Inc., 99 LRRM 1705 (NLRB 1978), *enforcement denied on other grounds.*

[199] C.K. Smith & Co., Inc., 95 LRRM 1617 (1977), *aff'd* 569 F.2d 162, 97 LRRM 2460 (1st Cir. 1977).

[200] Am. Tel. & Tel. Co., 231 NLRB No. 110, 96 LRRM 1144 (1977).

the courts often disagree on. In addition, refusal to cross a picket line because of fear may not be considered protected activity.[201]

[b] Picket Line at Another Employer's Premises

While the refusal to cross a picket line at another employer's premises is protected activity, employees who do so may be discharged if necessary to preserve the efficient operation of the employer's business.[202] The courts of appeals are split on this.[203] The rationale is that such a refusal is a partial strike, usually arising in delivery and trucking cases in which the company pleads the need to make deliveries to avoid business losses. Once the company meets its burden of proof, demonstrating a legitimate business necessity of discharging employees for refusing to cross such a picket line, the burden shifts to the NLRB and the worker to prove that the company's motivation was to penalize workers for honoring picket lines.[204]

Note that the First Circuit has denied enforcement of an NLRB order, holding that the company violated Section 8(a)(1) when it discharged a worker for refusing to cross a picket line.[205] The court analyzed the case as follows: Once the employer demonstrates a legitimate reason for the discharge, the burden shifts to the NLRB to establish that the employer's primary motivation was to penalize the employee for honoring the picket line. The decision rests upon a balancing of the right of the employee to express his/her sympathies and the right of the employer to conduct its business.

---

201 The courts will differ somewhat on this point. For examples of cases that hold such activity unprotected; *see* NLRB v. Union Carbide, 440 F.2d 54 (4th Cir. 1971); and G. & P. Trucking Co. v. NLRB, 539 F.2d 705 (4th Cir. 1976).

202 Newberry Eng'r Corp., *supra;* Redwing Carriers, Inc., *supra.*

203 *See* cases cited in note 197, *supra.*

204 NLRB v. William S. Carroll, Inc., 578 F.2d 1 (1st Cir. 1978).

205 NLRB v. William S. Carroll, Inc., 578 F.2d 1, 98 LRRM 2848 (1st Cir. 1978).

[c] Contractual Waiver of the Right to Respect Picket Lines

The inclusion of a clause in the collective bargaining agreement waiving the right to honor picket lines renders picket line observance unprotected activity.[206] The NLRB will not infer a waiver of the right to honor picket lines in the absence of clear and unmistakable language in the contract.[207] Even the standard broadly worded no-strike clause does not waive the workers' rights to refuse to cross the picket line of another union. In *C.K. Smith,*[208] the union had, during bargaining, specifically withdrawn a proposal authorizing the right of workers to honor picket lines; the court stated that this was not a waiver and simply left the parties covered under existing law.

[7] Standards for Imposing Discipline for Illegal Strike Activity

The gamut of disciplinary actions for illegal strike activity runs from warnings through suspension to discharge. Local union officials are often singled out for more severe discipline than that of other union members. This is a part of company efforts to make union officials police the activities of union members. Under what circumstances, if any, does more severe discipline imposed against union officials or other union members violate Section 8(a)(3) of the LMRA and/or applicable provisions of the collective bargaining agreement?

[a] Arbitration Decisions: Principles

Arbitration decisions are based upon applicable contractual

---

[206] NLRB v. Rockaway News Supply Co., 345 U.S. 71, 31 LRRM 2432 (1953).

[207] Keller Crescent Co., 217 NLRB 100, 89 LRRM 1201 (1975), *enforcement denied,* 92 LRRM 3591 (7th Cir. 1976). The Seventh Circuit refused to enforce without addressing this issue although it indicated that the issue should be arbitrated under the contract.

[208] C.K. Smith & Co., *supra.*

provisions and the history of the relationship between the parties. They will vary from contract to contract. However, there are some general lines of decisions and principles that can be rough guides. One warning: In a specific case, first check the contract and arbitration decisions under that contract.

Most arbitration decisions recognize the principle that workers who engage in the same type of misconduct should receive the same treatment unless there is a reasonable basis for variation. A reasonable basis for variation could include degree of fault, aggravating or mitigating circumstances, and prior offenses by the employee.[209] Management is not required to punish all those who engage in a strike or a slowdown. Some may escape punishment, while those with greater fault may be punished.[210] The dismissal of strike leaders is often upheld by arbitrators, even without proof of the extent of strike leadership.[211] Furthermore, there is no legal bar to the imposition of discipline against known leaders if the company is unable to identify other leaders.[212] *A warning note:* Should workers find it necessary to engage in a strike forbidden under the contract, no strikers should take open leadership, particularly in dealing with the media or the company. Furthermore, a small group of workers should not organize a strike themselves if they will be easily identified and will not receive the support of other members of the local union.

In *Homer Laughlin China,*[213] four workers who had participated in a wildcat strike were discharged. There had been four prior wildcat strikes but no prior discharges. The company's position was that it could selectively discharge; the union contended that it could not and that the discipline was too severe. The arbitrator ruled that (1) these were selective discharges in a situation in

---

[209] Arbitrator Murphy, 56 L.A. 880; Arbitrator Quinlan, 54 L.A. 1035; Arbitrator Dworkin, 46 L.A. 161; Arbitrator Turkus, 39 L.A. 823; Alan Wood Steel, 21 L.A. 843, 849 (1954).

[210] Arbitrator Murphy, 56 L.A. 880; Arbitrator Krimsley, 48 L.A. 257 (there should be a classification according to degree of participation in the strike and punishment should be imposed on that basis); Stoufer, 45 L.A. 943, 951.

[211] Arbitrator Pollack, 42 L.A. 142, 142-43.

[212] Arbitrator Schieber, 50 L.A. 487; Arbitrator Crawford, 49 L.A. 383; U.S. Steel Corp., 40 L.A. 598 (Arbitrator Seitz, 1963); Arbitrator Turkus, 51 L.A. 1228; Bethlehem Steel Corp., 39 L.A. 686 (Arbitrator Voltin, 1962).

[213] Homer Laughlin China Co., 67 L.A. 1251 (1977).

which a more sustained investigation would have revealed equal or more active involvement on the part of others; (2) the employer had failed to impose discipline on any employee in prior illegal strikes; and (3) the discharges should be reduced to suspension without pay. The general rule in arbitration is that the company can selectively discharge so long as the selection is not capricious.[214] Different degrees of punishment are permissible if they are based upon a reasonable difference between those penalized and those not penalized.

[b] Preparing the Arbitration Case Involving Allegedly Illegal Strike Activity

The following is an outline of matters to consider in such arbitration proceedings.

(1) Does the contract specifically address the issue or incorporate any arbitration decisions involving the issue? Does the strike constitute an exception to the contractual no-strike obligation?

(2) Examine the arbitration provisions in the contract; then examine other contracts with identical clauses and similar contracts in the same industry.

(3) What was the intent of the parties in negotiating the particular no-strike and/or mandatory grievance/arbitration clauses?

(4) Circumstances of the particular case: Does the company shoulder the blame for provoking a major confrontation over a minor dispute?

(5) Principles of progressive discipline: Have any of the disciplined employees been disciplined before? What has been the company's prior response to illegal strikes?

(6) Has the discipline been imposed in an even-handed way? What was the discipline in the past for the same acts?

---

[214] Oppenheim In Re: Acme Boot Co., 52 L.A. 1047; Le Winter In Re: Port Authority of Allegheny County, 1975 ARB Par. 8303; and In re Local 342 UAW v. T.R.W. Inc., 69 LRRM 2524 (6th Cir. 1968).

Was the discipline imposed according to degree of fault? Were union officials selected for special discipline?

(7) The fact that the offense may be dischargeable under the contract does not prevent the imposition of a lesser penalty.

[8] Liability of Union Officials for Allegedly Illegal Strike Activity

Not only may the local union face court injunctions and financial liability, but union officials who participate in a wildcat strike, or who take no affirmative steps to end the strike, may be disciplined more severely than are other union members. Many arbitrators have taken the position that union leaders have a special responsibility to promote the resolution of the dispute through the contractual grievance procedure rather than through striking. There is a split among arbitrators as to whether failure to fulfill this responsibility is in itself (as opposed to actual participation in an "illegal" strike) a proper basis for discharge or other discipline.

[a] Drawbacks of Arbitration

Arbitration is generally not a good forum in which to win a legal victory based upon charges of anti-union discrimination if union officials are disciplined. For example, one arbitrator held that the union president could be singled out for punishment because he should have attempted to end the walkout.[215] Another held that, although the company could not identify the slowdown leaders, it could suspend committeemen who had positions of leadership among the workers and had participated in the slowdown.[216] When the charge of anti-union discrimination is raised, arbitrators tend to require clear proof to sustain the

215 Arbitrator Klaman, 38 L.A. 928, 932-33.

216 Arbitrator Marshall, 38 L.A. 889.

charge.[217] Some arbitrators will deal with this issue in a thorough manner.[218] Arbitrators typically conclude that a union steward's duty to enforce the no-strike provisions of a collective bargaining agreement is greater than that of a rank-and-file member even though the steward may not be participating in the strike. In *Moraine Manufacturing,*[219] the arbitrator, referring to a union steward, stated: "He cannot with impunity turn his back on the agreement *which it is his duty to defend.* He is a leader and in participating—he set an example for others" (emphasis added). The arbitrator then concluded that status as a steward justified a serious penalty. In *Mack Truck,*[220] the arbitrator noted that union leadership has a *special responsibility* to honor the pledged word of the union to abide by the agreement's restraints in exchange for garnering its benefits. One supposes arbitrators would decide the same way even if there were a poorly negotiated agreement.

Unions must seek to negotiate contract clauses that limit the right of a company to discipline employees for failure to fulfill their responsibilities as employees and that bar the company from imposing discipline based upon an employee's failure to discharge his/her alleged responsibility as a union official. For example, in *Kennecott Copper,*[221] such a clause barred the company from imposing greater discipline upon a grievance committeeman for his participation in a walkout when the company contended he had exercised control over picketing. The rationale was that under that contract clause, the degree of control he exercised over picketing related to his responsibilities as a union representative and had nothing to do with his responsibility as an employee.

[b] NLRB Policy

Under certain circumstances, the NLRB will defer action on an

217 Arbitrator Katin, 49 L.A. 731; Arbitrator Livengood, 45 L.A. 495; Arbitrator Dworet, 43 L.A. 1070.

218 Arden Farms Co., 45 L.A. 1124 (1965).

219 Moraine Mfg. Co. & I.A.M., 63-2 CCH ARB 8797.

220 Mack Truck & UAW Local 71, 61-1 CCH ARB 8422.

221 Kennecott Copper Co. (Chino Mines Div.), 19:14, 334, FMCS File No. 75 K 12512 (John Phillip Linn, Nov. 10, 1975).

unfair labor practice charge pending arbitration, and will also defer to a final arbitration award, thus declining to process unfair labor practice charges under its jurisdiction.[222] This can be a crucial procedural area to understand when one is seeking to protect the rights of discharged union members and/or officials who have rights both under a contract and under the LMRA.

Arbitration decisions are less protective of the rights of union officials than is the NLRB, which will sometimes protect union officials under Section 8(a)(3), the section forbidding discrimination on account of union activity. However, the courts of appeals are not always inclined to enforce NLRB orders in this area.

In *Precision Castings*[223] the NLRB held that the selection of five stewards for discipline from among a group of illegal strikers on the ground that they failed to take reasonable steps to terminate the strike constituted discrimination against those employees based upon their status as union officers. This case was followed by *Indiana and Michigan Electric,*[224] in which the NLRB ruled that the greater responsibility that accompanies the holding of union office is not a sufficient basis for imposing greater discipline on union officials. However, the NLRB's reasoning and decision were reversed by the Seventh Circuit.[225]

The next blow came when the Third Circuit refused enforcement of the NLRB's order in the *Gould* case.[226] The NLRB had held that the company violated the Act by its discharge of a steward for his lack of action as a union official in attempting to stop an illegal work stoppage. In the appeal, the court took the view that the more severe punishment imposed upon the steward was based not merely on his status as a steward "but upon the breach of the higher responsibility that accompanies that status," a breach that made his misconduct more serious than that of the rank and file.[227] It must be emphasized that this is a developing

---

[222] Spielberg Mfg. Co., 112 NLRB 1080 (1955) (postarbitral deferral); Collyer Insulated Wire, 192 NLRB 837, 77 LRRM 1931 (1971) (prearbitral deferral).

[223] Precision Castings Co., 233 NLRB 183, 96 LRRM 1541 (1977).

[224] Ind. & Mich. Elec. Co. v. NLRB, 237 NLRB 35 (1978).

[225] Ind. & Mich. Elec. Co. v. NLRB, 599 F.2d 227 (7th Cir. 1979).

[226] Gould, Inc. v. NLRB, 237 NLRB No. 124 (1979) *rev'd,* 612 F.2d 729 (1980).

[227] Midwest Precision Castings Co., 102 LLRM 1074 (NLRB 1979) (steward may be disciplined for urging participation in a slowdown prohibited by the contract); NLRB v. Armour-Dial, Inc., 106 LRRM 2265 (8th Cir. 1981) (union's

area of the law and that results will probably continue to vary from case to case.

§ 3.06. Limitations on Tactics: Violence, Mass Picketing, etc.

Previous sections have described the legal limitations on the types of strikes that may be legally waged. Now we will look at the legal rights and limitations on the types of tactics used during a strike. The tactics utilized by the strikers themselves and the legal tactics utilized must be regarded as more important than the black letter legal principles, which simply outline the parameters of the courtroom battle. The litigation over picketing rights generally takes place in state court, and its importance is usually secondary to the negotiation of a collective bargaining agreement.

[1] Picketing Rights: The Legal Limitations

Thornhill v. Alabama,[228] marks the affirming of the right of workers to engage in peaceful picketing under the First and Fourteenth Amendments. It is generally accepted that state courts lack the jurisdiction to enjoin any peaceful activities of a union involved in a conflict with an employer if the dispute is arguably subject to the jurisdiction of the NLRB.[229] However, state courts do have jurisdiction to act and to issue injunctions in matters of traditional state concern. In situations involving mass picketing or picketing accompanied by violence, state courts have the power to issue injunctive relief against such activity and habitually and au-

---

executive committee lawfully suspended by employer for inducing an illegal work stoppage, reversing the NLRB); Hammermill Paper Co. v. NLRB, 108 LRRM 2001 (3d Cir. 1981) (discharge of steward for participation in wildcat strike was unlawful); C.H. Heist Corp. v. NLRB, 108 LRRM 2159 (7th Cir. 1981) (discharge of steward for participation in unlawful work stoppage was unlawful).

[228] 310 U.S. 88 (1940).

[229] San Diego Bldg. Trades v. Garmon, 359 U.S. 236 (1959); Broadcast Technicians v. Broadcast Serv., 380 U.S. 255; Garner v. Teamsters, 346 U.S. 485. The federal preemption doctrine is discussed in more detail below.

tomatically do so. The Supreme Court recognized this long ago in a number of cases,[230] stating in one of them, "[I]f picketing activity is counter to a valid state power in a domain open to state regulation . . . it can be restricted."[231] For example, state courts are free to enjoin mass picketing and threats of violence.[232]

While there is little disagreement about the authority of state courts to enjoin acts of violence, state courts will at times take an excessively broad view of violence, particularly courts not familiar with exuberant picket line conduct. The use by picketers of words like "scab" or "rat," without more, is generally legal, but the Supreme Court has held that the use of such words by large numbers of massed people justified a state court's holding that violence was imminent.[233]

[2] Mass Picketing

Courts routinely issue injunctions against mass picketing, even in the absence of violence. Mass picketing involves picketing in which strikers are massed in such a way as to block ingress and egress. Injunctions are issued on the rationale that "a picket fence is not the legitimate child of a picket line."[234] The courts typically deal with mass picketing allegations. In one such case, the court enjoined mass picketing (no violence was found); limited the number of pickets to three at each gate, spaced not less than 10 feet apart; and enjoined others from congregating nearby in large

---

230 Milk Wagon Drivers Union v. Meadowmoor Dairies, 312 U.S. 287 (1940); U.A.W. v. Wis. Employment Relations Bd., 351 U.S. 266 (1956); Teamsters Local 695 v. Vogt, 354 U.S. 284 (1957).

231 Teamsters v. Vogt, *supra* note 230, at 291. *See also* Allen Bradley Local v. Wis. Bd., 315 U.S. 740 (1942); Hughes v. Superior Ct. of Cal., 339 U.S. 460 (1950); I.B.T. Local #309 v. Hughes, 339 U.S. 420 (1950); Gen. Elec. Co. v. U.A.W. Local 997, 130 N.E.2d 759 (1955); Johnson Bros. v. United T.W.V., 92 LRRM 2302 (Minn. Sup. Ct. 1976).

232 U.A.W. v. Russell, 356 U.S. 634 (1958); United Constr. Workers v. Laburnum, 356 U.S. 634 (1958).

233 Youngdahl v. Rainfair, 355 U.S. 131.

234 Westinghouse Elec. Corp. v. U.E. Local 410, 139 N.J. Eq. 97, 49 A.2d 896 (1946).

numbers.[235]

[3] Restrictions on State Court Injunctions

The state court injunction must be "carefully limited to the protection of the compelling state interest in the maintenance of domestic peace."[236] The presence of some violence does not permit a court to enjoin all picketing. In one such case, the state court had enjoined peaceful picketing in addition to acts of violence, but the Supreme Court reversed, holding that the injunction against peaceful picketing entered the preempted domain of the NLRB.[237] State courts may enjoin peaceful picketing in very limited circumstances if a pattern of violence has been established that would reappear even if peaceful picketing were resumed.[238] When representing unions and rank-and-file groups in state court proceedings, take great pains to distinguish isolated acts of violence from peaceful picketing.

[4] Acts Not Constituting Violence but Still Subject to State Court Jurisdiction

State courts have consistently enjoined the use of language on picket signs that constitutes fraud, libel, misrepresentation, or inciting to a breach of peace. For example, the Supreme Court has held that state courts have jurisdiction if the complaint against the union involves a traditional state substantive law issue, such as libel.[239]

Further, in another case, it held that a state court could take jurisdiction over an allegation of intentional infliction of emotional distress.[240]

---

235 Westinghouse Elec. Corp. v. UE, Local 107, 383 Pa. 297, 118 A.2d 180 (1955).

236 UMWA v. Gibbs, 383 U.S. 715, 736 (1966).

237 Youngdahl v. Rainfair, 355 U.S. 131 (1957).

238 Milk Wagon Drivers Union v. Meadowmoor Dairies, Inc., *supra.*

239 Linn v. Plant Guard Workers, 383 U.S. 53 (1966).

240 Farmer v. Carpenter, 430 U.S. 290 (1977).

Such lawsuits and allegations are difficult to prove and involve potentially excessive interference by state courts in employer-employee disputes. In *Cafeteria Employees v. Angelos,* the Supreme Court recognized that "to use loose language or undefined slogans that are part of the conventional give-and-take in our economic and political controversies—like 'unfair' and 'fascist'—is not to falsify facts."[241] Lawsuits over such picket line activity simply ignore the occasional spontaneous exuberance and the give-and-take on picket lines.

There are instances in which silent forms of intimidation may be enjoined. The recording of customer license plate numbers was enjoined in one case because the court felt it implied a threat to do injury.[242] A request for an injunction against the same activity was rejected in a case in which the union had simply sent moderately worded letters describing the strike issues and requesting support.[243] The jurisdiction of the state courts was expanded in *Sears Roebuck v. Carpenters:*[244] The Supreme Court held that a company could maintain an action to enforce state trespass laws against peaceful picketing if the union had had the opportunity to present the issue to the NLRB and failed to do so and the conduct was not actually protected by the NLRB.

[5] Jurisdictional Issues

Companies often obtain ex parte temporary restraining orders against alleged union violence at the beginning of the strike. Some courts routinely grant them on the basis of extremely weak affidavits. Such injunctions usually expire within a few days after their issuance; adversary hearings must be held within that time. Consult your local court rules for the procedural issues.

The first step to take if a strike is imminent is to contact the

---

241 Cafeteria Employees Local 302 v. Angelos, 320 U.S. 293, 295 (1943). *See also* Paduach Newspapers Inc., v. Wise, 247 S.W.2d 989 (Ky. 1951), *cert. denied,* 343 U.S. 942 (1952) (involving libel allegations); Dinny & Robbins, Inc., v. Davis, 290 N.Y. 101, 48 N.E.2d 280 (1943).

242 Wallace Co. v. Machinists Local 1005, 155 Ore. 652, 63 P.2d 1090 (1936).

243 Loder Bus Co. v. Machinists Local 1506, 306 P.2d 411, 209 Ore. 305 (1957).

244 Sears Roebuck Co. v. Carpenters, 436 U.S. 180, 98 LRRM 2282 (1978).

company attorney (phone, certified mail, or telegram), informing him/her that you represent the union at all times and for all purposes and would like to be informed of any legal action the company may initiate. Also contact the local judge who is likely to hear the request for a temporary restraining order and inform him/her that you wish to be heard before any such order is issued. This may block the issuance of ex parte injunctive relief against the union; if it does not, use the company's actions in later proceedings as evidence of its bad faith. One question that always arises when one is faced with a request for an injunction in state court is whether the dispute is properly before that court. Two options are available: (1) Seek to remove the case from state court to federal court, or (2) seek to argue that neither court should hear the dispute because it is within the exclusive jurisdiction of the NLRB.

[a] Removal to Federal Court

There are two reasons for removing a state court proceeding to federal court: (1) The federal court is a more favorable forum for resolution of strike-related issues because removal sets up the Norris-LaGuardia Act's procedural standards making company attempts to obtain injunctive relief more difficult, and (2) removal, even if unsuccessful in the long run, delays the state court proceedings, minimizing the potential adverse impact an undesirable state court ruling would have on the strike effort.

A case may be removed from state to federal court on the ground of federal question jurisdiction.[245] The filing of the petition for removal effects the removal and stops the state court proceedings. The company will probably quickly file a petition to remand in the federal court, which will remand absent clear federal issues.

The content of the state court complaint, not the petition for removal, controls whether the district court has jurisdiction.[246] The removal petition is generally denied if the company's state court complaint seeks to enjoin violence, mass picketing, or other

[245] 28 U.S.C. § 1441(a).

[246] Jody Fair v. Dubinsky, 225 F. Supp. 695 (S.D.N.Y. 1964).

conduct forbidden by state law.[247] Employers frequently couch federal labor law violations under state law causes of actions, hoping to obtain relief in friendlier state court forums. If the complaint seeks damages for breach of the collective bargaining agreement or for illegal secondary boycott activity, then the federal court has jurisdiction.[248] This is so whether or not the complaint specifically uses the terms "secondary boycott" or "breach of the collective bargaining agreement." The factual allegations of the complaint control in determining if the federal court will take jurisdiction.

[b] Pendent Jurisdiction

Cases removed to federal court frequently involve claims under both state and federal law. A federal court may exercise jurisdiction over both claims if (1) both the state and federal claims for relief derive from a common nucleus of facts such that ordinarily all legal issues arising from the facts would be decided in the same lawsuit and (2) the federal issues present substantial questions under federal law.[249] The rationale for that decision is one that must be emphasized in any removal petition—the need to avoid a multiplicity of lawsuits and potentially conflicting decisions.

Company will oppose removal petitions because federal court proceedings set up much stricter procedural requirements under the Norris-LaGuardia Act. In this regard, see particularly Sections 6 and 7 of the Norris-LeGuardia Act[250] and *Kayser Roth v. Textile Workers.*[251]

---

[247] Woodland Nursing Home v. District 1199, 91 LRRM 3003 (S.D.N.Y. 1975); Beacon Mareney v. Teamsters, 362 F. Supp. 442 (S.D.N.Y. 1972).

[248] Bay Beverage, Inc. v. Teamsters Local 282, 83 LRRM 2078 (E.D.N.Y. 1973).

[249] United Mine Workers of America v. Gibbs, 383 U.S. 715 (1966).

[250] 29 U.S.C. §§ 106, 107.

[251] 479 F.2d 526 (6th Cir. 1973).

[c] Federal Court Jurisdiction over Mass Picketing and Acts of Violence

Federal courts have jurisdiction, if the appropriate federal diversity jurisdiction exists, to enjoin mass picketing and violence.[252] It is rare to see companies seeking such injunctive relief in federal court because the state court procedures are generally much less stringent if injunctive relief is requested.

When filed in federal court, the request for injunctive relief brings the Norris-LaGuardia Act into the picture. Section 7 of the Act[253] imposes rigid requirements for issuance of an injunction in addition to the requirement of absence of an adequate remedy at law. This has been construed very narrowly to limit the federal courts' authority to issue an injunction.[254] Section 6 of the Norris-LaGuardia Act alters normal agency principles by establishing an evidentiary standard of *clear proof* that the union participated in, authorized, or ratified the unlawful acts.[255] Companies generally go to state courts to obtain injunctive relief against picketing activities and/or violence to avoid the stringent procedural requirements of the Norris-LaGuardia Act. However, some states have anti-injunction acts with provisions very similar to those of the Norris-LaGuardia Act. (These are sometimes called little Norris-LaGuardia Acts.)

[d] NLRB Preemption

Jurisdictional questions arise throughout the whole spectrum of issues involved in strikes and are resolved through the application of the preemption doctrine. This doctrine is the basis of petitions to remove and of many arguments against the state courts' use of injunctions in labor disputes. The fountainhead of

---

252 Westinghouse Broadcasting Co. v. Dukakis, 92 LRRM 2729 (D. Mass. 1976).

253 29 U.S.C.A. § 107.

254 *See* UMWA v. Gibbs, 383 U.S. 715 (jurisdiction); Cimarron Coal Co. v. UMWA District 23, 72 LRRM 2409 (6th Cir. 1969); Ritchie v. UMWA, 71 LRRM 2267 (6th Cir. 1969); Emery Air Freight Corp. v. Local 295, Teamsters, 78 LRRM 2466 (2d Cir. 1971).

255 United Bhd. of Carpenters v. United States, 330 U.S. 395 (1947).

the doctrine is *Garmon v. San Diego Building Trades Council,*[256] in which the Supreme Court stated: "[W]hen an activity is arguably subject to Section 7 or 8 of the [LMRA] Act, the state as well as the Federal Court must defer to the exclusive competence of the NLRB if the danger of state interference with national labor policy is to be averted."[257]

The doctrine of primary jurisdiction was originally established in *Texas and Pacific Railroad v. Abilene Cotton Oil Company,*[258] a case not involving labor relations. In this case, the Supreme Court held that matters entrusted by Congress to the regulatory control of a federal agency must be litigated in the first instance under the procedures of that agency. In a later case, the court commented extensively on the specialized competence of administrative agencies and the need for uniformity and consistency.[259]

The basis of the federal preemption doctrine in its application to labor relations was explained by the Supreme Court in *Garner v. Teamsters:*

> Congress evidently considered that centralized administration of specially designed procedures was necessary to obtain uniform application of its substantive rules and to avoid these diversities and conflicts likely to result from a variety of local procedures and attitudes towards labor controversies. . . . A multiplicity of tribunals and a diversity of procedures are quite as apt to produce incompatible or conflicting adjudication as are different rules of substantive law.[260]

The scope of the preemption doctrine appears to be narrowing under recent Supreme Court decisions. A 1978 ruling indicates that an issue is preempted only if it is *identical* to the federal issue.[261]

---

[256] 359 U.S. 236 (1959).

[257] *Id. See also* Machinists Lodge 76 v. Wisc. Employment Relations Commr, 427 U.S. 132 (1976); Garner v. Teamsters Union, 346 U.S. 485 (1953).

[258] 204 U.S. 426 (1907).

[259] Far East Conference v. United States, 342 U.S. 570 (1952).

[260] Garner v. Teamsters Union, 346 U.S. 485, 490-91, 33 LRRM 2218 (1953).

[261] Sears, Roebuck Co. v. Carpenters, 436 U.S. 180, 98 LRRM 2282 (1978).

[e] Preparing Jurisdictional Arguments

Upon receipt of the employer's state court complaint, immediately consider the following issues:

(1) Do the employer's factual allegations spell out arguable violations under Section 8 or concern conduct protected under Section 7 or under Section 303 of the LMRA?
(2) Are proceedings pending between the parties before the NLRB, or was an NLRB charge filed at the beginning of the strike and then hastily withdrawn?
(3) Are suits pending between the parties in federal court?
(4) Even if the arguments for federal jurisdiction are weak, would the delay of a few days in state court proceedings effectuated by the petition for removal help the strike?

The removal petition should be filed *before* any further state court proceedings take place. You should note that, because the federal courts are more likely to consider the applicability of NLRB exclusive jurisdiction than are state courts, you may wish first to remove the state court case to federal court and then urge the federal judge to defer to the NLRB.

[6] Combating the Company Request for Injunctive Relief in State Court

[a] Notification of Company Attorney and Local Court

When a strike is imminent, notify the company attorney that you represent the union at all times and for all purposes and would like prior notification of any legal proceedings the company initiates. Similarly notify the local judge likely to preside over requests for injunctive relief in the state courts. Such notification should be by telephone and telegram or certified mail. Such notice will often block an employer's attempt to obtain ex parte injunctive relief and may also provide a slight delay in the eventual issuance of injunctive relief.

The existence of a temporary restraining order creates an immediate obstacle for the union, as even ex parte temporary restraining orders generally are converted into preliminary injunctions. If the company has obtained ex parte injunctive relief against the union, use it to advantage in two ways: (1) in arguments to the court, as an example of the unfairness of the company's actions during the strike, and (2) as an organizing tool, to expose the unfairness of the company's tactics.

[b] Meeting the Local Union and Named Individuals

It is crucial that such a meeting be held immediately to maintain morale and a solid front in the strike. The company's state court complaint frequently names not only the union but also individual officers and members. Many union members become intimidated when they are served with court papers by a uniformed officer—particularly if those papers state they are being sued for $100,000, say. Such an intimidating tactic by the company can drastically weaken a strike effort, although it often has the opposite effect.

At this meeting the following things must be done:

(1) Explain very carefully the significance of the court papers.
(2) Explain the legal rights and liabilities of union members for different types of picket line and strike activity. Also explain their reinstatement rights if the company has sent or is sending letters notifying them that temporary or permanent replacements are being hired.
(3) Describe the court papers you are filing: petition for removal, motion to dismiss, answer and counterclaim, etc.
(4) Instruct union officials and picket captains to keep a diary of the company's actions and activities.
(5) Discuss whether to pack the courtroom (usually desirable because of the public relations effect and potential impact on the judge). Also discuss who should stay away from court hearings—those who have been active but are not named in the court papers.
(6) Answer fully all questions.

After the meeting, conduct detailed interviews dealing with picket line activities, focusing on picket captains, union officers, and individuals named in the company's complaint. From these it is possible to know how much, if any, substance there is in the company's complaint.

[c] Do We Pack the Courtroom?

While the answer is usually yes, because of the reasons noted above, there are several crucial factors in making this decision. If no individuals have been named or identified in the company's pleadings and if no one has received a summons, do not bring any union members into the court hearings. (This set of circumstances is unlikely, although it occasionally occurs in the coalfields because of the inability to identify picketers.) Bringing individuals into court in such a situation invites very suggestive identification of union members by company personnel and police. The defense in such a situation should rest upon the failure of the company to identify any union members as engaging in acts of misconduct. The cross-examination of company witnesses in this instance should be very restrictive and should not give such witnesses the opportunity to explain why those engaging in misconduct had to be union members.

More commonly, the company's state court complaint specifically names and/or identifies a number of union members. In such a case, the courtroom should be packed for all hearings with union members and their families. This creates a display of a strong front, something both the court and the company will have to take seriously. It helps strengthen the union's bargaining position (regarding contract negotiations) and forces the judge fully to consider the union's legal position. It is also a good tool to use to build community support, helping the community realize that the strikers are fighting for their bread and butter.

Union members should sit in groups and stay in groups when in the hallways, particularly if they may have been involved in picket line activity. This will help avoid suggestive identification by company people. If a union member may have been involved in strike misconduct but is not named in the company's complaint, instruct that person to stay out of court.

[d] Petition for Removal to Federal Court

Considerations involving such a petition are discussed above. If you decide to attempt removal, do so immediately. Most removal petitions will be denied and the cases will be quickly remanded to the state court.

[e] Motion to Dismiss Complaint

This should be filed before any hearings on the company request for injunctive releif. The motion should cover the following areas:

[i] Federal Preemption

The state court lacks jurisdiction because of the preemption doctrine, since the company's factual allegations allege potential violations of Section 7 or 8 of the LMRA. If the state court is insistent upon issuing an injunction, emphasize that it has no jurisdiction to enjoin peaceful activities of a union involved in a dispute with an employer that is even arguably subject to NLRB jurisdiction.[262] Point out workers' free speech rights under both the First Amendment and Section 7 of the LMRA, emphasizing that the terms of any injunction should be strictly limited to enjoining violence and threats of violence. An improperly broad injunction that does not delineate specific illegal acts is subject to attack.

When a court insists on enjoining peaceful activities of union members, if the union members have been entirely peaceful and the activity is arguably protected or prohibited under the LMRA, it is possible, though risky, to ignore the overbroad aspects of the

[262] San Diego Bldg. Trades v. Garmon, *supra;* Broadcast Technicians v. Broadcast Service, 380 U.S. 255.

injunction. The Supreme Court has stated "a state court is without power to hold one in contempt for violating an injunction that the state court had no power to enter by reason of federal pre-emption."[263]

[ii] Vagueness

State that the company's request for injunctive relief is insufficient as a matter of law because the complaint consists of vague and conclusionary allegations. Complaints filed by companies in state courts frequently contain little in the way of specific allegations and often fail to identify times, places, and particular individuals. Historically, the law of equity governing the issuance of injunctions requires that positive averments of facts be made to support the request for injunctive relief. An old treatise on the subject states:

> Positive averments of fact necessary. . . . Thus it is well established that the mere allegation of irreparable injury will not suffice to warrant an injunction, but the facts must appear on which the allegation is predicated in order that the court may be satisfied as to the nature of the injury.[264]

Focus on the following issues in your oral and written arguments:

(1) Injunctive relief is an extraordinary remedy, which should be carefully considered before it is invoked.
(2) The company's complaint consists of a generalized shopping list of acts and is not tailored to any particular situation, certainly not the present one.
(3) Does the company particularize the individuals alleged to have committed certain acts, or does it simply name union officials and active union members?
(4) Are the days on and times at which certain acts are al-

---

[263] In re Green, 369 U.S. 689, 8 L. Ed. 2d 198. *See also* Ex parte George, 371 U.S. 72.

[264] High, On Injunctions, Vol. 1 (4th ed. 1905).

leged to have occurred listed on the complaint? Frequently, company pleadings and testimony recite "on or about x date" and go on to recite a shopping list of alleged atrocities committed by union members.

(5) The company has not presented facts sufficient to prove irreparable harm—only vague and generalized damages were presented.

(6) No threat of *continuing* injury exists—while there may have been some injury in the past, there is nothing to enjoin in the future.

(7) There is no immediate or impending injury.

(8) The company, if injured, has an adequate remedy at law. (There will generally be case law in your particular jurisdiction to support the equitable arguments listed above.)

(9) Irreparable injury is not established merely because it is difficult to prove damages.

(10) Injuries contingent upon uncertain future events are not the basis for injunctive relief.

[iii] Technical Deficiencies

Technical deficiencies in the company's pleadings should be raised before substantive arguments and will vary from state to state. Such arguments could include (1) clean hands argument because of the failure to provide notice of ex parte hearing on temporary restraining order, (2) improper service, and (3) improper verification.

[iv] Unclean Hands

Unclean hands because of company unfair labor practices should be raised in conjunction with jurisdictional arguments of federal preemption. Argue that the situation was provoked and aggravated by illegal company conduct.[265]

[265] *See* Advance Stamping Co. v. UAW, 38 LRRM 2382; Kohler v. UAW, 300 F.2d 699; David Adler v. Maglia, 200 Wis. 153, 228 N.W.2d 123; Cornellier v. Haverhill Shoe Mfg. Ass'n., 221 Mass. 554, 105 N.E.2d 643.

[f] Little Norris-LaGuardia Acts

The Norris-LaGuardia Act places judicial restraints on the issuance of injunctions by federal courts during labor disputes. Many states have passed anti-injunction legislation (so-called little Norris-LaGuardia Acts) aimed at curbing the abusive use of injunctions by state courts during labor disputes.[266]

Pennsylvania's Labor Injunction Act recognizes some key public policy points about the grant of ex parte injunctive relief:

> (1) The status quo cannot be maintained but is necessarily altered by the injunction;
>
> (2) Determination of issues of veracity and of probability of fact from affidavits of the opposing parties that are contradictory and under the circumstances untrustworthy rather than from oral examination in open court is subject to grave error;
>
> (3) Error in issuing injunctive relief is usually irreparable to the opposing party; and
>
> (4) Delay incident to the normal course of appellate practice frequently makes ultimate correction of error in law or in fact unavailing in the particular case.[267]

The Pennsylvania act does not establish the clear proof evidentiary standard[268] of the Norris-LaGuardia Act. Section 206(i) describes the prerequisites for issuance of injunctive relief in Pennsylvania; it is cited in full below because it provides a good outline of the procedural and substantive arguments that can be presented in opposing company attempts to get injunctive relief. Its arguments can be used in states that do not have little Norris-LaGuardia Acts because the law is simply a codification of general equitable principles. This section states:

> **§ 206i. Basis for labor injunctions**
>
> No court of this Commonwealth shall issue any restraining order or a temporary or permanent injunction in any case involving or

[266] *See, e.g.,* the Labor Injunction Act of Pennsylvania, 43 P.S. § 206 et seq.
[267] 43 P.S. § 206(b).
[268] *See* 43 P.S. § 206(h).

growing out of a labor dispute, except after hearing the testimony of witnesses in open court (with opportunity for cross-examination) in support of the allegations of a complaint made under oath, and testimony in opposition thereto, if offered and except after findings of fact by the court to the effect—

(a) That unlawful acts have been threatened and will be committed unless restrained, or have been committed and will be continued unless restrained, but no temporary or permanent injunction or temporary restraining order shall be issued on account of any threat or unlawful act, excepting against the person or persons, association or organization, making the threat or committing the unlawful act, or actually authorizing or ratifying the same after actual knowledge thereof.

(b) That substantial and irreparable injury to complainant's property will follow unless the relief requested is granted.

(c) That, as to each item of relief granted, greater injury will be inflicted upon complainant by the denial of relief than will be inflicted upon defendants by granting of relief.

(d) That no item of relief granted is relief which is prohibited under section six of this act.[1]

(e) That complainant has no adequate remedy at law; and

(f) That the public officers charged with the duty to protect complainant's property are unable to furnish adequate protection.

Such hearing shall be held only after a verified bill of complaint and a verified bill of particulars specifying in detail the time, place, and the nature of the acts complained of, and the names of the persons alleged to have committed the same or participated therein, have been served, and after due and personal notice thereof has been given, in such manner as the court shall direct, to all known persons against whom relief is sought, and also to the chief of those public officials of the county and city, within which the unlawful acts have been threatened or committed, charged with the duty to protect complainant's property. The hearing shall consist of the taking of testimony in open court with opportunity for cross-examination and testimony in opposition thereto, if offered, and no affidavits shall be received in support of any of the allegations of the complaint. 1937, June 2, P.L. 1198, § 9.

[1] Section 206f of this title.

One interesting point to emphasize is that there are no indications, despite past trouble, that the police are unable to preserve the public order. Very few police officials will concede their inability to preserve order; in such a situation a little Norris-LaGuardia Act will bar the issuance of an injunction.

[g] Counterclaim for Injunctive Relief and Damages

It is important to take offensive legal action against the company. Picket captains and union officials should keep a daily diary of company activities and have a camera available. It is likely that at some point company personnel will engage in some form of illegal activity.

Fire a specifically worded counterclaim against the company, specifying company violations of the law. Include all incidents of (1) violence, (2) threats of violence, (3) intimidation (physical threats and threats of losing jobs), and (4) surveillance. In any strike, company supervisors will have been instructed to keep a close watch on the picket line and to identify troublemakers. It is likely that they will use cameras.

It is common in court hearings on injunctive relief to hear the company attorney argue that an injunction will simply force the union and the union membership to comply with the law. Your response should be threefold: (1) If that is the case, then, of course, the company should have no objection to an injunction being issued against it. (2) Workers accused of violating a court order (injunction) have fewer procedural protections in contempt of court proceedings than they would in criminal proceedings for violation of the law. (3) The issuance of an injunction implies wrongdoing.

[7] Special Considerations in Fighting State Court Injunctions

[a] Extensions of Temporary Restraining Orders

Sometimes one may represent a number of different locals, or a particularly active one, and be defending company suits in several different courts. Set priorities of time, and focus on those suits that in the long run will have the greatest potential impact on the strike effort.

At times you may be buried under company proceedings and in a situation of defaulting in a case or of seeing a temporary restraining order extended. In such a situation, consent to only the extension, and specifically reserve objections to the order itself, the company's factual allegations, and the court's jurisdiction.

[b] Common Court Orders

State courts habitually issue injunctions against certain picket line activities even if there has been little or no violence. The activities most frequently banned by court injunction are—

(1) acts of violence to persons and property,
(2) threats of violence to persons and property,
(3) blocking of ingress and egress,
(4) mass picketing,
(5) large numbers of strikers congregating near the picket line,
(6) picketing beyond specified limits (number of pickets, so many per gate, spaced so many feet apart, etc.), and
(7) libelous statements (this is often vague).

At the point it becomes apparent an injunctive order will issue, clearly articulate that it must not interfere with the Section 7 or First Amendment free speech right of the workers publicly to state their grievances. Your counterclaim should also seek similar restrictions against company actions.

[c] Negotiations for a New Collective Bargaining Agreement

It is likely that state court proceedings will be pending at the time the contract is being negotiated. The union's negotiating position should stress the need to resolve all pending issues between the parties. There should be a stipulation filed in court, signed by both the union and the company, *dismissing the action with prejudice* to the union, union officers, and individually named defendants. The union should also attempt to resolve other pending legal actions, including Section 301 actions in federal court.

Amnesty should also be negotiated for all strikers (generally, this is not a problem with strikers who have not been identified as engaging in serious misconduct). If temporary or permanent replacements have been hired by the company, the union must take steps to ensure that the reinstatement rights of the strikers are fully protected. If the company is resistant on these points, make it completely clear that no contract will be ratified without amnesty for the strikers and full observance of reinstatement rights.

[d] Trial of Company's Damage Actions in State Court

The company's state court complaint frequently seeks damages for lost production, as will as for property damage. If the union is involved in a contract strike, the company is not entitled to damages for lost production caused by legal strike activity. The company may get damages for lost production during a legal strike if it proves that acts of sabotage to company machinery or physical intimidation of scabs led to lost production. Clearly distinguish between the two types of damages in the pleadings and in courtroom arguments.

The employer can also sue for damage to property caused by the actions of strikers, although to recover from the union on this basis, some form of participation, authorization, or ratification must be shown. The union might be found liable for damage done during mass actions on the picket line, but it is much less likely to be found liable for acts of an individual or for damage that simply "appears," with no one having been clearly identified.

§ 3.07. Organizing and Financing the Strike

The organization and the financing of the strike are matters best resolved by the union and rank-and-file organizations. However, it is important for attorneys to be aware of certain aspects of organization and financing in order to provide the most effective legal representation.

[1] Prestrike Meetings

It is crucial for the union to organize itself effectively. The prestrike meeting provides an opportunity for counsel to outline the legal rights and liabilities of union members who are on strike. The following matters should be dealt with in such a meeting:

(1) negotiation of the new collective bargaining agreement;
(2) discussion of the legal rights and restrictions the strikers and the union face, including—
   (a) rights under the First Amendment and Section 7, the limits of legal picket line conduct, and what constitutes illegal conduct;
   (b) the probability that the company will keep the strikers off company property and keep them under surveillance;
   (c) the possibility that the company will file a suit in state court; and
   (d) their reinstatement rights should the company hire temporary or permanent replacements (whether the company does so will in large measure be determined by the past relationship of the parties); and
(3) organizing disciplined picket lines, setting picket schedules, electing picket captains, and making signs.

Include the families of the strikers in these meetings; many families worry and weaken a strike simply because of lack of knowledge. Furthemore, strikers' families can actively strengthen a strike. (The coalfields provide some good examples of the effectiveness of support committees and women's clubs. For example, it is generally agreed that the strength of the Harlan County Women's Club was the main factor in winning the UMWA Brookside strike in Harlan County in 1975-76.)

[2] Negotiating the Contract

A separate prestrike meeting should be held to discuss matters the membership wants raised in the contract negotiations. Before this meeting, the union should leaflet every shift with questionnaires concerning the relative importance of various issues and new issues that should be raised. The completed questionnaires should be collected at the end of each shift. The meeting to discuss the contract proposal should be well publicized in the union newsletter, on union bulletin boards, and again with a leafletting of every shift. If the union can afford it, there should be a mailing sent out to every member and, at the very least, a mailing should go out to all the pensioners.

At the meeting a list of rank-and-file demands should be agreed upon and a rank-and-file bargaining committee that *participates* in negotiations should be chosen. A research group should prepare a memo on company finances, particularly outrageous company decisions, particularly outrageous arbitration decisions under prior contracts, and the history of past negotiations with the company. There should be careful renegotiation of key clauses dealing with management rights, grievance and arbitration machinery, right to strike, safety rights, etc.

[3] Legal Strategy

Specific responsibility should be taken for negotiations, civil actions, and a procedure for referring strikers accused of criminal activity. The union may want to avoid directly defending strikers accused of criminal activity because of potential civil liability.

[4] Financing the Strike

The following should be considered financial resources during a strike effort:

(1) accrued benefits owed by the company (vacation pay, etc.),
(2) strike benefits,
(3) strike fund,
(4) food stamps, and
(5) donations from other unions and gate collections at other union plants.

[5] Outreach to the Community

The following things should be done to communicate to other unions and to the community the fact of the strike and the strike issues in order to raise support for the strike:

(1) informational leaflets at plant gates, community meetings, and churches,
(2) press releases to local media,
(3) ads in community papers, and
(4) speaking at meetings of other unions and community groups.

§ 3.08. Maintaining Strike Discipline

The crucial factor in a solid and successful strike effort is the ability of the union to maintain a united front. Once the employer splinters the strike effort (e.g., by convincing some workers to cross the picket line), the employer will probably have a crucial advantage in any settlement negotiations. The importance of unity within a union's ranks can be seen historically in the national strikes in the coalfields. A union must do its groundwork in representing its members and in preparing them for a strike effort in order to prevent any splintering in its ranks. There are times when such efforts are not enough, with some union members crossing a picket line. In such a situation, the union retains a limited right to impose discipline on those members.

[1] Statutory Limitations on Union Discipline of Union Members

The statutory limitations on the union's rights to discipline its members are contained primarily in Section 8(b)(2) of the LMRA[269] and Title 1 of the Landrum Griffin Act.[270]

Section 8(b)(2) provides in part:

> It shall be an unfair labor practice for an labor organization or its agents to cause an employer to discriminate against an employee in violation of subsection (a)(3) or to discriminate against an employee with respect to whom membership in such organization has been denied or terminated on some ground other than his failure to tender the periodic dues and the initiation fees uniformly acquiring or retaining membership.

Under Section 7, an employee has the right to refrain from engaging in concerted activity, such as a strike. Therefore, an employee, whether a union member or not, has the right to cross a picket line free of fear of being discharged because of union pressure. The "except" provision of Section 7 is limited by Section 8(a)(3) and Section 8(b)(2) to the discharge of an employee who fails to pay the required dues. An employer may discharge a employee for failure to pay union dues but not for any other reason. A union that demands the discharge of a union member for crossing a picket line commits an unfair labor practice under Section 8(b)(2), which stipulates that a union may demand the discharge of a union member only for failure to pay union dues.

Title I of the Labor-Management Reporting and Disclosure Act (LMRDA) of 1959 sets forth the Bill of Rights of Members of Labor Organizations. Section 101(a)(5) of the Bill of Rights provides:

> No member of any labor organization may be fined, suspended,

---

[269] 29 U.S.C. § 158(b)(2).

[270] 29 U.S.C. § 411(a).

> expelled or otherwise disciplined except for nonpayment of dues by such organization or by any officer thereof unless such member has been (A) served with written specific charges; (B) given a reasonable time to prepare his defense; (C) afforded a full and fair hearing.[271]

It should be pointed out that this right—indeed, the entire Bill of Rights of the LMRDA—is granted only to union members and is granted to them only in their relationship to a union as its members. These rights in no way benefit union members in their relationship to management.

[2] What Action May a Union Take against Its Members?

Unions have the right to manage their own internal affairs;[272] in exercising that right, they may fine members, suspend them, and even expel them from the union. However, a union may not engage in conduct that restrains or coerces its members.[273] A union may fine its members for crossing picket lines and enforce this fine with a suit to collect.[274] The Act does not authorize the NLRB to determine the reasonableness of the fines.[275] The NLRB has ruled that local courts can best set standards of reasonableness of fines.[276]

A union member who resigns from the union may not be fined for crossing a picket line. The procedure for resigning may depend on the union's constitution and bylaws. However, if the procedure is too cumbersome or involves an unreasonable notice before the resignation is effective, the resignation procedure may

---

[271] 29 U.S.C. 411(a)(5).

[272] Section 8(b)(1) of the LMRA.

[273] Section 8(b)(1)(A).

[274] NLRB v. Allis-Chalmers Mfg. Co., 55 L.C. para. 11,972, 388 U.S. 811 (1967) (union lawfully fined supervisors for crossing picket lines); NLRB v. Typographical Union, San Francisco Typographical Union No. 21, 71 L.C. para. 13,713 (9th Cir. 1973).

[275] NLRB v. Boeing Co., 71 L.C. para. 13,668 (U.S. S. Ct. 1973).

[276] Machinists, Local 504 (Arrow Dev. Co.), 1970 CCH NLRB para. 22,260, 185 NLRB No. 22; Carpenters, Local 101, 1970 CCH NLRB para. 22,474, 186 NLRB No. 119.

be held to be a restraint on employees' rights, and an attempt to fine a union member may be held to be unlawful. If there are no restraints on the resignation of members, an ex-member who first resigned and then crossed a picket line may not be fined.[277] Absent resignation provisions in a union's constitution or bylaws, members can resign at will before or after a strike by notifying the union.[278] Such resignation is effective upon receipt by the union.[279] Resignation from the union before a strike may be accomplished by canceling dues checkoffs and returning membership cards to the union.[280] Union members may be lawfully fined if they first crossed the picket line, then resigned, and then were fined.[281] Before a union member can be fined or disciplined by the union for crossing a picket line he or she must first be afforded the rights stipulated in Section 101(a)(5) of the LMRDA.

Failure to pay a fine does not justify a union demand for the member's discharge. A union violates Section 8(b)(1) and Section 8(b)(2) of the Act if it causes or attempts to cause the discharge or layoff of an employee for failure to pay a fine.[282]

---

277 NLRB v. Textile Workers, Local 1029, 69 L.C. para. 13,199 (U.S. S. Ct. 1972).

278 District Lodge No. 99 (Gen. Elec. Co.), 1972 CCH NLRB para. 23,782, 193 NLRB No. 163.

279 Chem. Workers, Local 143 (Am. Cyanamid Co., Lederle Laboratories Div.), 1971 CCH NLRB para. 22,784, 188 NLRB 100.

280 Communications Workers, Local 6135 (S.W. Bell Tel. Co.), 1971 CCH NLRB para. 22,823, 188 NLRB 144.

281 Wash.-Baltimore Newspaper Guild, Local 85 (Wash. Post Co.), 1970 CCH NLRB para. 22,496, 186 NLRB 133.

282 NLRB v. Nat'l Automotive Fibres, Inc., 40 L.C. para. 66,465, 277 F.2d 779 (9th Cir. 1960); NLRB v. Carpenters and Joiners, Local 517, 29 L.C. para. 69,789, 230 F.2d 256 (1st Cir. 1956) (discharged); State, Tile & Composition Roofers, Local 4 (Damp & Waterproof Workers Ass'n), 1962 CCH NLRB para. 11,924, 140 NLRB 384 (lay-off); Custom Underwear Mfg. Co., 108 NLRB 117 (1954) (discharge); Miami Valley Carpenters' District Council of Dayton, Ohio, 1960 CCH NLRB para. 9356, 129 NLRB 517, *enforced,* 44 L.C. para. 17,390, 297 F.2d 920 (6th Cir. 1962).

§ 3.09. National Emergency Strikes—Taft-Hartley Injunctions

Title II of the Taft-Hartley Act (the Labor-Management Relations Act of 1947) contains provisions authorizing the president of the United States to intervene in strikes or potential strikes that create a national emergency as defined in the Act.[283]

Whenever the president is of the opinion that an actual or threatened strike or lockout affecting an entire industry, or a substantial part thereof, engaged in interstate or foreign trade, commerce, transportation, transmission, or communication or engaged in the production of goods for commerce imperils the national health or safety, s/he may appoint a board of inquiry to make a factual investigation of the dispute and to report to him/her. The report includes each party's statement of its position but cannot contain any recommendations.[284]

After the president receives the report of the board of inquiry, he may direct the Attorney General to petition any U.S. district court that has jurisdiction over the parties for an injunction. If the court finds that the strike meets two requirements—if it affects an *entire* or *substantial part* of the appropriate kind of industry to the required extent, *and* if it imperils the national health or safety—then the court has jurisdiction to enjoin the strike or lockout and to enter appropriate orders.[285] The court orders are subject to review by the U.S. circuit courts of appeal and the U.S. Supreme Court.

The industries covered include those engaged in trade, commerce, transportation, transmission, or communication among the several states or with foreign nations or engaged in the production of goods for commerce. This covers most basic industries as well as the transportation industry. The court is not required to find that the strike is industry wide; it need only find that a substantial part of the industry is or will be afflicted and that the strike, if allowed to continue, will endanger the national

---

283 These provisions are found at 29 U.S.C. §§ 176-82.

284 29 U.S.C. § 176.

285 29 U.S.C., § 178.

health or safety.[286] At times, a strike at a single plant might be considered sufficient to threaten national health and safety.[287]

Requests for a Taft-Hartley injunction are frequently accompanied by much publicity, creating political pressure on the court to issue the injunction. There is a tendency to consent to the request for the injunction. (International UMWA lawyers did this in 1978.) Fight the government's case each step of the way. In *United States v. International Longshoremen's Union, Local 418,*[288] the court ruled that (1) a strike at most of the grain elevators in Chicago did not affect an entire industry or a substantial part thereof and (2) its continuation would not imperil the national health and safety.

The Act requires the district court to specifically find that the national health and safety are imperiled before issuing an injunction.[289] Do not allow the government to present a case based upon conclusionary affidavits and statistics from government officials. Use thoroughly prepared cross-examination to break down the case presented by the government's witnesses, including those members of the board of inquiry who testify. Present your own expert witnesses (economists, etc.) to rebut the government's allegations that the national health or safety is imperiled. There will, of course, be disruptions in strikes but rarely are the national health and safety going to be endangered.

Once the injunction is granted, the Federal Mediation and Conciliation Service[290] is supposed to assist the parties in resolving the dispute, although no party is required to accept any proposal of settlement made by the Service.[291]

Upon issuance of the court's order, the president reconvenes the board of inquiry. If the dispute is not settled within sixty days of the court's order, the board of inquiry then reports to the president the positions of the parties and the offers for settlement that have been made and submits a statement of the parties

---

[286] *See* United States v. United Steelworkers of America, 202 F.2d 132 (2d Cir. 1953).

[287] United States v. Am. Locomotive Co., 109 F. Supp. 78 (W.D.N.Y. 1952).

[288] United States v. Int'l Longshoremen's Union, Local 418, 335 F. Supp. 54 (N.D. Ill. 1971), *stay denied,* 78 LRRM 2801 (7th Cir. 1971).

[289] 29 U.S.C. § 178.

[290] 29 U.S.C. §§ 172-74.

[291] 29 U.S.C. § 179(a).

explaining their positions and the employer's last offer. Within fifteen days, thereafter the NLRB takes a secret ballot of the workers on the question of whether they wish to accept the final offer, and within five days of the vote the NLRB certifies the results to the Attorney General.[292] Upon such certification or upon settlement, whichever happens sooner, the Attorney General has the court discharge the injunction. The president then reports to Congress and makes such recommendations for legislative actions as s/he sees fit.[293]

From 1947 through 1976, the national emergency provisions of the Taft-Hartley Act were used thirty times. Industries affected have been atomic energy, stevedoring, aircraft-aerospace, coal, maritime, steel, meat packing, shipbuilding, and telephones.[294]

Note that the government can obtain an ex parte temporary restraining order, which is enforceable, regardless of its merits, by civil or criminal contempt, even if the act on which the order is based is unconstitutional "and even if it is later determined that the court had no jurisdiction over the dispute itself, unless the court plainly usurps power."[295] Such a temporary restraining order is binding upon actual notice thereof and may bind others than the parties named in the pleadings. If it becomes apparent that the government may seek such an order, telegraph and send certified letters to the Attorney General stating that you represent the union and demand notification of any legal action.

Note also that the power to grant ancillary orders cannot be used by the district court to extend an injunction beyond eighty

---

[292] 29 U.S.C. § 179(b).

[293] 29 U.S.C. § 180.

[294] *See* Jenkins, Labor Law § 27.6 (1974) for a brief description of the parties and subject matter of the disputes in which boards of inquiry have been appointed. *See* Jenkins, Labor Law § 27.5 for a discussion and description of one case in some detail—the United Mine Workers case in 1948. For more detailed coverage of Taft-Hartley injunctions, *see* Jenkins 4 Labor Law ch. 27 (1974); Symposium on Labor Relations Law (Slovenko ed. 1961); Burnstein, Enarson & Fleming, Emergency Disputes and National Policy, esp. at 46-74, 129-46, 224-42 (1955); 5 Ind. & Lab. Rel. Rev. 3-19 (1951); 6 (Ind. & Lab. Rel. Rev. 352-67 (1953); 48 Am. Pol. Sci. Rev. 705-20 (1954).

[295] United Mine Workers v. United States, 177 F.2d 29 (D.C. Cir. 1949), *cert. denied,* 338 U.S. 871, 70 S. Ct. 140.

days.[296]

States are precluded from regulating local emergency disputes, because of the preemption doctrine.[297]

---

296 Seafarers Int'l Union of N. America v. United States, 304 F.2d 437 (9th Cir. 1962), *cert. denied,* 370 U.S. 924, 82 S. Ct. 1566.

297 Amalgamated Ass'n of Street, Elec. Ry. & Motor Coach Employees of America v. Wisc. Employment Relations Bd., 340 U.S. 383, 71 S. Ct. 359 (1951).

General Electric,[305] the primary employer can set up reserve gates to prevent pickets from reaching employees of allegedly neutral employers. (See Section 3.10(3)(b)(ii), *infra,* for a description of reserve gates.) Reserve gates can be used by those performing work (1) that is unrelated to the normal operations of the struck employer and (2) that, if performed during normal operations, would not necessitate curtailing these operations. A typical example of such a neutral employer would be a contractor building an addition to the primary employer's plant complex, so long as such construction does not require shutting down the existing operation.[306] The concept of related work is broadly defined. Since delivery persons and suppliers are traditional objects of primary picketing, they cannot be insulated by reserve gates.[307] Security and maintenance operations are also related.[308] Maintenance and repair work done by independent contractors during a periodic shutdown of a power plant is related work and thus open to picketing.[308.1]

The employer should not be allowed to take advantage of a strike to avoid a later shutdown for improvements. The construction workers can also be picketed if the improvements affect struck jobs, for example, mechanization.[309]

Although most of the primary situs cases involve plants owned or operated by the struck employer, an increasing number of companies operate entirely at another company's job site, for example, maintenance or security services. Although the primary employees typically constitute a minority of the workers at the site, they are stationed permanently at that site. Logically, the work site should be considered primary and all related functions open to picketing. A recent Board case applied the GE "related-work" test to a primary employer that neither owned the work

[305] Local 761 Electrical Workers v. NLRB, 366 U.S. 667, (1961).

[306] Jonesville Typographical Union Local 187, 173 NLRB 917 (1968).

[307] Linbeck Construction Corp. v. NLRB, 550 F.2d 311 (5th Cir. 1977).

[308] Oil, Chemical & Atomic Workers International Union, Local 2-5 v. Tosco Inc., 103 LRRM 1497 (Advice Memorandum of General Counsel, 1980).

[308.1] Construction & General Laborers, Local 721, 109 LRRM 1207 (Advice Memo of General Counsel, 1982).

[309] *See* Oil, Chemical & Atomic Workers Local 4-23 v. Firestone Synthetic Rubber Latex Co., 173 NLRB 1244 (1968).

site nor was the primary occupant of the site.[310] The union went on strike against one of three contractors performing flight dynamics testing at an air force facility. The union was held to have acted legally in picketing gates reserved for the use of the other two contractors since they were supplying "goods and services necessary for the day-to-day operations" of the primary. The ALJ held that the related-work test established in GE applies anywhere except transitory construction sites. There are some unique features to this case, e.g., the three contractors had associate contractor agreements with each other, which may cause later Board opinions to distinguish the holding. A few earlier Board decisions also support the argument that the GE test applies everywhere but at construction and ambulatory work sites.[311]

[b] Construction Sites

The Board and the courts have refused to apply the *General Electric* test to construction sites.[312] Instead, the standard first enunciated in *Moore Drydock*[313] has been applied. To meet the *Moore Drydock* test, picketing must (1) be limited to times when the situs of the dispute is on the secondary employer's premises, (2) be limited to times when the primary employer is engaged in normal business, (3) be reasonably close to the situs of the dispute, and (4) clearly disclose that the dispute is with the primary employer. The courts have repeatedly emphasized that these standards are only evidentiary tools to determine if the object of the picketing is to enmesh neutrals in the dispute.[314]

---

[310] Air Engineering Metal Trades (Pan-Am), 265 NLRB No. 19, 111 LRRM 1457 (198).

[311] United Assoc. of Journeymen and Apprentices of the Plumbing Industry, Local 60 (Circle, Inc.), 202 NLRB 99, 82 LRRM 1755 (1973); Local 32B-32J SEIU (The Dalton Schools), 248 NLRB 1067 (1980). But see Local 25, Nat. Assoc. of Broadcasting Employees & Technicians (Taft Broadcasting Inc.), 194 NLRB 162, 78 LRRM 1647 (1971).

[312] Building Trades Council v. Markwell & Hart, 60 LRRM 1296 (NLRB 1965), *enforced,* 66 LRRM 2712.

[313] Sailor's Union of the Pacific (Moore Drydock) 92 NLRB 547 (1958).

[314] Sherman Oaks Medical Center v. Local 1936, 680 F.2d 594, 110 LRRM 2971 (9th Cir. 1982).

Unions should be wary of the increasing number of factors used by courts in ruling that picketing was intended to enmesh neutrals in spite of compliance with the *Moore Drydock* standards, such as (1) statements by pickets that indicate the aim of reaching neutrals or shutting down the project,[315] (2) inconsistencies in the reasons given for picketing the primary employer, for example, area standards picketing when the primary meets the area standard for wages and benefits,[316] and (3) failure to picket at sites that would more effectively reach the primary employer.[317]

The Board has recently held that statements by union members that the strike would end if the primary were off the job are not sufficient to show a secondary object.[318]

However, a recent Eleventh Circuit case held that a union offical's statement was sufficient evidence for a jury to award damages in a § 303 case in spite of improperly marked reserve gates.[318.1] The union business representative had informed the secondary employees that the picket line was sanctioned in order to persuade them not to cross it. Although the standard of proof to sustain a jury verdict is low, this case points out the importance of instructing pickets and union representatives to avoid making any statements that indicate a desire to appeal to secondary employees. A common management tactic is to ask pickets what the purpose of the picket line is in hopes of obtaining such damaging evidence.

[i] Picketing Reasonably Proximate to Primary's Presence

If the primary employer is absent from the job site because of the effectiveness of the strike in closing down work, this should

[315] General Teamsters Local 126 (Ready Mixed Concrete), 200 NLRB 253 (1972).

[316] Lawhon Construction Co. v. Carpet Local 1179, 394 F. Supp. 520 (W.D. Mo. 1973), 513 F.2d 723 (8th Cir. 1975) (per curiam).

[317] Bexar Plumbing Co. v. NLRB, 536 F.2d 634 (5th Cir. 1976).

[318] Southern Sun Electric Corporation, 237 NLRB 829 (1978).

[318.1] Lane Crane Service v. Local 177 IBEW, 704 F.2d 550, 133 LRRM 2396 (11th Cir. 1983).

not negate factors 1 and 2 of the *Moore Drydock* test.[319] Continued picketing is usually necessary to maintain the effectiveness of the strike.

Minor deviations from the times that the primary is on the site should not render the picketing illegal. Thus, picketing during coffee breaks or at slightly different starting times should be allowed.[320] Similarily, if the employer works on an intermittent schedule, picketing should be allowed when the primary is not on the site, unless the union is accurately notified of the primary's schedule.[321]

Some general contractors may attempt to lessen the effect of picketing by confining the struck company to working at the site only at certain reserved times.[322] If these times are not complied with or if the union is not given adequate notice, then picketing can take place at other than the reserved times. If the struck employer has its business office at the work site, picketing should be allowed even if the employer is not at the site at that time.[323]

[ii] Reasonable Proximity to the Work Site

Most of the cases interpreting this standard involve reserve gates. The law on the adequacy of reserve gates is the same for both primary and neutral sites. The burden is on the employer to set up an adequate reserve gate.[324]

However, unlike primary situs cases, if an employer at a common situs does not establish adequate reserve gates, the union may still not be permitted to picket the entire work site. The union must still follow the *Moore Dry Dock* rules and picket only in reasonable proximity to the work site of the struck em-

---

319 Local 3 Electrical Workers v. New Power Wire and Electric Corporation, 144 NLRB 1089 (1963), *affirmed,* 340 F.2d 71, (2d Cir. 1965).

320 Plauche Electric, 135 NLRB 250 (1962).

321 Local 25 Electrical Workers v. Eugene Iovine, Inc., 201 NLRB 531 (1973).

322 Plumbers Local 519 v. H. L. Robertson & Associates, Inc., 171 NLRB 251 (1968).

323 Carpenters Local 345 v. The Kroger Company, 183 NLRB 1109 (1970).

324 Wire Service Guild Local 222 v. Herald Publishing Co., 218 NLRB 1234 (1975).

ployer.[324.1] Since suppliers and customers of the struck employer are also legitimate primary targets of picketing, a union can picket areas that are likely to be used by them.

The test of adequacy is whether the union has reasonable assurance that picketing only at the reserve gate will reach all within the legitimate direct appeal of the pickets.[325] The gate must be at a reasonable location not too remote from the work site.[326] The fact that the reserve gate is not on the main road most accessible to the public does not necessarily mean the location is unreasonable.[326.1] The union must establish that the remoteness impairs its ability to effectively communicate its message to its legitimate primary targets, including the public.[326.2]

If the site is not enclosed so that workers can enter at any location, the entire site should be open to picketing.[327] The site reserved for picketing should not be dangerous,[328] nor should it be set up so that adequate picketing is physically impossible.[329] If the reserve gates are locked, suppliers, etc., are likely to use other entrances. Locked gates have served as a basis to permit picketing of all entrances.[330] Similarly, if the access road to the reserve gate is inaccessible by motor vehicle, the union can reasonably assume that suppliers, etc., will use other gates and therefore need not confine picketing to the reserve gate.[330.1]

The signs on both neutral and primary gates must be clearly marked and legibly printed. Poorly marked gates open the entire site to picketing.[331] Under this standard, it is probably unreasonable for an employer to expect compliance with a typewritten

---

324.1 IBEW Local 323 (Renel Construction), 264 NLRB No. 81, 111 LRRM 1309 (1982).

325 IBEW Local 441 v. Jones & Jones, Inc., 158 NLRB No. 57 (1968).

326 Construction Drivers Local 83 v. Allied Concrete, 231 NLRB 1097 (1977), *enforcement denied,* 607 F.2d 827 (9th Cir. 1979).

326.1 IBEW Local 323 (Renel Construction), 264 NLRB No. 81, 111 LRRM 1309 (1982).

326.2 *Id.*

327 IBEW Local 441, *supra* note 325.

328 NLRB v. Ironworkers, 98 LRRM 2817 (5th Cir. 1978).

329 Wire Service Guild Local 222, *supra* note 324.

330 Local 32B-32J, SEIU, *supra* note 310.

330.1 Plumbers Local 398 (Robbins Plumbing Co.), 261 NLRB No. 72 110 LRRM 1093 (1982).

331 Local 32B-32J, SEIU, *supra* Note 310.

notice that is too small to be legible to, for example, a truck driver approaching the gate.

Suppliers of the picketed employer must be directed to the gates reserved for the primary.[332] In *Linbeck Construction,*[332.1] the leading case on this topic, the supplies were crushed rock that was to be used by the struck employer, a paving subcontractor. The rock belonged to the general contractor, who argued that since he had legal title, the supply trucks were neutrals. The Board rejected this argument, holding that anything essential to the primary employer's normal operations may not be insulated from picketing. The Board reached the same conclusion when electrical fixtures were delivered to a struck electrical subcontractor through neutral gates; this opened the neutral gates to picketing. The Board rejected the argued distinction between raw materials and finished products.[333]

A union does not have to confine its picketing to a reserve gate if the sign on the gate states that it is to be used by the primary employer only.[333.1] The likely effect of such a sign is to lead suppliers and delivery persons of the primary to use other gates.

Reserve gates have been held properly established if they state that the primary employer should use one set of gates, neutral employers another set and "all others" should call a telephone number on the signs.[333.2] The Board noted that suppliers and visitors of the primary called the telephone number and were directed to the primary gates. On the other hand, if a union can establish that the failure of such signs to clearly direct suppliers, etc., of the primary resulted in its using the wrong gates, all gates should be open to picketing.

---

[332] Linbeck Construction, *supra* note 307.

[332.1] *Id.*

[333] Local 323 Electrical Workers v. Hoff Electric, 241 NLRB No. 98, 101 LRRM 1132 (1979).

[333.1] Plumbers Local 398, *supra* note 330.1.

[333.2] Carpenters Local 1622 (Speciality Building), 262 NLRB No. 162, 111 LRRM 1059 (1982).

[iii] Tainted Gates

Once those within the legitimate primary appeal of pickets use neutral gates, the gates are tainted and may be picketed.[334] Isolated misuse does not taint the gates if the employer made reasonable efforts to enforce the reserve gate system.[335] Isolated violations will, however, reinforce the inadequacy of poorly marked gates.

[iv] Corrections

Once a reserved gate is breached, the employer can correct the problem and the union can no longer picket. The union can, however, insist on reasonable assurances of stricter enforcement before it ceases picketing.[336] Reasonable assurance is provided by, e.g., informing the union and pickets of the reestablishment of the gates and of policing the gates.[336.1] Repeated breach of such assurances can relieve the union of the obligation to respect the reserve gate.

[v] Adequate Signs

Unions should make sure that the struck employer's name is clearly disclosed, even at the reserve gates. Technical violations should not render the picketing illegal.[337] The union's failure initially to identify the primary employer properly has been excused if the signs were later corrected. Referring generally to the type of work done by the primary employer or merely stating

---

[334] Local 519 United Associate of Journeymen v. L&M Electric Company, 145 NLRB 215 (1963).

[335] Local 18 Operating Engineers v. Dodge & Ireland Inc., 236 NLRB 199 (1978).

[336] Mueller Anderson, Inc., 224 NLRB 316 (1976).

[336.1] Carpenters Local 1622 (Speciality Building), 262 NLRB No. 162, 111 LRRM 1059 (1982).

[337] Local 3 Electrical Workers v. Surf Hunter Electric Co., 172 NLRB 1101 (1968).

that the job is "unfair" will, however, violate the fourth *Moore Drydock* standard.[338]

[c] Primary Employer Located at Neutral Employer's Site: Ambulatory Picketing

Ambulatory picketing occurs if pickets follow the primary employer to neutral sites. A typical example would be following the delivery truck of the primary and picketing wherever the truck stopped. The Board has so far refused to apply the related-work test of *General Electric* when pickets follow the struck employer to a neutral's business. Instead, the pickets must observe the *Moore Drydock* standards. The pickets can follow the primary's trucks into the work site. If the neutral refuses to allow them access to the site they can picket at the entrances.[339] The Board and the courts have readily found a secondary objective in ambulatory picketing if the union did not strictly comply with the *Moore Drydock* rules. Additionally, the Ninth Circuit has imposed a duty to minimize the impact on the neutral by picketing only at reserve sites if the primary can be effectively reached there.[340]

[4] Ally Doctrine

The secondary boycott prohibitions are designed to protect third parties who have no concern in the primary dispute.[341] An employer who "allies" itself with the primary employer, so as to assist the primary employer weather the strike, is itself considered a primary target for union economic pressure.

There are two branches to the ally doctrine: (1) employers who are performing struck work and (2) employers who are a so-called alter ego of or joint employer with the struck employer. Either branch of the ally doctrine alone opens the second employer to picketing in the same fashion as the struck company may be

---

[338] Daniel Construction Co., 192 NLRB 272 (1971).

[339] Ready Mixed Concrete, *supra* note 315.

[340] NLRB v. Allied Concrete, 607 F.2d 827 (9th Cir. 1979).

[341] International Brotherhood of Electrical Workers Local 501 v. NLRB, 341 U.S. 694 (1951).

picketed.[342] Often there are aspects of both struck work and alter ego. The entire situation should be looked at as a whole to determine if the second employer is an ally. Thus, even though the

(*Text continued on page 3-107*)

---

342 Ironworkers Local 501 v. Oliver Whyte Co., 120 NLRB 856 (1958).

[c] Joint Employer

Related to the single employer doctrine is the concept that two companies can be allies despite the absence of any common ownership.[356] If another company has significant control over the performance of the employees' daily assignments, work stations, and hours, it should also be open to picketing if the employees go on strike. The concepts of joint employers and alter egos have been heavily litigated under Sections 8(a)(3) and 8(a)(5) regarding liability for unfair labor practice charges and duty to bargain. These cases are useful precedents for union attorneys seeking to defend picketing of an ally.

[d] *Hearst* Doctrine

In the case of alter egos, the question is whether two employers are really one. However, there are situations in which the Board and courts find one corporation to be really two "persons" within the meaning of the Act. They reason therefrom that union picketing of one company division to exert pressure on *another company division* is violative of Section 8(b)(4)(B). This is commonly referred to as the *Hearst* doctrine and is derived from a case in which employees of the Los Angeles Herald-Examiner, a Hearst publication, picketed the San Francisco Examiner, another Hearst publication. Certain benefit plans were available to employees of both publications; the same corporate labor relations representative negotiated for management of both publications; and neither publication was separately incorporated. The Board held, with Ninth Circuit approval, that the divisions were managed as if they were two separate corporate entities and were therefore separate "persons" for purposes of Section 8(b)(4)(B). The corporate benefits plans and labor relations representative were found to be merely optional services available at the request of local management and not indicative of centralized control of labor relations. The Board held that while there was clearly "potential"

[356] Highway Truck Drivers Local 107 v. Sterling Wire, 137 NLRB 1330 (1962).

control of day-to-day operations, actual control was not shown.[357]

The test for finding one corporation to be two persons is the reverse of that for finding two corporations to be one, that is, one must ascertain whether there is a lack of (1) common ownership, (2) common control (particularly of labor relations), (3) integration of operations, and (4) economic dependence for a substantial portion of the company's business.

In a combination of *Hearst* and ally concepts, the Board found one division of an employer to be an ally of another division if customer orders were cross-shipped and filled through central computers, thus making the performance of struck work a virtual certainty.[358]

It is usually impossible for a union to have sufficient facts to know in advance of picketing whether the company can successfully assert the *Hearst* doctrine. Almost any company document can be relevant to a *Hearst* doctrine claim. Therefore, one possible tactic is for the union, in advance of picketing, to serve an information request on the employer for disclosure of documents, records, or information from which the union can determine if a *Hearst* situation exists.[359] If the employer refuses to provide the requested information, the union can defend on the basis that it made good faith efforts to ascertain whether the employer it was picketing was in fact neutral but was denied access to the necessary information.[359.1]

Once picketing has occurred and a Section 303 action has been filed, discovery is available and should be used to its full potential to obtain company information, documents, procedures, etc. Most employers will drop a *Hearst* case simply to avoid the extensive discovery involved. Many employers are also afraid of an eventual ruling adverse to their position and therefore merely use the *Hearst* doctrine as a recurring threat hanging over the union without ever taking the issue to judgment.

---

[357] Los Angeles Newspaper Guild Local 69 v. San Francisco Examiner, Division of the Hearst Corporation, 185 NLRB 303 (1970), *enf'd,* 443 F.2d 1173.

[358] Curtin Matheson, *supra* note 343.

[359] *See* Section 11.05, *infra,* on information requests.

[359.1] Painters Local 829, 267 NLRB 136 (1983).

[5] Political Boycotts[360]

In 1982 the United States Supreme Court affirmatively an-

(*Text continued on page 3-111*)

---

360 *See also* Section 3.02[4], *supra.*

services in a building,[368] paper bags in a grocery store,[369] or bread in a restaurant.[370]

[b] Publicity Other than Picketing

Publicity other than picketing is typically in the form of handbills (leafletting), unfair lists, and media advertisements. Such activity directed toward consumers at the secondary site is accorded more liberal protection than is picketing. This is revealed in the expansive definition given the "produced" and "distributed" language of the proviso. The Supreme Court has recognized that not all employers manufacture tangible "products" and that services are "products" within the meaning of the proviso. In the leading case, *Servette,*[371] the union's dispute was with a company engaged in the business of distributing merchandise. The union leafletted grocery stores carrying goods distributed by the primary. The Court held, essentially, that the grocery stores were retail "distributors" of the primary's "product," which was wholesale distribution.

The Supreme Court has indicated that the "produced and distributed" language of the publicity proviso should not serve as a limitation on the type of labor disputes in which handbilling can be used.[371.1] In "almost any" primary dispute, a union can handbill companies which are responsible for the primary's products reaching the public. For example, in disputes with construction companies, a union can handbill the owner of the building constructed by the primary.[371.2]

Under its more liberal construction of the proviso in regard to nonpicketing publicity, the Board has permitted a union to go further than merely following the struck product. The union can

---

[368] K&K Construction Co. v. NLRB, 592 F.2d 1228 (3d Cir. 1979); Salem Building Trades Council (Cascade Employer Association), 163 NLRB 33 (1967), *enf'd,* 388 F.2d 987 (9th Cir. 1968).

[369] Kroger Co. v. NLRB, 105 LRRM 2897 (6th Cir. 1980).

[370] American Bread Co. v. NLRB, 411 F.2d 147 (6th Cir. 1969).

[371] NLRB v. Servette, 377 U.S. 46 (1964).

[371.1] Edward J. DeBartolo v. NLRB, 113 LRRM 2953 — U.S. — (1983).

[371.2] Operating Engineers Local 139 (Oak Construction Inc.), 226 NLRB No. 119 (1976); Edward J. DeBartolo v. NLRB, *supra.*

lawfully advocate a total boycott of the secondary "distributor." In the leading case, a union involved in a dispute with a radio station lawfully leafletted at the premises of a business that advertised on the station, asking consumers not to patronize the advertiser.[372] This rule has been followed in subsequent decisions.[373]

A recent Supreme Court decision, *Edward J. DeBartolo Co. v. NLRB,* [374] limited the extent to which secondary companies can be termed "distributors" under the publicity proviso. A union that had a dispute with a contractor building an addition to one store in a shopping mall distributed handbills urging a consumer boycott of the entire shopping mall. The Board[375] and Fourth Circuit[375.1] held the handbilling permissible, reasoning that the financial relationship between the mall owner and the tenants rendered the owners and all mall tenants "distributors" of one another's products. The Supreme Court found this "symbiotic relationship" between the various stores in the mall insufficient to create a business relationship between the primary contractor and the mall tenants who did not directly hire the contractor. Since a union is protected by the publicity proviso to § 8(b)(4) when it distributes handbills for the purpose of urging a customer boycott of a secondary employer, it is also protected by the proviso when it threatens to engage in such permissible activity.[375.2]

If the primary employer is a subsidiary of a parent company, the Board has held that a union call for a consumer boycott of the parent company's products and products of the parent's other subsidiaries is protected by the proviso.[376]

The proviso on its face requires that the union's publicity be

---

[372] Local 662, Radio & Television Engineers (Middle South Broadcasting Co.), 133 NLRB 1698 (1961).

[373] Honolulu Typographical Union, Local 37 (Hawaii Press Newspapers), 167 NLRB 1030 (1967), *enf'd,* 401 F.2d 952 (D.C. Cir. 1968); San Francisco Typographical Union Local 21 (California Newspapers, Inc.), 188 NLRB 673 (1971), *enf'd,* 465 F.2d 53 (9th Cir. 1972).

[374] Edward J. DeBartolo Co. v. NLRB, 113 LRRM 2953 — U.S. — (1983).

[375] 252 NLRB No. 99, 105 LRRM 1273 (1980).

[375.1] 662 F.2d 264, 108 LRRM 2727 (4th Cir. 1981).

[375.2] NLRB v. Servette, *supra,* note 371.

[376] Pet, Inc v. NLRB, 106 LRRM 2477 (8th Cir. 1981), *enforcing* 244 NLRB No. 6, 102 LRRM 1046.

truthful. If a union acts in good faith and takes reasonable steps to ensure the accurancy of its allegations, its publicity will not be held unprotected because it contains some inaccuracies.[377] If a union's allegations are publicized "with knowledge of, or reckless disregard for, the truth" the union will be stripped of the proviso's protection.[378]

A disturbing 3-2 decision, *Delta Airlines,*[379] recently emanated from the Board, holding that even a truthful leaflet may lose the protection of the proviso if it fails to identify the primary dispute and if it contains information about the secondary employer that is irrelevant to to publicizing the dispute. In *Delta Airlines,* the union's dispute was with a nonunion maintenance contractor used by Delta. The union distributed handbills asking consumers to boycott Delta and included in the handbill government statistics about Delta's safety record. The conduct was found to fall outside the proviso. The Board's decision presents obvious First Amendment problems, which will no doubt be the subject of appeals.

If both leafletting and picketing are used by a union, the picketing may be found unlawful while the leafletting is held protected by the proviso.[380] However, if the leafletting is found to be an integral part of the picketing," it will not qualify as "publicity other than picketing."[381] The Board decisions are not clear as to when leafletting becomes an extension of picketing and thus also illegal. If the pickets and handbills have the same message and take place at the same time and location, the leafletting probably will not be separated from illegal picketing.[382] The Board has, however, held picketing objectionable because it failed adequately to identify the struck product or the primary employer while

377 Milk Drivers & Dairy Employees Local 537, 132 NLRB 901 (1961).

378 Honolulu Typographical Union, *supra* note 373; Hoffman v. Cement Masons Local 337, 468 F.2d 1187 (9th Cir. 1972), *enforcing* 192 NLRB 377 (1971).

379 Service Employees Local 399 (Delta Airlines), 111 LRRM 1158 (1982).

380 Minneapolis House Furnishings, 132 NLRB 40, *enforcement denied,* 331 F.2d 561.

381 Nashville Building & Construction Trades Council, 188 NLRB 670 (1971).

382 Plumbers, Steamfitters & Pipefitters Local 155 v. The Kroger Co., 209 NLRB 341 (1974); Teamsters Local 732 v. Servair Maintenance Co., 229 NLRB 392, 96 LRRM 1128 (1972).

allowing simultaneous leafletting that did supply the missing information; the Board here refused to consider the picketing "cured" by the handbills.[383]

The issue of whether violative picketing taints otherwise lawful leafletting would appear to be relevant to a Section 303 action for damages, since it could be to the union's advantage to show that the damages alleged were the result of lawful leafletting and were not appreciably enhanced by the violative picketing.

§ 3.11. Lockouts

The term "lockout" has no clearly defined meaning under NLRB law. Almost any withholding of employment by an employer for the purpose of gaining some concession has been referred to as a lockout. Thus, mass discharges of union adherents,[384] brief shutdowns during a contract term[385] and plant closures during negotiations[386] have been referred to as lockouts.

Lockouts have traditionally not been a major concern of unions since most companies will not voluntarily shut down operations. However, in certain situations, employers may decide to forego operating revenue in order to gain leverage by controlling the timing of a threatened strike or in an effort to destroy or seriously weaken a union. Unions which feel they are susceptible to being locked out should make every effort during negotiations to gather evidence to support the filing of unfair labor practice charges in the event of a lockout.

Prior to 1964, lockouts were legal only if they were defensive; offensive lockouts, used as a bargaining weapon, were illegal. Defensive lockouts are used primarily to affect the timing of threatened union shutdowns so as to prevent potential losses from a sudden strike (e.g., spoilage of perishables) or to protect the integrity of a multi-employer bargaining association in the

---

[383] Local 248, Meat Cutters, *supra* note 366.

[384] Hopwood Refining Co., 4 NLRB 922 (1938).

[385] Carlson Roofing Co. v. NLRB, 105 LRRM 2145 (7th Cir. 1980).

[386] Smyth Manufacturing Co. (Dist 26, Inter. Assoc. of Machinists and Aerospace Workers), 247 NLRB 1139 (1980).

face of a whip-saw[387] strike.

In 1964, the Supreme Court decided *American Ship Building,*[388] which eliminated for most purposes the offensive/defensive distinction. The rule established in *American Ship Building* is that an employer can lock out its employees in support of a legitimate bargaining position. Thus, in order for a lockout to be illegal, a union must show that the goal the employer is attempting to further through the lockout is something other than a legitimate bargaining position. The general types of lockouts which the NLRB will hold illegal are:

(1) lockouts in support of bad-faith bargaining positions,[389]
(2) lockouts in support of an employer's position on a non-mandatory subject of bargaining, i.e., something other than wages, hours and working conditions of employment,[390]
(3) lockouts motivated by anti-union animus[391] and
(4) lockouts in which the employer's economic interests are too indirect to outweigh the harm to the employees' protected collective bargaining rights.[392]

In the first three situations, the union's case will be based primarily on the law governing the underlying unfair labor practice rather than decisions specific to lockouts. The fact that the lockout is contemporaneous with employer unfair labor practices may not be enough to render it illegal if the Board finds that the unfair labor practices are not the motivation for the lockout.[393]

387 "Whipsawing" is selectively striking a few of the employers in a multi-employer association. This tactic is designed to place additional pressure on the struck employer by allowing its competitors to continue doing business.

388 American Ship Building v. NLRB, 380 U.S. 300 (1964).

389 Smyth Manufacturing Co., *supra* note 3.

390 Movers and Warehousemen's Assoc. of Washington, D.C., 244 NLRB 356 *enforced,* 94 LRRM 2795 (4th Cir. 1977).

391 Bedford Cut Stone, 235 NLRB 269 (1978).

392 David Friedland Painting Co., 158 NLRB 571 (1966).

393 Golden State Bottling Co., 147 NLRB 410 (1964) *modified,* 353 F.2d 667 (9th Cir. 1965).

[1] Bad-Faith Bargaining

If the employer has been engaging in bad-faith bargaining, then it will not be privileged to lock out in support of its bargaining position.[394] The usual rules on bad-faith bargaining are applicable, i.e., an employer's overall conduct must indicate a lack of desire to reach an agreement. An employer's resort to a lockout early in the negotiations may indicate an intention of avoiding a contract.[395] However, lockouts prior to reaching impasse in negotiations are not illegal *per se.* An employer who locks out prior to impasse can prove good-faith bargaining by showing legitimate business reasons for the lockout, e.g., avoiding a sudden strike.[396]

[2] Non-Mandatory Subjects of Bargaining

Lockouts which are in support of non-mandatory subjects of bargaining will be determined by the Board on permissive and illegal subjects of bargaining.[397] If a lockout is a pressure tactic in support of both mandatory and non-mandatory subject of bargaining, it is illegal.[398]

[3] Anti-Union Animus

A lockout motivated by anti-union animus is also illegal.[399] One of the most common uses of the lockout is by an employer attempting to bust a union. Such an employer is more likely to bear the economic loss of a lockout than one merely seeking bargaining concessions. A number of the NLRB decisions on lockouts involve employers determined to resist bargaining with

---

394 Smyth Manufacturing Co., 247 NLRB 1139 (1980).

395 Edward J. Alexander, d/b/a, Strand Theatre, 235 NLRB 1500 (1978).

396 Darling and Company, 171 NLRB No. 95 (1968).

397 See § 11.04, *infra,* Subjects of Bargaining.

398 Movers and Warehousemen's Assoc. of Metropolitan Washington D.C., 244 NLRB 356, *enforced,* 94 LRRM 2795 (4th Cir. 1977).

399 Bedford Cut Stone Co., Inc, 235 NLRB 269 (1978).

newly certified unions.[400] Unions that fear an employer's union-busting campaign should begin documenting instances of anti-union statements or conduct to support an NLRB charge of illegal motivation.

[4] Indirect Economic Interest

Employers with closely allied interests but no formal bargaining association may have an agreement that in the event one of the employers is struck during negotiations, the others will lock out their employees. An employer may also decide that its interests are furthered by weakening a union's bargaining position in negotiations with other employers in the industry and lock out to place pressure on the union. Under current Board law, employers may be able to lock out their employees in these situations.

The mere absence of a formal multi-employer association is not sufficient to render a lockout in support of another struck employer illegal.[401] On the other hand, an employer is not justified in locking out its employees in regard to a labor dispute which only remotely impacts its bargaining position.[402] The test used by the court in *American Ship Building* is whether the lockout "is inherently so prejudicial to union interest and so devoid of significant economic justification"[403] that it should be held illegal without a showing of anti-union motivation.

The only case since *American Ship Building* in which the NLRB has considered the employer's bargaining interests to be too remote to justify a lockout is *David Friedland Painting Co.*,[404] in which a painting contractor locked out its employees who were members of a local on strike against an association of painting contractors. Friedland was not a member of the association and did not bargain with the striking local. It did hire members of the

---

400 *See, e.g.*, Maxwell's Plum (Amalgamated Service & Allied Industries Joint Board), 256 NLRB No. 211 (1981).

401 *See* Weyerhaeuser Co., 166 NLRB 229 (1967), *enforced*, 398 F.2d 770 (D.C. Cir. 1968).

402 David Friedland Painting Co., 158 NLRB 571 (1966) *enforced*, 377 F.2d 983 (3d Cir. 1967).

403 *Supra* note 388.

404 *Supra* note 392.

striking local on jobs within the local's jurisdiction. Friedland, therefore, would generally sign the association contract and follow its terms for some of its employees. Friedland did bargain with a sister local which represented most of its employees and presumably the results of the other area negotiations would affect its own upcoming contract negotiations. Thus, the employer argued that its economic interests were affected in two ways: (1) it would be required to follow the contract terms for a significant number of its employees and (2) its bargaining position in later contract negotiations would be weakened if the struck association acceded to union demands. The Administrative Law Judge, with the Boards' affirmation, rejected these reasons as being overweighed by the tendency of the lockout to discourage the exercise of the employees' protected rights.

> Respondent was seeking to intrude in a labor dispute not its own, involving a union other than the one with which it was then in untroubled relationship, for the reason that a settlement of the labor dispute favorable to the union could have an economic effect upon it. To allow this collateral or indirect interest in a labor dispute to be deemed a legitimate business interest sufficient to serve as justification for a lockout . . . would lead to a proliferation of the lockout so as to render it lawful in any situation where the employer . . . could arguably be affected economically by the outcome of particular negotiations . . . It would be an invitation to industrial chaos . . ..[405]

The *Friedland* decision rested in large part upon the fact that the employer was not currently engaged in negotiations and thus could not be deemed to be using the tactic in support of its *own* bargaining position. The Board had upheld the tactic if the employer were engaged in contract negotiations at the time it used a lockout as a reaction to a strike against another employer in spite of the absence of multi-employer bargaining. There are only a few of these cases. While there is no general Board rule that an employer is privileged to lock out a union striking another employer with a similar bargaining position, the Board has ruled on the particular facts of each case, that the lockout was in lawful furtherance of the employer's legitimate bargaining position.

[405] *Id.* at 578.

The leading Board case upholding a lockout in support of a second struck employer in the absence of a multi-employer association is the *Evening News Association.*[406] This case involved the News and the Free Press, the only members of an employer association which handled contract negotiations with most of the unions representing the employees of the two newspapers. Both papers had, however, bargained separately with the Teamsters local for 20 years. Both Teamsters' contracts expired at the same time and the union was pressing essentially the same demands upon both papers. After several bargaining sessions with the News, the Teamsters decided to concentrate on negotiations with the Free Press. The union eventually struck the Free Press and the News locked out its employees pursuant to an earlier agreement between the two papers. The Board found the News lockout lawful because "the circumstances of this case show both a significant economic justification and a lack of conduct prejudicial to union (or employee) interests."[407] While the Board specifically disavowed any intention of establishing a general rule that all supportive lockouts are legal, the facts in this case were sufficient to establish a significant economic justification, including:

(1) the parties had bargained for many months and were deadlocked on the significant issues,
(2) the two papers were bargaining at the same time, the contracts expired on the same date and the union was pressing its key demands on both simultaneously,
(3) the newspapers were in direct competition with each other as the only two daily newspapers in Detroit,
(4) the Teamsters' membership had authorized strike action against both papers and Mr. Hoffa had explicitly threatened the News with a strike, and
(5) the Teamsters' tactic was clearly to concentrate its strength on the Free Press on the assumption that the News would quickly sign a contract on the same terms.

Other NLRB cases upholding supportive lockouts involve

[406] The Evening News Association, 166 NLRB 219 (1967) *enforced,* 404 F.2d 1159.
[407] *Id.* at 222.

more direct economic interests of the employer utilizing the lockout and therefore add little clarification to the holding of *Evening News.*

In *The Hearst Corp., News America Division,*[408] the Board upheld a lockout during the contract term to protect the integrity of a no-strike clause contained in the multi-employer contract. The Hearst and Sun newspapers engaged in multi-employer bargaining with the Teamsters and ITU. Each paper negotiated separately with the Newspaper Guild. The Guild struck the Sun. The Teamsters and ITU refused to cross the picket line. Pursuant to an agreement with the Sun Papers, Hearst locked out its Teamster and ITU employees in support of the Sun. This was held lawful solely because the two employers had a multi-employer bargaining relationship with the two unions who were engaging in the sympathy strike.

Similarly, in *Capitol District Sheet Metal, Roofing and Air Conditioning Contractors' Association, Inc.,*[409] eight construction unions simultaneously pressed a demand for a shorter work day upon several employer associations belonging to one umbrella construction industry association. The unions selectively struck some employers in support of the shorter work day. The umbrella association thereafter called for a lockout by all of the individual associations. The Administrative Law Judge considered the interests of the employer associations in jointly resisting the shorter work day demand to be at least as inter-related as the employers in *News Association,*[410] and, therefore, upheld the legality of the lockout. However, the decision notes that "the fact that the lockout [is] to assist another employer in a dispute with its employees [is] relevant to a consideration of whether the lockout [is] so inherently prejudicial to union interest and so devoid of significant economic justification" as to be illegal without proof of unlawful intent.[411]

In view of these cases, multi-employer association bargaining

---

408 The Hearst Corp., News America Div., 161 NLRB 1404 (1966) *enforced,* 393 F.2d 673 (D.C. Cir. 1968).

409 Capitol District Sheet Metal, Roofing and Air Conditioning Contractors' Association, Inc., 185 NLRB 702 (1970).

410 *Supra* note 406.

411 *Supra* note 409, 185 NLRB at 717.

is not the sole justification available to employers for supportive lockouts. The NLRB also considers significant community of interest between the employers and similarity of union bargaining demands of the employers in ruling on the legality of lockouts. As the Board indicated in *Capitol District Sheet Metal,*[412] the fact that a lockout is in support of another employer is at least a factor in determining its illegality. Thus, a union should be able to strengthen a case of illegality based on anti-union animus, bad faith bargaining, etc., with evidence of indirect economic interests. In a jointly planned lockout, the anti-union animus of some of the employers involved should be imputed to the other employers as well.[413]

[5] Replacement of Locked Out Employees

Board law is currently unclear on whether an employer can operate with temporary replacements during a lockout. The use of scabs recruited from outside the employer's operation has been approved in several defensive lockout cases.[414] In *Inland Trucking,*[415] the Board held that the use of temporary replacements during an offensive lockout is a *per se* violation of Sections 8(a)(1) and (3). Subsequent decisions have retreated somewhat from this position, using a balancing test to determine whether the employer's legitimate business interests outweighed the harm to the employees' protected rights. Thus, in *Ottawa Silica,*[416] the Board dismissed charges against an employer for operating with replacements from non-bargaining unit positions within the plant during a five-day offensive lockout.[417]

Since the 1969 *Inland Trucking* decision, various Board members have favored three different approaches to the use of replacements during an offensive lockout: (1) *per se* illegality, and (2) *per*

412 *Supra* note 409.

413 Southern Beverage Co., 171 NLRB 296 (1968).

414 WGN of Colorado Inc., 199 NLRB 1053 (1972); Ralston Purina Co., 204 NLRB 23 (1973).

415 Inland Trucking Co. d/b/a Oskosh Readymix Co., 179 NLRB 350 (1969).

416 Ottawa Silica, 197 NLRB 449 (1972) *enforced,* 482 F.2d 945 (6th Cir. 1973).

417 Accord: Hess Oil Virgin Islands Corp., 205 NLRB 23 (1973).

se legality absent anti-union motivation and (3) the balancing of interests approach. Considering the pro-management trend of recent Board decisions and appointments, it is possible that the second cited approach will be adopted. However, since *Inland Trucking* has not yet been overruled, that decision remains the best precedent for a union attempting to challenge the use of scabs during an otherwise legal lockout.

Appendix 3A. Sample Local Union Instructions to Pickets

To be written and delivered to every person to do picket duty.

1. The right to peacefully picket is guaranteed by law.
2. Sign the picket roster and show the time your picketing starts and when it ends.
3. Picket at the assigned area only.
4. Do not carry or display arms, clubs, or any other weapon.
5. Do not stand in front of cars or pedestrians or block plant entrances or exits either with your person, blockade, parked cars, or other devices.
6. Do not scatter nails on roadways.
7. Do not trespass on private property.
8. Do not make verbal threats of bodily harm to those who cross the picket line, e.g., "I will get you when you come out," etc.
9. Shouting, taking license numbers, taking pictures, catcalls, boos, and yelling "scab" are usually lawful if not accompanied by threats of harm.
10. Do not throw objects at persons or cars or threaten to do so.
11. Do not damage property—hit cars, tear aerials off, break gates, fences, and the like. This can cause arrest and jail.
12. Do not follow cars that exit through the picket line without special permission from the picket captain.
13. Do not answer questions of anyone about the strike—police, reporters or individuals. Refer all questions to the picket captain.
14. Do not argue or fight on or near the picket line no matter what insults you experience—call your captain. If s/he is not present, call the police.
15. Your union may be financially responsible for you and your conduct while you are on picket duty—the success of the strike

depends upon you and your brother and sister pickets. Do your picketing with honor and dignity.

WARNING: Employers, supervisors, scabs, or others may try to bait or antagonize pickets to cause violence, police arrest, and court injunctions against your strike. Do not fall for it. Ignore them and call the police if indicated.

16. If you find that it is necessary to fight or engage in violent activity, wait until your picket shift is over, or get your captain to relieve you from picket duty, remove your banner, deliver it to your relief, get completely away from the picket line, and settle your private problems privately as best you can without involving the union or your companion pickets—preferably do not do it at all.
17. When you finish picket duty, leave the picket line. No one should be on the picket line without a banner and no one should have a banner unless actually serving on picket duty.
18. Keep a written record of time, place, and names for every unusual incident that may occur during picketing and report it to your picket captain—unusual congregations of persons near the picket line, "scabs" driving through the line threatening the safety of pickets with their cars, displaying weapons, and the like. If your captain is not available, report the incident immediately to the union and, if indicated, call the police.
19. Performing picket duty is an honor and a privilege. You will be protected by your union and the law. It is your duty to picket. Do it well and keep it peaceful.

CHAPTER 4

Stopping Runaway Shops

Plant shutdowns highlight the cruelest features of an unplanned economy. With little advance notice, workers who have spent a lifetime at a job find themselves unemployed. Often a worker is too old or has skills too specialized to find another job. At the same time, he or she may lose his/her pension, health insurance, and all the other benefits of accrued seniority. It is the worst of all possible worlds. This chapter will survey the different tactics an advocate might use in representing workers in such a situation.

§ 4.01. Contractual Protection

Workers will be in the best position if their union anticipates the danger of a runaway employer and negotiates clear language into the collective bargaining agreement. In *Joseph Schlitz Brewing Co.,*[1] the union had been concerned since 1947 with the growth of nationwide brewers. At successive negotiations, stronger language was incorporated into the labor contract. When in 1971 the employer decided to shift all production from its Brooklyn plant

[1] 58 L.A. 653 (1972).

to a new plant in Winston-Salem, North Carolina, it had agreed that "The Employer will not import beer from plants not covered by this contract to service areas traditionally served by the Employer from plants and depots covered by this contract which is the cause for layoff of employees covered by this contract," and "There shall be no layoffs except for lack of work." The arbitrator found that these contract provisions barred the employer from shifting production during the term of the contract.[2]

If the collective bargaining agreement contains a provision the union believes bars a transfer of work, the normal procedure is to seek arbitration of the issue. If the employer resists arbitration, it is necessary to bring a suit to compel arbitration under Section 301 of the National Labor Relations Act (NLRA).[3] Even if the employer accedes to arbitration, the union will want to enjoin any movement of either equipment or work pending the outcome of the arbitration. The courts in deciding whether to grant such injunctions will look at the specific contract provisions at issue and the relative hardship to the parties involved.[4]

In *UFI Razor Blades, Inc. v. District 65,*[5] the court of appeals reversed a district court order finding an employer in civil contempt for failure to comply with an arbitrator's award requiring it to reinstate laid-off employees and cease contracting out work. The court held that the lower court was in error in failing to consider

---

[2] For other examples of explicit contract provisions barring runaway shops, *see* Local 127 United Shoe Workers v. Brooks Shoe Mfg., 298 F.2d 277 (3d Cir. 1962); Allied Indus. Workers v. G.E. Co., 471 F.2d 751, 82 LRRM 2417 (6th Cir. 1973); Selb Mfg. v. IAM, District 9, 305 F.2d 177 (8th Cir. 1962); Jack Meilman, 34 L.A. 771 (1960); Pocketbook Workers Union of N.Y., 25 L.A. 804 (1956); Atomic Uniform Corp. v. Local 91, ILGWU, 72 L.C. para. 14.063 (S.D.N.Y. 1973).

[3] 29 U.S.C. § 185.

[4] Compare Lever Bros. v. Chem. Workers, Local 217, 554 F.2d 115 (4th Cir. 1976); UAW Local 408 v. Crescent Brass & Pin Co., 46 LRRM 2975 (E.D. Mich. 1960) (the court found an urgent need for injunctive relief); Teamsters Local 71 v. Akers Motor Lines, 99 LRRM 2601 (4th Cir. 1978); Local Div. 1908 v. E. Greyhound Lines, 225 F. Supp. 28 (D.D.C. 1965) (the cost of delay to the employer was minimal) *with* UAW v. Seagrave Fire Apparatus Div., 56 LRRM 2374 (E.D. Ohio 1964) (the company might have suffered large losses attributable to an inability to fulfill its contracts).

[5] 102 LRRM 2579, 610 F.2d 1018 (2d Cir. 1979).

changed economic and business considerations.[6]

The union may seek what had become known as a "reverse *Boys Markets*" injunction to enjoin the removal of work until after an arbitrator has ruled on whether the removal violates the contract.[7] Even if the union is unable to get a court injunction, if the suit is brought in sufficient time before the removal is scheduled, the court may pressure or order the employer to submit to expedited arbitration (an arbitration in which the grievance steps are waived, the hearing held promptly, the briefing schedule severely shortened or eliminated, and the arbitrator directed to rule shortly after the hearing is closed). If the company seeks to delay the arbitration, it may normally do so but usually will be enjoined from removing the work until after the arbitration process is completed.

Unfortunately, most collective bargaining agreements do not contain explicit provisions restricting the employer's right to move. In such circumstances, the courts are extremely hesitant to infer from other provisions of the collective bargaining agreement restrictions upon the employer's right to shut down a plant.[8] Typical is the statement of the Second Circuit that "the basic proposition . . . that seniority is a vested right finds no support in authority, in logic, or in the socio-economic setting of labor-management relations."[9]

In spite of this generally hostile, laissez-faire approach to the

---

[6] For a comprehensive discussion of injunctive relief, *see* Lever, *supra,* and its relationship to *Boys Markets* and *Buffalo Forge;* Payne, Enjoining Employers' Pending Arbitration, 3 Indus. Rel. (Rev. 169 (1979)). *See also* Fried v. Glenn Elec. Heater Co., 198 F. Supp. 248 (D.N.J. 1961); Allied Indus. Workers, *supra;* Johnson v. Archer-Daniels-Midland Co., 203 F. Supp. 636 (E.D. Mich. 1962); Local 2144, Bhd. of Ry. Clerks v. REA, 409 F.2d 312 (2d Cir. 1969); Lundgren v. Claytor, 619 F.2d 61 (10th Cir. 1980); Teamsters Local 961 v. Graves Truckline, 106 LRRM 2233 (D. Colo. 1980).

[7] Lever Bros. Co. v. Chem. Workers, Local 217, 554 F.2d 115 (4th Cir. 1976); Amalgamated Transit Union, Div. 1384 v. Greyhound Lines, Inc., 550 F.2d 1237 (9th Cir. 1977).

[8] *See e.g.,* UAW v. N. Telecom. 95 LRRM 2841 (E.D. Mich. 1977); Oddie v. Ross Gear, 305 F.2d 143 (6th Cir. 1962); Fraser v. Magic Chef-Food Giant Markets, 324 F.2d 853 (6th Cir. 1963); UAW Local 1251 v. Robertshaw Controls, 405 F.2d 29 (2d Cir. 1968); Local 2040, IAM v. Servel Co., 268 F.2d 692 (7th Cir. 1959); Wimberly v. Clark Controller Co., 364 F.2d 225 (6th Cir. 1966).

[9] Robertshaw Controls, *supra* note 8, at 33.

problem of job security, unions have in some cases successfully argued an implied prohibition against plant movement arising from other clauses in the collective bargaining agreement. In some cases an implied prohibition against moving or contracting out work has been derived from the recognition clause. For example, in *Vulcan Rivet & Bolt Co.*,[10] the employer began contracting out bargaining unit work while employees were on layoff. The arbitrator, relying on the recognition clause, found that the employer had guaranteed that work in bargaining unit classifications would be done by regular employees, noting that there had been no past history of contracting out bargaining unit work. One can argue that by recognizing the union and signing the collective bargaining agreement, the employer has implicitly agreed to have bargaining unit work done under the terms and conditions of the contract.[11]

In other cases, the union has argued that the employer, by transferring its operations, has violated an implied covenant of good faith and fair dealing. Often, when the threat of a plant shutdown looms, the union in negotiations will make material concessions with the understanding that this will forestall the cessation of operations. If an employer extracts such concessions with no intention of altering its plans to close the plant, it may have violated an implied covenant of fair dealing with the union.[12]

In *Steelworkers Local 1330 v. U.S. Steel Corp.*,[13] which involved the closing of the Youngstown steel facility, the plaintiffs asserted a theory based upon promissory estoppel and detrimental reliance that arose from managerial statements to production employees that productivity and profitability would be the controlling factor in deciding whether the plant would close. (The plaintiffs also requested injunctive relief for purposes of exploring the purchase of the facility and asserted that the corporation's failure to

---

[10] 36 L.A. 871 (1961).

[11] For other decisions finding the recognition clause a barrier to the movement of work, *see* Twin City Milk Producers, 42 L.A. 1121 (1964), and Celanese Corp. of America, 14 L.A. 31 (1950).

[12] *See* Ex-Cell-O Corp., 60 L.A. 1094 (1973); UAW v. Avis, 56 LRRM 2632 (E.D. Mich. 1964).

[13] 103 LRRM 2925 (N.D. Ohio 1980).

negotiate over sale of the facility constituted an antitrust violation.) The district court found that the employees should not have reasonably relied upon the statements and that the condition precedent of profitability was not fulfilled. The temporary restraining order (TRO) initially granted against the employer, was quashed after the preliminary injunction hearing. The court of appeals in *Steelworkers*[14] affirmed the district court's injunction denial and dismissal of plaintiffs' contract claims but reversed the dismissal of the antitrust claim.

Similar facts might also be used to support a theory of fraud and misrepresentation.[15] In other cases, courts and arbitrators have relied upon a union shop clause,[16] a clause specifying the procedure for filling job vacancies,[17] and frustration of the basic purposes of the collective bargaining agreement.[18] In *Kaiser,*[19] the arbitrator found a violation of the contract, since the employer failed to show a "sound business reason" for subcontracting work that had historically been done by members of the bargaining unit. Here, as elsewhere, it is important to know the bargaining history of the parties and the prevailing practices within the industry as a whole.

§ 4.02. Benefits That Survive the Plant Shutdown

Often in plant shutdowns, one's skills will be used at the negotiating table rather than in the courtroom. If there is little hope of preventing the plant from moving, an advocate will try to obtain the greatest compensation for the workers that she or he can. Crucial to this process will be the determination of which benefits in the collective bargaining agreement survive the shut-

---

[14] 105 LRRM 2312 (6th Cir. 1980).

[15] *See* UAW v. Cardwell, 94 LRRM 2149 (D. Kan. 1976) (this case also represents a successful effort to pierce the corporate veil and hold a parent corporation liable for obligations of its subsidiary). *Contra,* UAW Local 375 v. N. Telecom, Inc., 95 LRRM 2841 (E.D. Mich. 1977).

[16] UAW v. Webster Elec., 299 F.2d 195 (7th Cir. 1962).

[17] Martin-Marietta, 46 L.A. 430 (1966).

[18] Kaiser Steel Corp., 44 L.A. 24 (1965).

[19] Kaiser, *supra* note 18.

down. Here we will consider a few of the benefits to workers that are commonly at stake.

The union should take the position that the labor agreement runs for its full stated term regardless of the plant shutdown. Indeed, failure to give notice to terminate pursuant to the duration or termination provision may result in automatic renewal of the labor agreement.[20]

Active workers should be considered permanently laid off because of plant closing—thereby becoming entitled to benefits as laid-off workers through the term of the labor agreement, such as health and life insurance coverage.[21]

When a plant shutdown occurs, retirees represent a particularly vulnerable group of workers. They are the least able to relocate and least able to find other sources of income. Under the Supreme Court's holding in *NLRB v. Pittsburgh Plate Glass,*[22] the interests of retirees are only a permissible subject of bargaining, not a mandatory one. Thus, an employer may not legally be forced to bargain over the effect of a shutdown upon retired workers. This puts a premium on a construction of the existing collective bargaining agreement that provides for the continuation of retiree benefits. Often, employers will argue that such benefits exist only for the duration of the contract. In *Upholsterers Int'l v. American Pad & Textile Co.,*[23] such an argument was made by the employer with regard to retiree life insurance. The court held that the employer was obligated to maintain life insurance coverage for the full retirement of workers even though the plant had closed. Similarly, in *American Standard Co.,*[24] life and medical insurance were held to survive the termination of the contract through a clause that read, ". . . coverage will be maintained for the life of the employee." The key here is the particular interpretation of the contract accepted by the court. One's success will depend in part upon marshaling evidence of the bargaining history and past practices of the parties that will aid the court in its interpretation of the

---

20 Aaxico Airlines, Inc., 47 L.A. 289 (1966).

21 Teledyne Electro Finishing v. UAW Local 1546, 68 L.A. 36 (1977).

22 404 U.S. 157 (1971).

23 372 F.2d 427 (5th Cir. 1967).

24 57 L.A. 698 (1971).

contract.[25]

If the work force at a plant contains many high-seniority workers, a crucial issue will be the pension protection these workers will receive when they reach retirement age. The most frequently contested issue is whether the employer has properly funded the pension plan at the time of the plant shutdown. Often, the pension agreement will require only that the employer fund the plan on a "sound actuarial basis." What a "sound actuarial basis" is will depend in part on which expert testifies and what actuarial assumptions about the work force are made in computing the employer's funding obligation. If the employer has used unsound actuarial assumptions, it may be required to make compensatory payments even after the plant shutdown and the termination of the collective bargaining agreement.[26] One may resort to parol evidence to demonstrate that the funding of the pension plan was not consistent with what the parties meant by "a sound actuarial basis."[27]

Other cases have found an obligation to fund fully a plan for all vested pension rights.[28] However, in a 1974 case, parol evidence was used to show that the union understood that the employer had only a limited funding obligation.[29] Retirees have been in a number of other pension plan cases.[30]

If the shutdown occurs in mid-contract, one should argue that the pension plan does not terminate until the termination date of the collective bargaining agreement.[31] The additional time before the termination of the plan affects the company's funding obliga-

[25] *See* Schneider v. Elec. Auto-Lite Co., 456 F.2d 366 (6th Cir. 1972).

[26] Gould, Inc., 65 L.A. 1125 (1976); Briggs v. Mich. Tooling Co., 369 F. Supp. 920 (E.D. Mich. 1974).

[27] Gould, Inc., 65 L.A. 1125 (1976); IAM, Lodge 1194 v. Sargent Indus., 522 F.2d 280 (6th Cir. 1975). *But see* Int'l Union of United Brewery Workers v. Duke & Co., 373 F. Supp. 788 (W.D. Pa. 1974).

[28] UAW v. H.K. Porter, 93 LRRM 2917 (E.D. Mich. 1976) (justified reliance by an actuarial basis). IAM, Lodge 1194 v. Sargent Indus., 522 F.2d 280 (6th Cir. 1975).

[29] Int'l Union of United Brewery Workers v. Duke & Co., 373 F. Supp. 778 (W.D. Pa. 1974).

[30] Hurd v. Hutnick, 419 F. Supp. 630 (1976); Machinists v. Gulf & Western, 417 F. Supp. 191 (D. Me. 1976); Hardy v. H.K. Porter, 562 F.2d 42 (3d Cir. 1977).

[31] White Motor Corp., 61 L.A. 320 (1973); Keyless Lock Co., 59 L.A. 1125 (1972).

tion and the eligibility and benefit levels of many workers. Finally, of course, the funding obligations of an employer must today be seen against the backdrop of the minimum standards required by the Employee Retirement Income Security Act of 1974.[32]

Often in labor contracts, employees will be eligible for vacation pay as of a particular cutoff date, e.g., the first of the year or the date on which the employee was hired. If a plant closes before the cutoff date, the issue becomes whether an employee is entitled to at least a pro rata part of his or her anticipated vacation pay. The Sixth Circuit has said that this will depend on whether the vacation pay had been earned, or was due, only if one was eligible at the cutoff date.[33] Evidence that vacation pay is based on earnings will be taken to show employee entitlement for pro rata vacation pay.[34] If there is an unanticipated shutdown in midcontract, one is not required to be an employee at the cutoff date to be eligible for pro rata vacation pay.[35]

If an employer violates the collective bargaining agreement or statutory law, one remedy is transfer rights for the affected employees; this is also a common issue in negotiations surrounding a plant shutdown. This remedy provides workers with at least the opportunity to retain some economic security and makes the employer's probable desire to reopen as a nonunion shop more difficult to attain. A transfer agreement also has drawbacks. It may require workers to move long distances from family, friends, and other ties accumulated during a lifetime in one community. In some cases there will be no assurance of the same wages, benefits, and seniority rights. Many workers, therefore, will be unwilling to move. Some factors may make the right of transfer to distant areas less of a concession than it might first appear. Experience has shown that unions sometimes fight hard for transfer rights, giving up other monetary benefits, only to find that most workers who insisted they would move have changed their

---

[32] 29 U.S.C. § 1001 et seq.

[33] Local Union No. 186, Packinghouse Workers v. Armour & Co., 446 F.2d 610 (6th Cir. 1971); Smith v. Kingsport Press Co., 366 F.2d 416 (6th Cir. 1966).

[34] Schneider v. Electro-Autolite, *supra.*

[35] Baldwin Montrose v. Rubberworkers, 383 F.2d 796 (6th Cir. 1967); Telescope Folding Furniture, 49 L.A. 837 (1967).

minds.[36]

Other benefits to be considered and applied for are those provided under the Trade Act of 1972,[37] which provides for substantial benefits when the shutdown is related to imports. However, the continued funding of this act is subject to substantial question.

Generally, a union may extinguish or impair the rights of individual employees in negotiating a termination agreement.[38] However, one court has held that a union could not negotiate the distribution of funds in a pension trust in which vested pension rights existed.[39] Of course, in the negotiation of a termination agreement, a union must not violate its duty of fair representation and must not engage in conduct that is arbitrary, discriminatory, or in bad faith.[40]

§ 4.03. The Employer's Duty to Bargain

The Supreme Court, in *Fibreboard Paper Product Corp. v. NLRB,*[41] recognized the duty of an employer to bargain over the subcontracting of bargaining unit work. An employer's failure to bargain represents a violation of Section 8(a) (5) of the NLRA. The duty to bargain includes an obligation to give reasonable notice to the union of an employer's intention to shift work to another location.[42] This duty exists even if the contract is silent on subcontracting.[43] One problem with the *Fibreboard* decision has been in deciding the scope of its application. In *Fibreboard,* the company

---

36 For cases involving transfer rights, *see* Ex-Cell-O Corp., 60 L.A. 1094 (1973); Federal-Mogul Corp., 61 L.A. 745 (1973).

37 19 U.S.C. § 2101 et seq.

38 Int'l Longshoremen's & Warehousemen's Union v. Kuntz, 334 F.2d 165 (9th Cir. 1964); Cona v. Jim Walters Corp., 83 LRRM 2541 (E.D. Mich. 1973); Bosi v. USM Corp., 90 LRRM 2867 (D.N.J. 1975).

39 Hauser v. Farwell, Ozmun, Kirk & Co., 72 LRRM 2001 (D. Minn. 1969).

40 Vaca v. Sipes, 386 U.S. 171 (1967).

41 Fibreboard Paper Prod. Corp. v. NLRB, 379 U.S. 203 (1964).

42 Arnold Graphics v. NLRB, 505 F.2d 257 (6th Cir. 1974); Cooper Thermometer v. NLRB, 376 F.2d 684 (2d Cir. 1967); ILGWU v. NLRB, 463 F.2d 907 (D.C. Cir. 1972).

43 ACF Indus. Inc. v. NLRB, 100 LRRM 2710 (8th Cir. 1979).

had replaced union maintenance employees with those of an independent contractor. The majority opinion noted:

> The facts of the present case illustrate the propriety of submitting the dispute to collective negotiation. The Company's decision to contract out the maintenance work did not alter the Company's basic operation. The maintenance work still had to be performed in the plant. No capital investment was contemplated. . . . Therefore, to require the employer to bargain about the matter would not significantly abridge his freedom to manage the business.[44]

Justice Stewart, in a concurring opinion, distinguished this situation from those in which the employer's decision involves "larger entrepreneurial questions":

> This kind of subcontracting falls short of such larger entrepreneurial questions as what shall be produced, how capital shall be invested in fixed assets, or what the basic scope of the enterprise shall be. In my view, the Court's decision in this case has nothing to do with whether any aspects of these larger issues could under any circumstances be considered subjects of compulsory collective bargaining.[45]

The courts have generally adopted this distinction. If a company's decision to relocate does not alter the scope of the business, a duty to bargain arises.[46] In *ILGWU v. NLRB,*[47] the company relocated to Alabama principally to reduce labor costs. It manufactured the same products with the same machinery, sold to the same customers, and retained essentially the same management. Under such circumstances the decision to relocate was a mandatory subject of bargaining.[48] If, however, a plant is subject to urban renewal, the employer is not required to bargain over its decision to close the plant rather than to relocate. Such a decision involves a major change in the economic direction of the compa-

---

[44] 379 U.S. at 213.

[45] 379 U.S. at 225.

[46] ILGWU v. NLRB, *supra* at 916.

[47] *Id.*

[48] *See also* NLRB v. Plymouth Indus., 435 F.2d 558 (6th Cir. 1970); Weltronic v. NLRB, 419 F.2d 1120 (6th Cir. 1969).

ny.[49] Similarly, a security guard agency was not required to bargain over its decision to close all operations in one city.[50] During the 1960s, the National Labor Relations Board (NLRB) rejected any distinction based upon the scope of alteration. Rather, the Board would have required bargaining in either situation.[51] However, in a later case, the Board, over two dissents, adopted the "scope of alteration" test.[52] The Board reasoned that decisions involving significant investment or withdrawal of capital lie at the core of entrepreneurial control and, therefore, were not meant by Congress to be the subject of mandatory collective bargaining.[53] If the employer has a duty to bargain over the decision to alter its operations, bargaining with the union must begin before the employer has made a final decision to relocate.[54]

In *Brockway Motor Truck v. NLRB,*[55] the Third Circuit provided a new analysis of the duty to bargain over plant shutdowns; since *Brockway,* several other courts of appeals have adopted the same analysis. The *Brockway* court held that there is a presumption that the decision to close is a mandatory subject of bargaining. The court noted that the same factors that the Supreme Court considered in *Fibreboard* were present in a shutdown situation: (1) Both decisions are within the literal language of Section 8(d), since the termination of employment normally results from a facility shutdown and is necessarily a term and condition of employment. (2) Making the decision subject to bargaining will promote the NLRA goal of advancing peaceful resolution of labor disputes.

Next, the court's analysis requires examination of the facts in a given case and a balancing of the interests involved. On the one hand, there is the concern of the employees over losing their jobs.

---

[49] NLRB v. Royal Plating & Polishing Co., 350 F.2d 191, 195 (3d Cir. 1965).

[50] NLRB v. Burns Int'l Detective Agency, 346 F.2d 897 (8th Cir. 1965).

[51] Ozark Trailers, 63 LRRM 1264 (1966).

[52] Gen. Motors Corp., 77 LRRM 537 (1971), *review denied,* 470 F.2d 422 (D.C. Cir. 1972).

[53] Gen. Motors Corp., *supra,* at 1539; Kingswood Mining Co., 86 LRRM 1203 (1974). *But see* Am. Needle & Novelty Co., 84 LRRM 1526 (1973); Royal Typewriter Co., 85 LRRM 1501 (1974), *enforced,* 533 F.2d 1030 (8th Cir. 1976).

[54] Royal Norton Mfg. Co., 77 LRRM 1022 (1971); Ozark Trailers, *supra;* Am. Cyanamid Co. v. NLRB, 100 LRRM 2640 (7th Cir. 1979) (company failed to bargain over decision to subcontract made during strike).

[55] 582 F.2d 720 (3d Cir. 1978).

Here the court relied on *Ozark Trailers,*[56] a case that marked the Board's greatest protection of employees' rights during a plant closing. In *Ozark Trailers,* the Board stated:

> For, just as the employer has invested capital in the business, so the employee has invested years of his working life, accumulating seniority, accruing pension rights, and developing skills that may or may not be salable to another employer. And, just as the employer's interest in the protection of his capital investment is entitled to consideration in our interpretation of the Act, so too is the employee's interest in the protection of his livelihood.[57]

However, the court also considered the countervailing interests of the employer and its ability to make entrepreneurial decisions. The court cited two potential situations in which the employer's interests might outweigh the employees': (1) actions by a third party, such as condemnation by a municipal housing authority, and (2) dire financial straits. Since neither the employer nor the NLRB had presented evidence necessary to balance the interests of employees and employer, the case was remanded to the NLRB.[58] Decisions similar to *Brockway* have also been reached by the Second, Seventh, and Sixth circuits; the Ninth Circuit has refused to recognize a union's right to negotiate over the decision to relocate work.[59]

In 1980, the Supreme Court reversed the Second Circuit on the extent of an employer's duty to bargain over its economic decision to terminate a portion of its operations.[60] The Second Circuit had asserted a presumption of a duty to bargain over such a decision. This presumption could be rebutted by a showing by the employer that the purposes of the NIRA would not be furthered by the imposition of a duty to bargain (e.g., bargaining

[56] 161 NLRB 561, 63 LRRM 1264 (1966).

[57] *Supra,* 161 NLRB at 566.

[58] NLRB v. First Nat'l Maintenance Corp., 104 LRRM 2924 (2d Cir. 1980); Davis v. NLRB, 103 LRRM 2968 (7th Cir. 1980); NLRB v. Prod. Molded Plastics, 102 LRRM 2040 (6th Cir. 1979); NLRB v. Int'l Harvester Co., 104 LRRM 3098 (9th Cir. 1980).

[59] *Id.*

[60] First Nat'l Maintenance Corp. v. NLRB, 101 S. Ct. 2573 (1981), 107 LRRM 2705.

would be futile, existence of emergency financial circumstances, industry custom not to bargain over such decisions, bargaining would endanger the vitality of employer's entire business).

The Supreme Court held that an employer's economic decision to terminate a portion of its business is not a mandatory subject of bargaining, although the employer did have a duty to bargain over the "effects" of the termination. In this case, the employer provided maintenance and housekeeping work to commercial customers on contract. The employer terminated its contract with the customer, alleging that its company was losing money on the contract. While the Court's decision gives considerable weight to management prerogatives, the Court states that its decision is narrowly drawn and does not necessarily apply to other decisions, such as subcontracting, technological developments, plant relocation, sales, and corporate reorganization.

In summary, the law has evolved in the direction of holding employers to a duty to bargain about the decision to close a plant, relocate, or subcontract, except in the circumstances noted above. The recent Supreme Court decision in *First National Maintenance* will be used by employers to limit the duty to bargain, but advocates for workers will be expected to argue that that decision was narrowly drawn and that decisions to close involved other than economic reasons.

Whether or not an employer has a duty to bargain over the decision to relocate, it must always bargain over the effects of the relocation upon employees. This duty of the employer includes an obligation to give the union timely notice of the intended change in its operations. Failure to bargain over the effects or to give timely notice constitutes a violation of Section 8(a) (5) of the NLRA.[61]

Such bargaining over effects will include among other subjects severance pay, seniority, pensions, and transfer rights.[62] Howev-

---

[61] *See* Royal Plating & Polishing, 63 LRRM 1045 (1966), *enforced,* 350 F.2d 191 (3d Cir. 1965); Avila Group, Inc., 89 LRRM 1365 (1975); Elec. Prod. Int'l Corp., 85 LRRM 1268 (1974); Arnold Graphics Indus. v. NLRB, *supra;* NLRB v. Prod. Molded Plastics, 102 LRRM 2040 (6th Cir. 1979); Brockway Motor Trucks v. NLRB, 99 LRRM 2013 (3rd Cir. 1978).

[62] *See* NLRB v. Transmarine Navigation Corp., 380 F.2d 933 (9th Cir. 1967); Summit Tooling Co., 79 LRRM 1397 (1972); Cooper Thermometer, 63 LRRM 1219, *enforced in pertinent part,* 376 F.2d 684 (2d Cir. 1967).

er, the union must make a timely request to bargain over the effects of the change in the employer's operations. If it fails to do so, it waives the right to bargain over effects.[63]

The employer's duty to bargain includes a duty to provide the union with information about the movement of work. In one case, the employer committed an unfair labor practice when it refused to give the union information about the movement of machines out of the plant.[64] Other decisions have held that the union had a right to information about the relationship of the employer to its subcontractors[65] and information about customers of the employer.[66] If an employer claims the movement of operations is an economic necessity, the union has a right to see financial records that would substantiate this claim.[67] An employer must give the union sufficient information about the new location, the number and types of jobs at the new location, and the comparative costs of operation to permit the union to bargain effectively about the decision to move and its impact.[68] As an incidental benefit of such requests for information, they may aid the union in determining whether the employer's decision to move or partially close down operations is in fact a result of anti-union animus.

§ 4.04. Unfair Labor Practice Charges

In *Textile Workers Union v. Darlington Manufacturing Co.*,[69] the Supreme Court held that an attempt to chill unionism by means of the runaway shop is a violation of Section 8(a)(3) of the NLRA. In cases in which the Board has found a runaway shop, the remedy may include reinstatement with back pay, moving expenses, and reimbursement for the cost of commuting to the new

---

[63] NLRB v. Spun-Jee, 385 F.2d 379 (2d Cir. 1967); ABC Transnat'l Transp., 102 LRRM 1357; Raskin Packing Co., 102 LRRM 1489. *Contra,* First Nat'l Maintenance Corp., 101 LRRM 1178.

[64] NLRB v. Acme Indus., 385 U.S. 432 (1967).

[65] Herk Elevator Maintenance, Inc., 80 LRRM 1448 (1972).

[66] Fawcett Printing Co., 82 LRRM 1663 (1973).

[67] Am. Needle & Novelty Co., *supra.*

[68] Royal Typewriter Co., *supra.*

[69] 380 U.S. 263 (1970).

work location. At times the Board has even ordered resumption of the discontinued operation. Rarely, however, is it possible to provide sufficient evidence to establish that the employer's motivation was anti-union animus rather than "economic considerations."[70] However, in *Midland Ross Corp. v. NLRB,*[71] the Board was successful in enforcing its application of the principles of *Darlington*[72] to a plant closing intended to discourage an organizing effort. Similarly, Section 8(a)(3) and the principles of *Darlington* apply to partial closings and subcontracting motivated by anti-union animus.[73] The remedy for such a violation is an order for back pay and reopening of the plant.[74] It should be noted that such a remedy is often not enforced because of the burden to the employer.

If an employer violates its duty to bargain in a plant shutdown situation, the Board's order to bargain will normally include a back pay award. The NLRB will require the employer to pay employees their normal wages from the date of the Board's decision until (1) an agreement is reached between the union and the employer, (2) a bona fide impasse occurs in bargaining, (3) the union fails to request bargaining within five days of the Board's decision, or (4) the union fails to bargain in good faith.[75] The purpose of such an order is to put the union in a position in which meaningful bargaining can occur between it and the employer. If, however, the workers are on strike at the time of the plant closing, the Board will not award back pay.[76] One should recognize that "good faith bargaining" does not require the employer to make any concessions; a bona fide impasse may be reached in a relatively short period of time. For the criteria of a "bona fide

---

[70] *See* Johns Manville Prods. Corp., 557 F.2d 1129 (5th Cir. 1977), *cert. denied,* 436 U.S. 956 (1978).

[71] 617 F.2d 977 (3d Cir. 1980).

[72] *Supra.*

[73] *See* Smyth Mfg. Co., 103 LRRM 1432 (1980); Ethyl Corp., 231 NLRB 431 (1977).

[74] Smyth Mfg. Co., *supra.*

[75] Royal Plating & Polishing, *supra;* Automation Instit. of Los Angeles, Inc., 85 LRRM 1257 (1974). *See also* First Nat'l Maintenance Corp. v. NLRB, 627 F.2d 596 (2d Cir. 1980), *cert. granted,* 4905 L.W. 3493 (1981)(ordering reinstatement and back pay in a refusal to bargain over a partial closure).

[76] Royal Typewriter Co., *supra.*

impasse," see *Taft Broadcasting Co.*[77] When seeking remedial action before the NLRB, one must also recognize the opportunities for extensive employer delays inherent in the present procedures of the Board.

§ 4.05. Right to Strike

There are two basic situations in which the union may strike. First, if the contract has expired, the union may strike on the issue of the effects of the employer's decision to remove work. Second, if the contract has not expired, the right to strike is subject to the grievance arbitration process to the extent the employer's actions are so subject. For further information, see Chapter 3, *infra.*

§ 4.06. Problems with the Union

One of the most difficult problems arises in representing individual employees in a plant shutdown situation if the union has refused or failed to assert rights related to the shutdown or its effects. As the collective bargaining agreement is a contract between the union and employer, employees generally may not assert violations of the contract absent a showing of a breach of the duty of fair representation.[78] Furthermore, the ability to assert a contract claim against the employer and union in a plant closing situation requires, with few exceptions, the exhaustion of internal union remedies.[79]

Similar problems are posed by individual employee actions challenging plant removal as an unfair labor practice. As the central challenge to plant closure is for violation of Section 8(a)(5) for refusal to bargain with the union, it is obvious why the Board has not been receptive to employee claims if the union has failed to press a claim for violation of Section 8(a)(5). While the em-

[77] 64 LRRM 1386 (1967).

[78] Vaca v. Sipes, 386 U.S. 171 (1967); Motor Coach Employees v. Lockridge, 403 U.S. 274 (1971); Hines v. Anchor Motor Freight, 424 U.S. 554 (1976).

[79] Johnson v. Wilson Foods Corp., 102 LRRM 2149 (D. Kans. 1978); Bucholtz v. Swift Co., 102 LRRM, 2219 (8th Cir. 1979).

ployees' Section 8(a)(5) claim will not prevail without union support, the filing of an individual's charge may impact on potential union waiver problems if the union has not diligently pursued its options. Additionally, the filing of a Section 8(a)(5) charge as well as a charge against the union for failing to represent its members under Section 8(b)(2) may result in the union's asserting employee rights relative to the shutdown or relocation.

§ 4.07. Other Alternatives

If there are appropriate facts, one might also consider challenging an employer's plan to relocate on grounds of race or age discrimination.[80] For example, it may be possible to show that an employer is in effect trying to reduce costs by fleeing an older, high-seniority, high-benefit work force.

The heightening of the economic crisis has resulted in a significant increase in plant shutdowns and relocations. Responses to these developments have include somewhat novel union and community approaches to protect jobs. While these new approaches have had only limited success, they reflect an increasing tendency to confront the economic, social, and political problems of plant closure. In the *Youngstown Steelworkers* case,[81] the local union and community organizations asserted numerous theories to prevent the closing of the steel facility. Among the plaintiffs' claims were antitrust claims concerning the failure of U.S. Steel to negotiate over sale of the plant to the community organization and a vested rights theory based upon the vested interest of the community and workers in the long-established plant. The Sixth Circuit affirmed the dismissal of the contract and vested rights claims, but reversed and remanded the antitrust claim for trial. While the matter was eventually settled, many favorable concessions were gained through this effort.[82]

Outlined above are a number of different theories one might

---

[80] *See* Rock v. Norfolk & W. Ry., 332 F.2d 336 (7th Cir. 1975). *Cf.* Payne v. Bobbie Brooks, 24 FEP 1242 (N.D. Ohio 1980).

[81] *Supra.*

[82] *See* Corporate Ruthlessness and Community Despair, Staughton Lynd Labor Update Vol. 1, No. 4 (Feb. 1981).

use to challenge a plant shutdown. They should be seen as tools to obtain the best results possible in a particular situation for the affected workers. Ultimate vindication in the courtroom is the exception; negotiation is the rule.

Under the present state of the law, a plant shutdown requires the maximum use of an advocate's skills as a legal innovator and bargaining tactician. Rarely will one's efforts result in a total victory. Even if the employer's actions are clearly unlawful, vindication may come only after years of litigation—years the affected workers cannot afford.[83]

---

[83] In response to the large number of shutdowns and relocations in the recent period, there have been a number of community and legislative efforts directed against plant shutdowns. The legislative arena has largely been focused on the Ford-Riegle federal legislation (H.R. 5040 and 51608), which would require notice of intent to change operations, transfer rights, and numerous other benefits. For further discussion of legislation and community alternatives, *see Stop Runaway Shops,* available from the Citizens' Labor Committee on Plant Closures, 3600 Wilshire Boulevard, Suite 2200, Los Angeles, California 90010, and *Plant Closings and Runaway Industry,* available from the National Labor Law Center, Suite 612, 2000 "P" Street, N.W., Washington, D.C. 20036.

CHAPTER 5

Fighting for a Safe and Healthy Workplace

This chapter examines the legal tools available for increasing workers' control of safety on the job. It focuses on three fundamental issues: (1) gaining access to facts relevant to job hazards,

(2) controlling identified job hazards, and (3) job security. Section 5.01 presents the rights and remedies available under the National Labor Relations Act (NLRA) and the Occupational Safety and Health Act (OSH Act). Sections 5.02 through 5.05 discuss control of the workplace through the Occupational Safety and Health Administration (OSHA), review of OSHA's actions by the Occupational Safety and Health Review Commission (OSHRevCom), labor contracts, and court injunctions. Section 5.06 probes the protections for workers who refuse dangerous work and engage in safety-related activity. Section 5.07 capsulizes the emerging law on job protections for workers with or at risk of safety-related disabilities. The chapter's aim is to provide a legal framework through which workers' informed judgments about the safety of their working conditions can displace the judgments of the management-oriented personnel who presently dominate occupational safety and health decision making.

This chapter does not discuss workers' compensation or damage claims for workplace injuries, OSHA-approved state plans,[1] OSHA in the federal sector,[2] the Mine Safety and Health Act,[3] criminal liability for employers for safety violations,[4] or standard setting and variances under the OSH Act.[5]

The coverage of the OSH Act extends broadly over private employers, but it *excludes the public sector.* The definition of covered employers[6] includes any business with two or more employees that is "affecting commerce."[7] Only if the employer is already regulated by another federal agency controlling worker safety is

---

[1] Sections 18 and 23(g) of the OSH Act, 29 U.S.C. §§ 667, 672(g). 29 CFR, Parts 1902, 1908, 1950–56. *See also* AFL-CIO v. Brennan, 390 F. Supp. 972 (D.D.C. 1975), *aff'd,* 570 F.2d 1030 (D.C.Cir. 1978).

[2] Section 19 of the OSH Act, 29 U.S.C. § 668; Executive Order 12223 (June 30, 1980); 29 CFR § 1960 (as amended October 2, 1980).

[3] 30 U.S.C. § 801 et seq; 30 CFR, Parts 1–100; 29 CFR, Parts 2700–2701.

[4] Section 17(e)–(h), 29 U.S.C. § 666(e)–(h); OSHA Field Operations Manual, IX.D. *See generally* Levin, *Crimes against Employees: Substantive Criminal Sanctions under the Occupational Safety and Health Act,* 14 Am. Crim. L. Rev. 717 (1977).

[5] Section 6 of the OSH Act, 29 U.S.C. § 665.

[6] Section 3(5) of the OSH Act, 29 U.S.C. § 652(5).

[7] The courts interpret "affecting commerce" very liberally. U.S. v. Dye Constr. Co., 510 F.2d 78, 83 (10th Cir. 1975); Anchorage Plastering Co., 3 OSHC 1284, OSHD ¶19,720 (OSHRevCom 1975), *rev'd,* 570 F.2d 351 (9th Cir. 1978).

the employer possibly exempt.[8] If a quasi-public authority exists and the directors are political appointees, OSHA probably will not assert jurisdiction.[9]

The following terms and acronyms are used throughout this chapter:

- *ALJ*—Administrative Law Judge at the OSHRevCom or the NLRB.
- *ANSI*—The American National Standards Institute—OSHA officially recognizes this private agency as a source of "consensus" standards.
- *Citation*—OSHA's formal notice to an employer that it has violated the OSH Act.
- *Contest*—The common name for a legal proceeding before the OSHRevCom to review the sufficiency of an OSHA citation.
- *COSH*—Committees on Occupational Safety and Health. These committees usually have workers, unions, and occupational safety and health professionals as members.
- *FTC*—Failure to correct violation; a special type of OSHA citation which has very heavy penalties.
- *MSDS*—Material Safety Data Sheet—The OSHA Form-20, commonly used in industry to describe the hazards of chemicals.
- *NCI*—The National Cancer Institute.
- *NFPA*—The National Fire Protection Association—OSHA officially recognizes the NFPA as a source of standards.
- *NIOSH*—The National Institute for Occupational Safety and Health—The research agency created by the OSH Act.
- *NLRB*—The National Labor Relations Board.
- *OSH Act*—The Occupational Safety and Health Act of 1970.
- *OSHA*—The Occupational Safety and Health Administration—The safety and health "police" within the Department of Labor who inspect workplaces and issue citations.
- *OSHA FOM*—OSHA's Field Operations Manual.
- *OSHA IHM*—OSHA's Industrial Hygiene Manual.
- *OSHRevCom*—The Occupational Safety and Health Review

[8] Section 4(b)(1) of the OSH Act, 29 U.S.C. § 653(b)(1). *See generally* Section 5.03[a], *infra*.

[9] 29 CFR § 1975.5(d).

Commission—The independent safety and health "judges" who hear contests of OSHA citations.

- *PMA*—Petition for Modification of Abatement Date—The employer's formal request for additional time to correct a problem.
- *Private Right of Action*—A lawyer's phrase for the right to bring suit. The OSH Act did not create any private rights of action.
- *TOSCA*—The Toxic Substance Control Act.

§ 5.01. Getting Access to Relevant Facts: Exercising the Workers' Right to Know

Workers need quick and open access to the relevant facts about job hazards if they are to exericse meaningful control.[10] Those conducting a study of excessive cancer deaths in a particular department need to know what chemicals are being used and what information the company already has. Records showing that the employer has long known of a problem can be the basis for a "willful" OSHA citation, substantially increasing the penalties; however, workers need access to those records. Employer "recognition" of a hazard is needed to prove a violation of the general duty clause, and employer records can sometimes supply this proof. The employer's information can also be used in safety committee grievance handling or in establishing the need for a Health Hazard Evaluation by the National Institute for Occupa-

[10] The following handbooks are recommended for workers who are beginning to identify job hazards. The essential technical guide is: PHILAPOSH, *Health/Technical Committee Handbook: A Guide for Helping Workers Solve Job Health and Safety Problems,* 1979. This guide is available for $15 from: Philadelphia Area Project on Occupational Safety and Health, 1321 Arch Street, Philadelphia, Pennsylvania 19107. Also useful is: *A Worker's Guide to Documenting Health and Safety Problems* (1978), available from Labor Occupational Health Program Center for Labor Research, 2521 Channing Way, Berkeley, Cal. 94720. The NIOSH publication, *Occupational Diseases: A Guide to Their Recognition* (rev. ed., 1977, No. 77-181.) is useful and inexpensive. It contains an excellent summary of the vast literature and the range of institutional resources on job hazards, Section XI—"Sources of Consultation; Reference Aids." Finally, the UAW publishes *What Every UAW Representative Should Know about Health and Safety,* and *The Case of the Workplace Killers: A Manual for Cancer Detectives on the Job,* both of which are available from the UAW Purchase and Supply Department, 8000 E. Jefferson, Detroit, Michigan 48214.

tional Safety and Health (NIOSH), a procedure discussed more fully below. But often the employer will not readily grant workers access to its safety and health data base. The workers' right of access to information—their right to know—is the subject of this section.

For organizers and safety committee members, this "right to know" is a potent slogan. What employer can legitimately disagree with a worker's right to know about the safety of his workplace? Unionized shops with progressive safety leadership are in the best position to enforce this right. They can obtain access to relevant employer documents, inspect working conditions, obligate employers through bargaining, and use contract remedies and NLRB procedures to force compliance. Under OSHA regulations, both unorganized and organized workers have access rights to the employer's log of injuries and illnesses and to all the employer's medical surveillance and workplace exposure records. During OSHRevCom contests and state court litigation for injunctive relief, workers' representatives have the right to discovery of relevant employer data. Finally, government records on an employer can be reviewed under the Freedom of Information Act (FOIA). These remedies all have two major limitations: (1) the employer's trade secrets defense and (2) the worker's right to confidentiality. There are practical limitations, discussed below, such as the amount of trouble or expense involved in obtaining access.

Appendix 5A near the end of this chapter shows in tabular form the present legal scope of the worker's right to know. The first column lists common information requests. The second indicates whether the union has a right of access pursuant to Section 8(a)(5) of the NLRA. The third column indicates whether OSHA regulations cover the item. The fourth column covers access by way of the FOIA. Column five indicates whether the information item is available in discovery. An X on the chart indicates that a right to know exists; a O indicates no right. Labor contracts and state statutory rights are not on the chart; they vary so much that meaningful generalizations cannot be made. The right to a Health Hazard Evaluation by NIOSH is not on the chart, but it will be discussed below. The employer's duties to use labels or issue warnings[11] and to post notices[12] are not discussed.

[1] Unions' Right to Know in Organized Shops

Unions have two right to know remedies: (1) requiring the employer to disclose information about working conditions as a part of its "duty to bargain in good faith"; and (2) enforcing the labor contract to gain access to information.

To use the employer's duty to bargain, also called Section 8(a)(5),[13] a representative of the union—this is a union's right, not a worker's right—must make a reasonable request to the company for the information by certified mail, return receipt requested. The request or demand should clearly identify the information sought and set a reasonable time for the employer to respond. The request should also identify the section of any OSHA access regulation that has been violated.[14] Some tailoring of your initial request may be necessary if, for instance, you have unintentionally framed it too broadly. If trade secrets or worker's confidentiality are involved, it is necessary to bargain for a reasonable accommodation. The union must be prepared to file a Section

---

[11] The new comprehensive health standards, 29 CFR § 1910.1001–1046, all require signs and labels. Various other standards require labels and warnings, e.g., radiation warnings are required by 29 CFR § 1910.96(f), .97(a)(3), .145(d)(3), (d)(7). OSHA recently proposed a general rule on labeling; it is likely to take years before the final rule is enforceable. Section 5(a)(1) requires employers to warn workers of "recognized hazards" where the worker's exposure is forseeable. The duty to warn overlaps with the duty to train and supervise workers.

[12] Workers must be notified of OSH Act enforcement activity through employer posting of notices. *See* Section 5.03, *infra.* The employer must also post an official OSHA poster describing the OSH Act. During February of each year, the employer must post its Annual Summary of the preceding year's log of injuries and illnesses, 29 CFR § 1904.5(d)(1).

[13] 29 U.S.C. § 158(a)(5).

[14] *See* Section 5.03 *infra,* on "willfulizing" an OSHA complaint. Framing the request in this fashion puts the employer on notice that it is violating the OSHA access standard, which permits later use of this demand in OSHA proceedings to press for increased penalties when the employer has refused to comply.

8(a)(5) charge at the local National Labor Relations Board (NLRB) office after an impasse is reached with the employer.

The right to know under Section 8(a)(5) is very broad. In order for the union properly to perform its representative role in negotiating and enforcing its labor contract, it must be properly informed about the pertinent working conditions.[15] The relevancy standard is that of the Federal Rules of Civil Procedure.[16] The union's burden of proof is very light. Because plant safety and health issues are mandatory subjects of collective bargaining,[17] requests for information about safety and health are "presumptively relevant" to the union's proper performance of its job,[18] irrespective of the information's immediate connection[19] with the negotiation[20] or administration[21] of the labor contract. This presumption puts a very heavy burden of rebuttal upon the employer.[22]

Although the NLRB may modify its rules on the trade secrets defense,[23] the present favorable state of the law is worth review. Most important, the burden of proof is on the employer, which must show that the trade secret is indeed legitimate, that the union was apprised of this, that the union's request was overbroad, and that the employer indicated its willingness to reach an accommodation. In rebuttal, the union may show the employer's

---

[15] NLRB v. Truitt Mfg. Co., 351 U.S. 149 (1955); NLRB v. Acme Industrial Co., 385 U.S. 432 (1967).

[16] Westinghouse Elec. Co., 239 NLRB No. 19 (1978), *accord,* Acme Industrial, *supra* note 15, at 437.

[17] NLRB v. Gulf Power Co., 384 F.2d 822, 824–25 (5th Cir. 1967), *citing,* Fibreboard Paper Products Corp. v. NLRB, 379 U.S. 203, 222 (1964).

[18] Borden Chemical, JK-(SF)-87-79, 32-CA-551; Colgate Palmolive Co., JD-(SF)-61-79, 17-CA-331; Minnesota Mining & Mfg. Co., JD-12479, 18-CA-5710. These three cases were consolidated and argued before the NLRB in early 1980. All three involve union requests for information relating to toxic chemicals.

[19] For instance, some employers have complained that the union was seeking information about affirmative action plans for litigation, not collective bargaining. The courts have rejected this defense. *See, e.g.,* IUE v. NLRB, 105 LRRM 3337 (D.C. Cir. 1980).

[20] Western Mass. Elec. Co., 234 NLRB No. 19 (1978).

[21] Acme Industrial, *supra* note 15.

[22] *See* Borden Chem, *supra* note 18, slip opinion at 17–23.

[23] *See* cases cited note 18 *supra.*

laxity, e.g., inadequacy or absence of employer shop rules to protect trade secrets, failure to require new employees to sign covenants to preserve trade secrets, lack of tight control over plant access, and/or failure to take other meaningful steps to protect trade secrets formulae. In one case on cross-examination, the employer's witness admitted that he knew of only 1 out of 700 chemical products for which trade secrets protection had been claimed whose use, if known to outside competitors, would reveal any trade secrets.[24] Even if the employer does establish a trade secret defense, the risk of disclosure, which may be an element of the employer's proof, must then be balanced against the union's right to know. Often, a reasonable accomodation can be reached.

Worker consent to disclosure must be obtained if the information sought is personally identifiable and there is a strong privacy interest. In *Detroit Edison v. NLRB,*[25] the union sought individual psychological test scores of workers without their consent. Because the test scores showed their "competence," a matter of personal privacy, the Supreme Court held that the employer had not breached its duty to bargain in good faith by refusing to release the test results. Until *Detroit Edison,* however, the circuit courts generally rejected confidentiality claims.[26] The NLRB recently applied this case in the context of a request for the results of medical surveillance.[27]

Two final points about this remedy should be noted. First, the employer's duty should be extended to permit unions indepen-

---

[24] *Id.*

[25] 440 U.S. 301 (1979).

[26] *See* Curtiss-Wright Corp. v. NLRB, 347 F.2d 61 (3d Cir. 1965) (job evaluation and wage data); NLRB v. Item Co., 220 F.2d 956 (5th Cir. 1955), *cert. denied,* 350 U.S. 836 (1955), 352 U.S. 917 (1956) (wage data); Gen. Elec. Co. v. NLRB, 466 F.2d 1177 (6th Cir. 1975) (wage data); NLRB v. Frontier Homes Corp., 371 F.2d 974 (8th Cir. 1967) (selling price lists); *cf.* United Aircraft Corp., 192 NLRB 382, 390 (1971) (company physician's records not disclosable without worker's consent unless needed for a particular grievance), *modified on other grounds sub nom.,* Lodges 743 and 1746 v. United Aircraft Corp., 534 F.2d 422 (2nd Cir. 1975), *cert. denied,* 429 U.S. 825 (1976); Shell Oil Co. v. NLRB, 457 F.2d 615, 619 (9th Cir. 1975) (refusal to reveal workers' names without consent was proper when it was "establish[ed] beyond cavil that there was a clear and present danger of harassment and violence"); Detroit Edison, (dissent), *supra* note 25.

[27] Johns-Manville Sales Corp., 252 NLRB No. 56 (1980).

dently to investigate[28] health hazards of the job. Investigations by union personnel or outside consultants should be allowed, even if these may involve bringing equipment into the plant. Second, the duty is not found only in the NLRA, but also in organized shops covered by state labor boards[29] and in the federal sector.[30]

In a unionized shop, the labor contract may also be available to ensure the worker's right to know.[31] Enforcement of Section 8(a)(5) rights or OSHA record access regulations[32] may be cheaper and quicker if they are clearly set out in the union contract; the contract can also extend those rights. Before negotiating new language, assess the needs of the local and review Appendix 5A in this chapter and Chown's book of ideal contract language.[33] There are several areas in which the labor contract can improve upon the rights to know which exist under federal law. The union may be allowed access to the company's existing information system. Contract provisions can provide for immediate access to reports of accidents and accident files generated by company personnel, as well as independent investigation of incidents by the union, even if this requires the union to bring its own outside specialists into the plant. If the employer has not monitored workplace exposures, this duty can also be bargained for. Incidentally, neither the new OSHA Access Regulation nor Section 8(a)(5) requires the employer to monitor workplace exposures; only the new OSHA health standards require this.[34] Nor does OSHA require general medical surveillance. The vital questions for bargaining are: Who does the surveillance? Who interprets the results? How are the records segregated so that the employer

---

[28] *See* Fafai Bearing Co., 146 NLRB No. 179 (1974), *aff'd,* 62 LRRM 2415 (2d Cir. 1966); Winona Industries, Inc., JD-484-80, 18-CA-6509 (ALJ Stevenson, August 21, 1980).

[29] *In re* Board of Educ. City School Dist. of the City of Albany, 6 PERB 3029, 3039 (1973).

[30] 5 U.S.C. § 7116(b)(5).

[31] *See generally* Section 5.04, *infra.*

[32] CIBA Geigy Co. v. OCAW, 61 LA 438 (1973).

[33] Paul Chown, *Workplace Safety and Health: A Guide To Collective Bargaining* (1980), available from Labor Occupational Health Program, 2521 Channing Way, Berkeley, Cal. 94720.

[34] 29 CFR § 1910.1001 *et seq.*

does not misuse the medical information in making personnel decisions? Medical surveillance data can be used in making personnel decisions on removal of an employee from certain working conditions and in making disability determinations. Ideally, the employer should pay the costs for outside surveillance.

[2] OSHA Record Access Regulations

The new OSHA regulations on "Access to Employee Exposure and Medical Records"[35] are an important step forward. Any worker, whether organized or not, now has the right of access to the employer's existing records on the health hazards of the job, the levels of exposure and the health consequences of the exposure. The emphasis is on access; employers are *not* yet required to monitor exposures or worker health. The employer has to grant access within a "reasonable time" after the request, but no later than fifteen days afterwards.[36] Access means any of three options: provide the worker with a free copy (the worker pays for the second copy), provide the record and free access to a copying machine, or loan the original record for a reasonable time to permit a copy to be made.[37] Enforcement is provided through the routine OSHA citation system.

The definition of records is broad and the employer must preserve all records in existence from July 21, 1978, for thirty years.[38]

---

[35] 29 CFR § 1910.20 The OSH Act contains ample authority for OSHA to increase the worker's "right to know." Section 8(g)(2) grants OSHA and NIOSH rule-making authority, 29 U.S.C. § 657(g)(2); Whirlpool Corp. v. Marshall, 100 S.Ct. 883 (1980). Furthermore, the OSH Act specifies that (1) employers must notify workers of any overexposure to substances or hazards controlled by OSHA and of the corrective steps being taken, § 8(c)(3), 29 U.S.C. § 657(c)(3); (2) OSHA must issue regulations requiring employers to maintain records of workplace exposures of workers and allow workers to observe exposure monitoring, § 8 (c)(3), 29 U.S.C. § 657(c)(3); and (3) OSHA must issue standards requiring employers to inform workers of the OSH Act's protections, *but see* 29 CFR § 1903.2(c)(1). Eleven years after passage of the OSH Act, OSHA has yet to fulfill this mandate.

[36] 29 CFR § 1910.20(e)(1)(i).

[37] 29 CFR § 1910.20(e)(1)(ii).

[38] 43 Fed. Reg. 31019 (July 19, 1978).

The records covered fall into two classes: exposure records and medical records. Exposure records include workplace monitoring records, biological monitoring records, material safety data sheets (MSDSs)(OSHA Form 20; see Appendix 5B near the end of this chapter), or if none of these is available, any other record that reveals the identity of a health hazard.[39] Access need be granted only to exposure records relevant to the worker, including records of his or her exposure, records of similarly situated workers, and records relating to his or her present working conditions or to conditions to which s/he is being transferred.[40] Medical records include histories, examination results, opinions, treatments, and complaints; excluded are specimens, insurance records and records concerning worker counseling programs if the latter are separately maintained.[41] Limitations exist on access to medical records. Medical personnel may delete the names of those who have provided confidential information concerning a worker's health.[42] In cases of terminal illness or psychiatric conditions, a company physician may require that the worker designate a representative, and thus deny the worker direct access.[43] However, analyses utilizing exposure or medical records (to the extent that they do not identify individuals) must be made accessible to worker inquiry.[44]

The definition of covered health hazards is also broad. The regulation uses the phrase "toxic substance or harmful physical agent" to mean any chemical substance, biological agent (bacteria, virus, fungus, etc.), or physical stress (noise, heat, cold, vibration, repetitive motion, ionizing and nonionizing radiation, hypo- or hyperbolic pressure, etc.) that (1) is regulated by any federal law or rule because of a hazard to health; (2) is listed in the latest printed edition of the NIOSH Registry of Toxic Effects of Chemical Substances (RTECS); (3) has yielded positive evidence of an acute or chronic health hazard in human, animal, or

---

[39] 29 CFR § 1910.20(c)(5).

[40] 29 CFR § 1910.20(d)(2)(i).

[41] 29 CFR § 1910.20(c)(6).

[42] 29 CFR § 1910.20(e)(2)(ii).

[43] 29 CFR § 1910.20(e)(2)(iii).

[44] *Id.*

other biological testing conducted by, or known to, the employer; or (4) has an MSDS available to the employer indicating that the material may pose a hazard to human health.[45]

These regulations give workers significant control over record access. It is important to note that *no limitation* is placed upon who may act as a designated employee representative.[46] A worker may designate someone in the union, a *nonemployee* safety and health activist, or a personal physician. The only requirement is that the worker must designate his or her representative in writing if other than the union.[47] Employees may limit access to their personal medical records; the regulations require that before anyone, even the union (there is an exception for OSHA), may have access to personal medical records, he or she must have the specific written consent of the worker.[48] This consent requirement applies only to the medical records, however, not to exposure records.[49] When a worker wants to give a member of his local Committee on Occupational Safety and Health (COSH) group's health/technical committee access to all records pertaining to himself or herself, all s/he need do is to write a note to the employer naming the organization as his or her designated representative and granting permission for it to examine his or her personal medical records. A form consent letter appears as Appendix A to the regulation. An additional clause should be inserted in that form designating the representative for access to exposure records.

The regulations make some concessions to the employer's need to protect trade secrets, but these concessions are conditional.[50] If trade secret deletions are made, the worker or designated representative must be notified. If the deletion impairs the worker's evaluation of the exposure involved, the employer must provide alternative information to permit the worker to determine where and when the exposure occurred. Even if trade secret deletions are made, the employer must disclose the identities of chemical or

---

45 29 CFR § 1910.20(c).

46 29 CFR § 1910.20(c)(3).

47 *Id.*

48 29 CFR § 1910.20(e)(2)(ii)(B).

49 *See* 29 CFR § 1910.20(e)(2)(i).

50 29 CFR § 1910.20(f). OSHA's general authority for maintaining the confidentiality of trade secrets is Section 15 of the OSH Act, 29 U.S.C. § 664.

physical agents, including chemical names, levels of exposure, and employee health status data contained in the records requested.[51] Nevertheless, before granting access, the employer may require a written agreement not to disclose the trade secret to a competitor.[52]

OSHA has a second minor access regulation covering the log of "recordable" injuries and illness.[53] While there are reasons to doubt the reliability and validity of such logs,[54] they should nevertheless be periodically reviewed as a means of identifying job hazards. Before reviewing the log, you should prime yourself by quickly checking the pertinent OSHA regulations, paying particular attention to the requirements for coding injuries.[55] OSHA also requires that supplementary records be kept for each "recordable" case.[56] Although these records are an excellent source of facts, OSHA does not require employers to grant workers or their unions access.[57]

[3] The Freedom of Information Act

If the company has ever been inspected by OSHA, there may be some information in the OSHA compliance file useful for problem identification or control. Results of workplace sampling will be in the file, as will the company's plans for correction of major problems. Official citation forms list the corrections the company is supposed to have made. This checklist is useful in determining whether the employer has failed to correct hazards or has repeated violations. This is especially important, given the

---

[51] 29 CFR § 1910.20(f)(2).

[52] 29 CFR § 1910.20(f)(3).

[53] 29 CFR § 1904.2. "Recordable" injuries include all deaths and lost worktime cases, as well as injuries resulting in a transfer to different duties, termination of employment, more medical treatment in excess of first aid, loss of consciousness, restriction of work, or restriction of motion, 29 CFR § 1904.12(c). Access is granted by Section 1904.7, as amended July 21, 1978.

[54] The log underreports injuries, and significantly underreports illnesses. Ashford, *Crisis in the Workplace* (1976), at 92.

[55] 29 CFR § 1904.12.

[56] 29 CFR § 1904.4.

[57] *Compare* 29 CFR § 1904.7(a) *with* 29 CFR § 1904.7(b)(1).

new OSHA policy of not routinely doing follow-up inspections. A careful file review often indicates that OSHA failed to conduct an adequate inspection, a fact that can lead to a demand for either a reinspection or action by the company irrespective of the OSHA result.

The FOIA grants workers the right to inspect and/or copy the pertinent records.[58] Contact the OSHA area office in custody of the files and request copies. Ask for a waiver of the copying fees by explaining how the waiver will serve the public interest,[59] i.e., how it may help improve worker safety and health. Public interest organizations, such as unions and COSH groups, are supposed to have an easier time getting a fee waiver than individuals do. OSHA is liberal about fee waivers, partly because of the public policy of encouraging workers to work with OSHA in obtaining enforcement and partly because it has to make copies anyway since confidential material must be "sanitized" before the worker sees it.[60] If an area director fails to grant a fee waiver, appeal to the assistant regional administrator. Reasonableness in tailoring a request is a factor considered in granting fee waivers. In making the request, you may be unaware of the size of the files involved; therefore, be prepared to negotiate with the OSHA area director.

[4] Discovery

Workers' representatives have certain discovery rights during litigation (see Appendix 5A near the end of this chapter). Workers' representatives who have elected party status[61] in an employer's contest of an OSHA citation or contested the reasonableness

[58] 5 U.S.C. § 552. OSHA's FOIA Regulations—29 CFR § 70; OSHRevCom's FOIA Regulations—29 CFR § 2300.

[59] 5 U.S.C. § 552(a)(4)(A); 29 CFR § 70.65, .67; *See generally* Department of Justice, Office of Information Law and Policy, *Interim Fee Waiver Policy* (December 18, 1980).

[60] OSHA protects workers who make statements to it, even from fellow workers, under its "informant's privilege" (5 U.S.C. § 552(b)(7)(D); T.V. Tower, Inc., v. Marshall, 444 F. Supp. 1233 (D.D.C. 1978). OSHA will also hold back trade secrets and interagency memoranda (5 U.S.C. § 552(b)(4); *see also* 29 U.S.C. § 664; 29 CFR § 1903.9; 5 U.S.C. § 552(b)(5)).

[61] 29 CFR § 2200.20.

of the abatement date in an OSHA citation[62] have the right to discovery of the employer's case, as well as OSHA's, prior to the hearing. The scope of discovery before the OSHRevCom is the same as under the Federal Rules of Civil Procedure,[63] i.e., the material sought to be discovered should lead to admissible evidence.[64] While depositions and interrogatories require an OSHRevCom judge's approval,[65] requests for production of documents, inspections of premises,[66] or admissions to premises are freely allowed.[67] If there are any questions about how to make these requests, ask the judge or the OSHA lawyer for help. The most useful of these tools is the right to access to OSHA's files and the employer's records, with no charge for copies, including any records pertaining to a working condition that has been cited. If a penalty has been proposed by OSHA, the employer's good faith in complying with the OSH Act is an issue,[68] making records dealing with the employer's safety program subject to discovery. In addition, discovery is available in any other litigation over job hazards, whether brought under Section 301 of the Labor-Management Relations Act (LMRA) to enforce the labor contract or under the state common-law duty of employers to provide safe workplaces.[69]

[5] Choosing Your Approach

A worker in an organized shop with a strong union is in the enviable position of choosing remedies. Make Section 8(a)(5) requests of compliant companies, since that section has the broadest scope. If the company is not compliant with federal

---

62 29 CFR § 2200.35.

63 29 CFR § 2200.2(b).

64 Fed. R. Civ. P. 26.

65 29 CFR § 2200.53(a).

66 Because the OSHRevCom has no procedural rules governing requests for the production of documents or inspection of premises, F.R.C.P. 34 applies, 29 CFR § 2200.2(b).

67 The OSHRevCom shortens the time for answering requests for admissions to 15 days, 29 CFR § 2200.52(a).

68 Section 17(j), 29 U.S.C. § 666(j).

69 *See* Section 5.03 *infra.*

labor laws, then the OSHA access regulation can be used with a "willfulized" OSHA complaint[70] to increase the potential penalties. The problem is in getting quick action. The employer can delay compliance by contesting the OSHA citation;[71] this is even more likely if the OSHA complaint has been "willfulized". So if the employer is reluctant and time is of the essence, it may be advisable to file a Section 8(a)(5) unfair labor practice charge with the NLRB, hoping for settlement by the company before the thirty-day time limit for issuing the complaint has expired. At the time of this writing, the NLRB and OSHA do not have a memorandum of understanding concerning dual processing of right to know claims; presumably, you can dual-file and get action from both agencies.

If a contract clause expressly deals with the right to know issue, the NLRB may require exhaustion of the grievance/arbitration mechanisms.[72] This may be the simplest and most direct method of gaining access to the employer's data, especially if there is contract language expediting health and safety cases. A hitch is that the union must process the grievance and pay for the arbitration.

If the worker is in an unorganized workplace, OSHA is the only recourse. Luckily, the OSHA access regulations are relatively easy for OSHA to enforce. Read Sections 5.02 and 5.03 for tips on how to minimize delay. Remember that OSHA's files on the employer may contain useful background information; these files can be reviewed without revealing the worker's identity to the employer.

[6] Areas to Watch on the Right to Know

As far as Section 8(a)(5) is concerned, follow (1) the *Colgate* triplet of cases,[73] which the NLRB will use to outline its approach

---

[70] *Id.*

[71] *Id.*

[72] Collyer Insulated Wire, 192 NLRB 837 (1971); Gen. Am. Transportation Corp., 228 NLRB 102 (1977).

[73] *See* note 18 *supra.*

to trade secrets problems; (2) the post–*Detroit Edison*[74] cases, which will determine the limits of the workers' confidentiality exceptions; and (3) the cases on the union's right to have its own experts inspect working conditions.[75]

The proposal for a labeling standard for hazardous substances made in the last days of the Carter Administration[76] was pulled in February 1981 without public comment.

The progress of state legislation on the right to know is another interesting area to watch. California, New York, Maine, Michigan, Connecticut, and the city of Philadelphia have already passed a variety of statutes concerning this issue. The California law[77] requires manufacturers and users of hazardous substances to create and distribute MSDSs; it gives a state board discretion to define what is hazardous, and requires it to keep the MSDSs on file and to enforce compliance. The New York law[78] has a very broad statutory definition of hazardous substances; it requires employers to keep MSDSs and to maintain files on hazardous substances used. The law permits workers to refuse to work with substances if the employer fails to comply with information requests within seventy-two hours, but it has a trade secrets section of uncertain scope. The other statutes are narrower, some limiting their scope to the narrow list of substances controlled by OSHA and some having enforcement provisions of dubious value. These statutes serve mainly to cover all employers and to impose a duty on them to obtain adequately completed MSDSs for distribution, which they need not do now to comply with either Section 8(a)(5) or the OSHA access regulations.

[7] Health Hazard Evaluations by NIOSH

The workers have a right to request a Health Hazard Evalua-

---

[74] *See* note 22 *supra.*

[75] *See* note 28 *supra.*

[76] Daily Labor Report, January 14, 1981, at A-13.

[77] California Labor Code, Division 5, Part 1, Chapter 2.5, "Hazardous Substances Information and Training," (as amended, September 10, 1980).

[78] New York Statutes: Section 876 of the Labor Law; Section 4802 of the Public Health Law.

tion (HHE) by NIOSH. This is an important way for workers to get free medical and scientific assistance in identifying potential health hazards.

Because NIOSH has broad discretion to refuse requests on the ground that the complaint is not serious enough to deserve evaluation, workers should pay particular attention to preparing their HHE request. The three most important things to do are the following: (1) Obtain professional support during preparation of the request; (2) thoroughly research available data, such as employer records available under the OSHA access regulation and OSHA compliance files available at the OSHA area office, and use the data to justify the request; and (3) keep in close communication with the appropriate NIOSH officials before, during, and after you make your application. Expect NIOSH to take six to twelve months to complete the HHE after it indicates it will act on the request; be careful not to dissipate your organizational strength by playing the "waiting for NIOSH" game.

NIOSH has standard forms for making HHE requests.[79] Employees can ask to remain anonymous.[80] The NIOSH definition of an authorized employee representative requesting an HHE is much narrower than that used by OSHA for its complaints. NIOSH requires that employee requests come from an authorized union representative or officer, from an affected employee who is authorized in writing by at least two other employees affected by the potential hazard,[81] or from an employee who states that he or she is one of three or fewer employees employed in the workplace where the substance is normally found. This three-affected-employees standard drastically limits the program's use in nonunion shops. NIOSH seems to be willing to relax this rigid standard, however, where the hazard appears to be serious. NIOSH regulations require that the request be in writing and signed, and that it state the following: the requester's name, address, and telephone number; the employer's address; the spe-

---

[79] Write or call the regional NIOSH representative in the Department of Health and Human Services, or write the Hazard Evaluation Services Branch, NIOSH, Cincinnati, Ohio 45202.

[80] 42 CFR § 85.3(b)(5).

[81] These authorizations from fellow employees must be included in the request.

cific workplaces involved; the specific process that introduces or is the source of the substance in question; and, with "reasonable particularity," the grounds upon which the request is made.[82] Requesters must identify, if they are known, the potentially toxic substances involved, including the forms of the substances, their trade names and chemical names, and their manufacturer(s). The contents of any warning labels on the containers of the substance(s) must be quoted, and a description must be given of the respective exposures of the employees involved, including a list of their individual occupations.[83] The request should be filed with the Health Hazard Evaluation Services Branch.[84] If there is no reasonable cause to conclude that an investigation is warranted, the requestor shall be so notified in writing.

§ 5.02. Controlling Job Hazards Through OSHA

An overview of the OSH Act enforcement procedure and the proof of an OSHA case follow for those wholly unfamiliar with the statutory scheme.[85] Passed in 1970,[86] the OSH Act focuses on

---

[82] 42 CFR § 85.3(b)(2)–(b)(3).

[83] 42 CFR § 85.3(c).

[84] *See* note 79 *supra.*

[85] The following resources are essential for workers who want to control job hazards by using OSHA: Obtain a copy of the OSHA standards and regulations. The standards are the safety and health rules employers must follow; the regulations generally pertain to the administration of OSHA. These are available in the last two volumes of Title 29 of the Code of Federal Regulations; Part 1900 to Part 1919; and Part 1920 to End. Portions of the standards are available separately: Part 1910—General Industry Standards is also called the "White Book" and Part 1926—Construction Safety Standards is also separately available. You may get these free from the local OSHA office.

Next, get a copy of the OSHA *Field Operations Manual* (OSHA FOM) and the separate *Industrial Hygiene Manual* (OSHA IHM). These are rule books that OSHA put out for its own inspectors. They are indispensable for making sure the inspector is doing his job. They are available from the Government Printing Office.

[86] 29 U.S.C. § 651 *et seq.*

"prevention,"[87] with suprise inspections[88] and the potential award of penalties[89] as aids to enforcement. Employers must now comply with established OSH Act standards as well as maintaining a workplace free from "recognized" serious injury hazards.[90] OSHA was created as the safety police agency with the power to issue standards,[91] to cite employers for noncompliance,[92] and to propose penalties[93] for violations, even on the first inspection. The OSHRevCom was created to be the safety judiciary, hearing contests of OSHA citations.[94] This independent agency issues abatement orders, requiring employers to correct unsafe working conditions, and imposes penalties.[95] Workers cannot be cited or penalized by the OSHRevCom. Remedies exist whether or not an employee has already been injured or killed as a result of a hazard.

Enforcement cases are processed in the following sequence. First, OSHA conducts an inspection,[96] occasionally compelling production of evidence by subpoena.[97] When OSHA believes a violation exists, it issues a citation to the employer fixing a reasonable time for correction and proposing a penalty.[98] The penalties range up to $10,000 per violation, depending upon the gravity of the violation, the size of the business, the good faith shown by the employer, the history of prior violations,[99] and whether the violation is serious, willful, or repeated.[100] Additional penalties exist for employers who fail to correct a cited violation; they

[87] Nat'l Realty & Constr. Co. v. OSHRevCom, 489 F.2d 1257, 1265–66 (D.C. Cir. 1973).

[88] Sections 2(b)(10) & 17(f), 29 U.S.C. §§ 651(b)(10), 666(f).

[89] Sections 10(a) & 17, 29 U.S.C. §§ 659(a), 666.

[90] Section 5(a), 29 U.S.C. § 654(a).

[91] Section 6, 29 U.S.C. § 655.

[92] Section 9, 29 U.S.C. § 658.

[93] Sections 10 & 17, 29 U.S.C. §§ 659, 666.

[94] Section 12, 29 U.S.C. § 661.

[95] Sections 9 & 10, 29 U.S.C. §§ 658, 659.

[96] Section 8(a), 29 U.S.C. § 657(a); Section 8(f)(1), 29 U.S.C. § 657(f)(1).

[97] Section 8(b), 29 U.S.C. § 657(b).

[98] Sections 9(a) & 10(a), 29 U.S.C. §§ 658(a), 659(a).

[99] Section 17(j), 29 U.S.C. § 666(j).

[100] Section 17(a), 29 U.S.C. § 666(a).

can be fined up to $1000 a day for each uncorrected hazard.[101] Citations automatically become final orders if not contested within fifteen working days.[102] An employer's contest automatically removes its obligation to correct the violation until the hearing process is over.[103] A hearing is held before an Administrative Law Judge (ALJ) of the OSHRevCom.[104] OSHA has the burden of proving the elements of the violation,[105] the reasonableness of the time allowed for correction, and the appropriateness of the proposed penalty.[106] The ALJ can affirm, modify, or vacate OSHA's proposals. The ALJ's order becomes final within thirty days, unless it is reviewed by the three-member OSHRevCom.[107]

To fully appreciate how to make the most of the investigation and citation process, it is necessary to have a clear sense of the burden of proof in OSHRevCom cases. Remember that the employer can violate the OSHA standards *or* the general duty clause.[108]

There are two general types of standards. First are those that clearly specify the means the employer must use to correct the job hazard. For instance, all punch presses must have devices installed that prevent workers from having any part of their bodies exposed to the danger zone during the operating cycle. If an employer has failed to install such a device on its punch press, OSHA must prove (in addition to certain preliminary matters[109]) (1) that a safety standard does in fact apply to that particular machine, by specifically citing the applicable standard, i.e., that the employer was under a "duty"; (2) that the employer failed in fact to have the device in place, i.e., that the employer "breached" its duty; and (3) that some employee was exposed or had access to the violative condition that constituted the breach,

---

[101] Section 17(d), 29 U.S.C. § 666(d).

[102] Section 10(a), 29 U.S.C. § 659(b).

[103] *See* Section 10(b), 29 U.S.C. § 659(b).

[104] Section 12(j), 29 U.S.C. § 661(j).

[105] 29 CFR § 2200.73(b).

[106] Section 10(c), 29 U.S.C. § 659(c).

[107] *Id.*

[108] Section 5(a), 29 U.S.C. § 654(a).

[109] I.e., proof that the respondent is an "employer," and that it "affects commerce," Section 3(5), 29 U.S.C. § 652(5).

i.e., that there was "exposure" to the violation. The last element rules out citations where the employer stopped using the machine, or where the breach of the duty did not otherwise affect workers.[110] While the OSHRevCom rules impose the burden of proof on OSHA,[111] the fact that the violation creates a hazard is presumed. In the machine-guarding example mentioned above, OSHA and the worker representatives do not have to show how the lack of machine guards could cause harm. While this may seem trivial, it is important in toxic substance cases, since it eliminates the necessity of paying for an expert to testify that exposure to concentrations of the toxic substance in violation of the OSHA standard is hazardous to health; simply show the breach of the standard and a worker exposure to the toxic substance.

The second type of standards are those without specific requirements. For example, the personal protective equipment standard requires employers to provide equipment, such as face shields, "wherever it is necessary by reason of hazards of processes . . . encountered in a manner capable of causing injury . . . ."[112] Here the burden of proof is higher. For OSHA to show that the employer had a duty, it must now show that a hazard existed, i.e., "by reason of hazards . . . encountered," and that the employer knew, or should have known of them. The various ways of demonstrating the existence of a hazard are discussed in Section 5.03. Once the duty is established, OSHA must show the breach of the duty and worker exposure. Some circuits also require OSHA to prove that a particular means of complying was technologically feasible.[113]

If there is no applicable standard, OSHA may cite under the general duty clause. Here, however, OSHA will have more difficulty in establishing the employer's duty. OSHA must show that there was a "recognized," "preventable" hazard. A "recognized"

---

[110] A *de minimis* notice can be issued, but it does not require correction, Section 9(a), 29 U.S.C. § 658(a).

[111] 29 CFR § 2200.73.

[112] 29 CFR. § 1910.132(a).

[113] The OSHRevCom's approach, in which the employer must prove infeasibility, was adopted in S&H Riggers & Erectors, Inc., 7 OSHC 1260, OSHD ¶23,480. *Contra,* Diebold, Inc., v. Marshall, 585 F.2d 1327, 1333 (6th Cir. 1978).

hazard is one that should have been obvious, or known to exist by the employer, or known to exist by safety experts familiar with the general type of working condition. A "preventable" hazard exists where there is a technologically feasible means of freeing the workplace of the hazard. Besides recognition and preventability, OSHA must prove the hazard's potential for death or serious physical injury and that a worker was or could have been exposed. To participate effectively in OSH Act enforcement, workers must understand these essential elements of the burden of proof.

[1] Filing OSHA Complaints

The OSH Act grants workers the right to trigger an OSHA inspection merely by filing a complaint.[114] The worker filing the OSHA complaint has the right to remain anonymous.[115] There is no requirement to exhaust contract remedies first. OSHA is accountable to people filing OSHA complaints and must notify them of the reasons for any OSHA action.[116]

Workers should file "formal" complaints. Under OSHA's recently revised system of screening complaints and setting inspection priorities,[117] OSHA will investigate *all* complaints that are "formal," i.e., written, signed, and reasonably specific. Be specific about the likelihood of harm; inspection priorities are determined by OSHA's perception of the seriousness of the complaint. If an imminent danger is alleged, such as a trench in soft soil with no shoring or exposure to a carcinogen, an inspection "*shall* be investigated the same day received where possible, but not later than 24 hours after receipt of the complaint."[118] If a serious hazard is alleged, such as exposure to nonlethal levels of a toxic substance, the complaint should be investigated within three working days; those involving other conditions should be investigated within

---

[114] Section 8(f)(1), 29 U.S.C. § 657(f)(1).

[115] *Id.*

[116] Section 8(f)(2), 29 U.S.C. § 657(f)(2); 29 CFR. § 1903.12, .14(d).

[117] OSHA Instruction CPL 2.12A (September 1, 1979).

[118] CPL 2.12A - H.1.a.

twenty working days.[119] Only in "exceptional circumstances" will a "formal" complaint not result in an inspection.[120]

OSHA recognizes the potential validity of "nonformal" complaints, such as those filed by nonemployees, public interest groups, or employees fearful of giving their names even with a promise of anonymity. The complaint-screening process grades their seriousness; less serious "nonformal" complaints will not result in an inspection. Evaluations are done by an OSHA supervisor to determine the nature and severity of the alleged hazard, the number of employees potentially involved, and any injuries, illnesses, or symptoms attributable to the hazard.[121] A nonformal complaint leads to an inspection only if it involves an imminent danger, an extremely serious working condition, or some other special circumstance. When one of these exists, the complaint shall be evaluated and scheduled for an inspection within twenty-four hours. Otherwise, the OSHA area office will not inspect, but will write two letters: (1) one to the employer to advise him of the complaint and the action required and (2) one to the complainant to explain the letter to the employer and to request that the complainant notify the OSHA area director if the employer takes no action within thirty days or retaliates against the complainant. If the employer fails to correct a hazard after such notification, he may be cited for a willful violation and be subjected to substantially increased penalties.[122] OSHA expects that the possibility of willful citations will deter employers from ignoring nonformal complaint advice letters. Workers can avoid this latter procedure by filing formal complaints.

The form for filing an OSHA complaint may be obtained in person from the area or regional office or by letter. The complaint form used by OSHA (OSHA Form 7; see Appendix 5C near the end of this chapter) asks for identification of the employer, the workplace where the hazard exists, and the complainant and for a statement of facts constituting the alleged hazard. At the minimum, OSHA requires that the complaint allege a violation of the OSH Act in the workplace; in other words, the complaint should

[119] CPL 2.12A - H.1.b.
[120] CPL 2.12A - H.2.
[121] CPL 2.12A - G.
[122] CPL 2.12A - I.2.

not only pinpoint a hazard but should include a good faith allegation that the complainant believes the hazard amounts to a violation of the Act. As a practical matter, however, the complainant's primary focus should be on describing the hazard, not the possible applicable standards; the latter is one of OSHA's jobs. Every hazard of concern should be identified, its location should be specified, and the exposed workers should be identified so the OSHA inspector knows with whom to communicate.

The following kinds of supplemental information can also be included. If exposure to toxic substances is alleged, the complaint should include the trade name, the chemical name, the physical form, the manufacturer, the content of the warning label, the duration and manner of exposure, and the number of employees exposed. If the complainant has reason to believe that a general duty clause violation exists, include information indicating employer recognition of the hazard. This can take the form of a recitation of near-misses or accidents involving the hazard, any other history of employer knowledge of the problem, copies of workers' compensation awards indicating a hazard, any safety policy or manual that deals with the hazards, or any consensus safety standard that deals with the hazard (such as an American National Standards Institute (ANSI) standard). If possible, also indicate what practical steps the employer could have taken to correct the problem. If it is believed that the employer deserves no good faith credit, which might reduce the penalty, explain why. If the employer has had actual knowledge of the violation, yet has failed to correct it, explain this in detail; it can result in OSHA's issuing a "willful" citation, with a concurrent increase in penalties.

OSHA is generous in defining "employees or representatives of employees."[123] Any present employee is included, even if not exposed to the hazard alleged in the complaint. A former employee is permitted to file in the event he/she had to leave the job because of hazards. An employee of another employer may file if he/she is somehow exposed; this includes a construction worker exposed to industrial hazards while performing factory repairs under a construction contract. Also included in this category are: union business agents, international representatives,

[123] OSHA FOM, VI.C.

attorneys representing workers or their union and family members. Finally, OSHA has a catchall clause stating that any other representative, such as a COSH group, "shall be presumed to have authority to be the representative."

As mentioned above, the OSH Act guarantees workers the right to file a formal complaint and yet remain anonymous.[124] This right carries over into other stages of the proceedings as well. During inspections, the OSH Act guarantees workers the right to privacy when talking to the inspector. In OSHRevCom adjudications, case law holds that the "informant's privilege allows OSHA to withhold the names of employees interviewed by OSHA."[125] When the worker testifies at trial, anonymity is finally breached. OSHA will not disclose worker witness identities under the FOIA.[126] *While anonymity is a protection against employer retaliation, it can work at cross-purposes.* The employer may identify the complainant anyway and retaliate. Under either Section 11(c) of the OSH Act or Section 8(a)(1) of the NLRA, "employer knowledge" is a necessary element of proof. If the employer did not know who filed the OSHA complaint, how could he have retaliated against him/her? Thus, insisting on anonymity decreases or nullifies a complainant's legal protection against discrimination; being notorious in filing an OSHA complaint creates excellent evidence of "employer knowledge" of the worker's engaging in the protected activity.[127]

The OSH Act has a policy of surprise inspections,[128] but that policy has been significantly undercut. While most inspections

---

124 Section 8(f)(1), 29 USC. § 657(f)(1).

125 Stephenson Enterprises, Inc., v. Secretary and OSHRevCom, 578 F.2d 1021, 6 OSHC 1860, OSHD ¶22,964 (5th Cir. 1978); Quality Stamping Prods. Co., 7 OSHC 1285, OSHD ¶23,520 (RevCom 1979) (name and relationship to respondent of informant held privileged); Massman-Johnson (Luling), OSHD ¶23,520 (RevCom 1980) (need to cross-examine witness does not require disclosure of prior statements until after direct examination is complete; informant's privilege is not waived by submission of witness list and summary of proposed testimony).

126 OSHA's invocation of exception 7(d) to the FOIA was upheld in T.V. Tower, Inc., v. Marshall, 444 F. Supp. 1233 (D.D.C. 1978).

127 *See generally* Section 5.03, *infra*.

128 Section 17(f), 29 U.S.C. § 666(f) allows fines of up to $1000 and/or six months in jail for those who give unauthorized advance notice of OSHA inspections.

still surprise the employer, workers who believe that a surprise inspection is necessary now have a difficult time making sure that the employer is caught unawares. The two problems are (1) the Supreme Court inspection warrant case[129] and (2) the OSHA

---

[129] Marshall v. Barlow's, Inc., 436 U.S. 307 (1978). First the court pointed to the inspection regulation itself, which relied on civil court procedures, i.e., orders backed up by contempt proceedings to compel entry, instead of citing and fining employers for refusing entry or seeking the assistance of U.S. marshalls to compel entry. Then, without considering the surprise inspection policy in depth, the court commented, "[I]ndeed, the kind of process . . . apparently anticipated by the regulation provides notice to the business operator. If this safeguard endangers the efficient administration of OSHA, the Secretary should never have adopted it particularly when the act does not require it," 436 U.S. at 318–19.

The case spawned a remarkable amount of litigation—more than 150 reported cases by one recent count. The dust has settled on the following propositions. The probable cause standard for OSHA inspection warrants is quite relaxed, requiring (1) specific evidence of a violation, Section 8(f)(1); or (2) evidence of a reasonable administrative plan which has targeted the particular workplace, Section 8(a). Barlow's, 436 U.S. at 320. The OSHRevCom will now review the sufficiency of warrants in the administrative proceedings, Chromalloy Am. Corp., 7 OSHC 1547 (RevCom 1979), *rev'g* Electrocast Steel Foundry, Inc., 6 OSHC 1562, OSHD ¶22,702 (RevCom 1978), following the First Circuit opinion in Quality Prods., 592 F.2d 611 (1st Cir. 1979); and the judiciary will require exhaustion of those remedies, Babcock & Wilcox Co., 610 F.2d 1128 (3d Cir. 1979); Quality Prods., *supra;* Cent. Mine Equip. Co., 608 F.2d 719 (8th Cir. 1979). *Contra,* Weyerhauser v. Marshall, 592 F.2d 373 (7th Cir. 1979). The exclusionary rule will clearly not be applied retroactively by the OSHRevCom, Todd Shipyards, *infra;* Savina Home, *infra;* Daniel Int'l. Corp., 8 OSHC 1142, 1147 (RevCom 1980); but whether it will be applied prospectively is open. *Compare* Todd Shipyards Corp. v. Marshall 586 F.2d 683, 689 (9th Cir. 1978), *with* Savina Home Indus. v. Marshall, 594 F.2d 1358, 1363 (10th Cir. 1979). OSHA has a new regulation, 29 CFR § 1903.4(d) (as amended, November 3, 1980), permitting ex parte warrant applications without advance notice. *Compare* Cerro Metal Prods. v. Marshall, 8 OSHC 1196 (3d Cir. 1980), *with* Marshall v. W & W Steel Co., 604 F.2d 1322, 1326 (10th Cir. 1970) and S.D. Warren, 481 F. Supp. 491 (D. Me. 1979). The scope of OSHA warrants issued pursuant to Section 8(a) will probably be restricted in scope "only by the limitations imposed on Congress and the reasonableness requirement of the Fourth Amendment." Gilbert and Bennett Mfg. & Chromalloy Am. Corp. v. Marshall, 589 F.2d 1335, 1343 (7th Cir. 1979) (a result in accordance with established administrative subpoena law). *See,* Oklahoma Press v. Walling, 327 U.S. 186, 201, 208–10, 215–16 (1946). Whether Section 8(f)(1) warrants will be limited to the scope of the issues in the complaint is not clear.

regulations on advance notice.[130] The warrant requirement allows an employer to refuse to allow OSHA to inspect until it has obtained an inspection warrant from a court, which gives the employer an average of three weeks to clean up its workplace before the OSHA inspection. While OSHA has authority to seek a warrant *before* being refused entry, it rarely does so. Worker requests for advance warrants are usually not honored. Exceptions to the surprise inspection policy are also permitted by OSHA regulations when they will "enhance the probability of an effective and thorough inspection," a matter left up to the discretion of the OSHA area director. This regulation is commonly applied to OSHA inspections of health hazards.

[2] Tactics for Effective OSHA Complaints

[a] "Willfulizing" OSHA Complaints

OSHA has penalties as high as $10,000 for "willful" violations. To show a willful violation you must demonstrate that the employer (1) knew about the OSHA violation and (2) failed to correct it.[131] "Willfulizing" an OSHA complaint is easy. First, warn the employer of the hazard and be specific when describing the hazard. If possible, show the employer how the hazard violates a particular OSHA standard. To be sure the message gets through, communicate this by letter, return receipt requested. If this is not practical, orally warn a management official in the presence of dependable witnesses and then take the witnesses' written statements for future use. When the employer fails to correct the problem within a reasonable period of time, file an OSHA complaint, attaching proof of your warning to show its "willful" refusal to correct the condition. If OSHA agrees that there was a hazard, then it must propose "willful" penalties. Do not "willfulize" a complaint if you are not prepared for a fight or if you have dubious job security and are not willing to trust the local NLRB office to protect you against retaliatory discipline.

---

130 29 CFR § 1903.6(a).

131 For a more detailed discussion of "willful," see generally text accompanying notes 192-197, *infra.*

[b] Coping with Intermittent Hazards, Near-Misses, and Employer Evasion of Surprise Inspections

The OSHA inspector does not have to witness a violation to recommend a citation; OSHA has six months to act.[132] If the employer has done nothing to deal with a near-miss or if there is an intermittent problem, workers can file an OSHA complaint, including witnesses' statements and other information supporting an OSHA citation, and request an investigation of the incident. An employer who tries to escape OSHA liability by cleaning up violations while OSHA is obtaining a warrant, can still be cited for violations that existed before the cleanup on the basis of workers' testimony. Furthermore, where workers have their own capability to monitor workplace exposures to hazardous substances, they can even overcome faulty OSHA health inspections through careful documentation.

[c] Getting Quick Action

If an imminent danger or a very serious hazard is shown, you can get your complaint investigated within a day or two. Of course, some other workplace will be investigated *after* yours as a result of your complaint priority.

The definition of an imminent danger is very broad. It includes *any danger that could cause serious physical harm before it can be eliminated through the OSH Act's enforcement procedures.*[133] Since it can take up to three years for an employer contest to be defeated in the courts, and since the employer does not have to correct conditions being contested, the definition of "imminent" is very broad. The test of an imminent danger is the likelihood of something happening, not the gravity of the potential harm.[134] For exposures to toxic materials, OSHA makes "irreversible harm" the touchstone, "even though the resulting irreversible harm may not manifest

132 Section 10, 29 U.S.C. § 659.

133 Section 13(a) 29 U.S.C. § 662(a).

134 OSHA FOM, IX.A.

itself immediately."[135] *Any exposure to a carcinogen should be considered an imminent danger.* Imminent danger complaints can be filed by telegram provided that the telegram contains the elements of a formal complaint and is specific about describing the hazard and its imminence. Follow up, however, with a *signed* copy to satisfy all the elements of formality.

Even if a hazard is not likely to be imminent and thus be entitled to inspection within twenty-four hours, if a complaint documents conditions that affect large numbers of workers or could result in grave injuries, it will be given relatively higher inspection priority, even if the likelihood of injury is remote.[136]

In summary, always file a formal complaint as described above; this practically guarantees you an inspection and it makes OSHA accountable to you for its results. To make sure you are high on the list of inspection priorities, carefully describe the seriousness of the problem and the extent of worker exposure; use imminent danger allegations freely, but within the limits of common sense. If the employer deserves punishment by penalties, "willfulize" the complaint, but take care to avoid employer reprisals.

[3] Making the Most of OSHA Inspections

The OSH Act expressly encourages worker participation in inspections, for the obvious reason that "no one knows better than the working man what the conditions are, where the hazards are, where the failures are, and particularly, where there are safety hazards."[137] Section 8(e) grants workers their "walkaround" rights: A "representative authorized by his employees shall be given an opportunity to accompany [OSHA] during the physical inspection of any workplace . . . for the purpose of aiding such inspection."[138] OSHA regulations require employers to pay

---

[135] OSH FOM, IX.A.2.C.

[136] CPL 2.12A - 1.2.c.

[137] Remarks of Senator Williams concerning Section 8(e) at the time he introduced his bill onto the Senate Floor, *Legislative History of the Occupational Safety and Health Act of 1970,* Senate Committee on Labor and Public Welfare, 92nd Cong., 1st Sess., at 430. *See also* Legislative History, at 151.

[138] Section 8(e), 29 CFR § 657(e).

workers for time spent on the walkaround.[139]

Make the most of any OSHA inspection or possibly later have regrets. Get an effective sampling survey of a particular condition the first time around; otherwise, OSHA may not cite and a request for reinspection may be denied on the grounds that it duplicates the prior effort. By no means assume that the inspector can do the job alone. Lead the inspector to each hazard and explain it to him or her in detail. The best witnesses for the inspector to hear are those with personal knowledge of both the violation and the employer's knowledge of the hazard.

[a] Selecting the Workers' Representative

The first thing the inspector does when he or she arrives is to find the person in charge of the premises and to present his or her credentials. The inspector must obtain permission to inspect; otherwise, he or she must have an inspection warrant. Permission to enter must be unconditional; inspectors cannot make deals with the employer.[140]

Once admitted, the inspector must determine who will be in the inspection party. Management chooses its representatives. If the workers have a union, the inspector will ask it to name someone.[141] If there is no union, but there is a plant safety committee with employee members, they will be asked to designate a representative.[142] If there is neither a union nor a plant safety committee, the inspector will usually attempt to determine whether anyone else could suitably represent the workers' interest.[143] The standard for selection is whether the proposed walkaround representative appears loyal to his/her fellow workers and has the knowledge of the working conditions or expertise in safety and health matters to make a useful contribution to the inspection. If no employee representative can be identified, the inspector con-

---

[139] 29 CFR § 1903.8. (Effective February 17, 1981; however, the new administration has stayed implementation of this regulation.)

[140] 29 CFR § 1903.5.

[141] *See* 29 CFR § 1903.8(b); OSHA FOM, V.D.3.b.

[142] OSHA FOM, V.D.3.b.(2).

[143] OSHA FOM, V.D.3.b.(3).

sults "with a reasonable number of employees during the walk-around."[144] OSHA instructs inspectors that their "selection of random employees to interview should include the gang boss, supervisor, or other individual knowledgeable of the area or process being inspected."[145]

The employer has no legitimate input in the selection of the workers' walkaround representative. The regulations make it clear that the inspector controls who is in the walkaround party; he or she "shall have authority to resolve all disputes as to who is the representative authorized by the employer and employees for the purpose of the walkaround inspection."[146] The inspector can also "deny the right of accompaniment under the section to any person whose conduct interferes with a fair and orderly inspection."[147] If more than one union represents groups of employees at the worksite, a different employee representative may accompany the compliance officer during different phases of the inspection if it does not interfere with the inspection.[148] At construction worksites, where the walkaround party can become unwieldy in size, the inspector has three alternatives: attempt to have the participants thin their own ranks, divide the inspection into discrete phases, or discontinue the walkaround party and rely on interviews with a reasonable number of employees.[149]

A nonemployee may be a workers' walkaround representative. If good cause is shown why a nonemployee should be allowed to accompany the inspector on the physical inspection, the latter has the authority to permit the third party to accompany him/her.[150] The regulations mention two examples, an industrial hygienist and a safety engineer; other examples include an international or district safety representative and a COSH group health/technical committee person. The criterion for the inspector is whether the presence of the third party is reasonably necessary to an effective and thorough inspection of the workplace. Once again, the final

---

[144] Section 8(e), 29 U.S.C. § 657(c); 29 CFR § 1903.8(b).

[145] OSHA FOM, V.D.3.b.(3).

[146] 29 CFR § 1903.8(b).

[147] 29 CFR § 1903.8(d).

[148] 29 CFR § 1903.8(a); OSHA FOM, V.D.4.d.

[149] OSHA FOM, VII.F.4.

[150] 29 CFR § 1903.8(c).

decision rests with the inspector, not the employer.[151]

The worker who files the complaint may not necessarily have the right to accompany the inspector, especially if the union is interested in appointing the walkaround representative. But the complainant can request that the inspector include him or her, on the grounds that it is his/her complaint and s/he can best help the inspector understand the hazard. Again, the inspector has the final word. If there are any disputes, remember that OSHA gives workers the right to request an informal conference with the assistant regional administrator when necessary.[152] If the employer is illegitimately limiting the inspector, OSHA may obtain a warrant compelling the employer to accept the inspector's determination of how the inspection should be conducted.

[b] The Opening Conference

The inspector holds a brief opening conference with the inspection party[153] in an open place in view of the worksite, alert to any related attempts by the employer to correct violations. In cases of imminent danger, the inspector will get to the site of the alleged imminent danger as promptly as possible, leaving the niceties of the opening conference for the closing conference.[154] Otherwise, the opening conference is an opportunity for the inspector to explain the purpose and scope of the inspection,[155] to determine whether employees of outside employers are working at the site,[156] and to give the employer the opportunity to identify areas that contain trade secrets entitled to confidentiality.

The most important thing for the workers' representative to ask the inspector at the opening conference is "What is the scope of the inspection?" If it is to be a "wall-to-wall" inspection lasting several days, workers will have time fully to inform the inspector of their list of hazards. If, however, it is only a narrow

---

151 *Id.*

152 29 CFR § 1903.19.

153 OSHA FOM, V.D.2.

154 OSHA FOM, V.D.2.c.

155 OSHA FOM, V.D.2.a.&b.

156 OSHA FOM, V.D.2.g.

inspection, such as one dealing with conditions alleged in a complaint, the workers' representative must get help and move quickly. In either case, the workers should give the inspector a written "notice of violation" covering each hazard they want inspected.[157] The notice should specifically identify the hazard, its location, and the extent of worker exposure and give name and home telephone numbers of workers with personal knowledge of the problem; it should be signed.[158] Keep copies of your notices of violations.

[c] The Walkaround

The inspector is required to record all pertinent facts concerning apparent violations on a compliance worksheet.[159] These include a detailed description of the hazardous condition, including measurements, instrument readings, and identification of photographs taken. S/he must also detail employee exposure to the hazard, including the number of employees exposed, the duration and extent of exposure, and the names and addresses of exposed employees. It must be verified by the employer. Finally, he must detail employer knowledge of the condition: Did the employer know of the hazard, or did the employer consciously disregard knowledge that the hazard was a violation?

Once discussion is focused on a particular hazard, the workers' representative should make sure that the inspector hears all the reasons for the workers' belief that the condition is hazardous. The workers' representative should remind the inspector of his/her duty, when requested, to question *privately* any workers he or she interviews.[160] If reprisals are possible and *anonymity is the strategy,* the more workers he/she talks to in private, the harder it is for the employer to determine who has said what. Relevant infor-

---

157 Section 8(f)(2), 29 U.S.C. § 657(f)(2); 29 CFR § 1903.11.

158 29 CFR § 1903.11(c).

159 This form is called the OSHA-1B.

160 The OSHA FOM, V.D.a.5.c., requires that whenever an employee requests that an interview be held in private, the inspector should honor that request. In addition, even in the absence of such a request, the compliance officer should make an effort to conduct in-depth interviews with employees out of the view of employer representatives. Section 8(a)(2), 29 U.S.C. § 657(a)(2).

mation includes past incidents where workers became sick after exposure to a toxic substance, or a recital of accidents or near-misses with a particular piece of equipment. Employee testimony can also be excellent evidence of employer knowledge of the hazard, leading to increased penalties if the violation is willful or if the good faith of the employer is discredited. If properly included in the inspector's notes, workers' statements can be used as evidence at hearings even if the employee cannot appear to testify.[161] OSHA directs its inspectors to take written interview statements whenever a worker is willing to sign one, especially if some material facts are in controversy, if the alleged violations are willful or repeated, or if the violation occurred before the compliance officer arrived to inspect. The workers' representative should keep his own inspection log for use in preparing for a hearing, as well as for use at informal review conferences with OSHA.

[d] The Closing Conference

When the inspection is finished, the inspector must hold a closing conference with the employer, advising him/her of any apparent violation observed and explaining the citation, penalty, and abatement date procedure that may be followed. The inspector will also explain that the employer can request an informal conference and can contest any OSHA citation issued. Surprisingly, regulations do not require that the employee representative be present at this conference.[162] This has led to the obvious criticism that the closing conference is a one-sided affair favoring employers. An OSHA program directive compensates somewhat

[161] Rule 801(d)(2)(D) of the Federal Rules of Evidence, which is applicable in hearings before the OSHRevCom, 29 CFR § 2200.72, significantly liberalized the admissibility of vicarious admissions by employees. The old requirement that the statement must be authorized by the master was eliminated on the theory that requiring the admission to be made during the existence of the employment relationship would ensure trustworthiness to the fact finder, since the employee is still subject to the employer's control. Of course, if the statement is used at the hearing, the employee declarant must be identified if the admission is to have any weight.

[162] 29 CFR § 1903.7(e).

by directing the inspector to hold a separate closing conference with the workers' walkaround representative and to hold a joint labor-management closing conference wherever "practicable."[163]

[e] OSHA Accountability to Workers

Workers who have filed a formal complaint or a notification of a violation have the right (1) to a copy of any citation that issues as a result of the notification,[164] (2) to written notification of a determination not to issue a citation,[165] (3) to an informal review before the assistant regional administrator of an unfavorable determination by the area office, and (4) to written notification and explanation by the assistant regional administrator of a decision to uphold the area office, to order reinspection, or to issue a citation.[166]

[f] Checklist for OSHA Inspections

First, make sure the workers are well represented on the walkaround inspection. Next, determine the scope of the inspection and plan accordingly. Freely use notices of violations to focus the inspector's attention on each hazard on your hazards list and introduce the inspector to witnesses with personal knowledge of the problem. Finally, keep a careful inspection log.

[4] Limitations on Workers' Control over OSHA's Decision to Issue a Citation

While workers have the right to file a complaint to obtain an inspection and are encouraged to participate actively in the OSHA inspection, workers have little input into OSHA's deci-

---

163 OSHA PD #200-82 (August 15, 1978).
164 29 CFR § 1903.14(c).
165 29 CFR § 1903.14(d).
166 *Id.*

sion whether or not to issue a citation. Luckily for workers, OSHA's choice in the matter is limited by the OSH Act itself.

Citations are mandatory if OSHA has the evidence. The law requires that OSHA "shall" issue a citation if it "believes" there is a violation.[167] The legislative history makes it clear that this language is not accidental. Representative Steiger said he substituted the mandatory "shall" language to require "the Secretary to issue a citation *in every instance* where there is a violation of the act's requirements . . . ."[168] In conference, "belief" language was substituted for an earlier, stricter requirement that OSHA "determine" that a violation exists before citing.[169] If OSHA decides not to issue a citation, it must account to complaining workers for its reasons in writing.[170]

OSHA has an informal review procedure that workers can use to follow through on any disagreements they have with OSHA's conclusions. The assistant regional administrator decides the appeal after the workers and the company have exchanged position statements. He or she can hold a conference, if s/he chooses, before s/he "affirms, modifies, or reverses" the area director.[171] Supposedly, his/her decision is "final."[172]

If the area office fails to cite, workers should first find out why. A phone call or an informal discussion with area office officials may be sufficient. Carefully choose your approach. A diplomatic approach might involve the following. Approach the inspector's supervisor and discreetly suggest that the inspector just happened to be mistaken on this issue, but make it clear that you will take your "reasonable concern" to higher officials if the supervisor is not helpful. On the other hand, it may be tactically advantageous to bombard the area office with newspaper stories and congressional inquiries. The approach you take depends on the seriousness of the job hazard, your organizational strength, and the competence of the local OSHA officials. Workers may further request an informal conference with the assistant regional

---

167 Section 9(a), 29 U.S.C. § 658(a).

168 Legislative History, at 996 (emphasis added).

169 Legislative History, at 1191, 1202.

170 Section 8(f)(2), 29 U.S.C. § 657(f)(2).

171 29 CFR § 1903.12, .14(d).

172 29 CFR§ 1903.12(a).

administrator[173] without invoking the review process. While this may be an opportunity to find out OSHA's reasons for not citing, it may also harden its position before you have prepared your position statement for the informal review. The assistant regional administrator need not grant your request for an informal conference, but once s/he does, s/he is obligated to give the employer an opportunity to attend. Once it is known that OSHA failed to cite on the ground of insufficient reason, prepare a statement of position. In it, thoroughly marshal the facts concerning the hazard, including affidavits from employee witnesses and arguments concerning the applicability of the OSHA standards, or the OSHA general duty clause, to the particular hazard. Close with the statement that OSHA has a mandatory obligation to issue citations whenever it believes it has the facts. You may wish to send a carbon copy to your congressperson or to the labor liaison representative of the Assistant Secretary of Labor for Occupational Safety and Health in Washington, D.C.

The law is not settled on whether judicial review is available on OSHA's decision not to cite.[174] The following two paragraphs review the "pros and cons" of judicial review for lawyers considering this possibility. Workers' representatives can skip over them.

The OSH Act makes no provision for judicial review of negative citation decisions. It grants no review power to the OSHRevCom;[175] neither does it expressly grant review power to the U.S. district courts. Worker participation provided by the OSH Act, taken together with the well-established judicial presumption favoring review of an agency's action in the absence of an express congressional exclusion,[176] implies that OSHA is not insulated from judicial review. Section 8(f)(2) of the OSH Act, however, requires an informal review procedure without mentioning judicial review. Moreover, the Act's reference to the "finality" of the Secretary's position, although ambiguous, reinforces the implica-

---

173 29 CFR § 1903.19.

174 *Contra,* Marshall & IMC Chem. Group v. OSHRevCom, OSHD ¶24,990 (6th Cir. 1980).

175 *See* Sections 11 & 12, 29 U.S.C. §§ 660, 661.

176 *See, e.g.,* Abbott Laboratories v. Gardner, 387 U.S. 136, 140 (1967); Citizens to Preserve Overton Park v. Volpe, 401 U.S. 402, (1971).

tion that the decision is "committed to agency discretion by law."[177] This section also indirectly addresses the issues of scope of review and whether review rights should exist at all by requiring that OSHA issue a written statement of reasons justifying its final decision.[178] Notwithstanding these arguments, OSHA's duty to cite is clearly mandatory. Thus, once a "belief" that a violation exists is established, a failure to cite in that limited situation may be correctable through a mandamus-type action.[179]

Judicial review decisions often turn on an analysis of the institutional considerations apparently deliberated by Congress. Fruitful comparisons can be made here between the role of OSHA under the OSH Act and the roles of the General Counsel under the NLRA[180] and the Secretary of Labor under Title IV of the Labor-Management Reporting and Disclosure Act (LMRDA).[181] The OSH Act differs from these other labor laws in two significant respects, both of which indicate the lack of exclusiveness of OSHA decisions. First, the OSH Act clearly encourages decentralization of enforcement to the states through state plans and grants-in-aid.[182] Second, the OSH Act apparently sets only minimum safety and health standards,[183] i.e., there is no federal exclusion of more stringent standards set by the states.[184] These features show that OSHA does not occupy the central political position given to the General Counsel by the NLRA and to the Secretary of Labor by the LMRDA. It can therefore be argued that OSHA decisions not to cite should be fully reviewa-

[177] 5 U.S.C. § 701(a).

[178] *Cf.* Dunlop v. Backowski, 421 U.S. 560, 572–73 (1975).

[179] *Cf.* Leedom v. Kyne, 358 U.S.184(1958); Associated Builders&Contractors v. Irving, 610 F.2d 1221 (4th Cir. 1979), *cert. denied* (1980).

[180] Section 3(d), 29 U.S.C. § 153(d), Vaca v. Sipes, 386 U.S. 171, 183 (1967).

[181] 29 U.S.C. § 482; Calhoon v. Harvey, 379 U.S. 134, 140 (1964); Trbovich v. Mine Workers, 404 U.S. 528, 532 (1972).

[182] *See generally* Section 18, 29 U.S.C. § 667(b).

[183] Section 4(b)(4), 29 U.S.C. § 653(b)(4); Shimp v. N.J. Bell Tel., 145 N.J. Super. 516, 368 A.2d 408, 410–11 (Ch. D.1976).

[184] The primary concern of Section 18(c)(2), (4), (5) is that state plans be "at least as effective" as federal enforcement, 29 CFR §§ 1902, 1953; AFL-CIO v. Brennan, 390 F. Supp. 972 (D.D.C. 1975), *aff'd* 570 F.2d 1030 (D.C. Cir. 1978), *on remand,* 6 OSHC 2128, OSHD ¶23,117.

ble under the Administrative Procedures Act.[185]

[5] The Mechanics of OSHA Citations

OSHA citations contain "violations," which are usually grouped by the OSHA standard involved. Each violation may contain several "items," each item referring to a specific instance in which that OSHA standard was breached. The violations are usually numbered separately. Each violation contains three parts: (1) a specific reference to the OSHA standard or law violated, with a separate and specific description of the condition that has created the breach; (2) a date by which the employer must correct the condition;[186] and (3) a proposed penalty for the violation.[187] The OSHA citation form (see Appendix 5D near the end of this chapter) is perforated along the right edge to permit the proposed penalties to be torn off by the employer before posting.[188]

The proposed penalties depend on whether OSHA characterizes particular violations[189] as willful, repeated, serious, or nonserious.[190] A willful or repeated violation (there can be many violations in a citation) can be penalized up to $10,000; serious and nonserious ones can be penalized up to $1000 per violation. The employer's knowledge of the violation is particularly important in proving willful violations. OSHA's position is that the employer's knowledge is part of the OSHA burden of proof in willful violations only, and the lack of knowledge is a defense to a serious violation; otherwise, the employer's knowledge is irrelevant to penalty assessment.[191] OSHA defines "willful" as follows:

---

185 5 U.S.C. § 702.

186 Section 9(a), 29 U.S.C. § 658(a).

187 Section 10(a), 29 U.S.C. § 659(a).

188 *See* Sections 9(b) & 17(i), 29 U.S.C. §§ 658(b), 666(i); 29 CFR § 1903.2. *See* the OSHA citation form (Figure 3).

189 Section 17, 29 U.S.C. § 666. The OSHA FOM has two excellent chapters outlining the penalty system, Chapters VIII & XI.

190 There is no such thing as an "imminent danger" violation for purposes of penalties.

191 This is consistent with Cleary's dissent in D.R. Johnson Lumber Co., 3 OSHC 1124, OSHD ¶19,695 (RevCom 1975). The employer knowledge issue is confused in part because some employer knowledge issues arise in the context

> A 'willful' violation may exist under the Act where the evidence shows (1) that the employer committed an intentional and knowing, as contrasted with inadvertent, violation of the Act and the employer was conscious of the fact that what he was doing constitutes a violation of the Act, or (2) even though the employer was not consciously violating the Act, he was aware that a hazardous condition existed and made no reasonable effort to eliminate the condition. It is not necessary that the violation be committed with a bad purpose, or an evil intent, to be deemed 'willful' under the Act. It is sufficient that the act was deliberate, voluntary or intentional as distinguished from those which were inadvertent, accidental or ordinarily negligent.[192]

OSHA instructs its inspectors to look for evidence from workers that "an employer [was] advised by employees or employee representatives regarding an alleged hazardous condition and the employer [made] no reasonable effort to verify the condition."[193] OSHA also instructs that "before a violation can be classified as willful, the inspector must ascertain that the employer had specific knowledge of: the standard or its requirements, or of the particular hazardous working conditions to which the employee(s) were/are being exposed.[194]

The OSHRevCom has adopted both definitions.[195] The circuits

---

of penalty assessment, while other, equally important but analytically distinct, elements of employer knowledge arise as items of proof in general duty clause violations, i.e., "recognition," certain standards violations, (29 CFR § 1910.132(a)), or in particular affirmative defenses, such as the isolated employee misconduct defense. In Brennan v. OSHRevCom and Alsea Lumber, 511 F.2d 1139 (9th Cir. 1975), a case of intentional employee misconduct, the court confused these to reach the sweeping generalization that some element of employer knowledge must be proved in even a nonserious violation. This ignores the distinctions made by Section 17(c), (k) of the OSH Act. *See generally* Rothstein, *infra* note 210, at §§ 76–79.

[192] OSHA FOM, VIII.B.4.a.

[193] *Id.*

[194] OSHA FOM, XI.C.9.d.(1).

[195] Kent Nowlin Constr. Inc., 5 OSHC 1051, OSHD ¶21,550 (RevCom 1977); Nat'l Steel & Shipbldg. Co., 6 OSHC 1680, OSHD ¶22,808 (RevCom 1978), 607 F.2d 311 (9th Cir. 1979).

uniformly accept the first definition;[196] only the Third Circuit has rejected the second.[197]

A "serious" violation exists if there is a condition creating more than "a very remote possibility"[198] that a worker could be physically harmed. In health cases, OSHA often has difficulty proving seriousness.[199] "Repeated" violations are those that violated the same OSHA standard,[200] involved a "substantially similar" hazard,[201] and occurred in the same industrial complex.[202] Employer knowledge is irrelevant.[203]

---

196 F.X. Messina Constr. Co. v. OSHRev Com, 505 F.2d 701, 702 (1st Cir. 1974); Intercounty Constr. Co. v. OSHRevCom, 522 F.2d 777, 779–80 (4th Cir. 1975), *cert. denied,* 423 U.S. 1072 (1976); Ga. Elec. Co. v. Marshall, 595 F.2d 309, 318–19 (5th Cir. 1979); Empire Detroit Steel Div. v. OSHRevCom & Marshall, 579 F.2d 378, 384–85 (6th Cir. 1978); W. Waterproofing Co. v. Marshall, 576 F.2d 139, 143 (8th Cir. 1978), *cert. denied;* United States v. Dye Constr., 510 F.2d 78, 81 (10th Cir. 1975); Cedar Constr. Co. v. OSHRevCom, 587 F.2d 1303 (D.C. Cir. 1978). *Cf.* Coleman v. Jiffy-June Farms, 458 F.2d 1139, 1142 (5th Cir. 1972). *But see* Frank Irey, Jr., Inc., v. OSHRevCom, 519 F.2d 1200, 1206–07 (3d Cir. 1975), *aff'd on other grounds,* 430 U.S. 942 (1977) (the court added "deliberate flouting of the Act" to the elements of "willful").

197 Frank Irey, *supra* note 196. *Contra,* Intercounty, *supra* note 196; and Nat'l Steel, *supra* note 195. For an employer-oriented review of the cases, *see generally Annotation, What Constitutes "Willful" Violation for Purposes of §§ 17(a) and (e) of Occupational Safety and Health Act of 1970,* 31 ALR Fed 551 (1975).

198 Diamond Int'l Corp., 9 OSHC 1821, OSHD ¶19,333 (RevCom 1976); Shaw Constr., Inc., v. OSHRevCom, 534 F.2d 1183 (5th Cir. 1976).

199 Usery v. Hermitage Concrete Pipe Co., 584 F.2d 127, 132 (6th Cir. 1978).

200 George Hyman Constr. Co. v. OSHRevCom, 582 F.2d 831, 841 (9th Cir. 1978); Potlatch Corp., 7 OSHC 1061, OSHD ¶23,294 (RevCom 1979).

201 Potlatch, *supra* note 200, contains an excellent discussion of "substantial similarity."

202 Gen. Elec. Co., 3 OSHC 1031, OSHD ¶19,567 (RevCom 1975). This obviously limits the penalty exposure of large, multilocation employers. Commissioner Barnako's wish further to limit "repeats" to the same supervisor has been discredited, George Hyman, *supra* note 200, at 841 n. 41; Potlatch, *supra* note 200, at 1064. The OSHA FOM limits repeated citations against construction companies to citations in the same state, VIII.B. 5.e.

203 George Hyman, *supra* note 200, at 840; Todd Shipyards Corp. v. Secretary, 566 F.2d 1327, 1330–31 (9th Cir. 1977). *Contra,* Bethlehem Steel Corp., 540 F.2d 157, 162 (3d Cir. 1976). Of course, the employer must have received actual notice of the prior violation, George Hyman, *supra* note 200, at 841.

[6] Additional Penalties for Failures To Correct

The OSH Act's heaviest penalties are assessed on employers who fail to correct conditions cited: $1000 *per day per violation* is the upper limit.[204] Workers should consider using this section when the employer fails to comply with an OSHA citation. All the worker needs to do is to file a complaint. The complaint should—

(1) refer to the specific violation of the citation, indicating the correction date;
(2) include allegations or, better yet, witness statements that after the correction date the condition was still uncorrected; and
(3) include allegations or statements that after the correction date workers remained exposed to the violation.

This tactic can also be used by workers to control an employer who has filed a spurious contest solely to circumvent the abatement date. Note a critical feature of an employer contest of a citation: The contest stays correction of the problem until there is a final order of the OSHRevCom on the merits of the contest. Some unscrupulous employers have been caught buying time by filing phony contests. For instance, a construction contractor may be cited for allowing its workers to work in unshored trenches where they are exposed to cave-ins. The contractor may file a contest, thereby staying abatement. When the job is complete, it can then pay the penalty and withdraw the contest. If workers called in OSHA as soon as the proposed, but contested, abatement date elapsed, OSHA could issue a "failure to correct notice." Although the rules require that OSHA have a "final order" before issuing such a notice, the OSH Act contains another rule:

> [T]he period permitted for its correction . . . shall not begin to run until the entry of a final order by the Commission *in the case of any review proceedings under this section initiated by the employer in good faith and not solely for delay or avoidance of penalties* . . . . (emphasis added)[205]

[204] 29 U.S.C. §§ 659(b), 666(d).

[205] Sections 10(b) & 17(d); 29 U.S.C. §§ 659(b), 666(d). *But cf.* Potlach, *supra* note 200, at 1064.

Employee testimony on the good faith of the employer will obviously be crucial. There are no cases yet reporting the use of this tactic.

"Failure to correct" notices follow the procedure for citations and proposed penalties, but the title changes from "citation" to "notification of failure to correct violative condition," and the "proposed penalty" becomes the "proposed assessment of additional penalty." If the issue goes to a hearing, OSHA must prove that (1) the initial citation became a "final order"; (2) the condition on reinspection was the same as that described in the first citation; and (3) the condition on reinspection is in violation of the Act.[206] The OSHRevCom has allowed the following defenses: a challenge to the validity of the underlying citation if it became a final order by law, but not after a hearing;[207] a challenge to the specificity of the underlying citation, i.e., an allegation that the employer did not have adequate notice of his obligation;[208] and, finally, evidence that the condition was in fact corrected.

Workers should understand the attitudes of the OSHA personnel who enforce the penalty policies. Many OSHA compliance personnel separate the issues of control of a hazard from that of punishing employers. Control of hazards, or abatement, is their top priority; penalties are clearly secondary. Many settlements are made in which the employer promises to correct the hazard and OSHA reduces the proposed penalty. OSHA routinely reduces the penalty to as little as 50 percent of that initially proposed. The OSHRevCom ALJs generally reduce penalties even further. Commissioner Cottine, however, recently criticized his fellow commissioners for giving short shrift to the penalty policy of the OSH Act.[209]

---

[206] Kit Mfg. Co., 2 OSHC 1672, OSHD ¶19,415 (RevCom 1975).

[207] York Metal Finishing Co., 1 OSHC 1655, OSHD ¶17,633 (RevCom 1974).

[208] B.W. Harrison Lumber Co., 4 OSHC 1091, OSHD ¶20,623 (RevCom 1976), *aff'd,* 569 F.2d 1303 (5th Cir. 1978).

[209] Farmers Export Company, OSHD ¶24,569 (RevCom 1980) (Cottine dissenting).

§ 5.03. Controlling Job Hazards through the OSHRevCom

[1] Electing Party Status and Contesting Abatement Dates

Workers can become involved in OSHRevCom cases[210] in several ways. If an employer contests an OSHA citation, workers can elect party status to "meaningfully participate" in the contest

[210] The OSHRevCom's rules of procedure are located at 29 CFR § 2200. In the absence of an OSHRevCom rule, the Federal Rules of Civil Procedure apply, 29 CFR § 2200.2(b). In other than simplified proceedings, the Federal Rules of Evidence apply, 29 CFR § 2200.72.

If you expect to become involved in OSHRevCom proceedings, find out where you can use the following legal resources. The local OSHA area office or a well-equipped law library will have them:

The Commerce Clearing House (CCH) and the Bureau of National Affairs (BNA) have loose-leaf services on occupational safety and health. These include OSHA standards, regulations, directives, and operations manuals, together with digests of decisions of the ALJs, the full text of OSHRevCom and circuit court opinions, and numerous other materials, such as indexes and other finding aids and reports of current developments. The CCH cases are called the Occupational Safety and Health Decisions, and are cited as OSHD ¶24,409; the BNA cases are called the Occupational Safety and Health Cases, and are cited as 6 OSHC 2031.

The official reports of the OSHRevCom and its ALJs are called the Occupational Safety and Health Review Commission reports, and are cited as 4 OSHAHRC 1432 in the bound volumes; they are cited as 73/027/B07 on the more recent microfiche. Only the official reports include the full text of the opinions of the ALJs. The official reports can be researched using the OSHRevCom's Index to Decisions of the Occupational Safety and Health Review Commission, Citator of the Decisions of the Occupational Safety and Health Review Commission, and Table of Citations, which gives parallel citations to the CCH and the BNA for all cases by OSHRevCom docket number; all three are available by subscription.

The two commercially available law treatises on the OSH Act are: Rothstein, *Occupational Safety and Health Law* (1st ed., 1978)(West Handbook)("Rothstein"); and Hogan & Hogan, *Occupational Safety and Health Act* (2d ed., 1979)(Matthew-Bender)("Hogan & Hogan"). Hogan & Hogan, unlike Rothstein, discuss the case law interpreting the OSHA standards.

The worker's guide to OSHRevCom practice is Cottine, *Winning at the Review Commission* (Health Research Group, 1975). The forms in the back make this particularly useful. At last report, the manual is being revised. Copies of the old version are still available from HRG at their Washington, D.C., offices, and are a bargain.

proceedings.[211] If OSHA issues a citation that allows too much time for correction of the hazard, workers can contest the reasonableness of the abatement date.[212] Finally, if an employer files a Petition for Modification of the Abatement Date (PMA), workers can contest the reasonableness of the amount of time the employer is requesting.[213]

Before workers can do any of these things, however, they must first have notice that OSHA has issued a citation. The OSH Act requires employers to keep workers informed by posting notices of OSHA enforcement proceedings. OSHA citations must be prominently posted "at or near each place a violation which is referred to in the citation occurred."[214] Departures from this rule are allowed only if the workers are physically dispersed or if there are multiple worksites.[215] The citations must remain posted and unaltered[216] until the violation has been corrected or for three working days, whichever is later,[217] even if the employer has contested the citation.[218] Proposed penalties need not be posted.[219] Once the OSHRevCom has the case, the posting rules change. The employer's letter of contest must be posted only if the affected workers are not represented by a union. If there is a union, it may be served by ordinary mail. This system breaks down in two ways: (1) Only ordinary mail service is required,[220] which permits the unreliability of the U.S. Mails to cover the dishonesty of the employer, and (2) even if notice does reach the union, the union then ought to inform the affected workers, something it may fail to do. To avoid missing notification that the employer has contested the citation, simply call the OSHA office after the fifteen-working-day filing period has elapsed to verify whether the employer has contested the citation. The same notice

[211] Section 10(c), last sentence, 29 U.S.C. § 659(c); 29 CFR § 2200.20.

[212] Section 10(c), first sentence, 29 U.S.C. § 659(c); 29 CFR § 2200.35.

[213] Section 10(c), 29 U.S.C. § 659(c); 29 CFR § 2200.34.

[214] Section 9(b), 29 U.S.C. § 658(b).

[215] 29 CFR § 1903.16(a).

[216] *Id.*

[217] 29 CFR § 1903.16(b).

[218] *Id.*

[219] *Compare* Section 9(a), (b), 29 U.S.C. § 658(a), (b) *with* Section 10(a), 29 U.S.C. § 659(a); *see* 29 CFR § 1903.16(a).

[220] 29 CFR § 2200.7(c).

procedure is used to notify workers of the hearing date[221] or of any settlement reached between OSHA and the employer.[222] These postings must be maintained until the hearing.[223]

After learning that the employer has contested OSHA's citation, elect party status. To do so, write the OSHRevCom,[224] not OSHA. Identify yourself, the employer, the location, and the OSHA case number. State your intention to represent the affected employees[225] and request service of all legal papers at an address convenient to you.[226] If there is a union, it must designate you as the representative at the hearing. Otherwise you can only "intervene" in the case.[227] Even if your complaint led to the citation, if your union does not designate you as its representative, you cannot elect party status in the contest, even if the union sends no one else to represent the workers.[228] If there is no union, it is best if an "affected" worker elects party status.[229] The OSHRevCom permits nonattorneys to represent parties.[230] This allows nonemployees, such as COSH group representatives, to appear on behalf of affected workers who have elected party

---

221 29 CFR § 2200.7(1).

222 29 CFR § 2200.100(c), as amended, 43 Fed. Reg. 4604 (February 3, 1978), 44 Fed. Reg. 70105 (December 5, 1979).

223 29 CFR § 2200.7(n).

224 The address for the OSHRevCom is: Executive Secretary, Occupational Safety and Health Review Commission, 1825 K Street, N.W., Washington, D.C. 20006.

225 IMC Chem. Group, Inc., 6 OSHC 2075, 2076 n. 4, OSHD ¶23,149 at n. 4 (RevCom 1978).

226 Once party status has been elected, the worker representative has an unconditional right to a copy of all pleadings and motions filed, Harshaw Chem. Co., 8 OSHC 1138, 1140 (RevCom 1980). The ALJ must inform the Secretary and Respondent of worker elections of party status, Harshaw, *id.,* 8 OSHC at 1140; Reynolds Metals Co., 7 OSHC 1042, 1044 (RevCom 1979).

227 Babcock & Wilcox Co., OSHD ¶24,812 (RevCom 1980) (Cottine dissenting). While the OSHRevCom rules permit "intervention" in addition to election of party status, the rights attached are not self-evident. At the least "intervenors" have fewer rights than parties and probably have no right to block settlements. 29 CFR § 2200.20.

228 *Id.*

229 Int'l Harvester, 7 OSHC 2194, OSHD ¶24,216 (RevCom 1980).

230 29 CFR § 2200.22(d), .1(h).

status.[231] If the union has elected party status, an affected employee or a COSH group may request the right to intervene.[232]

Electing party status is important. It unconditionally guarantees you the right to "meaningful participation" in the OSHRevCom proceeding.[233] First, the OSHA attorney cannot withdraw or downgrade any item of a citation without your consent.[234] Second, the OSHA attorney cannot propose a settlement to the ALJ for approval until you have reviewed it and failed to object.[235] Third, at the hearing, you can offer evidence relevant to the issues raised by the employer's contest[236] and can press for increased penalties.

The OSHRevCom permits any party or intervenor to move for expedited proceedings.[237] This allows rulings without reference to the usual time periods and anything else the ALJ deems appropriate. A daily copy of the transcript is provided. The OSHRevCom also has elective procedures for "simplified proceedings."[238] Citations under the general duty clause and the health standards are generally *not* eligible for simplified proceedings.[239] A party must request simplified proceedings and there must be no objec-

---

231 Yaffee Iron & Metal Co. 5 OSHC 1057, OSHD ¶21,556 (RevCom 1977).

232 29 CFR § 2200.21.

233 Gurney Ind., 1 OSHC 1219, OSHD ¶15,685 (RevCom 1973). Commissioner Cleary, in his dissent in Southern Bell, 5 OSHC 1405, OSHD ¶21,840 (RevCom 1977), accepts that workers may be able to apply to the OSHRevCom for "a consultation order to help implement the Commission's abatement order," that they may apply for an order that "the costs of abatement be borne by the employer," and that they may apply for orders "enforcing the allocation of cost provision of section 6(b)(7) of the Act." This right to ask for increased penalties is a direct consequence of the allocation to the OSHRevCom of the sole power to assess penalties, Section 17(j), 29 U.S.C. § 666(j). This includes the power to characterize penalties as serious, willful, or repeated, as well as assessing the gravity of the violation and the size, history, and good faith of the employer.

234 IMC Chem. Group, *supra* note 22.

235 *See* Section 5.03[3], *infra.*

236 *Cf.* Int'l Union v. Scofield, 382 U.S. 205, 219 (1965).

237 29 CFR § 2200.101, as amended by 43 Fed. Reg. 4604 (February 3, 1978), 44 Fed. Reg. 70105 (December 5, 1979).

238 29 CFR § 2200.200–.211.

239 29 CFR § 2200.202.

tion to the request.[240] Once simplified proceedings have been elected, no pleadings beyond the citation and notice of contest are allowed,[241] discovery is generally not permitted,[242] the Federal Rules of Evidence do not apply,[243] and interlocutory appeals are not permitted.[244] A conference will be held to enter stipulations into the record and narrow the issues. Then a hearing will be held for the introduction of pertinent evidence.[245] Both the conference and the hearing will be transcribed.[246] The judge then renders a decision.[247]

Workers who wish to contest the abatement date proposed in the OSHA citation as unreasonably long have fifteen working days from the date on which the employer received the citation to file their contest with the OSHA office that issued it. If it is not known when the employer received the citation and you cannot find out at the plant, immediately contact the OSHA area office by telephone, state your intention to contest the abatement date, and find out how much time is available to confirm the telephone call with a written contest letter. This contest is of the abatement date proposed by OSHA, not the employer; OSHA will be your opponent in the hearing and the employer can elect party status and offer evidence to support OSHA's side. The scope of the contest will be limited to the abatement date itself; until the law changes, the reasonableness of the abatement plan on which the abatement date is based is immaterial.[248] Worker contests of abatement dates are automatically treated as expedited proceedings.[249]

Employers that have made good faith efforts to comply with OSHA citations but are unable to complete abatement on time for reasons beyond their control are allowed to file a PMA with

[240] 29 CFR § 2200.203.
[241] 29 CFR § 2200.204.
[242] 29 CFR § 2200.209.
[243] 29 CFR § 2200.206(c)(1).
[244] 29 CFR § 2200.210.
[245] 29 CFR § 2200.206.
[246] 29 CFR § 2200.207.
[247] 29 CFR § 2200.208.
[248] Int'l Union, UAW v. OSHRevCom, 557 F.2d 607 (7th Cir. 1977).
[249] 29 CFR § 2200.34.

OSHA.[250] Under both OSHA[251] and OSHRevCom[252] regulations, an employer's PMA must describe all the steps taken to comply; it must specify the amount of additional time needed, indicating the reasons it is needed; it must specify all interim measures that will be taken to protect the workers exposed; and it must certify that the affected employees have been notified of the PMA. The PMA must be filed with OSHA by the working day following the original abatement date, or else the employer will be subject to a failure to abate notice.[253] If either OSHA or a worker contests the PMA, the OSHRevCom will hear the case;[254] otherwise, OSHA will process the PMA. The burden of proof is on the employer.[255] PMA contests are automatically docketed and processed as expedited proceedings.[256]

[2] Preparation for the Hearing

Once party status has been elected, sit back for several weeks and watch. A contested abatement period will soon be on an expedited schedule.[257] The Secretary of Labor will switch control of the case from OSHA to the Solicitor's Office. This usually means a change in addresses. In the Solicitor's Office, an attorney will review the citation, the employer's contest, and the file. The attorney will make internal recommendations and will draft and issue a complaint.[258] This complaint consists mostly of legal boilerplate: (1) It recites the procedural history of the case, i.e., when the inspection took place, what in the citation was contested, and

---

250 Section 10(c), 29 U.S.C. § 659(c).

251 29 CFR § 1903.14(a).

252 29 CFR § 2200.34(b).

253 29 CFR §§ 1903.14(a), 2200.34(c).

254 29 CFR § 2200.34.

255 29 CFR § 2200.34(d)(3). The workers' contest will be upheld if the employer fails to justify its PMA, *e.g.*, Secretary v. IBEW, Local 1031 (Stewart-Warner), OSHRevCom Docket 78-5910-E.

256 29 CFR § 2200.34(d)(2).

257 29 CFR § 2200.101.

258 29 CFR § 2200.33 sets out the minimum standards for a complaint. While this should be issued within twenty days after receipt of the notice of contest, extensions of time are liberally granted. 29 CFR § 2200.5.

what penalty was proposed; (2) it alleges the procedural prerequisites for OSHA and OSHRevCom jurisdiction, namely, that an employment relation existed between an employer and two or more employees and that the employer "affected commerce"; (3) it recapitulates the allegations of the citation and notice of proposed penalty and alleges that the violations affected the health and safety of some employees; and (4) it closes with a request for relief. The OSHA attorney will sometimes amend the citation through the complaint, either to use a more appropriate standard to cover the violation or, where the applicability of a standard is dubious, to allege an alternative general duty clause violation. If an amendment is made, the changes must be explained.[259] If you have already elected party status, amendments cannot downgrade the citation without your consent.

The first major effort in the case should be made as soon as the employer's answer is filed. Review the scope of the contest, set priorities, and serve the discovery requests. The simple way to determine the scope of the dispute is to rely on the OSHA attorney. Do this by marking the citation or complaint with the admissions or denials contained in the employer's answer and noting the affirmative defenses raised.[260] Occasionally, however, the OSHA attorney will unnecessarily broaden the contest notice, or will be mistaken in reviewing the citation and contest letter.[261] Relying on the OSHA attorney ignores these remote risks.

Whether or not you double-check the scope of the contest, in

[259] 29 CFR § 2200.33(a)(3).

[260] An affirmative defense is one that tacitly admits the violation but claims facts amounting to an avoidance of culpability or legal liability.

[261] To check for these possible errors, which may expand the employer's contest, thoroughly assess the contest's scope yourself. First, check the filing date of the letter of contest, making sure that it was filed within the permissible fifteen-working-day period. Once you have determined that the contest is timely and there is no need to file a motion to dismiss the late contest, carefully review the contest to determine its scope. One practical way to do this is to mark the citation: Go through the whole citation, item by item, checking the contest letter to determine whether the violation, the abatement date, or the penalty is in contest. Using the citation as a checklist, indicate the scope of the contest, using your own letter code. Then compare your results with those of the OSHA attorney, as reflected in his or her complaint. To the extent the OSHA attorney is in error, your motion to amend the complaint should be granted.

marking the citation or complaint with the employer's admissions, denials, and defenses, you must indicate whether the violation, the abatement date, and/or the penalty is in contest. Otherwise, it is impossible to focus on the pertinent evidentiary issues.[262] For instance, if an employer has contested only the penalty for a serious citation for a machine-guarding violation, thereby conceding the underlying violation, then the issue of worker exposure to the violations, while relevant to the penalty, is no longer critical.[263] In contrast, the degree of employer knowledge of the violation is crucial: The more the employer knew, the more blameworthy it is. If you want to increase the penalty to a "willful"-grade violation, call as a witness the safety steward who repeatedly told the production foreman that there was a need for a guard, demonstrating the necessary employer knowledge for a "willful" violation; it might be unnecessary to call the machine operator who, although exposed to the hazard, had no testimony to give concerning the employer's knowledge. To repeat, if you have not clearly marked your copy of the pleadings, you may lose track of your proof objective; clearly mark whether the violation, abatement date, and/or penalty is in issue with respect to each item in the citation or complaint.

Once the pleadings have been marked and the scope of the contest has been determined, set priorities. Do you want to make sure that an abatement order issues; do you want to decrease the time allowed for abatement; and/or do you want to increase (or decrease) the penalty? This set of decisions must obviously be made with respect to each item in contest. If time is short and some issues have low priority, pick only the important ones. See how well the OSHA attorney is handling the case before narrowing the focus.

The next step is discovery. First, get a copy of OSHA's file. This is essential to preparation. The OSHA file not only reveals

262 Now is an excellent time to review the burden of proof in OSHRevCom cases; *see* Section 5.02 (text accompanying notes 108–13), *supra,* and Section 5.03[4]–[5], *infra.*

263 Worker exposure is a necessary element of any violation but is only one aspect of the gravity of the violation for purposes of penalty assessments, other aspects being the employer's good faith, size, and history of prior violations, Section 17, 29 U.S.C. § 666.

the strength of OSHA's case but also is an excellent practical vehicle for organizing preparation. To obtain a copy, serve a "Request for Production of Documents" on OSHA,[264] requesting an OSHA-1B Compliance Worksheet and Photo Mounting Worksheet (see Appendixes 5E and 5F near the end of this chapter) for every item of the citation that is in contest. These worksheets will repeat information contained in the citation; they will indicate evidence of the violations, worker exposure, and employer knowledge and spell out how the proposed penalties were calculated. Also ask for the OSHA-1A Narrative (see Appendix 5G at the end of this chapter); usually there is one to a case file, often with continuation sheets. Include a catchall clause in the request to cover any other relevant documents. Expect OSHA to delete the names of employee informants before forwarding the file. OSHA should simply send a free copy of the file within the required thirty days. Serve a copy of the request on the employer[265] and file a copy of the request with the OSHRevCom ALJ assigned to the case.[266] Keep a copy of the OSHA Field Operations Manual (FOM), Industrial Hygiene Operations Manual (IHM), and standards nearby during review of the OSHA files.[267]

The employer's case should be discovered, particularly if it has raised affirmative defenses. For instance, a common defense in accident cases is for the employer to blame the worker victim through the isolated misconduct defense. But, as is discussed below, the OSHRevCom's law on this defense is quite favorable to workers; essentially, the employer must put the adequacy of his safety program on trial before claiming that there was nothing more it could have done to prevent the hazard. If you have not discovered the details of this affirmative defense before the trial, you can get sandbagged. Therefore, for each affirmative defense, serve questions probing the defense,[268] securing the identification

---

264 The OSHRevCom rules incorporate Fed. R. Civ. P. 34.

265 29 CFR § 2200.7(a).

266 29 CFR § 2200.8.

267 If you have not obtained these manuals, visit any law library that carries either the CCH or the BNA OSH Act services, or visit the nearest OSHA area office.

268 When preparing these interrogatories, review the sections below on employer defenses to make sure that all pertinent proof elements have been covered.

of relevant witnesses, their expected testimony, and pertinent documents. Immediately follow with requests for production of those documents and depositions where needed. The OSHRevCom limits the use of interrogatories and depositions; they are permitted only upon a motion showing good cause.[269] Because of the quick pace of OSHRevCom proceedings, it is important to proceed to discover the employer's defenses *immediately* after the employer files its answer.

Also obtain copies of any employer documents or records that establish its prior knowledge or recognition of the hazards or otherwise pertain to the case. Lost-time accident reports, workers' compensation reports, or in-house engineering studies concerning a particular working condition can show employer knowledge in any of several contexts: (1) actual knowledge of a hazard for purposes of a vague standard, (2) recognition of a hazard in a general duty clause citation, (3) knowledge of the presence of the hazard for a serious citation, and (4) willful indifference to a known hazard for a willful citation. The employer's monitoring and surveillance records and consultant reports may be relevant in toxic substance cases. Thoroughly canvass relevant employer documents. Remember that the new OSHA access regulations[270] allow access within two weeks to the employer's exposure monitoring, medical records, and log of injuries and illnesses, whereas a "request for documents" takes thirty days. In an organized shop, additional access rights are available through Section 8(a)(5) and possibly under the labor contract. These rights are not lost in OSHRevCom cases; they are in addition to OSHRevCom discovery. Use the method that works best under the circumstances.

If the case requires expert testimony and the expert will need to inspect the premises, a "Request for Entry" is in order. Remember that experts are not necessarily needed to introduce uncontroversial scientific evidence into the record. A much less costly method is pretrial use of the evidence rule on judicial notice.[271] Write a motion to the judge requesting that he or she take judicial notice of certain facts contained in documents at-

---

[269] 29 CFR § 2200.53.

[270] 29 CFR §§ 1900.20, 1904.7.

[271] Fed. R.E. 201.

tached to the motion. If the facts cannot be genuinely disputed, s/he will "notice" them; contradictory evidence will be inadmissible at the hearing.[272] This saves the cost of an expert's fees. If the motion is denied, at least it will have forced the employer to reveal its side of the story before the expert is hired; this will help the expert focus on the disputed issues. To be effective, however, this motion must be made very early to allow time to hire an expert if it becomes necessary.

After obtaining the OSHA file and the employer's rationale for its affirmative defenses, plan the proofs. Consult and coordinate the case with the OSHA attorney. If time permits, review each item with him/her and determine what support is needed. An important backup role for workers' representatives is to provide witnesses for the OSHA attorney. Note that if you suggest a witness to the OSHA attorney and s/he acts on the suggestion, s/he will pay the witness and mileage fee for the appearance,[273] whereas if you subpoena the witness, you or your union will pay the fees. Note that the OSHRevCom rules implicitly require that ordinarily subpoenas for witnesses or documents must be served at least five days before the hearing date.[274] Pick up several subpoenas from the OSHRevCom ALJ to use later as necessary.

In planning the proofs, review the pertinent OSHA worksheets for the contested items, checking the applicability of the standard to the violation and reviewing the evidence available to substantiate the violation. Time permitting, review the standard cited by OSHA in its full context, instead of relying on the short excerpt in the OSHA citation. Analyze whether the standard's duties are unambiguous or vague; if they are vague, determine what evidence of industry standards may be admissible, e.g., check for applicable ANSI standards.[275] You may also wish to research the OSHRevCom decisions dealing with that standard. The quickest access aid to those cases, in either the Bureau of National Affairs

---

[272] *Id.*

[273] 29 CFR § 2200.63.

[274] This is implied by the requirement that a motion to quash or limit the scope of a subpoena be made within five days of the date of service, 29 CFR § 2200.55(b).

[275] The ANSI standards may be reviewed at the OSHA area office. These *may* be judicially noticed, Fed. R.E. 201.

(BNA) or Commerce Clearing House (CCH) reports, is the Index to Cases by Standards Cited. First review the RevCom cases (marked "RC"), turning to the digested ALJ opinions last.

If it is possible to establish that the employer breached a duty under the OSH Act, you can force an increase in the penalty imposed by introducing evidence that the violation was willful, i.e., that the employer was knowingly or negligently indifferent to the breach. Prior near-misses and warnings to the employer from workers about the breach are relevant here. If it can be shown that the employer knew about the OSHA standard, so much the better. The general penalty criteria, namely, the gravity of the violation, history of violations, and size and good faith of the employer, are additional criteria for evidence relevant to the penalty.

This is also the time to send out requests for admissions. The OSHRevCom rules shorten the time to fifteen days.[276] Use them to authenticate documents before trial. Make copies of all documents to be introduced; if the employer will not stipulate in writing to their authenticity, formally request that the employer admit to their authenticity.

The OSHRevCom has an unusual rule to consider using: "At any time prior to the commencement of the hearing . . . any person . . . may file a statement of position with respect to any or all issues to be heard."[277] Prior to the hearing, a prehearing conference can be requested.[278] If the employer has unreasonably refused to reach agreement on issues, this is an informal opportunity to explain why your views are the more reasonable ones and to enlist the aid of the judge in narrowing the dispute to the genuine issues.

To a large extent, the pretrial motion practice and the trial practice follow the Federal Rules of Civil Procedure and the Federal Rules of Evidence.[279] The exceptions are the OSHRevCom rules, which should be reviewed periodically during the case.

---

276 29 CFR § 2200.92.

277 29 CFR § 2200.36.

278 29 CFR § 2200.51.

279 29 CFR § 2200.2(b), .72.

[3] Settlements

Most OSHRevCom Cases are settled before the hearing occurs. The primary reason that workers elect party status is to obtain the rights meaningfully to participate in settlement discussions and to demand a hearing on any objectionable issues.

The OSHRevCom supervises all settlement agreements in contested cases;[280] the parties cannot avoid OSHRevCom scrutiny by consenting to a resolution. As a practical matter, the OSHRevCom ratifies most proposed settlements. In reviewing settlements, the OSHRevCom checks to make sure that affected employees or their representatives have been notified and given an opportunity to be heard.[281] The proposed settlement agreement must have been served on the workers.[282] Workers who have elected party status must be ensured an opportunity to participate by the ALJ, OSHA, and the employer.[283]

Workers with objections must file them *in writing* with the ALJ[284] within ten days of receipt of the proposed settlement agreement.[285] Always object to exculpatory language (e.g., "this agreement is not an admission of the validity of the OSHA citation") that will preclude the use of the settlement agreement in future OSH Act proceedings; it guts the penalty provisions for repeated citations and failure to correct notices.[286] Nonadmission language for purposes other than OSH Act proceedings is less important. Whether or not workers have a right to demand a hearing over settlement objections is an open question.

---

[280] Farmers Export Co., OSHD ¶24,569 (RevCom 1980). *Contra,* Marshall v. Sun Petroleum Prods. Co., 622 F.2d 1176, 1185 (3d Cir. 1980).

[281] 29 CFR § 2200.100(c); Am. Airlines, Inc., 2 OSHC 1391, OSHD ¶19,108 (1974); Davies Can Co., 4 OSHC 1237, OSHD ¶20,704 (1976); ITT Indus., Inc., 6 OSHC 1944 (RevCom 1978).

[282] 29 CFR § 2200.100(c).

[283] 29 CFR § 2200.7, 20(a), .66(m), .100(c), .102; ITT, *supra* note 281, at 1944–45.

[284] Reynolds Metals Co., 7 OSHC 1042, 1044 (RevCom 1979).

[285] Kaiser Aluminum & Chem. Corp., 6 OSHC 2172, 2173 (RevCom 1978), *accord,* 29 CFR § 2200.100(c). The ALJ must wait thirteen days from the date of service before ruling, Am. Cyanamid Co., 8 OSHC 1346, 1348 (RevCom 1980); Reynolds, *supra* note 284, at 1044 n. 9.; 29 CFR § 2200.4(b), .37.

[286] Farmers Export, *supra* note 280, dissent at 30,088. *See* Sun Petroleum, *supra* note 280; *cf.* NLRB v. Oil, Chem. and Atomic Workers, 476 F.2d 1031 (1973).

OSHA has recently instituted a policy on "Informal Settlements," which affects worker participation rights.[287] Under this conciliatory scheme, all citations will be accompanied by a letter inviting the employer to meet to discuss settlement with OSHA area office officials. The area director may make precontest settlements and, before the issuance of the OSHRevCom complaint, postcontest settlements. He or she has the authority to reduce the penalty, change the abatement date, or withdraw items of the citation. Postcontest informal settlements should follow the rules on worker participation outlined above. Workers can elect party status and object to a settlement even before OSHA's attorney at the solicitor's office has filed a complaint.[288] Precontest settlements, however, may limit workers' right to object. The new policy provides:

> Employee representatives shall be afforded the opportunity and encouraged to participate fully in the informal conference and negotiations. During the conduct of the informal conference, if matters of a delicate nature are brought up by either the employer or employee representative, separate or private discussions shall be permitted. In any event, the Regional Administrator or Area Director shall not amend or withdraw a citation or penalty without first attempting to obtain the views of the employee representative. When the employee representative disagrees with the Area Director's proposed amendment or withdrawal of a citation, the employee representative may appeal the proposal to the Regional Administrator. However, where the 15-working-day period for filing a notice of contest does not permit adequate time to appeal to the Regional Administrator in writing or in person, telephonic communication shall be utilized in order to expedite the resolution of the matter under consideration.[289]

Clearly, time pressure will be great. Workers should be wary of being quickly pressed into compromising. If time is too short to review the proposal adequately, suggest that the employer con-

---

[287] Memorandum of September 8, 1980, on "Settlement of Cases by Area Directors."

[288] IMC Chem. Group, Inc., OSHD ¶23,149 (RevCom 1978), *rev'd* OSHD ¶24,990 (6th Cir. 1980). But the OSHRevCom is not bound to acquiesce, Farmers Export, *supra* note 280, at n. 4.

[289] Memorandum, *supra* note 287, at 3.

test the citation to allow sufficient time for review. Once the employer contests, immediately elect party status and continue the settlement discussions.

[4] OSHA's Burden of Proof under OSHA Standards

When the OSHA Act was passed, Congress allowed OSHA to "grandfather" "any national consensus standard,"[290] and "any established Federal standard,"[291] unless "such a standard would not result in improved safety and health." The result was that the bulk of the Industrial Safety and Health Standards,[292] the Construction Safety Standards,[293] and the harbor workers' safety standards current around 1970[294] were adopted this way. The Industrial Safety and Health Standards include subparts on occupational health and environmental control,[295] including ventilation,[296] noise,[297] and radiation;[298] personal protective equipment,[299] including general requirements,[300] eye and face protection,[301] and respirators;[302] machinery and machine guard-

---

290 Section 6(a), 29 U.S.C. § 655(a); Section 3(a), 29 U.S.C. § 652(a). National consensus standards are those established by the American National Standards Institute and the National Fire Protection Association, 29 CFR § 1910.3(b)(1).

291 Section 6(a), 29 U.S.C. § 655(a); Section 3(10), 29 U.S.C. § 652(10). Established federal standards included those under the Walsh-Healy Act, 41 U.S.C. §§ 35 *et seq.;* the Service Contract Act, 41 U.S.C. §§ 351 *et seq.;* the Construction Safety Act, 40 U.S.C. § 333; the Longshoremen's and Harbor Workers Compensation Act, 33 U.S.C. § 941 and the National Foundation on Arts and Humanities Act, 20 U.S.C. §§ 951 *et seq.*

292 29 CFR § 1910. The subsection on mechanical power presses, § 1910.217, is a new standard. The health standards located after but not including § 1910.1000 are all new standards promulgated pursuant to Section 6(b), 29 U.S.C. § 655(b), rather than Section 6(a), 29 U.S.C. § 655(a).

293 29 CFR § 1926.

294 29 CFR §§ 1915–18.

295 29 CFR § 1910.94–.100.

296 29 CFR § 1910.94.

297 29 CFR § 1910.95.

298 29 CFR § 1910.96–.97.

299 29 CFR § 1910.132–.140.

300 29 CFR § 1910.132.

301 29 CFR § 1910.133.

302 29 CFR § 1910.134.

ing;[303] walking-working surfaces;[304] means of egress;[305] and toxic and hazardous substances.[306]

Many of the standards are specification standards, which govern the means the employer must use to correct the hazard. In enforcing specification standards, OSHA does not have to prove that a hazard exists as a result of noncompliance; the existence of the hazard is conclusively presumed.[307]

In contrast to specification standards, some standards are "vague;" here, OSHA's burden of proof is higher. A "vague" standard draws its content from the reasonable man test, which requires OSHA to prove what a reasonable employer would have done. The problem is well summarized in a leading First Circuit case on the subject.[308] The standard involved provided that protective equipment was required "wherever it [is] . . . necessary by reason of hazards . . . encountered in a manner capable of causing injury . . . through physical contact."[309] The court stated:

> A regulation without ascertainable standards, like this one, does not provide constitutionally adequate warning to an employer unless read to penalize only conduct unacceptable in light of the common understanding and experience of those working in the industry. (Citations omitted). Of course, if an employer is shown to have actual knowledge, an objective test may satisfy due process. In this case, an appropriate test is whether a reasonably prudent man familiar with the circumstances of the industry would have protected against the hazard. (Footnote and citation omitted). We would expect, most often, that reference to industry

303 29 CFR § 1910.211–.222.

304 29 CFR § 1910.21–.32.

305 29 CFR § 1910.35–.40.

306 29 CFR § 1910.1000–.1046.

307 The definition of a standard, which includes only those standards "reasonably necessary or appropriate" to provide for safety, is the basis for this presumption. *See, e.g.,* Greyhound Lines-W. v. Marshall, 575 F.2d 759, 762 (9th Cir. 1978). Of course, if there is no exposure of employees to potential injury, the citation may be *de minimis.* Section 9(a) provides that "a notice in lieu of citation [is appropriate] with respect to *de minimis* violations, which have no direct and immediate relationship to safety or health." Such notices are rarely, if ever, issued by OSHA; rather, no action will be taken at all.

308 Cape & Vineyard Div. v. OSHRevCom, 512 F.2d 1148, 1152 (1st Cir. 1975).

309 29 CFR § 1910.132(a).

> custom and practice will establish the standard of conduct. There may, however, be instances where industry practice fails to take reasonable precautions against hazards generally known in the industry; in such event it may be unfair to hold the employer to a standard higher than that of actual practice . . . .[310]

This approach has been widely adopted, with differences arising only over: (1) whether the standard of care should be limited to the custom in the trade or whether the higher standard of experts familiar with the trade will be applied,[311] and (2) whether OSHA has the burden of proving technological feasibility.[312]

Worker testimony on employee exposure to the violation can be important, whatever kind of standard is involved. Usually OSHA will rely on the inspector to demonstrate employee exposure to the condition. Under the access theory of exposure, OSHA need not actually observe workers in the danger zone; mere access to the danger zone is enough.[313] If the employer has a rebuttal witness who testifies that the noncomplying condition exists in a remote location where employees never work, the ALJ can vacate the citation. Only worker witnesses can make sure that the employer does not unfairly defeat the citation on the basis of this technicality.

[5] The Burden of Proof under the General Duty Clause

The employer may also be cited for hazards not covered by OSHA standards[314] under Section 5(a)(1) of the OSH Act:

(Text continued on page 5-64)

---

[310] Cape & Vineyard, *supra* note 308.

[311] *Compare* Bristol Steel & Iron Works v. OSHRevCom, 601 F.2d 717, 723–24 (4th Cir. 1979), *with* B & B Insulation, Inc., v. OSHRevCom, 583 F.2d 1364, 1367, 1371 (5th Cir. 1978).

[312] *See* cases cited note 113, *supra.*

[313] Brennan v. OSHRevCom & Dic-Underhill, 513 F.2d 1032, 1038 (2d Cir. 1975); Usery v. Marquette Cement & OSHRevCom, 568 F.2d 902, 910 (2d Cir. 1977); Winn-Dixie Stores, Inc., 6 OSHC 1598, OSHD ¶22,712 (RevCom 1978).

[314] The general rule is that if an OSHA standard applies to a hazard the general duty clause cannot be used, *e.g.,* Brisk Waterproofing Co., 1 OSHC 1263, OSHD ¶16,345 (RevCom 1973); Usery v. Marquette Cement Mfg. Co., 568 F.2d 902, 905 n.5 (2d Cir. 1977). Under the liberal pleading standards used by the OSHRevCom, alternative pleadings are encouraged where the choice is not clear, Fed. R. Civ. P. 8(c)(2); Marquette Cement, *id.,* at 909, n.11.

An important potential exception exists but remains undeveloped: *nonserious* Section 5(a)(1) abatement orders. To begin with, note that a Section 5(a)(1) violation is not necessarily "serious" for penalty purposes. Compare Section 5(a)(1), 29 U.S.C. § 654(a)(1), with Section 17(k), 29 U.S.C. § 666(k); *see also* Getty Oil Co. v. OSHRevCom, 453 F.2d 1143, 1145 (5th Cir. 1976); National Realty Constr., Inc., v. OSHRevCom, 489 F.2d 1257, 1268 n.41 (D.C. Cir. 1973). *But see* OSHA FOM, VIII.A.2.d; Rothstein, *Occupational Safety and Health Law,* § 127.

Where OSHA standards have become outdated by scientific and technological developments, but have not yet been modified to reflect such changes, a nonserious Section 5(a)(1) citation could be a fair and effective remedy. For instance, since the air contaminant standard was adopted, 29 U.S.C. § 1910.1000, at least 65 of the recommended exposure levels have been changed, while the pertinent OSHA standard has not itself been updated. *See* OSHA IHM, II. Yet the OSHA IHM only suggests *advising* the employer to reduce the exposure and does not recommend issuance of a citation.

This position is unnecessarily narrow and gives undue weight to the outdated standard. While the enforcement focus on standards is desirable, and "should be used instead of the general duty clause *wherever possible,*" Marquette Cement, *supra* note 314, at 905 n.5 (emphasis added), the OSH Act also provides, in another context: "In the event of conflict among any such standards, the Secretary shall promulgate the standard which assures the greatest protection of the safety or health of the affected employees," Section 6(a), 29 U.S.C. § 655(a). The policy of ensuring the greatest protection where there is a conflict in the standards could be extended to conflicts between outdated standards and newly recommended standards. It would be consistent with the general aim of the Act "to assure *so far as possible* every working man and woman in the Nation safe and healthful working conditions . . .," Section 2(b), 29 U.S.C. § 651(b)(emphasis added). Since the need for abatement has already been recognized in these situations, employers should not escape their duty merely because of OSHA's logjam in revising outdated standards. Importantly, an action to compel OSHA to update the standards would fail, since it is already established that OSHA has "open ended discretion" to set its own priorities in the standards area, Section 6(g), 29 U.S.C. § 655(g); Nat'l Congress of Hispanic Citizens v. Usery, 534 F.2d 1196 (D.C. Cir. 1977).

Penalties would be inappropriate under this type of citation. Employers are entitled to rely on existing standards, 29 CFR § 1910.5(f), and have a "due diligence" defense to a serious violation, Section 17(k), 29 U.S.C. § 666(k).

Moreover, this prospective use of Section 5(a)(1) is consistent with the legislative history of the early version of this clause. The Senate Committee Report accompanying S. 2193, the initial Senate proposal, said: "The general duty clause in this bill would not be a general substitute for reliance on standards, but would simply enable the Secretary to insure the protection of employees who are working under special circumstances for which no standard has yet been adopted. Moreover, the clause merely requires an employer to correct recognized hazards after they have been discovered on inspection and made the

> Each employer . . . shall furnish to each of his employees employment and a place of employment which are free from recognized hazards that are causing or are likely to cause death or serious harm to his employees.

The self-evident elements of this clause are "employment and a place of employment,"[315] "likely to cause death or serious physical harm,"[316] and the limitation to "his employees."[317] More difficult is defining "free from recognized hazards."

In *National Realty and Construction Co. Inc., v. OSHRevCom,*[318] Judge Skelly Wright analyzed this phrase in a landmark case. He found that construing the term "free" in the context of that case presented a dilemma:

> On the one hand, the adjective is unqualified and absolute: A workplace cannot be just "reasonably free" of a hazard, or merely as free as the average workplace in the industry. On the other hand, Congress quite clearly did not intend the general duty clause to impose strict liability: the duty was to be an achievable one. Congress' language is consonant with its intent only where the "recognized" hazard in question *can be* totally eliminated from a workplace. A hazard consisting of conduct by employees, such as equipment riding, cannot, however, be totally eliminated. A demented, suicidal, or willfully reckless employee may on occasion

---

subject of an abatement order. There is no penalty for violation of the general duty clause." Legislative History, at 150.

The remarks of Congressman Steiger, in introducing the final version of his substitute bill on the floor of the House, support this theory; his principal concern was with not penalizing employers under Section 5(a)(1), Legislative History, at 981. The Conference Report indicates that changes to Section 5(a)(1), which were adopted at the last stage, focused on "recognition," not the penalty issue. Legislative History, at 1186.

Finally, the courts have already recognized this possibility. The National Realty opinion noted: "While the Commission has the clear authority to impose a penalty even if the violation is not serious, a zero penalty, coupled with an abatement order, would obviously be the proper response where the Commission determined that the defendant-employer had no notice, i.e., no duty to know, that its safety regime was defective." 489 F.2d at 1268 n.41.

[315] Rea Express v. Brennan, 495 F.2d 822, 826 (2d Cir. 1974).

[316] R.L. Sanders Roofing Co., 7 OSHC 1566, OSHD ¶23,756 (RevCom 1979).

[317] *See,* Brennan v. OSHRevCom & Dic-Underhill, 513 F.2d 1032, 1037-8 (2d Cir. 1975). No such limitation exists for standards violations.

[318] 489 F.2d 1257 (D.C. Cir. 1973).

> circumvent the best conceived and most vigorously enforced safety regime. This seeming dilemma is, however, soluble within the literal structure of the general duty clause. Congress intended to require the elimination of preventable hazards. It follows, we think, that Congress did not intend unpreventable hazards to be considered "recognized" under the clause. Though a generic form of hazardous conduct, such as equipment riding, may be "recognized," unpreventable instances of it are not, and thus the possibility of their occurrence at a workplace is not inconsistent with the workplace being "free" of recognized hazards.
>
> Though resistant to precise definition, the criterion of preventability draws content from the informed judgment of safety experts. Hazardous conduct is not preventable if it is so idiosyncratic and implausible in motive or means that conscientious experts, familiar with the industry, would not take it into account in prescribing a safety program. Nor is misconduct preventable if its eliminination would require methods of hiring, training, monitoring, or sanctioning workers which are either so untested or so expensive that safety experts would substantially concur in thinking the methods infeasible. All preventable forms and instances of hazardous conduct must, however, be entirely excluded from the workplace. (footnotes omitted)[319]

This case is widely cited for the propositions that "free" means preventably free, and does not impose strict liability;[320] that "recognized" includes the imputation to the employer of the knowledge of safety experts familiar with the particular hazard,[321] a notion not limited by the custom and practice of the particular industry;[322] and finally that OSHA has the burden of proving the feasibility of particular measures to correct the condi-

---

319 *Id.*, at 1265–67.

320 Getty Oil Co. v. OSHRevCom, 530 F.2d 1143, 1145 (5th Cir. 1976); Brennan v. OSHRevCom & Republic Creosoting Co., 501 F.2d 1196 (7th Cir. 1974); Titanium Metals Corp. of America v. Usery, 579 F.2d 536, 543 (9th Cir. 1978).

321 The testimony of an OSHA inspector familiar with the particular industry can be proof of "recognition." Cormier Well Serv., 4 OSHC 1085, OSHD ¶20,583 (1976). State safety laws, Ford Motor Co. 5 OSHC 1765, OSHD ¶22,106 (1977), and ANSI consensus standards, Betten Processing Corp., 2 OSHC 1724, OSHD ¶19,481 (1975), are other possible sources of "recognition."

322 Nat'l Realty, *supra* note 314, at 1266 n.37.

tions cited.[323]

Since *National Realty,* two other approaches to the proof of "recognition" have emerged in addition to the use of expert knowledge. Actual knowledge is the second approach.[324] Worker testimony about employer knowledge of near-misses or accidents involving the same hazard can prove recognition as can an employer's safety manual, work rule, or contract clause that deals with the particular hazard. Common sense is a third standard for "recognition." In a case reviewed by the Second Circuit, the court found: "It scarcely requires expertise in the industry to recognize that it is hazardous to dump bricks from an unenclosed chute into an unbarricaded alleyway, twenty-six feet below, between buildings in which unwarned employees walk."[325] Whether a contract clause dealing with a particular hazard constitutes "recognition" has not been ruled on.

In addition to its notions of preventability and recognition, *National Realty* established the general requirement that, in addition to the particular standards requiring employers to maintain safety programs,[326] employers can be cited under § 5(a)(1) for failure adequately to train, instruct, and supervise their employees. This precedent has been followed in many OSHRevCom and circuit court cases.[327]

The general duty clause is of particular importance in coping with OSHA's delay in producing standards. In the early 1970s,

---

[323] But this burden was limited to the feasibility of preventing employee misconduct, excluding technological feasibility, in Jones & Laughlin Steel Co., 6 OSHC 1204, OSHD ¶22,380 (1977).

[324] Brennan v. OSHRevCom and VyLactos Labs, 494 F.2d 460, 464 (8th Cir. 1974).

[325] Marquette Cement, *supra* note 313, at 910.

[326] 29 CFR § 1910.96(i); 29 CFR § 1910.217(e)(3); 29 CFR § 1910.134(b)(3); 29 CFR § 1910.134(e)(5); 29 CFR § 1910.178(i). Brennan v. OSHRevCom & Gerosa, Inc., 491 F.2d 1340 (2d Cir. 1974). Many other standards contain specific training requirements. Supervision duties under standards are discussed in Brennan v. OSHRevCom & Hanovia Lamp Div., 502 F.2d 946, 949 (3d Cir. 1974).

[327] Thiele, Inc., 3 OSHC 1744, OSHD ¶20,079 (1975); Massman Constr., 5 OSHC 1027, OSHD ¶21,525 (1977); Old Bridge Chem. Co., 6 OSHC 1207, OSHD ¶22,450 (1977); Gen. Dynamics Corp., 6 OSHC 1753, OSHD ¶22,873 (1978); Brennan v. OSHRevCom & Republic Creosoting Co., 501 F.2d 1196 (7th Cir. 1974).

the ANSI consensus standards were incorporated in full into the OSHA enforcement machinery; since then, ANSI has continued to develop standards, which, if they had been developed at the time of the incorporation, would have already become OSHA standards. Of particular importance are health standards. The current OSHA policy, which can be changed by any new administration, instructs industrial hygienists as follows:

> Exposure to a substance which has been added to the ACGIH TLV list since 1968, or identified as a serious hazard by federal agencies such as NIOSH, EPA, or the National Cancer Institute, should be considered for a possible 5(a)(1) citation where an OSHA [standard] does not exist.[328]

Whether identification of carcinogens on the "candidate list" under the OSHA "cancer policy" will constitute "recognition" for Section 5(a)(1) purposes is an open question.[329]

Finally, Section 5(a)(1) is available if a standard has been knocked out by the courts as improperly promulgated. For instance, the air contaminant standard's provisions regulating the allowable levels of mixtures of air contaminants, any one of which does not exceed the OSHA PEL, could be enforced through Section 5(a)(1).[330]

[6] Employers' Affirmative Defenses

The principal defensive action in OSHRevCom contest proceedings is in the employer's denials that the OSHA standards in fact apply to the conditions cited. The phrases used in the standards specify the elements to which OSHA must adduce its

[328] OSHA IHM, II. A.12.

[329] Identification, Classification and Regulation of Potential Occupational Carcinogens, 29 CFR § 1990.121; 45 Fed. Reg. 5001, 5284–85, 5296 (January 22, 1980).

[330] *See* Durion Co., Inc., 8 OSHC 1701, OSHD ¶22,819 (1978). The only question of proof that might need to be resolved through expert testimony is whether the adverse health effect of the mixture of air contaminants increases additively or synergistically (e.g., mixing a gas with an aerosol often yields synergistic health effects).

proof. If the standard has limited its application to a specific type of hazard, OSHA may not apply it beyond its intended scope.[331] If the standard includes the phrase "feasible," as do the old Walsh-Healy standards for noise and air contaminants adopted by OSHA, it creates fertile ground for employers to argue for the application of cost-benefit analyses.[332]

In addition to mere denials of the facts cited or the applicability of the standard cited, employers often raise true affirmative defenses. A brief catalog of the more common of these, together with an indication of the critical elements of each, follows.

[a] Other Federal Agency Exemption

Employers subject to safety and health enforcement by more than one federal agency[333] can claim a Section 4(b)(1) exemption. The case law clearly sets out three elements for establishing this defense:[334] (1) The purpose of the other federal act must include protection of the safety and health of workers;[335] (2) the other authority must have actually exercised its power to protect workers, both by promulgating regulations and by enforcing them;[336] and (3) the other regulations must cover the specific working conditions governed by the OSHA regulation.[337] This last element's focus on "specific working conditions" means that there

---

331 E.g., a "roof" is not a "floor," allowing OSHA to apply a guardrail standard to roofs. Langer v. SOL, 524 F.2d 1337 (7th Cir. 1975).

332 E.g., Carnation Co., 6 OSHA 1730, OSHD ¶22,837(1978).

333 Section 4(b)(1) of the OSH Act provides: "Nothing in this Act shall apply to *working conditions* of employees with respect to which other Federal agencies, and State agencies acting under section 274 of the Atomic Energy Act 1954, as amended (42 U.S.C. § 2021), *exercise* statutory *authority* to prescribe or enforce standards or regulations *affecting occupational safety or health,*" 29 U.S.C. § 653(b)(1) (emphasis added).

334 Idaho Travertine Corp., 3 OSHC 1535, OSHD ¶20,013 (RevCom 1976).

335 Fineberg Packing Co., 1 OSHC 1598, OSHD ¶17,518 (RevCom 1974); Mushroom Transp. Co., 1 OSHC 1390, OSHD ¶16,881 (RevCom 1973).

336 S. Pac. Transp. Co. v. OSHRevCom, 539 F.2d 386 (5th Cir. 1976); Bettindorf Terminal Co., 1 OSHC 1695, OSHD ¶17,782 (RevCom 1974); Marshall v. N.W. Airlines, 574 F.2d 119 (2d Cir. 1978).

337 S. Ry. Co. v. OSHRevCom, 539 F.2d 335 (4th Cir. 1976); Mushroom Transp. *supra* note 335.

are no industry-wide exemptions.[338] Thus, the proworker theory of Section 4(b)(1) can be summarized as the "nook-and-cranny" doctrine—OSHA jurisdiction expands to fill the regulatory gaps left by other agencies, such as the Coast Guard, the Federal Aviation Administration, the Office of Pipeline Safety, the Bureau of Motor Carrier Safety, and the Federal Railroad Administration. Whether OSHA can rebut the employer's showing of an "exercise" of authority by demonstrating "exhaustion" or "futility" of the other agency's authority is open.

[b] Isolated Misconduct

This is a "blame the victim" defense. Since the OSH Act imposes "preventability" as the standard of care, employers cannot be cited for violations resulting from isolated, unpredictable employee misconduct; i.e., it was unpreventable. The isolated misconduct defense, also called the isolated occurrence or isolated event defense, is an affirmative defense with three major elements, the last of which itself has three elements.[339] First, the employer must show that the violation was isolated and brief. The OSHRevCom held that a violation involving six employees was not isolated.[340] Second, the employer must prove that it had no actual or constructive knowledge of the violation.[341] Finally, the employer must prove that the incident contravened its safety

---

[338] S. Pac., *supra* note 336; S. Ry., *supra* note 337.

[339] Standard Glass Co., 1 OSHC 1045, OSHD ¶15,146 (RevCom 1972); Floyd Pike Elec. Contractor, Inc., 6 OSHC 1675, OSHD ¶22,805 (RevCom 1975); S & H Riggers and Erectors, Inc., 7 OSHC 1260, OSHD ¶23,480 (RevCom 1978). *Contra,* Ocean Elec. Corp. v. Secretary, 574 F.2d 396 (4th Cir. 1979).

Isolated misconduct must be pleaded at the issue formulation stage of the OSHRevCom proceeding. Murphy Pac. Marine Salvage Co., 2 OSHC 1464, OSHD ¶19,205 (RevCom 1975).

[340] Miss. Valley Erection Co., 1 OSHC 1527, OSHD ¶17,098 (RevCom 1973).

[341] In Brennan v. OSHRevCom & Hendrix, 511 F.2d 1139 (9th Cir. 1975), the burden of proving employer knowledge was shifted to OSHA. As suggested by Rothstein, *supra* note 210, at § 90, a workable rule would require OSHA to prove actual knowledge only in rebuttal.

The knowledge of a supervisor is generally imputable to an employer, W. Waterproofing Co. v. Marshall, 576 F.2d 139, 144 (8th Cir. 1978), unless the employer shows the misconduct of the supervisor, Floyd Pike, *supra* note 339.

program. To prove that it had a safety program, the employer must demonstrate that (1) it established work rules effectively implementing the requirement of the OSHA standard; (2) it effectively communicated the work rules to employees through training, instruction, and publication of the rules; and (3) the work rules were effectively enforced through supervision and training.[342] When the employer raises the defense of isolated misconduct, it puts its safety program on trial. Use the OSHRevCom discovery process to prepare to meet this defense.

[c] Multi-Employer Worksite

On multi-employer worksites, the problem arises that one employer may create conditions hazardous to another employer's employees. OSHA cites all employers reasonably connected with a particular violation,[343] a policy that may soon be tempered by the OSHRevCom. Responsibility under the OSH Act then focuses on two issues: the creation and control of the hazards, and the exposure of employees to the hazards. The Second Circuit established the principle that an employer can be in violation of an OSHA standard even if none of its own employees are exposed if it nevertheless created or controlled the condition.[344] Complementing this is the OSHRevCom position that employers cited for *nonserious violations* who did not create or control the hazard but who had employees exposed to the hazard will be liable if they cannot show either that they could not have known of the hazard with the exercise of due diligence or that, knowing of the hazard, they took "realistic measures" other than literally complying with the standards to protect their employees.[345] Such

---

[342] Floyd Pike, *supra* note 339.

[343] Paramount Plumbing and Heating Co., 5 OSHC 1459, ¶21,820 (RevCom 1977). An employer's duties are nondelegable. Dayton Tire & Rubber Co. v. OSHRevCom & Secretary, 539 F.2d 242 (D.C. Cir. 1976).

[344] Brennan v. OSHRevCom & Dic-Underhill, 513 F.2d 1032, 1037–38 (2d Cir. 1975).

[345] Anning-Johnson Co., 4 OSHC 1193, OSHD ¶20,690 (RevCom 1976); Grossman Steel and Aluminum Corp., 4 OSHC 1185, OSHD ¶20,691 (RevCom 1976). For a successful employer use of this defense, *see* Dutchess Mechanical Corp., 6 OSHC 1795, OSHD ¶22,876 (RevCom 1978).

measures include attempting to have the general contractor or the responsible contractor correct the conditions, instructing employees to avoid the hazard, and providing alternative means of protection.[346]

[d] Greater Hazard

If compliance with the standard would create a greater hazard to employees than would noncompliance, the employer can raise this affirmative defense. The three elements of this defense[347] are the following: (1) The hazards of compliance are greater than those of noncompliance; (2) alternative protections are unavailable; and (3) a variance was sought or was inappropriate because the condition was recent or an emergency. This last element is necessary to prevent erosion of the Secretary's variance procedure by the OSHRevCom.[348]

[e] Impossibility

There are two kinds of impossibility defenses. The first defense requires proof of two elements:[349] (1) Compliance must be impossible, not merely difficult, inconvenient, or expensive and (2) available alternative protections must be in use. The second defense relies on a showing that literal compliance would be futile, as when an employer who installs guardrails will still have work to be performed outside their protection.[350]

---

346 Dutchess Mechanical, *supra* note 345.

347 Irwin Steel Erectors, Inc., v. OSHRevCom, 574 F.2d 222 (5th Cir. 1978); Gen. Elec. Co. v. Secretary, 576 F.2d 558 (3d Cir. 1978).

348 S & H Riggers and Erectors, Inc., 7 OSHC 1260, OSHD ¶23,480 (RevCom 1979), *appeal filed;* Gen. Elec., *supra* note 347, at 561, *accord,* Cleary's dissent in Republic Granite Co., 4 OSHC 1711, 1714, OSHD ¶21,167 (RevCom 1976).

349 Hughes Brothers, 7 OSHC 1830, OSHD ¶22,909 (RevCom 1978).

350 Universal Sheet Metal Corp., 2 OSHC 1061, OSHD ¶18,163 (RevCom 1974).

[f] Infeasibility

The affirmative defense of infeasibility must be carefully distinguished from denials that OSHA has met its burden of proving feasibility.[351] OSHA has this burden under Section 5(a)(1);[352] certain vaguely worded standards, such as the personal protective equipment standard;[353] and certain clearly worded standards, such as the noise and air contaminant standards.[354] Denying and rebutting that element of OSHA's burden of proof is different from alleging an affirmative infeasibility defense.[355]

A standard[356] can be attacked as infeasible "on its face," or as infeasible "as applied."[357] To the best of the author's knowledge, no facial attack on the feasibility of a particular standard has

---

[351] This burden does not extend to all OSHA standards; *see, e.g.*, Ace Sheeting and Repair Co. v. OSHRevCom, 555 F.2d 439 (5th Cir. 1977).

[352] Nat'l Realty, *supra* note 314, at 1268. *But see* the limitation to feasibility of preventing employee misconduct, thereby excluding technological feasibility. Jones & Laughlin Steel, 6 OSHC 1204, OSHD ¶22,380 (1977).

[353] 29 CFR § 1910.132(a); Diebold, Inc., v. Marshall, 585 F.2d 1327, 1333 (6th Cir. 1978).

[354] 29 CFR § 1910.95, .1000. Castle & Cook Foods, 5 OSHC 1435, OSHD ¶21,854 (RevCom 1977); Carnation Co., 6 OSHC 1730, OSHD ¶22,837 (RevCom 1978); Sampson Paper Bag Co., 8 OSHC 1515 (RevCom 1980); Republic Granite Co., 4 OSHC 1711, OSHD ¶21,167 (RevCom 1976).

[355] Even the broad proposition asserted by the Third Circuit in Atlantic & Gulf Stevedores, Inc., v. OSHRevCom, 534 F.2d 541, 551 (1976), is qualified by its statement that: "In an enforcement proceeding, invalidity is an affirmative defense to a citation, and the petitioning employer bears the burden of proof on the issue . . . To carry its burden the petitioner must produce evidence showing why the standard under review, *as applied to it*, is arbitrary, capricious, unreasonable or contrary to law . . .,"(at 551–52)(emphasis added). This broad notion may also be limited to substantive, not procedural, challenges. Nat'l Indus. Constrs., Inc., v. OSHRevCom, 583 F.2d 1048 (8th Cir. 1978).

[356] Feasibility deliberations in standards proceedings are arguably required by the Act's definition of a standard, i.e., that it be "reasonably necessary or appropriate," Section 3(8), 29 U.S.C. § 652(8); Am. Petroleum Inst. v. OSHA, 581 F.2d 493 (5th Cir. 1978), *aff'd on other grounds*, 100 S. Ct. 2844 (1980). In addition, the provisions regarding the generation of standards governing toxic materials use the phrases "to the extent feasible" and "feasibility" in specifying what OSHA must consider. Section 6(b)(5), 29 U.S.C. § 655(b)(5).

[357] 29 CFR § 1910.3.

succeeded.[358] There is emerging support for a carefully limited infeasible "as applied" defense.[359] To begin with, the employer should show exhaustion of other applicable remedies, such as the variance procedure, the procedure for modification of abatement dates, and the alternatives existing under other labor laws. Otherwise, the statute's centralization of the exemption power would be eroded.[360] Then the employer must develop its claim of technological or economic infeasibility and show that the application of the standard to its situation would be arbitrary or capricious.[361]

[g] Employee Resistance

Employee refusal to comply with a valid citation is no defense. Although Section 5(b) gives employees the responsibility of complying with the OSH Act, the Act provides no sanctions for employee noncompliance;[362] final responsibility for compliance rests with the employer. The result of the holdings[363] in this area is that employers must establish adequate programs of safety training and supervision, backed up by discipline. If an unorganized work force exists, the employer can do this through its own rules and procedures. If a union exists, an employer must bargain for the unilateral right to discipline workers for safety infractions and must use that right to enforce OSHA standards.[364]

---

358 Section 10(c), 29 U.S.C. § 659(c). There is no express power to create defenses.

359 *See,* Berger & Riskin, *Economic and Technological Feasibility in Regulation of Toxic Substances under the Occupational Safety and Health Act,* 7 Ecology L.Q. 285, 305 (1978).

360 *Id.,* at 326–34.

361 Atlantic and Gulf, *supra* note 355, at 551–52.

362 29 CFR § 1977.22 preserves the employers' right to impose discipline for safety infractions. Atlantic and Gulf, *supra* note 355, at 553–55. *Cf.* Fed. Coal Mine Health and Safety Act of 1969, 30 U.S.C. §§ 801, 819(a)(1)–(2).

363 Atlantic and Gulf, *supra* note 355, at 555–56; I.T.O. Corp. v. OSHRevCom, 540 F.2d 543 (1st Cir. 1976).

364 Such contract rights can be enforced under Section 301 and Boys Market injunctions should a job action result. Atlantic and Gulf, *supra* note 355. That case also suggests two other remedies, each of dubious value. "The employer can still apply to the Secretary pursuant to Section 6(d) of the Act, 29 U.S.C. § 655(d), for a variance from a promulgated standard on a showing that alternative methods for protecting employees would be *equally effective*" (emphasis

[h] Res Judicata and Collateral Estoppel

These doctrines are applicable to OSHRevCom contests.[365] To overcome this defense, OSHA must demonstrate that the violation is different from the previously adjudicated one, that the hazardous conditions have changed, or distinguish the prior determination as based on a condition that could have changed.[366] An employer has successfully used collateral estoppel to enjoin OSHA from enforcing its noise standard at any of its plants. After winning eight cases before the OSHRevCom on the basis of economic infeasibility, the employer won an injunction on the ground that requiring it to defend the remaining cases on economic infeasibility grounds would deny it due process.[367]

§ 5.04. Controlling Job Hazards through Labor Contracts

In an organized shop, the union has the right under the NLRA to bargain over workplace safety and health issues.[368] The rights

---

added) (at 555). In addition, "under § 10(c), 29 U.S.C. § 659(c), the Secretary has authority to extend the time within which a violation of a standard must be abated" (at 555).

[365] Ga. Power Co., 7 OSHC 1497, OSHD ¶21,199 (RevCom 1976). A prior failure to cite, in contrast to a prior determination by an ALJ, is no basis for a res judicata defense, Whirlpool Corp., 5 OSHC 1173, OSHD ¶21,659 (1977).

[366] Johnson Steel, 6 OSHC 1308, OSHD ¶22,484 (1977); Kaiser, 6 OSHC 1845, OSHD ¶22,845 (1978).

[367] Continental Can Co. v. Marshall, 455 F. Supp. 1015 (S.D. Ill. 1978), *aff'd,* 603 F.2d 590 (7th Cir. 1979).

[368] Section 8(d) of the NLRA mandates bargaining over "other terms and conditions of employment." 29 U.S.C. § 158(d). The NLRB holds that an employer that refuses to bargain over safety and health violates Section 8(a)(5). Gulf Power Co., 156 NLRB 622, *enforced,* 384 F.2d 822 (5th Cir. 1967). Furthermore, the courts will respect the result of the collective bargaining. Where an arbitrator's award found that an employer's unilateral change in work rules violated the labor contract, the court enforced the contract despite the employer's argument that the award contradicted the national policy against smoking in asbestos plants. Johns-Manville Sales v. IAM, 621 F.2d 756 (5th Cir. 1980).

obtained through collective bargaining are separate and independent from rights under the OSH Act.[369] When handling a grievance under the existing contract, consider OSHA in addition to the contract. Since OSHA has no "exhaustion" requirement, one can file an OSHA complaint without first filing a grievance. Some safety representatives report success in using the threat of calling in OSHA to resolve safety grievances on the floor. At bargaining time, carefully review applicable OSHA standards, thinking of them as the base from which to bargain, as you set up your strategy for bargaining over safety issues. Remember, OSHA standards only set minimums for safety and health, as the minimum wage and overtime laws create the minimum standards for wages and hours; neither prohibits unions from bargaining for better working conditions.

This section first discusses how to capitalize on existing contract language in grievance handling and arbitration, and then covers negotiation of new contract language about job hazards. (The role of the labor contract in obtaining access to data and in protecting workers' job security is discussed in Sections 5.01 and 5.06, respectively.)

[1] Working with Existing Contracts

If your contract has no safety and health language on which to file grievances, the only way to control job hazards through the contract is indirect and difficult: it is necessary to defend against discipline for insubordination on safety and health grounds. (Defending against discipline is discussed in detail in Section 5.06.)

The most important safety and health clause commonly found in labor contracts is the employer's general statement that it will provide a safe place to work, e.g., "The Company shall continue to make reasonable provisions for the safety and health of its employees."[370] The simplicity of this clause is deceiving; it is

[369] *Cf.* Alexander v. Gardner-Denver Co., 415 U.S. 36 (1974).

[370] Clauses like this are found in more than half of all labor contracts. Bureau of Labor Statistics, *Major Collective Bargaining Agreements: Safety and Health Provisions* (Bulletin 1425-16, 1976) at 3. Well over 90 percent of labor contracts have arbitration procedures with no exclusions for safety and health issues. BLS,

actually stronger than the OSH Act's general duty clause.[371] The only limit on its use is your ability to persuade the arbitrator that it is "reasonable" for the company to promote safety by doing what you have requested. One arbitrator, faced with a general clause similar to this one, was of the opinion that the union could use it to grieve the following:

(1) lack of a safe place to work;
(2) lack of safe machinery, tools, and equipment;
(3) lack of competent fellow employees;
(4) lack of instructions and warnings as to the dangers involved; and
(5) lack of rules for the conduct of the work.[372]

In another case involving workers exposed to toxic substances, the employer had agreed in the contract to "institute and maintain all reasonable and necessary precautions for the safety and health of its employees." The arbitrator used the word "reasonable" to find that the employer had a duty to supply the union with the identity of all toxic materials in use at the plant.[373] Recently, in a case involving drivers of unsafe vehicles, an arbitrator used the phrase "the employer agrees to strive to provide a safe and healthful workplace and environment for all employees" to compel the employer to repair a group of motor vehicles that had been so poorly maintained as to create a safety hazard to their drivers.[374]

In handling a grievance under such a general duty clause, base the first negotiations on the actual plant experience with the hazard. Document the history of the hazard, making sure to demonstrate clearly worker exposure to the hazard, including prior employer knowledge of the problem if possible. If offering

Characteristics Of Major Collective Bargaining Agreements, July 1, 1976 (Bulletin 2013, 1979), at 82.

[371] Section 5(a)(1) is limited to hazards that could cause death or serious physical harm. Furthermore, the hazard must be "recognized" by the employer. See Section 5.03[4]–[5], *supra,* on the burden of proof in OSHRevCom cases for a full explanation of Section 5(a)(1).

[372] Erie Mining Co., 36 LA 902, 912 (1961).

[373] Ciba-Geigy Corp., 61 LA 438 (1973).

[374] Ogden Air Logistics, 73 LA 1101 (1979).

a proposal for controlling the hazard, show why it is feasible. At later steps in grievance handling, consider the possibility of defining "reasonable" by reference to outside sources of standards. It should be possible to convince an arbitrator that OSHA violations can be grieved under such a general duty clause, i.e., that it is "reasonable" to obey OSHA. It may also be possible to convince him or her to apply other standards, such as state or local safety codes, ANSI Consensus Standards, or NIOSH Criteria Documents. These standards are "reasonable" because they represent the consensus of safety experts familiar with the particular hazard or because they were passed by government agencies. Before the arbitration, call the OSHA area office, the nearest safety library's reference librarian, or the local COSH group to determine whether the grievance is covered by one of these alternative safety standards.

Another common general-purpose safety and health clause is one in which the employer has promised to obey applicable federal, state, and local laws. This allows the union to grieve violations of OSHA standards in the grievance/arbitration machinery. To extend this clause further, argue that it includes the state common law, i.e., employer's general duty to provide a reasonably safe place to work.[375] This argument converts the promise to obey existing laws into a "general duty clause" and gives an arbitrator a basis to apply consensus standards that have not yet been adopted by OSHA.

What happens if the union fails to enforce the safety language in the contract? The duty of fair representation (DFR) is the same for safety and health grievances as for any other kind: If no grievance has been filed, the union will *not* be held liable for failing independently to push the employer into controlling job hazards, unless it has been arbitrary, discriminatory, or acting in bad faith.[376] As one court said,

> It would be a mistake of vast proportions to read every power granted the union by management as creating a corollary contract right in the employee as against the union. Such interpretation of collective bargaining agreements would simply deter unions from

[375] See Section 5.05 on injunctions, *infra.*

[376] Bryant v. UMW, 467 F.2d 1, 5 (1st Cir. 1972).

> engaging in the unfettered give and take negotiation which lies at the heart of the collective bargaining agreement.[377]

On that basis, the court found that the widows of coal miners killed in a mine explosion had no DFR claim against the union for failing to ensure the company's compliance with federal statutes. If, however, an employee has filed a grievance seeking to enforce a saftey clause in the contract, the union must fairly assess the claim's merits[378] and process the valid ones without being "perfunctory."[379]

[2] Bargaining to Control Job Hazards

To prepare for contract negotiations involving safety and health problems, allow enough lead time to study adequately the plant's problems and to prepare a list of specific safety and health priorities.[380] Temper these bargaining aims with a realistic assessment of the company's history of contract compliance and the union's track record at enforcing the contract. Remember that by bargaining for an issue but losing a bargaining history is created, which may return to haunt the union at arbitration.[381]

As a tactical consideration, it is harder for some employers to bargain against reasonable safety and health demands than against bread-and-butter issues; it is like opposing motherhood. Two major issues appear most amenable to this approach. The first is the right to open information on job hazards. In bargaining, the rhetorical posture is "Don't we have the right to know

---

[377] *Id.*

[378] Vaca v. Sipes, 386 U.S. 171, 190 (1967); Ruzicka v. Gen. Motors Corp., 523 F.2d 306, 309 (6th Cir. 1975), on remand, 649 F.2d 1207, action dismissed — F. Supp.—, 108 LRRM 2319 (1981).

[379] Hines v. Local 377, 421 U.S. 928 (1975); Curtis v. United Transp. Union, 102 LRRM 2961 (E.D. Ark. 1979).

[380] For resources on analyzing health and safety problems, see note 10. For a handbook of model clauses, *see* Paul Chown, *Workplace Health and Safety: A Guide To Collective Bargaining* (1980), available from Labor Occupational Health Program, 2521 Channing Way, Berkeley, Cal. *See generally* L. Marceau, *Drafting a Union Contract* (1965).

[381] S.W. Ornamental Iron Co., 38 LA 1025, 1028–29 (1962).

the composition of the materials we work with?" The second issue is getting the right to refuse hazardous work. In bargaining, the rhetorical posture is "Do we have to choose between our health and our jobs?"

These questions are of such great importance that they are treated separately in Sections 5.01 and 5.06 of this chapter; turn there for material on which to base detailed negotiating proposals.

The most important pair of clauses to bargain for are a strong general duty clause coupled with a broad safety exception to the no-strike promise.[382] The general duty clause allows you to grieve a multitude of unanticipated safety and health problems. Its shortcoming, however, is that without the safety exception to the no-strike promise, all safety and health disputes become subject to the "obey now, grieve later" principle. The crucial importance of the safety exception is to prevent this waiver of the workers' Section 7 rights.[383] In describing the employer's general duty, use words like "the best" or "optimum," e.g., "The employer agrees to provide the highest level of workplace safety and health."

In drafting, avoid the limiting word "reasonable" if at all possible. Two unfavorable arbitrators' decisions underscore the importance of this point. In one,[384] the arbitrator found that "reasonable provisions" meant the company had to correct only conditions that adversely affected a substantial number of employees. In the second case, the arbitrator found, among other things, that "reasonable efforts" did not impose a duty to prevent "risks normally inherent in the job.[385] This means that the worse the "normal" conditions, the lower the employer's duty. In arguing for better language, point out that the employer already has a duty under Section 5(a) of the OSH Act to be more than "reasonable"; it must "free" the workplace of all recognized hazards that are preventable.[386] By including this OSH Act "preventabili-

[382] Even if the contract contains no express no-strike promise, one is implied if the object of the strike is subject to arbitration. Gateway Coal v. UMW, 428 U.S. 317 (1974).

[383] *See generally,* Section 5.06, *infra.*

[384] Singer Co., 48 LA 1343 (1967).

[385] Brooklyn Union Gas Co., 48 LA 425 (1966).

[386] See text accompanying note 320, *supra.*

ty" duty in the contract, the company merely makes the OSH Act duty grievable, leading to fewer OSHA inspections.

Safety committees are another important subject of collective bargaining. They will become even more important in the 1980s as both the labor movement and employers press for reform of the OSHA enforcement system. The authors of a recent article[387] are convinced that properly established workplace enforcement committees can provide "more health and safety with less red tape" if workers are given training, government backup, real power to obtain information and control job hazards, and freedom from employer discipline for refusing to perform hazardous work. They report that in Sweden labor–management safety committees are mandatory and more than half of the health and safety committee members must be elected by the nonsupervisory employees. These union-dominated committees have the right to—

(1) veto any plans for new machines, materials, or work processes for health and safety reasons;
(2) decide how to spend the company health and safety budget, which is generally negotiated through local bargaining;
(3) approve the selection and direct the work of the company doctor, nurse, safety engineer, or industrial hygienist;
(4) review all corporate medical records, monitoring results, and other information on hazards;
(5) shut down dangerous operations until the hazards can be corrected (individual workers also have that right); and
(6) decide how much time they need to do their safety committee work, all of which must be paid for by the company.

The workers who belong to the committee are sent to safety institutes for training.

As a practical matter, generalizations about safety committees are difficult; no model can be applied in all workplaces. Accord-

[387] Matt Witt and Steve Early, *The Worker as Safety Inspector,* Working Papers, September/October, 1980, at 21.

ingly, set out below is a checklist of issues for review before negotiating safety committee clauses:

(1) Is the unit of representation well defined?
- — Plant, department, line

(2) Is membership well defined?
- — Number of members
- — Union-management mix
- — Selection
  - Union election, appointment
  - Joint appointment
  - Union veto over management choice
- — Qualifications of members
- — Duration of service

(3) Are meetings well defined?
- — Frequency and duration
  - Routine meetings
  - Emergency meetings
- — Quorum for action
- — Records

(4) Are functions well defined?[388]
- — Inspections and investigations
  - Regular, complaint response, and accident response
  - Monitoring equipment purchase, training, maintenance, and backup laboratory analyses
  - Outside consultants and experts
- — Recommendations for action[389]
- — Responsibility for grievance handling
  - Relation to other contractual grievance remedies
  - Final resolution of safety disputes
  - Safety exception to no-strike promise

(5) Is role of committee members well defined?
- — General safety officers or stewards
- — "Red tagging" of hazardous machines or lines

---

[388] See item (3) for additional functions.

[389] If the union completely takes over the safety function from management, it may be liable in some states when it negligently fails to carry out its duty. See text accompaning notes 402–06, *infra.*

- Follow-up on "red tagging"
- Protection for mistakes in "red tagging"

— Work refusals[390]

— Access to safety and health data[391]

— Training

- Provision, frequency, duration
- Type: first-aid, hazard recognition and control, monitoring equipment

— Compensation

Consider negotiating clauses covering ventilation, noise, sanitation, lighting, housekeeping, and other specific working conditions. First review the applicable OSHA standards in order to improve on the OSHA protections; avoid hard bargaining to win rights that are already in existence. For instance, if the OSHA standard's permissible exposure level for an air contaminant inadequately protects workers, improve on it by securing the employer's promise to adopt the NIOSH recommended standard instead. Generally, knowledge of the OSHA standard raises the level of discussion at the bargaining table.

Good ventilation control is worth pushing hard for. Unlike the tiresome and inadequate substance-by-substance approach to control used by OSHA to control air contaminants,[392] adequate ventilation can solve respiratory problems caused by many substances. If the employer is exposing workers to substances controlled by OSHA, potential OSHA liability can be used for leverage in exacting a promise to deal with ventilation. Hard information on actual workplace exposures at particular working stations, and an engineer's cost estimate for an adequate fresh air supply,[393] will prepare one to bargain over ventilation. The elegance of this approach is that the employer may be able to solve many potential problems with one solution.

Noise control is bound to become a more important bargaining topic because of OSHA's failure to make meaningful progress in enforcement. One of OSHA's few successes in the noise area has

---

390 *See* Section 5.06, *infra,* for work refusal materials.

391 *See* Section 5.01, *supra,* for a data checklist.

392 29 CFR § 1910.1000.

393 *See* Section 5.01, *supra,* on getting access to data for bargaining.

been to publish an excellent practical booklet on noise control.[394] This booklet should be mandatory reading for workers dealing with noise. Thoroughly review it before bargaining over noise problems. Also, review the OSHA noise standard and use it as a reference point, mindful of its limitations. Its 90-decibel, eight-hour exposure level is widely acknowledged to be inadequate to protect workers against hearing loss; its use of the word "feasible" has made it legally necessary for OSHA to perform a cost-benefit analysis to justify the imposition of controls, effectively carving out a large exception to the 90-decibel standard. OSHA has also recently promulgated a hearing conservation standard that must be reviewed.[395]

The preservation of pay and job rights is crucial. If workers lose pay as a result of plant safety and health activities,[396] or of being treated for a work-related condition, they will be discouraged from correction of the problems. Ideally, the worker with a partial disability as a result of work will have his job and his pay protected. The Department of Labor has two programs with relevant but limited standards. OSHA offers rate retention for eighteen months to those medically removed from excessive lead exposure under the new lead standard.[397] The Office of Federal Contract Compliance Programs requires federal contractors to make "reasonable accommodations" to the partially disabled to allow them to remain at work.[398] To cover this gap, Chown proposes the following contract language:[399]

(1) *Worker retains higher rate for duration of employment:*

---

[394] *Noise Control: A Guide for Workers and Employers* (U.S. Dept. of Labor, OSHA 1980).

[395] 46 Fed. Reg. 4078 (January 16, 1981).

[396] In a recent case, the arbitrator held that there was no wage protection for downgraded workers unable to wear respirators because of pulmonary dysfunction. Although the company gave "rate retention" to employees removed from lead exposure as a result of occupational disease, it did not have to extend it to workers physically incapable of wearing respirators. Globe Union, Inc., 80-2 ARB ¶8459 (1980).

[397] 29 CFR § 1910.1025(k)(2).

[398] 41 CFR § 60-741.6(d). *See also* § 60-741.54, app. B.2.; Notice of Proposed Rulemaking, 45 Fed. Reg. 86206, 86213-4 (December 30, 1980).

[399] Chown, *supra* note 380, at 32.

Rate retention: Any employee required to change a job because of an occupational injury or disease arising out of or in the course of employment shall retain the regular rate of pay if transferred to a lower-rated job. Subsequent raises in pay, cost of living adjustments or other upward pay adjustment applying to the former position shall be granted as though the original job were still being performed. Similarly, all other compensation-related benefits shall be maintained at the same or higher level.

(2) *Worker has right to transfer, including long training time on new job:*

Right to transfer: Any employee who suffers an industrial accident or illness which makes it impossible or medically unsuitable to perform the duties of the present job, shall have the right to transfer to another job. Every effort will be made to find an open position with comparable pay which the employee can do with little or no additional training. If necessary, however, the employer will train such an employee for the length of time necessary to qualify fully for the new job.

(3) *Worker given plant- or company-wide bump rights:*

Seniority rights: In the event there are no open jobs for an employee pursuant to Clause 2 above, then such employee may exercise seniority rights to bump an employee who is junior on the seniority roster. Such bumping shall be accomplished in such a manner that no one is laid off from work.

(4) *Modification of seniority rules:*

Where necessary to protect the employment rights of handicapped and otherwise medically disabled employees, the union and company agree to negotiate special rules of procedure to permit such employees to be assigned to and retained in jobs they are able to perform.

The following is a general checklist of safety issues for review before bargaining.[400] Use it in conjunction with the safety committee checklist.

[400] Adapted from BLS Bulletin, *supra* note 370.

(1) Compliance and inspection provisions
  (a) Employer compliance
    - Federal, state, and local laws should be distinguished as *minimum* standards.
    - ANSI and NFPA consensus standards can be adopted.
    - NIOSH recommendations and NCI, Environmental Protection Agency (EPA), and other government standards can be adopted.
    - Sanctions or penalties for employer noncompliance
  (b) Employee compliance
    - Duty to follow safety rules
    - Duty to wear protective gear
    - Duty to report job hazards
    - What disciplinary system is set up?

(2) Avoiding work under unsafe conditions
  (a) Who may refuse work? Union, worker, or both?
  (b) What is the scope of the no-strike promise here? Is there an exception?
  (c) Who may shut down a machine, line, or department? Union, safety committee members, or workers?
  (d) If line is shut down, what transfer and pay retention rights do workers have?
  (e) Who says what is unsafe? Is a good faith belief of danger enough, or must the hazard be abnormally dangerous as determined by a company expert after the fact?
  (f) What rights do individual work refusers have to assignment to other work and rate retention?

(3) Grievance/arbitration machinery for safety disputes
  (a) Who may file? Union, safety committee members, and/or workers?
  (b) Can they be filed at an advanced stage?
  (c) Which ones are referred to the safety committee?
  (d) Is there quicker grievance handling of safety disputes?
  (e) What is the final step for resolving remaining disputes? Special arbitrator, call in OSHA, union right

to call strike, joint union-management decision? Union choice of arbitration or strike?

(4) Safety equipment and related protection
  (a) General safety equipment clause
   - Who pays for,[401] who maintains, who replaces, which equipment?
   - Safe tools, equipment, and transportation
   - Crew size and working in isolation; is "buddy system" used on hazardous jobs?
  (b) Specific protections
   - Machinery guarding
   - Protection from electrical hazards
   - Lighting
   - Protective clothing, gloves, safety shoes, eye and face protection
   - Protection from falls and falling objects
   - Radiation
   - Fire protection

(5) Occupational illnesses and related provisions
  (a) Environmental monitoring
   - Who can request monitoring?
   - Who is trained to perform it?
   - Who directs studies?
   - Who has access to reports?
   - Who decides on budget for lab analyses?
  (b) Medical surveillance
   - Who conducts it?
   - Who interprets the results?
   - What confidentiality protections exist to prevent misuse of medical information?
   - Is there provision for second and third opinions on certain decisions, such as a worker's fitness to remain on a particular job?
  (c) What sanitation and personal hygiene provisions are made?

(6) Accident, injury, and disability procedures

---

[401] Some OSHA standards make payment for safety gear the subject of bargaining. Budd v. OSHRevCom, 513 F.2d 201 (3d Cir. 1975).

    (a) Accident reporting, investigating, and recordkeeping
    (b) Medical facilities, personnel, and transportation
    (c) Compensation for job-related injuries, illnesses, and disabilities
    (d) Leave, transfer, rate retention, and special seniority rights of disabled
(7) Hazardous duty pay

Negligence lawyers for the widows of workers killed in industrial accidents often sue unions for failing effectively to enforce safety and health clauses in labor contracts. The real problems are that employers are immune from suit despite their responsibility[402] and that workers' compensation benefits are disgracefully low. Our assessment is that, fortunately, unions need not seriously fear liability; it is wholly inconsistent with the federal labor policy. As one court commented,

> This Court is not unfamiliar with the difficult and longstanding problem of ensuring safety in the coal mines of this country. We recognize the harsh plight of those who have lost the family breadwinner through the all too frequent intervention of a mining disaster. The answer to their problem is not to pervert the collective bargaining process by reading into its instruments a liability which was never contemplated and duties which were never assumed in fact or in theory. To saddle labor unions with liability for the mine operators' failure to comply with standards introduced into the contract at the union's bidding would simply be to discourage the inclusion of similar or more effective standards in later contracts. Such a result would not serve the interest of miners and would retard rather than advance the goals of the national labor policy.[403]

In bargaining, the crucial point to remember is *not to bargain for exclusive control* over safety and health without clearly planning for

---

[402] Note that the employer has the final authority over safety and health matters under the common law, under Section 5(a) of the OSH Act, and under most management rights clauses in contracts.

[403] Bryant, *supra* note 376, at 5–6.

potential liability;[404] bargain for permissive language. If the contract provides that the union's role is the usual one of acting as safety advisor and grievance handler, it will be free of liability.[405] Reinforce these provisions by making sure that the contract assigns management the exclusive right to control workplace safety and health. The two cases holding unions liable under state law both relied on contract language giving the union mandatory duties. The courts also failed to understand the bedrock proposition of the federal labor law that the *only* enforceable duty arising under a labor contract is the federal duty of fair representation.[406] In bargaining, the DFR allows the union "a wide range of reasonableness."[407] Only where the union discriminates in bargaining on job hazards between members of the bargaining unit has it violated the DFR.

§ 5.05. Controlling Job Hazards through Injunctions

Getting a court to control a job hazard is possible but so expensive that it is a recourse only if OSHA and the labor contract fail. Court action can be based on either the state common-law duty of employers to provide a safe place to work or the employer's duties under its collective bargaining agreement.

While state court injunctions are not yet widely recognized,[408] they are based on a solid foundation—the nineteenth-century

404 Helton v. Hake, 564 S.W.2d 313 (Mo. Ct. App. 1978).

405 Brooks v. N.J. Mfrs. Ins. Co., 405 A.2d 466 (A.D. 1979); Bryant, *supra* note 376.

406 Helton, *supra* note 404; Dunbar v. United Steelworkers, 602 P.2d 21 (Idaho S. Ct. 1979), *cert. granted* (1980). *Contra,* House v. Mine Safety Appliances, 417 F. Supp. 939, 945 (D. Idaho 1976).

407 Ford Motor Co. v. Huffman, 345 U.S. 330, 338 (1953).

408 Shimp v. N.J. Bell Tel. Co., 368 A.2d 408, OSHD ¶21,421 (Ch. Div. 1976); Kaelin v. Goodrich, 88 LRRM 2282, 2283 (1974) (plaintiff refused to amend its complaint properly to allege a breach of this duty); Fed. Employees for NonSmokers' Rights v. United States, 446 F. Supp. 181 (D.D.C. 1978) (court requested briefs on federal jurisdiction to hear claim). *See generally* Blumrosen, Ackerman, Kligerman, van Schaick, & Sheehy, *Injunctions against Occupational Hazards: The Right*

duty of a master to provide his servants with a reasonably safe place to work,[409] coupled with the contemporary "prevention" policy of the OSH Act to temper the potential excesses of the tort standard of "reasonableness." The remedy is provided by the traditional principles of equity jurisprudence. While a court may require exhaustion of OSHA or of the grievance machinery where available and appropriate, neither the OSH Act nor federal labor law nor the workers' compensation acts preempt or exclude the matter from the jurisdiction of the state courts.

Briefly summarized, the master's general duty was to take reasonable care to provide a safe place to work, including safe machinery and equipment, instruction of workers where necessary, warnings of dangers not likely to be observed by the worker,[410] and provision of reasonably safe fellow workers.[411] While the safety practices and customs of the trade were evidence of reasonableness, laggard industries could not seek refuge in "custom" as a complete defense where ordinary judgment would recognize an unreasonable danger.[412] The master's three defenses—contributory negligence of the worker, the worker's assumption of the risk, and the fellow servant's negligence—drastically limited the workers' damage recoveries. These defenses, however, do not apply in injunction proceedings, since the injunction will issue before the harm has occurred, not after the fact as in damage actions.[413] In some decisions involving damage claims based on the employer's violation of safety statutes, judges recognized that workers should not have to face the choice between remaining at work under dangerous conditions or quitting, but should have the right to work under safe conditions.[414] To invoke equity jurisdiction, one must show irreparable injury and the inadequacy of legal remedies. Clearly bodily injury is irreparable injury that cannot adequately be compensated for through money dam-

to Work under Safe Conditions, 64 Cal. L. Rev. 702 (1976) [hereinafter cited as State Injunctions].

[409] *See generally* American Digest, Master-Servant, §§ 85–299.

[410] In an injunction action to enforce the duty to provide a safe place to work, the employer would have recourse to the state law of trade secrets as a defense.

[411] State Injunctions, *supra* note 408, at 708–10.

[412] *Id.*

[413] *Id.,* at 713.

[414] *Id.,* at 712.

ages. Since potential preventive remedies exist at law, namely, the OSH Act and the labor contract, a showing of exhaustion or of the futility of attempting exhaustion must be made.[415]

The continued availability of state court jurisdiction to issue such an injunction is preserved by Section 4(b)(4) of the OSH Act[416] and encouraged, in a general sense, the section of the OSH Act that allows states to assume enforcement responsibility under the Act.[417] While arbitration of contract disputes is favored under federal labor law,[418] since the common-law duty at stake here is an individual right, not a collective right, arbitration is not mandatory.[419] Finally, the workers' compensation statutes are essentially irrelevant, since they focus exclusively on money remedies, not prevention.

In the only decision accepting this theory,[420] the court injected a distinction that ignores the national "prevention" policy imposed by the OSH Act. The court said,

> In *Canonico* the court was presented with a byproduct which was a *necessary result* of the operation of the business . . . [whereas there] is no necessity to fill the air with tobacco smoke in order to carry on defendant's business, so it cannot be regarded as an occupational hazard which plaintiff has voluntarily assumed in pursuing

---

[415] *Id.*, at 715–20.

[416] Section 4(b)(4), 29 U.S.C. § 653(b)(4), provides: "Nothing in this chapter shall be construed to supersede or in any manner affect any workmen's compensation law or to enlarge or diminish or affect in any other manner the common law or statutory rights, duties, or liabilities of employers and employees under any law with respect to injuries, diseases, or death of employees arising out of, or in the course of, employment."

[417] Section 18(a), 29 U.S.C. § 667(a), provides: "Nothing in this chapter shall prevent any state agency or court from asserting jurisdiction under State law over any occupational safety or health issue with respect to which no standard is in effect under section 6." *See generally,* State Injunctions, *supra* note 408, at 720–27.

[418] The Steelworker Trilogy: United Steelworkers v. Am. Mfg. Co., 363 U.S. 564 (1960); United Steelworkers v. Warrior & Gulf Navigation Co., 363 U.S. 574 (1960); United Steelworkers v. Enterprise Wheel & Car Corp., 363 U.S. 593 (1960). The "industrial peace" rationale is pointed to as the aim of arbitration, 29 U.S.C. § 173(d).

[419] *See* Alexander v. Gardner-Denver Co., 415 U.S. 36, 58 (1974).

[420] Shimp, *supra* note 408, at 411–12.

a career as a secretary.[421]

This distinction can be argued against as an aberration of the national "prevention" policy.

The second approach to obtaining an injunction controlling a hazard is to seek a "reverse Boys Market" preliminary injunction based on the employer's breach of the labor contract. The role of this remedy in the safety area is limited to preventing physical harm to workers pending an arbitrator's decision on the alleged contract breach. Under the majority approach, the court asks whether an injunction is necessary to protect the arbitral process itself,[422] or whether failure to issue the injunction would "render the arbitral process a hollow formality."[423] Obviously if worker health and safety are at stake, the prospective harm is so irreparable that a preliminary injunction will be necessary to prevent frustration of arbitration.[424]

The second issue at the preliminary injunction hearing will concern how strong a showing the union must make on the probability of success on the merits of the arbitration. From the national labor policy favoring arbitration and the Supreme Court's "presumption of arbitrability" of safety disputes,[425] it can be argued that the judge should not usurp the arbitrator's function, an argument that compels a lower level of judicial scrutiny of the merits of the contract claim. Furthermore, the interest in protecting worker safety arguably outweighs any company claims to the implicit privilege initially to interpret and implement its version of the contract, subject only to later reversal by an arbitrator. Finally, argue that close scrutiny of the merits should not be made by the court because, in health and safety matters, the risk of error should favor worker safety. The *Lever Brothers* case articulated a useful standard: ". . . questions concerning the interpretation of collective bargaining agreements . . .

---

421 *Id.*, at 411.

422 Columbia Local v. Bolger, 621 F.2d 615, 617 (4th Cir. 1980).

423 Lever Bros. Co. v. ICWU, 554 F.2d 115, 123 (4th Cir. 1976).

424 United Steelworkers of America v. Fort Pitt Steel Casting, 598 F.2d 1273 (1979). *See* Gateway Coal v. UMW, 428 U.S. 317 (1974) (in Gateway the employer's request for an injunction was granted on the condition that the safety hazard be eliminated pending arbitration).

425 Gateway, *supra* note 424.

should not be predetermined by the courts on their rulings on the preliminary injunctions."[426]

§ 5.06. Job Protection: Defending Workers Disciplined for Work Refusals or Safety Activities

Workers faced with a job hazard that the employer has failed to prevent and OSHA and the union have failed to correct should be free to take reasonable self-help measures to protect themselves without fear of discipline. Luckily, Section 7 of the NLRA does protect workers who engage in concerted activities for mutual aid or protection, including protecting workers from discipline for walking off the job over safety disputes.[427] Section 7's protection is clearly superior to that of both the OSHA work refusal standard and Section 502 of the NLRA—the narrow safety exception to no-strike clauses. Under Section 7, the reasonableness of the workers' on-the-spot judgment is never questioned; the employer's only defense is that the workers acted in bad faith. With the exception of its limitation to "concerted activity," this standard is the best possible rule for protecting the jobs of workers who have been forced to defy an employer work order to protect their safety and health.

A recent circuit court opinion clearly demonstrates the continuing vitality of workers' Section 7 rights.[428] Three employees refused to melt and pour scrap lead that had been earlier used to store radioactive materials. At the hearing, the employer defended by saying that it had checked out the possible hazard, that it had told the employees the lead was safe, and that this should have ended the matter. In other words, the employees' fear was "unreasonable." The court, however, found that "the merits of the underlying dispute are *irrelevant* to the determination of whether a [protected] 'labor dispute' exists or not."[429] The circuit court's principal holding was that the only question of fact con-

[426] 554 F.2d, at 123.

[427] NLRB v. Washington Aluminum, 370 U.S. 9 (1962).

[428] NLRB v. Modern Carpet Indus., Inc., 611 F.2d 811 (10th Cir. 1979).

[429] *Id.*, at 814.

cerned the good faith belief of the workers, i.e., whether the employees acted upon a genuine fear.

This powerful precedent stands in sharp contrast to the work refusal standards under Section 502[430] of the NLRA and OSHA.[431] For the worker to prevail under these standards, he must have had a reasonable belief of an imminent danger of death or serious physical injury, and there can have been no alternative to refusing the work. These standards clearly contemplate that the worker's on-the-spot judgment will be stringently reexamined after the fact. Most courts interpreting Section 502 have taken the even more extreme position that for the worker to prevail he must introduce objective evidence not of the reasonableness of his belief but rather of an abnormally dangerous threat.[432] This means the worker bets his/her job on whether s/he is mistaken in his/her judgment as to the abnormality of the danger. These standards show such a shocking disregard for worker safety that one commentator[433] has wryly compared them to the language of the criminal defenses of coercion, necessity, and self-defense. She observes that a "closer parallel would have been difficult to achieve without copying this exact necessity defense provision."[434]

From the point of view of simple equity, as well as in contrast to the excellent protection offered by Section 7, both work refusal standards are ripe for reform. The OSHA standard was written narrowly before OSHA was sure of its power to write any work refusal standard. Now, after the *Whirlpool* case,[435] OSHA can be confident of its regulatory power in this area; its principal limitation is that it cannot write a regulation which gives workers the right to go on safety strikes *with pay.* Reform of the OSHA standard proceeds through rule making, which must wait for a change of administrations. Section 502 is also ripe for reform. A current, but narrow, view of the law was outlined in a recent opinion of

---

[430] 29 U.S.C. § 143.

[431] 29 U.S.C. § 660(c)(1); 29 CFR § 1977.12(b)(2).

[432] Redwing Carriers, Inc., 130 NLRB 1208 (1961), *enforced,* 325 F.2d 1011 (D.C. Cir. 1963).

[433] Nancy K. Frank, *A Question of Equity: Workers' "Right to Refuse" under OSHA Compared to the Criminal Necessity Defense,* 31 Labor L.J. 618 (1980).

[434] *Id.,* at 621.

[435] Whirlpool Corp. v. Marshall, 100 S. Ct. 883 (1980).

the NLRB's Division of Legal Advice.[436] The opinion concerned a worker who was fired after refusing on safety grounds to perform a painting job. The opinion accepted as given the following facts: (1) The employee had been warned of the hazard by his fellow workers; (2) the employee called OSHA immediately after his discharge; (3) OSHA had cited the employer for sixteen serious violations, including two violations directly related to the painting work in question; (4) the employer did not contest the citations; and (5) the employer had contractually bound itself to "make all reasonable provisions for the safety and health of its employees." The court also found that there was a no-strike clause that had no exception for safety disputes. This, it held, triggered application of Section 502; applying the "criminal necessity" version of Section 502, the court observed that the worker presented no objective evidence of an abnormally dangerous working condition and, therefore, the regional attorney should not issue a complaint. Luckily for workers, there are ways to avoid Section 502's application, even with a no-strike clause. Moreover, even if Section 502 is applied, persuasive arguments exist to temper its harshness through changes in the law. Unlike reform of the OSHA standard, Section 502 reform will slowly advance, case by case.

In the following discussion, the main aim is to give the practicing lawyer facing his or her first case of employee discipline for safety-related activity (1) a framework for analyzing the facts of the case; (2) a catalogue of rules and arguments to use along the way; and (3) a map for choosing the appropriate remedial route to follow. This includes discussion of arbitration and common-law claims. The section closes with a brief review on bargaining about safety discipline clauses.

Several recurring terms should be noted. Two basic types of fact patterns recur: work refusal cases and cases of retaliation for safety-related activity, such as filing an OSHA complaint. These fact patterns are analytically distinct. For example, Section 502 obviously applies only to work refusals; proof problems with employer knowledge only occur with retaliation cases. Keep these two types of problems separated in your thinking. Also understand the relationship between Section 7 and Section 502 of

[436] Economy Tank Line, Inc., 99 LRRM 1198 (1978).

the NLRA. Section 7 establishes the right to engage in concerted activity for mutual aid and protection, including striking over safety on the job. This right is often waived in collective bargaining by no-strike clauses. Section 502's role is limited; it is the statutory safety exception to no-strike clauses; it offers no protection itself. Finally, Section 7 has a major limitation around which the NLRB and the circuit courts are currently struggling: When is individual activity "concerted"? Clearly, some group interest in safety must be advanced for individual activity to be for "mutual aid and protection." This limitation to "concerted activities" applies to both NLRB work refusals and retaliation cases; the OSHA standard has no such limitation. If a case involves individual action, carefully analyze it and gather evidence of "concert."

[1] Fact Analysis Checklist

Take a thorough history as soon as possible in order to plan which remedies to use. Grievances usually have to be filed very soon after the action. OSHA permits filing within 30 days, with tolling allowed[437] if contract or NLRB remedies are being exhausted, the NLRB has a 180-day filing period, and state statutes of limitations vary from 6 months to 6 years. Once having determined the time limitations and the general nature of the situation the client has presented, then use the following checklist to take the analytical history of the event. The list attempts to cover the range of *relevant* evidence. Do *not* confuse it with the elements of evidence *material* to particular claims, which will be discussed in the following section.

[a] Work Refusal Cases

(1) What was the hazard?
- Unusual for workplace or common? Detail.

[437] 29 CFR § 1977.5(d)(3). To protect your right to file a Section 11(c) complaint later, you *must* file your NLRB or contract complaint within thirty days of the violation.

- Violation of contract or not? Detail.
- Violation of OSHA standard? Detail.
- Any past experience with hazard in plant? Detail.
- Any past experience with hazard in industry? Detail (e.g., international representative as witness).
- Any company work rules recognizing hazard?
- Any consensus standard recognizing the hazard? What degree of injury was threatened? How imminent was threat?
- How likely was harm before enforcement would be complete?
- If health hazard, is effect of exposure irreversible (e.g., does the "one-shot" theory of carcinogenesis apply)?

(2) Did worker have disabilities that contributed to situation? Did employer know of disabilities? How?

(3) What was worker's perception of the hazard?
- Use "objective" evidence from above to prove good faith or reasonableness of worker's belief.
- What was the basis for fear?
- Did worker know of possible OSHA or contract violation at time of incident? Detail.
- Can employer show bad faith? Trace the interaction between the worker and the supervisor that led to the refusal. Will fellow workers testify to worker's good faith?

(4) Is there a duty not to strike over safety disputes?
- Arbitration clause coverage? Is dispute arbitrable? Is language clear? Does arbitration clause cover all disputes between the parties or just disputes over the contract? If arbitrable, does arbitrator have power to compel correction of condition, or does s/he have the limited power to fine?
- Is arbitration mandatory or permissive?
- No-strike clause coverage? Is there an express no-strike promise? Does it cover work refusals? Is there any bargaining history pertaining to the scope of the clause? Is there an express waiver of the right to strike in safety cases?

(5) Did refusal amount to strike?
- Single concerted refusal or plan of intermittent action?
- Piecework or hourly?
- Brief interruption with no intent to disturb production?
- Was offer to accept alternative work tendered?
- Was work merely deferred?
- Was request made to call OSHA to file complaint?
- Was there any pressure to grant concessions other than to correct the condition?
- Was there any protest of general policies?
- Was production interrupted? If so, detail.

[b] Retaliation Cases

(1) Was the safety activity discriminated against protected?
- Did the worker participate in official activity? Complain of job hazards to OSHA, state plans, or health agencies? Participate in official proceedings to control job hazards (e.g., testimony to OSHRevCom)? File safety grievances under the labor contract? Take safety complaints to the employer? Participate in plant safety committee?
- Did employee engage in any unofficial safety-related activity? Belong to safety caucus? Distribute safety literature? Organize around and discuss safety issues? Educate fellow workers about safety and health issues?

(2) How did the employer know of the activity?
- Was the worker open and notorious in activity?
- Are there any relevant writings, e.g., signed OSHA complaint given to employer?
- Trace relationship between the disciplining official and the official with actual knowledge. Is imputation of knowledge reasonable? Is it a small plant with open communication?

(3) What is the employer's reason for the action?

- Is it in writing?
- What about statements in unemployment insurance proceedings?
- Is it a pretext or one of several reasons?
- Can you rebut employer's claim that action would have been taken even in absence of protected activity?

(4) How can you show causation?
- Actual evidence of animus or malice? How specific and reliable is it?
- Circumstantial evidence? Absence of any legitimate basis for action?
- Differential treatment of similarly situated workers
- Precipitous timing of action
- Breach of internal disciplinary rules
- Inconsistencies in employer's versions

[c] Was Activity "Concerted"?

(1) Was there a "controversy" over "conditions of employment," i.e., a "labor dispute" covered by Section 2(9) of the NLRA?

(2) Does the activity advance some group interest?
- Was worker, in fact, the designated spokesperson for others?
- Was worker enforcing contract provision?
- Did worker know of arguably applicable contract provision or OSHA standard at time of the activity?
- Did the claim affect fellow employees?
- Was worker enforcing public laws, such as OSHA?
- Was act for worker's sole benefit?
- Have fellow workers disavowed worker's action?
- Was there any related activity by other workers directed at same objective?
- Was there any union participation in the activity?

(3) What was the aim of the activity? Was it a specific safety objective?

(4) Was the activity lawful and proper?
- Was there an attempt to bargain with employer in derogation of union?
- Was activity illegal or disloyal?
- Did activity exceed "reasonable" bounds?
- Did activity amount to an unprotected "partial" strike?

[2] NLRA Protection

The NLRB offers protection to safety activists and those who refuse hazardous work if the following four criteria are met.[438] First, there must be a work-related conflict that amounts to a "labor dispute" within the meaning of the NLRA.[439] An argument with a foreman about a job hazard is a "labor dispute"; a fistfight with a foreman over a car accident in the parking lot is not. There is no requirement that the worker demand that the employer correct the condition before taking action. A group of workers walked off the job to protest a freezing cold shop; the Supreme Court found that there had been a labor dispute even though the workers had not made a demand before walking off.[440] The crucial feature of the definition of a labor dispute is that the reasonableness or the merits of the workers' side of the dispute are irrelevant to the determination that their activity was protected.[441]

Second, the activity must advance a group interest. This requirement stems from the language of Section 7, which protects "concerted activities" for "mutual aid and protection."[442] This precludes individual action for personal benefit.[443] The finding that the activity promoted a group interest is primarily a factual

---

[438] *See* Shelly & Anderson Furniture Co. v. NLRB, 497 F.2d 1200, 1202–03 (9th Cir. 1974).

[439] Section 2(9), 29 U.S.C. § 152(9).

[440] NLRB v. Washington Aluminum Co., 370 U.S. 9 (1962).

[441] *Id.*, at 16; NLRB v. Mackay Radio & Tel. Co., 304 U.S. 333, 344 (1938); Union Boiler Co., 213 NLRB 818, *enforced*, 530 F.2d 970 (4th Cir. 1975).

[442] 29 U.S.C. § 157.

[443] *See* Tabernacle Community Hosp. and Health Center, 233 NLRB No. 208 (1977).

finding; the following rules for interpreting those facts are of secondary importance. If an individual has acted alone to advance a matter of common concern, such as safe working conditions, the NLRB has two related rules that extend protection to the individual worker. The most important is that "common concern will be found with respect to [colorable] violations of a safety statute which created a general hazard for employees."[444] An earlier retaliation case involved a safety activist in an unorganized shop fired after individually filing complaints to a state OSHA program. He had not even discussed the problems with his fellow employees before filing charges. Even so, the NLRB found "concerted activity," explaining,

> [S]ince minimum safe and healthful employment conditions for the protection and wellbeing of employees have been legislatively declared to be in the overall public interest, the consent and concert of action emanates from the mere assertion of such statutory rights. Accordingly, where an employee speaks up and seeks to enforce statutory provisions relating to occupational safety designed for the benefit of all employees, in the absence of any evidence that fellow employees disavow such representation, we will find an implied consent thereto and deem such activity to be concerted.[445]

The beauty of this extension is that it applies to all workers protected by the NLRA, whether organized or not. This rationale has been applied by the NLRB in individual work refusal cases.[446] Individual workers are protected from discipline if they have a good faith belief that the job hazard is of the type protected by OSHA. Obviously, the more evidence that the job hazard was in fact a common concern, the better the chances for protection. Supplement evidence of the hazard, and the arguable applicability of OSHA, with evidence of how other workers were affected, e.g., by showing that the individual was one of several subject to assignment to the hazardous condition. The second way the NLRB protects individual conduct is if the individual acts to

[444] Diagnostic Center Hosp. Corp. 228 NLRB 1215, 1217 (1977).

[445] Alleluia Cushion Co., Inc., 221 NLRB No. 162 (1975).

[446] United States Stove Co., 245 NLRB No. 183 (1979).

enforce the labor contract.[447] Here, the theory is that contract enforcement is merely an extension of the concerted activity that led to the labor contract. Sometimes called the *Interboro* doctrine,[448] this approach has been rejected in many circuits;[449] it is ripe for review by the Supreme Court.[450] But, because the NLRB follows *Interboro* even in circuits in which their orders will not be enforced, counsel for workers should focus on the NLRB standards and on the primary task of building the factual basis for a finding of "concert," even without the help of the *Interboro* doctrine.

The third criterion is that the activity must seek some specific remedy or result. This removes protection from such things as mere griping.

The fourth criterion is that the activity must not be unlawful or otherwise improper. This excludes disloyal conduct,[451] strikes in derogation of the exclusive representative status of the union,[452] partial strikes,[453] and strikes or work refusals that violate the no-strike clause of the labor contract. This last exclusion has Section 502 as a statutory exception. In retaliation cases, illegal acts or egregious acts of disloyalty may be relevant. In cases of work refusals that violate no-strike promises, Section 502's stringent standards apply.

The application of Section 502 often can be avoided. Examine the contract to see if the underlying safety dispute was arbitrable. If it was not, i.e., if the worker did not have the choice of "working now and grieving later," then check the contract for a no-

447 Bunney Bros., 139 NLRB 1516, 1519 (1962); Snap-On Tools Co., 207 NLRB 238 (1973); John Sexton Co., 217 NLRB 80 (1975).

448 Interboro Contractors, Inc., 157 NLRB 1295, *enforced*, 388 F.2d 495 (2d Cir. 1967).

449 *Compare id.;* NLRB v. Ben Pekin Corp., 452 F.2d 205, 206 (7th Cir. 1971) *with* NLRB v. N. Metal Co., 444 F.2d 881, 884 (3rd Cir. 1971); Kohls v. NLRB, 104 LRRM 3049, 3051 (D.C. Cir. 1980).

450 The Supreme Court may be tipping in favor of the *Interboro* approach. NLRB v. Weingarten, Inc., 420 U.S. 251, 260–61 (1975); Anchortank, Inc., v. NLRB, 618 F.2d 1153, 1161 (5th Cir. 1980).

451 NLRB v. Local 1229, IBEW (Jefferson Standard), 346 U.S. 464 (1953).

452 Emporium Capwell Co. v. W. Addition Community Organization, 420 U.S. 50 (1975).

453 Valley City Furniture Co., 110 NLRB 1589 (1954), *enforced*, 230 F.2d 947 (6th Cir. 1956).

strike promise. If there was none, then none will be inferred because "absent an explicit expression . . . the agreement to arbitrate and the duty not to strike should be construed as having coterminus application."[454] Even if there is an ambiguous no-strike promise, if the underlying dispute is not arbitrable, the no-strike promise may be cut back to the scope of arbitrability.[455] If arbitration is not mandatory, or if the arbitrator only has the power to fine the employer rather than the power to order correction of the unsafe condition, the NLRB will not infer a no-strike obligation.[456] If a no-strike obligation does exist, the next step in avoiding Section 502 is to avoid characterization of the work refusal as a strike. A work refusal of brief duration or "deferred execution" of a task[457] is not a strike if it does not interfere with production or pressure the employer for other ends.[458] If the refusing worker indicates availability for other work or willingness to perform safe portions of the job, this is some evidence that there is no strike, but it is not conclusive. If the refusing worker states that s/he is refusing the work in order to take time to file an imminent danger complaint with OSHA, this is also evidence that the refusal is not a strike.

If there is a contractual duty not to strike and there has been a strike, Section 502 applies. However, a good faith refusal to work because of "abnormally dangerous conditions" is not considered a strike.[459] The first element, the good faith belief of the

---

[454] Gateway Coal Co. v. UMW, 414 U.S. 368, 382 (1974).

[455] Gary-Hobart Water Corp. 210 NLRB No. 87 (1974). Statutory rights can be waived only on clear and unmistakable showing that waiver occurred. Timken Roller Bearing Co. v. NLRB, 325 F.2d 746 (6th Cir. 1963), *cert. denied,* 376 U.S. 971 (1964). Pacemaker Yacht Co., 253 NLRB No. 95 (1980)(the particular matter causing the strike must be expressly covered by the waiver).

In individual work refusal cases involving no-strike promises, be careful not to make inconsistent arguments as to arbitrability. In arguing "concert," use *Alleluia,* not *Interboro.* Arguing *Interboro* relies on the arbitrability of the safety claim and concedes arbitrability somewhat for purposes of the Section 502 claim.

[456] Whitehouse & Sons Co., 252 NLRB No. 140 (1980).

[457] Anheuser-Busch, Inc., 239 NLRB No. 23 (1978).

[458] Shelly & Anderson, *supra* note 438, at 1203.

[459] 29 U.S.C. § 143 provides: ". . . nor shall the quitting of labor by an employee or employees in good faith because of abnormally dangerous conditions for work at the place of employment of such employee or employees be deemed a strike under this chapter."

worker, is essentially vestigial.[460] As to the second element, "abnormally dangerous conditions," the NLRB has ruled, ". . . the term contemplates . . . an objective . . . test. What controls is not the state of mind of the employee or employees concerned, but whether the actual working conditions . . . might . . . be considered "abnormally dangerous."[461] This test is particularly pernicious, since the worse the "normal" conditions, the higher the workers' burden of showing "abnormality."

The stringency of the "abonormally dangerous" element can be argued against on several grounds, all of which depend on "objective" evidence. The first position is that the OSH Act should be used to set the standard for "abnormally dangerous conditions." Section 502 has no legislative history defining this term. Given that Section 502 and the OSH Act are two pieces of remedial legislation with the same aim, the ambiguity of Section 502 should be construed *in pari materia* with the OSH Act. In particular, Section 502 should accept serious violations of OSHA standards or of the general duty clause as establishing standards of normality. Similarly, it can be argued that if the labor contract has a specific provision defining a safety duty of the employer, then the employer has defined its own standard of normality and any violations of the contract clause should be deemed "abnormally" dangerous conditions. The second position is that there is a *Mastro Plastics* exception to the employer's invocation of the no-strike promise if the employer has seriously violated OSHA or the contract standards. Both meet the requirement of an objective test. The OSHA standard approach will succeed only if OSHA inspects and vindicates the workers' initial judgment. The contract approach would do the same if the review of the discipline were stayed pending the arbitration of the arguable contract violation.

Another approach to ameliorating the effect of Section 502 relies on a crucial ambiguity of *Gateway.* Before opting for an objective test for Section 502, the Supreme Court posed a choice of two alternatives: a subjective good faith belief test or an objec-

---

[460] *Compare* Knight Morley Corp., 116 NLRB 140 (1956) *with* Redwing Carriers, Inc., 130 NLRB 1208, 1209 (1961).

[461] Redwing Carriers, *supra* note 460, at 1209.

tive abnormally dangerous conditions test;[462] the Court ignored the intermediate objective test of a reasonable belief. One circuit court has already used this ambiguity to construe *Gateway* as permitting objective evidence of the belief of the worker that there were abnormally dangerous conditions.[463] If confronted with a Section 502 case containing serious OSHA citations on the refused working conditions, and the regional attorney of the NLRB has questions about his/her authority to issue a complaint, remind him/her that s/he can request an opinion from the Division on Advice and submit a position paper on the issue for the NLRB's review.

Once having met the four criteria for a protected activity, it is still necessary to show that the employer was motivated by this bad reason in disciplining or discharging the worker. In retaliation cases, this necessitates proving employer knowledge of the activity; otherwise, how could it be retaliating? In both retaliation and work refusal cases, the employer may offer some other, legitimate reason for its conduct; the ostensible reason may be a pretext or dual motive. In either case, it is convenient to think of the employer's reason as an affirmative defense.[464] If the defense is rebutted, it is a pretext; if it is not rebutted, then it must be weighed against the protected conduct under the NLRB's new *Wright Line* test.[465] The employer prevails only if it demonstrates that its decision would have been the same even in the absence of the protected activity.[466]

Some procedural aspects of the NLRB remedies are worth pointing out. Charges must be filed within 180 days,[467] unlike OSHA's 30-day requirement for Section 11(c) complaints.[468] The ultimate decision makers are ALJs of the NLRB, who are experienced with unfair labor practice charges; whereas under the OSH Act, federal court judges, who rarely hear labor cases and who are busy with their criminal dockets, hear Section 11(c)

---

[462] Gateway, *supra* note 454, at 386–88.

[463] Banyard v. NLRB, 505 F.2d 342, 348 (D.C. Cir. 1974).

[464] New England Fish Co., 212 NLRB No. 44 (1974); Standard Boards, Inc., 196 NLRB No. 143 (1972).

[465] Wright Line, 251 NLRB No. 150 (1980).

[466] *Id.*, slip op. at 21.

[467] Section 10(b), 29 U.S.C. § 160(b).

[468] Section 11(c)(2), 29 U.S.C. § 660(c)(2).

cases. NLRA coverage is narrower than OSHA's; the NLRA does not apply to certain supervisory employees, whereas Section 11(c) protections apply to all employees.[469] The Board will not defer Section 8(a)(1) claims to arbitration without consent;[470] if, however, a claim has already been resolved by an arbitrator, the Board will dismiss the charge if the arbitration was fair and regular, the parties had agreed to be bound by the award, and the decision is not "clearly repugnant" to the aims of the NLRA.[471] The NLRB also defers to the OSHA Section 11(c) program if the charges allege retaliation for filing OSHA complaints or testifying in OSHA proceedings.[472]

[3] OSH Act Protection

Section 11(c) of the OSH Act protects workers who are involved in proceedings "under or related to" the OSH Act or have exercised "any right afforded by" the Act.[473] OSHA regulations further outline the standards to be used by OSHA in enforcing Section 11(c) cases in the district courts.[474] These regulations protect "complaints under or related to the Act"[475] and include complaints to non-OSHA enforcement units, such as state or local agencies,[476] as well as complaints to employers,[477] even if the complaints are oral. They protect participation in "proceedings under or related to the Act."[478] The regulations also protect the exercise of any right afforded by the Act, which includes requesting information from OSHA or giving information to the

---

469 *Compare* Section 2(3) of the NLRA, 29 U.S.C. § 152(3) *with* Section 3(6) of the OSH Act, 29 U.S.C. § 652(b).

470 Great Am. Transp., 228 NLRB No. 102 (1977).

471 Speilberg Mfg. Co., 112 NLRB 1080 (1955).

472 Memorandum 79-4 (January 17, 1979).

473 Section 11(c), 29 U.S.C. § 660(c).

474 Section 11(c) does not create a private right of action.

475 29 U.S.C. § 1977.9.

476 29 U.S.C. § 1977.9(b).

477 29 U.S.C. § 1977.9(c).

478 29 U.S.C. § 1977.10.

OSHA inspector during the course of the inspection.[479] The regulations do not protect safety activists who have spoken out or organized around safety issues, but who have not yet reduced their safety objective to participation in enforcement activity.

The OSHA Section 11(c) regulations grant workers the right to refuse dangerous work. Recently, the Supreme Court unanimously upheld these regulations as a valid exercise of OSHA's authority.[480] As mentioned in the introduction, the protection is much narrower than that of Section 7. Before a worker can invoke it, s/he must be able to show that a reasonable person would have the same apprehension of death or serious physical injury from exposure to the hazard that the worker had, that s/he was confronted with a choice between not working and running the risk of injury, that s/he was offered no alternative work, that the employer denied his/her request to correct the hazard (if the worker could have notified the employer), and, finally, that there was insufficient time to use the OSHA procedures.[481] This standard for protection against work refusal discipline is more favorable than the Section 502 standard in that it second-guesses only the "reasonableness" of the worker's apprehension, not the objective "danger" of the hazard itself. This provision may offer protection to individual work refusers in situations where Section 7 cannot be used because of its limitation to "concerted activity."

OSHA's burden of proof is outlined in the regulations.[482] Charges must be filed within thirty days of the discriminatory act.[483] OSHA is instructed by the statute to reach a preliminary result within ninety days and to notify the parties. The regulations also permit, but do not compel, OSHA to defer to arbitration[484] and unfair labor practice hearings;[485] these are

---

[479] 29 U.S.C. § 1977.12.

[480] Whirlpool Corp. v. Marshall, 100 S. Ct. 883 (1980).

[481] 29 CFR § 1977.12(b)(2).

[482] 29 CFR § 1977.6(b). Unlike the NLRB's *Wright Line* test, the burden of proof is on OSHA throughout.

[483] Section 11(c)(2), 29 U.S.C. § 660(c)(2); 29 CFR § 1977.15. This section of the regulation sets out allowable tolling arguments.

[484] 29 CFR § 1977.18; Alan Woodsteel Co., OSHD ¶20,136 (E.D. Pa. 1975); N.L. Indus., OSHD ¶24,354 (7th Cir. 1980).

[485] 29 CFR § 1977.18. Newport News v. Marshall, 8 OSHC 1393 (E.D.Va. 1980).

complemented by a Memorandum of Understanding with the NLRB.[486] The lack of a private right of action under Section 11(c)[487] is missed, given the notoriously poor administration of the program.

[4] Labor Contract Protection in Existing Contracts

In the landmark case of *Gateway Coal v. UMW,*[488] the Supreme Court followed the national labor policy favoring arbitration and upheld an injunction controlling a safety-related strike. The Court extended the presumption of arbitrability to safety disputes[489] and adopted an objective evidence test for Section 502.[490] Significantly, at the district court, the quid pro quo for the workers' return to work was the employer's agreement to arbitrate, coupled with the elimination of the hazard pending the outcome of the arbitration. In a general sense, the court held that the "obey now, grieve later" policy applies to safety disputes.

A major effect of this decision has been to force unions to examine closely how their labor contracts cover safety disputes. The worst contracts post-*Gateway* are those with broad arbitration clauses, general duty safety clauses, and no safety exception to the no-strike promise. Such contracts waive whatever Section 7 rights the workers had through the express or implied no-strike obligation, enforce the "work now, grieve later" policy that employers favor, and throw the choice of work refusal standard to arbitrators, who usually choose Section 502–type standards,[491] which almost invariably favor the employer.

Even before *Gateway,* arbitrators' results in safety discipline cases favored employers. One unpublished study[492] looked at

---

[486] NLRB Memorandum 75-29 (June 24, 1975); Memorandum of Understanding with Department of Labor Concerning Cases Arising under Section 11(c) of the OSH Act.

[487] Taylor v. Brighton Corp., 616 F.2d 256 (6th Cir. 1980).

[488] 414 U.S. 368 (1974).

[489] *Id.,* at 380.

[490] *Id.,* at 387–88.

[491] Bunker Hill Co., 65 LA 182 (1975).

[492] Steve Cuprey, John Listinski, and Paula Traffas, associated with the Cornell School of Industrial Relations, conducted the survey. *Contra:* Elkouri,

fifty-seven arbitration decisions reported between 1968 and 1979 in which a worker was "insubordinate" and defended on the ground that the management order threatened his safety or health. None of the cases involved work refusal contract language. Overall, workers lost 75 percent of the time; if they tried to use Section 502 to defend, their loss rate went up to around 90 percent. Closely examine the contract language and decide whether grievance/arbitration or the NLRB or OSHA offers more promise. The following award underscores the importance of this choice. *Waterloo Industries, Inc.,*[493] involved a three-day suspension of a chief electrician for refusing to obey an order to rewire a power press to permit installation of a foot pedal to replace two-hand palm buttons. The worker felt that a pedal device, which allowed both hands to be free during the operating cycle, violated OSHA and ANSI standards and created a hazard to his fellow workers. He did not walk off the job and the safety dispute was not clearly arbitrable. The sole issue presented to the arbitrator was whether the discipline was for "just cause." The arbitrator first restated the "longstanding industrial relations practice" that workers must "obey now and grieve later," except where there is an "unusual safety or health hazard."[494] He found that although the "grievant's concern and responsiblity for the safety of others is noted by the arbitrator and this concern certainly appears to be genuine," he did not have "reasonable grounds to believe that an imminent health and safety hazard existed."[495] If instead, Section 7's "subjective good faith" test had been applied, it is clear that the suspension would *not* have been upheld.

To keep options open, file a grievance and an NLRB charge. The NLRB no longer automatically defers to arbitration in Section 8(a)(1) cases.[496] Feed information to the NLRB investigator; if the charge goes to complaint, put a hold on the grievance/arbitration. If the NLRB does not issue a complaint, then press the grievance to arbitration.

How Arbitration Works (3d ed.), at 671–74; Atelson, *Threats to Health and Safety: Employee Self-Help under the NLRA,* 59 Minn. L. Rev. 647, 712–13 (1975).

[493] 62 LA 605 (1974).

[494] *Id.,* at 609.

[495] *Id.,* at 610.

[496] Great Am. Transp., 228 NLRB No. 102 (1977).

If proceeding to arbitration on a work refusal case, the framing of the submission is crucial. Strive for a joint submission of the issue that includes the "good faith belief" or the "reasonable belief" test for the worker's conduct, instead of a simple "just cause" standard. If contract language governs, however, this may be impossible. Avoiding an "objective" test of the worker's belief or of the seriousness of the danger not only helps protect the worker but also cuts costs—"objective" expert testimony need not be paid for.

[5] State Common-Law Protection

The present common law of the individual employment contract holds that it is presumptively terminable at the employer's will.[497] The statute of frauds requires that any exceptions be written. One court has said that employers have the right to fire a worker for "good cause, for no cause, or even for cause morally wrong."[498] Recently, some states have tempered this harsh rule. In Massachusetts, the Supreme Court recently found that "in *every* [employment] contract there exists an implied covenant of good faith and fair dealing."[499] Courts that have followed this theory have often limited it to discharges in retaliation for the worker's advancing some public policy.[500] Others have looked to bad faith or malice on the part of the employer.[501] Personnel manuals often become controlling adjuncts to the oral employment contract.[502]

While none of these recent cases has dealt with discharges

[497] Martin v. N.Y. Life Ins. Co., 148 N.Y. 117 (1895).

[498] Payne v. W. & Atl. Ry. Co., 81 Tenn. Rptr. 506, 519020 (1884).

[499] Fortune v. Nat'l Cash Register Co., 364 N.E.2d 1251, 1257 (1977) (emphasis in original), *accord,* McKinney v. Nat'l Dairy Council, 491 F. Supp. 1108 (D. Mass. 1980).

[500] Tameny v. Atl. Richfield Co., 610 P.2d 1330 (1980); Sheets v. Teddy's Frosted Foods, Inc., 41 C.L.J. 30 (S. Ct. Conn. 1980); *see* Pierce v. Ortho Pharmaceutical Corp., 417 A.2d 505 (S. Ct. N.J. 1980).

[501] Monge v. Beebe Rubber Co., 316 A.2d 549 (S. Ct. N.H. 1974).

[502] Toussaint v. Blue Cross & Blue Shield, 292 N.W.2d 280 (S. Ct. Mich. 1980). *But see* Edwards v. Citibank, 418 N.Y.S.2d 269, *aff'd,* 425 N.Y.S.2d 327 (1st Dept. 1980).

involving health and safety problems, related safety cases have rejected application of the common-law defenses of the assumption of risk[503] and contributory negligence[504] in damage actions based on an employer's violation of a safety statute. These decisions, arrived at without specific statutory authority, tacitly hold that a worker should not have to choose between working under dangerous conditions or quitting. They are common-law authority for the right to work under safe conditions.

[6] Suggestions

In *all* work refusal cases, file a formal OSHA complaint to get an objective assessment of the hazard. If the worker's judgment is vindicated by OSHA's issuing a citation, you are in a superior position to defend him/her. If OSHA does not cite, follow the informal review procedure to determine the reasons.[505] Proof problems, not the worker's incorrect judgment, may be the reason. The inspector can be subpoenaed at a later hearing if he or she is called as a fact witness.[506] You may even be able to get the inspector's opinion as a "reasonable man" as to the worker's good faith belief. Failure to cite is not an adjudication and has no evidentiary value.

Unemployment insurance hearings should be utilized in all discharge cases to prepare for later hearings. If the employer is approached carefully, it may be lulled into a sense of false security, only to be sandbagged at the hearing into clearly stating its reasons for its conduct without adequate preparation. For clients with limited resources, this hearing is an inexpensive opportunity for discovery. If there is a work refusal discharge, argue that the hazardous working conditions should be construed as having discharged the worker. If the state statute and precedent are ambiguous on this point, make an analogy to the "national labor

---

503 American Zinc Co. v. Graham, 179 S.W. 138, 139–40 (Tenn. 1915).

504 Koenig v. Patrick Constr. Corp., 63 N.E.2d 133, 135 (N.Y. 1948).

505 See, Section 5.02, *supra.*

506 29 CFR § 1906.5.

policy" as articulated in *Washington Aluminum,*[507] and the OSH Act.[508]

Absent adverse information about the competence of the local NLRB office, the following rules of thumb should be followed in choosing where to file charges. In *all* retaliation cases, and in work refusal cases in shops without a no-strike promise, persevere to get the NLRB to issue a complaint. The NLRB will defer to OSHA only if the case involves retaliation for filing an OSHA complaint *and* a charge has been filed with OSHA. File your NLRB charge first, within 30 days of the discharge, rather than the normal 180 days allowed by the NLRA. This protects the right to use the OSHA procedure as a backup, since OSHA regulations permit tolling of the Section 11(c) filing period if NLRB relief has been sought first. Only if the NLRB does not go to complaint should you then file your OSHA complaint.

[7] Negotiating Contract Protection

Cuprey[509] suggests the following considerations in drafting work refusal contract language. First, define conditions under which workers may refuse work. There are two issues here: the degree of the hazard and the workers' perception of the hazard. In defining unsafe conditions, use a phrase like "any condition which might cause injury or harm," rather than strict phrases such as "imminent danger," "abnormally dangerous," or "would cause serious physical injury." Do not use safety standards to define the hazard; this mandates that the worker's initial judgment be second-guessed. If this is unavoidable, expressly incorporate NIOSH criteria documents, ANSI consensus standards, and any other well-accepted safety standard in addition to OSHA standards. The second definitional problem involves the weight given to the worker's on-the-spot judgment. It is best for workers if their *honest belief* that a hazard existed is sufficient. The employer can only rebut this at arbitration by showing that the worker

---

507 370 U.S. 9 (1962).

508 29 U.S.C. § 651.

509 In an unpublished fact sheet entitled *Collective Bargaining and the Right to Refuse.*

acted in bad faith. As an intermediate position, require that the worker have a *reasonable belief* that a hazard existed, which permits the employer to introduce objective evidence that the worker was unreasonable. This standard forgives workers' "reasonable" mistakes. Finally, requiring *actual evidence* that a hazard existed is worst for workers; it makes their initial judgments essentially irrelevant.

The second major consideration in drafting refusal language is to specify the employer's disciplinary rights. Ideally, discipline should not be allowed until the underlying safety dispute has been finally resolved; otherwise, the worker suffers the discipline in the interim, chilling other workers' safety activity. The employer's reason for discipline should be limited to the honesty or the reasonableness of the worker's belief that a hazard existed, or the worker's failure to abide by the contract procedures for resolving safety disputes.

Third, pay and work assignment issues should be resolved. Coverage of these provisions should extend to workers who are indirectly affected by the work refusal, as well as those actually refusing work. Employers can be required to assign workers to other available work at the same rate of pay with the right to return to the original job as soon as the hazard is corrected. If no other work is available, the worker should not be penalized by loss of pay. If the contract does not require that the job be shut down pending a final safety decision and the employer is allowed to replace the refusing workers, then the contract should require the employer to notify the replacements of the refusal and the workers' reason for so refusing.

Short of express language protecting workers from discipline for refusing dangerous work, the most direct way to avoid Section 502 and to gain Section 7 protection is to reserve the right to strike over safety disputes.[510] Thus, the ironic result of the

---

[510] If you have no-strike language that is unclear, bargaining for clarification and losing creates an inference that the no-strike language does apply. NLRB v. Rockaway News Supply Co., Inc., 345 U.S. 71 (1953). One way to avoid this problem is to make a proposal to shift safety grievance handling to the safety committee and leave open the question of how the committee finally resolves grievances. If accepted, there will be no *quid pro quo* for the arguably applicable express no-strike clause and Section 502 will be inapplicable. *See* note 455, *supra.* No unfavorable bargaining history on the scope of the no-strike clause will be created if the proposal is rejected.

Gateway push to arbitration of safety disputes is to press unions into bargaining for contract language that avoids mandatory arbitration of safety disputes or otherwise preserves workers' Section 7 rights.

§ 5.07. Job Protection: Defending "Disabled" Workers

The OSH Act promise of "safe and healthful working conditions" for "every working man and woman in the Nation"[511] is limited by "feasibility." "[T]he statute was not designed to require employers to provide absolutely risk-free workplaces whenever it is technologically feasible to do so."[512] The OSH Act permits some risk to workers. Moreover, the degree of risk varies from worker to worker, with more vulnerable workers labeled "hypersusceptible" by employers. Blacks and Mediteranean peoples may carry the sickle-cell trait, making them sensitive to hemolytic chemicals. Pregnant women carry fetuses sensitive to teratogens. Employers otherwise in compliance with OSHA standards argue for the right to exclude "hypersusceptibles" from toxic workplaces. Luckily for workers, the employer's right to discriminate against such workers can sometimes be checked.

Title VII law most commonly applies where the employer's screening policy[513] has an adverse numerical impact on wo-

---

[511] Section 2(b), 29 U.S.C. § 651(b).

[512] Indus. Union Dep't AFL-CIO, v. Am. Petroleum Inst., 100 S. Ct. 2844, 2864 (1980).

[513] At this time, the author knows of only two Title VII cases dealing with a company policy excluding female employees of childbearing ability from certain work. In Doerr v. B.F. Goodrich Co., 484 F. Supp. 320 (N.D. Ohio 1979), the court denied the plaintiff's application for a preliminary injunction largely because of plaintiff's failure to show irreparable injury. The court was impressed with the fact that the company had granted plaintiff rate retention for at least a year, and it found that claims that her career would be impaired not only were speculative but, should they occur, could be redressed under Title VII principles. The first case squarely to address the issue is EEOC v. Olin Corp. — F. Supp. — (W.D.N.C., December 29, 1980). There, the court apparently rejected the argument that the employer's "fetal vulnerability" policy amounted to a Title VII violation.

men,[514] blacks, or some national origin group. Under traditional Title VII principles, an employer's flat bar to employment of members of a protected class is a prima facie violation of Title VII; thus, an employer that simply bars all women of childbearing age from particular working conditions is prima facie in violation. Similarly, if the selection procedure has a statistically adverse impact on a protected group, the prima facie violation shifts the burden of proof to the employer, requiring it to demonstrate business necessity.[515] An employer in prima facie violation must show that its policy serves a compelling business purpose,[516] that the policy effectively carries out that business purpose, and that the policy is the least discriminatory of the available alternatives.[517] Contact the local office of the Equal Employment Opportunity Commission to file complaints on this ground.

Under the OSH Act, screening can be controlled through standards or through the general duty clause.[518] The lead standard is the only standard, so far, that offers protection. Its "medical removal protection" does not prevent a firm from screening out certain "unfit" workers; it does, however, protect workers' pay, seniority, and other benefits for up to eighteen months if they are screened out because their bodies have accumulated too much

---

[514] *See generally* Samuelson, *Employment Rights of Women in the Toxic Workplace,* 65 Cal. L. Rev. 1113 (1977).

[515] Griggs v. Duke Power Co., 901 U.S. 424 (1971); Robinson v. Lorillard Co., 444 F.2d 791 (4th Cir. 1971); Albermarle Paper Co. v. Moody, 422 U.S. 407 (1975); Uniform Guidelines on Employee Selection Procedures, 29 CFR § 1607.

Title VII's bona fide occupational qualification defense is probably inapplicable because its focus is on employee performance, not potential harm to the employee or a fetus.

[516] Protection of the employees' health is potentially a legitimate business purpose. The employer may not, however, select certain groups for this attention, while ignoring others: An employer may not act to protect women's reproductive systems from harm, while ignoring potential harm to male reproductive systems.

[517] *See* Albermarle, *supra* note 515. The proposed *Guidelines of Employment Discrimination and Reproductive Hazards,* jointly proposed by the Department of Labor and the Equal Employment Opportunity Commission, 45 Fed. Reg. 7514 (February 1, 1980), were withdrawn on January 16, 1981. The Guidelines contain an excellent checklist for use in reviewing an employer's "business necessity" defense. 45 Fed. Reg., at 7515.

[518] Section 5(a), 29 U.S.C. § 654(a). Section 11(c) only protects employer discrimination based upon the safety activities of employees; it is essentially inapplicable to screening "hypersusceptible" workers.

lead or, for women, because they are pregnant.[519] Unfortunately, this provision does not require an employer to keep a worker in its employ; after eighteen months, or earlier if a medical determination is made that the worker will never be able to return to the hazardous environment, the lead standard permits the employer to dismiss the worker as "unfit."[520] Despite this, the rate retention provision in the lead standard does remove the major financial disincentive to worker participation in medical surveillance under the standard.

The general duty clause is an awkward enforcement tool to use in "screening cases." The first case using this approach involved an employer's sterilization policy.[521] The violation was that "the employer adopted and implemented a policy which required women employees to be sterilized in order to be eligible to work in those areas of the plant where they would be exposed to toxic substances . . .." The general duty clause's phrase "shall provide employment and a place of employment" became crucial because the harm, i.e., sterilization, actually occurred in a hospital, not the workplace. To show that the hazard is "preventable," the record should include testimony on the range of reasonable alternatives. In future general duty cases involving exclusions, proof that the hazard is "recognized" will be simplified by the employer's tacit admission that a "recognized" hazard is the justification for the exclusionary policy. Whether the general duty to provide "employment and a place of employment" implies that the "unfit" have a right to employment is an open question.

Labor contracts may have language protecting "unfit" workers;[522] but where there is no contract protection the company may dismiss the permanently disabled worker. One arbitrator has said:

> When a worker's health is permanently impaired and he lacks the physical ability to regularly attend his job and perform his assigned work duties, his condition will justify a non-disciplinary discharge for just cause.[523]

---

[519] 29 CFR § 1910.1025(k)(2).

[520] *See* 29 CFR § 1910.1025(j)(3)(iii).

[521] Am. Cyanamid, OSHD ¶24,720 (ALJ 1980).

[522] *See* Chown, *supra* note 380, at 30, for model contract language.

[523] Kurtz Bros., Inc., 43 LA 678, 682 (1964).

The employer has no implied duty to accommodate the partially disabled worker.[524] In reaching its decision, the employer can rely on the opinion of its own doctor.[525] Blanket exclusions, however, are impermissible; fitness must be decided on an individual basis. [526]

The most important potential job protections for "unfit" workers are the new state and federal handicap laws. Under Section 503 of the Rehabilitation Act of 1973,[527] it appears clear that when an employer makes the determination that an otherwise qualified worker is physiologically unfit to work in certain job conditions, that the employer has created some evidence, if not conclusively determined, that the worker is an "impaired"[528] worker with a "substantial handicap to employment"[529] for whom the employer has a duty to make a "reasonable accomodation."[530] Section 503 imposes obligations on essentially all federal contractors. A complaint response system is enforced by the area offices of the Department of Labor's Office of Federal Contract Compliance Programs.[531] Implied private actions are unavailable.[532] Section 504 imposes parallel requirements on all federal grantees. The Department of Health and Human Services enforces these provisions.[533] In contrast to Section 503, implied private actions *are* available to enforce Section 504.[534] State remedies are also commonly available.

---

524 Reynolds Metals Co., 43 LA 734 (1964); Cominco Am. Inc., 52 LA 1152 (1969).

525 Lamson & Sessions, 43 LA 61 (1964).

526 Bethlehem Steel Corp., 66 LA 194 (1976).

527 29 U.S.C. §§ 701 *et seq.*

528 29 U.S.C. § 706(7); E.E. Black, Ltd., v. Marshall, 24 EPD ¶31,260 (D. Hi. 1980).

529 *Id.*

530 41 CFR § 60-741.6(d); 41 CFR § 60-741, Appendix B. For the proposed amended definition, *see* 45 (251) Fed. Reg. 86213, 86214 (December 30, 1980).

531 41 CFR § 60-741.

532 Rogers v. Frito-Lay, 611 F.2d 1074 (5th Cir. 1980).

533 45 CFR § 84.

534 United Handicapped Fed'n v. Andre, 558 F.2d 413 (8th Cir. 1977); Kampameier v. Nyquist, 553 F.2d 296, 299 (2d Cir. 1977); Lloyd v. Regional Transp. Auth., 548 F.2d 1277 (7th Cir. 1977); *cf.* Cannon v. University of Chicago, 441 U.S. 677 (1977) (Title IX of the Education Act Amendments of 1972 uses language parallel to Section 504).

Appendix 5A. Table: Legal Scope of Workers' Right to Know

Type of Information	Right to Know through: § 8(a)(5) (Unionized Shops)	OSHA Regs. (All Covered Workplaces)	FOIA	Discovery (If Relevant to Case)
(1) OSHA log of injuries and illnesses—Form 200	X	X	O	X
(2) OSHA Form 101 or equivalent—injury or illness report to compensation carrier	X	O	O	X
(3) Material or Product Safety Data Sheets issued by manufacturers or designers	X	MSDS only if kept	O	X
(4) Medical surveillance records	X	X	O	X
(5) Exposure or monitoring records	X	X	If collected by OSHA	X
(6) Plant access for experts	X	O	O	X
(7) Questioning of company witnesses	O	O	O	X
(8) Employer's reports to government (e.g., TOSCA reports)	X	O	X	X
(9) Company safety and health policies	X	O	O	X
(10) Company safety and health training programs	X	O	O	X
(11) Copies of OSHA standards	X	Only if employer has copy	X	Not applicable
(12) Access to the employer's safety and health library	X	O	O	O
(13) Plans for modification of working conditions	X	O	If collected by OSHA	X
(14) Information on toxic substances, (e.g., generic name, Chemical Abstract Service number, physical characteristics, health effects data)	X	Only if kept by employer	X	X

Appendix 5B. Material Safety Data Sheet (MSDS)—OSHA Form 20

U.S. DEPARTMENT OF LABOR
Occupational Safety and Health Administration

Form Approved
OMB No. 44-R1387

MATERIAL SAFETY DATA SHEET

Required under USDL Safety and Health Regulations for Ship Repairing, Shipbuilding, and Shipbreaking (29 CFR 1915, 1916, 1917)

SECTION I

MANUFACTURER'S NAME	EMERGENCY TELEPHONE NO.
ADDRESS *(Number, Street, City, State, and ZIP Code)*	
CHEMICAL NAME AND SYNONYMS	TRADE NAME AND SYNONYMS
CHEMICAL FAMILY	FORMULA

SECTION II - HAZARDOUS INGREDIENTS

PAINTS, PRESERVATIVES, & SOLVENTS	%	TLV (Units)	ALLOYS AND METALLIC COATINGS	%	TLV (Units)
PIGMENTS			BASE METAL		
CATALYST			ALLOYS		
VEHICLE			METALLIC COATINGS		
SOLVENTS			FILLER METAL PLUS COATING OR CORE FLUX		
ADDITIVES			OTHERS		
OTHERS					

HAZARDOUS MIXTURES OF OTHER LIQUIDS, SOLIDS, OR GASES	%	TLV (Units)

SECTION III - PHYSICAL DATA

BOILING POINT (°F.)		SPECIFIC GRAVITY (H_2O=1)	
VAPOR PRESSURE (mm Hg.)		PERCENT, VOLATILE BY VOLUME (%)	
VAPOR DENSITY (AIR=1)		EVAPORATION RATE (________ =1)	
SOLUBILITY IN WATER			
APPEARANCE AND ODOR			

SECTION IV - FIRE AND EXPLOSION HAZARD DATA

FLASH POINT (Method used)	FLAMMABLE LIMITS	Lel	Uel
EXTINGUISHING MEDIA			
SPECIAL FIRE FIGHTING PROCEDURES			
UNUSUAL FIRE AND EXPLOSION HAZARDS			

PAGE (1) (Continued on reverse side) Form OSHA-20

SECTION V - HEALTH HAZARD DATA

THRESHOLD LIMIT VALUE
EFFECTS OF OVEREXPOSURE
EMERGENCY AND FIRST AID PROCEDURES

SECTION VI - REACTIVITY DATA

STABILITY	UNSTABLE		CONDITIONS TO AVOID
	STABLE		
INCOMPATABILITY *(Materials to avoid)*			
HAZARDOUS DECOMPOSITION PRODUCTS			
HAZARDOUS POLYMERIZATION	MAY OCCUR		CONDITIONS TO AVOID
	WILL NOT OCCUR		

SECTION VII - SPILL OR LEAK PROCEDURES

STEPS TO BE TAKEN IN CASE MATERIAL IS RELEASED OR SPILLED
WASTE DISPOSAL METHOD

SECTION VIII - SPECIAL PROTECTION INFORMATION

RESPIRATORY PROTECTION *(Specify type)*		
VENTILATION	LOCAL EXHAUST	SPECIAL
	MECHANICAL *(General)*	OTHER
PROTECTIVE GLOVES		EYE PROTECTION
OTHER PROTECTIVE EQUIPMENT		

SECTION IX - SPECIAL PRECAUTIONS

PRECAUTIONS TO BE TAKEN IN HANDLING AND STORING
OTHER PRECAUTIONS

PAGE (2) Form OSHA-20
GPO 930-540 Rev. May 72

Appendix 5C. OSHA Complaint—OSHA Form 7

Occupational Safety and Health Administration
Complaint

U.S. Department of Labor

This form is provided for the assistance of any complainant and is not intended to constitute the exclusive means by which a complaint may be registered with the U.S. Department of Labor.

Form Approved
O.M.B. No. 044R1449

Sec. 8(f) (1) of the Williams-Steiger Occupational Safety and Health Act, 29 U.S.C. 651, provides as follows: Any employees or representative of employees who believe that a violation of a safety or health standard exists that threatens physical harm, or that an imminent danger exists, may request an inspection by giving notice to the Secretary or his authorized representative of such violation or danger. Any such notice shall be reduced to writing, shall set forth with reasonable particularity the grounds for the notice, and shall be signed by the employees or representative of employees, and a copy shall be provided the employer or his agent no later than at the time of inspection, except that, upon request of the person giving such notice, his name and the names of individual employees referred to therein shall not appear in such copy or on any record published, released, or made available pursuant to subsection (g) of this section. If upon receipt of such notification the Secretary determines there are reasonable grounds to believe that such violation or danger exists, he shall make a special inspection in accordance with the provisions of this section as soon as practicable, to determine if such violation or danger exists. If the Secretary determines there are no reasonable grounds to believe that a violation or danger exists he shall notify the employees or representative of the employees in writing of such determination.

NOTE: Section 11 (c) of the Act provides explicit protection for employees exercising their rights, including making safety and health complaints.

For Official Use Only		
Area	Date Received	Time
Region	Received By	Formal ☐ Non Formal ☐

The undersigned *(check one)*

☐ Employee ☐ Representative of Employees ☐ Other *(specify)* __________

believes that a violation at the following place of employment of an occupational safety or health standard exists which is a job safety or health hazard.

Employer's Name

Employer's Address *(Street)* *(City)*

(State) *(Zip Code)* Telephone

1. Kind of business

2. Specify the particular building or worksite where the alleged violation is located, including address.

3. Specify the name and phone number of employer's agent(s) in charge.

4. Describe briefly the hazard which exists there including the approximate number of employees exposed to or threatened by such hazard.

OSHA-7 (Rev. October 1977)

CONTINUED ON REVERSE SIDE

5. (a) To your knowledge is this condition being considered by any other Government agency, or has it been considered by any other Government agency?

Yes ☐ No ☐

5. (b) If yes, and you know, which Government agency?

6. Has this condition been brought to the attention of the employer?

Yes ☐ No ☐ Don't know ☐

7. Please indicate your desire: ☐ I *do not* want my name revealed to the employer. ☐ My name *may be* revealed to the employer.

NOTE: It is unlawful to make any false statement, representation or certification in any document filed pursuant to the Occupational Safety and Health Act of 1970. Violations can be punished by a fine of not more than $10,000, or by imprisonment of not more than six months, or by both. (Section 17(g))

Signature ______________________ Date ____________

Typed or Printed Name ______________________

Address *(Street)* ______________________ *(City)* ____________

(State) ____________ *(Zip Code)* ____________ Telephone ____________

If you are an authorized representative of employees affected by this complaint, please state the name of your organization and your title. ______________________

GPO 923-242

Appendix 5D. OSHA Citation Form

U.S. DEPARTMENT OF LABOR
OCCUPATIONAL SAFETY AND HEALTH ADMINISTRATION

CITATION and NOTIFICATION OF PENALTY

1 ISSUANCE DATE	2 OSHA NUMBER	
3 REGION	4 AREA	5 PAGE OF

6 TYPE OF VIOLATION(S)	7 CITATION NO.

INSPECTION DATE:

INSPECTION SITE:

TO:

THE LAW REQUIRES that a copy of this Citation be posted immediately in a prominent place at or near the location of the violation(s) cited below. The Citation must remain posted until the violations cited below have been corrected, or for 3 working days (excluding weekends and Federal holidays) whichever is longer.

PENALTIES ARE DUE WITHIN 15 DAYS OF RECEIPT OF THIS NOTIFICATION UNLESS CONTESTED (See enclosed Booklet)

This Section May Be Detached Before Posting

OSHA AREA OFFICE MUST DETACH THIS SECTION BEFORE MAILING OR FILING IN CASE FILE

This citation describes violations of the Occupational Safety and Health Act of 1970. The penalty(ies) listed below are based on these violations. You must correct the violations referred to in this citation by the dates listed below and pay the penalties proposed, unless within 15 working days (excluding weekends and Federal holidays) from your receipt of this citation and penalty you mail a notice of contest to the U.S. Department of Labor Area Office at the address shown above. (See the enclosed booklet which outlines your responsibilities and courses of action and should be read in conjunction with this form.)

8 ITEM NUMBER STANDARD, REGULATION OR SECTION OF THE ACT VIOLATED; DESCRIPTION	9 DATE BY WHICH VIOLATION MUST BE CORRECTED	10 PENALTY	11 NBR INST.	12 REC	13 MOD

14 AREA DIRECTOR

15 TOTAL PENALTY FOR THIS CITATION Make check or Money Order Payable To: "DOL-OSHA" Indicate OSHA No. on Remittance	16 TOTAL PENALTY FOR THIS PAGE

NOTICE TO EMPLOYEES – The law gives an employee or his representative the opportunity to object to any abatement date set for a violation if he believes the date to be unreasonable. The contest must be mailed to the U.S. Department of Labor Area Office at the address shown above within 15 working days (excluding weekends and Federal holidays) of the receipt by the employer of this citation and penalty.

EMPLOYER DISCRIMINATION UNLAWFUL – The law prohibits discrimination by an employer against an employee for filing a complaint or for exercising any rights under this Act. An employee who believes that he has been discriminated against may file a complaint no later than 30 days after the discrimination with the U.S. Department of Labor Area Office at the address shown above.

EMPLOYER RESPONSIBILITIES AND COURSES OF ACTION – The enclosed booklet outlines employer responsibilities and courses of action and should be read in conjunction with this notification.

CITATION AND NOTIFICATION OF PENALTY

OSHA-2 REV. 5/76

DETACH HERE

Appendix 5E. OSHA Compliance Worksheet—OSHA Form 1B

OCCUPATIONAL SAFETY AND HEALTH ADMINISTRATION
U.S. DEPARTMENT OF LABOR

WORKSHEET

1. CSHO No.	2. Report No.	3. Date/Time	4a. Type	4b. Number	Page / of

5. Item No.	6. Instance	7. Standard Allegedly Violated	8. Abatement Period	9. No. of Inst.	10. REC

11a. SAVE ID Code Tape Ref. No. b. AVD/Variable Information:

Cont'd

12. INSTANCE DESCRIPTION (a. Hazards-Oper./Cond.-Acc.; b. Equip.; c. Location; and d. Injury/Ill.):

Cont'd

e. Measurements:

13. PHOTO

Y

14. EMPLOYEE EXPOSURE

a. Occupation (& Employer)	b. No.	c. Total Duration	d. Frequency	e. Exposed Employee – Name, Address & Phone

Cont'd

15. EMPLOYER KNOWLEDGE:

16. COMMENTS (Employer, Employee, Closing Conf.):

Cont'd

17. OTHER EMPLOYER INFORMATION

18. CLASSIF.:	a Failure to Correct?	b Serious H or D?	c Knowl.?	d S or O?	e R?	f W?

19. PENALTY

a. Prob. of Injury/Ill. or a. No. Cal. Days Uncorr.	b. Gravity-Based Penalty	c. Times Repeated/ Degree Of Willful	d. Adjustment Factors 1) Size	2) Good Faith	3) History	4) Total	e. Proposed Adjusted Penalty

Form OSHA-1B

Appendix 5F. OSHA Photo Mounting Worksheet

Occupational Safety and Health Administration
Photo Mounting Worksheet

U.S. Department of Labor

CSHO No.	Report No.	Page ____ of ____
1. Photo ID No.	2. Date/Time	
3. Citation No.	4. Item No.	5. Instance No.

6. Location: ***(Photo and Photographer)***

7. Description

8. ☐ CONFIDENTIAL MATERIALS — CONTINUED

1. Photo ID No.	2. Date/Time	
3. Citation No.	4. Item No.	5. Instance No.

6. Location: ***(Photo and Photographer)***

7. Description:

8. ☐ CONFIDENTIAL MATERIALS — CONTINUED

1. Photo ID No.	2. Date/Time	
3. Citation No.	4. Item No.	5. Instance No.

6. Location: ***(Photo and Photographer)***

7. Description:

8. ☐ CONFIDENTIAL MATERIALS — CONTINUED

OSHA-89B (April 1978)

Appendix 5G. OSHA Narrative—OSHA Form 1A

U.S. DEPARTMENT OF LABOR
OCCUPATIONAL SAFETY
AND HEALTH ADMINISTRATION

NARRATIVE

1. CSHO No.	2. Report No.

3. Employer Name:

4. Type Of Legal Entity | 5. Type Of Business Or Plant

6. NAMES AND ADDRESSES OF ALL ORGANIZED EMPLOYEE GROUPS:		7. AUTHORIZED REPRESENTATIVES OF EMPLOYEES:		W A
Name		Name	Tele. No.	☐ Y
Local No.	Tele. No.	Organization	Title	
Address		Home Address		☐ N
	Zip Code		Zip Code	
Name		Name	Tele. No.	☐ Y
Local No.	Tele. No.	Organization	Title	
Address		Home Address		☐ N
	Zip Code		Zip Code	

8. EMPLOYER REPRESENTATIVES CONTACTED: (I - Credentials Presented; O - Opening Conf; C - Closing Conf; M - Other Mgmt. Official)

Name	Title	Function	W A
			☐ Y
			☐ Y
			☐ Y
			☐ Y

9. OTHER PERSONS CONTACTED:

Name, Occupation & Affiliation	
Home Address	Tele. No.
	Zip Code
Name, Occupation & Affiliation	
Home Address	Tele. No.
	Zip Code
Name, Occupation & Affiliation	
Home Address	Tele. No.
	Zip Code

10. COVERAGE INFORMATION

11. Date & Time of Entry:	12. Date & Time Walkaround Began:	13. Date & Time Closing Conference Began: (1) (2)	14. Date & Time of Exit:

15. EVALUATION OF SAFETY AND HEALTH PROGRAM: (Codes: 0 = Nonexistent 1 = Inadequate 2 = Average 3 = Above Average)

Comprehensiveness of Safety & Health Program		0 1 2 3
Written?	Y N	
Copy Enclosed?	Y N	
Communication of Program to Employees		0 1 2 3
How?		
Safety Meetings		0 1 2 3
Frequency?		
By Whom?		
Enforcement		0 1 2 3
How?		
Safety Training Program		0 1 2 3
Health Training Program		0 1 2 3
Safety Staff	Y N	
Health Staff	Y N	
Accident/Injury Investigations Performed		0 1 2 3
Preventative Action Taken	Y N	

Health Monitoring Program		0 1 2 3
Hazard?		
Medical Programs		0 1 2 3
Frequency?		
Agent?		
Extent?		
Content?		
Hazard Control — Engineering & Administration		0 1 2 3
— Personal Protective Equipment		0 1 2 3
— Regulated Areas		0 1 2 3
— Emergency Procedures		0 1 2 3
Records: 100 — 101 — 102 — Supplementary Health		
If SH, specify		
Notice to Employees (Poster)	Y N	
Add'l Comments:		

16. FOLLOW-UP INSPECTION RECOMMENDED: Yes ☐ No ☐ Reason:

17. CSHO Signature & Date: | 18. Accompanied By:

Form OSHA-1A
(11/76)

19. CLOSING CONFERENCE CHECKLIST ☐ No Violations Observed

1) Review Hazards Observed/Standards Allegedly Violated ☐ | 2) Encourage Compliance ☐

20. ADDITIONAL COMMENTS

CHAPTER 6

Obtaining Benefits for the Disabled Worker

§ 6.01. Social Security Disability Benefits

Social Security Disability Insurance (SSDI) and Supplemental Security Income–Disability (SSI) are two payment programs administered by the Social Security Administration (SSA) for disabled people. SSDI is only for individuals who have a substantial enough work history to be paid up on their Social Security insurance. SSI has no work requirement. Instead, eligibility for benefits is based upon financial need. An applicant for either program must meet these technical requirements and prove that s/he is unable to engage in any substantial, gainful activity because of medically verifiable physical or mental impairments that have lasted one year, are expected to last one year, or will result in death.

Legal assistance is always helpful, and often necessary, for applicants at both the administrative and the federal court levels of appeal. This chapter will discuss the requirements and procedures of both programs and will also provide some practical suggestions for advocates working on these cases.

Given this state of affairs, it is crucial that advocates keep abreast of the changes in this area by regularly consulting knowledgeable sources, such as those listed in the bibliography at the end of this chapter.

For the past two years the Reagan administration has made vigorous efforts to cut back drastically on the SSI and SSDI programs. Legislation had been proposed which would significantly affect the substantive and procedural rights of current and future claimants. In addition, the SSA, not content to wait for the outcome of these legislative efforts, has undertaken so-called continuing disability investigations, with the result that substantial numbers of beneficiaries have been terminated.

[1] Social Security Disability: Title II Benefits

The benefits variously referred to as SSDI, Title II, DIB, or "regular disability" are received in the form of a green monthly

determination of disability was made by state agencies rather than the Social Security Administration. These two aspects of the program continue today.

It should be recognized that the term "insurance" is misleading in the context of the whole Social Security program. The relation of benefits to wages earned and the fact that eligibility for these benefits is unaffected by financial need, or the lack of it, give the Old Age, Survivors and Disability Insurance (OASDI) programs an insurancelike character. On the other hand, there are aspects of the program unrelated to any insurancelike programs. For instance, there is currently an ensured minimum income for aged citizens, spouse's benefits, etc. (This may change under the Reagan administration.) The insurance concept distinguishes these programs from both the SSI program and various state and county public assistance programs.[2]

The 1960 Amendments to the Social Security Act lifted the age requirement. In 1967, Congress amended the Act to add benefits for certain disabled widows, widowers, and divorced wives. At the same time, Congress tightened the definition of disability, which had been somewhat liberalized by federal court decisions.

[a] Coverage Requirements

In addition to meeting the definition of disability, a claimant of disability insurance benefits under Title II must have sufficient Social Security coverage to qualify. For workers aged over 31, the person must have worked in employment covered by the Act for twenty of the forty quarters prior to the date of onset of the disability. Also, the worker must have earned at least $50 in each such quarter. If the claimant is younger than 31, s/he must have coverage in one-half (but not less than six) of the quarters after s/he reached age 21 prior to the onset date.[3] Analogous require-

---

[2] For a full discussion of Social Security, *see* Liebman, *The Definition of Disability in Social Security and Supplemental Security Income: Drawing the Bounds of Social Welfare Estates,* 89 Harv. L. Rev. 833 (1976).

[3] 20 CFR § 404.115-116.

ments exist for self-employed people.[4] (This quarters-of-coverage requirement may be made stricter by Congress.)

Sometimes a claimant will have the necessary coverage, but the Social Security record will not reflect it. This is often true of former domestic workers whose employers had not paid Social Security for them. If one encounters this problem, the representative can obtain the claimant's past IRS records, get affidavits from former employers regarding the employment (though they may be uncooperative, since it means IRS liability for them), or obtain other affidavits as to the claimant's work history.

[b] Amount of Benefits

The amount the disabled worker[5] receives in monthly benefits is dependent on the amount of average prior earnings. The amount is often adjusted for cost-of-living expenses.[6]

Benefits are not payable until the expiration of a five-month waiting period after onset of disability.[7] A claimant may apply for benefits prior to that time, but payments will not start until the sixth month. The cases most often seen by representatives involve significant retroactive payments, since the appeals procedures are often quite lengthy. Such retroactive payments will be made dating back to the sixth month after onset, but they are limited to one year prior to the date of application for benefits.[8]

[c] Workers' Compensation Offset

If a disabled worker is also receiving workers' compensation benefits, Social Security disability insurance has an offset provision so that the total benefits received by a worker do not exceed

[4] *See* 20 CFR § 404.103 for requirements.

[5] See also 20 CFR § 404.313-314 *re* wives' benefits; 20 CFR § 404.320-320(a) *re* children's benefits; 20 CFR § 404.328-334 *re* widows' and widowers' benefits.

[6] The method used in making these computations is detailed in Subpart C of Title 20 of the CFR.

[7] 20 CFR § 404.308.

[8] 20 CFR § 404.308.

80 percent of the person's average monthly past earnings.[9] The Social Security Administration will adjust the amount of the disability check after computing the information. The workers' compensation offset provisions have been held constitutional by several courts.[10]

[d] Definition of Disability

As well as meeting the quarters-of-coverage requirements, the claimant must prove that s/he meets the Social Security definition of disability in order to be eligible for this program. The definition of disability is the same under both the Title II program and the Title XVI one. Generally, disability is defined as the inability to perform regular, sustained employment. The standard is *not* one of hireability, i.e., it is irrelevant whether or not the claimant could actually get a job.[11] The Social Security Administration will not look at such factors as high unemployment rates, effects of race discrimination, hiring practices, employers, etc.[12] In the early sixties, a number of courts ruled that hireability was an issue, but the 1967 amendments explicitly stated that hireability was not an issue, thus overruling these cases.

Age, education, and work experience are taken into account in determining disability. This generally works in favor of a claimant who is over age 50 and has worked in unskilled medium to heavy work. For younger workers, the test is not just whether the person is unable to perform his/her former work, but whether s/he would be unable to perform any other substantial, gainful activity as a result of his/her physical or mental problems. Again, it does not matter whether the claimant realistically would be hired, but whether s/he could perform the work *if* hired. For older workers, the test becomes more complex in terms of former

[9] The details of this offset provision are found in 20 CFR § 404.408.

[10] Richardson v. Belcher, 404 U.S. 78, 92 S. Ct. 254, 30 L. Ed. 2d 231 (1971); Bartley v. Finch, 311 F. Supp. 876 (E.D. Ky. 1970); Gambill v. Finch, 309 F. Supp. 1 (E.D. Tenn. 1970).

[11] Whiten v. Finch, 437 F.2d 73 (1971); Fing v. Finch, 428 F.2d 709 (1970).

[12] Hoffman v. Weinberger, 383 F. Supp. 592 (D.C. Pa. 1974); Alvarado v. Weinberger, 511 F.2d 1046 (1st Cir. 1975); Ihnen v. Gardner, 253 F. Supp. 441 (D. S.C. 1966).

work.[13]

[e] Vocational Rehabilitation Provisions

There is a limited connection between the disability program and vocational rehabilitation efforts. The initial determinations of disability or nondisability are made by state agencies, which can make mandatory referrals of claimants to state rehabilitation agencies.[14]

Once a worker is receiving disability benefits, s/he may participate in the program's "trial work period," during which s/he may attempt to work and still receive disability benefits.[15] The Social Security Administration would then terminate that person from disability if the work attempt is successful. This is somewhat of a Catch-22 program, however, since the fact that a person is working may not *itself* be grounds for termination before the end of the nine months, but in fact may lead to further evaluation that will lead to termination.

[2] Supplemental Security Income–Disability: Title XVI

Title XVI of the Social Security Act is the SSI program that provides benefits to certain blind, aged, and disabled workers.[16] This chapter will discuss only the SSI-Disability program. Claimants for SSI must fall within the same definition of disability as for Title II benefits. Instead of a quarters-of-coverage requirement, however, the SSI program is similar to a welfare program, with income and resource restrictions. The amount of monthly benefits received is thus not related to past earnings, but is based on the amount of a claimant's other income, as well as the living

[13] *See* detailed description of the definition, the "grid" regulations, the burden of proof, and related issues, *infra.*

[14] 42 U.S.C. § 422.

[15] For a description of this program, *see* 20 CFR § 404.1591-1592.

[16] The law is found in Title XVI of the Social Security Act, 42 U.S.C. §§ 1381 et seq.; 20 CFR §§ 416 et seq.

and the Title XVI one. Generally, disability is defined as the inability to perform regular, sustained employment. The standard is *not* one of hireability, i.e., it is irrelevant whether or not the claimant could actually get a job.[11] The Social Security Administration will not look at such factors as high unemployment rates, effects of race discrimination, hiring practices, employers, etc.[12] In the early sixties, a number of courts ruled that hireability was an issue, but the 1967 amendments explicitly stated that hireability was not an issue, thus overruling these cases.

Age, education, and work experience are taken into account in determining disability. This generally works in favor of a claimant who is over age 50 and has worked in unskilled medium to heavy work. For younger workers, the test is not just whether the person is unable to perform his/her former work, but whether s/he would be unable to perform any other substantial, gainful activity as a result of his/her physical or mental problems. Again, it does not matter whether the claimant realistically would be hired, but whether s/he could perform the work *if* hired. For older workers, the test becomes more complex in terms of former work.[13]

[e] Vocational Rehabilitation Provisions

There is a limited connection between the disability program and vocational rehabilitation efforts. The initial determinations of disability or nondisability are made by state agencies, which can make mandatory referrals of claimants to state rehabilitation agencies.[14]

Once a worker is receiving disability benefits, s/he may participate in the program's "trial work period," during which s/he

---

11 Whiten v. Finch, 437 F.2d 73 (1971); Fing v. Finch, 428 F.2d 709 (1970).

12 Hoffman v. Weinberger, 383 F. Supp. 592 (D.C. Pa. 1974); Alvarado v. Weinberger, 511 F.2d 1046 (1st Cir. 1975); Ihnen v. Gardner, 253 F. Supp. 441 (D. S.C. 1966).

13 *See* detailed description of the definition, the "grid" regulations, the burden of proof, and related issues, *infra.*

14 42 U.S.C. § 422.

may attempt to work and still receive disability benefits.[15] The fact that a claimant has made several unsuccessful attempts to return to work does not disqualify him.[15.1] The Social Security Administration would then terminate that person from disability if the work attempt is successful. This is somewhat of a Catch-22 program, however, since the fact that a person is working may not *itself* be grounds for termination before the end of the trial work period, but in fact may lead to further evaluation that will lead to termination.

[2] Supplemental Security Income–Disability: Title XVI

Many disabled individuals will not be eligible for SSDI benefits because they worked in employment not covered by Social Security, worked sporadically, or worked too long ago to meet the quarters of coverage requirements. They may, however, be entitled to benefits under Title XVI of the Social Security Act, which provides SSI benefits to certain blind, aged, and disabled individuals.[16]

This chapter will discuss only the SSI-Disability program. Claimants for SSI must fall within the same definition of disability as for Title II benefits. Instead of a quarters-of-coverage requirement, however, the SSI program is similar to a welfare program, with income and resource restrictions. The amount of monthly benefits received is thus not related to past earnings, but is based on the amount of a claimant's other income, as well as the living situation (whether s/he has cooking facilities, lives with others, etc.). Those eligible for SSI receive a monthly *gold* check.

The SSI program went into effect in 1974, replacing State Aid to the Totally Disabled program. It is a federal program enacted by Congress and administered by the Social Security Administration. It is not an insurance program; the federal portion is paid for by the general fund, not by payroll deductions. Many states make

---

[15] For a description of this program, *see* 20 CFR § 404.1591-1592.

[15.1] Milton v. Schweiker, 669 F.2d 554 (8th Cir. 1982).

[16] 42 U.S.C. §§ 1381 et seq.; 20 CFR §§ 416 et seq.

additional contributions to the basic federal payment; therefore, the monthly benefit amount will vary from state to state.

The program is a supplementary one: Benefits are reduced on the basis of other income received by the applicant and/or family.[16.1] In addition, if the applicant and family members have more than a certain amount in assets and resources, no benefits will be paid.[16.2] Advocates should be aware that as of March 1981 a transfer of assets law applies to cases in which claimants have transfered nonexempt assets to others for less than fair market value within the previous twenty-four months. The law provides that these assets will be included in the applicant's resources for purposes of determining eligibility unless the applicant can prove that the transfer was "exclusively" for another purpose.[16.3]

Many disabled workers receiving DIB benefits will also be eligible for SSI because past wages will result in a DIB check low enough to be supplemented by SSI if the worker does not have a working spouse or other financial resources. This is called a concurrent Title II/Title XVI claim. Many apply for both programs at the same time; the two cases are usually consolidated for hearing, since the definition of disability is the same.

A potential problem with concurrent Title II/Title XVI claims can occur if the claimant has been receiving state public assistance payments based on disability. The problem arises because of the interrelationship of two statutes. One is the so-called windfall offset provision, which requires that a claimant's SSDI retroactive benefits be reduced by the amount of SSI received for months included in the retroactive award, which would not have been payable if the SSDI had been paid when originally due rather than retroactively.[16.4] The second is the requirement, which many states have, that a person applying for public assistance based on disability must apply for SSI and agree to reimburse the state for the amount of public assistance it provided out

---

16.1 Not all income is counted. *See* 20 CFR § 416, Subpart K.

16.2 Some resources are excluded. *See* 20 CFR § 416, Subpart L, for the applicable rules on exclusions.

16.3 42 U.S.C. § 1382b(c)(1)(1981). *See Transfer of Assets: New Penalties in SSI and Medicaid,* 15 Clearinghouse R. 259 (July 1981).

16.4 42 U.S.C. § 1320a-6 (1981), as amended by Pub. L. 96-265, § 501; 20 CFR § 404.408b.

of the first (retroactive) SSI check. The two rules taken together can sometimes have the effect of reducing the claimant's retroactive SSI/SSDI benefits by the amount of public assistance received. It also may result in reducing the amount from which an attorney may receive a fee, making it more difficult for such claimants to obtain representation.[16.5]

Some advocates are dealing with the problem by "withdrawing" the SSI application after a favorable decision on the claim, pursuant to 20 CFR § 416.355(b). There may be problems with this approach, including the possibility it may run afoul of state public assistance regulations if they require "application." Another approach is to dismiss the SSI appeal any time before the decision. In some cases, the Office of Hearings and Appeals will notify state public assistance, with the likely effect that such assistance will be terminated. In many cases, this is a risk not worth taking. Advocates are cautioned to evaluate the usefulness of dismissing the SSI appeal in the context of the state's public assistance regulations and decisions as well as the facts of each particular case.

Prison inmates cannot receive SSI, although they currently can continue to receive DIB. United States citizens and foreign citizens residing here legally may receive SSI, though the latter's immigration status may be detrimentally affected by the receipt of these benefits. A United States citizen or resident residing abroad may not receive SSI.

An important difference between SSI and SSDI is that eligibility for SSI benefits begins with the date of application. Therefore, although there is no five-month waiting period, there also are no retroactive benefits for any period of disability prior to the date of application.[16.6]

The program is administered by the Social Security Administration in generally the same way as is the DIB program. As with other welfare programs, a recipient can expect periodic review of his/her financial situation. Also, the complicated nature of the financial rules and the slowness of the bureaucracy often result in an overpayment of SSI benefits. (This chapter will not describe the procedures by which one can appeal an overpayment deci-

---

16.5 *See* section on attorneys' fees, *infra.*

16.6 20 CFR § 416.501.

sion, but the advocate can consult the bibliography for other resources on this subject.) Some states have special programs for SSI recipients, such as Medicaid, funds for moving expenses, home care programs, etc.

[3] Prehearing Administrative Procedures

These procedures are the same for the DIB and SSI programs.

[a] Initial Application

Benefits are applied for at a District Office (DO) of the SSA. A claims representative will take the initial application and related forms and will determine whether or not the claimant meets the technical, nondisability requirements. The forms filled out by the claims representative include the initial Application, Medical Report, Vocational Report, and medical record releases.[16.7] There is space on the forms for the claims representative to record his/her personal observations of the applicant. It is important that the applicant be prepared to give all the needed information, since many claims representatives will not pursue the questions with the client to ensure that all information is obtained. For DIB applicants, the claims representative will obtain a computer printout listing the applicant's earnings record, insurance coverage status, and potential monthly benefit amount.[16.8] For SSI claimants, the claims representative will ask for proof of certain financial aspects of the case. For instance, s/he may ask the claimant to bring in a bankbook, copies of other documents, etc. The claims representative has the power to, and often will, check some of the financial information.

If the applicant does not meet the technical requirements, the claim will be denied by the DO on these grounds. Otherwise, the file will be sent to the state agency that has been delegated the function of making disability determinations by the SSA.

16.7 *See* reprinted SSA forms, *infra.*

16.8 *See* SSA forms, *infra.*

[b] State Agency Role

At the state agency, a team consisting of a physician and a lay disability analyst makes the actual decision as to disability. The agency is first to gather medical information on the claimant by requesting reports and/or records from the doctors and other medical sources listed on the claimant's application form. In addition, the claimant may be sent for "one shot" examinations with one or more private consulting physicians paid for by the SSA.[17] The state agency may also send the applicants for vocational rehabilitation screening.

Eventually, a physician at the state agency reviews the medical evidence in the file and makes a determination as to whether the claimant is disabled. Inserted into the claimant's file is a "Disability Determination and Transmittal Form" detailing the decision and its rationale.[17.1] In practice, this decision is often made without the agency having obtained much, if any, of the relevant medical information. This happens both because the agency does not write for all records (or often does not follow up on such requests) and because many doctors will not provide the requested information.

Not only is the medical evidence available to the state agency physician at the time of the decision often limited, but the standard applied to the evidence is extremely strict. The state agencies do not apply the disability standards developed through Social Security regulation and case law. Rather, they follow the much stricter standards contained in the SSA's own internal claims manual, known as the "Program Operations Manual System" (POMS), a large, frequently updated loose-leaf compendium.

The POMS standards are based primarily on the Listing of Impairments contained in the regulations.[17.2] But while the regulations provide that the Listings are to be only one factor in the disability evaluation process,[17.3] under the POMS standards if the claimant does not meet the Listings criteria, it is unlikely that a

---

[17] 20 CFR § 404.1517; 20 CFR § 416.917.

[17.1] *See* SSA forms, *infra.*

[17.2] 20 CFR Part 404, Suppart P, Appendix 1. *See* discussion on proper use of the listings, *infra.*

[17.3] 20 CFR § 404.1520(d); 20 CFR § 416.920(d).

finding of disability will be made. Individuals with impairments that are not easily diagnosed by "objective" testing, such as those with psychiatric, back, and arthritic conditions, have a particularly difficult time qualifying under the POMS standards. The POMS standards also do not consider vocational, age, and educational factors, which can be crucial in evaluating whether a given medical impairment disables a person from working. Many advocates have found that, in practice, under the POMS, applicants who are not bedridden, are relatively mobile, and can carry on a conversation will be found "not disabled" by the state agency.

After the DDS makes its decision, it is sent to the Office of Disability Operations (ODO) for possible review. While in SSI cases the ODO may reverse or modify either a grant or denial of benefits,[18] in SSDI cases it may only make a decision less favorable to the claimant than the one made by the state agency.[18.1] If the determination is favorable at this stage, an award letter is sent to the claimant, benefits are computed, and payments should commence in about eight weeks. If the claim is denied, the applicant will receive a "Notice of Disapproved Claim" form letter with a personalized attachment giving some explanation of why the claim was denied.[18.2] The claimant then has sixty days to appeal the decision by requesting reconsideration.

[c] Reconsideration

If an applicant for either DIB or SSI is denied initially, the claimant appeals by filing a Request for Reconsideration form with the DO.[18.3] This can be done in person at the DO or by mail, either by the applicant or his/her representative. An applicant may submit new evidence with this request and will often be asked by the DO to update the medical information already on file by completing a Reconsideration Disability Report[19] and additional medical authorizations so that the state agency can ob-

[18] 20 CFR § 416.903(d).

[18.1] 20 CFR § 404.1503(d).

[18.2] *See* SSA forms, *infra.*

[18.3] 20 CFR § 404.907-.921; 20 CFR § 416.1407-.1421. *See* SSA forms, *infra.*

[19] *See* SSA forms, *infra.*

tain any new information. Recently enacted legislation requires SSA to provide the opportunity for a face-to-face evidentiary hearing during reconsideration of any decision that a recipient is no longer disabled. This will be effective with respect to reconsiderations requested on or after a date to be specified, but no later than January 1, 1984.[19.1]

The file is then sent once more to the state agency. Usually a different analyst team will reconsider the claim. The team may send for further medical evidence or request a consultative report. Thus, it is important for a claimant to note on the request form any medical information sources that the state agency did not contact previously.

Upon making the decision on the reconsideration request, another "Disability Determination and Transmittal Form" is placed in the claimant's file, and the case is again forwarded to the ODO for review. If the determination at this stage is favorable, a notice to that effect is sent and the claimant's benefit payments processed accordingly. If the claim is again denied, a "Notice of Reconsideration"[19.2] is sent and the claimant has sixty days to request a hearing before an Administrative Law Judge (ALJ) from the SSA Office of Hearings and Appeals (OHA). Because the same standard is applied on reconsideration as on initial application, very few cases are reversed.

In general, because of the great difficulty in being granted benefits at the state agency level, many clearly disabled people

---

19.1 PL 97-455, signed January 12, 1983.

19.2 *See* SSA forms, *infra*.

physicians to specify the expected length of recovery when filling out forms. It is also important to obtain, if possible, older records showing that the claimant's problems have already lasted the twelve-month period. If a claimant is recovering from an illness that lasted longer than twelve months but from which s/he has now recovered, it is possible to win a period of disability called a "closed period of disability." The claimant would thus be awarded disability benefits with both a closing and an ending date at the same time to cover the period when s/he was in fact disabled. One check will be issued for that period, and no monthly benefits would be paid.[34]

[b] Combination of Impairments

It is important for representatives to remember that a combination of impairments may be disabling where a single impairment alone may not be of the requisite level of severity.[35] This frequently happens if a claimant has both physical and mental impairments (which often are interrelated) or has multiple physical problems that in combination are simply too much for him/her to continue working.

[c] Remediability

If an impairment is considered remediable, then it is not disabling.[36] "Remediable" means treatable by some reasonable means. A claimant need not submit to all treatment no matter how painful, dangerous, or uncertain. A claimant's age, background, and medical history should be considered in determining whether there was justifiable cause to refuse treatment. A history of unsuccessful treatment may justify refusal. However, the more

---

[34] 20 CFR § 404.1539(a)(i).

[35] Hicks v. Gardner, 393 F.2d 299 (4th Cir. 1968); Oppenheim v. Finch, 495 F.2d 396 (4th Cir. 1971); Prestigiacomo v. Celebrezze, 234 F. Supp. 999 (E.D. La. 1964).

[36] 20 CFR § 404.1530 and 20 CFR § 416.930.

debilitating the problem, the less reasonable the refusal.[37] For instance, a spinal fusion operation will not be required, since it is dangerous and not guaranteed to be successful. However, if the physicians state that a disease would be controlled by medication and the claimant refuses that medication, a finding of nondisability will be made on the basis of remediability. Another example of a remediable condition, as seen by the Social Security Administration, is obesity—a related condition is not considered disabling if it is treatable through weight loss.[38] (It may be useful in such a case to show that the obesity is related to emotional problems.) The remediability provisions may penalize a claimant without sufficient funds to purchase medication or to pay for physical therapy treatments or other medical care. (See discussion, *infra,* for the applicability of the remediability criteria to alcoholism and drug addiction.)

[5] Practical Considerations in Specific Cases

Many applicants for disability benefits experience severe pain that interferes with their functional abilities, to the extent that they are unable to perform work activity. Many of these claimants suffer from orthopedic problems and will not have complete diagnoses of their problems; the doctors will see the pain as disproportionate to the objective medical findings. Or the diagnosed problem will impose certain objective limitations, such as limits on lifting in order to avoid further problems, but the claimant's experience of pain imposes even more restrictions. Further, everyone's individual experience of pain differs. It is difficult to *prove* that a person is actually experiencing severe pain. There is new medical research being done in this area, and pain clinics using a variety of techniques to help people live with and lessen their experience of pain have opened in many areas.

For an average disability client, the issue often comes down to his/her credibility and whether his/her experience of pain ren-

---

[37] Nichols v. Califano, 556 F.2d 931 (9th Cir. 1977); Smith v. Weinberger, 394 F. Supp. 1002 (D. Md. 1975); Chester v. Mathews, 403 F. Supp. 110 (D. Md. 1975).

[38] Wilson v. Califano, 453 F. Supp. 79 (N.D. Texas 1978).

substantial gainful activity because of medically verifiable impairment(s) that have lasted one year, can be expected to last one year, or will result in death.[21] The level of severity of each impairment is crucial, that is, it is not enough that a person simply have high blood pressure; it must be severe enough to interfere with work activity. The impairment must be a medically determinable physical or mental one that is demonstrable by medically acceptable clinical and laboratory diagnostic techniques.[22] The regulations list and describe the impairments and their level of severity[23] that qualify an individual for disability benefits on the basis of medical evidence alone without any consideration of vocational factors (age, education, work experience) or combinations of impairments.[24] If an impairment meets the listings the applicant will be found disabled. These cases are often seen at the first two administrative levels, since they are the more extreme. It is also acceptable for an impairment to "equal" instead of exactly meet the listings (for example, the level of severity of one or a combination of problems may equal although not exactly meet the listings).[25]

Most claimants who seek representation have problems that will not readily appear to meet the listings. However, with full documentation, an impairment or a combination of impairments will often meet or equal the listings. It is also useful to consult the listings for general guidelines with respect to mental impairments. If an individual's impairment does not meet or equal the listings, s/he may still be found to be disabled if the impairment is severe enough to keep her/him from working, taking into account age, education, and vocational experience.

In determining whether a person meets the statutory standard of disability, it is crucial to review the functional and exertional limitations caused by the impairments. The question is, how is the claimant limited in his/her activities by the impairments? For physical impairments, how are exertional activities (lifting, carrying, bending, standing, walking, etc.) affected? For emotional

---

[21] 20 CFR § 404.1505; 20 CFR § 416.905.

[22] 20 CFR § 404.1508; 20 CFR § 416.908.

[23] The listing of impairments is at 20 CFR Part 404, Subpart P, Appendix 1.

[24] 20 CFR § 404.1520; 20 CFR § 416.920-925.

[25] 20 CFR § 404.1526; 20 CFR § 416.926.

problems, as well as pain syndromes, how are concentration, relations with others, outside interests, daily activities, etc., affected?

One must look at the individual as a whole in considering the question of disability.[26] The test is whether a job is realistically within the physical and mental capabilities of a claimant.[27] Courts have ruled that the factors to be considered in determining disability are (1) the objective medical facts, (2) diagnoses or medical opinions based on those facts, (3) subjective evidence of pain and disability testified to by the claimant and his/her family or others, and (4) the claimant's educational background, age, and work experience.[28]

One must look at both objective and subjective factors. In other words, many people experience pain that may not be adequately explained by a doctor's diagnosis. This is especially true in orthopedic cases, where physicians often do not know the cause of a problem. A doctor is simply not able precisely to assess the level of pain, which is a subjective matter. The case law in this area conflicts somewhat. Some courts have held that no objective findings are necessary and a finding of disability may be made on subjective evidence alone.[29] The regulations state that the medical signs or findings must indicate a medical problem that could be reasonably expected to produce those symptoms.[30] The regulations also state that there must be "medical findings" to support a finding of disability. These consist of symptoms, signs, and laboratory findings. With respect to symptoms, the regulations state: "Your statements alone are not enough to establish that there is a physical or mental impairment."[31] Many cases state that there must be some objective findings but subjective evidence must be examined and explicit findings must be made.[32] These

[26] Landess v. Weinberger, 490 F.2d 1187 (8th Cir. 1973).

[27] Timmerman v. Weinberger, 510 F.2d 439 (8th Cir. 1975).

[28] Gold v. Secretary of H.E.W., 463 F.2d 38, 41 (2d Cir. 1972); Walden v. Schweiker, 672 F.2d 835 (9th Cir. 1982).

[29] E.g., Walston v. Gardner, 381 F.2d 580 (6th Cir. 1967); Aubeuf v. Schweiker, 649 F.2d 107 (2d Cir. 1981).

[30] 20 CFR § 404.1529; 20 CFR § 416.929.

[31] 20 CFR § 404.1528; 20 CFR § 416.928.

[32] Thorne v. Weinberger, 530 F.2d 580 (4th Cir. 1976); Storck v. Weinberger, 402 F. Supp. 603 (D. Md. 1975); Hargen Rader v. Califano, 575 F.2d 434 (3d Cir. 1978).

cases are quite clear on this latter point. The Social Security Administration must look at the subjective evidence and make explicit findings on whether the pain is severe enough to disable the person. (See further discussion of proving these cases, *infra.*)

The stress *is,* however, on objective evidence, such as laboratory tests, X-ray results, etc. This often puts working-class people at a disadvantage, since they have often not had the chance to receive regular, consistent high-quality medical care.

[a] Twelve-Month Requirement

Some claims are denied because, even though a claimant's problems meet the requisite levels of severity, they are not expected to last for twelve months.[33] For example, the Social Security Administration will often conclude that a claimant will recover from surgery within twelve months. It is thus important for physicians to specify the expected length of recovery when filling out forms. It is also important to obtain, if possible, older records showing that the claimant's problems have already lasted the twelve-month period. If a claimant is recovering from an illness that lasted longer than twelve months but from which s/he has now recovered, it is possible to win a period of disability called a "closed period of disability." The claimant would thus be awarded disability benefits with both a closing and an ending date at the same time to cover the period when s/he was in fact disabled. One check will be issued for that period, and no monthly benefits would be paid.[34]

[b] Combination of Impairments

It is important for representatives to remember that a combination of impairments may be disabling where a single impairment

[33] 20 CFR § 404.1509; 20 CFR § 416.909.

[34] 20 CFR § 404.1539(a)(i).

alone may not be of the requisite level of severity.[35] This frequently happens if a claimant has both physical and mental impairments (which often are interrelated) or has multiple physical problems that in combination are simply too much for him/her to continue working.

[c] Remediability

If an impairment is considered remediable, then it is not disabling.[36] "Remediable" means treatable by some reasonable means. A claimant need not submit to all treatment no matter how painful, dangerous, or uncertain.[36.1] A claimant's age, background (including religious beliefs),[36.2] and medical history should be considered in determining whether there was justifiable cause to refuse treatment. A history of unsuccessful treatment may justify refusal. However, the more debilitating the problem, the less reasonable the refusal.[37] For instance, a spinal fusion operation will not be required, since it is dangerous and not guaranteed to be successful. However, if the physicians state that a disease would be controlled by medication and the claimant refuses that medication, a finding of nondisability will be made on the basis of remediability. Another example of a remediable condition, as seen by the Social Security Administration, is obesity—a related condition is not considered disabling if it is treatable through weight loss.[38] (It may be useful in such a case to show that the obesity is related to emotional problems.) The remediability provisions may penalize a claimant without sufficient funds to purchase medication or to pay for physical therapy treatments

---

[35] Burnam v. Schweiker, 682 F.2d 456 (3d Cir. 1982); Hicks v. Gardner, 393 F.2d 299 (4th Cir. 1968); Oppenheim v. Finch, 495 F.2d 396 (4th Cir. 1971); Prestigiacomo v. Celebrezze, 234 F. Supp. 999 (E.D. La. 1964).

[36] 20 CFR § 404.1530 and 20 CFR § 416.930.

[36.1] Blankenship v. Califano, 598 F.2d 1041 (6th Cir. 1979).

[36.2] Lewis v. Califano, 616 F.2d 73 (3d Cir. 1980).

[37] Nichols v. Califano, 556 F.2d 931 (9th Cir. 1977); Smith v. Weinberger, 394 F. Supp. 1002 (D. Md. 1975); Chester v. Mathews, 403 F. Supp. 110 (D. Md. 1975).

[38] Wilson v. Califano, 453 F. Supp. 79 (N.D. Texas 1978).

or other medical care. (See discussion, *infra,* for the applicability of the remediability criteria to alcoholism and drug addiction.)

[d] Widows' And Widowers' Benefits

Individuals applying for benefits as disabled widows or widowers (or surviving divorced spouses) of deceased workers who were "fully insured" at the time of their disability or death[38.1] must meet a stricter test of disability than do regular DIB applicants. Applicants to this program must have medical problems that meet or equal the listing of impairments. For these claimants, unlike claimants who are applying for disability benefits on their own earnings records, the SSA will not consider their age, education, training, or experience in determining whether they are disabled.[38.2] In addition, certain other requirements of this program differ from the regular disability program, including age, insurance coverage, etc.

[5] Practical Considerations in Specific Cases

Many applicants for disability benefits experience severe pain that interferes with their functional abilities, to the extent that they are unable to perform work activity. Many of these claimants suffer from orthopedic problems and will not have complete diagnoses of their problems; the doctors will see the pain as disproportionate to the objective medical findings. Or the diagnosed problem will impose certain objective limitations, such as limits on lifting in order to avoid further problems, but the claimant's experience of pain imposes even more restrictions. Further, everyone's individual experience of pain differs. It is difficult to *prove* that a person is actually experiencing severe pain. There is new medical research being done in this area, and pain clinics using a variety of techniques to help people live with and lessen their experience of pain have opened in many areas.

[38.1] 20 CFR § 404.335-338.

[38.2] 20 CFR § 404.1577-1580.

For an average disability client, the issue often comes down to his/her credibility and whether his/her experience of pain ren-

(*Text continued on page 6-19*)

ders him/her totally disabled. One court has stated that the Social Security Administration must rule on the credibility of the client, not on whether or not s/he falls into a textbook definition of pain syndromes.[39] In some circuits, pain may be recognized as disabling even if there is no supporting objective medical evidence.[39.1] The ALJ should not reject an allegation of pain based on the observation the claimant did not appear to be in pain during the hearing.[39.2] It is important to examine some of the factors that typically appear with persons suffering from pain syndromes, such as complaints of sleep disturbance, loss of weight, loss of appetite, impairment of concentration, etc. Also, the representative should explore whether the claimant suffers from side effects of the medication that interfere with normal activities and should examine a possible interplay between the pain and any existing emotional impairments.

It is often useful in a hearing to use corroborating witnesses or psychological reports to verify the existence of this level of pain. For instance, the claimant may have suffered from such severe pain that s/he withdraws from social contacts. Often a psychiatrist or a witness well acquainted with the claimant can provide detailed evidence as to how this pain has affected his/her day-to-day life. Also, the claimant at the hearing should testify as fully as possible about the frequency, level of severity, location, and nature of the pain, how it varies from day to day, what activities will produce severe pain that may render him/her bedridden, etc. For instance, if attending church will bring on such severe pain that the claimant will be in bed for a day, it is hard to imagine that the claimant could sustain regular seated work; if the claimant is able to attend church on some Sundays, but misses other days because of pain, this is relevant evidence as to the level and effect of pain. Often, the claimant will not want to be seen as a "complainer" especially in front of a judge, so caution against minimizing the complaints, as well as against maximizing them. It is often helpful to have a witness who can realistically describe the situation if the claimant tends to minimize the effects of pain.

---

[39] Day v. Weinberger, 522 F.2d 1154 (9th Cir. 1975).

[39.1] Wiggins v. Schweiker, 679 F.2d 1387 (11th Cir. 1982); Myers v. Califano, 611 F.2d 980 (4th Cir. 1980); Marcus v. Califano, 615 F.2d 23 (2d Cir. 1979).

[39.2] Freeman v. Schweiker, 681 F.2d 927 (11th Cir. 1982).

One of the philosophical issues raised by the disability program is that those who continue to function despite severe pain will often be denied disability benefits, whereas someone with less motivation to work or keep busy may have a lower pain threshold or fewer psychological resources to fight off the pain. The former will often be denied benefits even if s/he is not working because his/her level of activities is so high that s/he is found not to be disabled, though s/he may in fact be totally incapable of performing substantial, gainful work activity. S/he may be unable to admit this, however, since that would be admitting defeat.

[a] Emotional Impairments

A representative should read the relevant sections in the listings of impairments for general guidelines as to the proof and level of severity needed for emotional impairments in disability cases. Generally, it is possible to receive disability on the basis of neuroses, but the problems must be significant.[40] The Medical-Vocational Guidelines do not apply to emotional impairments.[40.1]

People with emotional difficulties are often denied compensation at the initial stages. The responses of ALJs to psychological problems vary widely, so it is useful to obtain as much information as possible about the particular ALJ's attitude toward these impairments before the hearing. A representative in such a case should submit a report from a psychologist or psychiatrist, either from a treatment source or on a consultative basis. Psychological tests are often useful. (IQ tests can also work favorably for people who do not score well on them, especially in combination with other problems. See the listings requirements.) Some ALJs will be more impressed by a psychiatrist's M.D. than by a psychologist's credentials. Generally, a report from a licensed psychologist or a psychiatrist will carry more weight than will one from a social worker or other mental health care worker. Also, a narrative

---

[40] Dean v. Gardner, 393 F.2d 327 (9th Cir. 1968); Dressel v. Califano, 558 F.2d 504 (8th Cir. 1977).

[40.1] Tennant v. Schweiker, 682 F.2d 707 (8th Cir. 1982).

report from a psychiatrist should disclose the findings of the mental status exam, since these are considered objective findings.

Of course, emotional difficulties may be inextricably tied to socioeconomic factors. If the Social Security Administration finds that the claimant is depressed only because s/he is out of work, such a "reactive" depression will not be disabling because returning to work will remedy it. However, such depression in an orthopedic patient may worsen the experience of pain. Often people fall into pain/emotional difficulty feedback loops; in such cases, psychiatric evidence is useful in showing disability. It should also be remembered that if a judge is trying to say that the claimant is simply not motivated to work, a lack of motivation may be a symptom of neurosis.[41]

In interviewing a client, the representative must often act as a diagnostician of emotional problems. Many working-class people are not psychiatrically oriented and will rarely have seen a therapist unless they have acted out in a significant way. Questions to ask claimants are whether they feel they have problems with their nerves, how they would describe their relations with others, whether there are times they cannot cope with being around people, whether they have sleep problems, etc. It is crucial to characterize such problems as psychological in nature. For instance, "cultural deprivation" is not a medical impairment contemplated by the Social Security Act.[42]

The Social Security Administration seems less inclined to grant benefits to younger people on the basis of emotional problems. One must also be very aware of the twelve-month requirement with respect to these problems. For instance, someone who has had a spouse die recently may suffer disabling depression, but it must be expected to last one year to meet the requirements of the disability program.

[b] Alcoholism

Alcoholism and drug abuse are disabling if the level of severity prevents the claimant from performing substantial, gainful ac-

---

[41] Branham v. Gardner, 383 F.2d 614 (6th Cir. 1967).

[42] Laffoon v. Califano, 558 F.2d 253 (5th Cir. 1977).

tivity. Even if it has reached this level of severity, however, one has to look at whether or not it is remediable. Many denials of alcoholic disability cases are based on the simple premise that if the claimant stops drinking s/he will no longer be disabled.

This question has been addressed more and more by the courts and by the Social Security Administration. In the past, alcoholism required organ damage or some underlying mental problem to be considered a disabling impairment. It was not seen as a disabling impairment on its own. But recent court cases have changed these requirements, and the regulations have been rewritten so that organ damage is no longer required.

The case law[43] is inconsistent. The more progressive rulings state that some people are unable to seek or benefit from treatment and that their alcoholism is therefore not remediable. Sometimes the fact that a claimant has repeatedly tried to stop drinking in various programs and failed is evidence of nonremediability. For others, the fact that they have never gotten themselves to a treatment center is evidence of their inability to seek and receive successful treatment. Some of the factors to review in showing the required level of severity and nonremediability of alcoholism are (1) duration and level of drinking problem (it is obviously easier for an older, longtime alcoholic than for a younger one to receive benefits), (2) loss of employment attributable to drinking, (3) related arrests, (4) divorces or other relationship problems attributable to alcoholism, (5) any underlying physical or mental problem that is being self-medicated by alcohol, (6) resulting physical problems such as pancreatitis or alcoholic gastritis, and the continuation of drinking despite such painful problems, (7) past attendance or nonattendance at rehabilitation programs, (8) experiences with DTs or withdrawal seizures, (9) impairment of daily activities (e.g., what assistance is needed from other people), and (10) loss of a driver's license.

Alcoholics frequently deny their problems, both to a representative at an office interview and in a hearing. If the claimant

[43] For discussion of alcoholism, *see* Griffis v. Weinberger, 509 F.2d 837 (9th Cir. 1975); Adams v. Weinberger, 548 F.2d 239 (8th Cir. 1977); Badichek v. Secretary of H.E.W., 375 F. Supp. 940 (E.D.N.Y. 1974); Gray v. Califano, 448 F. Supp. 1142 (S.D. Cal. 1978); Swaim v. Califano, 599 F.2d 1309 (4th Cir. 1979); Veal v. Califano, 610 F.2d 495 (9th Cir. 1979).

denies the problem at a hearing, the representative may have to impeach that testimony.[43.1] A witness is often useful in such a case, for s/he can often testify to the level of severity of a drinking problem much better than the claimant can. The witness can often identify the alcohol as the real culprit in the loss of spouse, employment, etc.

If SSI is granted on the basis of alcoholism, the regulations require the appointment of a representative payee to receive the benefits. The regulations also require that the claimant obtain

(*Text continued on page 6-23*)

43.1 McShea v. Schweiker, 700 F.2d 117 (3d Cir. 1983).

regular treatment as a condition of receiving the benefits.[44]

There are few cases on drug abuse, but the considerations should be analogous.

[6] Evaluation of Disability and Consideration of Vocational Factors

[a] Sequential Evaluation

The Social Security Administration follows certain sequential steps in evaluating disability.[45] These steps are—

(1) Is the claimant working? If so, and the work is considered substantial, gainful activity, then a finding that the claimant is not disabled will be made, regardless of the his/her medical condition, age, education, work experience.

(2) Does the claimant have a severe impairment? If the Social Security Administration determines that there is no impairment that significantly limits the claimant's physical or mental ability to perform basic work activities, then it will find him/her not disabled. It will not consider his/her age, education, and work experience.

(3) Does the claimant's impairment meet or equal a listed impairment, and meet the twelve-month duration requirement? If so, the Social Security Administration is to make a finding of disability.

(4) Is the claimant precluded from performing his/her past work by a severe impairment? If so, the Social Security Administration will then consider the claimant's residual functional capacity, plus the claimant's age, education, and experience to see if s/he can perform other work. If not, then it will find the person disabled. If the claimant has performed arduous, unskilled, physical work over a long work history (i.e., thirty-five years or more), has only a marginal education, and is no longer able to perform such work, the Social Security Administration is to find

---

[44] 20 CFR § 404.935-939.

[45] 20 CFR § 404.1520; 20 CFR § 416.920.

that claimant disabled.[46]

The vocational factors of age, education, and work experience are thus considered at the fourth step of this process. Such factors are not sufficient on their own to obtain benefits, but they are taken into consideration with the evidence of medically severe impairments.

[b] Burden of Proof

A claimant has the burden of proof of showing disability.[47] However, once s/he has shown the inability to perform his/her prior usual occupation, the court cases hold that the burden of proof shifts to the Social Security Administration, which must show work that the claimant could do.[48] The shifting burden means that the Social Security Administration must produce some actual evidence of some other job (1) that the plaintiff could perform and (2) that exists in significant numbers in the economy. It is important to remember that *openings* need not exist, nor must the Social Security Administration show that the claimant would be hired. The Social Security Administration must show only that jobs themselves exist and that the claimant has the physical and vocational capacity to perform them. Many district courts have held in the past that in order to meet this shifted burden, the Social Security Administration must have a vocational expert testify at a claimant's hearing, as to both whether the claimant could perform the work and in what numbers the jobs exist. Other cases state that administrative notice could be taken of the number of jobs, but not of a claimant's *ability* to perform the work. The case law is split on what would be sufficient to meet the burden of proof by the Social Security Administration, with some cases saying that a vocational expert is not necessary in each such case. Many court remands on appeal have been granted on these issues.

---

[46] 20 CFR § 404.1562.

[47] Jenkins v. Gardner, 430 F.2d 243 (6th Cir. 1970).

[48] Dressel v. Califano, 558 F.2d 504 (8th Cir. 1977); May v. Gardner, 362 F.2d 616 (6th Cir. 1966).

ing observation of the patient's condition.[48.2] It can also be argued that any report by a nonexamining state agency physician or medical advisor is entitled to only limited, if any, weight if it contradicts the opinion of an examining physician and if the nonexamining physician does not testify at the hearing.[48.3] In general, opinions by the treating physician can be very valuable, and the failure of the ALJ to consider them, especially if they are uncontradicted, can be ground for reversal or remand.[48.4] The opinion of a treating physician is entitled to more weight than a one-time examiner.[48.5] The ALJ must give clear and convincing reasons for rejecting uncontroverted medical opinion from a treating physician.[48.6]

Once evidence on the claimant's RFC is introduced, the SSA must produce evidence of specific jobs in the national economy that the claimant has the ability to perform.

It is important to remember that *openings* need not exist, nor must the Social Security Administration show that the claimant would be hired. The Social Security Administration must show only that jobs themselves exist and that the claimant has the physical and vocational capacity to perform them.

The SSA attempts to meet its burden on the issue of vocational capacity through the use of testimony by vocational experts as well as by using the Medical-Vocational Guidelines (otherwise known as the "grid" regulations).[48.7] Before the introduction of the grids, many courts had held that in order to meet its burden the SSA had to introduce expert testimony of specific jobs that the claimant could perform and that existed in the national economy. The United States Supreme Court has held that the use of the "grids" neither conflicts with the Social Security Act nor

48.2 Vitek v. Finch, 438 F.2d 1157 (4th Cir. 1977).

48.3 Browne v. Richardson, 468 F.2d 1003 (1st Cir. 1972); Strickland v. Harris, 615 F.2d 1103 (5th Cir. 1980). *See also* Richardson v. Perales, 402 U.S. 389 (1971).

48.4 Day v. Weinberger, 522 F.2d 1156 (9th Cir. 1976); Walker v. Matthews; 546 F.2d 814 (9th Cir. 1976); Golofski v. Califano, 607 F.2d 1063 (3d Cir. 1979).

48.5 Arnold v. Secretary, 567 F.2d 258 (4th Cir. 1977); Jones v. Harris, 497 F. Supp. 161 (E.D. Pa. 1980).

48.6 Rhodes v. Schweiker, 660 F.2d 722 (9th Cir. 1981).

48.7 20 CFR Part 404, Subpart P, Appendix 2.

is arbitrary and capricious.[48.8] There may remain, however, a certain flexibility, particularly with respect to the age category.[48.9]

[c] Use of a Vocational Expert by the ALJ

The vocational expert is usually a vocational counselor or psychologist specializing in the vocational area who reviews the claimant's file and listens to the claimant's testimony at the hearing. Then the ALJ poses hypothetical questions to the vocational expert, basically asking whether a claimant with the claimant's age, education, training, experience, and impairments (as viewed by the ALJ) could perform the claimant's former job or any other job that exists in significant numbers in the economy. The vocational expert would then describe specific jobs s/he felt the claimant could perform. How these vocational factors are dealt with not only varies in the district court cases but also varies from ALJ to ALJ, from vocational expert to vocational expert, and from region to region. The manner in which an ALJ utilizes a vocational expert can vary considerably depending on the particular expert, the ALJ, and the region. A full discussion of dealing with the vocational expert is beyond the scope of this chapter.[48.10] However, in general, the advocate should cross-examine the vocational expert by stating all the claimant's limitations in detail and then trying to get the expert to acknowledge that someone with those limitations would not be able to hold any of the jobs that the expert had previously mentioned.

[d] The "Grid" Regulations

In part to cut down on the use of vocational experts in hearings (it is quite expensive) and to attempt to provide a more uniform

48.8 Heckler v. Campbell, 51 USLW 4561 (May 16, 1983).

48.9 20 CFR § 404.1563(a); Broz v. Schweiker, 677 F.2d 1351 (11th Cir. 1982).

48.10 For examination and cross-examination of vocational experts, *see* Babitsky, *The Vocational Expert in Social Security Disability Cases,* Trial, January 1979, for suggested approaches to vocational experts. Also, see articles on this subject in back issues of the NOSSCR Social Security Forum.

consideration of vocational factors, new regulations involving use of standardized grids to assess disability were promulgated in 1979.[49] These regulations instruct ALJs to take administrative notice of the existence of certain unskilled jobs in the national economy, as well as the exertional requirements of these jobs. They also require ALJs to take notice of the impact of age, education, and work experience on the ability to perform these jobs.

The grids are meant to be applied as part of the SSA's "sequential analysis" of disability,[50] discussed earlier in this chapter. They are to be utilized only if the ALJ finds that the claimant is disabled from performing her/his past relevant work, but has the RFC to perform other, less strenuous work.[51] The ALJ then makes a finding as to the exertional level of the claimant's "maximum sustained work capability" (for example, sedentary, light, or medium), taking into account her/his exertional impairments (limitations on lifting, bending, stooping, standing, etc.).[52] The grid chart for that exertional level is then consulted and the claimant is placed on the appropriate line of the grid, depending on the ALJ's findings as to the claimant's age, education, and transferable work skills, if any.

These classifications and how they are applied (for example, what is "closely approaching advanced age") are discussed in the regulations accompanying the grids. Some of the categories utilized in the grids, such as "transferable skills," are not clearly defined in the regulations and are the subject of ongoing judicial interpretation. In some cases, a vocational expert's testimony may be necessary on the issue of transferability.

Once a claimant is located on the correct grid, the chart will direct a finding of disabled or not disabled. However, the grid's finding is not dispositive if the claimant has nonexertional impairments, such as mental problems or the need to lie down frequently during the day.[52.1] In these cases, the ALJ must then determine how these further restrictions affect the claimant's

---

49 Medical-Vocational Guidelines, 20 CFR, Part 404, Subpart P, Appendix 20b.

50 20 CFR § 404.1520; 20 CFR § 416.920.

51 20 CFR § 404.1569; 20 CFR § 416.969.

52 20 CFR § 404.1545,.1549; 20 CFR § 416.945,.949.

52.1 *E.g.,* Roberts v. Schweiker, 667 F.2d 1143 (4th Cir. 1981).

ability to perform the jobs administratively noticed by the grids. The advocate should make a prehearing request for a vocational expert if there are nonexertional impairments and if the expert's testimony could prove helpful.

The effect of the grids is to take away much of the former discretion of the ALJs. In some cases, the grids prove to be advantageous to a claimant; in others, they are not advantageous. In general, the grids tend to favor older workers by not expecting them to switch to different, even if less strenuous, jobs. Younger workers, on the other hand, will probably be found to be not disabled under the grids if they have the ability to do at least sedentary work, regardless of their education or vocational background.

Even if the grids are used by an ALJ to determine whether a claimant is disabled, specific findings based on substantial evidence in the record must still be made on each of the factors to be assessed on the grid. Therefore, advocates should keep the criteria of the grids in mind when preparing and presenting their clients' cases. The advocate should attempt to show that the claimant qualifies under the grids or, alternatively, that the grids are not determinative in the claimant's situation because of the effect of nonexertional limitations or because the person cannot perform a wide range of sedentary work. An example of the latter situation would be the case of the younger worker who has the RFC to perform sedentary work. In that case, the advocate would want to emphasize any nonexertional restrictions, such as environmental restrictions, mental impairments, or the need for several naps during the day because of pain-related fatigue.

As noted previously, if medical impairments on their own are of sufficient severity to establish disability, the grid is not looked at. Also, if the claimant has done manual labor for thirty-five years and is no longer able to perform that work because of his/her impairments, the regulations direct a finding of disability.[52.2]

[52.2] 20 C.F.R. § 404.1562; 20 C.F.R. § 416.962.

[7] Substantial, Gainful Activity Defined

In this definition, "substantial" modifies "activity" as opposed to "gainful." If a person is doing some work, however, the Social Security Administration must determine whether or not it is substantial, gainful activity. The amount of wages received determines in part whether the activity is defined as substantial and gainful. There is a presumption that the work is substantial, gainful activity if the person receives more than a certain dollar amount per month. (The exact amount changes from time to time.) There is a presumption that the work is *not* substantial, gainful activity if the wages are under a certain amount per month. If the amount of wages is in between those two figures, there is no presumption either way.[53]

The amount of actual wages is almost always less important than the amount of time spent in work activity and the regularity with which the person performs such work. Part-time work can be substantial, gainful activity, but intermittent work generally is not. The whole situation must be examined in making this determination.[54] Therefore, it is crucial to show that the claimant is incapable of sustained, regular employment.

If a person is regularly attending school, s/he should show why such attendance does not mean that s/he could perform in an employment situation. A representative should try to point out any irregularity of attendance, problems with concentration resulting in poor grades, or other problems with school as documented by school records, letters from teachers, or other evidence.

Claimants for disabled widows' or widowers' benefits, discussed *supra,* have to meet a higher standard of disability.[54.1] For these claimants, doing *any* work will probably result in benefits being denied.

---

[53] For these amounts, as well as a general description of how substantial, gainful activity is determined, *see* 20 CFR § 404.1574; 20 CFR § 416.910. *See* CFR § 404.1575 for definition of substantial, gainful activity for self-employed persons.

[54] Cornett v. Califano, 1979 CCH UIR 16008 (4th Cir. 1978); Prevette v. Richardson, 316 F. Supp. 144 (D. So. Car. 1970).

[54.1] 20 CFR § 404.1572(b); .1577.

[8] Initial Interview with Client

[a] Purpose of Interview

The representative must first decide whether or not to take the claimant's case, assuming of course that the claimant wants to hire the representative. If the representative works in a legal services office, then office guidelines will often determine which cases may be accepted.

For private law offices, the question is more difficult and troubling, since the economics of the situation must enter into that decision. Most Social Security cases are taken on a contingency fee basis; thus, the attorney must decide whether or not to take a case with an eye toward whether or not s/he will get paid. If the claimant has recently applied for benefits and/or has had a recent onset of disability, there may not be sufficient past due benefits from which a representative may be paid. Thus, a lawyer must either believe that there is a good enough chance that the client will win or feel that there are other reasons besides financial ones to take the case. The client may be represented by the lawyer in another matter, or there may be political or legal reasons for assisting in the case.

The main purpose of the first interview is to obtain enough information and sense of the client to be able to decide whether or not to take the case and also to start to gather the evidence and plan a strategy for the claim.

[b] Conduct of the Interview

Before the interview, the client should be told to bring in all correspondence from the Social Security Administration and a list of medications or the medications themselves. It is often helpful to have a special intake form so that all relevant questions will be asked of the claimant. The representative should remember to get the client's birthdate and any other names used by the client so that there will be no problem in tracking down medical records.

In the interview, the representative often needs to diagnose the

(*Text continued on page 6-29*)

client's problems, especially with alcoholism or emotional problems, which are difficult for clients to describe. Also, since doctors often do not give direct and clear explanations of impairments to patients, many clients will not know the medical diagnoses and resulting functional limitations.

The representative should try to obtain as much detailed information as possible about treatment sources, e.g., doctors, clinics, therapists, rehabilitation centers, physical therapists, etc. It is also helpful to know the names of the medications taken by a client to determine the client's diagnosed problems. The representative can check the *Physicians' Desk Reference* for description of the medications.

The representative should get information as to the client's work history and his/her reasons for leaving work. If the client received unemployment insurance benefits, one will need to deal with the possible contradiction of holding oneself out as able to work as required by that program. Often, a person left a job for another reason and became disabled at a later date.

It is also important to ask the client about his/her daily activities and how they have changed since the disability. For instance, if s/he has a back problem, is s/he now able to sit through church or a movie? Does s/he mow the lawn, and, if so, is that inconsistent with his/her type of disability? Has his/her disability affected his/her social relationships? In short, the representative should obtain as many details as possible about each impairment and how it limits the person in his/her daily activities.

The representative should have the claimant sign medical releases, a fee agreement, and the Appointment of Representative form so that the representative may begin work. If a representative is undecided about taking on the claimant's case, one option is to review the person's Social Security file before making the decision to see the content of the medical evidence. The client should sign an authorization form allowing the representative to examine the file in this situation.

[9] Review of File

After a representative has been retained by a client, it is necessary to develop a strategy for the case. A review of the client's Social Security exhibit file is crucial. The representative should examine the Disability Transmittal form to see why the claim was initially denied. This will usually help to determine a strategy for the case. The application forms filled out initially will give the representative more information about the client and will also point out any past contradictory statements made by the claimant. A review of the file will also show what records are missing.

[10] Development of Case

After deciding on a strategy, the representative will need to develop the case. The most important aspect of working on a disability case is usually gathering strong written documentation. Hearsay is permissible.[55] Decisions are based on written medical evidence, as well as the oral testimony of the claimant and other witnesses.

The representative should try to obtain a complete report from the claimant's doctors. Each report should contain information about the client's symptoms, diagnoses and severity of each impairment, nature and degree of resulting functional loss, clinical findings, recommended or current treatment, and prognoses. In addition to such narrative reports and records, questionnaire forms detailing residual functional limitations are very helpful. It is crucial that medical reports contain such detailed information since a conclusory statement of a doctor that a person is disabled is not sufficient to show disability.[56] Other documentary evidence in a given case may include letters or affidavits from a client's past employers showing problems on the job or reasons for ending work, records from vocational rehabilitation centers, records from alcohol or drug rehabilitation programs, records from the welfare department, a letter from a social worker as to his/her observations of a client, etc.

Since the claimant has the burden of proof of showing disability, one should obtain all possible medical evidence. The representative should request records of office visits to clinics or other

[55] Richardson v. Perales, 402 U.S. 389, 91 S. Ct. 1420, 38 L. Ed. 2d 842 (1971).
[56] 20 CFR § 404.1527.

treatment centers, as well as requesting narrative reports. Hospital in-patient and emergency room records should also be requested.

If the treating doctor does not write a report, or does not write a complete or strong enough report, the representative may want to send the client for a consultative examination to a doctor who will write a comprehensive report. This is probably most frequent with clients who have psychiatric problems, since they will usually not have a treating psychiatrist or psychologist. (Payment for such reports is discussed in the sections on attorney's fees and costs.)

Often a treating doctor will be willing to write a complete narrative report after having direct contact with the representative. Thus, it is often a good idea to phone the doctor to discuss the client's case. Also, if a doctor is reluctant to write a narrative report, the representative could compose a form with the appropriate questions to be answered, similar to those used by the Social Security Administration. The treating doctor's report is especially important since it can be used to show the long-standing nature of the disability.[57]

It may be necessary to make follow-up phone calls to doctors' offices and institutions to inquire why records have not been sent. In some instances, it may be necessary to subpoena the records through the ALJ.

[11] Administrative Hearing

A hearing is scheduled after a claimant fills out a request for a hearing. This request must be filed within sixty days of receipt of the reconsideration denial.[58] When requesting the hearing, the claimant should state that s/he wishes to appear personally at the hearing. The Request for Hearing form can be filled out and filed by either the claimant or the representative. It should be sent or taken to the DO, which will then forward the client's file to the appropriate Office of Hearings and Appeals (OHA). At that

[57] For discussion of the weight to be given a treating doctor's report, *see* Hayes v. Gardner, 376 F.2d 517 (4th Cir. 1967).

[58] 20 CFR § 404.933; 20 CFR § 416.1433.

office, the case will be assigned to an ALJ, who will hear the case. There must be ten days' notice given to a claimant of the hearing date. There are also set rules now as to when the hearing must be scheduled, though a representative may wish to waive these limits.

The ALJ has the duty to develop the evidence fully and fairly.[59] This means that s/he will often send the claimant for consultative examinations, request further medical evidence from treatment sources, and/or have a client fill out forms concerning vocational history, current medications, etc. The administrative hearing is a hearing *de novo;* prior decisions of the Social Security Administration do not bind the ALJ. S/he may also make a decision on the record that is favorable to the claimant without the need for a hearing.

The ALJ represents both the government and the claimant, and is also a neutral arbiter. (This is the "three-hat" doctrine.) There have been many decisions remanded by the federal court because the ALJ failed properly to develop the evidence or otherwise acted to deny a full and fair hearing. This burden on an ALJ is necessarily higher when a claimant is not represented by counsel.[60]

ALJs are federal employees working for the OHA. They are appointed under the Administrative Procedure Act from a special civil service register and can be removed only for good cause. They are not included in the annual civil service rating programs. There are over 600 ALJs in 126 hearing offices.

Hearing assistants and other staff people at the OHA help to develop the exhibit files, schedule cases, oversee and tape the hearing, etc. When a representative wishes to see a client's file, s/he should call the OHA and find out which ALJ has been assigned to the case. Then, the representative should make the necessary arrangements to review and/or obtain photocopies of the exhibits.

The representative may wish to discuss the case with the ALJ before the hearing. Most ALJs will be amenable to such a discussion. The representative may wish to point out an aspect of the

---

[59] 20 CFR § 404.944.

[60] Cox v. Califano, 587 F.2d 988 (9th Cir. 1978); Gachette v. Weinberger, 551 F.2d 39 (3d Cir. 1977); Gold v. Secretary of H.E.W., *supra* note 27.

case that has not appeared to be determinative in the past development of the evidence or may wish to argue for a decision on the record. It is often helpful to clarify issues before the hearing if possible. The case may be assigned to a visiting ALJ, since regions with lighter case loads often send their ALJs to areas with backlogs.

[a] Conduct of the Hearing

The representative should meet with the client before the hearing to review the case, elicit any further relevant information, and describe to the client the procedures of the hearing. The conduct of the hearing may vary from region to region and from ALJ to ALJ. However, the testimony is always taken under oath and the proceedings tape-recorded. The hearing should be understandable to the layperson, should not necessarily be stiff and comfortable only for the trained attorney, and should be liberal in its tone and operation.[61]

The ALJ will generally make an opening statement describing the proceedings, which s/he may ask the representative to waive. The ALJ will ask the representative if there are objections to any of the exhibits in the file. (Objections are usually overruled unless the evidence is clearly improper.) During the hearing, the claimant is questioned by both the ALJ and the representative. The ALJ may ask a representative if s/he wants to give an opening statement. This may be wise, especially if the ALJ seems unfamiliar with the file. Sometimes the better practice is to save any argument for an oral or written closing statement.

Topics to cover in the questioning are work history, educational and vocational-training background, current living situation, complete description of impairments (including symptoms and resultant limitations), treatment sources, and description of daily activities (contrasting latter with prior activities). The representative should have questions prepared for the claimant and should be sure to cover any areas not covered by the ALJ's questions. The claimant's representative should also attempt to controvert or qualify any damaging statement made by the claimant in re-

---

[61] Richardson v. Perales, *supra* note 55.

sponse to the ALJ's questioning. (In some cases, the ALJ will ask questions first; in others, the representative will start the questioning.)

The representative is entitled to have the record kept open to submit a written brief after a hearing. This is the forum in which to make any relevant legal arguments. The representative may need to ask for more time to submit further medical evidence, but it is best to have all evidence submitted by the time of the hearing since this request may not be granted and, also, since the ALJ will be more favorably inclined toward a complete file at a hearing. The representative may wish to ask the Social Security Administration to send the client for a consultative examination, especially if there are no funds to obtain a private consultative report. In some cases it may be error for the ALJ to deny the request for a consultative exam.[61.1]

[b] Medical Advisor as Witness

Medical advisors are physicians hired per appearance to testify at certain disability hearings. They are usually specialists in various medical fields and are called upon to "translate" the meaning of various medical reports and to explain apparent conflicts in the evidence.[62] They often give their opinion as to whether or not a claimant is disabled, and though their testimony is not supposed to determine a case, it often does. This is true even though they have not personally examined the client.

Such medical testimony is very difficult for the advocate to deal with. The testimony may be fully favorable to the client, which obviously poses no problem, but if it is not favorable the representative should fully cross-examine the doctor. First, clarify whether or not the comments made are within the doctor's field of specialty. Also, question the doctor about the client's subjective experience and how this might change his/her opinion. If the representative is well prepared, s/he may be able to point out medical evidence ignored by the medical advisor in his/her testimony. Of course, the style of examination will vary

---

[61.1] Ford v. Secretary, 659 F.2d 66 (5th Cir. 1981).

[62] Richardson v. Perales, *supra,* Note 55.

depending on the situation, but a nonadversarial approach is often the most useful in trying to have a medical advisor be sympathetic to the client's position.

[c] Vocational Expert as Witness

The use of vocational experts by the SSA in its efforts to deny benefits has been discussed *supra.* Some advocates call their own vocational experts to testify to the relevant issues. This can be particularly effective if the vocational expert has met with the claimant personally prior to the hearing or performed a vocational evaluation. For example, expert testimony that a person is incapable of a wide range of even sedentary work, as it is defined, on a sustained basis can (at least arguably) render the grid regulations inapplicable.

[d] Physician as Witness

It is usually not financially feasible for a client's treating doctor to testify at the hearing, although it would be helpful in many cases, provided that the representative has spoken at length with the doctor before the hearing. Often in a judicial hearing, a doctor will be unwilling to describe total disability, even if s/he has already done so in a written report. It is also possible to subpoena a physician, a method usually used for doctors who have written a consultative report unfavorable to the client. The subpoena should be requested from the ALJ with the reasons for the request, since the ALJ is not required to issue it.[63]

[e] Lay Witnesses

It is often helpful to have lay witnesses appear at a hearing. The testimony of a social worker who has worked closely with the claimant may be useful in providing further evidence of disability. Such a person should give concrete testimony with specific

---

63 20 CFR § 404.950.

examples of how the claimant has been affected, since conclusions as to diagnoses, etc., will not be accepted without appropriate credentials. Likewise, a vocational rehabilitation worker may provide excellent testimony.

Family members or close friends may be able to provide information that the claimant cannot provide. For instance, some claimants may deny alcoholism or simply be unable to describe the devastating effects of the disease. A relative of the alcoholic can often testify to the severity of the disease, e.g., retrieving the alcoholic from the police, and can verify the effects of pain or emotional problems: "We will be playing cards and all of a sudden he will get up and go to his room and not come out for six hours. This happens daily." In general, the representative should carefully determine who, if anyone, should be called as a witness.

[f] Submission of Case

As stated, supra, the representative may submit a written summary of the case after the hearing. After the case is submitted for decision, the ALJ will complete a written decision and send one copy each to the claimant and the representative.[64] These decisions are not precedents for any other cases, nor do they become a public record.

If the decision is favorable to the claimant, the Appeals Council has sixty days in which to decide whether to review the decision on its own motion for possible reversal, remand, or modification.[65] If a decision is unfavorable, the claimant has sixty days to file a written appeal, called "Request for Review of Hearing Decision."[66]

[11.1] Termination Cases

An increasing number of SSDI recipients are being terminated, pursuant to an accelerated schedule of continuing disability

[64] 20 CFR § 404.953.

[65] 20 CFR § 404.969; 20 CFR § 416.1469.

[66] 20 CFR § 404.968; 20 CFR § 416.1468.

investigations. There is authority for the argument that, since a recipient has previously proved that s/he was under a disability, there exists a presumption the condition continues to exist.[66.1] At least one court has recognized that the Secretary has the burden of producing evidence (for example, at a hearing contesting the termination) that the person's condition has improved.[66.2] If there is no evidence establishing improvement, the claimant should not be terminated.

Recently enacted legislation provides that a recipient who is terminated because disability has ceased may receive continuing benefits.[66.3] The continued benefits would be treated as overpayments and subject to the recovery requirements, including waiver rights, if the ALJ upholds the termination decision. The last month for which such continuing payments could be made is June, 1984. It appears that if the appeal of termination is made in "good faith" the overpayment should be waived.[66.4]

[12] Appeals Council Review

The request for review should be sent to either the DO or to Appeals Council. If the client has missed the filing deadline, an extension can be requested.[67]

After the request for review is made, the Social Security Administration will send the claimant's exhibit file and folders to the Appeals Council. The branch there will review the case to determine whether or not to give the case a more complete review. A claimant may submit a brief with arguments counter to the hearing decision. The Appeals Council may consider additional evidence it believes is material to the record. There is authority that in reviewing an unfavorable ALJ decision, the Appeals Council is obliged to consider new evidence which has become available

66.1 Miranda v. Secretary, 514 F.2d 996 (1st Cir. 1975).

66.2 Patti v. Schweiker, 660 F.2d 582 (9th Cir. 1982).

66.3 PL 97-455, signed January 12, 1983.

66.4 42 U.S.C. § 223(g)(2)(B).

67 *See* 20 CFR §§ 404.968, 404.911.

since the hearing.[67.1] The Appeals Council has the power to overturn the decision and actually grant benefits (although this is rare) or to remand the case to the OHA for further proceedings (more common).[68] A strong written argument with concrete examples of the mistakes made at the hearing level can be persuasive at the Appeals Council. Denial is made in writing and usually takes one month or more. If the claimant is again denied at this level, the only appeal left is a lawsuit in a U.S. district court.

[13] Federal Court Review

Again, the client has sixty days from the receipt of the denial from the Appeals Council to file suit in federal court.[69] This is a very strict time limit, though in certain instances the client may obtain an extension from the Appeals Council.[70] (It usually takes so long to get this extension from the Appeals Council, however, that it may not make sense to ask for permission.)

The federal court case is commenced by the filing of a summons and complaint. Different district courts have their own forms, so contact the court prior to filing the suit. After filing, the suit is served by the U.S. Marshal on the U.S. Department of Health and Human Services and the U.S. Attorney. The government generally has sixty days in which to respond to the complaint. (Some districts have differing rules specific to disability cases with varying time limits, so check with the court.) With the answer, the government must file a complete transcript of the case, including a typed transcript of the hearing. This takes the Social Security Administration approximately three months to prepare, so extensions of time to answer are often granted. A representative may wish to submit new evidence that might be persuasive in showing disability and an informal summary of why benefits should be granted or why the case should be remanded to the local Health and Human Services attorney or U.S. Attorney prior to the time the transcript is filed. The attorney will

---

[67.1] Epps v. Harris, 624 F.2d 1267 (5th Cir. 1980).

[68] 20 CFR § 404.979.

[69] 20 CFR § 404.981.

[70] 20 CFR § 404.982.

then often send this material to the Social Security Administration in Baltimore and the case may be remanded without briefs having to be filed.

These cases are frequently determined by cross-motions for summary judgment and motions by plaintiffs for remand. Some courts, however, simply set a briefing schedule and no motions are filed. It is advisable to determine the preference of the judge assigned. A remand motion may be made in addition to, or instead of, a plaintiff motion for summary judgment. Such a remand is a request to send the case back to the Social Security Administration for further proceedings to consider new evidence or correction of legal errors. The standard for review is whether there was substantial evidence supporting the Secretary of Health and Human Services' decision.[71] If there is found to be substantial evidence, the Secretary will prevail on the motion for summary judgment.

The standard for remand is whether or not good cause is shown. Common grounds for remand are legal errors made by the ALJ that denied the client a full and fair hearing, failure to use the correct standards in evaluating such problems as alcoholism, etc.[72] Sometimes SSA will request a remand in order to obtain additional evidence, for example, a consultative examination. A strong argument exists that remand in this situation is appropriate only if good cause exists for failure to offer the evidence initially.[72.1]

If a case is remanded, it will usually return to the OHA, often with the same ALJ, who is instructed by the Appeals Council on how to proceed. For instance, the Appeals Council may instruct the ALJ to obtain a specific type of consultative report. These instructions should conform to the order of the court.

The defendant in these cases is represented by the U.S. Attorney. The motions are usually prepared by Health and Human Services attorneys but presented by the U.S. Attorney. A lawyer preparing a motion in a disability case can obtain sample briefs

---

[71] Reyes Robles v. Finch, 409 F.2d 84 (1st Cir. 1969).

[72] Estep v. Richardson, 465 F.2d 969 (6th Cir. 1972); Arms v. Gardner, 353 F.2d 197 (6th Cir. 1965); Parker v. Califano, 441 F. Supp. 1174 (N.D. Cal. 1977).

[72.1] 42 U.S.C. § 405(g).

from the National Organization of Social Security Representatives or from other local attorneys.

If a remand is granted, the ALJ makes a recommended decision

(*Text continued on page 6-39*)

to the Appeals Council, which issues the final decision. If that decision is favorable, then the federal court case will be dismissed and payments processed. If the decision is unfavorable, then the transcript of the second hearing is prepared and filed with the court. Another set of motions is then made and argued.

Attorneys are often wary of taking cases at this level. There are significant time delays in the process. Such case may not be financially remunerative in relation to the number of hours spent in preparing memos or making court appearances in a courthouse often far from the lawyer's office; moreover, there is no assurance of receiving a favorable decision. Remands are more usual than the granting of summary judgment, so further time delays are necessary for a remanded hearing to be held. Often, a lawyer may take only a case with a very strong legal argument, or a case in which there are other, legal or political reasons to appeal. However, there are many very worthy claimants whose cases are denied both at the hearing and at the Appeals Council, and representatives should not balk at filing such a case.

It may sometimes be better, depending on the situation, for a claimant to request a reopening of his/her case.[73] It is difficult to advise a client not to appeal, since once appeal rights are lost res judicata applies to that application unless there are sufficient grounds for reopening. This means that if the person reapplies later after neglecting to file a civil suit, s/he may no longer have the requisite quarters of coverage and all rights to disability insurance may thus be lost. Therefore, a federal court suit may be the only way to protect the onset date in disability cases. The Appeals Council is not often favorably disposed to reopening cases.

[14] Process after a Favorable Decision

After a claimant receives a favorable decision at any level of these administrative proceedings, the Social Security Administration will process the claim for payment. The amount of past due benefits will be computed and paid. It will normally take several weeks for a disabled worker to start receiving payments, though

[73] *See* 20 CFR § 404.987-989.

there are often delays in the process. It also routinely takes much longer to process payment to dependents or to a worker who is also receiving workers' compensation or had worked for a railroad.

Before payment, the DO will often have a claimant come to the office to provide further documents and/or update financial information. This is particularly true with SSI cases; the DO will want to know about the claimant's current financial and living situation.

Also, the welfare nature of the SSI program means that the receipt of past due benefits (under either Title II or Title XVI) will often result in the claimant having been overpaid for that quarter and having too much money to receive SSI. In that case, a claimant will be cut off for some period of time (usually a quarter), or until the his/her bank account is low enough. The claimant will often be asked to show proof of how a large back benefits check was spent. These computations mean that a recipient should report the receipt of the past due benefits check, even though it was issued by the Social Security Administration.

Also, a representative should be aware of the policy of many welfare departments to have recipients assign their past due benefits check on SSI to the welfare department. This is generally done by a written agreement signed by the recipient when applying for welfare, (i.e., the welfare is seen as a loan). In such cases, the welfare department deducts its past payments and sends the balance to the recipient. This is only true with SSI, because of its nature as a welfare program. Disability insurance benefits under Title II are not assignable or attachable.[74] If the recipient is in such a situation with his/her SSI, the attorney can assist by making certain that the correct agreement was signed and that the correct amount was withheld.

Eventually, the recipient will receive an Information Notice setting forth the amount of past due benefits. The form for DIB will state the amount withheld for attorney's fees. The check will arrive in a separate envelope at about the same time as the notice. SSI recipients will also receive a Notice of Decision stating the amount of monthly benefits and DIB recipients will receive an award certificate setting out the monthly benefits. The award

[74] 42 U.S.C. § 407.

certificate will follow the first notice regarding past due benefits in DIB cases. In SSI cases, the recipient will often receive the monthly amounts before receiving the past due benefits, because the local office can compute the monthly benefits. But if the check for past due benefits exceeds a certain amount (currently $3000), it must be sent to Baltimore for processing and payment. The processing for each program is done separately, which is why a client must report the receipt of the DIB benefits to the SSI program.

It is often very difficult to track down the status of the processing of payment. Sometimes SSI processing occurs in various regional payment centers, or the folder may be in Baltimore or in the local office. Usually, the DIB portion is processed at the Bureau of Disability Insurance in Baltimore, but railroad-related cases are sent to Chicago. One cannot call these offices, but must go through the DO. Depending on the person at the DO s/he may be able to trace the status and possible problems with the case. The claims representative first checks the Social Security Administration computer, which has little information as to the status but does state the location of the file. The DO claims representative often has great difficulty in calling the appropriate office and will often have to write to it or send a memo. It may take quite a while to obtain a response. It is very important to be able to speak to a helpful person at the DO who will persistently look into problematic cases. Sometimes the file will simply be sent to the wrong place and will not be processed for payment, or the attorney's fees will not be withheld, or the amount will be computed but for some reason payment will not be made.

If such bureaucratic problems cannot be resolved with the DO, the representative may have the client ask the local Congressperson for assistance. That official generally has a staff person assigned to assisting people with Social Security snafus. This "Congressional inquiry" is taken quite seriously by the Social Security Administration.

[15] Right to Representation

Although clients have the right to be represented at a disability hearing, such representation is not required. Nonrepresentation alone is not grounds for a remand after a hearing. However, it may be grounds for remand if the client had mental problems, did not speak English, or had some other impairment that would have kept him/her from being able to represent him/herself adequately. The ALJ's burden is necessarily higher when a claimant is not represented.[75]

A representative need not be an attorney, but may be a legal worker who is trained in Social Security cases. A formal degree is not required.[76]

[16] Attorneys' Fees

The Social Security Administration has the authority to set attorneys' fees (and legal workers' fees) in all work done before it. This means that a representative must obtain the Social Security Administration's approval (or court approval) for the award of fees for all but SSI federal court cases.[77]

In DIB cases, the government will withhold 25 percent of the worker's and dependents' past due benefits in anticipation of payment of attorney's fees. "Past due benefits" means the total amount of benefits payable under Title II of the Act to all beneficiaries that have accumulated because of a favorable decision up to, but not including, the month in which the decision was made. (Nonattorney's fees will not be withheld, but must be collected directly from the client.) In SSI cases, no monies are withheld; the money must be paid by the client to the representative.

The amounts withheld are not sent to the attorney until a fee petition has been filed and approved by the appropriate person. The amounts paid directly to a representative from the client (usually in an SSI case) can be deposited only in a trust account and cannot be spent by the representative until the filing and approval of a fee petition. Because approval of the fee petition

---

[75] Alamo v. Richardson, 355 F. Supp. 314 (D.P.R. 1972); Arms v. Gardner, *supra* note 72; Rayborn v. Weinberger, 398 F. Supp. 1303 (N.D. Ind. 1975); Gold v. Secretary of H.E.W., *supra* note 27.

[76] 20 CFR § 404.1705.

[77] 42 U.S.C. § 406(a); 20 CFR § 404.1720; 20 CFR § 416.1520.

monthly check. This notice is especially important for attorneys in SSDI cases; otherwise, the SSA may release any benefits which, as discussed *infra,* may have been withheld for payment of the fee.

The fee petition describes in detail the dates, time spent, and nature of the work done on the claimant's case, as well as the amount of the fee being requested.[78] A copy of the petition must be sent to the claimant, who has the right to contest the amount being requested.

If benefits were awarded at the hearing level, the ALJ who heard the case should be sent the fee petition for approval. If the case was decided at the Appeals Council, the petition should be sent to the Attorney Fee Branch in Washington, D.C. If benefits were awarded in federal court or following a remand from federal court, the procedure is to file two fee petitions: one to the Attorney Fee Branch for work done before the SSA and one to the federal court for work done before it. Local practice should be checked for the procedure to be used in the federal court for requesting a fee.

Recently, federal courts have considered the applicability of the Equal Access to Justice Act to social security cases. The Act provides that the United States shall pay fees to a prevailing plaintiff unless the court finds that the government's position was "substantially justified or that special circumstances would make an award unjust."[78.1] Courts have awarded fees under the Act in social security cases.[78.2]

[b] Approval of the Fee Petition

After the petition is filed, it will be reviewed by the ALJ or, where appropriate, by the Attorney Fee Branch or federal court judge. The ALJ is not bound to approve the amount requested by

---

78 20 CFR § 404.1725; 20 CFR § 416.1525. *See* SSA forms, *infra.*

78.1 28 U.S.C. § 2412(d)(1)(A).

78.2 Shumate v. Harris, 544 F. Supp. 779 (W.D.N.C. 1982); Occasio v. Schweiker, 540 F. Supp. 1320 (S.D.N.Y. 1982); Wolverton v. Schweiker, 533 F. Supp. 420 (D. Ida. 1982); Berman v. Schweiker, 531 F. Supp. 1149 (N.D. Ill. 1982).

the representative. Rather, the amount authorized will depend on the ALJ's determination of the type of services rendered, amount of time spent, degree of complexity of the case, level of skill and experience of the representative, and results achieved.[78.3] Thus, although a representative may have a fee agreement with the claimant providing for a contingent fee of 25 percent of past due benefits or for a specified hourly rate, the SSA is not required to authorize that amount.

Another variable is the extent to which fees will be approved for work performed by a paralegal. As this depends on the individual ALJ, it is best, if possible, to check with the ALJ before a paralegal works on such a case. It would also be wise to set out the paralegal's status as a nonattorney in any fee agreement. Once the fee is authorized, notice will be sent to the claimant and representative, either of whom may request review of the determination within thirty days.[79]

[c] Collecting the Fee

Once a fee has been approved, attorneys in SSI cases and nonattorneys in both SSI and SSDI cases must look to the claimant for payment of the entire fee. However, for attorneys representing successful SSDI claimants the SSA will withhold 25 percent of the claimant's past due benefits (and those of her/his dependents) in anticipation of payment of the fee.[79.1] When the claimant receives the Award Certificate, it will state the amount of retroactive benefits accrued and the amount withheld for fee payment. After the fee petition is approved, the amount up to the amount withheld will be forwarded to the attorney. If the fee authorized is less than the amount withheld, the balance is sent to the claimant.

In calculating the amount to be withheld, the SSA counts only Title II benefits payable to the claimant and her/his dependents that have accumulated up to, but not including, the month in which the favorable decision was made. Thus, in concurrent Title

[78.3] 20 CFR § 404.1725(b); 20 CFR § 416.1525(b).

[79] 20 CFR § 404.1720(d); 20 CFR § 416.1520(d).

[79.1] 20 CFR § 404.1730(b).

II/Title XVI claims, the amount withheld will not include 25 percent of any accrued SSI benefits. In addition, the amount of the SSDI benefits that are withheld may be greatly reduced because of the SSA's application of the SSI "windfall offset" statute.[79.2] This provision was intended to prevent claimants' double recovery of retroactive SSI and SSDI benefits for the same period by providing that any retroactive SSDI payable would be reduced by the amount of SSI already received that the claimant would not have been paid if the SSDI had been paid when due rather than retroactively.

The problem of withholding attorneys' fees arises because the

(*Text continued on page 6-45*)

[79.2] 42 U.S.C. § 1320a-6 (1981); 20 CFR § 404.408b.

costs is a very serious one for clients who are not affluent as well as for attorneys who are not affluent. This is one specific area where working-class clients are at a disadvantage compared to wealthier clients who can afford to pay for medical reports and exams.

A representative should explore the possibility of receiving medical reports from doctors who have evaluated the client for other purposes. For instance, a claimant who is also receiving workers' compensation will often have been to many specialists, as will a plaintiff in a personal injury suit. These reports can generally be obtained by the advocate for the cost of photocopying.

[18] Disability Determinations from Other Programs

[a] VA Benefits

DIB benefits are not currently offset by the receipt of VA benefits. (SSI benefits will be offset, since VA benefits are other income to be considered.) The Social Security Administration must examine and take into account a VA determination of disability, but such a determination does not direct the Social Security Administration to make a similar decision. (This is true of other agencies' determinations of disability as well.)[80] The VA test is different from the Social Security Administration one. The VA looks at whether an average person with the claimant's impairments would be disabled, whereas the Social Security Administration is supposed to look at that particular person as an individual.

[b] Workers' Compensation

As noted, *infra,* there is an offset provision so that a claimant receiving workers' compensation may receive a reduction in DIB benefits.

---

[80] Skeels v. Richardson, 433 F.2d 882, *cert. denied,* 93 S. Ct. 137, 409 U.S. 857, 34 L. Ed. 2d 101.

[c] Welfare Programs

As stated, *infra,* the client may have had to sign a repayment agreement with a welfare department in order to receive those payments. Such agreements in California require that the recipient follow through all SSI appeals. Again, this only applies to SSI. Generally, SSI will also mean the person will be eligible for the state medical insurance program. The claimant may still be eligible for food stamps.

[d] Private Disability Insurance

Clients often have disability insurance through their union or employer. Many of these plans define total disability in the same fashion as does the Social Security Administration and many require that the client actually be adjudged disabled by the Social Security Administration before these benefits are paid. This comes as a shock to many workers who may be disabled from their regular employment but not disabled from all work, and so may be denied by the Social Security Administration. Further, many disability insurance plans have offset provisions of their own and decrease their payments according to the amount of Social Security benefits received. A representative should request the policy or brochure describing the plan to assist a client in this situation.

[19] Overpayments

Often the Social Security Administration will determine that it has overpaid a client and will attempt to recover this overpayment. This chapter cannot cover all procedures or reasons for this. This happens, of course, most frequently with the SSI program, since the financial resources and income requirements are strict and the person's situation may change more quickly than the computer can adjust. The representative should refer to the appropriate CFRs and other resources for a discussion of the possible remedies. Appeals procedures are very similar to those for applications and should be followed. Often a legal services office can represent a client faced with an overpayment case.

[20] Bibliography

[a] Law Review Articles

Steven Babitsky, *The Vocational Expert in Social Security Disability Cases, Trial,* January, 1979.

David S. Bloomfield, *Disability Claims under the Social Security Act: A Practitioner's Guide to Administrative Procedures,* 6 Capital U.L. Rev. 340 (1977).

Anthony Champagne & Amos Danube, *An Empirical Analysis of Decisions of Administrative Law Judges in the Social Security Disability Program,* 64 Georgetown L. J. 43 (1975).

Coffman, *Social Security Offset, Trial,* March 1974.

Dixon, *The Welfare State and Mass Justice: A Warning From the Social Security Disability Program,* Duke L. J., 1972, p. 681.

Haviland & Glomb, *The Disability Insurance Benefits Program and Low Income Claimants in Appalachia,* 73 W. Va. L. Rev. 109 (1971).

Larson, *The Social Security Workmen's Compensation Offset Practice,* 13 William & Mary L. Rev. 539 (1972).

Lance Liebman, *The Definition of Disability in Social Security and Supplemental Security Income: Drawing the Bounds of Social Welfare Estates,* 89 Harv. L. Rev. 833 (1976).

Laurence Locke, *Upgrading Disability Benefits,* 12 Trial 34 (1976).

Peter W. Martin, *Social Security Benefits for Spouses,* 63 Cornell L. Rev. 789 (1978).

William D. Popkin, *The Effect of Representation in Non-Adversary Proceedings: A Study of Three Disability Programs,* 62 Cornell L. Rev. 989 (1977).

Elliot L. Sagal, M.D., *Social Security Disability,* 9 Trial 63 (1973).

Anne Silverstein, *Relitigating Social Security Claims,* 13 Trial 46 (1977).

Jerome Smith, *Social Security Appeals in Disability Cases,* 28 Ad. L. Rev. 13 (1976).

Peter G. Warren, *Administrative Delay in Providing Hearings for Social Security Disability,* 6 Hofstra L. Rev. 565 (1978).

[b] Books and Reporters

Practice Manual for Social Security Claims, by Dennis M. Sweeney, James J. Lyko. Published by Practising Law Institute, 1980. Describes various programs, with practice tips. Includes copies of regulations and forms.

Social Security Claims and Procedures, by Harvey C. McCormick. General comprehensive book on all Social Security programs and black lung benefits, with citations to statutes and cases. Published by West Publishing Co.

Social Security Disability Benefits: Legal Issues for Mentally Disabled Claimants, by Barbara L. Hawley, Debbi Kay, Ann McGowan, David L. Norman. Published by the A.B.A. Commission on the Mentally Disabled, 1979.

Social Security Explained. Published by Commerce Clearing House, Inc., 1980.

Social Security Handbook, published by U.S. Govt. and available from the U.S. Govt. Printing Office. This is a useful summary of the OASDI programs.

Unemployment Insurance Report. Published by Commerce Clearing House, Inc. Vols. 1 and 1(a) cover Social Security benefits. This reporter provides up-to-date information on cases and new legislation.

[c] Organization Materials and Newsletter

The National Organization of Social Security Claimants' Representatives publishes an excellent monthly newsletter, "Social Security Forum," covering cases, proposed and enacted changes in the law, discussion of relevant issues, etc. The organization also has an extensive list of materials which may be ordered for the copying cost. Executive Director: Nancy Shor, P.O. Box 794, Pearl River, New York 10965; (914) 735-8812.

§ 6.02. Workers' Compensation

Workers' compensation is a form of wage-loss insurance that

Haviland & Glomb, *The Disability Insurance Benefits Program and Low Income Claimants in Appalachia,* 73 W. Va. L. Rev. 109 (1971).

Larson, *The Social Security Workmen's Compensation Offset Practice,* 13 William & Mary L. Rev. 539 (1972).

Lance Liebman, *The Definition of Disability in Social Security and Supplemental Security Income: Drawing the Bounds of Social Welfare Estates,* 89 Harv. L. Rev. 833 (1976).

Laurence Locke, *Upgrading Disability Benefits,* 12 Trial 34 (1976).

Peter W. Martin, *Social Security Benefits for Spouses,* 63 Cornell L. Rev. 789 (1978).

William D. Popkin, *The Effect of Representation in Non-Adversary Proceedings: A Study of Three Disability Programs,* 62 Cornell L. Rev. 989 (1977).

Elliot L. Sagal, M.D., *Social Security Disability,* 9 Trial 63 (1973).

Anne Silverstein, *Relitigating Social Security Claims,* 13 Trial 46 (1977).

Jerome Smith, *Social Security Appeals in Disability Cases,* 28 Ad. L. Rev. 13 (1976).

Peter G. Warren, *Administrative Delay in Providing Hearings for Social Security Disability,* 6 Hofstra L. Rev. 565 (1978).

[b] Books and Reporters

Clearinghouse Review. Published by the National Clearinghouse for Legal Services, 500 North Michigan Avenue, Chicago, Illinois. This legal services–oriented journal covers both SSI and SSDI with articles and case summaries.

Practice Manual for Social Security Claims, by Dennis M. Sweeney, James J. Lyko. Published by Practising Law Institute, 1980. Describes various programs, with practice tips. Includes copies of regulations and forms.

Social Security Claims and Procedures, by Harvey C. McCormick. General comprehensive book on all Social Security programs and black lung benefits, with citations to statutes and cases. Published by West Publishing Co.

Social Security Disability Benefits: Legal Issues for Mentally Disabled Claimants, by Barbara L. Hawley, Debbi Kay, Ann McGowan,

David L. Norman. Published by the A.B.A. Commission on the Mentally Disabled, 1979.

Social Security Disability Claims, by Ronald R. Gilbert and J. Douglas Peters. Published by Bancroft-Whitney Co. One looseleaf volume with updates. New.

Social Security Explained. Published by Commerce Clearing House, Inc., 1980.

Social Security Handbook. Published by United States Government and available from the U.S. Govt. Printing Office. This is a useful summary of the OASDI programs.

Social Security and SSI Disability: A Legal Services Practice Manual. Published by Legal Council for the Elderly 1909 K. Street, N.W., Washington D.C. A very thorough and well-organized handbook.

Unemployment Insurance Report. Published by Commerce Clearing House, Inc. Vols. 1 and 1(a) cover Social Security benefits. This reporter provides up-to-date information on cases and new legislation.

West's Social Security Reporting Service. Published by West Publishing Co. Five bound volumes, including cases, codes, rulings, etc., along with monthly pamphlets. New.

[c] Organization Materials and Newsletter

The National Organization of Social Security Claimants' Representatives publishes an excellent monthly newsletter, "Social Security Forum," covering cases, proposed and enacted changes in the law, discussion of relevant issues, etc. The organization also has an extensive list of materials which may be ordered for the copying cost. Executive Director: Nancy Shor, P.O. Box 794, Pearl River, New York 10965; (914) 735-8812.

§ 6.02. Workers' Compensation

Workers' compensation is a form of wage-loss insurance that provides benefits to workers and their dependents for injuries, diseases, or death arising out of and in the course of the worker's employment. Workers' compensation legislation is unique in its radical departure from the common law liability doctrine of fault or negligence. Under workers' compensation statutes, a worker need not prove fault or negligence on the part of the employer in order to recover benefits. At common law, a worker had to prove not only negligence or intentional misconduct on the part of the employer but also that the worker himself/herself had not contributed to the injury (contributory negligence) and that the negligence of a fellow worker was not the cause of the injury (fellow servant doctrine). Further, if an employer showed that the worker knew or should have known of the risks inherent in the employment and assumed those risks upon accepting such employment, the worker was barred from recovery for a work-related injury (assumption of the risk).

For the most part, recovery at common law was unusual and at best, grossly inadequate. Although estimates vary, they indicate that between 70 and 90 percent of all workers with occupationally related injuries who sought recovery at common law prior to the end of the nineteenth century received no relief. Toward the close of the nineteenth century, juries began to find in favor of the worker/plaintiff in these civil suits and began to make extremely high awards. This change in the outcome of common law suits, as well as the increased organization of labor and labor's demand that the employer absorb the cost of these injuries, compelled industry to accept the limited and determinable liability of workers' compensation programs. Support for these programs also came from the American Federation of Labor (AFL) and the National Association of Manufacturers (NAM). Between 1910 and 1920, most states enacted some form of workers' compensation statute. By 1963, every state had substituted such legislation for common-law recovery. The worker, under this type of legislation, is forced to accept benefits that are more limited and smaller then those awarded in common-law suits in exchange for not being required to prove negligence or fault on the part of the employer, or the lack thereof on the part of him or herself or a fellow worker.

There is no uniform, national workers' compensation act for those who fall under state coverage rather than under the jurisdiction of the Federal Employees Compensation Act[81] or the Longshoremen's and Harborworkers' Act.[82] (Railroad workers are covered, but only for employer negligence.)[83] Requirements and benefits vary throughout the country, depending on the statutes and case law governing each jurisdiction's act; states with stronger labor movements usually provide higher and more extensive benefits for their workers.

This section on workers' compensation is written with the warning that the laws, requirements, procedures, and benefits may vary significantly from state to state. Each issue should be checked against the law governing in each state.

[1] Basic Elements

Although the variance may be great between the various state workers' compensation laws, certain characteristics are common to all or most such compensation schemes:

[a] Exclusivity

Rights, remedies, and procedures under the acts are exclusive. A worker covered by the act cannot sue an insured employer at common law for any injury compensable under the act. Some states provide for an election of remedies, but this is very rare and should be checked carefully. Suits against employers can be brought in some states under the dual capacity doctrine. If an injury is caused by employer negligence but does not arise out of the employer/employee relationship, this narrow doctrine may apply. Also, in some states, employees can sue employers for intentional torts.[83.1]

(*Text continued on page 6-53*)

---

[81] 5 U.S.C. § 8102.

[82] 37 U.S.C. 90A.

[83] Railroad and Railway Act, 45 U.S.C. § 51.

[83.1] Blackenship et al. v. Cincinnati Malacron Chemicals, Inc., # 81-402 (employees and spouses can sue an employer in Ohio for intentionally using chemicals that employer knew were harmful and failing to warn employees); Burdette v. Burlington Industries, Inc., — F. Supp. — (D.S.C. 1981), No. 79-2116-2 (fraudulent misrepresentation as to safety of cotton mill to induce continued work states a claim for conspiracy to deprive of statutory benefits); Johns-Mansville Products Corp. v. Contra Costa Superior Court, 165 Cal. Rptr. 858 (Sup. Ct. 1982) (fraudulent concealment of disease caused by ingeston of asbestos states a claim for aggravation of the disease).

[ii] Arising in the Course of Employment

Not only must a worker prove that his or her injury arose out of the employment, but also must prove that it arose in the course of employment. Again, jurisdictions vary on this requirement. In general, the term refers to the time, place, and circumstances in which the injury occurred. What is required is some work relatedness to these factors. Obviously, the further away from the worker's duties or the employer's premises that the injury occurs, the greater the question as to whether the injury arose in the course of employment.

Primarily, workers are not protected for injuries that occur going to or coming from work. However, in many states, this is not the case if the injury occurs on the employer's premises, in areas under the employer's control, or in areas made accessible to the worker by the employer. There have been several cases applying an even broader standard. Injuries that occur while the worker is on an errand for the employer, between two workplaces, traveling as a worker, or using his or her own vehicle on the job may all be compensable. The key factor is whether the injury occurs while the worker is engaged in the performance of his or her duties. However, many states do not accept such a broad interpretation; again, the law in each jurisdiction must be carefully examined.

[2] Benefits

The workers' compensation acts provide for the following benefits (the extent and duration of the benefits vary greatly from jurisdiction to jurisdiction);

(1) weekly compensation disability payments (tax free),
(2) dependent benefits (added to weekly compensation),
(3) medical expenses (direct and incidental),
(4) compensation for disfigurement and loss of function of extremities and certain organs,
(5) rehabilitation,
(6) death benefits, and

(7) burial benefits.

[a] Payments for Medical Care

When a worker is injured on the job, a question arises as to what medical treatment s/he is entitled, and when. Under all compensation laws, injured workers must be given medical treatment. Usually this is mandatory even if the worker has not lost the work time required to be eligible for disability payment for lost wages. Most states provide for full medical aid, and many have no limitation as to the amount of medical treatment that may be given for a covered injury or the time in which it may be given. In some states where there are such limitations, the state compensation agency may approve indefinite extensions. In addition, some states have limitations on the amount of coverage for certain occupational diseases (e.g., Arkansas, Illinois, Vermont). In several states, there are absolute cost and/or time period limitations (e.g., Alabama, Colorado, Kansas).

States vary as to the administration of medical treatment to the worker. Some states (Tennessee, Arkansas, Florida) require the worker to be treated only by doctors authorized by the employer, while others allow workers to choose their own doctors only if the company has failed to provide a doctor or needed medical services within a specified period of time and only after notice to the employer. Still other states allow a worker to choose his or her own physician and medical facilities from the very start of the necessary treatment; even in these states, the state act may require a worker to submit to periodic examinations requested by the insurer during the course of treatment. Continued receipt of benefits may be conditional upon consent to examinations.

Hospitalization is usually covered, although, again, there may be limitations on the amount or the time. Nursing care is also included. Some states permit nursing care at home provided by a member of one's own family.

Medical benefits often cover incidental effects of an injury or disease as well as the direct effects. For example, a worker who has suffered serious scarring in an injury is entitled not only to medical treatment directly related to the injury itself, but also (depending on the jurisdiction) to psychological treatment necessitated by depression related to the injury. The only condition in this instance is that the worker prove a causal relation between the injury and the ensuing depression. Almost all laws guarantee payment for artificial limbs or other appliances. State laws often include payment for transportation for medical treatment. Payment for drugs is also usually included, as is medically supervised weight reduction necessary before the primary condition can be treated. Drug addiction related to treatment of the injury may be the responsibility of the employer.

[b] Weekly Compensation Disability Payments

Weekly disability payments are to compensate a worker for the loss of his or her earning capacity as a result of the injury or disease. However, these benefit payments are not adequate compensation to a worker who has lost (temporarily or permanently) his or her ability to earn wages, even with the additional benefits for dependents.

Weekly benefits are computed on a fixed percentage (usually 66 2/3 percent) of the worker's average weekly wage. All states set a maximum weekly amount; thus, even if two thirds of a worker's weekly wage is more than the state's weekly maximum, that worker can collect only the maximum amount provided by statute.

The "average weekly wage" is usually based on earnings for the year prior to the injury if the worker was fully employed for that period of time. However, the states have different methods of computing this figure. For example, some states use the wage level at the time of the injury instead of over the previous fifty-two weeks. State laws also vary as to when a determination is to be made for a worker who did not work for a full year before the injury or who switched jobs (and whose income changed as a result). Some states total the amount of income earned for the number of weeks actually worked and then divide by the number of weeks, after dropping the first and last weeks worked; others base the average weekly wage on an industry "average wage," for a worker in the same job classification. In some states, the percentage will also vary according to the worker's marital status and number of dependents (e.g., Washington). Many states also base the payments to the family of a worker killed on the job on a percentage of the worker's average weekly wage; in about one-third of the states this percentage is lower than that paid to injured workers who are still alive.

Differences also exist among the states as to what kind of compensation may be included in determining the average weekly wage. For example, some states permit bonuses, overtime, tips, laundry, value of meals or room, and other benefits to be computed into the average weekly wage. As in all matters pertaining to workers' compensation, one must check the laws governing in the particular jurisdiction and be innovative.

A feature common to most state acts is that a worker must be out of work as a result of the injury or disease for a specified period of time before he or she is eligible to collect disability payments. This time period ranges from two to seven days. Once this time requirement has been met, many states allow the worker to collect disability benefits from the date of injury or the commencement of the disability. Although most impose this condition, they usually will allow a worker to recover medical and other benefits (for loss of function and disfigurement) even if the worker is not out of work long enough to collect weekly disability benefits.

The nature of the worker's disability is classified; this affects the amount and duration of payments. These classifications fall into two categories: total disability and partial disability.

[i] Total Disability

The category of total disability is further broken down into temporary and permanent. A worker can be totally disabled temporarily or permanently. Often it is not possible to determine which category applies in a given situation because it may not be possible for many years to determine the permanent effect of the injury.

The case law on what constitutes total disability varies greatly among jurisdictions. If a worker is not capable of performing any work at all, the case is clear. The more difficult questions arise if a worker is capable of performing some work, but not his or her prior job or a similar activity, or if a worker has regained the physical ability to perform work yet cannot get a job because of the injury. This may be a situation in which a worker has sustained a back injury or a heart attack and no employer will hire him or her because of these medical problems. (To be eligible, however, the worker is usually required to look for work, except under unusual circumstances.) In many states, a worker can get compensation for total disability under these circumstances.

Under some laws, the determination of total incapacity to work is based only on the extent of the injury, whereas other jurisdictions consider the age, experience, training, and capabilities of the worker.[86] If the worker is unable to pursue his or her customary job (or work of the same or a reasonably similar type) or is unable to obtain or perform any substantial amount of work in his or her field, then he or she should be considered totally disabled. Moreover, some definitions of total disability do not disqualify a worker who is able to perform some menial work. For example, in Massachusetts it has been held that total disability may be found if the "disability is such that it prevents [the worker] from performing remunerative work of a substantial and not merely trifling character. . . "[87]

The fact that a worker has tried to work, or has in fact worked, does not necessarily disqualify the worker from being considered totally disabled:

> Pinched by poverty, beset by adversity, driven by necessity, one may work to keep the wolf away from the door though not physically able; and . . . the fact the woman (injured in this case) worked to earn her living did not prevent (a finding) that she was totally and permanently disabled even while working.[88]

Similarly, many states allow a worker to go back to work after a period of total disability to see if s/he is capable of working. Theoretically, if a worker goes back to work for some time (one,

---

[86] C.J.S. Workmen's Compensation § 299.

[87] Frennier's Case, 318 Mass. 635, 639.

[88] Mabry v. Travelers Ins. Co., 193 F.2d 497, 498 (5th Cir. 1952). *See also* Tex. Employers Ins. Ass'n v. Smith, 374 S.W.2d 287, 293 (Tex. 1964).

two, or even three weeks,) and finds that s/he is still affected by the injury or disease and is unable to work, s/he should be able to collect disability payments upon leaving work. Very often the insurance company will refuse to continue payments, forcing the worker to argue his or her case before the state agency administering the act in order to regain the benefits.

[ii] Temporary Total Disability

Most claims under workers' compensation are for injuries that result in a temporary total disability. This means that the worker fully recovers after a period of total disability (which can be weeks or a matter of years) or recovers sufficiently to gain a partial ability to work. Most states limit the amount of time during which benefits for a temporary total disability may be paid or limit the amount collectable as a result of a temporary total disability. The length of time and monetary amounts vary greatly and should be carefully checked.

[iii] Permanent and Total Disability

The second category of total disability is called permanent and total disability. Such a disability exists after it becomes obvious over a period of time (years) that the disability will continue indefinitely although there may be a remote possibility of recovery[89] and the injury is severe enough to prevent the worker from earning a living. Both these factors are factual questions to be determined by the agency administering the workers' compensation act (if the insurance company or self-insurer does not agree to the workers' claim of permanent and total disability; standards vary among jurisdictions).

[iv] Permanent Partial Disability

The category of partial compensation covers "schedule" and

[89] *See, e.g.,* Ford Motor Co. v. Indus. Comm'n, 189 N.E.2d 488 (Ill.) .

"nonschedule" disabilities (the latter are disabilities of a more general nature, such as a back disability that does not totally incapacitate the worker). The worker is paid benefits for schedule disabilities on the basis of a percentage of the average weekly wage (often the same percentage as that paid for total temporary disability) for a specified number of weeks (varying from 100 to more than 600 weeks) or a specific amount set by the statute. Some states (e.g., California) provide for a small life pension if the permanent disability is greater than 70 percent; if the permanent disability is total (100 percent), the weekly payments continue at the same rate as temporary disability indemnity for life. (Some states do not provide for compensation in this manner; rather, they provide for total or partial compensation only.)

"Nonschedule" partial disabilities are typically those that result in reduced earning capacity. For example, a worker who suffers a back injury may no longer be able to do the heavy work for which he or she was receiving $200 per week at that time of the injury. But s/he may be capable of doing a lighter job that pays only $150 per week. For this partial disability, the worker will be entitled, under many statutes, to receive the difference between the former wage and the wage earned after the injury. However, compensation for this is limited to the same weekly maximum amount one could receive for total disability. There is also a maximum collectable amount for partial compensation; after this amount is exhausted, the worker is not entitled to further weekly compensation payments. Furthermore, if a worker was first out of work for a period of time and received compensation for partial disability after returning to work, the amount received for total disability will be included when computing the maximum the worker can eventually be awarded for partial disability.

It should be mentioned that one of the gross inadequacies of these statutes (and this is true in every state) is the failure to provide for cost of living increases. A worker who received $25 per week for a total disability because that was the maximum at the time of the injury, still receives that same amount today.[90]

[90] California now provides that if the statutory rate of *temporary* disability indemnity increases after an injury, the worker is entitled to receive the higher rate after two years from the date of injury.

Needless to say, this works a hardship on any worker who has received a serious injury and is either totally or partially incapacitated for the rest of his or her life.

Minors who are legally employed are generally covered in the same or similar manner as are adults in cases of temporary disability. However, in cases of permanent disability, many states make special provision for such injured minors because of the low earnings which such workers usually receive; special consideration is taken of the minor's future earning capacity.

[c] Benefits for Disabled Workers with Dependents

As mentioned above, many states, but not all, provide extra payment to an injured worker for dependents, i.e., those who rely on the worker for their support. This amount is added to the amount received for weekly compensation. The states that pay such benefits have different standards for determining who is a dependent. Various standards and statutory restrictions govern which offspring are dependents, whether a husband living with his injured worker wife is a dependent, and under what circumstances (many statutes are highly discriminatory in this regard); those who do not fall into either of these two categories can be classified as a dependent. Oftentimes, classification as dependent will be determined by dependency in fact. These additional payments are always low (e.g., $6 per dependent in Massachusetts). Several states also restrict such benefits to those workers who are receiving compensation for total disability, either permanent or temporary.

Most states make some provision for reduced benefits to nonresident alien dependents, i.e., dependents living outside the U.S. The state acts, for the purpose of compensation benefits to the injured worker, do not, however, make any distinction between alien and citizen workers, nor is any distinction made between citizen dependents and resident alien dependents.

[d] Disfigurement and Loss of Function

Scarring or other disfigurement or loss of function of extremities and certain organs covered under the workers' compensation law will entitle the injured worker to additional benefits in more than half of the states. Sometimes the laws place a maximum limit on the amount receivable for such benefits, ranging from $550 to $7000. Usually, each part of the body is assigned a monetary amount, and such specific compensation is based on these schedules. Some states do not follow this schedule method but award such benefits by assigning a number of weeks for which permanent partial disability benefits are awarded.

[e] Rehabilitation

A majority of states include coverage for programs or plans for the rehabilitation of injured workers, i.e., the retraining of the injured worker either to allow him or her to return to a former job or to obtain new skills for work suitable for the worker's current physical capacities. Sometimes such plans provide for the state to operate its own rehabilitation facility under the direction of a state agency or of the state agency that administers the workers' compensation act. In other states, arrangements are made to provide rehabilitation through insurance carriers, private organizations, or other government agencies. Many of these state programs place limits on the amount of compensation, the number of weeks covered, or both.

[f] Death Benefits

An award of benefits to the surviving dependents of a worker is available in almost every state. The amount of such benefits will vary on the basis of the number of dependents. All states set a limit on the number of weeks or the monetary amount for which these benefits may be paid, or else allow them until widowhood is ended and the children reach age 18. Several states provide for a specific dollar amount to be paid to the survivors either in installments or as a lump sum. Some states (e.g., California) provide that if there is no dependent, either total or partial, the full death benefit is paid to the state. This creates the situation of the insurer trying to locate a partial dependent in order to pay a little money rather than the full death benefit. Furthermore, the survivors must prove dependency and extent thereof. In California, the state supreme court recently held that the conclusive presumption of total dependency, previously applicable to the widow only, would be available neither to the widow nor the widower; both must prove extent of dependency.[91]

The California Workers' Compensation Appeals Board recently held that a woman who had living with a man for three months would qualify as a dependent for death benefits. This case is currently being appealed through the courts.

[g] Burial Expenses

Almost all states provide for payment of burial expenses of the worker who dies as a result of a covered injury or disease. The amounts vary from state to state, ranging from $200 to $1000. Some states only allow such payments if there are no dependents, while other states increase the amount for burial if there are dependents.

[3] Procedure for Recovery of Benefits

[a] Notice of Injury

Before a worker can receive benefits under the state act, he or she must satisfy two conditions: (1) Notice of the injury or disease must be given to the employer; and (2) the worker must file a claim with the appropriate state agency (see Section 6.02[3][b], *infra*) unless the insurer or self-insurer has agreed voluntarily to compensate the worker for the injury or disease.

The first step an injured worker should take is to report the injury to his or her foreperson, superintendent, or supervisor, to

[91] Arp v. WCAB, 19 Cal. 3d 395; 138 Cal. Rep. 293, 563 P.2d 849 (1977).

any other agent of the employer, or to the employer directly. Injuries need not be the result of accidents in order to be compensable; thus, all injuries or symptoms that a worker feels that may have some relationship to his or her conditions of work should be reported.

In addition to reporting the injury to the employer, the worker should also notify his or her union representative, if there is a union, and s/he should tell as many co-workers as possible about the injury and the resulting condition. This is not a legal requirement, but a helpful measure for the preparation of the worker's case. If co-workers witnessed the injury or the physical condition developing from the injury, statements should be solicited. In any event, the worker should make sure that s/he takes the names and addresses of co-workers who witnessed the incident(s) causing the injury or disease as soon as possible.

Most states require the employer to fill out a first report of injury, whether or not such injury is compensable. For instance, in Massachusetts, employers must fill out and file a report of all injuries with the Massachusetts Division of Industrial Accidents. Although filing these reports is required by law and is the responsibility of the employer, the employee should and can make sure the employer complies with this requirement. If this report is in the worker's file, it will thwart any attempt on the part of the employer to deny that notice was given or that the injury arose out of and in the course of employment.

Two issues regarding notice must be taken into consideration: what constitutes notice and when notice must be given. In general, the law requires that the employer be given notice sufficient to enable it or the insurer to investigate the injury or disease and mitigate damages by providing prompt medical attention which might minimize eventual disability. Moreover, it is meant to protect the employer from unrelated or stale claims by the worker.[92]

Notice must be given "forthwith" or "as soon as is practicable."[93] In some jurisdictions, notice may be written or oral; others require notice to be given in writing. If written notice is required, failure to give it will not absolutely bar a later claim, so long as the worker can show that the employer had actual knowledge of

---

[92] West v. N. Tree Co., 365 Mich. 402, 112 N.W.2d 567 (1965).

[93] Peabody Coal Co. v. Harp, Ky., 351 S.W.2d 170 (1961).

the injury. This must be more than mere knowledge that the worker was ill, out of work, or had an injury. It must be enough to indicate that the employer has not been prejudiced and had comparable opportunity to investigate the incident and fill out the necessary report, as the law may require.[94]

A basic defense arises in the allegation that the employee's notice, be it oral or written, was not timely. In cases in which the employer or insurer asserts this defense, provisions that excuse late notice will be relevant in sustaining the worker's case. First, there must be a showing that the employer has or has not been prejudiced by the lateness of notice (with the burden of proof falling either on the employer or the claimant, respectively). Other possible excuses for late notice or absence of notice include a mistaken belief that the injury was too trivial to constitute a basis for recovery, latent injuries, a mistake of fact, duress or threats made to the worker, and fraudulent representations as to the worker's rights or the necessity of notifying the employer. Lack of knowledge of the law is generally held insufficient to excuse failure to give timely notice.[95] Timeliness of notice is considered a jurisdictional issue; the power to excuse late notice by the employee lies within the discretion of the administrative body hearing the claim.[96] Generally, a tardy notice will not be excused unless a showing is made by the employee that the compensation payer was not prejudiced by reason of his/her tardiness.[97]

[b] The Claim

Filing a claim, along with the giving of proper notice, is a statutory requirement imposed by the state acts. For purposes of statute of limitations provisions, a claim is established if a statement of the claim is filed with the administrative body handling

[94] Cofield v. Liberty Mutual Ins. Co., 110 Ga. App. 225, 138 S.E.2d 115 (1964).

[95] Reinhold v. Indus. Comm'n, 253 Wis. 606, 34 N.W.2d 814 (1948).

[96] Sante Fe Trailways Co. v. Marshall, Okla., 391 P.2d 784 (1964).

[97] Thayer's Case, 346 Mass. 36, 185 N.E.2d 292 (1962); Liscomb v. Halloran Constr. Co., 86 R.I. 159, 133 A.2d 759 (1957).

compensation claims. A letter for advice[98] or correspondence regarding benefits[99] is not considered a claim.

Most states are not rigid as to the form a claim must take (most states provide their own forms), so long as it is clear that compensation is sought.[100] At the least, a claim should include (1) the name of the claimant, (2) the fact that an injury occurred and (3) a clear statement that benefits are desired.[101] Most jurisdictions are liberal in permitting amendments to claims. In most states, there is a fixed period, usually one or two years, during which claims must be filed. Claims are generally considered to be filed at the time of delivery to the administrative body.[102]

Jurisdictions vary considerably on the issue of whether or not excuses for failing to file within the statutory period will be adequate to revive a tardy claim. Some states afford no provisions for excusing late claims.[103] In jurisdictions that provide for exemptions from the required statutory limit, the specific circumstances constituting sufficient excuse differ. As with late notification to the employer or insurer, the power to excuse late claims is within the discretionary power of the administrative body.[104]

There is no uniformity on the question of when the statute of limitations begins to run on a (potential) claim. Statutes fall into two categories: those that maintain the statutory period begins to run from the time the injury becomes apparent to the worker (or otherwise manifests itself) and those that maintain it begins from the time of the occurrence of the injury or event giving rise to the

---

98 Morgan v. Kays Laundry & Cleaning, Inc., 332 S.W.2d 248 (1960)(letter requesting advice).

99 Powell v. Bestwall Gypsum Co., 255 Iowa 937, 124 N.W.2d 448 (1963)(correspondence regarding rights to benefits).

100 Peschka v. Wilkinson Drilling Co., 192 Kan. 126, 386 P.2d 509 (1963)("so long as it is sufficient to apprise other parties involved that a claim has been made"); A.B. Taff & Sons v. Clark, 110 So. 2d 428, 433 (Fla.)

101 Workmen's Compensation Law Larson, Vol. 3, Ch. XV, p. 9.

102 Parrish Esso Serv. Center v. Adams, 237 Ark. 560, 374 S.W.2d 468 (1964).

103 Santa Fe Trailways Transp. Co. v. Marshall, Okla., 391 P.2d 784 (1964). (Act provides for excusing notice, but no discretion or equitable power in Commissioner to enlarge limitation period for filing claims).

104 Escarra v. Winn Dixie Stores, Inc., 131 So. 2d 483 (Fla. 1961).

injury or the date of last exposure (in the case of industrial diseases).

This distinction is particularly crucial in the instances of latent injuries—those that initially may seem trivial but develop into serious conditions or disabilities over time. Many of the states that have adopted the view that the statutory period begins at the occurrence of the event permit liberal exemptions from the limited time period if a claimant can show good cause for the delay in registering his or her claim.[105] These statutory exceptions should be carefully checked. The statutes regarding death benefits for dependents have various provisions for notice and claim requirements. These, too, should be carefully checked.

[c] Investigation and Agreements to Compensate

Once an injury has been reported by the worker, s/he should demand compensation from the insurance company or, in the case of a self-insurer from the employer. (It is always a good idea to file a claim, even if the worker is almost certain that the insurer will not contest the case). Most states have provisions requiring the employer or its insurer to come to an agreement over compensation with the injured worker within a specified period of time. In addition, an act may require failure to reach a voluntary agreement to be reported to the governing administrative body after passage of the specified amount of time. The effect of such regulations should be to compel prompt investigation of claims or payment of benefits.

In the course of the insurer's investigation, the worker will often be asked to sign a statement regarding the circumstances surrounding the injury and possibly the extent of the injury. Most jurisdictions do not require that the worker sign such a statement; however, practically speaking, a worker may expedite

[105] *E.g.,* W.R. Grasle Co. v. Alaska Workmen's Compensation Board, 517 P.2d 999 (1974) (regular statute of limitations does not apply to latent injuries whose presence becomes known only at later date); Bird v. Indus. Comm'n, 14 Ariz. App. 322, 403 P.2d 63 (1971) (late claim okay since claimant got incomplete diagnosis of condition so could not be held to know of cause of problem prior to one year before filing of claim). *See* Larson, 78.41 n.23, for others.

receipt of compensation payments by doing so. In these situations, it is desirable to have legal advice as to the contents, use, and consequences of such a statement. A worker should never sign a statement the contents of which s/he does not understand or is in disagreement with; under no circumstances, should a worker sign blank papers submitted by the insurer or employer. Also, a worker should not give the insurer authorization for release of medical records.

Should a written statement have been signed by a worker and a claim is later heard before the administrative board, the laws of evidence relevant to procedures under that state's act will govern. The statement may be inadmissible under the state's law unless the claimant, or his or her attorney, is afforded the opportunity upon proper notice to obtain a statement. If any statement is signed by a claimant, s/he should be sure to get a copy. If a worker has difficulty speaking English, he or she should have a trustworthy person present who is bilingual, especially for the purpose of translating written statements into English.

After investigation, the insurer will determine whether to pay compensation or to deny liability. Should the insurer agree to pay compensation, most states provide that such voluntary agreements be filed with the administering agency.

[d] Disputed Claims

If an insurer or self-insurer denies liability, or accepts initial liability, the administrative agency takes on a quasi-judicial function and decides the issues of the case. At the first level of hearings a commissioner, referee, or administrative law judge hears the case and the disputed evidence, may make inquiries and otherwise investigate, and finally will issue an order accepting or denying the worker's claim in whole or in part. Upon acceptance of the claim, the hearing officer will issue an order to the insurer or self-insured to pay compensation; the insurer or self-insurer must comply. This first round of hearings is usually informal, and the case is presented in a more or less summary fashion. If either party is aggrieved by the decision, most states provide for a more complete hearing on the merits of the case. Often, this formal hearing will not be held for months after the initial determination. Many states also provide for a third opportunity to be heard within the administrative agency: the administrative appeal from the hearing level. If necessary after this appeal within the administrative agency, the case must be taken to the appropriate state court. One should be careful to check what benefits the administering agency can order at what level of proceedings: for instance, can a claimant be awarded medical benefits pursuant to an order issued at the informal level of proceedings?

The trial, or hearing, level is the form in which the issues of the case are formally litigated within the administrative agency. The main issues addressed at these proceedings are the insurer's liability, length of disability (and, in the case of continuing disability, current disability), and medical findings. At this stage, the claimant testifies about the relevant issues, as does any witness with material evidence, and the claimant's medical expert also testifies (or is deposed by the parties). (Some states, e.g., California, indicate a preference for receiving written medical reports in evidence.)

[4] Discontinuation of Compensation

Once a worker is receiving compensation, either by agreement or by an award, there are several specified ways in which that weekly compensation can be discontinued. If the worker returns to work, compensation is discontinued. Some states, however, allow a worker to return to work on a so-called trial basis. If a worker finds that he or she is still disabled and the return to work was premature, theoretically s/he should be able to continue to collect weekly benefits. The amount of time a worker can work under this type of arrangement varies from jurisdiction to jurisdiction.

Another way compensation can be discontinued is by an order from the agency or board administering the act. For such an order to be issued, the insurer or self-insurer must petition for an informal or formal hearing on the matter of current disability and a decision then must be rendered. (What constitutes total disability should be carefully checked in each state.)

A third way to discontinue weekly compensations is by the exhaustion of time or money for the particular injury. For example, a worker can continue to collect total temporary disability payments as long as he or she is disabled and as long as the amount of money allotted for a total but temporary disability is not exhausted. In order to continue to collect weekly compensation benefits once the statutory amount has been collected by the worker, the worker must prove to the state agency that he or she is permanently and totally disabled.

Two cautions should be noted: First, even though a worker may no longer be receiving weekly compensation benefits, s/he may still be eligible for medical and other benefits. A case is not closed upon the resumption of work and/or the cessation of weekly compensation. Second, the insurer or self-insurer can not unilaterally decide that a worker is capable of working and on the basis of that decision discontinue weekly compensation payments.

[5] Coverage of Diseases under Workers' Compensation

Historically, employers have tried to distinguish occupational diseases from accidental injuries to deny compensation to workers who suffer from job-related diseases. The argument was that such diseases were not accidents because they were acquired gradually over a period of time. "Accidents," it was argued, had a fixed date of onset. This argument is no longer useful in that most occupational diseases now fall within the scope of most workers' compensation acts.

In some industries, almost all workers contract occupational diseases attributable to manifestly unsafe working conditions. The semantic debates over the inclusion of occupational diseases as compensable injuries were attributable to the frequency of claims for benefits (e.g., for black lung disease).

Currently, all states provide some coverage under workers' compensation acts for occupational diseases. Basically, there are two ways in which states cover occupational diseases. Nine states have a list (schedule) of diseases for which a worker may receive compensation. The majority of the states have general coverage that includes any disease arising out of exposure to harmful conditions of employment. The coverage is accomplished by different means in different states. Some states have a separate act for occupational diseases. Others have a general definition of the term, and others cover occupational diseases through a broad definition of "injury" as it appears in the workers' compensation statute.

The harmful conditions of employment must be present to an increased extent as compared to employment in general. This is so because the disease must arise out of employment to be classified as an occupational disease, and must further be distinguishable from contracting an ordinary disease of life. Having a preexisting weakness, condition, or predilection to an occupational disease does not disqualify a worker from receiving coverage under the acts if conditions of employment exacerbated the condition. In a few jurisdictions, a preexisting allergy disqualifies a worker from receiving compensation.

Some workers are covered for occupational diseases under federal legislation. The Black Lung Act[106] covers mine workers. The Federal Employees Compensation Act[107] and the Longshoremen and Harbor Workers Compensation Act[108] also provide coverage for occupational diseases.

Occupational diseases pose one of the most problematical situations. So little is known about so many chemicals in industrial use that many diseases go undiagnosed as having any relationship to a worker's working conditions. Also, many diseases have latent effects and it may be very difficult to establish or trace a connection to toxic substances that a worker came into contact with at one time or another.

Also included in most states are psychiatric conditions related to the work and its stresses, as well as heart conditions, ulcers, skin conditions, and orthopedic problems resulting from exposure to particular work situations over a period of time.

---

[106] 30 U.S.C. § 901.

[107] 5 U.S.C. § 68102.

[108] 33 U.S.C. § 901.

[6] Lump Sum Payments and Agreements

Normally, compensation is paid in weekly installments. However, all statutes provide for a one-time lump sum payment in lieu of payments ordinarily made in the future. Technically, there are two types of lump sum payments, although a state's act may consider them together.

The first kind of lump sum payment covers the situations in which there is no dispute as to (1) liability, (2) the extent of disability, (3) the length of time that the worker will be disabled, and (4) any other material factor in figuring the amount of compensation due. Thus, the lump sum award accurately reflects the amount to which the worker would be entitled if he or she were to receive installment payments. This form of lump sum payment is a "commutation" of future installments to a single payment,[109] and the case is open, including entitlement to future medical care. Usually either the worker or the employer must petition the state agency or a court for approval. The statutory standard for approval is generally whether the lump sum payment is in the "best interests" of the worker.

The second type of lump sum payment occurs if there is a dispute as to liability (the employer may insist that the worker was not injured on the job) or as to disability (whether it is total or partial, or either).[110] Just as in other types of tort actions, there are negotiations between the two sides over these issues and an attempt is made to resolve the dispute by settling on a sum of money without a hearing. Employers and insurers often dispute claims simply to stall proceedings and thus prevent the out-of-work employee from obtaining any money during this time in order to force him or her to settle for less than s/he is entitled to. Often, approval is required by the state agency; again, the standard of the "best interests" of the worker is applied.

Some statutes do not contain any specific provision concerning the validity of such agreements that affect statutory rights to full benefits. In a majority of states without such a provision, courts have held invalid agreements that would give the worker less

---

[109] Cretella v. N.Y. Dock Co., 45 N.E.2d 429, 289 N.Y. 254, *motion denied,* 47 N.E.2d 444, 289 N.Y. 848.

[110] *See* Sourthern v. Dept. of Labor & Indus., 236 P.2d 548, 550 (Wash. 1951).

than he or she is entitled to under the statute. The minority view allows such settlements on the rationale that such claims may be compromised like any other claim.[111]

In states with statutory prohibitions against the waiving of compensation rights by an employee, there is the same split in the courts as to what such prohibitions mean in regard to a settlement. Again, the majority have interpreted such a statutory clause as forbidding settlement for less than the full amount to which the worker is entitled. Some of these statutes also provide for the submission of such settlements to the compensation agency for approval. Similarly, in some jurisdictions, payments made under such an agreement can be discontinued only with the consent of the agency.

Jurisdictions also differ as to whether a lump sum payment of either type cuts off medical benefits.[112] This often depends on the wording of the agreement. In some jurisdictions, moreover, there are differences in the method of allowing lump sum payments for temporary, as opposed to permanent, disability.

Workers and attorneys should be very cautious in deciding to settle a case with a lump sum payments. Sometimes it may be in the worker's interests to do so, but it should be done with a very clear idea of the state of the injury, the possibility of future damage, and, if appropriate, the strength of the case legally. Often a worker will be induced to settle a case by the prospect of what appears to be (at the time) a substantial amount of money, especially if s/he has suffered financial hardship, many times brought on by the insurance company's refusal to compensate a legitimate claim. In many states, both insurance companies and state agencies encourage settlement of claims so that the matter can be removed from the insurer's books and from the agency's crowded docket.

---

[111] Bahan v. Raziano, 58 So. 2d 341 (La. App. 1952); Gray v. Indus. Comm'n, 24 Ariz. App. 499, 539 P.2d 973 (1975), *aff'd,* 133 Ariz. 296, 552 P.2d 766 (1976).

[112] *See, e.g.,* Wehmeir v. W.E. Wood Co., 139 N.W.2d 733 (Mich. 1966).

[7] Misconduct by Employer or Employee

[a] Misconduct by Employer or Employer's Supervisory Personnel

In a number of states, penalties may be levied against an employer for serious misconduct. The effect of establishing such misconduct varies from state to state. In some states, the injured worker may be entitled to sue the employer under common law for willful misconduct (Arizona), intentional injury (Kentucky and West Virginia), or willful acts of gross negligence causing death (Texas). Some statutes allow a worker to recover a percentage increase for failure to provide safety devices or to obey safety regulations or for failure to comply with statutory or regulatory safety duties (Kentucky, Ohio). If an employer commits what is called "serious and willful misconduct," an employee may collect a percentage increase over what s/he is awarded for his or her claim. The California statute provides for a 50 percent penalty, with a maximum of $10,000, and the Massachusetts statute provides a 100 percent increase (a "double compensation" claim). In these cases, the penalty is assessed directly against the employer, not the insurer or self-insurer.

Courts have set high standards for what constitutes an "intentional," "serious and willful," etc., injury. A worker may also have to prove that the employer knew or should have known that a particular working condition was dangerous, yet required the worker to work in such a situation with the intention of causing injury. "Serious and willful misconduct" and "willful misconduct" are also difficult to establish. The definitions also vary from state to state. What is common to most of the statutes is that they are strictly interpreted. Thus, a worker is most often forced to rely solely on the benefits established under statute for injuries caused by the dangerous and hazardous conditions created or maintained by the employer.

Some states have established standards against which the employer's conduct can be measured. Some states set out a vague standard. California, for example, will consider the general duty of the employer to provide a safe place to work along with other elements, such as the employer's knowledge of the danger, in order to determine whether serious and willful misconduct exists. Some states provide for increased penalties for failure to abide by statutory or regulatory safety provisions or to provide safety devices. However, the application of such standards has not been very strict, and very often violation of safety standards alone will not satisfy the burden of proof imposed by the categories such as "serious and willful," or "intentional" injuries.

Especially if the statutory requirements or safety regulations do not set out objective and clear specification, the legal test may be whether the safety devices or procedures used by the employer were reasonable. As to the reasonableness of its actions, the employer might argue that the devices or procedures used were standard or common in the particular industry, that safety inspectors had seen the device prior to the accident and had not requested any changes or made any objections, that the accident occurred because of momentary negligence, or that another employee or the injured worker had been negligent or guilty of willful misconduct.[113]

Careful warning should be given. The standards set are particular to the individual statutes, their intent, and the law decided under them. No blanket pronouncements can be given. However, attorneys and legal workers should exclude the possibility of a viable suit based on misconduct of the employer only after very careful scrutiny, for it provides benefits not usually available to workers who suffer serious consequences. Attention should also be given to special statutes of limitation applicable to these claims.

[b] Employee Misconduct

Although the entire scheme of workers' compensation generally removes the question of fault or negligent conduct from the granting of compensation to an injured worker, certain statutory provisions create either a defense for the employer or a reduction in the amount of the benefits the worker may receive. Although

---

[113] Ex rel Barrett v. State Indus. Comm'n, 175 Ohio St. 255, 193 N.E.2d 516 (1963)("generally used device"); Icke Constr. Co. v. Indus. Comm'n, 30 Wis. 2d 63, 139 N.W.2d 841 (1966)("momentary negligence").

most jurisdictions do not have any provisions relating to employee misconduct (except for intoxication or intentional self-injury), some statutes either make "willful misconduct" a complete defense, i.e., the employer will have to pay no compensation, or cite certain kinds of misconduct as grounds for a reduction of the award.

It should be noted that, even in the absence of a specific statutory provisions, certain activities that result in injury may also result in the denial of benefits. Such instances are based on the broad theory that such conduct takes the worker out of the scope of employment. For example, Massachusetts and Illinois deny benefits to workers injured while acting in such a way. Other states look to whether the "misconduct" involves work done for the employer or for the worker's personal benefit unrelated to the job. However, if the work is still of the type the worker is assigned to do and only the method used is prohibited, this satisfies the "in the course of employment" standard and compensation will not be denied.[114] States are divided as to whether compensation will be awarded to an injured worker who performs his or her assigned work but does it at a forbidden location and/or at a forbidden time.[115] Conduct is not deemed "willful" if it is "instinctive or thoughtless, rather than intentional and deliberate," such as driving a truck too fast or wiping oil from a machine without first shutting it off. "The worker must understand the seriousness of the consequences" of a violation of a safety rule before this defense will be allowed. In some cases, intentional violation of a safety rule has been held to be in the "willful

---

[114] Kilgore v. Fragola, 14 A.D.2d 612, 218 N.Y.S.2d 146 (1961); Cadsner Iron Works v. Beadsley, 249 Ala. 115, 30 So. 2d 10 (1947); Bennett's Case, 140 Me. 49, 33 A.2d 799 (1943).

[115] For awards in forbidden location cases, *see* Chila v. N.Y. Cent. R.R., 251 App. Div. 574, 297 N.Y. Supp. 850 (1937), *aff'd without opinion,* 275 N.Y. 585, 11 N.E.2d 766 (1937); Harkness v. Olcott-Stone Motors, 203 La. 947, 14 So. 2d 773 (1943). For denials in forbidden location cases, *see,* Lange v. Minn. St. Paul Metropolitan Airports Comm'n, 257 Minn. 54, 99 N.W.2d 915 (1959); City of Pembroke v. Jones, 109 Ga. App. 296, 136 S.E.2d 139 (1964). For awards in forbidden-time cases, *see* Turner Elkhorn Mining Co. v. Goble, 506 S.W.2d 521 (Ky. 1974). For denials in forbidden-time cases, *see* Gonzales v. Indust. Comm'n, 23 Ariz. App. 179, 531 P.2d 555 (1975).

misconduct" category.[116]

Voluntary intoxication of the worker either may be treated as a departure from the course of employment or may be defense under a specific statutory provision. Under the statutes that make intoxication a defense, standards for intoxication and its effect in causing the injury vary from state to state. In some states, the mere fact of intoxication will provide a complete defense; in others, the intoxication must be the sole cause of the injury.

Some states also make violation of a statute or commission of a crime by the worker a defense. Suicide is also a defense to a claim for death benefits in most states; however, if the suicide was closely related to and followed from a work-related injury or experience, then compensation may be awarded. Again the attorney must be cautioned that the facts are very important and cases may be won or lost by very important details.

§ 6.03. Welfare Benefits

People who have exhausted other sources of state or private insurance compensation or who have been unable to collect compensation for other reasons are eligible for welfare programs. Eligibility for welfare programs requires both fitting into a category for which benefits are provided, (such as Aid to Families with Dependent Children AFDC), and being in financial need. Financial need is determined by looking at income, resources that may be available, and resources that were available within the last two years that have been disposed of. Frequently, welfare payments can be obtained more quickly than other forms of compensation, which require proof of disability. In some states, welfare benefits may have to be paid back if other compensation or personal injury damages are obtained.[117]

Welfare programs include AFDC and Aid to Families with Dependent Children—Unemployed Parent (AFDC-UP), state or local general assistance programs (also known as general relief),

[116] Klein v. Trinity Indus. Inc., 201 N.W.2d 200 (Neb. 1972).

[117] When the welfare benefits must be repaid from the compensation or damages, the welfare department will impose a lien on the benefits, thereby giving notice to the other agencies involved.

Medicaid, and food stamps. Welfare benefits are obtained from local welfare offices. Local legal services offices are good sources of information and assistance for problems and questions about welfare programs.[118] The following is a brief summary of the welfare programs for which unemployed or disabled workers and their families may qualify.

[1] Aid to Families with Dependent Children

AFDC is a federally established program administered by the state that provides both state and federal funds to needy families with dependent children (under age 18) who are deprived of parental support and care because of the death, the continued absence from home, or the physical or mental incapacity of one parent.[119] More than half the states also provide benefits to two-parent families in need because of the unemployment of one of the parents.[120] In some states, families with children between the ages of 18 and 21 who are still in school may also be eligible for AFDC. Families of workers who are receiving other disability compensation benefits may be eligible for AFDC if the AFDC grant for that size family exceeds the amount of compensation benefits that the worker is receiving. For those who qualify, AFDC benefits are likely to be more quickly available than some other forms of compensation.

In some states a welfare recipient must pay back benefits if new

[118] Several programs provide backup legal assistance on welfare law issues. The following centers are generally funded by the Legal Services Corporation. They can provide advice and pleadings. Food: Food Research Action Project, 2011 Eye Street, N.W., Washington, D.C. 20006; (202) 452-8250. Welfare: Center on Social Welfare Policy and Law, 95 Madison Avenue, New York, N.Y. 10016 or 1029 Vermont Avenue, N.W., Washington, D.C. 20005. Medicaid: National Health Law Program, W.401 Main Street, Santa Monica, California 90505; (213) 392-4811.

[119] 42 U.S.C. § 601 et seq.; 45 CFR § 201 et seq.

[120] For a two-parent family to qualify for the AFDC-UP program, one of the parents must meet a test of having worked a certain number of quarters in the past few years. The work history of either parent (not just the father's) can be used to meet this test.

resources become available; some states provide for liens against damages or benefits received for personal injuries.

In addition to fitting into one of the categories for AFDC eligibility, a family must also be in financial need. This is determined by looking at the income and resources of the family; the specific financial requirements, as well as the amount of benefits, vary considerably from state to state.

[2] General Assistance

General assistance, or relief, can be obtained in every area of the United States and its territories. It is funded by state or local government; about half the programs are administered by local governments. Anyone who is poor enough can qualify for benefits, but payments tend to be very low, and in one-third of the states they provide only short-term or emergency assistance. Disabled workers waiting for other types of compensation may receive general relief.

[3] Medicaid

Medicaid is a federal program administered by state welfare departments that provides medical assistance to welfare recipients and other needy individuals.[121] AFDC recipients and disabled recipients of Supplementary Security Income (SSI) are automatically eligible for Medicaid. People who fit into one of the AFDC or SSI categories but cannot qualify for the financial assistance because of excess income or resources may still be eligible for Medicaid. Financially needy children may qualify even if their family does not meet the AFDC category requirements. The benefits vary considerably from state to state, but when the state does offer a program, it is bound by certain federal requirements.

---

[121] 42 U.S.C. § 1396 et seq.; 42 CFR §§ 430 et seq.

[4] Food Stamps

Food stamps are coupons for buying food obtained through the local welfare office.[122] Recent changes in the program have eliminated obstacles that prevented people from obtaining benefits. Recipients no longer need to purchase the coupons; instead, they receive a smaller amount of coupons at no cost. Also, cooking facilities are no longer required for one to be eligible for food stamps. Unlike the welfare programs described above, there are no categories into which one must fall in order to be eligible for food stamps. The only test is that of the income of the entire household; the household must consist of those who shop, cook, and eat together. Emergency food stamps are available on just a few days' notice to anyone who has no income and does not immediately expect any income.

[5] Supplementary Security Income

SSI is a federal program that provides a minimum income to individuals who are disabled, over age 65, or blind.[123] It is listed under the welfare programs because, unlike the other social security programs, one of the major tests is financial need. Thus, people are eligible for SSI only if they have no other income or their other income does not add up to the amount they would receive on an SSI grant. Therefore, SSI can supplement any disability insurance, pension, social security, workers' compensation, or welfare payments.

Although SSI is funded and administered through the federal government by the Social Security Administration (SSA), many states supplement the federal monies with a state portion of the grant. This state portion is usually also administered by the SSA, but in some states it may be administered separately through the state welfare system and may require a separate application at the local welfare office.

The standards for meeting the disability test and the procedures for applying for SSI are the same as those for social security

---

[122] 7 U.S.C. § 2011 et seq.; 7 CFR § 250 et seq.

[123] 42 U.S.C. § 401 et seq.

disability benefits. These standards and procedures are discussed extensively in the section on disability insurance benefits.

The additional requirement for SSI eligibility is the financial need test. This is a test both of current income and of assets, or resources. The size of the SSI grant that one receives will depend on whether the applicant contributes to food and shelter costs. The income test varies from state to state, depending upon the amount of SSI grant provided by each state when the state supplement is added to the federal base amount. The resources test is uniform throughout the country. An individual is entitled to have up to $1500 ($2250 for a couple) of resources and still be eligible for SSI. In determining what resources are available to a person, the following resources are exempted from consideration: a home, an automobile up to $4500 in value, household goods and personal effects up to a value of $2000, certain life insurance policies, and certain resources that are used to produce income.

§ 6.04. Third-Party Suits

Most states provide for suits against a third party,[124] although there are important variations. The purpose of a third-party suit is to allow an injured worker to sue a third party (a party other than the employer or the employer's agents) in a civil damage suit for negligently or intentionally causing the injury or disease suffered. Since the recovery in a third-party action is not limited to the scheduled benefits of the workers' compensation statutes,[125] third-party suits provide greater relief and should be brought whenever feasible.[126]

---

[124] Only Georgia, Ohio, and West Virginia have no third-party statutes, although third-party suits are now permitted in Georgia by case law. White v. Liberty Mutual Ins. Co., 206 S.E.2d 576 (Ga. App. 1974).

[125] A third-party suit, like any tort action brought in civil court, allows for full recovery of lost wages (rather than a reduced percentage). It also includes damages for pain and suffering not available in compensation claims. Also, loss of function, loss of limbs, and disfigurement are compensated at a much greater rate.

[126] For a thorough outline on recognizing a third-party case, preparing it, and trying it, with bibliography, *see* Products Liability Third Party Tort Actions by Victoria Heldman and Linda Miller-Atkinson (paper presented at Women and the Law Conference, Detroit, 1978).

Third-party actions can arise out of a wide variety of situations. If a worker traveling on the road in the course of his or her job is negligently struck by another vehicle, that constitutes a third-party cause of action. If a worker is injured when his or her machine malfunctions because of negligence in the manufacturing, design, or installation of the machine, a third-party suit is viable. If a chemical manufacturer sells an improperly or insufficiently tested or labeled product that causes harm to the workers who come into contact with it, a third-party suit will lie. These are only some examples of third-party actions; others are discussed below.

The workers' compensation lawyer must be alert to the existence of a third-party cause of action. Letting the statute of limitations run on a valid third-party claim has been found to be legal malpractice.[127]

Whether or not a third-party suit should be brought depends in large part on what the worker will recover. The injury must be serious enough to enable the worker to recover enough money (after the insurer is reimbursed[128] and the attorney fees are deducted) to make such a suit worthwhile.

States have different provisions as to who can bring a third-party suit. Some states give the right to sue to the entity paying compensation; some give it to the worker; some provide for suits by either the worker or the payer of insurance, but with certain time restrictions (if one does not sue within a specified period of time, then the other may); some permit either party to sue. Some very complicated situations can arise where a worker was injured in a state other than the one in which s/he is employed.

Most states do not require that a worker choose at the outset between filing a workers' compensation claim under the state statute or suing a third party in a civil action. However, some states still do require the worker to elect either remedy. It is therefore important to know the procedure in your state, as the

---

127 *See* case discussed at 23 ATLA L. Rep. 58 (March 1980)(a California court awarded $400,000 to an injured worker against his workers' compensation attorney).

128 If a worker or insurer prevails in a third-party action, the insurer must be reimbursed for any money or other benefits furnished, and the insurer may be allowed credit against future benefits.

election of a remedy could have serious consequences if the appropriate action is not taken.

The available defenses to a third-party action vary. However, common defenses are contributory negligence (or comparative negligence) of the worker or employer, the statute of limitations, and, as a defense to a suit by a worker, subrogation.

[1] Context in Which Injuries Arise

Injuries arise in a number of contexts. The most common causes of injuries giving rise to products liability actions are machines, chemicals, and defective facilities. Liability in these different contexts may lie with a number of possible defendants.

[a] Machine-Caused Injuries

If the injury was caused by a defective machine or tool, investigate potential third-party liability of—

(1) the manufacturer or designer of the defective machine or tool causing the injury;
(2) the installer of the defective machine;
(3) the maintainer or repairer of the defective machine or tool;
(4) the manufacturer, designer, supplier, installer, repairer, or maintainer of machine parts or point-of-operation devices employed with the machine or tool; and
(5) the compensation carrier who has undertaken safety advice and given it negligently or misrepresented its expertise.

[b] Injuries by Chemicals or Toxic Substances

If the worker's injuries were caused by the action of chemicals or other harmful toxic substances, investigate potential third-party liability of

(1) the manufacturer of the toxic substance;
(2) the shipper, packager, or supplier of the toxic substance;
(3) the designer, installer, or maintainer of the chemical storage facility in which the toxic substance was stored or transported (e.g., tanks, vats, piping);
(4) the manufacturer, designer, installer, or maintainer of the plant machinery that applies or employs the toxic substance (e.g., spray machines, dusting equipment);
(5) the manufacturer, designer, supplier, installer, or maintainer of safety devices that were or should have been used with the toxic substances (e.g., respirators, warning badges, ventilation systems, filters, smoke inhibitors, toxic alarm systems); and
(6) the compensation carrier who has undertaken safety advice and given it negligently or misrepresented its expertise.

[c] Injuries Attributable to Defective Industrial Facilities

If the worker's injuries were caused by defects in the plant, place of work, or other major capital installations, investigate potential third-party liability of—

(1) the builder, contractor, or subcontractor of the defective industrial facility (e.g., roof beam, water drain, stairway, concrete floor, ventilation system, electrical wiring);
(2) the architect or designer of the defective or inadequate industrial facility (e.g., loading dock, storage area, conveyor belt);
(3) the installer or supplier of the defective industrial facility (e.g., assembly line, overhead transporter, pulley);
(4) the maintainer of the defective industrial facility (e.g., roofer, painter, plumber, custodial contractor, electrical contractor); and
(5) the compensation carrier.

[2] Areas of Liability

An industrial injury may be caused by a variety of errors of omission or commission that give rise to liability. The following are some examples of areas to consider:

(1) true drawing board errors in design for function (e.g., the press designed too short for the operator, making guards ineffective);
(2) failure to install adequate safety devices, such as guards, fail-safe switches, interlocks, monitoring devices, safety valves, and the like;
(3) employment of safety devices that fail in use, (e.g., pull-back devices, sweep guards);
(4) deficient inspection processes, quality control, and testing before and after manufacture (e.g., the 1961 Pontiac Tempest, which had a front-end cross-member so low that it got caught on railroad and trolley tracks; the Dalkon Shield intrauterine device; the oral contraceptive);
(5) personal protection equipment that fails in use;
(6) construction from unsafe or unsuitable materials (e.g., lightweight aluminum ladders, which buckle);
(7) manufacturing processes that result in a defective product (e.g., the proper heat treat, which is destroyed later on in manufacture by a welding operation);
(8) failure to plan for foreseeable uses unintended by the manufacturer (e.g., forklifts without overhead protections used for heavy loading);
(9) failure to foresee the consequences of ordinary wear and tear and improper maintenance on the part of the user (e.g., scaffold cables or sheaves that fail);
(10) the addition of an unnecessary part to the product (e.g., injury-producing tail fins or rearview mirrors);
(11) absence or inadequacy of labelling, warning, and instruction as part of basic design, or labels and warnings that fade or disappear before the machine's useful life ends;
(12) selling as opposed to overselling (e.g., chemical components, engine cleaners, toxic chemical supplies);
(13) employing a negligent contractor;

(14) dangerous conditions on land; unsafe workplace.

[3] Suing the Manufacturer or Seller of Faulty Products

The most common causes of action for a third-party action for parties other than the employer or doctor include negligence, breach of warranty, and strict liability in tort.

In a negligence action, the injured party must show that the defendant owed him or her a duty of reasonable care and that such duty was breached. In the products liability area—our chief concern, since machines cause most worker injuries—the following rule has developed: "[t]he seller is liable for negligence in the manufacture or sale of any product which may reasonably be expected to be capable of inflicting substantial harm if it is defective."[129] It may be difficult or impossible to prove negligence in a products liability case because actual negligence by the manufacturer must be proved. Even with the aid of the res ipsa loquitur doctrine, the plaintiff must show that the accident would not have occured in the absence of the defendant's negligence.[130]

An action for breach of warranty against a third-party manufacturer eliminates the necessity of proving negligence. Where it can be shown that a breach of either an express warranty or an implied warranty of merchantability or fitness for a particular purpose was the proximate cause of the injury, recovery will lie.[131] The main difficulty in this type of action is in determining whether the warranty extends from the manufacturer to the injured party—i.e., whether there is privity between the parties. In those states that have adopted either Alternative B or Alternative C of § 2-318 of the Uniform Commercial Code, seller's express and implied warranties extend to "any natural person who may reasonably be expected to use, consume or be affected by the goods and who is injured. . . ." In California, where Alternative

---

129 Prosser, The Law of Torts § 96 (4th Ed.).

130 *Id.* § 40. It is, however, useful to note that in two areas of products liability litigation, negligence is still the main theory relied on—cases involving unsafe design and cases involving failure to warn. Prosser § 96.

131 Prosser, *supra* § 97. The U.C.C. should be examined for a definition of these types of warranties.

A to § 2-318 was adopted and seems to extend warranty protection only to members of the family, household, or guests, the California Supreme Court has held that an employee is part of the employer's "industrial family" and thus in privity with the manufacturer of the machine that caused his or her injury.[132] In other states with Alternative A, the privity requirement has been abolished by other statutes.[133] The code does not set up vertical privity as a bar to actions and thus has been cited as permitting suit of manufacturers of component parts as well as the manufacturer, final assembler, and seller or distributor.[134] Pitfalls and complications with warranty actions, which vary from jurisdiction to jurisdiction, include notice of injury requirements under the code or within the contract and disclaimers set up by the seller in the contract with the buyer.[135]

Strict liability in tort is recognized in the common law of about two-thirds of the states in the products liability setting.[136] It eliminates the contract limitations present in warrant actions, such as strict privity, lack of notice, and disclaimers. There is conflict among the jurisdictions as to the applicability of the traditional bars to recovery present in negligence actions, such as contributory or comparative negligence, abnormal use, failure of an intermediate party to warn, etc.[137] Nevertheless, all that it is necessary to show under this theory in order to hold the seller liable is that the product was sold "in a defective condition unreasonably dangerous to the user . . .," who was thereby injured, and that the product was substantially unchanged between the seller

---

[132] Peterson v. Lamb Rubber Co., 353 P.2d 575 (Cal. 1960).

[133] American Law of Products Liability 2d § 10:6 [hereinafter cited as ALPL]. ALPL § 10:43 has an excellent jurisdiction-by-jurisdiction summation of privity requirements in warranty actions.

[134] ALPL § 10:6.

[135] Prosser § 97.

[136] Prosser § 98. The first case in which the court found strict liability on the part of the manufacturer was Greenman v. Yuba Power Products, 377 P.2d 897 (Cal. 1963)(plaintiff was injured by a power tool he was using but had not bought; the court allowed recovery, Chief Justice Traynor declaring that a warranty was unnecessary and the manufacturer would be held strictly liable). This case is very influential and widely cited.

[137] Prosser § 102.

and the consumer.[138] "Defective" has been defined to mean that the product does not meet the reasonable expectations of the consumer as to its safety.[139] Liability extends to the seller, maker of component part, assemblers, etc. The trend in the products liability area is that those plaintiffs who would be eligible to bring a negligence action, as well as those who are forseeably injured, would be able to bring their action in strict liability in tort.[140]

[4] Suing the Employer

Although all workers' compensation statutes generally bar a common law action by an injured worker against the employer, it may be possible to bring such an action where the injury is caused by the employer while he or she is acting not in the capacity of employer but rather as a third party. Such an action is analogous to the common law action allowed in all jurisdictions against third parties where liability is not determined by statute. This common law action against the employer, referred to as the dual capacity doctrine, has been recognized in a few jurisdictions and by the Supreme Court.[141] Analogous reasoning would call for

---

138 Restatement of Torts 2d § 402A.

139 Prosser § 99.

140 Prosser § 100. *See* Elmore v. Am. Motors Corp., 451 P.2d 84 (Cal. 1969)(manufacturer of defective auto which ran into plaintiff was held liable).

141 Comment, *Workmen's Compensation and Employer Suability: The Dual Capacity Doctrine,* 5 St. Mary's L.J. 818. This paper discusses the rationale of the doctrine and the cases decided under it. On page 831, the author offers the rationale that there is no justification for going beyond the intent of the compensation statutes by exonerating culpable negligence outside of the employer-employee relationship. Cases cited include Duprey v. Shane, 241 P.2d 78 (Cal. Dist. Ct. App.) *aff'd,* 249 P.2d 8 (Cal. 1952)(a chiropractor was held suable by his nurse for his negligent treatment of her since, by giving treatment himself rather than paying for it, he was taking on the responsibilities of the doctor-patient relationship and the common law liabilities that accompany it); and Reed v. The Yaka, 373 U.S. 410 (1963)(plaintiff, a longshoreman, was held entitled to a common law recovery against his employer as well as statutory compensation because the employer, a stevedoring company, had assumed non-delegable duties of providing a seaworthy vessel when it became a bareboat charterer of the vessel on which the plaintiff was injured).

The test is not whether separate departments or functions are involved but whether the second function generates obligations not related to the employer

holding liable the worker's compensation insurance carrier for its negligence when acting in the capacity of a third party, but, with very few exceptions, the courts that have decided this question have held against such recovery.[142]

[5] Suing the Malpracticing Doctor

The workers' compensation statute in effect in the state will govern the maintainability of a civil suit for physician malpractice if the worker's injuries are compensable under the workers' compensation act.[143]

Jurisdictions that grant civil immunity to the employer or any agent, servant, or employee of that employer acting within the course of the employer's business have almost uniformly held that a company doctor who treats a worker injured on the job falls within the definition of employee and will, therefore, dismiss a civil suit for damages brought by the injured worker.

---

obligations of the first or original function. 5 St. Mary's L.J. 818 at p. 825. *See* A. Larson, 2 The Law of Workmen's Compensation § 72.80, at 226.23 (1970).

Some courts have held the general contractor liable for injuries of the employee of a subcontractor where the general contractor was the owner of the site on which the work was performed and the injury was incurred. State v. Luckie, 145 So. 2d 239 (Fla. Dist. Ct. App. 1962); Bright v. Reynolds Metal Co., 490 S.W.2d 474 (Ky. 1973).

Where the employee of a subcontractor is injured, the suability of the contractor may hinge on the issue of control. Hickman v. Fairleigh, 459 F.2d 790, 793 (10th Cir. 1972); Ray v. Monsanto Co., 473 F.2d 219, 220 (9th Cir. 1973).

Cases rejecting the doctrine where the test seems to have been met include Hudson v. Allen, 161 N.W.2d 596 (Mich. Ct. App. 1968); Lewis v. Gardner Eng'r, 491 S.W.2d 778 (Ark. 1973).

It should be pointed out that the "dual capacity" doctrine has gained only very limited acceptance, most states rejecting it. The precise language or provisions of a jurisdiction's compensation statute may be determinative.

[142] Generally, courts have held that the exclusive remedy provisions of the statute have barred this type of remedy. The few cases decided on this point are collected under 93 A.L.R.2d 598. *See also* Larson, *Workmen's Compensation Insurer as Suable Third Party,* 1969 Duke L.J. 1117; Comment, *Workmen's Compensation Insurance Carrier as Third Party Tortfeasor,* 1 Conn. L. Rev. 183 (1968).

[143] *See generally* 28 ALR3d 1066, superceding 82 ALR 932 and 139 ALR 1010; 101 CJS, Workmen's Compensation § 1043, at 625-26; 2 Larson, 72.61; 41 Am. Jur., Phys. Surg. 136.

Those cases that have denied a right of action against a physician under the fellow servant doctrine have analyzed the relationship of the doctor to the employer along the traditional tests for evaluating employee status to determine whether the doctor is an employee within the meaning of the workers' compensation statute or a third person who would generally be amenable to suit.[144]

Most states, whether the workers' compensation statute re-

(*Text continued on page 6-91*)

---

[144] Hayes v. Marshall Field Co., 351 Ill. App. 329, 115 N.E.2d 99 (1953). Plaintiff got a dust particle in her eye while at work. She was sent to the company doctor who pierced her eye in the course of treatment, causing blindness. The doctor was paid an hourly rate of compensation by the Marshall Field Co. for providing first aid to injured employees. The court distinguished this case from others where a damage action was maintainable against a company doctor in that in this case the medical treatment was pursuant to an injury that arose out of the employment situation.

Jones v. Bouza, 75 Mich. App. 561, 152 N.W.2d 561 (1967), *aff'd*, 381 Mich. 299, 160 N.W.2d 881 (1968). Plaintiff suffered a back injury on the job and was sent to the plant physician. The physician gave him pain tablets and heat treatment and told him to return to work. Later in the day the plaintiff became partially paralyzed and was taken to the hospital. The court held that the fact that the doctor exercised independent judgment in rendering medical treatment did not prevent him from also obtaining the status of employee of the Ford Motor Company as he "worked regular hours at a place designated by Ford Motor Co., for a fixed salary. Furthermore, his professional practice was exclusively at Ford Motor Company" (152 N.W.2d at 395). The plaintiff unsuccessfully raised an equal protection argument, claiming that company-employed physicians were placed in a protected category different from that of all other physicians.

Proctor v. Ford Motor Co., 36 Ohio 2d 3, 302 N.E.2d 580 (1973). The Ohio court held that "the exercise of professional judgment and freedom in treating the workers of Ford" does not take physicians outside the definition of an employee of the employer. The Ohio statute additionally excludes for civil immunity ". . . any person whose employment is casual and not in the usual course of trade, business, profession, or occupation of his employer . . ." (at 581). The court held that the "operation of a medical facility is work which serves Ford's business interest and doctors are not excludable as being outside of the employer's usual course of business" (at 583).

Bergen v. Miller, 104 N.J. Super. 350, 240 A.2d 49 (1969). Defendant doctor was employed by General Motors as medical director of the dispensary. His duties included treating employees injured on the job and performing certain medical examinations. At the time of the incident the doctor was salaried by General Motors. This salary constituted substantially all of his income. The court found the defendant doctor to be an employee. Immunity applies to all employees even those in supervisory positions or "uniquely talented" as in the

case of the plant physician.

Golini v. Nachtigall, 347 N.Y.S.2d 981 (1973). Defendant doctor was employed full-time and salaried by the Pepsi-Cola Company as the Associate Director of the medical department. The court found that the availability of a medical facility provides better working conditions for the employees of Pepsi and is in furtherance of the company's business purposes and therefore workers' compensation is the exclusive remedy.

Garcia v. Iserson, 33 N.Y.2d 421, 309 N.E.2d 420 (1974). The plaintiff was treated at the infirmary on the employer's premises by Dr. Iserson. The doctor was salaried and worked regular hours, normal salary deductions were taken from the doctor's paycheck, and he was covered under the employer's medical plan and workers' compensation insurance policy. The court held that if the injured worker receives professional services not as a member of the general public but only in consequence of his/her employment, a damage suit against the company physician is barred and the remedy available under the workers' compensation system is the exclusive remedy. That portion of Volk v. City of New York, 284 N.Y. 279, 30 N.E.2d 596, that is inconsistent with the holding in *Garcia* was overruled. In reaching its decision in Silverstein v. State of N.Y., 19 N.Y.2d 698, 278 N.Y.S.2d 886, 225 N.E.2d 572, the court, in reliance on *Volk*, held that "workmen's compensation was not the exclusive remedy where the plaintiff employee was injured while receiving care provided for all patients at Creedmoor State Hospital (at 422)." In a footnote, the *Garcia* court left open the question "whether workmen's compensation would be the exclusive remedy if an employee were injured while availing himself of services or facilities furnished by his employer to the general public if the employee's access to such services was a benefit regularly furnished by the employer in consequence of a union contract, an individual agreement or otherwise" (at 422).

Martin v. Consol. Casualty Ins. Co., 138 F.2d 896 (5th Cir. 1943). Doctor who examined plaintiff at the "direction and control of the company . . . was not . . . an independent contractor but . . . a mere servant or agent of the company, and under the Texas Workmen's Compensation law, no recovery could be had against him" (at 899).

Contra, Duprey v. Shane, 109 Cal. App. 586, 241 P.2d 78 (1951), *aff'd,* 39 Cal. 2d 781, 249 P.2d 8 (1952). Plaintiff was a practical nurse employed by a chiropractor. She was treated by her employer and a co-employee. The court found the Industrial Accident Commission did not have exclusive jurisdiction over the matter and that the plaintiff could bring the action because "when the employing doctor elected to treat the industrial injury, the duties and obligations growing out of the employer-employee relationship terminate, and the doctor assumed the same responsibility that any doctor would have assumed had he been called in on the case" (at 82).

Duprey was decided prior to California's amending its statute to include fellow servant immunity. In a post amendment case with facts similar to those in *Duprey,* Hoffman v. Rogers, 22 Cal. App. 2d 655, 99 Cal. Rptr. 455 (1972), the doctor-defendant was found amenable to suit.

quires an election of proceeding under the act or suing in civil court, will allow a malpractice suit against a physician who attends to the injured worker. A doctor who is paid by the insurance company or the employer is not deemed to be a third party to the workers' compensation scheme and is not immune from civil suit if his/her relationship to the employer is not that of employee-employer. In cases where the worker's suit against the doctor prevails, generally the employer or the insurer will have a right to reimbursement through subrogation for monies already paid out as a result of aggravation of the original injury caused by the negligent physician.[145]

(*Text continued on page 6-94*)

However, in Deauvill v. Hall, 188 Cal. App. 2d 535, 10 Cal. Rptr. 511 (1961), the injured employee could not sue the employer for the negligence of a first-aid station attendant who was also an employee of the employer. The maltreatment aggravations were foreseeable consequences of the original injury and were compensable.

Garrison v. Graybeel(r), 202 Tenn. 567, 308 S.W.2d 375 (1957). The company doctor gave the plaintiff a tetanus shot, the reaction to which caused paralysis in the plaintiff. The court did not find a bar to a civil suit against the doctor in the fellow servant immunity afforded by the workers' compensation statute because the plaintiff was a carpenter and the defendant a skilled physician whose services were wholly foreign to the work the plaintiff or any other employee was doing for the employer and, therefore not related to the employer's business.

[145] DeHaven v. Caulfield, 314 F.2d 269, 114 U.S. App. D.C. 264 (1963). Plaintiff received a compensable injury under the D.C. workers' compensation act. She was sent to defendant doctor by the employer. The court held that the defendant doctor is a person other than the employer and therefore amenable to a malpractice action by the injured worker.

Duprey v. Shane, *supra.*

Indus. Com. v. Standard Ins. Co., 149 Colo. 587, 370 P.2d 156 (1962). The insurer is subrogated only to the extent of the amount of compensation it is required to pay for the aggravation of the original injury caused by the doctor. The insurer has no right to reimbursement for monies paid out to cover medical bills because the bills are not compensation.

Froid v. Knowles, 95 Colo. 223, 36 P.2d 156 (1934).

Pyles v. Bridges, 259 So. 2d 724 (Fla. App. 1972). Doctors and hospital rendering services to an injured worker paid for by the employer pursuant to the workers' compensation act do not share in the immunity afforded to the employer.

Gay v. Greene, 91 Ga. App. 78, 84 S.E.2d 847 (1954). The defendant physician was engaged in his own profession as an independent contractor. His liability arises from the doctor-patient relationship and not from an employer-employee relationship. Nothing in the workers' compensation act places the attending physician in a class with the employer.

Hancock v. Halliday, 67 Idaho 119, 171 P.2d 333 (1946). The subrogation statute gives the employer the right to bring an action to recover monies paid out to the employee, with any excess going to the employee. In giving the employer this right, however, the workers' compensation statute does not extinguish the common law action of the employee to recover for negligence of the doctor.

Huntoon v. Pritchard, 371 Ill. 36, 20 N.E.2d 53 (1939). The injured worker has a right of action against a negligent physician. However, the employer has a right of subrogation for amounts paid out.

Bradshaw v. Iowa Methodist Hosp. 251 Iowa 375, 101 N.W.2d 167 (1960). Any common law action the employee may have survives unless explicitly repealed by the statute.

Cooke v. Bunten, 135 Kan. 558, 11 P.2d 1016 (1932).

Morrison v. Carbide & Carbon Chems. Corp., 278 Ky. 746, 129 S.W.2d 547 (1939). The doctor, not the employer, is liable for the aggravation of the injury.

Turner v. Guiliano, 350 Mass. 675, 216 N.E.2d 562 (1966). The employee may sue the negligent physician if the employer fails to do so within the time prescribed in the subrogation statute.

Steeves v. Irwin, 233 A.2d 126 (Me. 1967). The employer's right of subrogation may be waived and the action reverts back to the employee.

Wood v. Vroman, 215 Mich. 449, 184 N.W.2d 520 (1921). The physician's treatment was subsequent to the claim for which compensation was paid; therefore, the employee's right of action is not transferred to the employer.

Viita v. Dolan, 132 Minn. 128, 155 N.W. 1077 (1916). The doctor, not the employer, is liable for the malpractice.

Schumacher v. Leslie, 360 Mo. 1238, 232 S.W.2d 913 (1950). Doctor furnished by the employer or carrier is a third person and amenable to suit for malpractice. Employer has a right to subrogation for any monies paid to the worker for the aggravation of the injury caused by the physician.

Dettman v. Goldsmith, 11 N.J. Super. 571, 78 A.2d 626 (1951). Injured workers have a right of action against third party tortfeasors but must reimburse the employer for monies paid out.

Brum v. Int'l Terminal Operating Co., 125 N.J. Super. 558, 312 A.2d 507 (1973). Reimbursement is limited to the amount paid out by the employer attributable to the aggravation.

Schreckinger v. York Distributors, Inc., 9 App. Div. 2d 333, 194 N.Y.S.2d 67.

Bryant v. Dougherty, 148 S.E.2d 548 (1966), 28 ALR 3d 1057, *app. after remand* 270 N.C. 748, 155 S.E.2d 181 (1967). North Carolina has a statute similar to that of Virginia; the *Bryant* court decided in accord with Fauver v. Bell, *infra.* The court further stated that "where, as here, the physician is carrying on an independent practice of medicine or surgery . . . he is not conducting the business of an industrial corporation merely because the manager of the plant sends to him, for examination and treatment, those who, from time to time, sustain injuries in the plant" (at 553).

Wimer v. Miller, 235 Ore. 25, 383 P.2d 1005 (1963). "The right to elect between remedies was granted to the injured workman as a benefit rather than a burden. To thrust upon the average worker the dilemma of choosing between damages which might take several months or years to realize and the certain payments to be received under the Act would convert the benefit into a burden. In some cases the evidence of a physician's malpractice might not manifest itself until some time after a final award had been accepted." (at 1010).

Peterson v. State Farm Mutual Auto Ins. Co., 238 Ore. 106, 393 P.2d 651 (1964). A victim's recovery under the uninsured motorists' statute cannot be limited because he is collecting benefits under the workers' compensation statute.

Greenstein v. Fornell, 143 Misc. 880, 257 N.Y.S. 673 (1932). The election doctrine will not bar a civil suit if it is not stated in the award whether the amount included the effects of doctor malpractice.

Lemonovich v. Klimoski, 315 F. Supp. 1290 (W.D. Pa. 1970). Where, apart from a letter written by the company's medical director indicating that the defendant doctor was to be regarded as surgical liaison officer and would be responsible for attending to hospitalized employees and refer employees to qualified specialists, all on a fee for service basis, the doctor was an independent contractor and not an employee of the company, and, therefore, the injured worker could bring a malpractice action against the doctor.

Garrison v. Graybeel(r), *supra.*

McKelvy v. Barber, 381 S.W.2d 59 (Tex. 1964), *rev'g* 368 S.W.2d 38 (Tex. Civ. App. 1963). A doctor who treats an injured worker pursuant to an arrangement with the employer or its insurance carrier and who is paid for services as they are rendered is not an agent, servant, or employee of the employer who is immune from an action for malpractice. The test for establishing whether a person is an agent, servant, or employee is whether the employer would be legally responsible under the doctrine of respondeat superior. The fact that the doctor is generally regarded as the company doctor and paid for by the insurer does not establish that the employer or the insurer has ultimate control over the doctor's treatment of industrial injuries.

Fauver v. Bell, 192 Va. 518, 65 S.E.2d 575 (1951). The injured worker's common law right to bring a malpractice action against a treating physician is not extinguished by Virginia's compensation law. Virginia's statute limits liability of one who is conducting the employer's business; the attending physician is not engaged in the business pursuit of the employer but in his own business or calling.

Jones v. Laird Foundation, Inc., 195 S.E.2d 821 (W. Va. 1973), *rev'g* Makarenko v. Scott, 132 W. Va. 430, 55 S.E.2d 88.

Lakeside Bridge & Steel Co. v. Pugh, 206 Wis. 62, 238 N.W. 872 (1931). The employee has a cause of action for malpractice, less the amount received under the act, and the employer has a cause of action for amounts paid out because of the doctor's malpractice.

A few states bar suit against an attending physician if the injured worker proceeds under the workers' compensation system.[146]

[6] Preparation of Third-Party Products Liability Actions

In developing sources of information and allies for a third-party action, there are a number of sources to examine.

Counsel for the injured worker should first determine what information can be obtained from the client's coworkers or union. For example, have there been grievances filed regarding the hazard in question? Does the union have notes from collective bargaining sessions dealing with the provision of a safe workplace? The fellow workers and the worker's representatives may be of great assistance in helping you get access to witnesses material to your case. They would have the best knowledge of who is familiar with the machine or chemical in question and what the history of use of that machine or chemical is at the workplace.

The workers' compensation disability carrier may also be helpful since the compensation carrier is generally entitled to receive

---

[146] Duvardo v. Moore, 98 N.E.2d 855 (Ill. 1951). The Illinois statute transfers the employee's cause of action to the employer if all the parties are under and subject to the act. Here, the injured worker was treated by a physician who owned the hospital and he and all his employees were covered by a workers' compensation policy.

Markly v. White, 168 Okla. 244, 32 P.2d 716 (1934).

Alexander v. Von Wedel, 169 Okla. 341, 37 P.2d 252 (1934).

But see Walker v. Von Wedel, 108 Okla. 292, 237 P.2d 86 (1925). An action against a doctor was permitted because the doctor maliciously malpracticed so as to protect the employer from liability for the loss of the worker's hand, thus causing her to lose her fingers, and suffer extreme bodily harm and mental anguish.

Manda v. DeWitt, 261 Mich. 246, 246 N.W. 199 (1933).

Overbeck v. Nex, 261 Mich. 156, 246 N.W. 196 (1933). In accepting compensation from the employer, whatever right of action plaintiff had against the defendant doctor passed by subrogation to the employer.

Ross v. Erickson Constr. Co., 89 Wash. 634, 155 P. 153 (1916). The workers' compensation statute abolishes all civil actions.

Carmichael v. Kirkpatrick, 185 Wash. 609, 56 P.2d 686 (1936); ltd. by Shortridge v. Bede, 51 Wash. 2d 391, 319 P.2d 277 (1957). Dicta point to statutory provision allowing for an election.

back all it has paid out for first-party benefits to or on behalf of the worker from any recovery the worker receives. Therefore, the compensation carrier may be willing to assist with the costs of preparation of the action and with gaining access to the worksite or company documents. Further, the compensation carrier may be willing to make available the entire compensation file regarding the injury in question.

However, in states where the law provides for added penalties to the employer in the case of serious and willful claims, the employer's compensation carrier will probably be unwilling to cooperate without a waiver of this additional liability. Case-by-case evaluation of the possible benefits to be gained by employer cooperation as against the extent of benefits and likelihood of recovery in a "serious and willful" claim is necessary.

In such states another factor affecting cooperation with the employer on a third-party claim, is that the employer cannot recover its lien to the extent that the employer was responsible for the accident occurring. Care must be taken to make certain that the financial and other assistance of the employer does not constitute an implied waiver of an assertion of employer's negligence. This concern, however, is pertinent only to settlement of the case.

A third possible ally is the industrial safety and health agency responsible for inspecting the worksite. Through OSHA or the state agency, you may be able to obtain access to prior inspection files on the employer. You may be able to initiate investigations of various health or safety hazards at the employer's workplace. The OSHA investigators may be helpful in explaining and providing standards regarding complex chemical injuries, toxic gases, guarding, or electrical injuries.

A final possible ally would be the worker's treating physician. However, care must be taken where the treating physician is experienced in compensation cases. Such physician must be educated regarding the minimal usefulness of percentage rating approaches in products liability cases, where the real question is the effect of the disability on the plaintiff's earning potential. Further, the physician must be educated as to the limited usefulness of workers' compensation theories of apportionment and aggravation. In a workers' compensation case where there is a preexisting injury, the physician must apportion the percentage of disability to the work-related injury. In a third-party claim where there is a preexisting injury, if the aggravating injury is the last straw that rendered the worker unable to continue in his or her work, then the damages in the third-party case must be measured by the fullest extent of the worker's disability.

[7] Trial of Common-Law Actions by Injured Workers against Third Parties[147]

Generally, courts have held that it was improper to bring before the jury information that the plaintiff was entitled to a workers' compensation award. If the jury hears such information, its presentation is generally held to be prejudicial error necessitating reversal or a new trial. The decision on whether such information is prejudicial is generally within the discretion of the trial court; some jurisdictions have held that error in admitting such information may be cured by instruction.[148]

Generally, findings material to the decision of a workers' compensation board are res judicata in subsequent proceedings involving the same parties. Thus, a finding by a workers' compensation board of denial of compensation on the ground that the employee's activity at the time of injury was outside the scope of employment would not be a bar in a subsequent negligence action by the employee against the employer on the negligence issue, while the employer would be estopped from claiming that the action was barred on the ground that the injury occurred within the scope of employment since this issue was previously adjudicated. A few jurisdictions, contrary to the general rule, have held that decisions of administrative tribunals do not have res judicata effect on the courts. The parties in subsequent proceedings must be identical or in privity with those in the proceed-

[147] For a detailed and excellent account of a products liability action successfully brought by an injured worker, *see* Sullivan, *Trial of a Punch Press Case,* 19 Trial Law. Guide 249. The case discussed is Wells v. Web Mach. Co., 315 N.E.2d 301 (Ill. 1974).

[148] The cases on this point are collected in Annot., 77 ALR2d 1154.

ing relied upon for its res judicata effect. Generally, a decision by a workers' compensation board that it has jurisdiction is res judicata. Other determinations by a board that are generally considered to have a res judicata effect in a subsequent action at law between the same parties are the existence of an employer-employee relationship, the nature of the employment, that the injury arose out of and in the course of employment, the fact and cause of the injury, and the employer's status as an insured.[149]

---

149 The cases on this point are collected in Annot., 84 ALR2d 1036.

CHAPTER 7

Rank and File Rights in the Shop

In many workplaces, there is already an established union. But the existence of a union does not mean that the union is doing an effective job of representing its membership. Increasingly, rank-and-file workers have organized committees or caucuses to press their union to fight more vigorously on their behalf, to oppose employment discrimination, or even to change the union that is representing them. Often, these caucuses may run candidates for union office or take up particular demands for improvements in collective bargaining agreements.

The activities of such groups are protected under Section 7 of the Labor Management Relations Act (LMRA) regardless of whether they are part of any official union activities or are undertaken by a union official.[1] Since the nature of workers' Section 7 rights is discussed elsewhere in this book, this chapter will deal only with the questions of caucus concerted activity, independent participation in grievance/arbitration, rival union organizing, protections for communists and radicals, and access to the Board.

§ 7.01. Caucus Concerted Activity: Unauthorized, Dissident Activity at the Plant

[1] Economic Action by Dissident Unionized Employees

Dissident union members subject to a collective bargaining agreement run two major risks when they undertake economically coercive activities[2] that have not been authorized by their union. One risk is that the dissident's actions will be deemed unprotected because they violate the arbitration or no-strike provision in the collective bargaining agreement.[3] (This factor can be problematic whether the action is taken by the whole union or just by a dissident minority).[4] Another risk is that the actions may be seen as undermining the authority of their exclusive bargaining representative and therefore undeserving of statutory

[1] *See* Chapter 1, *supra.*

[2] In its broadest sense, economically coercive activity comprises strikes and other interferences with production, picketing, and appealing to the public to engage in a consumer boycott.

[3] The gravity of this risk will in many cases depend on the extent of the participation in the work stoppage. But it must be kept in mind that the employer's right to fire for striking in violation of a collective bargaining contract is unqualified. *See* Mackey Radio & Tel. Co. v. NLRB, 304 U.S. 333 (1938).

[4] This subchapter on caucus concerted activity is confined to the special problems encountered by dissident unionized employees. Questions of contract interpretation (i.e., whether certain activity violates a no-strike clause) and the right to engage in economic action despite the existence of a no-strike clause will not be considered here. For a general discussion of strike action, *see* Chapter 3. Therefore, as used here, the term "economically coercive activity" refers to picketing and appealing to the public but does not include strikes and other interferences with production.

protection under the National Labor Relations Act (NLRA). This factor has particular significance for dissidents and was considered by the Supreme Court in *Emporium Capwell Co. v. Western Addition Community Organization.*[5] In that case, the Supreme Court dealt a major blow to unauthorized economic activity by dissidents. Since *Emporium,* one question still unresolved is whether any economically coercive activity by dissidents will be considered protected activity by the National Labor Relations Board (NLRB). and the courts. This section will address that question.[6]

Briefly, the facts in *Emporium* involved four employees who picketed their employer (a large department store) on a Saturday and distributed handbills urging consumers not to patronize the store. The dissidents were protesting what they believed to be the store's racially discriminatory employment practices. Prior to the picketing, the dissidents had disagreed with their union's decision not to picket the store but instead to process every grievance through to arbitration. The dissidents demanded to speak directly to top management; their professed goal was to work out a broad agreement to correct the racial inequities. They were discharged for their activities, and the NLRB refused to reinstate them. When the case eventually reached the Supreme Court, the Court adopted the NLRB's finding that the discharged dissidents had attempted to bargain with their employer concerning working conditions affecting minority employees. In labeling their activity as an attempt to bargain, the Court found that the exclusivity principle of Section 9(a)[7] had been violated and, consequently, Section 7[8] protection could not be extended. The Court rejected

---

[5] 420 U.S. 50 (1975). *See also* NLRB v. Pincus, 104 LRRM 2001 (3d Cir. 1980).

[6] It appears that many people feel that this question will be answered in the negative. Very little dissident activity that is economically coercive in nature has been undertaken since *Emporium.* Case law on this point, subsequent to *Emporium,* is minimal. The *Emporium* decision has already had a significant chilling effect on dissident activity against the employer.

[7] Section 9(a) provides, among other things, that the representative designated by the majority shall be the exclusive representative of all the employees in the unit. For the complete text of Section 9(a), *see* note 42, *infra.*

[8] Section 7 of the NLRA, 29 U.S.C. § 157 (1970), provides: "Employees shall have the right to self-organization, to form, join or assist labor organizations, to bargain collectively through representatives of their own choosing, and to engage in other concerted activities for the purpose of collective bargaining or other mutual aid or protection, and shall also have the right to refrain from any

the employees' argument that a limited exception to the exclusivity principle should be fashioned for dissidents seeking to eliminate racial discrimination. In reaching this conclusion, the Court reasoned that dissident activities in opposition to the majority representative undermine the very principles upon which national labor policy is founded.[9] According to the Court, satisfactory safeguards against tyranny by the majority already exist.[10] The grievance process adequately handles discrimination disputes,[11] and other legal processes are available to the employee who seeks to eliminate discrimination.[12] Furthermore, the Court suggested that separate bargaining is in fact counterproductive to the progress of the whole union because of potential fragmentation of the bargaining unit. The Court asserted that such fragmentation may result when certain groups are allowed to employ economic tactics while the others must resort to established procedures.[13]

Strictly speaking, the *Emporium* decision did not address the question of whether unauthorized, dissident activity economically coercive in nature but not accompanied by a demand to speak with management will be extended Section 7 protection.[14] However, it appears likely that, using the *Emporium* decision as precedent, the NLRB will find that dissident employees have demanded separate bargaining even if in a technical sense they have not done so. But concerted action to spur the union to better representation, rather than to pressure the employer directly, may be engaged in.

This result has already occurred in *United Parcel Service.*[15] In that

---

or all of such activities except to the extent that such right may be affected by an agreement requiring membership in a labor organization as a condition of employment as authorized in Section 8(a)(3)."

[9] 420 U.S. at 62-64.

[10] *Id.* at 64.

[11] *Id.* at 66-67.

[12] *Id* at 70.

[13] *Id.* at 67-69

[14] For a detailed discussion of the *Emporium* decision and its ramifications, *see* Cantor, Dissident Worker Action after the Emporium, 29 Rutgers L.J. 35 (1975).

[15] 205 NLRB 991, 84 LRRM 1098 (1973). This case was decided after the Court of Appeals decision in *Emporium* but before the case reached the Supreme Court.

case, fifteen to twenty employees (including two union stewards) protested working conditions and slowness in employer grievance dispositions by picketing on a Saturday. A majority of the NLRB held that the picketing was not protected by Section 7 because the dissidents circumvented the contractual grievance procedure by trying to initiate direct negotiations with their employer over matters that were subject to agreed-upon procedures.[16] The facts stated in the dissenting opinion show that the dissidents never demanded separate talks with management and never repudiated their union representatives.[17] Furthermore, the dissenting NLRB members asserted that the dissidents' protest was not economically coercive in that appeals to the public were not made and the employer's business operation was not impeded.[18]

Given the factual situation in *United Parcel,* the NLRB, if it had been so inclined, could have deemed the activity protected by Section 7 and could have characterized the protest as merely an expression of employee dissatisfaction rather than a demand to meet with the employer to negotiate separate terms and conditions of employment.[19] This case illustrates the NLRB's reluctance to condone the use of what it deems to be economically coercive tactics whenever channels have been established for the peaceful resolution of disputes. After *United Parcel,* it will not be much of a departure for the NLRB to state that dissidents implicitly attempt to initiate direct negotiations whenever tactics such as picketing or picketing accompanied by appeals to the public are used.[20] This extension of *Emporium* would be consistent with

16 For a complete discussion of *United Parcel, see* Cantor, *supra* note 14, at 52-53. The majority stated that the dissidents attempted to negotiate with management but did not state what facts led them to their conclusion. No facts are given in the majority opinion which relied on the dissent's statement of the facts.

17 205 NLRB at 991-993 84 LRRM at 1101.

18 205 NLRB at 993-994, 94 LRRM at 1102.

19 205 NLRB at 993-994, 84 LRRM at 1101. The dissenting members stated: "[T]his lack of economic pressure is consistent with the thesis that the pickets were merely attempting to talk to management rather than negotiate with management as in *Emporium.*"

20 For a theoretical discussion of why the Board and the courts needn't pursue this course, see Cantor, *supra* n. 12 at 53 et eq.

the underlying rationale of that decision.[21]

At the *United Parcel* decision illustrates, the NLRB is more than willing to proscribe dissident activity even in the absence of express appeals to the public and interference with production.[22] Needless to say, an appeal to the public in the form of a boycott by a dissident minority exerts significant economic pressure on the employer and thus is that much more likely to be condemned by the NLRB. In addition to a finding of interference with the exclusivity principle of Section 9(a), dissident employees also run the risk of a finding that their discharge is valid on grounds of disloyalty. For instance, when handbills disparaging an employer's product with no mention of a labor controversy are distributed, employees can be lawfully discharged.[23] A call for a consumer boycott can also be viewed as a violation of a contractual no-strike provision.[24]

Thus, dissident employees seeking advice before engaging in any activity that could later be construed as economically coercive, should instead be encouraged to pursue intraunion channels and established grievance procedures. It would be exceedingly difficult, if not impossible, to chart a strategy involving picketing and/or leafletting with appeals to the public that would not result in discharge. Although the law is technically unsettled, an employer would probably suppress the dissidents by discharging them as soon as the coercive activity was undertaken. Given the NLRB's propensity to follow vigorously, if not extend, *Emporium*, the employer would have little reason to fear that the dissidents would eventually be reinstated.

However, if the labor practitioner is approached after the dissidents have already engaged in economically coercive activity and

---

21 *See* discussion of *Emporium supra. See also,* 420 U.S. at 67-69.

22 *See* United Parcel, dissenting opinion, 205 NLRB at 993-994.

23 NLRB v. Elec. Workers, 346 U.S. 464 (1953). However, disparagement of the employer's product, if a by-product of a legitimate labor controversy, does not cause an employee to lose Section 7 protection. Circle Bindery, Inc., 218 NLRB 123, 89 LRRM 1421 (1975). *See also,* Eastex, Inc. v. NLRB, 473 U.S. 556, 98 LRRM 2717 (1978)

24 Moore v. Sunbeam Corp., 459 F.2d 811 (7th Cir. 1972). (In this case, the no-strike clause was interpreted to apply to curtailment of all economic warfare. An employee's discharge for picketing and calling for a consumer boycott was therefore upheld.

have been discharged, an attempt could be made to persuade the NLRB to issue a complaint against the employer on the basis of a Section 8(a)(1) violation. An argument could be made that the dissidents were not attempting to bargain, but were merely expressing their opposition to certain employment practices, had not, in fact, rejected the union as their bargaining representative, and were not trying to negotiate with their employer.[25] There is some case law in other areas to support the contention that not all presentations of employee dissatisfaction through picketing involve attempted negotiation.[26] Of course, the success of such an argument will depend on the factual situation at hand.

One could also argue that the dissidents were simply presenting grievances pursuant to Section 9(a) in a demonstrative fashion.[27] However, this argument will probably fail if the dissidents' actions have been economically coercive. The NLRB will no doubt find footnote 12 in *Emporium* controlling,[28] in which the Court rejected the employees' argument that they were only presenting their grievances within the meaning of the first proviso of Section 9(a). The Court reasoned that Section 9(a) cannot be read to "authorize resort to economic coercion."[29]

If the dissidents have protested discriminatory employment practices proscribed by Title VII of the 1964 Civil Rights Act,[30] one can file a charge with the Equal Employment Opportunity Commission (EEOC) or pursue Title VII remedies in federal court.[31] An argument could be presented that Section 704(a) of

---

25 *See* Cantor, *supra* note 14, at 53 et seq.

26 *See* Local 259, UAW, 133 NLRB 1468 (1961) (nonunionized employees who picketed their employer to obtain reinstatement of a discharged employee were not attempting to bargain with their employer or to compel recognition of the group as a labor organization); Shell Chem. Co. v. NLRB, 495 F.2d 1116 (5th Cir. 1974), *cert. denied*, 421 U.S. 963.

27 For discussion of presentation of grievances pursuant to Section 9(a), see notes 42-52 accompanying text.

28 420 U.S. at 50, n. 12 (1975).

29 *Id.*

30 42 U.S.C. § 2000a et seq. (1970), as amended, 42 U.S.C. § 2000a et seq. (Supp. III, 1973).

31 Section 706(b) of the Equal Employment Opportunity Act of 1972, 42 U.S.C. § 2000-e5(b) (Supp. III, 1973), amending 42 U.S.C. § 2000e-5(b) (1970); Section 706 (f)(1) of the Equal Employment Opportunity Act of 1972, 42 U.S.C. § 2000a-5(f)(1).

Title VII was violated when the employees were discharged.[32] Several court and EEOC decisions could be cited to support this contention.[33] However, the precedential value of these decisions is probably limited in light of *Emporium.* It is doubtful that the courts would utilize Title VII to condone economically coercive activity given the Supreme Court's unequivocal relegation of employment discrimination disputes to established collective bargaining channels.

Economic action by dissident unionized employees is clearly frowned upon by the NLRB and the courts. Dissidents are caught in a bind because activity that puts any pressure on the employer (i.e., activity that can be effective) will probably be proscribed by the NLRB as being an attempt to bargain. This holds true even if the dissident's demands support the overall position of the union and do not undercut it. By exaggerating the importance of majoritarian principles, the Court has forced the union to deal with the employer on one front through the channels set up according to the terms of the collective bargaining agreement. The Court has shown that it will not tolerate circumvention of the collective bargaining agreement by a union's back-door use of coercive methods through the actions of its members. Therefore, the dissident unionized employee, whether his or her disagreement with the union is strategic or substantive, must assert a voice in labor-management relations by resorting to intraunion channels or by presenting grievances to the employer within the

[32] Section 704(a) of the Civil Rights Act of 1964, 42 U.S.C. § 2000a-3(a) (1970), as amended, 42 U.S.C. § 2000e-3(a) (Supp. III, 1973). Section 704(a) provides: "It shall be an unlawful employment practice for an employer to discriminate against any of his employees or applicants for employment, for an employment agency, or joint labor management committee controlling apprenticeship or other training or retraining, including on-the-job training programs, to discriminate against any individual, or for a labor organization to discriminate against any member thereof or applicant for membership, *because he has opposed any practice made an unlawful employment practice by this subchapter,* or because he has made a charge, testified, assisted, or participated in any manner in an investigation, proceeding, or hearing under this subchapter." (*emphasis added*).

[33] McDonnell Douglas Corp. v. Green, 411 U.S. 792 (1973); Pettway v. Am. Cast Iron Pipe Co., 411 F.2d 998, 1006 n. 18 (5th Cir. 1969); EEOC Decision No. 71-1804, 1973 CCH EEOC Decisions ¶ 6264 (April 19, 1971); EEOC Decision No. 74-56, 2 CCH Emp. Prac. G. ¶ 6438 (Nov. 16, 1973).

parameters of Section 9(a). Problems associated with the presentation of grievances are examined in § 7.01[3].

[2] Free Speech Rights within the Union

Although *Emporium* presents problems in nonunion concerted activity, dissidents may still legally press through their union for aggressive efforts to remedy the problems.

If there is a contract clause that the dissident can invoke, he or she can file a grievance. Speeches and resolutions at union meetings and letters to union officers can demand prompt, vigorous action (including arbitration) on the grievance. Should the union be inattentive or show signs of violating its duty of fair representation through perfunctory treatment of the grievance, the dissident can picket the union.[34] The dissident can, in all probability, picket the plant if the signs and leaflets make it clear that this is not an effort at economic action against the employer but rather an effort to protest, at a place where the union functions and where the employees involved can be most effectively reached, the failure of the union properly to process the grievance.

If there is no contract provision to invoke, the dissidents can demand that the union obtain such protection by collective bargaining. This effort could utilize all the methods just reviewed. Timing is important because the existing contract may, for its term, define the areas in which the employer can be compelled to bargain, but picketing the union, letters, and leaflets can be used to build up to the time when the contract can be opened for further bargaining.

The rights of dissidents to criticize union officers and union programs are broadly protected under Section 411 of the Labor-Management Reporting and Disclosure Act of 1959 (LMRDA).[35] The explicit and central purpose of this provision is to safeguard the right to "unbridled discussion and criticism of the management of . . . union affairs without fear of being silenced by disciplinary powers of union officials." So crucial are these rights

[34] *See* Samsonite, Massey-Ferguson, McDonnell-Douglas. *See also* 29 U.S.C. § 411(a)(1).

[35] 29 U.SC. § 411(a)(2).

that they extend to expressions that are false and libelous.[36] This provision is designed to achieve "greater democracy within unions"; democracy cannot flourish "where freedom of speech and assembly are hindered by threats of reprisal."[37] The protection accorded by the statute embraces discussion of the fitness of union leaders, their policies, and their administration.[38] The proviso protects criticism of the union and its conduct, which of necessity thrusts at the conduct, policies, and administration of its officers.[39] The protection extends to the act of soliciting members not to pay a tax the union was collecting under circumstances giving good cause to the claim that it was unlawful.[40] Also protected are the holding of meetings and the calling into question of the union's conduct of a strike.[41]

Dissidents should be prepared to exercise these rights and to invoke the statutory protection wholly apart from, but perhaps in conjunction with, the use of picketing of the employer's place of business in order to get a maximum hearing among the persons most directly concerned with the dissidents' message.

[3] The Right to Present Grievances

The first proviso in Section 9(a) preserves the right of an individual employee, or a group of employees, to present grievances to the employer and to have the grievances adjusted without the intervention of the union.[42]

---

[36] Salzhander v. Caputo, 316 F.2d 445, 451 (2d Cir. 1963); Archibald v. Local 57, 276 F. Supp. 323, 329-330 (D. R.I. 1967).

[37] Kuebler v. Cleveland Lithographers, 473 F.2d 359, 364 (6th Cir. 1973).

[38] Semancik v. United Mine Workers, 466 F.2d 144, 153 (3d Cir. 1972).

[39] Giordani v. Upholsterers Int'l Union, 403 F.2d 85, 89 (2d Cir. 1968); Farnum v. Kurtz, 2 Cal. App. 3d Supp. 1 (1969); Pearl v. Tarantola, 361 F. Supp. 288 (S.D.N.Y. 1973).

[40] Farowitz v. Associated Musicians, 330 F.2d 999, 1002 (2d Cir. 1964).

[41] Farnum v. Katz, *supra;* Kuebler v. Cleveland Lithographers, *supra.*

[42] Section 9(a) of the NLRA, 29 U.S.C. § 159(a) (1970), provides: "Representatives designated or selected for the purposes of collective bargaining by the majority of the employees in a unit appropriate for such purposes, shall be the exclusive representatives of all the employees in such unit for the purposes of collective bargaining in respect to rates of pay, wages, hours of employment, or other conditions of employment: *Provided,* that any individual employee or a

Certain requirements must be satisfied before any activity will be construed as within the ambit of Section 9(a). First, one must be presenting a grievance, i.e., a dispute relating to the meaning or proper application of a collective bargaining agreement already in effect.[43] A major dispute pertaining to the acquisition of future rights is not the proper subject of a grievance and thus does not fall under Section 9(a).[44] For example, one court held that the fixing of wages and rates of pay was not the proper subject of a grievance because a grievance refers to a secondary dispute, not one concerning a broad issue, such as wage rates.[45] Second, an individual employee or a group of employees cannot obtain an adjustment of a grievance that is inconsistent with the collective bargaining agreement in effect. Thus, in *Ingalls Shipbuilding Corp.*,[46] an adjusted grievance was set aside because the employer had given the grievants rights that had been sacrificed by the union during negotiations.[47]

In addition to the foregoing considerations, the courts have not viewed the "right" to present grievances in Section 9(a) as a right at all. Instead, it has been characterized as a privilege to approach the employer.[48] Once the grievance has been communicated to

---

group of employees shall have the right at any time to present grievances to their employer and to have such grievances adjusted, without the intervention of the bargaining representative, as long as the adjustment is not inconsistent with the terms of a collective-bargaining contract or agreement then in effect: Provided further, that the bargaining representative has been given opportunity to be present at such adjustment."

[43] Elgin, J. & E. Ry., v. Burley, 325 U.S. 711 (1945).

[44] *Id.*

[45] W. Texas Util. Co. v. NLRB, 206 F.2d 442 (D.C. Cir. 1953), *cert. denied*, 346 U.S. 855 (1953).

[46] 143 NLRB 712 (1963).

[47] In *Ingalls*, the NLRB held that an employer violated Section 8(a)(5) when it reinstituted wage incentives. The employer had restored the incentives when a dissident group had approached it on the subject. The incentives had originally been eliminated pursuant to an agreement with the union.

[48] Black-Clawson Co. v. Machinists, 313 F.2d 179 (2d Cir. 1962) (the court said that the proviso on Section 9(a) was merely intended to safeguard the employer who voluntarily processed an individual's grievance not taken up by the union from unfair labor practice charges).

An employer cannot fire employees for filing grievances on behalf of themselves or others as this is protected concerted activity, NLRB v. Quality Mfg. Co., 481 F.2d 1018 (4th Cir. 1973), *rev'd on other grounds*, 420 U.S. 276 (1975).

the employer, the employer is under no obligation to entertain it.[49] In *Emporium,* the Supreme Court expressly stated that dissidents may not undertake economically coercive tactics in support of the presentation of grievances.[50] Thus, it is clear that Section 9(a) cannot be utilized by dissidents who desire to do more than communicate their grievances to management.[51]

In reference to communicating grievances and publicizing their existence within the plant, one Seventh Circuit case may provide an argument for protection of dissidents who present grievances and engage in concerted activity not economically coercive in nature. In *Dreis and Krump Manufacturing Co. v. NLRB,*[52] the union had filed a grievance on behalf of an employee. Several weeks later, but before the grievance was resolved, the employee distributed copies of a leaflet to fellow employees at the entrance of the company parking lot to call attention to his grievance. The leaflet stated that the grievance, which involved a supervisor who was careless about worker safety, concerned all workers. The employee was fired for distributing the leaflet. The Seventh Circuit affirmed the NLRB's ruling that the discharge was violative of Section 7. The court found that the employee's conduct was concerted within the meaning of Section 7 and that it served to complement, rather than circumvent, the established grievance procedure. The *Emporium* decision was distinguished on the grounds that the employess in *Emporium* had sought to exert economic pressure to compel separate bargaining and had acted contrary to their union's advice.

On the basis of *Dreis,* one could argue that leafletting by a dissident minority seeking employee support in the presentation of grievances is permissible in the absence of economic coercion or a demand to bargain. However, the employee in *Dreis* did enjoy the support of his union in the prosecution of his grievance. The NLRB may be reluctant to extend *Dreis* to situations in which the

---

[49] Black-Clawson Co. v. Machinists, 313 F.2d 179 (2d Cir. 1962); Emporium Capwell Co. v. W. Addition Community Organization, 420 U.S. 50, n. 12 (1975).

[50] Emporium, 420 U.S. 50. n. 12 (1975). *See* notes 9-13 and accompanying text, *supra.*

[51] Communicating grievances to management often means nothing more than talking to the department foreman. Black-Clawson, 313 F.2d 179, 183.

[52] 544 F.2d 320, 93 LRRM 2739 (7th Cir. 1976).

union refused to process the grievance. At any rate, the labor law practitioner should be aware that the question of non-economically coercive dissident activity in support of the presentation of grievances has not been conclusively resolved.[53]

In conclusion, caucus concerted activity at the workplace, whether economically coercive or more akin to simply expression of dissident employees' dissatisfaction in conjunction with the direct presentation of grievances to the employer, is not really a viable legal tactic at this time. Union exclusivity has become a fundamental tenet of the collective bargaining process; consequently, dissidents must ultimately resort to intraunion channels to exert a sustained influence on the labor relations process.

§ 7.02. Independent Participation in Grievance/Arbitration

One of the most common problems facing the rank-and-file union activist is how to assert his/her rights in the grievance/arbitration procedure independent of his/her union. The problem must be considered in the context of a possibly bureaucratic, unresponsive, or hostile union leadership that may attempt to suppress the just demands of its members.[54] The problem arises in the following three ways: (1) The union leadership refuses to arbitrate a case, and the grievant seeks to force it to do so. (2) The union leadership is politically at odds with the grievant and cannot be expected to represent him/her adequately. (3) The compa-

---

[53] *See* Section 7.02[1], *infra.*

[54] In some contexts, circumventing union leadership can be a tool of reactionaries within and outside the union or of members who merely seek to advance their own personal interests over the collective, e.g., in seniority or promotion disputes. For the purposes of this subsection, however, we will assume that those who seek independent participation are acting out of a motive to make the union more responsive to collective needs. Also, circumventing established channels for redress of grievances has been vitally important to black and other minority union members. There is a long history of failure to respond—and in many cases active support of Jim Crow—on the part of union leadership, which has forced blacks to seek other avenues. *See generally,* Phillip Foner, Organized Labor and the Black Workers (International Publishers, New York, 1974). *See also* Alexander v. Gardner-Denver Co., 415 U.S. 36 (1974).

ny and the union agree on the issue presented, and the grievant is the only party in controversy with the company.

The present law in this area is most unfavorable to the dissident activist. The incumbent union is considered the sole representative of its membership in enforcing the contract.[55] A union member cannot generally participate in grievance/arbitration unless his/her union permits it. His/her recourse is to elect other leadership or to file internal union charges against the offending union officals.[56]

Despite the negative state of the law, union members continue to come to progressive lawyers for advice on how to enforce their rights under the contract independent of the union. The practitioner, in devising arguments in support of this position, should look to three sources of law: (1) the duty of fair representation, (2) Section 9(a) of the NLRA, and (3) hostility between the union leadership and the grievant or absence of controversy between the union and the company.

[1] The Duty of Fair Representation

This duty itself covers the entire collective bargaining agreement, as well as the process of collective bargaining itself.[57] Violations of the duty of fair representation are usually charged if the union (1) arbitrarily fails to arbitrate a case, (2) arbitrates a case, but merely goes through the motions, or (3) in handling the case,

---

[55] Emporium Capwell Co. v. W. Addition Community Organization, 420 U.S. 50 (1975). *See generally* Section 7.02[3], *infra.*

[56] Most union bylaws and constitutions require a member to file internal union charges before taking legal action. *See, e.g.,* By-laws of Local Union 1011, United Steelworkers of America, AFL-CIO (Youngstown Sheet & Tube, East Chicago, Ind.) Article IX, Discipline: Section 1: "Any member may be penalized for committing any one or more of the following offenses: . . . . (c) instituting, or urging, or advocating that a member of any Local Union institute action outside the Union against the International Union, Labor Union or any of their officers without first exhausting all remedies through the forms of appeal of the International Union." *But see also* Title I, Section 101(4) of the Landrum-Griffin Act, 29 U.S.C. § 411(a), which puts a four-month time limit on a member's duty to exhaust internal procedures and also protects the member's right to sue.

[57] *See generally* Julia Penny Clar, *The Duty of Fair Representation: A Theoretical Structure,* 51 Tex. L. Rev. 1119 (1973).

does something else that indicates conduct ranging from bad faith to perfunctory treatment.[58]

Alleged violations of the duty of fair representation are most often raised in a Section 301 suit brought by the individual union member against the company for breach of the contract that formed the basis of the contested grievance. For the contract issue to be reached, the plaintiff must demonstrate that the grievance/ arbitration procedure set out in the contract has been exhausted and/or that the union has breached its duty of fair representation.[59] Thus, if a union has refused to arbitrate a discharge case, for instance, the plaintiff must prove that the refusal had no reasonable basis and/or was done in bad faith by the defendant union.[60]

The result is that in a case in which the union has declined to arbitrate a case and a breach of the duty of fair representation is found, a court is inclined to order that the case be arbitrated by the parties and to retain jurisdiction pending the decision of the arbitrator.[61] Courts are also inclined to order that the plaintiff be permitted to obtain his/her own representative (usually a lawyer) and to participate independently of the union.[62] The reason is obvious: there is already enough ill will between the union leadership and the plaintiff as the result of the suit to render the union incapable of representing him fairly and adequately. There is a developing body of law that allows courts to review allegations of procedural irregularities in arbitration proceedings, including

---

[58] *See, e.g.,* Vaca v. Sipes, 386 U.S. 171 (1962); Savel v. Detroit News, 435 F. Supp. 329 (D.C.Mich. 1977); Baldini v. Local Union No. 1095, 435 F. Supp. 264 (D.C.Ind. 1977); Hershman v. Sierra Pac. Power Co., 434 F. Supp. 46 (D.C.Nev. 1977).

[59] Section 301, 29 U.S.C. § 185(a) reads: "Suits for violation of contracts between an employer and a labor organization representing employees in an industry affecting commerce as defined in this Act, or between any such labor organizations, may be brought in any district court of the United States having jurisdiction of the parties, without respect to the amount in controversy or without regard to the citizenship of the parties." *See also* Republic Steel Corp. v. Maddox, 379 U.S. 650 (1965).

[60] Clark, *supra;* Simpson & Berwick, *Exhaustion of Grievance Procedures and the Individual Employee,* 51 Tex. L. Rev. 1201 (1973).

[61] Mitchell v. Hercules Inc., 410 F. Supp. 560 (S.D. Ga. 1976).

[62] *Id.*

inadequate representation.[63] This law provides a basis for the court to fashion relief, including independent participation to ensure fairness.

It is not easy to prove a violation of the duty of fair representation, especially if the case has been arbitrated and the claim of such violation arises from union misconduct at the hearing.[64] On the other hand, these suits are a nuisance and very costly to unions. Thus, union legal advisors often tell the union leadership to bend over backwards to prevent allegations of violations of the duty of fair representation in the grievance/arbitration procedure.[65] This often may mean that a demand to bring an independent representative to arbitration is granted by the union leadership.

[2] Section 9(a) of the NLRA

Another possible source of law for the union member seeking independent participation in grievance/arbitration is the proviso at the end of Section 9(a) of the NLRA:

> Representatives designated or selected for the purposes of collective bargaining by the majority of the employees in a unit appropriate for such purposes, shall be the exclusive representatives of all the employees in such unit for the purposes of collective bargaining in respect to rates of pay, wages, hours of employment, or other conditions of employment: *provided, That any individual employee or a group of employees shall have the right at any time to present grievances to*

---

63 *See, e.g.,* Bethlehem Steel Corp. v. Fennie, 55 A.D.2d 1007, 391 N.Y.S.2d 227, 95 LRRM 2099 (1977); Teamsters, Local 11 v. Abad t/a Gen. Grocery Warehouse Co., 144 N.J. Super. 239, 365 A.2d 209, 93 LRRM 2791 (1976).

64 *See, e.g.,* Hardee v. N.C. Allstate Servs. Inc., 92 LRRM 3342 (4th Cir. 1976); Warren v. Teamsters, 92 LRRM 2734 (8th Cir. 1976); Siskey v. Teamsters, Local 261, 419 F. Supp. 48, 93 LRRM 2200 (D.C. Pa. 1976).

65 *See, e.g.,* the comments of Lester Asher of the law firm of Asher, Greenfield, Gubbins & Segal (Chicago), reported at the Proceedings of the 23rd Annual Meeting, National Academy of Arbitration, at 31-38. Mr. Asher, whose firm represents a number of local unions in the Chicago area, states quite candidly that he advises his clients to let a member bring whomever s/he wants to an arbitration hearing as a representative. The reason he cites is the fear of duty of fair representation suits.

their employer and to have such grievance adjusted, as long as the adjustment is not inconsistent with the terms of a collective-bargaining contract or agreement then in effect: Provided further, That the bargaining representative has been given opportunity to be present at such adjustment.[66] (emphasis added).

This language was originally designed and used to inhibit effective unionism.[67] Most of the cases in this area deal with the right of an employee not to be discharged for presenting grievances directly to the employer.[68] Only a few deal with a member's right to carry a grievance by himself/herself through the entire grievance procedure, including arbitration.

In *Mitchell v. Hercules, Inc.*,[69] a union member sued the company for wrongful discharge and other relief. The court held that there was a factual issue as to whether the refusal to arbitrate amounted to a violation of the union's duty of fair representation and, on that ground, denied the company's motion for summary judgment. Instead of scheduling a hearing on the issue, however, the court ordered the plaintiff to present a request for arbitration to the company. The court's order was not based on Section 9(a); indeed, it found that most of the authorities did not interpret Section 9(a) as permitting an individual to process a grievance by himself/herself absent specific contractual language to that effect.[70] In this case, the court found that the contract did authorize the union member to request arbitration *pro se.* As a corollary, the court held that the member would be entitled to use his own representative or proceed *pro se* in front of the arbitrator.[71]

There are other cases in which courts or arbitrators have relied

---

[66] 29 U.S.C. § 159(a).

[67] *See* 1947 U.S. Code Cong. Serv. p. 1135; NLRB v. Sands Mfg. Co., 306 U.S. 332 (1939); NLRB v. Jones & Laughlin Steel Corp., 310 U.S. 1 (1937).

[68] *See e.g.*, NLRB v. Union Pac. Stages, 99 F.2d 153, (C.C.A. 1938); NLRB v. Lundy Mfg. Corp., 316 F.2d 921 (2d Cir. 1963), *cert. denied*, 375 U.S. 895.

[69] 410 F. Supp. 560 (S.D. Ga. 1976).

[70] 410 F. Supp. at 570.

[71] 410 F. Supp. at 571. The *Mitchell* decision also held that the plaintiff, in order to exhaust his contractual remedies, had to make his own demand on the company for arbitration. The practitioner should therefore advise his client to do this even absent clear contractual authority for independent prosecution of grievances.

on Section 9(a) as authority for independent participation.[72] Their number is limited, however, and it will be some time before courts and arbitrators will routinely order independent participation absent contractual language to that effect.

[3] Member-Union Hostility; Absence of Controversy between Company and Union

Often, there is so much subjective antagonism (or objective conflict of interest) between a grievant and his/her union representatives that it can be predicted with reasonable certainty that the grievant will not obtain adequate representation. This is especially true if the issue concerns exactly which part of a bargaining unit is to receive a contract benefit (e.g., new work, seniority, etc.). On other occasions, the union representatives will agree with the company on the issue presented, and the individual grievant will be the sole party at issue with the company. These fact situations compromise the adversary nature of arbitration; thus, courts and the NLRB have felt justified in ordering independent participation as an antidote.

Clark v. Hein Werner Corp.[73] is the leading case on the right of independent participation on the ground of objective grievant-union antagonism. In that case, the issue was whether supervisory personnel who had been returned to nonsupervisory jobs have continuous service running from the time they were made supervisors. Naturally, the bargaining unit members were opposed to

---

[72] Donnelly v. United Fruit Co., 40 N.J. 61, 190 A.2d 825 (1963). This case is relied upon by the *Mitchell* court, 410 F. Supp. at 569, as authority for the proposition that an employee is entitled to carry through a grievance to arbitration by himself/herself if the union refuses. However, its force is somewhat blunted by language in Vaca v. Sipes, 386 U.S. 171, 185-86 (1962), that explicitly states that even where a contract authorizes independent prosecution of grievances, national labor policy requires that the union be the sole representative. *See also* Hillner v. Liquor Salesmen's Union, 55 LRRM 2310, 226 F.Supp. 161 (S.D.N.Y. 1964), *rev'd,* 338 F.2d 778 (2d Cir. 1964). The district court allowed independent participation, but the Second Circuit reversed, holding that Section 9(a) requires the company to arbitrate a case only with the union. This reading of Section 9(a) appears to be indefensibly narrow.

[73] 8 Wis. 2d 264, 99 N.W.2d 132 (1959), *rehearing denied,* 8 Wis. 2d 264, 100 N.W.2d 317, *cert. denied,* 362 U.S. 962 (1960).

the idea. The union filed a grievance on behalf of the bargaining unit members. As the result of their demotion, the ex-supervisors had become union members. However, the union leadership failed to notify them of the time and place of the arbitration hearing. The union won the arbitration, and the former supervisors filed an action in state court. On appeal, the Supreme Court of Wisconsin held that the union had violated its fiduciary duty to the former supervisors by not notifying them of the arbitration and thus not permitting them to intervene. The court held, in pertinent part:

> However, where the interests of two groups of employees are diametrically opposed to each other and the union espouses the case of one in the arbitration, it follows as a matter of law that there has been no fair representation of the other group. This is true even though, in choosing the cause of which group to espouse, the union acts completely objectively and with the best of motives. The old adage, that one cannot serve two masters, is particularly applicable to such a situation.[74]

This decision has been criticized. The case most often cited as contrary authority is *Ford Motor Co. v. Huffman.*[75] In that case, the Supreme Court, faced with conflicting seniority claims similar to those in *Clark,* held that majority rule should prevail. In other words, the union leadership is immune from liability for violation of the duty of fair representation if it makes a reasonable decision as to which of two or more conflicting bargaining unit interests to espouse at an arbitration. The clear implication is that unrepresented groups have no right to independent participation.

In *Maier Brewing Co.,*[76] the arbitrator permitted the grievant to be represented by his own counsel and to participate fully in the proceeding upon a finding that the union and the employer were in agreement concerning the grievance. The grievance involved long-haul truck driver rates. The union representatives and the company had entered into a local agreement setting the rates. The

---

[74] 8 Wis. 2d at 272. *Accord,* In re Iroquois Beverage Corp., 14 Misc.2d 290, 159 N.Y.S.2d 256, 28 L.A. 906 (1955); Soto v. Lenscraft Optical Corp., 7 A.D.2d 1, 180 N.Y.S.2d 388, 31 L.A. 715 (1958).

[75] 345 U.S. 330 (1953).

[76] 49 L.A. 14 (1967).

grievant, therefore, was the only party who had a dispute with the company as to the rates. Although it is almost certain that other cases such as *Maier Brewing Co.* have arisen, none of these cases appear to have been reported.[77] Perhaps many such cases have been settled informally by granting some form of independent participation to the grievant.

[4] Practitioner Recommendations

Although the three principles—duty of fair representation, Section 9(a), and grievant-union hostility—are separate sources of law, in practice they are invoked in overlapping fashion. Accordingly, the practitioner should rely on all three until such time as one of these principles has developed as the primary authority for independent participation.

A union member seeking independent participation should preserve that request either by letter or by making a record somewhere during the course of the grievance/arbitration procedure. A separate request should also be made to the company for arbitration (if the union refuses to take the case to arbitration) or for independent participation.[78] Unless the request is granted by the company and the union, another request should be made to the arbitrator at the hearing. Arguments in favor of independent participation are stronger in conflicting seniority cases, in cases in which different sectors of the bargaining unit are in competition for contract benefits, and if it is apparent that the union really does not disagree with the company and is just going through the motions, confident that its position will be upheld by the arbitrator. The most difficult cases will be the common discharge cases, in which, despite demonstrable hostility to the grievant, the union can argue that it will make a good faith effort to represent the dischargee. Also, it is obvious that an arbitrator—who is, after all, selected by the company and the union, not by the grievant—

[77] Neither the L.A. nor the LRRM Digest system report any similar cases. See Digest headings §§ 94.553, 94.59 and 94.80. Arbitrations have been terminated by agreement of the parties if the arbitrator granted a right of participation to the grievant.

[78] *See* discussion of this tactic in notes 71 and 72.

will be loath to compromise his/her position with his/her "employers" unless a clear-cut case for independent participation is presented to him/her.

The difficult cases must be taken either to state or federal court via a Section 301 suit. The cases teach that it is sometimes beneficial to file before the arbitration in the hope that the court will order independent participation. Of course, the grievant still faces the formidable task of proving a violation of the union's duty of fair representation, which might entitle him or her to independent participation in the ensuing arbitration.

§ 7.03. Law of Rival Union Organizing

Labor organizations have repeatedly fought one another for collective bargaining agent status. The most significant competitions have involved progressive unions and their reactionary rivals. The old AFL and the CIO (and their predecessors) competed for status in the late twenties, thirties, and forties.[79] The United Electrical Workers and the International Electrical Union Workers fought many battles in the late forties.[80] The Teamsters and the UFW locked horns in the late sixties and seventies until peace was imposed by the AFL-CIO. More often than not, the reactionary rival—or the union that objectively was doing the work of management—prevailed. Progressive unionists are not without defenses, however. This section is an attempt to summarize some of the more common legal defenses.[81]

---

[79] *See generally* Richard O. Boyer & Herbert M. Morais, Labor's Untold Story (United Electrical, Radio and Machine Workers of America, N.Y., 1955), pp. 329-65; James J. Matles & James Higgins, Them and Us (Beacon Press, Boston, 1974) pp. 153-244.

[80] *See generally* William Z. Foster, American Trade Unionism (Int'l Publishers, N.Y., 1947), pp. 62-80, 143-85.

[81] An uncommon legal defense to rival organizing has been the use of antitrust laws against a pattern of employer conduct involving use of a company union or a compliant union. *See* Heat & Frost Insulators v. United Contractors, 483 F.2d 384 (1973); Carpenters Dist. Council v. United Contractors, 484 F.2d 119 (1973). An antitrust complaint filed by the United Farm Workers (UFW) against the Teamsters and various growers alleging treble damages of $84 million was settled after five years of protracted litigation to the benefit of the UFW. For discussion of this case and the general use of antitrust in this setting

The problem varies according to the historical period. When the progressive CIO unions were incumbents in many sections of basic industry, employers, the government and the right wing of the CIO conspired to oust them.[82] Today, when lack of organization in the South significantly impedes the labor movement, employers frequently use the device of the "independent" union to avoid recognition of an international union. There is a seemingly endless array of tactics available to the employer.

The practitioner will most frequently be called upon to (1) block an election bid by a rival union to oust a progressive incumbent, (2) take legal action against an employer who has unlawfully withdrawn recognition from an incumbent and recognized and executed a contract with a rival union, (3) take legal action against an employer who is attempting to keep a progressive union from replacing the "independent" it has already recognized, or (4) provide legal protection for a union during an NLRB election.

[1] Avoiding an Election

There are two basic scenarios here. In the first, an employer senses that an incumbent is losing its majority status and peti-

---

of rival union organizing where employer collaboration is present, *see* John T. McTernan, Anti-Trust and Labor Relations: Union Concerns, 12th Annual Pacific Labor Law Conference, Seattle, Wash., 1979.

[82] Matles & Higgins, *supra,* at pp. 153-244. In 1946, there were massive strikes in the steel, auto, and electrical industries. These strikes were highly successful because of the unity of the CIO. Management and its allies set out to destroy this unity. One tactic was the passage of the Taft-Hartley Act. Another was Red-baiting the CIO. Among other things, Taft-Hartley required officers of local unions to sign affidavits that they were not communists. Any local union whose officers failed to do so could not participate in an NLRB election. In addition, the Act permitted employers to petition for elections. The electrical industry union, the UE, refused to have its officers sign the affidavits. Phillip Murray, the head of the CIO, decided that the CIO would, and the UE left the CIO. As a result, Murray called into being a "dual" union, the IUE, and sent messages to employers where the UE was recognized asking them to cease dealing with the UE. In concert with Murray, the big electrical manufacturers petitioned for NLRB elections. As the local UE officers had not signed the affidavits, they were barred from the election. As a result, the IUE replaced the UE in many places.

tions the NLRB for an election as authorized by Section 9(a)(ii) of the Act.[83] In so doing, the employer commits myriad unfair labor practices, usually in the process of setting up a "rival" union to take the place of the incumbent. In the second, when an outside union petitions for a certification election, the employer commits several unfair labor practices in attempting to prop up the "independent" incumbent. In both cases, the usual tactics are to file a "blocking" unfair labor practice charge with the NLRB.

[a] Technical Requirements

The NLRB recognizes six types of election petitions.[84] For the purposes of this subsection only four are relevant: certification (RC), employer filed (RM), decertification (RD), and withdrawal of union shop authority (UD). Except for the UD election, all of them are governed by the same rules, i.e., certain technical requirements must be satisfied before the NLRB will order an election.

The Act requires that an election be conducted only when a "question concerning representation" (QCR) arises.[85] The question may be raised by the employer (RM), a union (RC), or an individual (RD). The technical requirements to be satisfied before an election will be ordered are the certification rule, the contract bar rule, the showing of interest rule, and the election bar rule. The first line of defense against a "raiding" rival union, then, is to convince the NLRB that one or more of these conditions have not been satisfied.

---

[83] 29 U.S.C. § 159(c)(A)(ii).

[84] *See generally* NLRB Field Manual (rev. ed., June 1971).

[85] NLRB certification is not an absolute requirement. An employer can recognize a union without an election, so long as no rivals present themselves and there is clearly no question that the union has a majority. However, after the passage of the Taft-Hartley Act in 1947, employers found it increasingly easy not to bargain with a union by asserting "good faith doubt" as to the union's majority. The Supreme Court, in NLRB v. Gissel Packing Co., 395 U.S. 575, 603 (1969), in effect rendered irrelevant the "good faith doubt" standard as a consideration and expressly relegated the card check to a status "admitted inferior" to the NLRB-conducted election. *See also* Linden Lumber Division, Summer & Co. v. NLRB, 419 U.S. 301 (1974).

The NLRB has established the doctrine that a current and valid contract will ordinarily prevent it from holding an election, but the doctrine is complex. Stated roughly, the rule is that a rival petition must be filed no more than ninety and no less than sixty-one days before the expiration date of the existing contract (called the "window" period). A post-expiration petition may be filed if the company and the incumbent union do not reach an agreement within sixty days (provided, of course, that the employer is not guilty of any unfair labor practice, e.g., refusal to bargain). The rule applies to any contract of less than three years' duration. Contracts executed within sixty days prior to the contract expiration date (called the "insulated" period) will bar election petitions unless filed in the window period. The company and the incumbent union cannot rely on agreements to renew the contract automatically if either party wishes to change any term thereof. Contracts that discriminate on racial lines will never bar an election petition.[86] Of course, collusion by the employer and the incumbent union to manipulate the rule will be grounds for an unfair labor practice charge.

The election bar rule simply forecloses an election until at least twelve months have elapsed since the preceding unsuccessful election. Elections that have been overturned because of objections filed do not bar new elections. As a matter of policy, the NLRB considers any contract executed during the certification year a bar to rival petitions during its term, up to a maximum of three years.[87]

The certification bar rule is essentially the same as the election bar rule, except that it applies if the union won the election; it can be extended for more than a year if the employer engages in bad faith bargaining.

For certification (RC), decertification (RD), and withdrawal of union shop authority (UD) petitions, the NLRB requires the petitioner to show that at least 30 percent of the members of the bargaining unit have unequivocally demonstrated that they sup-

---

[86] Pioneer Bus Co., NLRB 1962, 51 LRRM 1546 ("Execution of such a contract 'is in patent derogation' of the union's certification and 'would warrant revocation of the certification"). *See also* Cent. Cal. Ice Co., 1949, 85 NLRB 1205.

[87] *See, e.g.,* Cent. Cal. Ice Co., 85 NLRB 1205, 24 LRRM 1274 (1949).

port the petition.[88] This is usually accomplished by the use of authorization cards. Prior to the Taft-Hartley Act, an employer could file only if confronted with recognition demands from two or more unions. The Act gives the employer the right to file a representation (RM) petition if there are objective considerations leading the employer to believe the union has lost its majority.

The place to raise challenges to an election—election bar, contract bar, showing of interest, bargaining unit—is at the preelection hearing. While the hearing is essentially a fact-finding process, it is the place where opposing points of view can be aired. For instance, even though the employer's RM petition is not subject to the showing of interest requirement, it must nevertheless show reasonable grounds for believing that the incumbent has lost its majority status.[89] Sometimes a representation hearing is consolidated with an unfair labor practice hearing, especially if the same parties are involved and the same facts must be determined in both cases.

[b] Blocking Charges

The second line of defense is the filing of the so-called blocking unfair labor practice charge.[90] Typically the employer, in attempting to oust a troublesome incumbent union, will be guilty of a Section 8(a)(5) violation. The incumbent union is well advised to file an unfair labor practice charge immediately. Likewise, if an outside union is launching an organizing compaign to oust an "independent" incumbent union, an unfair labor practice charge should be filed at the first sign of employer or rival union misconduct. With certain exceptions, a pending unfair labor practice charge will block any of the four election petitions (RC, RM, RD, and UD).

The blocking charge procedure is embodied in the NLRB's

---

88 *See generally* for types of election petitions NLRB Field Manual (rev. ed., June 1971).

89 Gissel, *supra,* at pp. 595-600.

90 *See generally* 18 ALR Fed. 420 (unremedied unfair labor practice charge against party to NLRB election as ground for postponing election ("blocking charge" procedure)).

Field Manual.[91] Specifically, the doctrine will be invoked if there are concurrent representation (R) and unfair labor practice (C) cases pending, provided that the R case involves a charge under Section 8(a)(2), Section 8(a)(5), Section 8(b)(3), or Section 8(b)(7). When the C case is disposed of, the R case will be "unblocked," and the election can proceed. In addition, the charging party can file a request to proceed or can withdraw the unfair labor practice charge if it wishes the election to go forward. The latter procedure is sometimes used by an outside union if it thinks it can win an election despite the employer's unfair labor practices. If the election is lost after a request to proceed has been filed, the union may still claim that the unfair labor practice requires that the election be overturned.

Late-filed unfair labor practice charges will not be considered blocking, as many courts have commented on the potential for abuse of this procedure,[92] although the regional director has the discretion to block the election, or hold it and impound the ballots in certain cases. Thus, as long as the unfair labor practice charge(s) is a viable one, an election can be blocked until the NLRB disposes of it. And, as noted above, representation and unfair labor practice proceedings are often consolidated, expediting disposition of blocking charges.

[2] Employer Recognition of an "Independent" Union

If there is no incumbent union, an employer often attempts to avoid a representation election by unilaterally recognizing an "independent" union. Very often, these "independents" are creations of management and, thus, are vulnerable to Section 8(a)(2) unfair labor practice charges.

In a Texas case, the company hastily recognized a union called the "Independent Employees Union of Packerland" when it was notified that the Amalgamated Meat Cutters and Butcher Workers Union (AMCBW) was about to petition for an election.[93] Not

---

[91] Section 11730.

[92] 18 ALR Fed. 420 at § 19, for collected cases.

[93] NLRB v. Packerland Packing Co. of Texas, 537 F.2d 1343, 93 LRRM 2128 (5th Cir. 1976).

only did the company recognize this "union"; it also negotiated and executed a three-year contract with it, all in the space of two and one-half hours. Not surprisingly, the NLRB and the 5th Circuit found that this conduct violated the LMRA. However, the legal process took three years, and it is very likely that the employer accomplished its objective of keeping the union out.

The settled rule is that unless the employer can show that no real question of representation exists, it will have violated the *Midwest Piping*[94] rule. The case held that an employer confronted with conflicting claims of two or more rival unions giving rise to a real question concerning representation may not recognize one of the rivals until its right to represent employees has been established in an NLRB election. This rule is now strictly enforced.

Another non-election tactic open to an employer is to attempt to undermine recognition based on authorization cards. This often happens when the incumbent is an "independent" created when the company began and an outside union has launched a rival organizational campaign.[95] The employer may also call meetings and interrogate the employees when it learns an outside union is soliciting cards,[96] or it may refuse to bargain with the incumbent or newly certified union and instead urge its employees to form an "independent" union.[97] Moreover, the employer may just decide not to bargain with the incumbent union, hoping thus to undermine its majority status and instigate a decertification petition from its employees. However, the incumbent union is entitled to a presumption of majority status, which may be rebutted only by an affirmative showing that (1) the union in fact no longer enjoys majority status or (2) the employer has a "good faith and reasonable doubt" of the union's actual

---

94 Midwest Piping Supply Co., 63 NLRB 1060, 17 LRRM 40 (1945). For an exception, *see also* Buck Knives v. NLRB, 549 F.2d 1319, 94 LRRM 2813 (9th Cir. 1977).

95 *See, e.g.,* Huskey Mfg., Inc., 196 NLRB 683, 80 LRRM 1215 (1972); Distribution Centers of Detroit, Inc., Subsidiary of Distribution Centers, Inc., 197 NLRB 1, 80 LRRM 1257 (1972).

96 Ring Metals Co., 198 NLRB 143, 81 LRRM 1001 (1972).

97 Am. Bldg. Components Co., 203 NLRB 811, 83 LRRM 1297 (1973). However, not all interrogation is violative of the Act.

majority.[98] All these tactics are unlawful, and a bargaining order may eventually issue. However, the employer gains precious time in which to dissipate union strength, at practically no cost. The practitioner will be left with the familiar NLRB unfair labor practice remedies. The best defense, however, is an energetic and dedicated union that can retain the loyalty of a majority of the workers during the time it takes to obtain relief.

[3] The Election

The NLRB has exclusive power not only to decide whether an election should be held in a particular bargaining unit but also to conduct the election at whatever time and in whatever manner it sees fit. Thus, an NLRB order in an election case is not subject to judicial review, unless (1) that order happens to be the basis of an unfair labor practice case that is before the court or (2) the NLRB's action is arbitrary and capricious. However, the employer can test the NLRB's certification by refusing to bargain and by appealing the Section 8(a)(5) charge to the Court of Appeals.

Once the election is scheduled, the practitioner's role is to detect and record unfair labor practices committed by the employer and the rival unions and to seek redress either by a post-election challenge or by unfair labor practice charges.

The rules governing employer activity during an election have changed dramatically since the passage of the Taft-Hartley Act in 1947, particularly during the early 1950s.[99] Before 1941, the NLRB usually held that an anti-union statement made by an employer during an organizational campaign was coercive *per se*.[100] The NLRB felt that, since an employer speaks from a position of weight and authority, any anti-union statements by the employer were bound to be interpreted as threats to an employee's job and thus were forbidden. In 1941, the Supreme Court modified this *per se* approach, allowing the employer a limited

[98] *See* note 85, *supra*.

[99] *See generally* Bernard T. King, *Pre-Election Conduct—Expanding Employer Rights and Some New and Renewed Perspectives*, 2 Ind. Rel. L. J. 185 (Summer 1977).

[100] *See, e.g.*, Citizen-News Co., 21 NLRB 1112 (1940), *enforcement denied*, 134 F.2d 962 (9th Cir. 1943); Rockford Mitten & Hosiery Co., 16 NLRB 501 (1939).

right to express anti-union views.[101] The Taft-Hartley Act permitted employer "free speech" absent threat of reprisal or force or promise of benefit.[102] The NLRB has recently relaxed the rule against employer pre-election interrogation of employees.[103] Generally speaking, there has been a shift by the NLRB from *per se* to "context" rules as to employer speech and conduct.[104] This shift has found a rationale in the so-called Getman Study, which recommends that the NLRB remove itself from certification elections to an even greater extent.[105] In addition, employers now have an ever-expanding pool of anti-union "professionals" from which to draw for help in winning elections.[106]

After a brief interlude, the NLRB recently returned to its earlier position—that it would set aside elections on the basis of misleading campaign statements.[107] A misrepresentation, whether deliberate or not, that involves substantial departure from the truth and occurs at a time that prevents rebuttal by the opposition may be expected to have an effect on the election; consequently the NLRB will set aside the election.[108]

The fact that propaganda statements by employers, either written or oral, are not in themselves coercive and do not, there-

---

[101] NLRB v. Va. Elec. & Power Co., 314 U.S. 469 (1941).

[102] Taft-Hartley Act, Pub. L. No. 101, 61 Stat. 136 (1947) codified at 29 U.S.C. §§ 141-87 (1970 & Supp. V. 1975). § 8(c).

[103] *See* Rock Island Franciscan Hosp., 226 NLRB 46, 94 LRRM 1048 (1976); NVF Co., Hartwell Div., 210 NLRB 663, 86 LRRM 1200 (1974) (small group interrogation); Jerome J. Jacomet, 222 NLRB 899, n.1, 91 LRRM 1370 (1976) (polling just before election day).

[104] *See* Airporter Inn Hotel, 215 NLRB 824, 88 LRRM 1032 (1974), *overruling* Trojan Battery Co., 207 NLRB 425, 84 LRRM 1619 (1973) (statement advising employees not to sign authorization cards); Computer Peripherals, Inc., 215 NLRB 293, 88 LRRM 1027 (1974), *overruling* Raytheon, Co., 160 NLRB 1603, 63 LRRM 1180 (1966) (employer's petition to dismiss proceedings granted), 408 F.2d 681 (9th Cir. 1969), *rev'd & remanded,* 398 U.S. 25 (1970) (threat of rescinding benefits).

[105] Getman & Goldberg, *The Behavioral Assumptions Underlying NLRB Regulation of Campaign Misrepresentations: An Empirical Evaluation,* 28 Stan. L. Rev. 263 (1976). For a good discussion of this study, see King, *supra* note 99.

[106] *See, e.g.,* Charles Hughes, Making Unions Unnecessary, (Executive Enterprises, Inc., N.Y., 1976). Executive Enterprises also runs anti-union campaign seminars for labor relations people for $450 a seminar.

[107] Gen. Knit of California, 239 NLRB 101 (1978).

[108] Hollywood Ceramic Co., Inc., 140 NLRB 221 (1962).

fore, constitute unfair labor practices under Section 8(c) does not mean that such statements may not void an election, since Section 8(c)'s "free speech" privilege does not apply in representation proceedings.[109] The test is whether such statements, taken in total context, tend to impede a free election.

Acts of employers that have been held to interfere with their employees' freedom of choice so as to justify setting aside an election have included announcement of a profit-sharing plan just before election day,[110] grants of wage increases shortly before a scheduled election,[111] promise of favored treatment to employees who vote against the union,[112] favoring one union over another,[113] and threats of economic reprisals or of unqualified refusal to bargain in the event of a union victory.[114]

On the other hand, an employer can show the virulently anti-union movie *And Women Must Weep* to its employees without voiding an election.[115] Likewise, employers can give "captive audience" anti-union speeches as long as they are not within twenty-four hours of the election and the union has an opportunity to respond.[116] Management can even take small groups of employees into the office for anti-union talks (or speeches in favor of one rival) without necessarily voiding an election. Racial propaganda calculated to inflame employee prejudices warrants setting aside an election, although a truthful, noninflammatory statement of position on a racial matter does not if it is pertinent

---

109 Dal-Tex Optical Co., NLRB 1962, 50 LRRM 1489. The Board added, however, that "the strictures of the First Amendment, to be sure, must be considered in all cases."

110 Spengler-Loomis Mfg. Co., 102 NLRB 47, 31 LRRM 1314 (1953).

111 Bradley Lumber Co., 34 NLRB 610, 9 LRRM 25 (1942); Fairchild Camera & Instrument Co., 169 NLRB 11, 67 LRRM 1126 (1968).

112 Sherman Distribution Co., 171 NLRB 194, 68 LRRM 1284 (1968).

113 NLRB v. Wagner Iron Works, 220 F.2d 126, 35 LRRM 2588 (7th Cir. 1955), *cert. denied,* 350 U.S. 981, 37 LRRM 2639 (1956).

114 *See, e.g.,* Duvernoy & Sons, 177 NLRB 83 (1969).

115 Litho Press of San Antonio, 211 NLRB No. 143, 86 LRRM 1471 (1974).

116 Peerless Plywood Co., 107 NLRB 106, 33 LRRM 1151 (1953). *See also* Bonwit Teller, Inc., 96 NLRB 608, 28 LRRM 1547 (1951), *enf. denied & remanded with directions,* 197 F.2d 640, 30 LRRM 2305 (2d Cir.) *cert. denied,* 345 U.S. 905, 31 LRRM 2444 (1953).

to the issues of the election.[117]

Once the election is over, the parties have the right to file objections that relate either to election procedure or to conduct of the parties that may have affected the results of the election. Decisions of the NLRB on objections are subject to judicial review.

The practitioner is advised to pursue the post-election challenge route, rather than filing unfair labor practice charges. The main reason is that the former procedure is far speedier. Favorable decisions on unfair labor practice charges must be enforced by a Court of Appeals decision if the company fails to comply. Decisions on objections may lead to NLRB orders for new elections.

In sum, the trend of the law in this area is decidedly in favor of management. The practitioner is well advised to pursue all available remedies, but the ultimate strength, as always, lies with a strong and loyal rank and file that is clear as to its wishes and not subject to ingenious anti-union (anti-progressive union) tactics.

§ 7.04. Protections for Communists and Radicals

It was once clear that an employer did not automatically violate the Act if it refused to hire, or otherwise discriminated against, a person because he or she was a communist.[118] The rule has been substantially weakened, however, by Supreme Court decisions striking down certain sections of the Taft-Hartley Act.[119] The cases have generally held that the term "communist"

[117] Allen-Morrison Sign Co., 138 NLRB 11, 50 LRRM 153 (1962); Sewell Mfg. Co., 140 NLRB 24, 51 LRRM 1611 (1962); S. Car & Mfg. Co., 106 NLRB 144, 32 LRRM 1418 (1953).

[118] Administrative Decision of NLRB General Counsel (1953), Case No. 683. See also Title VII of the 1964 Civil Rights Act, 42 U.S.C. §§ 2000(e) et seq., Section 703(f), which specifically excludes Communists from the protections of the Act.

[119] *See, e.g.*, Keyishian v. Board of Regents, 385 U.S. 589 (1967); Baggett v. Bullitt, 377 U.S. 360 (1964); Elfbrandt v. Russell, 384 U.S. 11 (1966); Aptheker v. Secretary of State, 378 U.S. 500 (1964) (passports); United States v. Brown, 381 U.S. 437 (1965) (defense plant employment); United States v. Robel, 389 U.S. 258 (1967).

represents too broad a proscription and to take adverse action against a person on that basis may well infringe upon important First and Fifth Amendment liberties.[120]

However, while the law may not be as inflexible as it was during the McCarthy era, the way the issue presents itself has changed. Indeed, it is difficult to find any communist-discharge cases reported in the last twenty years. The obvious reason for this is that employers have found other means by which to discharge radicals and communists.

Whatever the grounds for discharge, the aggrieved worker must prove an anti-union motive on the part of the employer to establish a Section 8(a)(3) violation. However, motive is irrelevant if a Section 8(a)(1) violation is alleged. Any action that deters concerted activity is a violation of Section 8(a)(1).

Once that hurdle is cleared, the aggrieved dischargee or person not hired must deal with the employer rationale for the contested action. The most common employer technique is discharge for application falsification.[121] That problem is discussed in Chapter 2, *supra.*

In summary, while it is certain the issue will be presented directly sometime in the future, at present very few cases deal with it. Indeed, it is far more common to find the issue raised in union disciplinary proceedings.[122]

§ 7.05. Access to the NLRB

As mentioned previously, if a plant is already organized and its collective bargaining agreement includes a provision prohibiting retaliation for union activities, the aggrieved worker may be forced to rely on the contract's grievance/arbitration procedure for relief from what would commonly be an unfair labor practice. Although the NLRB has the power to decide unfair labor practice

---

120 *See* U.S. v. Brown, *supra* note 119.

121 *See, e.g.,* Whittaker Knitting Mills, 207 NLRB 1019 (1973); Chrysler Corp., Inc., 242 NLRB No. 71 (1979), 101 LRRM 1268.

122 Turner v. Machinists Lodge 1894, 100 LRRM 2055 (1978) (union violated LMRDA by expelling member of the Progressive Labor Party campaigning for steward election).

charges regardless of the existence of any other judicial or administrative power, it has adopted the policy of deferring to the contract's grievance/arbitration procedure if (1) the contract clearly provides for grievance/arbitration machinery, (2) the employer's unilateral action is not patently erroneous or designed to undermine the union, but is based on a substantial claim of contractual privilege, and (3) it appears that the arbitrator's ruling will resolve both the unfair labor practice issue and the contractual interpretation issue in a manner compatible with the purposes of the Act.[123]

In *Collyer*,[124] decided in 1971, the NLRB held that it would defer a refusal-to-bargain case (Section 8(5)(a)) and would retain jurisdiction over the case for the limited purpose of entertaining a motion for further consideration upon a showing that either (1) the dispute was not resolved with reasonable promptness after the issuance of the NLRB's deferral decision or was not resolved by agreement or promptly submitted to arbitration or (2) the grievance or arbitration procedures were not fair and regular or reached a result repugnant to the Act.

The *Collyer* rule was modified in a 1977 case, in which the NLRB majority stated that it would no longer defer in cases involving alleged violations of Section 8(a)(3) or other unlawful interference with employees' Section 7 rights.[125] In addition, if it can be shown that the interests of the union—as representative of the employee—and those of the grievant are at odds, either objectively or subjectively, the NLRB will not defer.[126] Thus, the NLRB may take jurisdiction of a Section 8(a)(5) refusal to bargain case if it also involves Section 8(a)(3) allegations.[127]

---

[123] Section 10(a) of the Act provides that the power of the NLRB to prevent unfair labor practices "shall not be affected by any other means of adjustment or prevention that has been or may be established by agreement, law or otherwise." *See, e.g.*, NLRB v. Wagner Iron Works, 35 LRRM 2588 (7th Cir. 1955), *cert. denied*, 37 LRRM 2639.

[124] Collyer Insulated Wire, NLRB 1971, 77 LRRM 1931.

[125] Gen. Am. Transp. Corp., NLRB 1977, 94 LRRM 1483. *See also* Roy Robinson Chevrolet, NLRB 1977, 94 LRRM 1474.

[126] Kansas Meat Packers, NLRB 1972, 80 LRRM 1743.

[127] *See, e.g.*, Gen. Am. Transp., *supra* note 125 at 1484, which states: "[O]ur Act explicitly protects employees from on-the-job discrimination because they have engaged in, or have refrained from engaging in, union activities. The

In summary, the doctrine seems to be that the aggrieved worker will have access to the NLRB in contrast to being forced to go to contract grievance/arbitration in cases of alleged employer discrimination or interference or in cases of alleged union coercion.[128]

---

protection thus afforded employees by the Act is clearly an individual, as contrasted with a union or group, right. In the instant case, instead of pursuing arbitration, a route which for a myriad of reasons he concluded would prove futile, Charging Party Soape chose to seek vindication of his statutory rights before the Board. Were we to order deferral in these circumstances there would be nothing voluntary about the arbitration to which the Charging Party Soape would be forced. Hence the voluntary nature of arbitration, long trumpeted by the Collyer enthusiasts as the main reason for deferral, is revealed as a sham in cases, like the instant case, where the charging party is an individual discriminatee seeking to enforce his individual rights." The battle between the pro-Collyer and anti-Collyer forces on the Board continues.

[128] *But see* NLRB v. Pincus Bros., 104 LRRM 2001 (3d Cir. 1980) (finding the NLRB required to defer to an arbitrator's decision upholding the discharge of a dissident for disloyalty).

CHAPTER 8

Rights of Union Members within Their Unions

Title I of the Labor-Management Reporting and Disclosure Act (LMRDA) of 1959,[1] the most litigated title of the Act, concerns the fundamental democratic rights of the individual within a labor union. Although entitled Bill of Rights of Members of Labor Organizations it is not nearly as broad as the Bill of Rights of the U.S. Constitution. Its stated purpose is to ensure the right of labor union members to participate freely in the government and affairs of their unions.

When it enacted the National Labor Relations Act (NLRA) of 1935 (predecessor of the present Taft-Hartley Act), Congress felt it necessary to protect the rights of workers to organize, choose their own representatives, bargain collectively, and engage in other concerted activities. In so doing, Congress imposed a system of exclusive representation upon individual employees, granting solely to the labor organization power to represent employees in negotiating with the employer concerning wages, hours, and working conditions. As a consequence, member employees are denied some freedom of individual action. Some union officials began abusing their power by engaging in corruption, breaches of trust, collusion with management, denial of members' rights, and other unethical conduct that failed to represent the real interests of union members. In an effort to stop such abuses, Congress, through Title I of the LMRDA, granted power to members to protect and engage in those rights essential to

[1] 73 Stat. 552, 29 U.S.C. §§ 411-528, P.L. 86-257.

democratic participation in the affairs of their unions. Through protection of internal democratic processes, Congress intended that unions should best represent their membership.

Title I strikes a balance between the union's need for unity in the face of management and the union member's democratic rights to individual expression and dissent. Congress did not intend for the courts to intervene at will in the internal affairs of the unions,[2] nor is Title I a catch-all provision for dissatisfied union members.[3] The stated purpose is to protect individual union members' interests from the danger of overreaching by entrenched union leadership[4] exercising arbitrary, despotic control.[5] The law is remedial in nature and should be liberally applied,[6] but reasonable restraints are allowed by a union constitution and bylaws consistent with the statute.[7]

Of course, it is important for rank-and-file activists and their lawyers to remember that the LMRDA is far less helpful than its lofty statement of goals implies. Its enactment represented a compromise among those seeking to reform unions, union officials seeking to retain their hitherto unquestioned power and authority, and employers trying to undermine unions by advocating "union democracy." Consequently, most sections of the LMRDA

---

[2] Gurton v. Arons, 339 F.2d 371 (2d Cir. 1964); Smith v. Sheet Metal Workers Int'l Ass'n, 500 F.2d 741 (5th Cir. 1974).

[3] Horn v. Amalgamated Ass'n of Street, etc., 194 F. Supp. 560 (D.C. Mich. 1961).

[4] Rota v. Bhd. of Railway, etc., 489 F.2d 998 (7th Cir. 1973), *cert. denied* 414 U.S. 1144, 39 L. Ed. 2d 99, 93 S. Ct. 896, *and on remand* 64 FRD 699 (D.C. Ill.); Smith v. Sheet Metal Workers Int'l Assn, *supra* note 2.

[5] Russo v. United Ass'n of Plumbing & Pipefitting Indus., 372 F. Supp. 1265 (D.C. Conn. 1974), *aff'd without opinion,* 493 F.2d 1398 (2d Cir.); Wittstein v. Am. Fed'n of Musicians, 223 F. Supp. 27 (D.C. N.Y. 1963), *aff'd,* 326 F.2d 26 (2d Cir.), *rev'd on other grounds,* 379 U.S. 171, 13 L. Ed. 2d 214, 85 S. Ct. 300; Thomas v. United Mine Workers of America, 422 F. Supp. 1111 (D.C.D.C. 1976); Green v. Hotel & Restaurant Employees & Bartenders Int'l Union, 220 F. Supp. 505 (D.C. Mich. 1963); Stout v. Constr. & Gen. Laborers Dist. Council, 226 F. Supp. 673 (D.C. Ill. 1963); Schuchardt v. Millwrights & Mach. Erectors Local Union, 380 F.2d 795 (10th Cir. 1967).

[6] Kiepura v. United Steelworkers of America, 358 F. Supp. 987 (D.C. Ill. 1973).

[7] Rosen v. Bhd. of Painters, Decorators & Paperhangers, 198 F. Supp. 46 (D.C. N.Y. 1961), *appeal dismissed* 326 F.2d 400 (2d Cir.).

strike compromises between union authority and members' rights. In addition, many courts react unfavorably to suits aimed at strengthening "militant" or "radical" caucuses at the expense of union leadership known for its cooperation with management.

This chapter is divided into two main parts. First, a systematic description of Title I law will be presented in the order followed by the statute. Fact situations taken from the case law will illustrate its application. Second, a discussion of the procedures involved in Title I litigation will be presented. Attention will be given to the requirement of exhausting internal union procedures before filing suit and other procedural problems.

The attorney should be aware of the risk inherent in filing Title I suits. If brought for harassment or in poor judgment, such suits can weaken a union and dissipate its assets. But suits brought to ensure that the democratic voice of the union members is heard can substantially strengthen a union—for only by responding to the changing needs of its constituency can a union command the full respect and support of its membership, from which comes the power for forceful bargaining.

§ 8.01. The Bill of Rights of Members of Labor Organizations

[1] Equal Rights

> Sec. 101 (a)(1) Equal Rights—Every member of a labor organization shall have equal rights and privileges within such organization to nominate candidates, to vote in elections or referendums of the labor organization, to attend membership meetings, and to participate in the deliberations and voting upon the business of such meetings, subject to reasonable rules and regulations in such organization's constitution and bylaws.

Section 101(a)(1) is an obviously vague section of the Act, resulting in a wide variety of court opinions and interpretations. Creative attorneys have used this section, with mixed success, to challenge, among other things, union contract ratification procedures, weighted voting within various union bodies, the failure to provide members with information or with even the right to vote on union action merging one or more locals into one, and various actions pertaining to the nomination and election of union officers.

[a] Nature of Rights

In a referendum held to ratify a local union's affiliation with an international, one court held that members had a right not only to a vote but also to a *meaningful* vote, one that was reasoned and informed.[8] This decision suggests the duty of a union to send and the right of the members to receive all relevant information, perhaps translated, necessary for such an informed vote. It also held that any member should be permitted to mail his or her views to the membership at any time so long as he or she bears the expense.[9] Section 101(a)(1) might be interpreted further to expand rights of members relative to activities in all phases of the voting process and its preliminary activities. However, most cases hold that a plaintiff may not attempt to assert as a cause of action under Section 101(a)(1) a complaint that falls within the scope of Title IV of the LMRDA, which deals specifically with the election of union officers.[10]

Equal rights and privileges were held to have been violated when a union tried to exclude from the remainder of its meeting those members who refused to salute and pledge allegiance to the flag (an act required by the union's meeting agenda) in exercise of their free speech rights.[11]

[b] Who Is a Member?

A question arises under this section and the remainder of the

---

[8] Blanchard v. Johnson, 532 F.2d 1074 (6th Cir. 1976), *cert. denied,* 429 U.S. 834, 50 L. Ed. 2d 100, 97 S. Ct. 100, and *cert. denied,* 429 U.S. 869, 50 L. Ed. 2d 149, 97 S. Ct. 180.

[9] *Id.*

[10] *But see* for exceptions to this rule chapter on union elections; *especially* Depew v. Edmiston, 386 F.2d 710, 66 LRRM 2663 (2d Cir. 1967); and Kupau v. Yamamoto, 662 F.2d 449, 105 LRRM 2260 (9th Cir. 1980).

[11] Stachan v. Weber, 535 F.2d 1202 (9th Cir. 1976).

union members' bill of rights regarding who is a "member of a labor organization." Section 3(o) gives the statutory definition:

> 'Member' or 'member in good standing,' when used in reference to a labor organization, includes any person who has fulfilled the requirements for membership in such organization, and who neither has voluntarily withdrawn from membership nor has been expelled or suspended from membership after appropriate proceedings consistent with lawful provisions of the constitution and bylaws of such organization.

Once an employee has fulfilled the requirements, whatever they are, that person is a member and remains one until suspension or voluntary withdrawal. A suspension, and the requirement of due process in any disciplinary action, is covered later in this chapter. It must be remembered, though, that one of the requirements of membership may be to have been elected by a percentage of the union's members.[12] Although a person may meet various fixed standards and pay a membership fee or dues, he or she may still not become a member without the union vote.[13] The union retains the right to choose its members.[14] Thus, it would appear that an employee meeting the fee and dues provisions of an agency shop provision but not joining or being voted in does not possess the rights vis-à-vis the union granted by the LMRDA.

However, membership can ordinarily be denied only if an applicant fails to meet membership or dues requirements. But if an applicant meets such requirements, there is a question as to whether he or she may be arbitrarily denied membership by vote or otherwise. The traditional view is that a union is a voluntary and private organization and has sole control over its choice of members.[15] However, a California court has held that, where there was a union or closed shop, the union could not arbitrarily

---

[12] Moynahan v. Pari-Mutual Employees Guild, 317 F.2d 209 (9th Cir. 1968), *cert. denied,* 375 U.S. 911, 11 L. Ed. 2d 159, 84 S. Ct. 207.

[13] *Id.*

[14] *Id.;* Stone v. Int'l Bhd. of Boilermakers, etc. 262 F. Supp. 961 (D. Mass. 1967); Axelrod v. Stoltz, 264 F. Supp. 536 (D.C. Pa. 1967), *aff'd,* 391 F.2d 549 (8th Cir.).

[15] Oliphant v. Bhd. of Locomotive Firemen & Enginemen, 156 F. Supp. 89 (1957), *aff'd,* 262 F.2d 359 (6th Cir. 1958), *cert. denied,* 79 S. Ct. 648 (1959).

restrictions. On the other hand, if an identifiably progressive plaintiff challenges an identifiably conservative union administration, or challenges union accommodations to employers, courts may rapidly shed their "democratic" sympathies.

The fact that litigation necessarily taxes union institutions, depleting both the treasury and the energies of officers, which might otherwise be devoted to the struggle against employers, is by no means a reason to forswear LMRDA litigation.[19] However, this danger and the danger of entrusting a decision to antiunion or proemployer judges, are reasons to consider carefully the desirability of litigation at all, the tactics to be employed, and the relief to be sought. At various points in this chapter and the following chapter on union elections, ways in which such considerations bear on the uses of the law are mentioned. Union members and their counsel should carefully consider these dangers at every juncture of their proceedings.

§ 8.03. Who Is a Union "Member"?

A basic question in any LMRDA proceeding is whether a person is a union member. The LMRDA creates rights and the ability to sue for "members"; thus, an individual who works in an agency shop but does not belong to the union except for the payment of dues cannot seek the protections of the statute.[20] The statutory definition is contained in Section 3(o), 29 U.S.C. § 402(o):

> "Member" or "member in good standing", when used in reference to a labor organization, includes any person who has fulfilled the requirements for membership in such organization, and who neither has voluntarily withdrawn from membership nor has been expelled or suspended from membership after appropriate pro-

[19] *See* Cox, *Internal Affairs of Labor Unions Under the Labor Reform Act of 1959*, 58 Mich. L. Rev. 819, 853 (1960).

[20] Klemens v. ALPA, 500 F. Supp. 735 (W.D. Wash. 1980); MacKenzie v. Operating Engineers Local 624, 102 LRRM 2910, 2913 (N.D. Miss. 1979). It has also been held that termination of status as an applicant for membership, based on actions protected by Title I, is not a violation. Wallace v. IOMMP, 547 F. Supp. 155 (S.D.N.Y. 1982).

ceedings consistent with lawful provisions of the constitution and bylaws of such organization.

In many industries, one of the most important functions of the union is to limit entry into the trade in order to protect standards by restricting the number of available workers. Moreover, Congress was persuaded by the contention, advanced by union supporters seeking to kill Title I on the Senate floor, that an open-ended provision barring limitations on membership would force racial integration of unions.[21] Accordingly, the statute was written to allow unions to adopt whatever restrictions they wish on access to membership. However, once an individual is admitted, even to a subordinate form of membership, the rights accorded by Title I become applicable.[21.1]

One who has met the requirements, however, is deemed a member despite the fact that the union has not issued a membership card or otherwise not recognized formal membership status.[22] The question naturally arises, then, whether a lack of formal admission might not be a failure to fulfill the requirements. The distinction depends on whether the missing step is a mere formality, or whether the union bylaws explicitly grant discretion to grant or withhold membership.[23] For example, many unions require a membership vote, by a majority or more, before a member may be admitted; such a requirement is not voided by the LMRDA, and one who has not obtained such a vote cannot rely upon the LMRDA's protections.[24] These issues commonly arise both when an individual is seeking admission to a union

---

[21] McAdams, Power and Politics in Labor Legislation 102-04 (1964).

[21.1] *See* Young v. Asbestos Workers Local 17, 112 LRRM 3289 n.2 (N.D. Ill. 1981) (apprentice member paying half dues and lacking right to vote is member for purpose of § 101(a)(5) suit against expulsion).

[22] Hughes v. Ironworkers Local 11, 287 F.2d 810, 816 (8th Cir.), *cert. denied,* 368 U.S. 829 (1961). Although joint councils and other regional bodies frequently describe local unions or elected delegates as their "members," the members of component locals are members of the regional body as well. Roddy v. UTU, 479 F. Supp. 57 (N.D. Ala), *aff'd mem.,* 608 F.2d 522 (5th Cir. 1979).

[23] Moynahan v. Parimutual Employees Local 280, 317 F.2d 209 (9th Cir. 1973).

[24] Axelrod v. Stoltz, 264 F. Supp. 536, 539 (E.D. Pa.), *aff'd on other grounds,* 391 F.2d 549 (3d Cir. 1967); Gavin v. Ironworkers Local 1, 553 F.2d 28, 31 (7th Cir. 1977).

initially and when a member of one local seeks admission to another local in which he or she is working.

There is also authority for the position that a union cannot be compelled to provide formal recognition, but only to afford individuals the specific rights conferred by the statute as if they were members.[25] Certainly if a union entity purports to exercise power over an individual or over his or her contract rights, the individual must be deemed a "member" at least insofar as that may be a prerequisite of participating either within the union or in litigation concerning the propriety of the union's actions.[26] Other courts would go still further and actually require the union to issue membership cards.[27]

Once a person has become a member, that status continues until a voluntary withdrawal or valid suspension or expulsion. Actions of a member will be construed against a finding of voluntary withdrawal, but a clearly stated withdrawal will be recognized and LMRDA rights consequently denied.[28] Presumably, however, even in the case of a "clear" withdrawal, a doctrine of constructive expulsion would be available to preserve the LMRDA rights of one who was forced to withdraw, just as the doctrine of constructive discharge preserves the remedies of an employee who has been forced to "quit" a job.[29]

If the withdrawal has not been voluntary, membership status is lost only if the member was validly suspended or expelled.[30] The validity is tested both against the union constitution

---

25 *See* Ferger v. Ironworkers Local 483, 356 F.2d 854 (3d Cir.), *cert. denied,* 384 U.S. 908 (1966).

26 Harris v. Plasterers Local 406, 619 F.2d 1164, 1167 (7th Cir. 1980); Alvey v. General Electric Co., 622 F.2d 1279, 1284-1287 (7th Cir. 1980).

27 Woods v. IBEW Local 613, 404 F. Supp. 110, 117 (N.D. Ga. 1975). Other statutes forbid discriminatory refusals to grant membership on certain grounds. *E.g.,* Section 703(c) of the Civil Rights Act of 1964, 42 U.S.C. §§ 2000 e-2 (race, color, religion, sex, national origin); LMRA § 8(b)(5), 29 U.S.C. § 158(b)(5) (discriminating or excessive fees).

28 Basilicato v. IATSE, 479 F. Supp. 1232, 1243 (D.Conn. 1979). *See* Bradley v. IUE Local 119, 236 F. Supp. 724 (E.D.Pa. 1964) (revocation of dues checkoff authorization is not tantamount to resignation, where member continues to pay dues in person). *Cf.* Local 1 (ACA) v. Teamsters, 543 F. Supp. 1321 (E.D. Pa. 1982) (retiree is not a member for purposes of diversity jurisdiction).

29 J.P.Stevens & Co. v. NLRB, 461 F.2d 490, 494 (4th Cir. 1972).

30 Stone v. Boilermakers, 262 F. Supp. 961, 963 (D. Mass. 1967); Carroll v.

and against the procedural and substantive requirements of the LMRDA.[31] If the deprivation of membership is based on discharge from employment, good standing continues so long as the discharge is being actively contested.[32] Presumably, the same rule applies while a union expulsion is being contested.[33] If the discipline is not a complete expulsion, all rights not specifically denied are retained, and membership status continues to permit suit under the LMRDA to protect those rights.[34] Finally, the dormancy of a local after it has been decertified as a collective bargaining representative does not deprive its members of their status as such.[35]

§ 8.04. Definition of "Employer" and "Employee"

Another basic term of the LMRDA is "employer." The definition is important, not only because it defines the entities obligated to comply with various portions of the act, such as the second proviso of Section 101(a)(4), Section 481g, and the reporting provisions of Title II, but also because "labor organization" is defined by reference to its relationship with employers and employees. The statutory definition follows:

Musicians Local 802, 235 F. Supp. 161, 173 (S.D.N.Y. 1963).

[31] *See* Addison v. Machinists, 318 F.2d 504, 508 (9th Cir. 1963); Agola v. Hagner, 113 LRRM 2421, 2425 (E.D.N.Y. 1982) (dictum). *See also* 29 C.F.R. § 452.50.

[32] Brennan v. Independent Lift Truck Bldrs., 490 F.2d 213, 217-218 (7th Cir. 1974); Marshall v. Postal Workers, 105 LRRM 3384, 3385-86 (D.D.C. 1980). These protections do not apply to a member who quits a job, however, Taylor v. Steelworkers Local 5000, 701 F.2d 590 (6th Cir. 1983). These cases are based on the definition of "employee," which specifically includes those who have ceased work because of a labor dispute or unfair labor practice. Although the definition of "member" does not include such specific protections, the courts assume that they are implicit.

[33] *See* Schuchardt v. Carpenters Local 2834, 380 F.2d 794 (10th Cir. 1967).

[34] Axelrod v. Stoltz, 264 F. Supp. 536 (E.D. Pa.), *aff'd on other grounds,* 391 F.2d 549 (3d Cir. 1967). But *cf.* Brennan v. Teamsters Local 357, 113 LRRM 3390 (9th Cir. 1983) (member suspended for non-payment of dues may not complain under § 101(a)(5) about procedure used to deny reinstatement).

[35] Erkins v. Bryan, 663 F.2d 648 (5th Cir. 1981).

"Employer" means any employer or any group or association of employers engaged in an industry affecting commerce (1) which is, with respect to employees engaged in an industry affecting commerce, an employer within the meaning of any law of the United States relating to the employment of any employees or (2) which may deal with any labor organization concerning grievances, labor disputes, wages, rates of pay, hours of employment, or conditions of work, and includes any person acting directly or indirectly as an employer or as an agent of an employer in relation to an employee but does not include the United States or any corporation wholly owned by the Government of the United States or any State or political subdivision thereof.[36]

(*Text continued on page 8-11*)

[36] Section 3(e), 29 U.S.C. § 402(e).

that he or she remains free as a member openly to criticize the union's leadership and policies and provided that the removal was not done to chill or inhibit the free speech rights of that person as a union member. (On appeal, the Second Circuit found that the evidence presented did not establish that Newman's criticism of the union's leadership inhibited his ability to act as an effective shop steward.[38]

Another court held that appointed officers and other employees may be discharged from their positions because a newly elected official has the right to a duty of loyalty from those working under him.[39] However, where removal or reassignment is done in retaliation for prior intra-union political activity, such action constitutes discipline and violates Section 101(a)(1) and (2), since these provisions are applicable to union officers and employees. A union employee so disciplined meets his or her burden of proof if he or she shows that the reassignment was not related to a legitimate desire of the union leadership to ensure management in accord with the mandate of its election, but was done rather in retaliation for internal union activity.[40]

However, the right to free expression does not require union officials to give space to union dissidents in union periodicals.[41]

[b] Assembly

Freedom of speech and assembly includes the right to meet and assemble freely with other members. Union members may meet outside the regular union meetings and discuss union affairs without fear of reprisal by union officials.[42] This right does not

---

38 Newman v. Communications Workers, Local 1101, 597 F.2d 833, 101 LRRM 2265 (2d Cir. 1979).

39 Wambles v. International Brotherhood of Teamsters, etc., 488 F.2d 888 (5th cir. 1974).See also, Cehaish v. UAW, 496 F. Supp. 912 (E.D. Mich. 1980); Weyhmueller v. SEIU Local #1, 509 F. Supp. 992 (N.D. Ill. 1981).

40 Cooke v. Orange Belt Dist. Council of Painters No. 48, 529 F.2d 815 (9th Cir. 1976).

41 Sheldon v. O'Callaghan, 497 F.2d 1276 (2d Cir. 1974), *cert. denied,* 419 U.S. 1090, 42 L. Ed. 2d 682, 95 S. Ct. 681.

42 Yanity v. Benware, 376 F.2d 197 (2d Cir. 1967), *cert. denied,* 389 U.S. 874, 19 L. Ed. 2d 158, 88 S. Ct. 167.

require the union to call special meetings or to depart from procedures concerning proper motions to be made from the floor during meetings.[43] Local union members may meet without interference from the international union, except where the international union acts lawfully through established procedures to set up a trusteeship over the local union.[44] A union cannot take action against its members for assembling to petition for a local charter or to discuss negotiation of a strike settlement.[45]

[3] Dues, Initiation Fees, and Assessments

> Sec. 101. (a)(3) Dues, Initiation Fees, and Assessments—Except in the case of a federation of national or international labor organizations, the rates of dues and initiation fees payable by members of any labor organization in effect on the date of enactment of this Act shall not be increased, and no general or special assessment shall be levied upon such members, except—
>
> (A) in the case of a local labor organization, (i) by majority vote by secret ballot of the members in good standing voting at a general or special membership meeting, after reasonable notice of the intention to vote upon such question, or (ii) by majority vote of the members in good standing voting in a membership referendum conducted by secret ballot; or
>
> (B) in the case of a labor organization, other than a local labor organization or a federation of national or international labor organizations, (i) by majority vote of the delegates voting at a regular convention, or at a special convention of such labor organization held upon not less than thirty days' written notice to the principal office of each local or constituent labor organization entitled to such notice, or (ii) by majority vote of the members in good standing of such labor organization voting in a membership referendum conducted by secret ballot, or (iii) by majority vote of the members of the executive board or similar governing body of such labor

---

[43] *Id.*, Scovile v. Watson, 338 F.2d 678 (7th Cir. 1964), *cert. denied,* 380 U.S. 963, 14 L. Ed. 2d 154, 85 S. Ct. 1107.

[44] Navarro v. Gannon, 385 F.2d 512 (2d Cir. 1967), *cert. denied,* 390 U.S. 989, 19 L. Ed. 2d 1294, 88 S. Ct. 1184, *rehearing denied,* 390 U.S. 1046, 20 L. Ed. 2d 310, 88 S. Ct. 1634.

[45] Johnson v. Int'l Bhd. of Elec. Workers, 181 F. Supp. 734 (D.C. Mich. 1960).

> organization, pursuant to express authority contained in the constitution and bylaws of such labor organization: *Provided,* That such action on the part of the executive board or similar governing body shall be effective only until the next regular convention of such labor organization.

Rates of dues and initiation fees payable by members may not be increased except in conformity with the LMRDA provisions. As will be explained below, the statute prescribes one set of procedures for local unions and another for district, conference, national, or international labor organizations. The LMRDA also defines what a labor organization is:

> Sec. 3 (i) "Labor organization" means a labor organization engaged in an industry affecting commerce and includes any organization of any kind, any agency, or employee representation committee, group, association, or plan so engaged in which employees participate and which exists for the purpose, in whole or in part, of dealing with employers concerning grievances, labor disputes, wages, rates of pay, hours, or other terms or conditions of employment, and any conference, general committee, joint or system board, or joint council so engaged which is subordinate to a national or international labor organization, other than a State or local central body.

One court has held that a council of sugar workers that was a coordinating body for the International Longshoremen's Association's local of sugar workers and the association itself was required to impose dues according to part (B) of Section 101(a)(3), because it was neither a local nor a federation.[46]

"Dues" includes dues paid by a member to the local;[47] a per capita tax paid by each local to the international but levied on union members by being withheld from their pay;[48] and a per capita tax imposed by an international and payable by union members to a subordinate council.[49] "Dues" does not include a

---

[46] King v. Randazzo, 346 F.2d 307 (2d Cir. 1965).

[47] Ranes v. Office Employees Int'l Union, 317 F.2d 915 (7th Cir. 1963).

[48] Int'l Bhd. of Tel. Workers v. Int'l Bhd. of Tel. Workers, 362 F.2d 891 (1st Cir. 1966), *cert. denied,* 385 U.S. 947, 17 L. Ed. 2d 226, 87 S. Ct. 321.

[49] King v. Randazzo, 234 F. Supp. 388 (D.C. N.Y. 1964), *aff'd,* 346 F.2d 307 (2d Cir. 1965).

per capita tax paid by a local to a district council or an international if the increase involved does not result in increasing the total amount paid by each member.[50]

The statute deals with dues increases, not with decreases or changes in the collection procedures.[51] Not included are increments regarding classification changes, provided that they are not rate increases.[52] A fine is not a dues increase.[53] If an independent union joins an international with a higher dues standard, then the local must follow the rules in Section 101(a)(3).[54] But if a union had already observed the procedures before a new local became affiliated, it need not repeat the process after affiliation.[55]

Fees may not be increased nor (in the case of a local) assessments levied unless one of two procedures is followed. In either case, those who may vote are members in good standing. The first procedure requires notice. It requires that an increase be approved by a majority of the members voting on the proposal at either a general or special meeting. The vote must be by secret ballot, not by standing vote.[56] The notice must be reasonable and given before the vote and it must specify the question to be voted upon. A notice is not reasonable if it fails to do this; it fails if a member is not aware of the particular issues or if a member is notified with too little time before the meeting.[57] Another question may arise regarding whether notice given in a language foreign to the member is reasonable, considering both the members' inability to read it and the time and practicality of the union's being able to translate it.

The second procedure, a secret ballot vote in a membership

---

[50] Sawyers v. Grand Lodge, Int'l Ass'n of Machinists, 279 F. Supp. 747 (D.C. Mo. 1967).

[51] Schwartz v. Associated Musicians of Greater N.Y., 237 F. Supp. 149 (D.C. N.Y. 1963), *aff'd,* 340 F.2d 228 (2d Cir.).

[52] Williams v. Int'l Typographical Union, 423 F.2d 1295 (10th Cir. 1970), *cert. denied,* 400 U.S. 824, 27 L. Ed. 2d 53, 91 S. Ct. 47.

[53] Kalish v. Hosier, 364 F.2d 829 (D. Colo. 1965), *cert. denied,* 386 U.S. 944, 17 L. Ed. 2d 874, 87 S. Ct. 972.

[54] Am. Bridge Div., United States Steel Corp. v. NLRB, 457 F.2d 660 (3d Cir. 1972).

[55] King v. Randazzo, *supra* note 46.

[56] White v. King, 319 F. Supp. 122 (D.C. La. 1970).

[57] Gates v. Dalton, 67 FRD 621 (D.C.N.Y. 1975).

referendum, does not require advance notice. But a ballot must be delivered to each member who is eligible and he or she may not be required to attend a membership meeting in order to obtain the ballot.[58] The ballot in a membership referendum must be clear and must not link the dues or assessment with some other issue. For instance, where it was impossible to vote down a dues increase without also turning down negotiations for a wage increase with the same vote, a court ruled the vote invalid.[59]

A local need not allow non-local members to vote even if the non-locals are working within the bargaining unit served by the local, if the local was authorized by its international to require the same payments of its members.[60] It has been held that an international may increase dues or assessments of members to their local by a proper international union vote,[61] and the local members cannot reject it through a vote of their own.[62] However, there is conflict on this issue, and a few courts have held that where an international or other higher union body votes to increase dues paid by members to their locals—as opposed to an increase in the per capita tax paid to the international or other higher body—the provisions of Section 10(a)(3)(A) must be followed.[63]

A labor organization other than a local may raise dues or levy assessments in three different ways. The first is through a majority vote of delegates voting at a regular convention or at a special convention held with at least thirty days' written notice to each local or constituent labor organization. There is no requirement of a secret ballot here. The delegates to an international may vote with unequal weight if, through proper constitutional procedure, the weight reflects the number of members in the local which the

---

58 Int'l Bhd. of Tel. Workers v. Int'l Bhd. of Tel. Workers, *supra* note 48.

59 Sertic v. Cuyahoga, Lake, Geauga & Ashtabula Counties Carpenters Dist. Council, etc., 423 F.2d 515, (6th Cir. 1970), *rev'd & remanded,* 459 F.2d 579 (6th Cir. 1972).

60 Zentner v. Am. Fed'n of Musicians, 237 F. Supp. 457 (D.C. N.Y. 1965), *aff'd,* 343 F.2d 758 (2d Cir.).

61 Ranes v. Office Employees Int'l Union, *supra* note 47.

62 United Bhd. of Carpenters & Joiners v. Brown, 343 F.2d 872 (10th Cir. 1965).

63 *See, e.g.,* Mori v. Boilermakers, 482 F. Supp. 838 (N.D. Cal. 1979).

delegate represents.[64] The approval at a special convention of a labor council composed of locals representing the workers of a particular industry may allow an international to increase dues.[65]

The second method requires a majority vote of the members in good standing of such a labor organization in a membership referendum conducted by secret ballot. This does not allow an international to use a secret ballot at membership meetings because each member must receive a ballot whether at a meeting or not.[66]

The third allows a majority vote of the members of an executive board or similar international governing body pursuant to express authority contained in the constitution and bylaws of the organization. One court has held that in order to impose additional dues in this way there must be express authority in the international constitution to do so.[67]

An illegally collected dues increase cannot be retroactively ratified. Although the requirements of Section 101(a)(3) seem straightforward, one issue involving its interpretation has given the courts trouble. If an international or intermediate labor organization increases not only the dues that must be paid to it but also the dues that the member pays to the local and the local retains, which procedure must be followed? Logic suggests that the increase should be divided and both procedures employed. A further wrinkle occurs when the action of the international or intermediate labor organization increases the dues in a non-uniform manner.[68]

[4] Protection of the Right to Sue

Sec. 101 (a)(4) Protection of the Right to Sue—No labor organization shall limit the right of any member thereof to institute an action in any court, or in a proceeding before any administrative agency, irrespective of whether or not the labor organization or its

[64] Am. Fed'n of Musicians v. Wittstein, 379 U.S. 171 (1974).

[65] King v. Randazzo, *supra* note 46.

[66] Int'l Bhd. of Tel. Workers v. Int'l Bhd. of Tel. Workers, *supra* note 48.

[67] King v. Randazzo, *supra* note 46.

[68] For one approach to these questions, see Mori v. Boilermakers, *supra* note 63.

[1] Restrictions on the Scope of Section 101(a)(1)

Both proposed restrictions on the scope of Section 101(a)(1) have been adopted in reliance on the Supreme Court's decision in *Calhoon v. Harvey.*[62] In that case, the Marine Engineers had bylaws forbidding a member to nominate for union office anyone except him- or herself and providing that only members with a minimum amount of sea time were eligible for office. Plaintiff members contended that, in tandem, these rules deprived them of the right to nominate candidates for office of any substance. The Supreme Court held, however, that, although the right to nominate had been limited by the self-nomination rule, that limitation had been applied without discrimination among members.[63] Moreover, it was improper to raise the issue of the unreasonableness of the eligibility rule in a preelection suit under Section 101(a)(1). Rather, such issues may be raised only in proceedings initiated by the Secretary of Labor under Title IV of the Act.[64] The meaning of this brief opinion has been the source of great debate ever since.

[a] Use in Preelection Suits

The first limitation that has been applied in light of *Calhoon v. Harvey* will not be discussed at length here because it is examined in the chapter on union elections.[65] In sum, the distinction that has emerged is that if union members attack the reasonableness of a rule that limits the right to vote, nominate, or run in union officer elections, then the action must be filed by the Secretary of Labor under Title IV. If, however, the members complain that a rule that is valid, for Title I purposes at least, has been applied discriminatorily against them, they may sue under Section 101(a)(1) prior to the election. The extent of discrimination that must be shown in these circumstances is open to question; in any event, it is clear that the scope of Section 101(a)(1) is broader

62 379 U.S. 134 (1964).

63 379 U.S. at 138-39.

64 379 U.S. at 139-41.

65 Section 9.03[2], *infra.*

outside the context of union officer elections. It should be noted, however, that the exclusivity provision in Title IV applies only to officer elections. Thus, if a union convention votes on dues, a challenge to the system of representation pursuant to which the delegates voted may be filed under Section 101(a)(3).[65.1] Even a suit which is based on conduct during an officer election may be filed, as long as no relief is sought which would overturn the election.[65.2]

[b] The Distinction between Direct and Indirect Attacks

In applying the principle of equality, courts encounter a basic problem—what is the basis for determining when "equality" is abridged? Just as it may be a breach of the principle to treat identical situations differently, it may also be a breach to treat different situations in the same manner.

Another way of approaching the problem is to note that the function of a rule is to discriminate between like and unlike cases. Thus, a claim that a rule is "discriminatory" is simply a tautology. Nevertheless, such complaints are often made. What they mean is that the rule does not accurately divide situations that *ought* to be treated the same from those that ought to be treated differently. The court then confronts the original question: Which situations are the same and which are different?

These considerations are important to the analysis of Section 101(a)(1), because they indicate that, at its broadest construction, the subsection could simply authorize courts to substitute their judgments for those of unions every time a member asks for help. This would be desirable for neither unions nor the courts. Accordingly, many courts have sought an easy rule to distinguish cases that warrant application of Section 101(a)(1) from those that do not.

65.1 Denov v. Musicians Local 10-208, 703 F.2d 1034, (7th Cir. 1983).

65.2 Weisen v. Reichett, 111 LRRM 3136 (W.D. Pa. 1982) (counterclaim in suit by members sought restitution of local union funds allegedly diverted to use in election campaign). *See also* Steelworkers v. Sadlowski, 457 U.S. 102, 117-118 n.10 (1982) (suit may be filed under Title I to block use of rule on contributions in campaign for election to union office).

One such rule is the requirement that in order to have a cause of action under Section 101(a)(1), a member must show that the union has "directly" denied the right to vote, nominate, or participate. If the union permits the exercise of the right to vote, but then fails to take the action required by the vote or otherwise frustrates the right "indirectly," there is be no cause of action. This analysis was originally proposed by Chief Judge Lumbard, concurring in *Gurton v. Arons,* who concluded that *Calhoon* limits Section 101(a)(1) to "relatively direct attack[s] on the right to vote."[66] The distinction has been repeated in several other cases, notably in the Second Circuit.[67]

Other courts, however, have rejected the limitation, explicitly or implicitly, and it must be regarded as the minority rule.[68] The distinction is unpersuasive, because under it a union could allow members to enter the balloting area but throw the ballots cast by opponents of the regime into the garbage or fail to send them notice of the impending balloting without contravening Section 101(a)(1).

The availability of such easy subterfuges has led even courts that have espoused the direct/indirect dichotomy to weaken it or ignore it altogether in appropriate cases.[69] Rather, the dichotomy represents a determination not to allow the courts to be drawn into every internal union dispute. This determination is adequately served by some of the limitations discussed below.

---

66 339 F.2d 371, 377 (2d Cir. 1964).

67 *E.g.,* Fritsch v. Painters District Council 9, 493 F.2d 1061, 1063 (2d Cir. 1974); Keck v. Employees Indep. Ass'n., 387 F. Supp. 241, 247 (E.D. Pa. 1974).

68 *E.g.,* Bunz v. Moving Picture Mach. Operators, 567 F.2d 1117 (D.C. Cir. 1977); Aguirre v. Teamsters Local 165, 633 F.2d 168, 173 (9th Cir. 1980); Beckman v. Ironworkers Local 46, 314 F.2d 848, 850 (7th Cir. 1963); Christopher v. Safeway Stores, 644 F.2d 467, 470-71 (5th Cir. 1981).

69 *E.g.,* Ford v. Philadelphia Dist. Coun. of Carpenters, 323 F. Supp. 1136, 1139 (E.D. Pa. 1970) (in deciding whether to invalidate dues vote, looks to see whether union letter was intentionally or actually misleading); Sheldon v. O'-Callaghan, 497 F.2d 1276, 1281-82 (2d Cir. 1974) (both sides must be allowed to circulate propaganda for vote to be fair); Fritsch v. Carpenters District Council 9, 493 F.2d 1061, 1063 (2d Cir. 1974) (appears to sanction claim based on union's counting votes of some members more than others).

[2] Right to Vote on Contracts

One of the ways in which Section 101(a)(1) has frequently been applied is in cases where union members sued for the right to vote on contracts. The courts have generally held that Section 101(a)(1) does not, in itself, give members the right to vote on contracts.[70] However, if the union allows votes on some contracts, it cannot unreasonably refuse to allow votes on other contracts unless it is able to justify the distinction.[71] Similarly, Section 101(a)(1) may be used in some cases to protect the right to vote on contracts or contractual changes if the union constitution provides that right.[71.1]

[3] Right to Have Votes Implemented

There is substantial conflict among various courts as to whether Section 101(a)(1) gives union members the right to insist that votes taken lawfully, fairly, and in the manner prescribed by the union's constitution and bylaws must be implemented. Refusal to do so would be discriminatory because the union in effect would be counting the votes of the minority more heavily than the votes of the majority. Thus, in *Pignotti v. Sheet Metal Workers Local 3,*[72] the members of the local voted three times to reject a pension plan; yet the union nevertheless signed an agreement for the plan. The court found a violation of Section 101(a)(1), reasoning that the union leadership had denied the equal right to vote "as effectively as if they had stuffed the ballot box itself. . . ."[73] On the other hand, in *Vincent v. IBEW*[74] the members of a local voted to adopt a particular pension plan, but the union leadership decided to seek a different plan in collective bargaining

---

[70] *E.g.,* Cleveland Orch. Comm. v. Cleveland Fed'n of Musicians, 303 F.2d 229 (6th Cir. 1962); Stelling v. IBEW Local 1547, 587 F.2d 1379, 1385 (9th Cir. 1978).

[71] Trail v. Teamsters, 542 F.2d 961 (6th Cir. 1976); Postal Workers Local 6886 v. Postal Workers, 665 F.2d 1096 (D.C. Cir. 1981).

[71.1] Frenza v. Sheet Metal Workers, 113 LRRM 2619 (E.D. Mich.).

[72] 343 F. Supp. 236 (D. Neb. 1972), *aff'd,* 477 F.2d 825 (8th Cir. 1973).

[73] 343 F. Supp. at 243.

[74] 622 F.2d 140 (5th Cir. 1980).

negotiations. The court found no violation because "the fact that the vote was not translated into action consistent therewith does not in and of itself give a cause of action to the plaintiffs. . . ."[75]

Probably the best solution for this conflict is to defer to the union's constitution and bylaws. If these governing instruments commit a decision on a particular matter to the membership, then it is unreasonable discrimination to refuse to heed a proper vote. On the other hand, if the constitution and bylaws leave a question to the leadership's discretion, then disobedience to the vote is implicitly sanctioned by the membership and thus would not be unreasonable unless the decision were so fundamental as to require membership action by its very nature.

[4] Right to Fair Decision-Making Procedures

Section 101(a)(1) has frequently been used to protect the right of union members to have decisions made, particularly to have votes conducted, by fair procedures.[75.1] The first source of the definition of fairness is the union's constitution and bylaws. If there has not been substantial compliance with such rules, a vote may be overturned and implementation of the decision enjoined. For example, the balloting on a proposed constitutional amendment authorizing the officers to move the union's headquarters was conducted in violation of the procedures set forth in the union constitution; the court found a violation and enjoined the move until such time as defendants could show that a valid vote had been taken.[76] In another case, the union constitution required a two-thirds vote before an assessment could be imposed; Section 101(a)(1) was violated when the union sought to collect the as-

[75] 622 F.2d at 143. *See also* Alexander v. Operating Engineers, 624 F.2d 1235 (5th Cir. 1980).

[75.1] The fair procedures must be applied in membership meetings and referenda. It has been held, however, that the section does not govern votes at union conventions. Denov v. Musicians Local 10-208, 703 F.2d 1034, 1038-39 (7th Cir. 1983).

[76] Stettner v. Printing Pressmen, 278 F. Supp. 675 (E.D. Tenn. 1967).

sessment after only a simple majority had voted in favor.[77]

Even in the absence of a violation of an explicit requirement of the union constitution, Section 101(a)(1) may be used to ensure that a vote produces "a fairly determined expression of the will of the union. . . ."[78] Thus, if the ballot boxes have been stuffed, or some other voting fraud has occurred, the result of the vote may be invalidated.[79] In another case, the union leadership proposed forty-seven amendments to the constitution, required that all amendments be voted up or down together, and informed the membership that the changes were made "necessary" or "mandatory" by the LMRDA. The union admitted in the litigation that followed the vote that the amendments were not in fact required by law. The court invalidated the vote, because the misleading propaganda had led to a "forced choice" which deprived the members of an equal right to vote.[80] The "forced choice" analysis has also led to invalidation of a referendum vote because the issue of a wage increase was tied to a dues increase; otherwise, the courts have been relatively unsympathetic to claims based on requirements that certain issues be voted on together or in a particular order.[81]

The importance of an informed vote has led the courts to require union leaders who espouse one position on a pending vote to permit other members to mail statements of their own

---

[77] Bunz v. Moving Picture Mach. Operators, 567 F.2d 1117 (D.C. Cir. 1977).

[78] Rota v. BRAC, 64 F.R.D. 699, 702 (N.D. Ill. 1974).

[79] Aguirre v. Teamsters Local 165, 633 F.2d 168, 173 (9th Cir. 1980), *citing* Beckman v. Ironworkers Local 46, 314 F.2d 848, 850 (7th Cir. 1963).

[80] Young v. Hayes, 195 F. Supp. 911 (D.D.C. 1961). *See also* Christopher v. Safeway Stores, 476 F. Supp. 950, 954 (E.D. Tex. 1979), *aff'd,* 644 F.2d 467 (5th Cir. 1981). Although no cases have discussed in detail the standards that should be applied to "misleading" leadership conduct cases, in similar suits under Section 101(a)(3), the courts have examined both the intent to mislead, and whether the materials were actually misleading. Ford v. Philadelphia Dist. Coun. of Carpenters, 323 F. Supp. 1136, 1139 (E.D. Pa. 1970); Brooks v. Roofers Local 130, 187 F. Supp 365 (E.D. Pa. 1960). Moreover, in a Section 101(a)(1) case a court found no violation because it deemed the confusing statements not to have been material. Soto v. Masters, Mates and Pilots, 466 F. Supp. 1294 (S.D. N.Y. 1979).

[81] *Compare id. and* Sertic v. Carpenters, 423 F.2d 515 (6th Cir. 1970), *with* Black v. Transport Workers, 454 F. Supp. 813 (S.D.N.Y. 1978), *and* Davey v. Fitzsimmons, 413 F. Supp. 670 (D.D.C. 1976).

views to the membership by using union mailing lists.[82] In all these cases, the union members themselves offered to pay the expenses of the mailings; there has been no decision as to the union's obligation to pay for the mailing. However, inasmuch as members may have the right under Section 101(a)(2) to mail views at their own expense even absent a previous mailing by the leadership,[83] equal treatment would seem to require that if union funds have been used to express one view, publication of the opposing view should also be supported by the treasury.[84] Such a requirement that the exchange of views be facilitated seems greatly preferable to a rule that depends on post hoc evaluations

(*Text continued on page 8-23*)

82 Sheldon v. O'Callaghan, 497 F.2d 1276, 1281-82 (2d Cir. 1974); Blanchard v. Johnson, 532 F.2d 1074, 1079 (6th Cir. 1976).

83 BRAC Lodge 1380 v. Dennis, 625 F.2d 819 (9th Cir. 1980). *But see* NALC Knox Cy. Local v. King, 110 LRRM 2541 (E.D. Tenn. 1982) (plaintiffs could have expressed view by mail, no right to buy ad in union journal on theory that it would be less expensive).

84 Although this issue has never been litigated to a final decision on the merits, it has been held that a consent order embodying such a requirement conferred a common benefit on the union membership as a whole. Pawlak v. Greenawalt, 713 F.2d 972, 980 (3d Cir. 1983). 29 C.F.R. § 452.67 (similar rule under LMRDA Title IV in union elections); Bonner-Lyons v. Boston School Comm., 480 F.2d 442 (1st Cir. 1973) (U.S. Constitution); 17 C.F.R. § 240.14-8 (proxy rules in corporate government).

[b] What Constitutes Discipline

The threshold question in any case arising under Section 101(a)(5) or Section 609 is what acts constitute discipline under the statute. Not every act by a union toward a member will constitute discipline that calls into play procedural protections. Certain zones of autonomy have been reserved to the union. Further, some objectionable union actions may be dealt with under other sections of the Act.

[i] "Fine, Suspend, Expel, or 'Otherwise Discipline' "

How construed: Courts tend to give the term "otherwise discipline" a relatively narrow scope as to Section 101(a)(5), limiting the phrase to actions that conform to the specifically enumerated types of discipline—i.e., fine, suspension, and expulsion.[100] The court will therefore look to the motivation of the union's action and to the manner in which the penalty is enforced.[101] In other words, the punishment suffered must relate to the plaintiff's union membership in order to constitute discipline.[102] Therefore, discharge from employment is discipline when employment status is a function of some internal union status, such as a hiring hall or, conversely, a union blacklist.[103]

When the union's act appears to be in retaliation for the exercise of rights protected by the Act, however, courts *may* construe "otherwise discipline" more broadly.[104]

Who is protected: The guarantees afforded extend only to union members as members.[105] Thus, a union has greater latitude when discharging an employee of the union even though the employee

---

100 *See* Miller v. Holden, 535 F.2d 912 (4th Cir. 1976).

101 *Id.* at 915.

102 *See* Seeley v. Bhd. of Painters, 308 F.2d 52, 59-60 (5th Cir. 1962).

103 Miller v. Holden, *supra* note 100, at 915.

104 *See* Grand Lodge of Int'l Ass'n of Machinists v. King, *supra* note 36; Wood v. Dennis, 489 F.2d 849 (7th Cir. 1973). *But see* Murphy v. Operating Eng'rs Local 18, 18A, 18B, 18C, 18RA, 99 LRRM 2074 (D.C. Ohio 1978) (the court stated that the phrase is entitled to the same construction of scope in both § 105(a)(5) and § 609).

105 Conlon v. Teamsters, Chauffeurs, etc., 409 F. Supp. 1165 (D. Mass. 1976); Gabauer v. Woodcock, 520 F.2d 1084 (8th Cir. 1975), *cert. denied,* 423 U.S. 1061.

is also a union member. The LMRDA does not cover the relationship of employer and employee, and a complaint alleging that procedural safeguards were not followed when a union employee was discharged will probably be dismissed.[106]

Again, while the Act may not cover discharge of union officers generally, when such discharge is in retaliation for the officer's exercise of his or her LMRDA rights, a court may nevertheless find that the Act forbids removal from office for such exercise of rights.[107]

What acts are included/excluded as discipline: Certain union acts have been ruled to be clearly discipline or non-discipline; others represent gray areas, with a number of interrelated elements to consider.

Clear-cut cases include the following. Discipline has been held to include (1) expulsion from the union;[108] (2) prohibiting a member from attending local meetings for a five-year probationary period;[109] and (3) a union's unlawful refusal to reinstate dissident member after conclusion of suspension, since the member was entitled to procedural due process prior to expulsion.[110] Discipline has been held to exclude (1) union action that results in recommending expulsion after finding a member guilty of certain charges;[111] (2) a verbal reprimand for filing charges;[112] (3) the action of removing a supervisor from membership pursuant to a NLRB trial examiner's decision, as opposed to punishment;[113] (4) intimidation, physical violence, and/or economic discrimination by officers against a union member (although such conduct is not "discipline" subject to the procedural safeguards of Section

[106] Bennett v. Hoisting and Portable Eng'rs Local 701, 207 F. Supp. 361 (D. Ore. 1960).

[107] *See* Grand Lodge of Int'l Ass'n of Machinists v. King, *supra* note 36.

[108] Deluhery v. Marine Cooks and Stewards Union, 199 F. Supp. 270 (D.C. Cal. 1961).

[109] Krulikowsky v. Metropolitan Dist. Council, 212 F. Supp. 338 (D.C. Pa. 1962); Rosario v. Dolgen, 441 F. Supp. 657 (D.C. N.Y. 1977).

[110] Murphy v. Operating Eng'rs, *supra* note 104.

[111] Deluhery v. Marine Cooks and Stewards Union, 211 F. Supp. 529 (D.C. Cal. 1962).

[112] Bougie v. Carpenters, 57 CCH Lab. Cases 12435 (D.C. Ind. 1968), 67 LRRM 2402.

[113] UMW v. UMW, 475 F.2d 906 (D.C. Cir. 1973).

representative.[92] The use of unfair voting procedures not only invalidates the vote, but threatens to invalidate the new representative.[93]

Finally, even if a decision is to be made by an international or by certain officers, they may in turn allow the membership to decide by offering to hold a binding vote. When this happens, union members may invoke the rule that once a discretionary decision has been delegated to others it is a violation of due process to ignore the decision if it is unfavorable.[94] Thus, even if a court could have approved a decision had it been made by one route, it should not defer on such grounds if the union has used a different procedure.[95]

[6] Exclusion of Classes of Members

The protections of Section 101(a)(1) may also be invoked if the union has, pursuant to its bylaws or otherwise, excluded a class of members from any participation in a vote or other form of deliberative process; this constitutes the "direct attack" to which the court of appeals for the Second Circuit has sometimes limited the provision.[96] Given the need to avoid substitution of the court's judgment for that of the union concerning which distinctions should be recognized, and given the express proviso permitting "reasonable rules and regulations in [union] constitution and bylaws," an exclusion will be permitted if it appears to be reasonable.[97] For example, a rule that nonworking members, or members who only "moonlight" at the trade, may not vote on wage scales is reasonable, given the much greater interest in the matter on the part of working members;[98] a decision to restrict the au-

---

92 North Elec. Co., 165 NLRB No. 88, 65 LRRM 1379 (1967).

93 Steelworkers, 253 NLRB No. 129, 106 LRRM 1129 (1980).

94 United States ex rel. Accardi v. Shaughnessy, 347 U.S. 260 (1954); Service v. Dulles, 354 U.S. 363 (1957).

95 *Cf.* SEC v. Chenery Corp., 318 U.S. 80 (1943).

96 *See* Section 8.11(B)(2).

97 *E.g.*, Allen v. IATSE, 338 F.2d 309, 319 (5th Cir. 1964); Cleveland Orch. Comm. v. Cleveland Fed'n of Musicians, 303 F.2d 229 (6th Cir. 1962).

98 Williams v. ITU, 423 F.2d 1295, 1298 (10th Cir. 1970). *See also* Myers v. Carpenters, 684 F.2d 225 (2d Cir. 1982) ("contracting members" who contract

tonomy of districts that are not financially self-supporting is also reasonable.[99]

Several principles must be borne in mind when considering the reasonableness of an exclusion. First, there must in fact be a rule. If decisions are made without any standards, the discrimination is per se unreasonable.[100] This is in accord with the general principle that important constitutional rights, among which the right to vote or otherwise participate in political affairs certainly ranks high, may not be denied absent clear standards that severely limit discretion.[101]

Second, the creation of a long-standing class of members who are deprived of the right to vote or participate fully in union affairs is particularly suspect.[102] This is not to say that it is improper to divide a union along craft lines or between skilled and unskilled workers with each group electing its own representatives; it would be improper, however, to award the more powerful offices to one section.[103]

In considering the reasonableness of excluding a class of members, the court normally considers the effect of the exclusion on democracy in the union as a whole. As in Title IV cases, if the issue is the propriety of a rule of eligibility to hold office, a rule that restricts the participation of a large portion of the union should be treated with great skepticism—the greater the exclusion, the less likely it is to be reasonable.[104]

However, the fact that a class of union members may properly be excluded from the consideration of certain or even most matters does not mean that they may be entirely deprived of the right

---

for work and hire other members may be denied right to vote in officer elections).

[99] Smith v. UMW, 493 F.2d 1241, 1244 (10th Cir. 1974).

[100] Burch v. Machinists, 337 F. Supp. 303, 306-07 (S.D. Fla. 1971), *aff'd*, 454 F.2d 1170 (5th Cir. 1971).

[101] *E.g.*, Kunz v. New York, 340 U.S. 290 (1953); Louisiana v. United States, 380 U.S. 145, 153 (1965).

[102] O'Brien v. Paddock, 246 F. Supp. 809 (S.D.N.Y. 1965); Acevedo v. Bookbinders Local 25, 196 F. Supp. 308, 311 (S.D.N.Y. 1961). *But cf.* Allen v. IATSE, 338 F.2d 309, 319 (5th Cir. 1964).

[103] *See* Acevedo v. Bookbinders Local 25, 196 F. Supp. 308, 311 (S.D.N.Y. 1961). *Cf.* 29 C.F.R. §§ 452.42, 452.4.

[104] Usery v. Steelworkers District 22, 543 F.2d 744, 748-49 (5th Cir. 1976).

to participate. For example, in a contract that had to be ratified by the union membership, with one of the key issues concerning the treatment of recall rights, a court held that union members on extended layoff had to be allowed to participate in the decision, although they could properly be excluded from voting on most other matters.[105]

[7] Right to Have Union Meetings

Although, as previously noted, Section 101(a)(1) does not give union members the right to have particular decisions submitted to the membership for a vote, a court recently held that in conjunction with Section 101(a)(2) the subsection does create a requirement that unions hold membership meetings.[106] The court found in the legislative history and in the repeated statutory references to rights which would be exercised that there *must* be membership meetings.[107] The court also concluded that there are some minimum standards for such meetings. Merely providing a space at which members can gather is not sufficient; rather, the meetings must be called, convened, and conducted by the union's officers, and there must be reasonable allowance for membership discussion of matters affecting union policy.[108] However, in appropriate circumstances, meetings may be conducted either on a divisional basis (craft by craft, or shop by shop) or on a union-wide basis.[109]

§ 8.08. Freedom of Speech and Assembly

> Sec. 101(a)(2) Freedom of Speech and Assembly—Every member of any labor organization shall have the right to meet and assemble freely with other members; and to express any views, arguments, or opinions; and to express at meetings of the labor organization

105 Alvey v. General Elec. Co., 622 F.2d 1279 (7th Cir. 1980).

106 Wade v. Teamsters Local 247, 527 F. Supp. 1169, 1174-75 (E.D. Mich. 1981).

107 *See* Bausman v. NCR Indep. U., 74 LRRM 2950 (Ohio Ct. App. 1970).

108 Wade v. Teamsters Local 247, 527 F. Supp. 1169, 1178 (E.D. Mich. 1981).

109 *Id.;* Birthwright v. Karsch, 413 F. Supp. 119 (S.D.N.Y. 1976).

> his views, upon candidates in an election of the labor organization or upon any business properly before the meetings, subject to the organization's established and reasonable rules pertaining to the conduct of meetings: *Provided,* That nothing herein shall be construed to impair the right of a labor organization to adopt and enforce reasonable rules as to the responsibility of every member toward the organization as an institution and to his refraining from conduct that would interfere with its legal or contractual obligations.

Although the language of Section 101(a)(2) is different from that of the First Amendment to the United States Constitution, the legislative history clearly makes it a model on which Congress drew. Congress believed that by adopting a free speech right with provisos it was essentially applying the constitutional right of free speech to the context of union affairs.[110] Because there has been so much litigation under the First Amendment and the courts have been able to develop a large body of rules for deciding such claims, courts faced with Section 101(a)(2) actions have naturally turned to the First Amendment cases for principles to be be applied by analogy.[111] However, specific differences between unions and governments may warrant different rules in a particular context.[112]

[1] Types of Expression Protected

Section 101(a)(2) protects union members' right to express their views in union meetings.[113] However, the right also extends

[110] 2 NLRB, Legislative History of LMRDA 1103, 1294 (1959) (Sen. McClellan).

[111] *E.g.,* Steelworkers v. Sadlowski, 457 U.S. 102, 111, 113, 118 (1982); Mallick v. IBEW, 644 F.2d 228 (3d Cir. 1981).

[112] Steelworkers v. Sadlowski, 457 U.S. 102, 111 (1982). For example, although a government may penalize false statements made with malice, New York Times v. Sullivan, 376 U.S. 254 (1964), unions have not been permitted to do so because internal disciplinary proceedings are not deemed sufficiently fair or careful to apply technical doctrines governing free speech. Cole v. Hall, 339 F.2d 881, 883 (2d Cir. 1965).

[113] Navarro v. Gannon, 385 F.2d 512 (2d Cir. 1967), *cert. denied,* 390 U.S. 989 (1968).

to discussions held in public or with reporters[114] and to discussions about public issues, as opposed to union affairs.[115]

Expression in union affairs is often rough-and-tumble. Accordingly, courts have been reluctant to approve discipline of members simply because they speak in strong terms. For example, the leading case on expression of union members is *Salzhandler v. Caputo*,[116] in which the union's financial secretary found indications among the canceled checks that the president had embezzled funds. He was disciplined for calling the president a "petty robber" and calling others "thieves, scabs, robbers, scabby bosses, bums, pimps, f—— bums, jailbirds." The court of appeals held, however, that his speech was protected.

Other courts have followed *Salzhandler*, finding speech protected even if it is false, malicious, or libelous.[117] This rule applies even if the criticism is directed at the union or the membership itself,[118] because the rule is based in large part on the fear that union tribunals, normally controlled by the targets of an attack, cannot be trusted to apply fairly the definition of malice.[119] Some courts have suggested in dicta, however, that expression may be protected only so long as it is primarily directed either at the union's leadership or at the policies for which the leaders are effectively responsible.[120]

Similarly, speech is not deemed unprotected simply because it may express great hostility to a listener. Physical threats are not protected;[121] however, the dividing line between inexcusable behavior and protected expression can be difficult to detect, and most courts are anxious to avoid the suppression of speech on a

---

114 Machinists Fulton Lodge No. 2 v. Nix, 415 F.2d 212 (5th Cir. 1969); Deacon v. Op. Eng. Local 12, 273 F. Supp. 169 (C.D. Cal. 1967).

115 Mitchell v. Machinists, 196 Cal. App. 2d 796, 16 Cal. Rpt. 813 (Ct. App. 1961).

116 316 F.2d 445 (2d Cir.), *cert. denied*, 375 U.S. 946 (1963).

117 Cole v. Hall, 339 F.2d 881 (2d Cir. 1965); Machinists Fulton Lodge v. Nix, 415 F.2d 212 (5th Cir. 1969); Semancik v. UMW, 466 F.2d 144 (3d Cir. 1972); Keeffe Bros. v. Teamsters Local 592, 562 F.2d 298 (4th Cir. 1977).

118 Giordani v. Upholsterers, 403 F.2d 85, 89 (2d Cir. 1968).

119 Cole v. Hall, 339 F.2d 881, 882 (2d Cir. 1965).

120 Farnum v. Kurtz, 2 Cal. App. Supp. 3d 1, 81 Cal. Rptr. 924 (1969). *See also* Loekle v. Hansen, 551 F. Supp. 74 (S.D.N.Y. 1982); Archibald v. Op. Eng. Local 57, 276 F. Supp. 326, 329 (D.R.I. 1967).

121 Reyes v. Laborers Local 16, 327 F. Supp. 978 (D.N.M. 1971).

"threat" theory.[122] Verbal abuse of a member by an officer is also protected by the act,[123] although some sensitivity is needed to the possibility that threats from a person in power may be more intimidating than those from a member.[124]

As under the First Amendment, activities that facilitate expression, such as picketing, are protected by Section 101(a)(2).[125] Moreover, members have the right to refuse to engage in speech or other expressive activity, for example, a refusal to stand and pledge allegiance to the flag at a union meetings.[126]

[2] Right of Assembly

In addition to protecting the right to express views, Section 101(a)(2) protects members' rights to meet with others, either at union meetings[127] or elsewhere.[128] The provision may not confer the right to call a special meeting of the union;[129] however, as discussed in Section 8.11, *infra,* the act does give members the right to have periodic meetings.[130] As under the First Amendment, the rights of speech and assembly have together been con-

---

[122] *E.g.,* Kelsey v. IATSE Local 8, 419 F.2d 491 (3d Cir. 1969), *aff'g* 294 F. Supp. 1398 (E.D. Pa. 1968). *But see* Generalis v. Local 25, 101 LRRM 2088 (D.D.C. 1979) (verbal abuse of office worker held unprotected).

[123] Marshall v. Textile Workers Local 815, 479 F. Supp. 613, 615 (E.D. Tenn. 1979); Broomer v. Schultz, 239 F. Supp. 699 (E.D. Pa. 1965).

[124] *See* Parker v. Steelworkers Local 1466, 642 F.2d 104 (5th Cir. 1981).

[125] Graham v. Soloner, 220 F.2d 711, 714 (E.D.Pa. 1963).

[126] Stachan v. Weber, 535 F.2d 1202, 1203 (9th Cir. 1976); Loekle v. Hansen, 551 F. Supp. 74 (S.D.N.Y. 1982) (failure to report election violation to incumbents).

[127] Navarro v. Gannon, 385 F.2d 512 (2d Cir. 1967), *cert. denied,* 390 U.S. 989 (1968).

[128] Kuebler v. Cleveland Lithog. & Photo, Local 24-P, 473 F.2d 359 (6th Cir. 1973).

[129] Yanity v. Benware, 376 F.2d 197, 200 (2d Cir. 1967). *But see* Parker v. Steelworkers Local 1466, 642 F.2d 104 (5th Cir. 1981) (violation where officers failed to enforce member's right to bring issue before special meeting). However, if the constitution or bylaws of the union provide a method for calling meetings, or require that particular meetings be held, those rules may be enforced by a lawsuit under such provisions as 29 U.S.C. §§ 301 or 501, or under state law.

[130] Wade v. Teamsters Local 247, 527 F. Supp. 1169 (E.D. Mich. 1981).

strued to include a right of association. Thus, members have a protected right to join organizations, such as caucuses or political groups[131] and may also collaborate with organizations in the pursuit of activities protected by Section 101(a)(2).[132]

[3] Acts That May Violate Section 101(a)(2)

Obviously, the imposition of discipline in the traditional sense (fine, expulsion, loss of the right to attend meetings or to run for union office) will violate Section 101(a)(2) if it is imposed because of the exercise of protected rights. However, it is not necessary that the action constitute "discipline" within the meaning of Section 101(a)(5). Nor is the issue whether a union member has a right to a particular status or to have a particular action taken or not taken. Rather, any action that is taken or omitted because of an exercise of a protected right is deemed to "infringe" upon the right and thus to be actionable.

Thus, a physical attack on a union member done either to teach the member a lesson for having exercised or to prevent the exercise of speech or assembly rights will violate Section 101(a)(2).[133] Also forbidden are (1) refusing to refer a member to jobs, (2) refusing to readmit a member to union membership because of such exercise,[134] and (3) calling the police and having a member arrested for leafleting at the union hall.[135] Similarly, a threat to use the powers of office may so "chill" the exercise of free speech

---

131 Retail Clerks Local 648 v. Retail Clerks, 299 F. Supp. 1012, 1024 (D.D.C. 1969); Turner v. Machinists Lodge 1894, 590 F.2d 409 (2d Cir. 1979. This case raises the possibility that membership in the Communist Party—but in no other radical organization—might be unprotected. However, the LMRDA's ban on Communists as officers of unions (Section 504) has been struck down as unconstitutional, United States v. Brown, 381 U.S. 437 (1965), and it is unlikely that it would stand in the Section 101 (a)(2) context.

132 Ostrowski v. Utility Workers Local 1-2, 530 F. Supp. 208, 217-20 (S.D.N.Y. 1980).

133 *E.g.*, Shimman v. Frank, 625 F.2d 80, 90 (6th Cir. 1980). *But see* Maier v. Patterson, 113 LRRM 3424, 3428 (E.D. Pa. 1982) (no violation if attack is a mere "personal feud").

134 Vandeventer v. Op. Eng. Local 513, 579 F.2d 1373 (8th Cir. 1978); Keeffe Bros. v. Teamsters Local 592, 562 F.2d 298 (4th Cir. 1977).

135 Morrissey v. NMU, 544 F.2d 191 (2d Cir. 1970).

as to be a violation.[136] Thus, even the initiation of disciplinary proceedings to hear charges that a member has exercised free speech rights may be a violation warranting immediate relief.[137] In this regard, however, many courts will be inclined to require the member to submit to the proceedings on the chance that the charges may be dismissed or that no protected conduct will be punished, pursuant to the doctrine of exhaustion of union remedies.[138] As a practical matter, unless the very conduct of the disciplinary proceedings is likely to disrupt a protected activity, a member is best advised to go through at least the trial portion of the proceedings, inasmuch as the union may well either make more actionable mistakes or decide against imposing discipline that will lead to a lawsuit.

The majority view is that removal or suspension from union office because of the exercise of protected rights is a violation of Section 101(a)(2).[139] This controversy and the exceptions to the rule are discussed elsewhere.[140]

Actions taken against a local as a whole may also violate this provision. Thus, an international union that sought to control the conduct of a local meeting, without following the constitutional procedures for imposing a trusteeship or other supervision, was enjoined in one case.[141] This is not to say, however, that a valid trusteeship necessarily suspends Title I rights.[142] Moreover, if a merger is imposed in retaliation for the exercise of Section

---

136 Mallick v. IBEW, 644 F.2d 228, 236 (3d Cir. 1981).

137 Sheridan v. Liquor Salesman Local 2, 303 F. Supp. 999, 1006 (S.D.N.Y. 1969). *See also* Semancik v. UMW District 5, 466 F.2d 144, 157 (3d Cir. 1972) (injunction against hearings where provision violates Section 101(a)(2) and trial body is biased); Tincher v. Piasecki, 520 F. 2d 851, 853 (7th Cir. 1975) (citing without comment unpublished decision below).

138 Baron v. Newspaper Guild Local 173, 342 F.2d 423, 424 (3d Cir. 1965). Although there is an exception to the exhaustion doctrine for free speech cases, Pearl v. Tarantola, 361 F. Supp. 288, 292 (S.D.N.Y. 1973), courts are normally willing to give the union a chance to make its own decision not to impose any discipline at the trial level.

139 *E.g.*, Maceira v. Pagan, 649 F.2d 8 (1st Cir. 1981).

140 *Infra* notes 182-87 and accompanying text.

141 Navarro v. Gannon, 385 F.2d 512, 518-20 (2d Cir. 1967), *cert. denied*, 390 U.S. 989 (1968).

142 *See* Pignotti v. Sheet Metal Workers Local 3, 477 F.2d 825, 832 (8th Cir. 1973).

101(a)(2) rights, it may be enjoined as illegal.[143]

All of the acts discussed above involve the imposition of penal-

(*Text continued on page 8-33*)

---

143 Teamsters Local 1 (ACA) v. Teamsters, 419 F. Supp. 263, 272-74 (E.D.Pa. 1976).

a provision inapplicable to him or her and find him/her guilty of that charge.[156]

Right to a hearing before an unbiased, disinterested tribunal: An essential element of a fair hearing with due process is the impartiality, i.e., open-mindedness, of the tribunal.[157] Often litigated under Section 101(a)(5) is the question of whether the accused has been fairly tried before an unbiased tribunal. Denials of the right to a full and fair hearing have been found when a member of the tribunal had prejudged the guilt of the accused[158] and when the prosecutor was present and actively participated in the hearing panel's deliberation.[159]

But a trial is not per se unfair simply because trial board members were present at a previous informal hearing on those charges, absent a showing of actual unfairness.[160] Nor will a hearing be deemed unfair because the member's accusers were members of influence (business agents) within the union.[161]

However, in a few cases the courts have held that due process was denied when a member was tried by a hearing panel consisting of members who were the political allies of the member's accusers and his own opponents.[162]

Evidence—rights of the accused: The accused union member must see, hear, and have an opportunity to rebut the evidence admitted against him or her.[163] He or she has the right to cross-examine all pertinent witnesses and is not confined to examining the charging parties.[164] The accused must be given a reasonable opportunity to prepare rebuttal witnesses and other defense evidence.[165] Further, a member has the right to make his or her own record of the proceedings by tape recorder or stenographer at his/her own

---

[156] Allen v. Int'l Alliance of Theatrical, etc., *supra* note 22.

[157] Falcone v. Dantinne, *supra* note 149; Parks v. IBEW, *supra* note 123.

[158] Falcone v. Dantinne, *supra* note 149; Stein v. Mutuel Clerks, *supra* notes 91, 141.

[159] *See also* Addison v. Grand Lodge of Int'l Ass'n of Machinists, 318 F.2d 504 (9th Cir. 1963).

[160] Falcone v. Dantinne, *supra* note 149.

[161] Cornelio v. Metropolitan Dist. Council, *supra* note 153.

[162] Tincher v. Piasecki, 520 F.2d 851 (7th Cir. 1975).

[163] Kiepura v. United Steelworkers of America, *supra* note 6.

[164] Ritz v. O'Donnell, *supra* note 132.

[165] Gleason v. Chain Service Restaurant, *supra* note 140.

expense[166] if the union does not supply a certified court reporter to transcribe the proceedings.[167]

The union must follow its own rules: Regarding selection of tribunal, imposition of fines, etc., due process requires that a union follow its own internal rules.[168]

Rights on appeal: On appeal, the accused is entitled to copies of the charges against him or her, the names of the executive board members who tried him or her, the tribunal's decision showing how each member voted, and the transcript of the evidence and proceedings at the trial.[169]

Waiver: A member who knowingly fails to exercise rights guaranteed or offered in connection with the union disciplinary hearings is considered to have waived those rights.[170]

Sufficiency of the evidence: The requirement of a full and fair hearing mandates that there be *some* evidence to support the charges made.[171] If there is no substantial evidence to support the charges *and* the charges are found to be a pretext to expel the member because he or she is a critic and opponent of union officers and their policies, it is a denial of a full and fair hearing even if the hearing complies with all the procedural requisites.[172]

Standard of review: The leading case articulating the standard of review of union disciplinary proceedings is *Boilermakers v. Hardeman,*[173]

In this case, the U.S. Supreme Court held that when hearing a Section 102 suit that challenges a disciplinary hearing, the court will not substitute judicial for union interpretation of union regulations in determining the scope of offenses warranting discipline. A court's scope of review is limited and the court must uphold

---

166 Rosario v. Dolgen, *supra* note 109; Kiepura v. United Steelworkers of America, *supra* note 6.

167 Feltington v. Stage Employees, Local 306, 97 LRRM 2517 (S.D.N.Y. 1978).

168 Stein v. Mutuel Clerks, *supra* notes 91, 141; Kiepura v. United Steelworkers of America, *supra* note 6.

169 Kuebler v. Cleveland Lithographers, etc., *supra* note 32.

170 Ritz v. O'Donnell, *supra* note 132.

171 Int'l Bhd. of Boilermakers, etc. v. Hardeman, *supra* note 145.

172 Leonard v. M.I.T. Employees Union, 225 F. Supp. 937 (D. Mass. 1964). *See also* Vars v. Int'l Bhd. of Boilermakers, etc., *supra* note 142.

173 Int'l Bhd. of Boilermakers, etc. v. Hardeman, *supra* note 145.

[5] Defense under the Provisos

[a] Standards for Application of Provisos

Section 101(a)(2) permits unions to defend their adverse treatment of protected activities pursuant to reasonable rules pertaining to three subjects: (1) "the conduct of meetings," (2) "the responsibility of every member toward the organization as an institution," and (3) "conduct that would interfere with [the union's] performance of its legal or contractual obligations." The courts have developed several principles governing the application of these provisos.

First, the provisos specifically require that there be a "reasonable rule" that was violated.[155] The provisos have no application unless the rule has in fact been adopted;[156] Section 101(a)(2) is thus unlike the procedural protections of Section 101(a)(5), which do not require that the union constitution describe all offenses that may be punished.[157] Moreover, the adoption must have been accomplished by the "labor organization," that is, by the membership's using proper procedures set forth in the constitution and bylaws; mere fiat by an officer will not suffice.[158]

Second, the rule must have been "reasonable"; otherwise, it is void pursuant to Section 101(b) of the act and cannot be cited as an affirmative defense.[159] If a rule is vague or overbroad, it is unreasonable and therefore void.[160] Reasonableness will be de-

155 *E.g.*, Maceira v. Pagan, 648 F.2d 8, 15 (1st Cir. 1981); Loekle v. Hansen, 551 F. Supp. 74 (S.D.N.Y. 1982).

156 Leonard v. MIT Employees Union, 225 F. Supp. 937, 940 (D. Mass. 1964).

157 Boilermakers v. Hardeman, 401 U.S. 233, 243-45 (1971). The difference is attributable to the principle of constitutional law that, because political expression is easily chilled, the regulation of speech must be accomplished through formal standards that eliminate official discretion and give clear notice of what is prohibited. *E.g.*, Gooding v. Wilson, 405 U.S. 518 (1972).

158 Morrissey v. NMU, 544 F.2d 9, 24 (2d Cir. 1976), *aff'g* 397 F. Supp. 659, 664-65 (S.D.N.Y. 1975).

159 Turner v. Machinists Lodge 1894, 98 LRRM 2522, 2525 (E.D.N.Y. 1978), *aff'd*, 590 F.2d 409 (2d Cir. 1979). *See also* NEA v. Dade Cy. Classroom Teach. Ass'n., 407 F. Supp. 539 (S.D. Fla. 1974), *aff'd*, 527 F.2d 1388 (5th Cir. 1976).

160 *E.g.*, Semancik v. UMW Dist. 5, 466 F.2d 144, 153 (3d Cir. 1972); Mallick v. IBEW, 644 F.2d 228, 235-36 (3d Cir. 1981); Sadlowski v. Steelworkers, 645 F.2d 1114, 1125 (D.C. Cir. 1981). In reversing the latter decision, the Supreme

termined by comparing the purportedly legitimate interests served by the rule with the interests Congress showed concern to protect.[161]

Third, merely hypothetical threats to the union's legitimate interests will not suffice to justify reliance on the provisos. Rather, the union must demonstrate that the member's conduct posed a serious threat to the interests protected by the provisos.[162] The burden in this regard is on the union,[163] which must produce strong evidence in order to justify abrogation of the protected activity.[164] In addition, the threat to the union's interests must be imminent[165] and such that counterspeech by the union, or other measures short of censorship, would be insufficient to ward off the serious threat.[166] In sum, the union's showing must approach the imminent and likely harm test that is required in First Amendment cases.[167] This showing will obviously be easier if the action comes at a sensitive point in collective bargaining or during a strike when the union membership has already formulated its position.[168]

Fourth, in order to be valid, a rule must protect not the interests of individual officers who happen to be in a position to exercise disciplinary powers but rather the interests of the organization as

---

Court used an overbreadth analysis, but ruled that the relationship between the challenged rule and the legitimate union interest need not be so precise as under the First Amendment. Steelworkers v. Sadlowski, 457 U.S. 102 (1982).

161 *Id.*

162 Stachan v. Weber, 535 F.2d 1202, 1203 (9th Cir. 1976); Turner v. Machinists Lodge 1894, *aff'd,* 590 F.2d 409 (2d Cir. 1979).

163 Kuebler v. Cleveland Litho, and Photo. Local 24-P, 473 F.2d 359, 363 (6th Cir. 1973).

164 Archibald v. Op. Eng. Local 57, 276 F. Supp. 326, 330 (D.R.I. 1967).

165 Morrisey v. NMU, 397 F. Supp. 659, 665 (S.D.N.Y. 1975), *aff'd,* 544 F.2d 19 (2d Cir. 1976).

166 The facts of such cases as Degan v. Tugmen's and Pilots Ass'n, 84 LRRM 2569 (N.D. Ohio 1973), and Sawyers v. Machinists, 279 F. Supp. 747 (E.D. Mo. 1967), are instructive.

167 Brandenburg v. Ohio, 395 U.S. 444 (1969); Healy v. James, 408 U.S. 169 (1972). *See also* Degan v. Tugmen's and Pilots' Ass'n. 84 LRRM 2569, 2571 (N.D. Ohio 1973) (court relies on three First Amendment cases in requiring "immediate danger to its very existence").

168 *See* Falcone v. Dantinne, 288 F. Supp. 719, 728 (E.D. Pa. 1968), *rev'd on other grounds,* 420 F.2d 1157 (3d Cir. 1969); Leonard v. MIT Employees U., 225 F. Supp. 937 (D. Mass. 1964).

members' rights is to study the constitution of the international union and the bylaws of the local union involved. The sections of the constitution and bylaws dealing with the issue at hand should be identified. Next, it is important to determine what the constitution and bylaws establish as to the procedure set out for redress of members' grievances. Care must be taken here, because constitutions and bylaws often establish time limits for processing members' complaints. If a member is late in meeting such deadlines, the union may refuse to hear the grievance. When suit is filed, the court may also refuse to hear the issue on the ground that the member has failed to fulfill his or her obligation to exhaust union procedures before asserting an alleged right or injustice in court.

Since a court also may refuse to entertain the member's suit because the member has not exhausted internal union remedies for a period of up to four months, it is important to begin the union process as soon as possible. In most unions, these processes begin with a letter from the member to an officer of the union setting out the member's grievance and identifying the sections of the union constitution or bylaws that have been violated. The union constitution and bylaws probably will require that the letter be sent and signed by the member (not an attorney). The letter should be sent by certified mail with return receipt requested; a copy should be retained.

[1] Civil Enforcement

Sec. 102. Any person whose rights secured by the provisions of this title have been infringed by any violation of this title may bring a civil action in a district court of the United States for such relief (including injunctions) as may be appropriate. Any such action against a labor organization shall be brought in the district court of the United States for the district where the alleged violation occurred, or where the principal office of such labor organization is located.

[2] Jurisdiction

The language of the statute makes it clear that any person whose rights have been infringed under "this subchapter" may bring a civil action in a federal district court for relief, including injunctions, as may be appropriate. Bringing this action in federal court does not require diversity of citizenship.[183] Further, such action is not precluded because the NLRB has jurisdiction[184] or has acted in some way concerning it.[185] For violations of the union member's bill of rights (Sec. 101), federal jurisdiction is exclusive and state courts cannot entertain a suit.[186]

Claims brought under Section 102 must be based upon allegations that a labor organization or officer or agent thereof acting in an official capacity has violated one of Sections 101 through 105.[187]

Jurisdiction under Section 102 also extends to claims arising under Section 609, which forbids the disciplining of a union member for exercising any of his or her LMRDA rights:

> Sec. 609. It shall be unlawful for any labor organization, or any officer, agent, shop steward, or other representative of a labor organization, or any employee thereof to fine, suspend, expel, or otherwise discipline any of its members for exercising any right to which he is entitled under the provisions of this Act. The provisions of Section 102 shall be applicable in the enforcement of this section.

---

[183] Addison v. Grand Lodge of Int'l Ass'n of Machinists, 300 F.2d 863 (9th Cir. 1962).

[184] Int'l Bhd. of Boilermakers, etc. v. Braswell, 388 F.2d 183 (5th Cir. 1968), *cert. denied,* 391 U.S. 935, 20 L. Ed. 2d 854, 88 S. Ct. 1848; Int'l Bhd. of Boilermakers, etc. v. Hardeman, *supra* note 145; Rekant v. Shochtay-Gasos Union, etc., *supra* note 176; Parks v. Int'l Bhd. of Elec. Workers, *supra* note 123.

[185] Bailey v. Netter, 266 F. Supp. 165 (D.C. La. 1967); Boggs v. Int'l Bhd. of Elec. Workers, 326 F. Supp. 1 (D. Mont. 1971).

[186] Safe Workers' Organization, etc. v. Balinger, 389 F. Supp. 903 (D.C. Ohio 1974).

[187] Calhoon v. Harvey, 379 U.S. 134, 13 L. Ed. 2d 190, 85 S. Ct. 292 (1964), *rehearing denied,* 379 U.S. 984, 13 L. Ed. 2d 577, 85 S. Ct. 639, *motion denied,* 380 U.S. 901, 13 L. Ed. 2d 793, 85 S. Ct. 878; Thompson v. N.Y.C.R. Co., 361 F.2d 137 (2d Cir. 1966).

sometimes cited if the interference with the union's operations might inhibit its performance of its obligations.[181] However, in these circumstances the defense seems merely duplicative of the second proviso.

[6] Rights of Union Officers

Most courts hold that elected union officers are protected against removal from union office in retaliation for their exercise of Section 101(a)(2) rights.[182] However, as with other adverse actions, unions may raise the provisos in defense, and the courts may properly take into consideration the fact that an officer is in a much better position than is a rank-and-file member to cause serious harm to a union's legitimate interests.[183] Thus, removal will be permitted if the union shows that the officer's otherwise protected activities were inconsistent with the duties of the position held.[184]

A similar rule may be applicable to appointed union officials, but the courts are more evenly split on the question. Some courts have concluded that most of the reasons supporting the rights of elected officers also apply to appointed officers.[185] Other courts have expressed the belief that the election of union officers who may than remove appointees on the basis of their expression both provides adequate guarantees of union democracy and is indeed necessary to permit the members' will, as expressed at elections,

---

181 Rutledge v. Aluminum Workers, 528 F. Supp. 892 (N.D. Ala. 1981).

182 *E.g.*, Lamb v. Miller, 660 F.2d 792 (D.C. Cir. 1981); Maceira v. Pagan, 649 F.2d 8 (1st Cir. 1981); Miller v. Holden, 535 F.2d 913 (5th Cir. 1979). *Contra*, Sheridan v. Carpenters Local 626, 306 F.2d 152 (3d Cir. 1962). Even under the minority rule, however, actions other than removal from office (such as fines or a bar against running for office) are forbidden by Section 101(a)(2). *E.g.*, Martire v. Laborers Local 1058, 410 F.2d 32 (3d Cir. 1969).

183 Levy, *Legal Responses to Rank-and-File Dissent: Restrictions on Union Officer Autonomy*, 30 Buff. L. Rev. 663, 694 (1981).

184 *Id.*; Maceira v. Pagan, 649 F.2d 8 (1st Cir. 1981); Ostrowski v. Utility Workers Local 1-2, 530 F. Supp. 208 (S.D.N.Y. 1980).

185 *E.g.*, Weyhmueller v. SEIU Local 1, 509 F. Supp. 992 (N.D. Ill. 1981); Cooke v. Orange Belt Dist. Council of Painters, 529 F.2d 815 (9th Cir. 1978). *See* Levy, *supra* note 183, at 694-700.

to be implemented.[186] At least in the case of full-time union officers whose positions are so important that the elected administration could not implement its program without being able to fill those positions on the basis of political stances, the Supreme Court, in *Finnegan v. Leu,* made it clear that appointees are not protected against removal for exercise of Section 101(a)(2) rights.[187] Availability of statutory protections to other appointees was expressly left undecided.[188] Since *Finnegan* was decided, lower courts have, by and large, been hospitable to claims by elected officials[188.1] but fairly inhospitable to suits by appointees.[188.2]

§ 8.09. Dues, Initiation Fees, and Assessments

> Section 101(a)(3) Except in the case of a federation of national or international labor organizations, the rates of dues and initiation fees payable by members of any labor organization in effect on the date of enactment of this Act shall not be increased, and no general or special assessment shall be levied upon such members, except—
>
> (A) in the case of a local labor organization, (i) by majority vote by secret ballot of members in good standing voting at a general or special membership meeting, after reasonable notice of the intention to vote upon such question, or (ii) by majority vote of the members in good standing voting in a membership referendum conducted by secret ballot; or
>
> (B) in the case of a labor organization, other than a local labor organization or a federation of national or international labor organizations, (i) by majority vote of the delegates voting at a regular

[186] *E.g.,* Cehaich v. UAW, 496 F. Supp. 912 (E.D. Mich. 1980), *app. pend.,* No. 81-1134; Wambles v. Teamsters, 488 F.2d 888 (5th Cir. 1974).

[187] 456 U.S. 431 (1982).

[188] *Id.* at 441 n.11 and 442–43.

[188.1] *E.g.,* Howard v. IBEW, 113 LRRM 3460 (S.D. Ohio 1983) (Magistrate); Brett v. Sohio Constr. Co., 113 LRRM 2345, 2346–47 (D. Alaska 1983); Mojica v. UFW, No. C-82-0512-WAI (S/J) (N.D. Cal. November 16, 1982). No relief can be obtained under § 609, however. Childs v. IBEW Local 18, 113 LRRM 3313 (9th Cir. 1983); Runyan v. Carpenters, 554 F. Supp. 859 (D. Colo. 1982).

[188.2] *E.g.,* Cehaich v. UAW, 113 LRRM 3220 (6th Cir. 1983); Rutledge v. Aluminum Workers, 681 F.2d 1352 (11th Cir. 1982).

convention, or at a special convention of such labor organization held upon not less than thirty days' written notice to the principal office of each local or constituent labor organization entitled to such notice, or (ii) by majority vote of the members in good standing of such labor organization voting in a membership referendum conducted by secret ballot, or (iii) by majority vote of the members of the executive board or similar governing body of such labor organization, pursuant to express authority contained in the constitution and bylaws of such labor organization: *Provided,* That such action on the part of the executive board or similar governing body shall be effective only until the next regular convention of such labor organization.

Actions to enforce members' democratic rights with respect to dues and assessments are a double-edged sword. On the one hand, the rights declared in this subsection represent a vital means of control over the affairs of the union. On the other hand, thoughtless use of this weapon can imperil the union's very existence in a more direct way than perhaps any other legal attack. The democratic importance of Section 101(a)(3) rights is easy to understand. Fights over taxation historically have been closely linked with complaints about the quality of representation. Yet, unlike every other union vote except officer elections, membership votes on dues must be conducted by secret ballot. Moreover, it is unnecessary to find members who are willing to take the financial risks that are often involved in being nominated against an incumbent officer. Thus, the right to elect officers is no substitute for direct control over dues.[189] Indeed, dues campaigns offer an attractive vehicle for building an opposition movement that may ultimately produce a slate of candidates.[190]

Yet dues are a labor union's lifeline. When a union's strike funds are depleted, when its solvency is imperiled, a dues increase may be necessary for survival. Furthermore, the relief that may be obtained in a dues suit (refund of an illegal increase) may require a union to pay out millions of dollars despite the fact that expenditures have already been made in reliance on the increase.

---

189 King v. Randazzo, 346 F.2d 307, 310 (2d Cir. 1965).

190 This happened, for example, when the Dues Protest Committee led to the Rarick slate's campaign in the Steelworkers. *See* Herling, Right to Challenge 41-57 (1972).

There is no proviso to Section 101(a)(3), as there is to Section 101(a)(2), restricting its application if the union may be seriously harmed as an institution. Rather, this factor must be weighed by the membership when voting on the dues proposal. Of course, even after an increase is invalidated, the membership may decide to impose a special assessment to replace the lost dues. However, members should be wary of using the dues weapon at times when the union's effectiveness is endangered.

Moreover, it is particularly desirable to raise all relevant objections during the campaign and to exhaust internal remedies and file suit quickly. This will permit the leadership to conform the procedures to the law; any violations will be willful ones, and the consequences will be clearly the leadership's fault. Finally, the extent of the damages payable by the union will be minimized because judgment will be entered more promptly.

[1] "Dues" and "Assessments"

The principle to remember in determining whether a financial exaction is "dues" or an "assessment," and therefore subject to the procedural requirements of this subsection, is that the label attached by the union is not determinative; rather, the question is whether it imposes a direct financial burden on the members.[191] The basic rule seems to be that if a financial obligation is incurred by members generally, by a class of members on a regular basis, or in every month in which the member has work, the obligation is "dues."[192] An obligation that is to be paid once by all or a class of members is an "assessment." An obligation imposed on a single individual is neither dues nor an assessment within the meaning of the requirements of Section 411(a)(3).[193]

The distinction between dues and fines occasionally arises. The requirement that a specific sum of money be paid whenever a member misses a membership meeting or fails to perform picket

---

[191] Steib v. ILA Local 1497, 436 F.2d 1101 (5th Cir. 1971).

[192] Denov v. Davis, 61 LRRM 2203, 2205-06 (N.D. Ill. 1966).

[193] Williams v. Typographers, 423 F.2d 1295, 1293-99 (10th Cir. 1970) (whether there is an "increase" depends on effect on class of members, not on individuals).

duty is generally considered to be covered by the voting requirements of Section 101(a)(3).[194] A union that seeks to create a schedule of fines to be imposed for specific violations may thus be required to take a Section 101(a)(3) vote. It should be noted that the procedural requirements of Section 101(a)(5) need not be followed each time a member fails to pay dues, although this exception does not apply to assessments.[195]

The most frequently litigated issue concerning the definition of "dues" and "assessments" is whether per capita taxes, payable to internationals or other bodies at a fixed rate per member, must be approved pursuant to Section 101(a)(3) procedures. Like the above issues, the general rule depends on whether an obligation is imposed on the *members,* as opposed to the local to which they belong. Inasmuch as most unions simply ask members to pay all dues to the local, and the local in turn sends a check to the international or region, Section 101(a)(3) is usually held not to apply.[196] However, if the international receives the dues payments directly from the members or pursuant to an employee checkoff, the per capita tax must have been approved pursuant to Section 101(a)(3).[197] A minority view is that because the per capita tax amounts to a burden on the membership—in effect, the local simply increases its own dues rate to a level sufficient to meet its own needs, plus the amount it must pay per member to the international—the tax is covered by the provision.[198] In response to the logic of this view, some courts following the majority rule have stated that, even if the financial burden is not directly imposed on the member, the per capita increase may be so great as to force the local to increase its own dues; in those circum-

---

194 Gravenstein v. HRE Local 879, 110 LRRM 2346 (D. Alaska 1981). *See also* Kalish v. Hosier, 2356 F. Supp. 853, 856 (D. Colo.), *aff'd mem.,* 364 F.2d 829 (10th Cir. 1965).

195 *See* Section 8.11.

196 *E.g.,* Sawyers v. Machinists, 279 F. Supp. 747, 757-759 (E.D. Mo. 1967); King v. Randazzo, 234 F. Supp. 388, 394 (E.D.N.Y. 1964), *aff'd,* 346 F.2d 307 (2d Cir. 1965).

197 Telephone Workers Local 2 v. Telephone Workers, 362 F.2d 891 (1st Cir. 1966).

198 Jennette v. Ammons, 60 LRRM 2154, 2158 (M.D. Tenn. 1965).

stances the subsection would apply.[199]

[2] "Increased" or "Levied"

The procedures of Section 101(a)(3) are applicable only if dues and initiation fees are "increased," and assessments are "levied." The general rule is that there is a levy or an increase at the time when the decision is made that all, or a certain group of, members will have to pay a certain amount or certain fraction of their wages, not when the decision becomes applicable to an individual.[199.1] Thus, a work tax is not levied anew each time members earn wages and thus incur the obligation to pay 2 percent of their basic scale.[200] Nor does a single member have dues "increased" simply because his/her membership classification changes to one imposing the obligation to pay a higher rate.[201] On the other hand, if a dues exemption for a class of members is removed, the increase must be accomplished in accordance with the statute.[202] Similarly, if a previous resolution provides for an increase of a specified amount that the union has the discretion to "waive," the decision whether or not to forgo the increase must be made according to Section 101(a)(3).[203] When a local union joins a larger body that has higher dues, it must conduct the appropriate secret ballot vote; however, the larger body apparently need not

---

[199] *E.g.*, Seybert v. Lowen, 623 F.2d 780, 785-86 n.11 (2d Cir. 1980).

[199.1] *See generally* Burroughs v. Operating Eng. Local 3, 686 F.2d 723 (9th Cir. 1982).

[200] Denov v. Davis, 61 LRRM 2203 (N.D. Ill. 1966).

[201] Williams v. Typographers, 423 F.2d 1295, 1298-99 (10th Cir. 1970). Nor must a change in the manner of collecting dues be approved by secret ballot. Schwartz v. Musicians Local 802, 237 F. Supp. 149 (S.D.N.Y. 1963), *aff'd*, 340 F.2d 228 (2d Cir. 1964).

[202] Wesling v. Waitresses Local 305, 74 LRRM 3068 (D. Ore. 1970).

[203] Burroughs v. Operating Eng. Local 3, 686 F.2d 723 (9th Cir. 1982). Painters Local 127 v. Painters Dist. Council 16, 423 F.2d 515 (9th Cir. 1969), *aff'g* 278 F. Supp. 830 (N.D. Cal. 1968). However, the existence of limited discretion to waive an increase on the petition of individual locals may not subject the waiver decisions to § 101(a)(3) standards. Denov v. Musicians Local 10-208, 703 F.2d 1034, 1041–42 (7th Cir. 1983).

readopt the dues in order to collect them from its new members.[204]

[3] Required Procedures

The statute sets out different procedures to be followed in voting by local unions and by other bodies. The statute does not state whether local procedures must be followed in order to increase local dues: "[T]he rates of dues . . . payable by members of any labor organization . . . shall not be increased . . . except (A) in the case of a local labor organization, [by specified procedures]; or (B) in the case of [other] labor organizations, [by specified procedures]." The question is whether parts (A) and (B) govern the manner in which certain union bodies may increase dues, or instead govern the manner in which dues payable by members of the specified union bodies can be increased. The clear majority rule adopts the former analysis of the bill, and thus permits an international to increase the dues payable by members of all locals.[205] However, a nonuniform increase must be approved by the local procedures.[206]

Related to this issue is the rule that members are required to pay dues only to a union body that qualifies as a labor organization under Sections 3(i) and (3)(j) of the act.[207] By the same token, a union body cannot require the payment of dues except by its own members, who were entitled to vote on the issue or at least to choose the nonlocal representatives who did vote.[208] According to an alternative holding in one court, however, a local need not allow traveling members of other locals in the same national union to vote on working dues assessed against all who work

---

204 *Compare* Am. Bridge Div. v. NLRB, 457 F.2d 660, 666 (3d Cir. 1972) *with* King v. Randazzo, 346 F.2d 307, 310 (2d Cir. 1965).

205 Ranes v. Office Employees Local 28, 317 F.2d 915 (7th Cir. 1963); Mori v. Boilermakers, 653 F.2d 1279 (9th Cir. 1981). *Contra,* Steib v. ILA Local 1497, 436 F.2d 1101 (5th Cir. 1971).

206 White v. Laborers Local 207, 387 F. Supp. 53 (E.D. La. 1974).

207 *See* Roddy v. UTU, 479 F. Supp. 57 (N.D. Ala.), *aff'd mem.,* 608 F.2d 522 (5th Cir. 1979).

208 *See id.*

within its jurisdiction.[209] This seems inconsistent with the language of the statute, but may be explained by the fact that the national had properly adopted a rule allowing nondiscriminatory work taxes up to 4 percent of the scale wage.[210]

At the local level a decision may be made at a membership meeting or by referendum. Under the former procedure, the union must issue a notice that identifies the specific issue to be decided at the meeting; it is not sufficient simply to state that some unspecified dues issue may be raised.[211] The notice must be given sufficiently in advance of all votes to permit all members to discuss and debate the matter among themselves, and must be distributed in a way calculated actually to be read and understood by most members.[212] A referendum is not specifically required to be preceded by notice; however, in some circumstances, a failure to provide notice might provide grounds for attacking the election as unfair. Whether the vote is at a meeting or by referendum, it must be done by secret ballot.[212.1]

At the international level, or in any other nonlocal body, three different procedures are permissible. The vote may be taken at a convention, in which case there is no secret ballot requirement. If the convention is a regularly scheduled one, there are no specific rules in Section 101(a)(3) governing the vote.[213] If it is a special convention, however, notice must be given to the offices

---

[209] Zentner v. Musicians, 237 F. Supp. 457 (S.D.N.Y.), *aff'd on other grounds,* 343 F.2d 758 (2d Cir. 1965).

[210] This explanation would, however, be inconsistent with the rule that adoption of an indefinite dues level does not excuse noncompliance with Section 101(a)(3) when the specific level is adopted. *Supra* note 203.

[211] Gates v. Dalton, 67 F.R.D. 621, 628 (E.D.N.Y. 1975); Gates v. Dalton, 441 F. Supp. 760 (E.D.N.Y. 1977). One case suggests that notice of a special convention at the international level need not specify the dues proposal, or that dues will be considered at all. Cole v. UAW Local 509, 68 LRRM 2097 (C.D.Cal. 1968). There is no basis for requiring less complete notice at the international than at the local level, however.

[212] Hummel v. Brennan, 469 F. Supp. 1180 (E.D.Pa. 1979).

[212.1] *E.g.,* Kelly v. IATSE Local B-183, 113 LRRM 3486 (S.D.N.Y. 1983).

[213] For example, no advance notice that dues will be considered need be given. Telephone Workers Local 2 v. Telephone Workers, 362 F.2d 891, 895 (1st Cir. 1966).

of the locals, although not to the members themselves.[214] The vote may also be taken by referendum, in which case ballots must be sent to all members individually; they may not be required to come to meetings in order to exercise the right to vote.[215] Finally, if the union constitution or bylaws specifically so provide, a majority on the executive board may vote a temporary increase effective until the next regular convention. The constitutional authority must be quite specific and, indeed, must relate solely to dues.[216]

At whatever level the vote is taken, the specific requirements of Section 101(a)(3) are supplemented by a general rule of fairness. Thus, in one case a dues increase was set aside because the ballot was presented in such a way that it was impossible to vote against the dues increase without also rejecting a proposed wage increase.[217] Moreover, the fair voting procedures required under Sections 101(a)(1) and 101(a)(2) will be read into Section 101(a)(3),[218] and, as under those sections, the more thoroughly elaborated case law under Title IV concerning officer elections serves as a guide both to substantive rules and to adjudicatory standards.[219] Thus, dues votes have been invalidated for such violations as unfair counting procedures and ballot box stuffing.[220]

All methods must produce a majority vote in favor of the increase. This does not prohibit the use of weighted voting in which the number of votes cast by each delegate is proportional to the number of members represented; thus an increase can be

---

214 Cole v. UAW Local 509, 68 LRRM 2097, 2099 (C.D. Cal. 1968).

215 Telephone Workers Local 2 v. Telephone Workers, 362 F.2d 891, 895 (1st Cir. 1966).

216 King v. Randazzo, 346 F.2d 307, 309 (2d Cir. 1965).

217 Sertic v. Cuyahoga Dist. Council of Carpenters, 423 F.2d 515 (6th Cir. 1970).

218 Denov v. Musicians Local 10-208, 703 F.2d 1034, 1039 (7th Cir. 1983). Rota v. BRAC, 64 F.R.D. 699, 702 (N.D. Ill. 1974).

219 *E.g.*, Hummel v. Brennan, 469 F. Supp. 1180 (E.D.Pa. 1979) (uses Title IV as analogy for secret ballot precautions and union burden to rebut inference that violations "may have affected" the result). *See also* White v. King, 319 F. Supp. 122, 124 (E.D. La. 1970) (without citing parallel rule under Title IV, court says no prejudice must be shown because of lack of secret ballot).

220 *E.g.*, Teas v. Teamsters Local 413, 504 F. Supp. 12, 16 (S.D. Ohio 1978); Rota v. BRAC, 489 F.2d 998 (7th Cir. 1973).

valid even if the number of actual *delegates* voting for the increase is smaller than the number voting against it.[221] The requirement of a majority sets only a minimum; the union's constitution may validly require a super-majority of some kind.[222] The statute may not require a system of proportional representation for dues votes, as long as meaningful representation is achieved.[222.1]

A union may delay implementation of a voted dues increase for a short period of time if the circumstances so warrant; however, it cannot simply hold the increase in abeyance until it chooses to put it into effect.[223] Similarly, a local that has been directed to increase dues by a proper international vote must comply separately with Section 101(a)(3) if it wishes to take an increase in circumstances other than those specified by the international.[224]

[4] Relief

Issues of relief under all provisions of Title I are generally treated elsewhere.[225] However, some issues specific to dues increases are briefly discussed here. For example, one might expect that, inasmuch as the principal relief sought under Section 101(a)(3) is rescission of unlawful monetary exactions and refunds of money collected, preliminary relief might not be available, unlike other Title I cases.[226] However, the courts have held that Section 101(a)(3) involves crucial voting rights that cannot

---

221 Musicians v. Wittstein, 379 U.S. 171 (1964).

222 Bunz v. Moving Picture Mach. Oper., 567 F.2d 1117, 1119 (D.C. Cir. 1977).

222.1 Denov v. Musicians Local 10-208, 703 F.2d 1034, 1040 (7th Cir. 1983). The court upheld as reasonable a dues vote in which larger locals had some extra votes, but not enough to be proportioned to their membership. It relied in part, however, on the fact that a roll call, in which each local casts a vote proportional to the size of its membership, could be forced by petition of fifteen locals or thirty delegates. This limitation was justified by the difficulties which would be imposed if every issue had to be decided by a role call vote.

223 Brooks v. Roofers Local 30, 187 F. Supp. 365, 368 (E.D. Pa. 1960) (four-month delay justified by strike); Painters Local 125 v. Painters Dist. Council 16, 415 F.2d 1121 (9th Cir. 1969), *aff'g* 278 F. Supp. 830 (N.D. Cal. 1968).

224 Crowley v. Teamsters Local 82, 521 F. Supp. 614, 633 (D. Mass. 1981).

225 *Infra*, Sections 8.20-8.22.

226 *See infra* Section 8.21.

be measured in monetary terms alone.[227] Moreover, because nonpayment of dues can easily lead to termination of membership and employment, preliminary relief against collection of the increased dues is particularly appropriate.[228]

The other principal issue concerning relief involves the disposition of the unlawfully collected dues. Courts tend to apply a "may have affected" standard, borrowed from Title IV, in deciding whether to order that dues approved in an unlawful election be repaid to the membership.[228.1] The law is clear that an unlawful vote cannot be cured by a later valid vote, even if the later vote purports to be retroactive.[229] Nor can the union claim that because the illegally collected money was spent for the benefit of all members, the members are estopped from obtaining refunds.[230] Thus, the majority rule is that the proper remedy is to require the union to reimburse all members who were required to pay the increase.[231] In one case, however, the court reasoned

(*Text continued on page 8-49*)

---

227 Hummel v. Brennan, 469 F. Supp. 1180 (E.D. Pa. 1979).

228 Stieb v. ILA Local 1497, 436 F.2d 1101, 1106-07 (5th Cir. 1966). *See also* White v. King, 319 F. Supp. 122, 126 (E.D. La. 1970) (damages awarded for lost wages).

228.1 Kelly v. IATSE Local B-183, 113 LRRM 3486, 3488 (S.D.N.Y. 1983); Thompson v. Flight Attendants, 109 LRRM 2870 (C.D. Cal. 1980). *Contra,* White v. King, 319 F. Supp. 122, 124–25 (E.D. La. 1970).

229 *E.g.,* Telephone Workers Local 2 v. Tel. Workers, 362 F.2d 891, 896 (1st Cir. 1966).

230 Teas v. Teamsters Local 413, 504 F. Supp. 12, 17 (S.D. Ohio 1978). This case involved an additional issue because the increased dues were collected during a trusteeship. The court held that because the international had the power to cease collection of the unlawful increase, it was properly held liable to repay the dues. *Id.* at 18-19.

231 *E.g.,* Peck v. Food Distrib. Local 138, 237 F. Supp. 113, 115 (D. Mass. 1965). This reimbursement includes persons who did not exhaust internal union remedies, and therefore might not have been qualified to be plaintiffs in the action. *Id. But cf.* Barnes v. Sanzo, 680 F.2d 3 (2d Cir. 1982) (retroactive vote among members who were in union at time of illegal increase, plus retired

individual members. Rather, the decision must involve the application of general rules or principles to the disadvantage of an individual.[270]

Third, due process is not required prior to the purely ministerial application of the general principles to an individual. If, pursuant to a collective bargaining agreement, a union refuses to refer a member for employment or reclassifies a member for referral or seniority purposes because the member is an alcoholic or has not worked recently or is so incompetent that employers have refused to accept the referrals, it need not hold a hearing.[271] This principle has also been applied to exempt from a due process hearing the union expulsion of supervisor members pursuant to an NLRB decision that their participation in union affairs violated the NLRA.[272] If, however, there is a dispute concerning the facts that make the general principles applicable to the particular individual, then the procedures required by Section 101(a)(5) must be followed.[273]

[b] Actions Related to Employment

It is in the decisions relating to union actions affecting a member's employment that the greatest contradictions confounding

---

270 Scovile v. Watson, 338 F.2d 678 (7th Cir. 1964), *cert. denied,* 3809 U.S. 963 (1965); Figueroa v. NMU, 342 F.2d 400, 406 (2d Cir. 1965).

271 *E.g., id.;* Williams v. ITU, 423 F.2d 1295, 1297 (10th Cir. 1970); Caravan v. ITU Local 86, 381 F. Supp. 14 (E.D. Pa. 1974); Turner v. Boilermakers Local 455, 528 F. Supp. 1008 (N.D. Ala. 1981). *See also* Rekant v. Meatcutters Local 446, 320 F.2d 271 (3d Cir. 1963).

272 UMW Local 13410 v. UMW, 475 F.2d 906, 911 (D.C. Cir. 1973).

273 *E.g.,* Figueroa v. NMU, 342 F.2d 400, 406 (2d Cir. 1965); Driscoll v. Op. Eng. Local 139, 484 F.2d 682, 689 (7th Cir. 1973). *See also* Macaulay v. Boston Typographers, 692 F.2d 201 (1st Cir. 1982). *Contra,* Hackenburg v. Boilermakers, 694 F.2d 1237 (10th Cir. 1982), *criticized,* 34 Union Democ. Rev. 4 (1983). In Galke v. Duffy, 645 F.2d 118 (2d Cir. 1981), the majority suggests that no hearing was required where the union was "uniformly and fairly" enforcing its rules on status for employment purposes, and the member's testimony in support of his former status was "incredible." In dissent, Judge Oakes said that the question should not turn on whether the union was correct on the merits; rather, if the employee *disputes* the underlying facts, there should be a hearing. Judge Oakes seems to have the better of the debate.

attempts to state general principles for interpretation of "otherwise discipline" are found. Courts have been reluctant to apply Section 101(a)(5) in this area for two reasons. First, employers are not subject to the Bill of Rights of Union Members; thus, in most cases, a remedy pursuant to Section 101(a)(5) will be incomplete. Yet, because employer decisions are implicated, the employers will necessarily be drawn into the litigation; most judges' proemployer prejudices militate against the cause of action. Second, and more important, unions make so many decisions concerning members' employment and these decisions are so frequently subject to dispute that a general application of Section 101(a)(5) would substantially increase the frequency of litigation under the LMRDA. Courts frequently seek to avoid increases in the number of cases filed.

If a union actively seeks the discharge of one of its members and the company acts at its behest, these considerations apply but weakly; thus, a court will find "discipline" requiring due process.[274] The same result obtains if the union puts a member's name on a blacklist.[275] On the other hand, if a member complains that the union has refused to process a grievance or to take it to arbitration, the courts are steadfast in denying a cause of action under Section 101(a)(5).[276] Although these courts normally leave open the possibility that a refusal to arbitrate might be discipline subject to due process in unspecified circumstances,[277] the only ruling that actually said so characterized the union decision as

---

[274] *E.g.,* Duncan v. Peninsula Shipbuilders Ass'n, 394 F.2d 237 (4th Cir. 1968).

[275] Detroy v. AGVA, 286 F.2d 75, 81 (2d Cir. 1961). *But see* Hackenburg v. Boilermakers Local 101, 694 F.2d 1237 (10th Cir. 1982), which states that employment related sanctions imposed at the hiring hall are governed by § 101(a)(5), *citing* Finnegan v. Leu, 456 U.S. 431 (1982). *Criticized,* 34 Union Democracy Rev. 4 (1983).

[276] *E.g.,* Allen v. Teamsters Local 820, 185 F. Supp. 492, 494 (D.N.J. 1960); Scovile v. Watson, 338 F. 2d 678 (7th 1964), *cert. denied,* 380 U.S. 963 (1965). *See also* Hall v. Pacific Maritime Ass'n, 67 LRRM 2756, 2758-59 (N.D. Cal. 1968) (provision does not apply to actions of a joint committee through which employers must hire and fire).

[277] *E.g.,* Catanzaro v. Teamsters Local 812, 65 LRRM 2092, 2094 (E.D.N.Y. 1967).

taking the member off the job.[278]

[c] Nonpayment of Dues

The statute expressly excludes sanctions imposed for nonpayment of dues.[279] Many unions make suspension or expulsion automatic upon delinquency of a specified duration, and the exception extends to late payment as well as to a flat refusal to pay.[280] However, if there is a real question concerning the facts that made the member liable for the dues, notice and hearing are required to determine the facts.[281]

[d] Treatment of Union Entities and Officers

Several early decisions found that Section 101(a)(5) procedures were required before an international union could revoke a local union's charter and order one local merged into another local.[282] These courts relied on the effects of the merger on members' pension and employment rights, on the hostility of the officers or members of the new local to the members of the old, and on the loss of influence when a small local was joined with a much larger one. In more recent merger cases, courts recite the same factors, but tend to be less sympathetic to claims that members' rights are being affected.[283]

---

278 Gross v. Kennedy, 183 F. Supp. 750, 756 (S.D.N.Y. 1960).

279 Brady v. Transport Workers Local 551, 96 LRRM 3281, 3285 (S.D.N.Y. 1977).

280 Burch v. Machinists, 433 F.2d 561, 563 (5th Cir. 1970).

281 Caravan v. ITU Local 86, 381 F. Supp. 14, 20 (E.D. Pa. 1974). If the question is not whether the facts are those required pursuant to union rules, but rather whether union rules as applied to given facts require the dues, or whether the rules are lawful, then Section 101(a)(5) does not apply.

282 Pittman v. Carpenters, 251 F. Supp. 323 (M.D. Fla. 1966); Parks v. IBEW, 314 F.2d 886, 920-22 (4th Cir. 1963); Calabrese v. Carpenters, 211 F. Sup. 609 (D.N.J. 1962), *aff'd,* 324 F.2d 955 (3d Cir. 1963).

283 *E.g.,* Sheet Metal Workers Local 37 v. Sheet Metal Workers, 655 F.2d 892 (8th Cir. 1981). *Compare* Parks v. IBEW, 314 F.2d 886, 922 (4th Cir. 1963) (unclear what effect will be on members' rights, but those rights will be "touched"), *with* Teamsters Local 1 (ACA) v. Teamsters, 416 F. Supp. 263, 273 (E.D. Pa. 1976)

The legislative history makes clear that a hearing would not be required *before* a union officer was summarily suspended.[284] Early authorities suggested that a hearing was required before the suspension or removal could be made permanent;[285] however, the clear majority rule is to the contrary.[286] This is contrasted with the rule that a union decision barring a member from seeking or holding office for a given term is discipline.[287]

[2] Prehearing Requirements

[a] Notice

Section 101(a)(5)(A) requires that a member be given written notice that a hearing will be held on given charges on a certain date. The notice must indicate that a formal hearing will be held, that the accused will have the opportunity to present witnesses and confront adverse witnesses, and that serious penalties may be imposed.[288] It must be sent in a manner reasonably calculated to

---

(dilution of voting power doesn't make merger discipline where members can vote in new, larger union).

[284] Conference Report on LMRDA, H. Rep. No. 1147, 86th Cong., 1st Sess., at 31, 1 NLRB, Legislative History 935 (1959).

[285] *E.g.*, DeCampli v. Greeley, 293 F. Supp. 746, 753 (D.N.J. 1968); Dunau, *Some Comments on the Bill of Rights of Members of Labor Organizations,* 14 N.Y.U. Conf. on Labor 77, 94 (1961). *See also* 2 NLRB, Legislative History 1295 (Sen. McClellan), 1667 (Rep. McCormack) (1959).

[286] *E.g.*, Machinists v. King, 335 F.2d 340, 341-43 (9th Cir. 1964), *cert. denied,* 379 U.S. 920 (1964); Martire v. Laborers' Local 1058, 410 F.2d 32, 35 (3d Cir.), *cert. denied,* 396 U.S. 903 (1969); Miller v. Holden, 535 F.2d 912, 915 (5th Cir. 1976).

[287] *E.g.*, Martire v. Laborers Local 1058, *supra;* Sullivan v. LIUNA, 707 F.2d 347, 350 (8th Cir. 1983). Hartner v. Clothing Workers Jt. Bd., 80 LRM 2246 (D. Md. 1972). When the decision is made in the context of an eligibility determination prior to a union election, Title IV may be the exclusive remedy. *See* Driscoll v. Op. Eng. Local 139, 484 F.2d 682 (7th Cir. 1973). *See also* Chapter 9, *infra.*

[288] Reilly v. Sheet Metal Workers, 488 F. Supp. 1121, 1127 (S.D.N.Y. 1980). In one case, the penalty for the offense charged was $25. When the accused failed to attend, the union imposed forty fines on the theory that there were forty separate violations. The court held that the notice was insufficient because there was no indication that $1000, not $25, was at stake. OPEIU v. Sabetay, 98 LRRM 3167, 3170 (N.J. Dist. Ct. 1978).

reach the member; if the union learns that delivery has not been effected, it must try again.[289]

The notice must specify the conduct with which the member is charged. Although the strict requirements of a criminal indictment do not apply, at a minimum the notice must specify (1) the minimum circumstances surrounding the infraction, (2) the time and place, as nearly as can be determined, and (3) the names of other members connected with the violation if the names are reasonably necessary for the member to identify the material events.[290] If this description is clear, it is not necessary to identify the specific rule violated.[291] Section 101(a)(5) does not impose any requirement that the union's constitution or bylaws specify what conduct may be punished.[292]

The burden is upon the union to provide a specific notice; the member need not seek a bill of particulars. A member who does obtain the specifics sufficiently in advance of the hearing may not complain of the inadequacy of the original notice.[293] Similarly, if the member concedes that he or she had independent knowledge of the specifics, or that the factual allegations underlying the discipline are correct, minor inadequacies in the notice will be excused.[294]

[b] Reasonable Time to Prepare Defense

Section 101(a)(5)(B) requires that a union member must be given a reasonable time between the notice and the hearing to

---

[289] Reilly v. Sheet Metal Workers, 488 F. Supp. 1121, 1126 (S.D.N.Y. 1980).

[290] The leading case stating the standard is Gleason v. HRE Local 12, 300 F. Supp. 1241, 1251-52 (S.D.N.Y. 1969), *aff'd,* 422 F.2d 342 (2d Cir. 1970). *See also* Berg v. Watson, 417 F. Supp. 806, 810 (S.D.N.Y. 1976); Cefalo v. Moffett, 78 LRRM 2112, 2114 (D.D.C. 1971).

[291] Messenger v. Op. Eng. Local 4, 79 LRRM 2626 (1st Cir. 1977).

[292] Boilermakers v. Hardeman, 401 U.S. 233, 245 (1971).

[293] Megellsen v. Plasters Local 518, 233 F. Supp. 459, 461 (W.D. Mo. 1964); Null v. Carpenters Houston Dist. Coun., 239 F. Supp. 809 (S.D. Tex. 1965).

[294] *E.g.,* Vars v. Boilermakers, 215 F. Supp. 943, 948 (D. Conn.), *aff'd,* 320 F.2d 576 (2d Cir. 1963); Carroll v. Musicians Local 802, 236 F. Supp. 161 (S.D.N.Y. 1963). However, substantially inadequate notice cannot be cured in this fashion. Strom v. National Ass'n of Basketball Refs., 113 LRRM 3433, 3437 (E.D. Pa. 1983).

prepare a defense. Although a disruptive union member may be removed from a meeting if necessary to continue the meeting, the union cannot summarily impose any punishment during the meeting.[295] There are few decisions as to how much more time must be allowed. One decision held that a letter mailed twenty-four days before the hearing allowed sufficient time.[296] Another decision held that seven days' notice was insufficient; however, the court appeared to rely on the fact that the union's bylaws specifically required twenty days' notice.[297] It is wise to seek any continuances in advance of the scheduled hearing; such a request made at the hearing may be disregarded as a mere delaying tactic.[298]

[3] Full and Fair Hearing

Section 101(a)(5)(C) requires that the union afford the member a "full and fair hearing." This provision precludes trial by a biased tribunal, governs the procedures which must be followed at trial, and permits a limited review of the findings of the trial body.

[a] Biased Tribunals

Compliance with procedural requirements that are fair on their face will not validate discipline imposed by a biased tribunal. Thus, an accused member may not be tried by his or her recent electoral and political opponents[299] or by persons allied with or

---

[295] Ford v. Kammerer, 287 F. Supp. 853, 856-85 (E.D. Pa. 1968).

[296] Falcone v. Dantine, 288 F. Supp. 719, 727 (E.D. Pa. 1968), *rev'd on other grounds,* 420 F.2d 1157 (3d Cir. 1969).

[297] Jacques v. ILA Local 1418, 246 F. Supp. 857, 859 (E.D. La. 1965). *See also* Vars v. Boilermakers, 215 F. Supp. 943, 948 (D. Conn.), *aff'd,* 320 F.2d 576 (2d Cir. 1963).

[298] *Id.*

[299] *E.g.,* Kiepura v. Steelworkers Local 1091, 358 F. Supp. 987 (N.D. Ill. 1975); Loekle v. Swayduck, 94 LRRM 2442, 2445-46 (S.D.N.Y. 1976). This rule has been extended to require disqualification of a trial committee member who has been the subject of a charge by the accused. The court was at pains to note,

related to those opponents.[300] On the other hand, the bias of the accuser does not make the resulting discipline unlawful under Section 101(a)(5). Nor will the fact that the biased accusers are influential in the local suffice to invalidate resulting discipline, absent a showing that the members of the tribunal were especially influenced.[301]

However, the members who file a charge or testify against the accused may not themselves sit in judgment.[302] Nor may an individual who has prejudged the guilt of the accused participate in the tribunal.[303] Courts have also held that participation in a previous trial pursuant to which the accused was found guilty or in an informal prehearing settlement hearing creates a conclusive presumption of prejudgment, which bars membership in a subsequent trial body on the same charges.[304]

Participation in the hearing by even one biased person violates the hearing requirement,[305] although if the trial is before the membership as a whole, the fact that some members are biased is not alone sufficient to invalidate the discipline.[306] One early

---

however, that an accused member will not be permitted to force disqualifications by attacking members of the trial committee. Tincher v. Piasecki, 520 F.2d 851, 855 (7th Cir. 1975).

300 Semanick v. UMW Dist. 5, 466 F.2d 144, 157 (3d Cir. 1972); Falcone v. Dantinne, 420 F.2d 1157, 1163 n.8 (3d Cir. 1969).

301 Burke v. Boilermakers, 302 F. Supp. 1345, 1353 (N.D. Cal. 1967), *aff'd,* 417 F.2d 1063 (9th Cir. 1969); Cornelio v. Carpenters Phila. Dist. Coun., 243 F. Supp. 126 (E.D. Pa. 1965), *aff'd,* 358 F.2d 728 (3d Cir. 1966).

302 Cornelio v. Carpenters Phila. Dist. Coun., 243 F. Supp. 126 (E.D. Pa. 1965), *aff'd,* 358 F.2d 728 (3d Cir. 1966). *But cf.* Gabauer v. Woodcock, 520 F.2d 1084, 1094 (8th Cir. 1975) (no violation where head of audit department who conducted audit, presided at hearing of charge by union president based on audit).

303 Falcone v. Dantinne, 420 F.2d 1157, 1161-63 (3d Cir. 1969); Stein v. Mutuel Clerks, 560 F.2d 486, 491 (1st Cir. 1977).

304 Rosario v. ILGWU Local 10, 605 F.2d 1228, 1242-44 (2d Cir. 1979); Falcone v. Dantinne, 420 F.2d 1157, 1163 n. 8 (3d Cir. 1969).

305 *Id.* at 1161-63; Myers v. IATSE Local 144, 667 F.2d 817 (9th Cir. 1982).

306 Curtis v. IATSE Local 125, 687 F.2d 1024 (7th Cir. 1982) (no violation where member chose trial by membership instead of by executive board, although prosecutor and witnesses voted on discipline); Murphy v. Op. Eng. Local 18, 99 LRRM 2074, 2128 (N.D. Ohio 1978) (court found a violation because the officers sought to stack the deck by packing the meeting with prejudiced members). Myers v. IATSE Local 44, 667 F.2d 817 (9th Cir. 1982), also involved an attempt by the prosecutor to stack the deck.

decision held that it was insufficient to show a structural bias attributable to the mixing of functions of prosecutory and adjudicatory functions; rather, this court held that the plaintiff must show that the apparent bias actually affected the result.[307] The great weight of authority, however, is that actual effect need not be shown.[308] This rule is tempered by a de minimis requirement for showing the presence of bias.[309]

[b] Procedures at Trial

The basic requirement of a full and fair hearing is that members be able to present witnesses in their own defense[310] and to cross-examine witnesses against them.[311] If the members who file the charges do not testify as witnesses, it is unnecessary that they be presented for cross-examination, so long as the accused be given the opportunity to call them as hostile witnesses; indeed, if guilt is shown by documents of admitted authenticity and accuracy, it has been held that no witnesses are required at all.[312] However, it is necessary that evidence be put on the record; the trial body may not rely on its own knowledge of the events.[313] It has also been held to be permissible to require all cross-examination questions to be propounded by both accuser and accused through a hearing officer if the defense was in no way limited.[314] The complete hearing must take place in the presence of the accused; it is improper for the accuser or prosecutor to meet ex

---

[307] Parks v. IBEW, 314 F.2d 886, 912-13 (4th Cir. 1963).

[308] *E.g.*, Myers v. IATSE Local 44, 667 F.2d 817 (9th Cir. 1982); Tincher v. Piasecki, 520 F.2d 851, 855 (7th Cir. 1975).

[309] *E.g.*, Ritz v. O'Donnell, 413 F. Supp. 1365, 1371 (D.D.C. 1976), *quoted*, Murphy v. Op. Eng. Local 18, 99 LRRM 2074, 2117 (N.D. Ohio 1978).

[310] Reilly v. Sheet Metal Workers, 488 F. Supp. 1121, 1127 (S.D.N.Y. 1980).

[311] Allen v. IATSE, 338 F.2d 309, 317 (5th Cir. 1964); Anderson v. Carpenters, 53 LRRM 2795 (D. Minn. 1963).

[312] Ritz v. O'Donnell, 566 F.2d 731, 736 (D.C. Cir. 1977).

[313] Kiepura v. Steelworkers Local 1091, 358 F. Supp. 987, 991 (N.D. Ill. 1973).

[314] Nelms v. Plumbers, 405 F.2d 715 (5th Cir. 1968). This may be the right result if all properly requested questions are in fact asked, although the tendency of such a procedure to inhibit the defense is troubling.

parte with the trial body.[315] However, if the accused refuses to participate in an otherwise valid proceeding, the union may conduct the trial in absentia.[316]

The union must offer the accused an opportunity to make an accurate record of the trial by bringing a tape recorder into the sessions.[317] However, if the union has arranged for the transcription of the proceedings by an independent certified court reporter, it has been held that no substantial rights are violated if the union member is refused permission to use a tape recorder.[318] Another court has deemed the prohibition of a tape recorder to be lawful if the member did not dispute the facts underlying the discipline.[319]

Union members are generally not permitted to bring outside legal counsel into disciplinary hearings.[320] The courts reason that it is required only that accuser and accused be on roughly the same footing. Unions have an interest in keeping disciplinary proceedings on a lay level; if the accused brings in a lawyer, the accuser will be forced to do so too. Moreover, the union members who form trial bodies will probably be on approximately the same level as the accused.[321] Although no cases have decided this point, it seems likely that the rule on lawyers is limited to this underlying reasoning. If union counsel participates, or if the prosecutor is a member who happens to be a lawyer, or if the level of complexity of the procedures or the sophistication of accuser and trial body is so great that the accused is at a substantial

---

315 Stein v. Mutuel Clerks, 560 F.2d 486, 491 (1st Cir. 1977).

316 Feltington v. IATSE Local 306, 605 F.2d 1251, 1256 (2d Cir. 1979). *But cf.* OPEIU v. Sabetay, 98 LRRM 3167, 3170 (N.J. Dist. Ct. 1978), discussed *supra* note 288.

317 Rosario v. ILGWU Local 10, 605 F.2d 1228, 1240-42 (2d Cir. 1979); Deacon v. Op. Eng. Local 12, 59 LRRM 2706 (S.D. Cal. 1965); Kiepura v. Steelworkers Local 1091, 358 F. Supp. 987 (N.D. Ill. 1973).

318 Feltington v. IATSE Local 306, 605 F.2d 1251, 1256 (2d Cir. 1979).

319 Pawlak v. Greenawalt, 464 F. Supp. 1265, 1271 (M.D. Pa. 1979). This ruling seems to be akin to the harmless error rule that applies to due process violations in criminal prosecutions. Chapman v. California, 386 U.S. 18 (1967).

320 Winterberger v. Teamsters Local 162, 89 LRRM 2737, 2739 (D. Ore. 1975); Cornelio v. Carpenters Phila. Dist. Coun., 243 F. Supp. 126, 129 (E.D. Pa. 1966), *aff'd,* 358 F.2d 728 (3d Cir. 1966).

321 Curtis v. IATSE Local 125, 687 F.2d 1024 (7th Cir. 1982).

disadvantage, then it may be unlawful to deny the accused the right to bring a lawyer as a representative.

[c] Fair Determinations

A court may not review the decision of the trial body to determine whether the conduct that has been punished falls within the prohibition of the union rules alleged to have been violated.[322] However, the decision must be limited to the offenses described in the charge and the notice to the member.[323] Section 101(a)(5) also does not require that there be sufficient evidence to support the decision; so long as there is some evidence in the record to support the result, due process has been satisfied.[324]

One court has held that Section 101(a)(5) imposes no limits on the kinds of discipline which may be imposed.[325] However, under the common law there is a requirement that the punishment not be unduly excessive by comparison with the crime.[326] By analogy with the constitutional due process limitations of excess punishment,[327] it seems appropriate that a similar rule be applied, albeit with caution, under Section 101(a)(5).

[4] Internal Union Review of Trials

[a] Appeals

The union has no obligation under Section 101(a)(5) to afford its members the right to take an appeal; the only required "full

---

322 Boilermakers v. Hardeman, 401 U.S. 233, 244-45 (1971).

323 Allen v. IATSE, 338 F.2d 309 (5th Cir. 1964); Eisman v. Clothing Workers Balt. Jt. Bd., 352 F. Supp. 429 (D. Md. 1972), *aff'd,* 496 F.2d 1313 (4th Cir. 1974).

324 Boilermakers v. Hardeman, 401 U.S. 233, 246 (1971). As previously noted, this evidence must be in the record, inasmuch as the trial body may not rely on its own knowledge of the events at issue. *Supra* note 313.

325 Rosario v. ILGWU Local 10, 605 F.2d 1228, 1238 (2d Cir. 1979) (penalty may include exclusion from membership meetings).

326 Gulickson v. Forest, 290 F. Supp. 457, 467 (E.D.N.Y. 1968).

327 Rummel v. Estelle, 445 U.S. 263 (1980).

and fair hearing" is the trial.[328] Further, if appeals are permitted, the member has no right to present or cross-examine witnesses unless the union constitution provides otherwise.[329] It has also been held that a union may, if the member is not indigent, condition the right to appeal on payment of a small deposit toward fines higher than a certain amount.[330]

Nevertheless, if appeals are allowed, certain minimum due process requirements must be met. If the accused is acquitted and the accuser appeals, the accused must be given timely notice of that fact, of his or her right to oppose the appeal, and of the manner for doing so.[331] If the appeal will be considered on the record of the trial below, the member must be furnished with a copy of that record.[332]

[b] De Novo Review

Sometimes in response to an appeal, sometimes in response to litigation, and sometimes on their own motion, unions may provide a member who has been subjected to unlawful proceedings with a de novo trial. If properly conducted, such a trial cures the defects of the previous trial and validates the sentence.[333] In order to be proper, however, the new proceeding must take testimony from witnesses, create a new record, and otherwise be in compliance with Section 101(a)(5).[334] If the second trial body considers the record and report of the invalid first trial body, the second

---

328 Kiepura v. Steelworkers Local 1091, 358 F. Supp. 987, 992 (N.D. Ill. 1973).

329 *Id.*

330 Hart v. Carpenters Local 1292, 341 F. Supp. 1266, 1271 (E.D.N.Y. 1972), *aff'd on other grounds,* 497 F. 2d 401 (2d Cir. 1974).

331 Reilly v. Sheet Metal Workers, 488 F. Supp. 1121, 1127-28 (S.D.N.Y. 1980).

332 *Id.* at 1127; Kuebler v. Lithographers Local 24-P, 473 F.2d 359 (6th Cir. 1973).

333 Perry v. Teamsters Local 302, 656 F.2d 536, 539 (9th Cir. 1981); Ehrlich v. Maggiore, 61 LRRM 2041 (N.Y. App. Div. 1965). However, as noted *infra,* text accompanying notes 350-53, the union may still be liable for damages based on the original trial.

334 Perry v. Teamsters Local 302, 656 F.2d 536, 539 (9th Cir. 1981).

trial is invalid,[335] even if there is an opportunity to present new evidence in addition to the existing record.[336]

[5] Effect of Rights in Union Constitution

If a union constitution contains provisions that violate the rights afforded by Section 101(a)(5), such provisions are void.[337] If, however, the union constitution provides an accused with greater rights, the courts are divided on the issue of whether the greater rights may be enforced pursuant to Section 101(5)(5). Some courts have held that rights in union constitutions are not incorporated into the procedural protections of Title I.[338] The better rule, which seems to be followed by a slight majority of courts, is that internal rules may be enforced pursuant to Section 101(a)(5).[339] This is analogous to the due process requirement that administrative agencies follow their own rules until they are repealed.[340] In any event, the controversy has lost some significance in light of the recent decisions permitting union members to sue their unions under Section 301 of the NLRA to enforce union constitutional rights.[341]

[6] Waiver of Procedural Rights

There is no question that rights under Section 101(a)(5), like constitutional due process rights, may be waived. However, a

---

[335] Tincher v. Piasecki, 520 F.2d 851, 856 (7th Cir. 1975).

[336] Reilly v. Sheet Metal Workers, 488 F. Supp. 1121, 1128 (S.D.N.Y. 1980).

[337] Section 101(b), 29 U.S.C. § 411(b).

[338] Buresch v. IBEW Local 24, 343 F. Supp. 183, 190 (D. Md. 1971), *aff'd mem,* 460 F.2d 1405 (4th Cir. 1972); Ritz v. O'Donnell, 413 F. Supp. 1365, 1370 (D.D.C. 1976), *aff'd on other grounds,* 566 F.2d 731 (D.C. Cir. 1977).

[339] Jacques v. ILA Local 1418, 246 F. Supp. 857 (E.D.La. 1965) (amount and specificity of notice); Kiepura v. Steelworkers Local 1091, 358 F. Supp. 987, 991 (N.D.Ill. 1973) (composition of trial board); Stein v. Mutuel Clerks, 384 F. Supp. 444, 449 (D.Mass. 1974), *aff'd on other grounds,* 560 F.2d 486 (1st Cir. 1977) (fines exceeded constitutional limits).

[340] Service v. Dulles, 354 U.S. 363 (1957).

[341] Plumbers v. Plumbers Local 334, 452 U.S. 615 (1981).

waiver will not be found unless there is affirmative and clear evidence showing that the accused member was aware of the right, yet chose not to exercise it.[342] The analysis will depend, of course, on the circumstances and the type of right. Thus, a member need not affirmatively state that he or she does not wish to cross-examine witnesses expressly made available for cross-examination in order to waive the right to do so.[343] On the other hand, a member need not alienate those who are about to hear the case by suggesting that they are biased; rather, the members of the trial body are affirmatively obligated to disqualify themselves.[344] The courts disfavor attempts by unions to avoid due process challenges by asking a charged party at the hearing whether procedural safeguards, such as adequate notice, have been observed.[344.1]

[7] Relief

Although issues of relief for Title I violations are treated elsewhere,[345] a few issues are particularly pertinent to Section 101(a)(5). First, with respect to equitable relief, it is normally required that rescission of the unlawful discipline be awarded.[346] The injunction against implementation of the sentence will ordinarily not prevent the union from refiling the charges and imposing the same sentence, so long as the rights accorded by Section 101(a)(5) are respected in the postlitigation proceedings.[347] If procedurally correct discipline has been imposed during the litigation, it is improper to enjoin execution of the new

---

342 Rekant v. Meatcutters Local 446, 205 F. Supp. 284, 289 (E.D. Pa. 1962), *rev'd on other grounds,* 320 F.2d 271 (3d Cir. 1963); Loekle v. Swayduck, 94 LRRM 2442, 2446 (S.D.N.Y. 1976). This is the same as the constitutional standard. Johnson v. Zerbst, 304 U.S. 458 (1938).

343 Ritz v. O'Donnell, 566 F.2d 731, 735-36 (D.C. Cir. 1977).

344 Falcone v. Dantinne, 420 F.2d 1157, 1162 (3d Cir. 1969); Tincher v. Piasecki, 520 F.2d 851, 855 (7th Cir. 1975).

344.1 *See* Strom v. National Ass'n of Basketball Refs., 113 LRRM 3433, 3437–38 (E.D. Pa. 1983).

345 *Infra,* Sections 8.20-8.22.

346 Feltington v. IATSE Local 306, 636 F.2d 890, 892 (2d Cir. 1980).

347 Magellsen v. Plasterers Local 518, 233 F. Supp. 459 (W.D.Mo. 1964).

sentence,[348] although it may still be necessary to enjoin future due process violations. Although there is disagreement on this question, the better view is that equitable relief may be obtained against procedurally improper hearings before they are held, as well as against the consequent invalid discipline.[349]

Damages may be awarded both for injuries caused by the discipline and for injuries caused by the improper hearings themselves. Thus, if a member is ultimately subjected to a lawful discipline, damages may nevertheless be recovered for the improper procedures.[350]

One court has also held that, even if no proper discipline is later imposed, the union must be given an opportunity to prove, without relying on the results of the improper trial, that the member would have been convicted and disciplined had the trial been conducted in a proper manner.[351] This rule, although analogous to a similar recent development under the constitutional right to due process,[352] is troubling, particularly in light of the manner in which the "but-for" would have to be proved. The court suggested that the results of a second, properly conducted proceeding would be probative.[353] Yet it is difficult to imagine a clearer case of structural bias than a trial board that considers a case knowing that unless it both convicts and imposes the same sentence as an earlier trial board, the union is likely to be liable for substantial damages.

---

[348] Rosario v. ILGWU Local 10, 605 F.2d 1228, 1244-45 (2d Cir. 1979).

[349] *Compare* Semancik v. UMW District 5, 466 F.2d 144, 157 (3d Cir. 1972) *with* Flaherty v. Steelworkers, 46 LRRM 3007 (S.D.Cal. 1960). The latter court declined to issue relief on the theory that the language of Section 101(a)(5) requires that discipline already have been imposed before the right attaches. However, the words "No member may be [disciplined]" do not seem to preclude prospective relief. On the other hand, the exhaustion doctrine certainly encourages members to go through the trial and seek to overturn the trial on appeal, absent some basis for applying an exception to the exhaustion doctrine.

[350] Rosario v. ILGWU Local 10, 605 F.2d 1228, 1245 (2d Cir. 1979).

[351] Feltington v. IATSE Local 306, 605 F.2d 1251, 1258 (2d Cir. 1979).

[352] Carey v. Piphus, 435 U.S. 247, 260 (1978).

[353] Feltington v. IATSE Local 306, 636 F.2d 890, 892 (2d Cir. 1980).

§ 8.12. Retention of Existing Rights

> Section 103. Nothing contained in this title shall limit the rights and remedies of any member of a labor organization under any State or Federal law or before any court or other tribunal, or under the constitution and bylaws of any labor organization.

This section preserves the rights and remedies that exist independently of Title I of the LMRDA.[354] Thus, Title I rights are enjoyed in addition to, rather than supplanting, other rights.[355]

(*Text continued on page 8-71*)

---

354 Tirino v. HRE Local 164, 202 F. Supp. 809 (E.D.N.Y. 1968); Mills v. Collier, 56 LRRM 2894 (S.D. Ind. 1964).

355 Rekant v. Meatcutters Local 446, 205 F. Supp. 284 (E.D. Pa. 1967), *rev'd on other grounds,* 320 F.2d 271 (3d Cir. 1963); Ferger v. Ironworkers Local 483, 229 A.2d 532 (N.J. Super. Ct. 1967), *aff'd,* 235 A.2d 482 (N.J. Super Ct.).

for the union to have done the act.[388]

The greatest controversy arises over the question of whether a violation occurs where it takes effect on the member. Several courts have said that this is so.[389] Other courts have denied this, stating that in cases accepting the rule there were other factors favoring venue in the district where the member was affected.[390]

§ 8.17. Exhaustion of Internal Union Remedies

The most unusual aspect of the enforcement of the LMRDA, as compared not only to most federal litigation but also to proceedings before the NLRB, is the requirement that the union member exhaust available internal union remedies for a reasonable period, not exceeding four months, before filing suit.[391] There are a number of exceptions to the requirement. Some would argue that the exceptions are so numerous and broad as to swallow the rule.[392]

Reliance on the exceptions, however, is dangerous. The courts have great discretion in whether to require exhaustion and are extremely inconsistent in applying the exceptions; indeed, it often appears that a court will use exhaustion as an excuse to avoid a difficult case or to deny relief that it does not want to give for some reason that it chooses not to state. Moreover, although courts are not supposed to deny relief altogether when exhaustion has improperly been skipped, but rather simply "stay their hands for four months, while the aggrieved person seeks relief within the union,"[393] many courts will dismiss for lack of juris-

---

388 Daniels v. National Post Office Mail Handlers, 454 F. Supp. 336, 340 (E.D. Va. 1978).

389 Giordani v. Upholsterers, 403 F.2d 85, 88 (2d Cir. 1968); George v. Bricklayers, 255 F. Supp. 239, 242 (E.D. Wis. 1966); Vestal v. Teamsters, 245 F. Supp. 623, 625 (M.D. Tenn. 1965).

390 *E.g.*, Rota v. BRAC, 338 F. Supp. 1176 (E.D. Pa. 1972). This is not true, however, with respect to George v. Bricklayers, *supra* note 389.

391 Section 101(a)(4), first proviso.

392 Detroy v. AGVA, 286 F.2d 75, 79 (2d Cir. 1961).

393 NLRB v. Marine Workers, 391 U.S. 418, 426 (1968). This rule was applied in reversing a dismissal for failure to exhaust in Chadwick v. IBEW, 674 F.2d 939 (D.C. Cir. 1982). *See also* Phillips v. Teamsters Local 560, 209 F. Supp. 768,

diction.[394]

Internal procedures provide a better focus for organizing by a dissenting caucus than do court proceedings; thus, the member's political victory will be all the better if the union has been given an opportunity to correct its errors. In addition, of course, both the member and the union will have saved both time and legal expenses. For all these reasons, a union member is best advised to begin exhausting union remedies as soon as possible and to continue to use union remedies without filing suit for as long as possible without unduly prejudicing the prospect of obtaining prompt and necessary relief. Even after suit is filed, it may be useful to continue to press within the union for relief.

[1] What Exhaustion Is Required?

[a] Available Adequate Procedures

Because exhaustion is an affirmative defense, the union must raise it and show that adequate internal procedures existed and were not followed.[395] This is accomplished by making a factual showing concerning remedies and their availability for the vindication of the asserted statutory rights.[396] The union also has the burden of showing that the exceptions to the exhaustion doctrine, such as futility, do not apply.[397] If the remedy does not appear expressly in the union's constitution, the union must bring the existence of the remedy to the attention of the membership.[398]

769-70 (D.N.J. 1962); Adams v. Rear, 424 F. Supp. 1115, 1118 (W.D. Okla. 1976); Richardson v. National P. O. Mail Handlers, 442 F. Supp. 188, 189-91 (E.D. Va. 1977).

394 Harris v. Plasterers Local 406, 619 F.2d 1164 (7th Cir. 1980). Such a dismissal should be without prejudice. Packer v. Teamsters Local 249, 428 F. Supp. 145, 149 (W.D. Pa. 1977).

395 Murphy v. Teamsters, 56 LRRM 2885 (W.D. Ky. 1964).

396 Forline v. Helpers Local 42, 211 F. Supp. 315, 317 (E.D. Pa. 1962); Teamsters Local 760 v. Morely, 378 F.2d 738, 745 (9th Cir. 1967).

397 *Id.*

398 Steib v. ILA Local 1497, 436 F.2d 1101, 1106 (5th Cir. 1971). *See also* Weisen v. Reichett, 111 LRRM 3136 (W.D. Pa. 1982) (International need not

The most commonly used remedies involve the procedures for internal union charges and appeals. Thus, if a member complains that the union has illegally imposed certain discipline, the remedies to be exhausted are the appellate procedures invoking the assistance of higher authorities within the union.[399] If the action about which the member complains does not involve an action that may be appealed, then the proper remedy is to file charges against the errant officer or entity.[400]

[b] Four-Month Limitation

The statute imposes a limit of four months, beyond which a court may not require exhaustion of union hearing procedures. Only if less than four months is involved does a court have discretion to require exhaustion or not, depending on the circumstances.[401]

If the plaintiff's exhaustion was initiated by filing charges, the time starts to run when the charges were filed. However, if the plaintiff's complaint concerns discipline imposed pursuant to charges, some courts have counted four months beginning with the decision of the trial body,[402] while others seem to begin with the date of the hearing.[403] The latter view seems more sensible in light of the statutory language requiring exhaustion of "hearing procedures"; on the other hand, the former view may be supported if the alleged violation is not the hearing, but rather the decision.

---

exhaust before filing counterclaim in Title I suit because constitution allows members, not union, to institute proceedings.). *But cf.* McKeon v. Teamsters Local 107, 223 F. Supp. 341, 345-46 (D. Del. 1963) (where constitution lists chargeable offenses, but provides that list is not exclusive, members should file charges even if ground is not listed).

399 *E.g.,* Deluhery v. Marine Cooks and Stewards, 199 F. Supp. 270 (S.D. Cal. 1963); Tirino v. Hotel and Restaurant Employees, 282 F. Supp. 809, 816 (E.D.N.Y. 1968).

400 *E.g.,* McKeon v. Teamsters Local 107, 223 F. Supp. 341, 345 (D. Del. 1963).

401 Semancik v. UMW Dist. 5, 466 F.2d 144, 150 (3d Cir. 1972).

402 Hart v. Carpenters Local 1292, 341 F. Supp. 1266, 1269 (E.D.N.Y. 1972), *aff'd,* 497 F.2d 401 (2d Cir. 1974).

403 McCraw v. Plumbers, 341 F.2d 705, 711 (6th Cir. 1965).

The mere fact that all union appeals cannot be exhausted within four months or that it is not certain that a decision will be forthcoming within the four-month period does not excuse a failure to exhaust so long as it is likely that at least some decision will be made within that time.[404] However, if the only remaining appeal could not be completed within the statutory period, the member need not file such an appeal before suing.[405] If the union provides more than one way to appeal, a member need not choose the speediest remedy; if the slow way is chosen, suit may be filed once the four-month period has expired.[406]

[c] What Is Satisfactory Exhaustion?

Some cases under state law hold that a member who fails to comply with all procedural requirements pertaining to the union's appeal system fails to exhaust union remedies.[407] Because the exhaustion proviso of Section 101(a)(4) was intended to preserve the common law exhaustion doctrine,[408] it has sometimes been argued that this principle applies to Title I actions as well.

If, as at common law, the theory of the case is that the member seeks to enforce the union constitution as a contract, it may be proper to restrict the member to contractual remedies, and thus to bar enforcement if the member has not followed the contractual appellate procedures. However, the federal exhaustion doctrine is not a slavish imitation of the state common law; rather, it has been necessary to formulate a federal rule.[409] Thus, if the member seeks to enforce supervening statutory rights, almost every court has rejected this common law rule and has concluded that "a liberal attitude should be adopted to sustain an appeal rather than

[404] Harris v. ILA Local 1291, 321 F.2d 801, 805 (3d Cir. 1963); Monroe v. UAW, 540 F. Supp. 249 (S.D. Ohio 1982) (dictum).

[405] Ornellas v. Oakley, 618 F.2d 1351, 1354 (9th Cir. 1980).

[406] Giordani v. Upholsterers, 403 F.2d 85 (2d Cir. 1968).

[407] Couie v. Carpenters Local 1849, 51 Wash.2d 108, 316 P.2d 473 (1957); Allander v. Carpenters District Council, 145 Colo. 164, 358 P.2d 8 (Colo. 1960).

[408] *E.g.*, 105 Cong. Rec. 16414 (1959) (Sen. Kennedy).

[409] Detroy v. AGVA, 286 F.2d 75, 78-79 (2d Cir. 1961).

a technical attitude to defeat it . . .."[410] This is analogous to the rule applied under Title IV that the exhaustion requirement is satisfied so long as the union has been given fair notice of the complaint about its conduct.[411]

Similarly, the fact that a particular union member has not exhausted union remedies will not preclude a suit brought by that member based on issues similar to those raised by another appeal.[412] If the union member did conduct some exhaustion, the union may not complain about failure to exhaust on the basis of the member's alleged failure vigorously to press all possible objections to the accusations against him or her absent a showing that exhaustion was not conducted in good faith.[413] However, if the member's suit was based on a claim that the union's constitution forbade certain conduct and if the leadership had never been given an opportunity to construe the constitutional provision because the member failed to raise that point in the course of the union's proceedings, the court will decline to consider that particular claim for failure to exhaust.[414]

The rejection of the general proposition that all union procedural requirements must be satisfied does not mean that all such requirements may be disregarded. For example, a union member who refused to post a fifty-dollar appeal bond, required by the union bylaws for appeals of fines greater than that sum, was held to have failed to exhaust reasonable internal union proce-

---

410 Sheridan v. Carpenters Local 126, 191 F. Supp. 347, 354 (D. Del. 1961), *rev'd on other grounds,* 306 F.2d 152 (3d Cir. 1962). *See also* Boilermakers Local 455 v. Terry, 398 F.2d 491, 493-494 (5th Cir. 1968); Woods v. IBEW Local 613, 404 F. Supp. 110, 114-15 (N.D. Ga. 1975); Maxwell v. UAW Local 1306, 489 F. Supp. 745 (C.D. Ill. 1980). The only known decision that adopted as a general principle the rule of the common law cases cited in note 407, *supra,* was reversed on appeal. Chadwick v. IBEW, No. 80-2642 (D.D.C. May 21, 1981), *rev'd,* 674 F.2d 939 (D.C. Cir. 1982). *See also* Chadwick v. Pillard, 536 F. Supp. 73, (E.D. Tenn. 1982).

411 Hodgson v. Steelworkers, 403 U.S. 333, 340-41 (1971); Hodgson v. Liquor Salesmen's Local 2, 444 F.2d 1344 (2d Cir. 1971); Schultz v. ILA Local 1921, 429 F.2d 592, 597-98 (3d Cir. 1970).

412 Parks v. IBEW, 314 F.2d 886, 924 (4th Cir. 1963).

413 McCraw v. Plumbers, 52 LLRM 2516, 2520-21 (E.D. Tenn. 1963), *aff'd,* 341 F.2d 705, 711 (6th Cir. 1965).

414 Reilly v. Sheet Metal Workers, 488 F. Supp. 1121, 1125 (S.D.N.Y. 1980).

dures.[415] This holding may have been justified, as the court stated, by the union's interest in avoiding frivolous appeals. However, it must be borne in mind that the exhaustion doctrine extends to unions the privilege of obtaining a first hearing on the member's objections. Thus, the reasonableness of the refusal to hear an appeal should be judged in light of the federal interest in vindicating the purposes of Title I, not of the union's extrinsic interests.[416]

[2] Exceptions to the Exhaustion Requirement

Even if the union has shown that an internal procedure was available for the vindication of the statutory rights asserted, the district court has discretion not to require resort to that procedure. The courts frequently state that there are no formalized exceptions to the requirement and that each case must be evaluated on its own facts.[417] It is for this reason, in part, that the courts' behavior in this area is erratic and that the member is well advised to accomplish as much exhaustion as possible before and even during the suit. However, several broad principles guiding the exercise of judicial discretion recur in the decisions and are here set forth with the warning that they are extremely flexible in practice. They are best argued in conjunction with one another.

[a] Futility

Exhaustion is not required if resort to internal union procedures would be futile. Futility can be shown if the union has consistently taken a position in opposition to that which the

---

[415] Hart v. Carpenters Local 1929, 341 F. Supp. 1966, 1271 (E.D.N.Y.), *aff'd*, 497 F.2d 401, 402 (2d Cir. 1974).

[416] Thus, refusal to consider a claim because a member failed to post a $1,000 bond seems unjustified. Carroll v. Musicians Local 802, 235 F. Supp. 161, 171 (S.D.N.Y. 1963). The court ultimately heard the claim because remedies were exhausted with respect to other objections.

[417] *E.g.*, Detroy v. AGVA, 286 F.2d 75, 79 (2d Cir. 1961).

plaintiff seeks to accomplish by the lawsuit.[418] It is also shown if the internal procedure involves a hearing before or an appeal to the union officer about whose conduct the union member complains, or who appointed the members of, or otherwise controls, the trial or appellate body.[419] This exception bears some

(*Text continued on page 8-83*)

---

418 Farowitz v. Musicians Local 802, 330 F.2d 999, 1002-03 (2d Cir. 1964).

419 Wood v. Dennis, 489 F.2d 849, 856 (7th Cir. 1973); Machinists Fulton Lodge v. Nix, 415 F.2d 212, 216 (5th Cir. 1969).

Some early decisions held that punitive damages, not being "directly and proximately" caused, were not available under Title I.[484] However, the great weight of authority allows an award of such damages, intended to punish the wrongdoer and to deter future violations, against a defendant who has acted either with malice or with reckless or wanton indifference to the rights of the plaintiff.[485] Punitive damages should not be awarded against the union, however, unless it either ratified the officers' actions or gave the officer the authority to commit the wrongful actions.[486] Inasmuch as a punitive damage award against the union must ultimately be paid by the membership, although the officers may pay a political price for the financial harm they helped cause to the union, a court should be reluctant to give such an award unless the membership really does share the blame.[487]

§ 8.21. Equitable Relief

[1] Types of Relief Available

Section 102 specifies that injunctions are available, and, from a political perspective, this is usually the most important form of relief available. Plaintiffs may obtain such injunctive relief requiring the discipline imposed to be lifted[488] or requiring the union to undertake or to refrain from specific acts.[489] In addition,

---

484 Burris v. Teamsters, 224 F. Supp. 277, 280 (W.D.N.C. 1963).

485 *E.g.*, Boilermakers v. Braswell, 388 F.2d 193, 200 (5th Cir. 1968); Cooke v. Painters Orange Belt Dist. Coun. 529 F.2d 815, 820 (9th Cir. 1975); Vandeventer v. Operating Eng. Local 513, 579 F.2d 1373, 1380 (8th Cir. 1978).

486 Morrissey v. NMU, 397 F. Supp. 659, 667 (S.D.N.Y. 1975), *aff'd in part and rev'd in part on other grounds,* 544 F.2d 19 (2d Cir. 1975).

487 In IBEW v. Foust, 442 U.S. 42 (1979), the court held that punitive damages could not be assessed against a union for violations of the duty of fair representation, but was careful to leave open the question under the LMRDA. *Id.* at 47 n.9.

488 *E.g.*, Kuebler v. Cleveland Lithog. & Photo. Local 24-P, 473 F.2d 359 (6th Cir. 1973) (reinstatement to membership); Maceira v. Pagan, 649 F.2d 8 (1st Cir. 1981) (reinstatement to office).

489 *E.g.*, Wade v. Teamsters Local 247, 527 F. Supp. 1169 (E.D. Mich. 1981) (hold meetings); Petrazullo v. Lowen, 534 F. Supp. 173 (S.D.N.Y. 1982) (refrain from conducting vote unless information has been furnished to membership);

defendants may be ordered generally to refrain from interfering with Title I rights.[490]

Union members may obtain a judgment declaring that a provision in the union's constitution or bylaws is contrary to Title I and is therefore void.[491] The court may also enjoin the union from enforcing the provision or may require the union to revise the rule.[492]

[2] Preliminary Relief

A member may also obtain a temporary restraining order[493] or preliminary injunction.[494] Although normally preliminary relief is issued to maintain the status quo pending the resolution of the lawsuit and to ensure that defendants do not frustrate plaintiffs' objective during that time,[495] in some cases preservation of the status quo will perpetuate a wrong. Thus, preliminary relief may take the form of an order compelling affirmative acts that minimize the irreparable harm to all parties, such as requiring that a previously scheduled election be held pursuant to specific rules.[496]

The test for preliminary relief requires a preliminary determination of the chances for success, a consideration of the public interest, and a balancing of the irreparable injury to the parties. Irreparable injury to the plaintiff is injury that would be caused if preliminary relief were mistakenly denied and could not later be rectified by permanent relief (such as damages). The balance

---

Canez v. Guerrero, Civ. 82-811 PHX-EHC (D. Ariz. June 5, 1982) (conduct election under specified rules and post notices).

490 *E.g.*, Burns v. Painters Local 1503, 90 LRRM 2824, 2829 (D. Conn. 1975).

491 LMRDA Section 101(b), 29 U.S.C. § 411(b).

492 *E.g.*, Pawlak v. Greenawalt, 628 F.2d 826 (3d Cir. 1980); Boswell v. IBEW, 106 LRRM 2713 (D.N.J. 1981). *See generally* Note, *Facial Adjudication of Disciplinary Provisions in Union Constitutions,* 91 Yale L.J. 144 (1981).

493 *E.g.*, Sheridan v. Carpenters Local 626, 191 F. Supp. 347 (D. Del. 1961).

494 *E.g.*, Navarro v. Gannon, 385 F.2d 512 (2d Cir. 1967); Semancik v. UMW, 466 F.2d 144 (3d Cir. 1972); Kupau v. Yamamoto, 622 F.2d 449 (9th Cir. 1980).

495 Maceira v. Pagan, 649 F.2d 8 (1st Cir. 1981); Gartner v. Soloner, 220 F. Supp. 115 (E.D. Pa. 1963).

496 Crowley v. Teamsters Local 82, 679 F.2d 978, 995-99 (1st Cir. 1982), *cert. granted,* 51 U.S.L.W. 3552 (Jan. 24, 1982).

of the irreparable injuries is most important because the more the plaintiffs' outweigh the defendants', the less sure the court needs to be that the plaintiff will ultimately prevail; conversely, if the irreparable injury to the defendant seems greater, the court will want to be all but certain that the plaintiff will ultimately prevail before granting preliminary relief.[497]

Accordingly, although the cases hold that the deprivation of Title I rights in itself constitutes irreparable injury,[498] a member is ill advised to rely on that theory alone. Emphasis should be placed instead on the decisions that will be made without the plaintiff's input or vote,[499] or the effect of discipline on job rights, for the loss of which the union may not be able to compensate the member in damages.[500]

It is customary for a bond to be posted to indemnify a preliminarily enjoined party against injuries caused by the order in case it is later determined that the order should not have been granted.[501] However, courts have discretion to require only a nominal bond, or indeed to require no bond at all. If individual rank-and-file members have obtained preliminary relief against a union and its officers whose attorneys' fees have been borne by the union treasury, the congressional purpose of encouraging full participation militates against requiring a bond.[502]

---

497 These general considerations are discussed in such cases as *id.;* WMATA v. Holiday Tours, 559 F.2d 841 (D.C. Cir. 1977); Blackwelder Furn. Co. v. Seilig Mfg. Co., 550 F.2d 189 (4th Cir. 1977); Canal Auth. v. Callaway, 489 F.2d 567 (5th Cir. 1974). If the balance tips decidedly in favor of the plaintiff, it is necessary only to show that grave or serious questions are presented on the merits.

498 *E.g.,* Ostrowski v. Utility Workers Local 1-2, 530 F. Supp. 208, 215 (S.D.N.Y. 1980); Hummel v. Brennan, 469 F. Supp. 1180, 1187 (E.D. Pa. 1979). This argument is particularly strong where free speech rights are involved, by analogy with Elrod v. Burns, 427 U.S. 347, 373 (1976).

499 *E.g.,* Gartner v. Soloner, 220 F. Supp. 115 (E.D. Pa. 1963).

500 *E.g.,* King v. Randazzo, 234 F. Supp. 388, 393 (E.D.N.Y. 1964), *aff'd on other grounds,* 346 F.2d 307 (2d Cir. 1965).

501 Rule 65(c), F.R. Civ. P. The restrained party may not cover damages in excess of the bond. 7 Moore's Federal Practice, ¶ 65.10[1], at 65-98 to 65-99 (1973).

502 Crowley v. Teamsters Local 82, 521 F. Supp. 614, 635-36 (D. Mass. 1981), *aff'd,* 679 F. 2d 978, 999-1001 (1st Cir. 1982), *cert. granted,* 51 U.S.L.W. 3552 (Jan. 24, 1983). Similar reasoning suggests that costs should not be awarded against

§ 8.22. Attorneys' Fees

One form of relief available in Title I suits is attorneys' fees. In *Hall v. Cole,*[503] the Supreme Court ruled that if a union member obtains relief against violations of Title I rights, the court order benefiting the plaintiff also provides the membership at large with a reassurance that if the union violates their rights, they can obtain relief, too. The order also encourages the union to obey the law in the future. In both ways, the plaintiff's pursuit of the litigation provides a benefit to other members, and so it is fair to ask the members to pay for the benefits by having the attorneys' fees paid from the union treasury.

Although the court has the power to deny an award of fees, the invalidation of the union's acts effectively establishes a presumption favoring attorneys' fees. Fees will be awarded for all services that were necessary or beneficial to the litigation, including time spent on exhaustion of union remedies or other prelitigation services.[504] However, if the union granted the relief sought before litigation was initiated, or if the litigation otherwise has no effect on obtaining the relief, no fees should be awarded.[505] By similar reasoning, the court may consider a failure to exhaust reasonable remedies in fixing the amount of fees in order to encourage union members to avoid unnecessary litigation.[506]

Because an award of attorneys' fees itself encourages union members to protect their rights and encourages unions to respect those rights, the general rule that time spent on the fee application is compensable applies in Title I litigation.[507] One court, however, denied such relief because the award would have to be paid indirectly by the membership.[508] This argument is unpersuasive, because all Title I relief against the union is indirectly against the membership.

---

plaintiffs who sue in good faith. *See* Baker v. Newspaper & Graphic Comm. U.; 461 F. Supp. 109, 116 (D.D.C. 1978), *aff'd,* 628 F.2d 156, 160 n.2 (D.C.Cir. 1980).

[503] 412 U.S. 1 (1973).

[504] Mezo v. Steelworkers, 558 F.2d 1280, 1283 (7th Cir. 1977).

[505] *Id.*

[506] Evans v. Local 8-86, 501 F. Supp. 93, 95 (E.D. Pa. 1980).

[507] Pawlak v. Greenawalt, 713 F.2d 972 (3d Cir. 1983); Cole v. Hall, 356 F. Supp. 460 (E.D.N.Y. 1974).

[508] Colpo v. Teamsters Local 326, 531 F. Supp. 573, 576-77 (D. Del. 1982).

Generally, the factors governing the amount of attorney fees in Title I suits are the same as those governing fees in civil rights or other federal litigation.[509] The standard sources should be consulted on this issue.[510]

509 *See, e.g.,* Christopher v. Safeway Stores, 644 F.2d 467, 472 (5th Cir. 1981); Kerr v. Screen Extras Guild, 526 F.2d 67, 70 (9th Cir. 1975).

510 *E.g.,* Larson, Federal Court Awards of Attorney Fees (1981).

Appendix 8A. United States Department of Labor Report Forms

U.S. DEPARTMENT OF LABOR
Office of Labor-Management
Standards Enforcement
Washington, D.C. 20216

OFFICIAL BUSINESS

POSTAGE AND FEES PAID
U.S. DEPARTMENT OF LABOR

FIRST CLASS MAIL

LAB 441

U.S.MAIL

LABOR ORGANIZATION INFORMATION REPORT

Form LM-1 and Instructions

A MESSAGE TO OFFICERS OF LABOR ORGANIZATIONS COVERED BY THE LABOR-MANAGEMENT REPORTING AND DISCLOSURE ACT OF 1959 AND EXECUTIVE ORDER 11491, AS AMENDED

This packet contains forms and instructions to assist you in complying with the requirements of the Labor-Management Reporting and Disclosure Act of 1959, Executive Order 11491, as amended, and Regulations issued thereunder. These forms have been prescribed by the Assistant Secretary of Labor for Labor-Management Relations pursuant to authority under the Act delegated by the Secretary of Labor and pursuant to authority granted to the Assistant Secretary under the Executive Order.

An original plus one copy of the LM-1 form, properly signed, and two copies of all attachments, must be filed with the Office of Labor-Management Standards Enforcement, U.S. Department of Labor, Washington, D.C. 20216.

You can make your task, and ours, easier by reading the instructions carefully, by completing the form accurately, and by filing your report promptly.

We will be glad to give you help if you visit or communicate with the nearest Area Office of the Labor-Management Services Administration at the address shown on the back cover.

U.S. DEPARTMENT OF LABOR

LABOR-MANAGEMENT SERVICES ADMINISTRATION
OFFICE OF LABOR-MANAGEMENT STANDARDS ENFORCEMENT

DEPARTMENT OF LABOR · UNITED STATES OF AMERICA ·

CHAPTER 9

Internal Union Elections

The Labor-Management Reporting and Disclosure Act of 1959 (LMRDA) was enacted by Congress "to eliminate or prevent improper practices on the part of labor organizations, employers, labor relations consultants, and their officers and representatives

. . ."[1] Congressional investigations had revealed shocking abuses —"a number of instances of breach of trust, corruption, disregard of the rights of the individual employees, and other failures to observe high standards of responsibility and ethical conduct . . ."[2]—which, although confined to a few unions, were sufficient to require legislation. Because of the public interest in a strong and independent labor movement, the LMRDA is to provide a mechanism for ensuring democratically run labor organizations[3]

The provision of the LMRDA of concern here is Title IV—Elections. This title's function is to ensure free and democratic union elections in this country.[4] Within Title IV, Congress sought to balance the public's interest in democratic unions and the unions' right to control their own elections.[5] To this end, Title IV enumerates democratic principles with respect to election procedures and lists the means of enforcement. Note that throughout the following text, all references within Title IV will be made to its public law section: Section 401 for procedures and Section 402 for enforcement. This is the approach taken in court opinions and in federal regulations. All references to the regulations will be made to the Code of Federal Regulations (CFR).

Title IV provides only minimum safeguards or guidelines by which elections should be conducted and assigns implementation of those safeguards to various parties: the union, the members, the Secretary of Labor, and the courts. The union, i.e., its officers, is given the primary role in enforcing compliance with the Act.[6] Elections are to be conducted in accordance with its constitution and bylaws.[7] And, in almost all cases, the union must be given

[1] 29 U.S.C. § 401(c).

[2] 29 U.S.C. § 401(b).

[3] 29 U.S.C. § 401(b).

[4] Steelworkers v. Usery, 429 U.S. 305, 309, 50 L. Ed. 2d 502, 97 S. Ct. 611 (1977).

[5] Wirtz v. Hotel, Motel and Club Employees Union, Local 6 [hereinafter cited as Wirtz v. Hotel], 391 U.S. 492, 496, 497 20 L. Ed. 2d 763, 88 S. Ct. 1743 (1968).

[6] Wirtz v. Hotel, *supra* note 5, at 497 n.6; Wirtz v. Local 153, Glass Bottle Blowers Ass'n, 389 U.S. 463, 472, 19 L. Ed. 2d 705, 88 S. Ct. 643 (1968).

[7] 29 U.S.C. § 481(e).

the first opportunity to redress any violation of Title IV.[8] A member of a labor organization has two basic responsibilities: to participate in the electoral processes[9] and to initiate enforcement procedures.[10] In certain situations, a member may also participate in the Secretary of Labor's enforcement action in the U.S. District Court.[11]

The Secretary of Labor, hereinafter referred to as the Secretary, has been assigned a special role in the administration of the Act. With one exception (29 U.S.C. 481(c)), the Secretary has exclusive enforcement responsibility.[12] The Secretary promulgates regulations (see 29 CFR 452.1-452.136) that interpret the Act and takes the necessary steps to ensure democratic elections;[13] however, the Secretary is restricted to post-election enforcement. This promotes a congressional policy of minimal governmental interference in the internal affairs of unions, thereby preserving maximum independence and self-government for unions.[14] Moreover, to carry out enforcement of Title IV, "the statute relies upon the special knowledge and discretion of the Secretary . . ."[15] Note, however, the primary interest that the Secretary is to protect: ". . . vital public interest in assuring free and democratic union elections that transcends the narrower interest of the complaining union member."[16]

To implement enforcement decisions, the Secretary must institute civil action in a U.S. District Court. If, after a trial upon the

---

[8] *See* 29 U.S.C. §§ 481(c), 482(a)(1).

[9] *See* Steelworkers, *supra* note 4, at 312.

[10] *See* 29 U.S.C. §§ 481(c), 482(a)(2).

[11] Trbovich v. United Mine Workers of America, 404 U.S. 528, 30 L. Ed. 2d 686, 92 S. Ct. 630 (1972); Usery v. Local Union 639, Int'l Brotherhood of Teamsters, Chauffeurs, Warehousemen and Helpers of America, 543 F.2d 369, 79 CCH Lab. Cas. 11570, 93 LRRM 2113 (D.C. Cir. 1976), *cert. denied,* 429 U.S. 1123 (1977).

[12] Steelworkers, *supra* note 4, at 313; Wirtz v. Hotel, *supra* note 5, at 498; Wirtz v. Glass Bottle Blowers, *supra* note 6, at 473; Calhoon v. Harvey, 379 U.S. 134, 140, 13 L. Ed. 2d 190, 85 S. Ct. 292 (1964).

[13] 29 U.S.C. § 481(i).

[14] Wirtz v. Glass Bottle Blowers, *supra* note 6, at 472; Calhoon, *supra* note 12, at 140.

[15] Dunlop v. Bachowski, 421 U.S. 560, 571, 44 L. Ed. 2d 377, 95 S. Ct. 1851 (1975).

[16] Steelworkers, *supra* note 4, at 309.

merits, the court agrees with the Secretary, it will set aside an election, if any, and order a new election under the Secretary's supervision.[17] The court has the basic responsibility for fashioning the ground rules for the election[18] and may also provide injunctive relief where a private (by a union member) pre-election suit is brought under 29 U.S.C. 481(c). Finally, the court provides very limited judicial review of discretionary decisions by the Secretary—either the decision not to file a complaint[19] or the decision relating to certification.[20]

Basically, the Act extends to all labor organizations and employers engaged in industries affecting commerce. The Act defines a "labor organization" to include

> any organization of any kind, any agency, or employee representation committee, group, association, or plan so engaged in which employees participate and which exists for the purpose, in whole or in part, of dealing with employers concerning grievances, labor disputes, wages, rates of pay, hours, or other terms or conditions of employment, and any conference, general committee, joint or system board, or joint council so engaged which is subordinate to a national or international labor organization, other than a state or local central body.[21]

An "employer"

> includes any group or association of employers engaged in an industry affecting commerce . . . but does not include the United States or any corporation wholly owned by the Government of the United States or any State or political subdivision thereof.[22]

Note, however, that employees of the U.S. Postal Service are included within the Act.[23] Also, as of October 13, 1978, the Civil Service Reform Act of 1978, Pub. L. No. 95-454, 92 Stat. 1198, Title VII, replaced those presidential executive orders, which for-

---

[17] 29 U.S.C. § 482(c).

[18] Usery v. Teamsters, *supra* note 11, at 377.

[19] Dunlop, *supra* note 15.

[20] Usery v. Teamsters, *supra* note 11.

[21] 29 U.S.C. § 402(i).

[22] 29 U.S.C. § 402(e).

[23] Postal Reorganization Act of 1970.

merly governed labor-management relations in the federal service.

Furthermore, a national or international labor organization composed of both government locals and nongovernment or mixed locals is covered, as well as its mixed or nongovernment locals.[24] Also, a "labor organization" is determined by its actual functions and practices in addition to its constitution and bylaws.[25] Consequently, most labor organizations are within the coverage of the Act. For a more precise interpretation of a "labor organization," see 29 CFR 451.2-451.6.

§ 9.01. Procedural Safeguards

Within Section 401 are the minimum electoral safeguards to ensure "'free and democratic' union elections . . . where 'the assumption is that voters will exercise common sense and judgment in casting their ballots.' "[26] These safeguards relate to frequency of officer election, electoral processes, campaign methods, and other adequate safeguards for fair elections.

[1] Election Frequency

Title IV specifies the particular elective offices covered: officers of every local, intermediate, national and international labor organization, except a federation of national or international labor organizations.[27] The frequency of elections depends on the type of labor organization. Every local must hold its election at least once during each three-year period. The period for an intermediate body is four years, and the period for a national or international organization is five years. A period is measured from the date of the last election.[28] There are three exceptions to these time requirements: (1) a vacancy may be filled by any method pre-

---

[24] 29 CFR § 451.3(a)(4).

[25] 29 CFR § 451.3(a)(2).

[26] Steelworkers, *supra* note 4.

[27] 29 U.S.C. § 481(a),(b), (d).

[28] 29 U.S.C. § 481(a)-(c); 29 CFR § 452.23-24.

scribed in the organization's constitution and bylaws.[29] (2) A newly formed or merged organization is required to hold its first election "within a reasonable period after the organization begins to function" (of course, this election is subject to Title IV; therefore, the maximum period would be that provided for in the statute).[30] (3) The establishment of a valid trusteeship may result in the suspension of elections—in fact, the effect may be to suspend all election provisions of Title IV (note, however, that Title IV provisions may be applicable to elections held during the trusteeship).[31]

[2] Officers

The officers who are to be elected periodically are defined in the Act: "any constitutional officer, any person authorized to perform the functions of president, vice president, secretary, treasurer, or other executive functions of a labor organization, and any member of its executive board or similar governing body."[32]

A constitutional officer is one identified as an officer by the organization's constitution and bylaws. This identification is irrespective of the actual function and duty of the individual; however, certain positions that the constitution and bylaws may require to be filled by the election process are not necessarily "officer" positions within the meaning of the Act.[33] A person authorized to perform executive functions is one "who in fact has executive or policy-making authority or responsibility." The authorization "may be inferred from actual practices or conduct. . . ." Thus, a distinction is to be drawn between one performing ministerial acts and one who has the requisite authority or responsibility.[34] The phrase "any member of the executive board or similar governing body" pertains to members of any unit vest-

---

[29] 29 CFR § 452.25.

[30] 29 CFR § 452.14.

[31] 29 U.S.C. § 461; 29 CFR § 452.15.

[32] 29 U.S.C. § 402(n).

[33] 29 CFR § 452.18.

[34] 29 CFR § 452.19.

ed with executive functions.[35]

Thus, the focus is on requiring elections for those possessing authority or responsibility for determining organizational policies or implementing executive functions. The Act does not cover many important union elections, such as those of shop stewards; members of or delegates to negotiating committees; delegates to conventions, county labor councils, or similar bodies.

[3] Electoral Processes

The procedures by which officers are elected may be quite different, depending on whether the organization is local or otherwise. Local elections must be determined by secret ballot among the members in good standing. But the intermediate, national, and international bodies may choose either the procedure required of local units or a convention of delegates or other representatives chosen by secret ballot.[36] Also, those rights granted to members in Section 401(e) (nomination, candidacy, etc.) are applicable only to individuals, not organizations: "For example, while locals may be members of an intermediate body, they are not entitled to the rights granted 'members' in section 401(e)."[37]

[a] Secret Ballot

The secret ballot process is the basis of any election, whether it is used by members, delegates, or representatives. This process is defined in the Act as

> the expression by ballot, voting machine, or otherwise, but in no event by proxy, of a choice with respect to any election or vote taken upon any matter, which is cast in such a manner that the person expressing such choice cannot be identified with the choice expressed.[38]

---

[35] 29 CFR § 452.21.
[36] 29 U.S.C. § 481(a), (b), (d); 29 CFR § 452.119.
[37] 29 CFR § 452.96.
[38] 29 U.S.C. § 402(k).

The regulations suggest that secrecy be maintained by use of voting machines, by physical arrangements to preserve privacy in polling places using paper ballots, or by use of double envelopes for mail ballots.[39] Challenged ballots are subject to the same secrecy requirements.

Courts have applied varying standards of strictness to the conduct of a secret ballot election. In one instance, election procedures that conceivably could have led to a violation of secrecy but had been followed for many years without objection were approved by the court as being in "substantial compliance" with the Act.[40] In another case, the validity of an election was sustained where the procedure used, involving numbered ballots, was open to abuse but it was not shown that it had actually been abused by using the ballots to identify the voters.[41] However, a more recent decision analyzed the secret ballot more closely. An election was invalidated because of a possible invasion of privacy although no actual abuse was indicated. The court noted that the use of a secret ballot was mandatory, not optional. In rejecting the union's argument that secrecy could be maintained by the voter moving to the back of the hall, the court noted that "in many cases, requiring a union member to make a great show of securing his secrecy may be tantamount to indicating his vote."[42] It has also been held that the requirement of secrecy is applicable after the ballots are cast. Any post-voting method by which a voter can be identified with his or her choice is a violation of the secret ballot provision.[43]

[b] Election Notice

In addition to the secret ballot provision, the Act requires a

---

[39] 29 CFR § 452.97.

[40] Shultz v. Local 420, Aluminum Workers, 62 CCH Lab. Cas. 10867, 74 LRRM 2281 (N.D. N.Y. 1970).

[41] Wirtz v. Local 11, Laborers Union, 211 F. Supp. 408, 46 CCH Lab. Cas. 17865, 51 LRRM 2280 (W.D. Pa. 1962).

[42] Brennan v. Steelworkers Local 3489, 520 F.2d 516, 522, 77 CCH Lab. Cas. 11140, 89 LRRM 3211 (7th Cir. 1975).

[43] Bachowski v. Brennan, 413 F. Supp. 147, 99 CCH Lab. Cas. 11729, 92 LRRM 3623 (W.D. Pa. 1976).

notice of the election: "Not less than fifteen days prior to the election notice thereof shall be mailed to each member at his last known home address."[44] This is a mandatory provision, which may not be circumvented by any other means of notice, however reasonable.[45] This provision also applies to a "primary election" at which nominees are chosen and to any runoff election. As to the latter, notice for the first election may suffice for the runoff election.[46]

A mailed notice can be in the form of a separate notice, a conspicuously displaced notice in a labor organization's newspaper, a sample ballot, or an actual ballot in a mail ballot election.[47] The content of the notice must be such as to inform the members of the impending election. At the minimum, this would include the date, time and place of the election and the office to be filled. Where absentee voting is available, the notice must include that information.[48]

Although the fifteen-day requirement is a minimum standard, a notice mailed too far in advance of the election may be in violation of the Act because the intent of Congress was that a notice should reasonably precede the date of the election. Also, if any material change (e.g., a change in date) is made after the mailing, another fifteen-day notice must be mailed.[49]

Finally, to ensure that all the members will in all likelihood receive the notice, each notice must be mailed to its recipient's last known address. (The last known address includes an extended temporary address of definite duration of which the labor organization was aware.[50]) Further, notices must be sent to all members, rather than to just a substantial number.[51] Thus, it is a violation if not all the members received notice and the labor

---

[44] 29 U.S.C. § 481(e); *see also* 29 CFR § 452.96.

[45] Brennan v. Local Union 639, Int'l Bhd. of Teamsters, Chauffeurs, Warehousemen and Helpers of America, 494 F.2d 1092, 73 CCH Lab. Cas. 14353, 85 LRRM 2594 (D.C. Cir. 1974); *see* Wirtz v. Local 169 Int'l Hod Carriers, etc., 246 F. Supp. 741, 52 CCH Lab. Cas. 16752, 60 LRRM 2540 (D. Nev. 1965).

[46] 29 CFR § 452.103.

[47] 29 CFR § 452.99-102.

[48] 29 CFR § 452.99.

[49] 29 CFR § 452.104.

[50] 29 CFR § 452.99.

[51] Brennan v. Teamsters, *supra* note 45.

organization knew or had reason to know that not all members would receive the notice.[52]

Therefore, the labor organization is restricted in the method of notice (mailed), in the content (date, time, place, and offices), and in the time of notice (reasonably prior but at least fifteen days prior) and it is required to exercise reasonable care to ensure that all members receive notices. Note that these requirements are applicable only to the local organization for rights granted to members in Section 401(e); e.g., requirements concerning notice are applicable only to individuals, not organizations.[53]

[c] Additional Safeguards

Once election day arrives, there are additional safeguards. One is the requirement that a candidate be permitted "to have an observer at the polls and at the counting of the ballots."[54] The regulations state that this right encompasses every phase and level of the counting and tallying process. The number of observers may be as many as necessary to observe the actual counting of ballots. They may also note the names of those voting in order to ascertain whether the individual is authorized to vote, but the observers must not compromise or give the appearance of compromising the secrecy of the ballot. Unless otherwise specified in the labor organization's constitution and bylaws, the observer need not be a union member. Finally, in mail ballot elections, an observer is entitled to be present at the preparation, mailing, receipt, opening and counting of the ballots.[55]

When the votes are cast Section 401(e) requires that the "votes cast by members of each local labor organization shall be counted, and the results published separately." The counting of ballots must account for all ballots, not just valid ballots. Publication ensures that the results are made known to interested members. This could be accomplished by the entry of an election report in the minutes of a regular local membership meeting, provided the

---

52 *Id.*

53 29 CFR § 452.96.

54 29 U.S.C. § 481(c).

55 29 CFR § 452.107.

minutes are available for inspection by the membership. Separate publication of the results has significance where the members elect by secret ballot officers for levels above the local (e.g., intermediate bodies). Here, the votes of each local must be tabulated and published separately.[56] Note, however, that the union is not required to elect an official by majority vote. It may by its constitution and bylaws provide for election of the candidate who receives the greatest number of votes.[57]

In addition to counting and publication of ballots, "(t)he election officials . . . shall preserve for one year the ballots and all other records pertaining to the election."[58] This responsibility is assigned by the Act either to the election officials designated in the constitution and bylaws or to the labor organization's secretary. Also, this preservation requirement cannot be satisfied by an independent certification.[59]

Lastly, along with the other safeguards mentioned above, the Act specifies a broad requirement: "Adequate safeguards to ensure a fair election shall be provided. . . ."[60] In this regard, the regulations note that a labor organization's discretion concerning the conduct of election is "circumscribed by a general rule of fairness."[61] This is applicable to all aspects of the election. Conduct by a labor organization or its officers that would violate "a general rule of fairness" includes the following: failure to provide adequate instructions for properly casting ballots;[62] permitting one candidate the use of his nickname on the ballot without affording a similar privilege to other candidates;[63] failure to preclude officers from counting the votes or retaining custody of the ballots;[64] failure to inform candidates of the location of polling places, thereby precluding candidates' right to have observers

---

[56] 29 CFR § 452.108.

[57] 29 CFR § 452.117.

[58] 29 U.S.C. § 481(e).

[59] 29 CFR § 452.106.

[60] 29 U.S.C. § 481(c); *see also* 29 CFR § 452.96.

[61] 29 CFR § 452.110(a).

[62] 29 CFR § 452.110(b).

[63] 29 CFR § 452.110(a).

[64] Hodgson v. District No. 5, United Mine Workers of America, 353 F. Supp. 108, 70 CCH Lab. Cas. 13421, 82 LRRM 2352 (W.D. Pa. 1973).

present;[65] and permitting campaigning within a polling place.[66]

Therefore, the Act dictates the minimum standards as to the mechanics of the election: secret ballot; election notice; observers at the polls; counting, publication, and preservation of ballots; and a broad rule of fairness.

[4] Candidacy

The guarantee of "free and democratic" union elections not only covers the election itself but also extends to the various aspects of candidacy. In a secret ballot election, "every member in good standing shall be eligible to be a candidate and to hold office (subject to Section 504 and to reasonable qualifications uniformly imposed). . . ." [67] What qualifies a member in good standing is discussed in connection with the right to vote.

If one is a member in good standing, there are still two other limitations. The first is that Section 504 prohibits certain persons from holding office: a member of the Communist Party or one convicted of a criminal offense listed in the section. However, persons convicted of the specified criminal offenses become eligible after completing a five-year probationary period after conviction or end or imprisonment, whichever is later, and former Communist Party members become eligible after termination of Communist Party membership.[68] Note, as to the latter, that the U.S. Supreme Court has held unconstitutional as a bill of attainder the Section 504 provision that imposes criminal sanctions on Communist Party members for holding union office.[69] Other courts have ruled that it is illegal for a union to penalize a member for membership in a Communist organization.[70]

The second limitation is one of "reasonable qualifications." Legislative history and the wording of the statute require a nar-

---

[65] Hodgson v. United Mine Workers of America, 344 F. Supp. 17, 68 CCH Lab. Cas. 12622, 80 LRRM 2145 (D.D.C. 1972).

[66] *Id.*

[67] 29 U.S.C. § 481(e); *see also* 29 CFR § 452.96.

[68] 29 U.S.C. 504.

[69] U.S. v. Brown, 381 U.S. 437, 14 L. Ed. 2d 484, 85 S. Ct. 1707 (1965).

[70] Turner v. Machinists Lodge 1894, 590 F.2d 409, 100 LRRM 2055 (2d Cir. 1978).

row construction of reasonable qualifications uniformly imposed.[71] Reasonable qualification "must be measured in terms of its consistency with the Act's command to unions to conduct 'free and democratic' union elections."[72] The main interest sought to be protected is not that of the individual union member but that of the public in "free and democratic" elections. Thus, an eligibility rule must be judged "by its effect on free and democratic processes of union government."[73]

The effects "on free and democratic processes" must be determined on a case-by-case basis.[74] In this regard, the standard must be flexible, i.e., the "reasonableness must be gauged in the light of all the circumstances of the particular case. . . ."[75] It would appear, however, that any rule that deprives a substantial number of members of the right to be a candidate is per se unreasonable.[76] Thus, a meeting attendance rule that renders ineligible 93 percent or 96.5 percent of the members is in violation of the Act. In any event, the percentage of members denied eligibility by the application of a rule is an important factor.[77] Note that rules reasonable on their face may not be applied in an unreasonable or inconsistent manner.[78] Rules applied retroactively may be reasonable, depending on the nature of the rule. A retroactive application would be unreasonable if the members had no opportunity to satisfy the rule, e.g., a retroactive meeting attendance rule.[79]

The Secretary, in establishing guidelines for determination of reasonableness, paraphrased the Supreme Court in *Wirtz,*[80] noting:

> Union qualifications for office should not be based on assumptions that certain experience or qualifications are necessary. Rather it

---

[71] Wirtz v. Hotel, *supra* note 5, at 492, 499.

[72] Steelworkers, *supra* note 4, at 309; Wirtz v. Hotel, *supra* note 5, at 499.

[73] Steelworkers, *supra* note 4, at 310 n.6; Wirtz v. Hotel, *supra* note 5, at 499.

[74] Steelworkers, *supra* note 4, at 313.

[75] *Id*, at 313.

[76] Steelworkers, *supra* note 4; Wirtz v. Hotel, *supra* note 5.

[77] *Id.*; 29 CFR § 452.38.

[78] 29 CFR § 452.53.

[79] 29 CFR § 452.54.

[80] Wirtz v. Hotel, *supra* note 5, at 504.

> must be assumed that the labor organization members will exercise common sense and judgment in casting their ballots.[81]

In addition, the Secretary listed some factors to be considered when making a determination of reasonableness:

> (1) The relationship of the qualification to the legitimate needs and interests of the union; (2) The relationship of the qualification to the demands of union office; (3) The impact of the qualification, in the light of the Congressional purpose of fostering the broadest possible participation in union affairs; (4) A comparison of the particular qualification with the requirement for holding office generally prescribed by other labor organizations; and (5) The degree of difficulty in meeting a qualification by union members.[82]

The Secretary has promulgated various specific guidelines as to what may be considered reasonable or unreasonable.[83] Meeting attendance rules are measured by considering

> all the circumstances of the particular case, including not only the frequency of meetings, the number of meetings which must be attended and the period of time over which the requirement extends, but also such factors as the nature, availability, and extent of excuse provisions, whether all or most members have the opportunity to attend meetings, and the impact of the rule, that is, the number or percentage of members who would be rendered ineligible by its application.[84]

A requirement of prior service in a lower office is considered by the Secretary to be unreasonable. This appears to be based upon *Wirtz.*[85] However, in that ruling, the Court implicitly approved a similar restriction in the International Ladies Garment Workers Union because "that Union provides members with the alternative of a union-conducted course in union manage-

---

[81] 29 CFR § 452.36(a).
[82] 29 CFR § 452.36(b).
[83] 29 CFR § 452.37-452.52.
[84] Steelworkers, *supra* note 4, at 313; 29 CFR § 452.38.
[85] Wirtz v. Hotel, *supra* note 5, at 504.

ment."[86] Also, it may be unreasonable to limit eligibility to particular branches or segments of the union. But a union may limit eligibility to members of a unit defined on a geographic, craft, shift, or similar basis where the position is representative of that unit (e.g., a geographical vice president).

A reasonable period of prior membership or continuous good standing may be a reasonable qualification as well as a requirement that a candidate be employed in the trade of the union or actively be seeking such employment if the member has previous experience in the trade. Apprentices may be barred from candidacy until they complete their apprenticeship. A rule barring anyone holding an additional membership in a rival labor organization is a permissible qualification. And, as in the construction industry, supervisors or employers holding valid union membership must be barred from candidacy. Members who are full-time non-elective employees may be prevented from being candidates. Other regulations state that personal characteristics that have a direct bearing on fitness for a particular office may form the basis for reasonable restrictions, e.g., a minimum age requirement. But age requirements may conflict with the Age Discrimination in Employment Act of 1967.[87]

A breach of union rules may result in a candidate's disqualification, but such disqualification must conform to the provisions of Section 101(a)(5) of the Act. Requiring a filing fee is not permitted. Multiple office holding is permitted under the Act. Finally, it is not a reasonable qualification to require candidates to be registered voters or to have voted in public elections or to have voted in prior union elections.

Therefore, the policy of the Act, in order to ensure that knowledgeable and dedicated union leaders are elected, "is to leave the choice . . . to the membership in open democratic elections, unfettered by arbitrary exclusions.[88] Although labor organizations may impose qualifications on candidacy for elective office, the qualifications must be reasonable. Whether any particular qualification is reasonable depends on the facts of the particular case and is assessed by its anti-democratic effects.

---

[86] *Id.*, at 505.

[87] 29 U.S.C. § 623 et seq.

[88] Steelworkers, *supra* note 4, at 313.

[5] Nomination

Accompanying the right to be a candidate is a requirement that "a reasonable opportunity . . . be given for the nomination of candidates. . . ."[89] The Act does not prescribe any particular nomination procedures but it does require the employment of reasonable procedures that conform to the labor organization's constitution and bylaws.[90] To meet this requirement, the regulations require members (in good standing) to be fully informed, i.e., timely provided with the following information: the offices to be filled, the time and place of nomination, and the form of nomination.[91]

To be timely, notice of nomination need only reach the members in sufficient time to permit them to nominate a candidate of their choice. Unlike the election notice, a minimum of fifteen days prior notice is not required. But both the election and nomination notice could be combined, provided the combined notice conforms to the requirements of an election notice.[92] Thus, any notice that sufficiently enables members to participate in the nomination process will satisfy the statute.

As to the procedure of nomination, the labor organization may use any procedure that provides a reasonable opportunity for making nominations.[93] There are several limitations implicit in the Act. Procedures be uniformly applied, e.g., procedures for obtaining forms must be uniformly imposed on incumbents and challengers alike.[94] Certain requirements for candidacy are illegal because they deprive members of the opportunity to nominate candidates: filing fee for candidates;[95] filing a declaration of intention to run 5 ½ months prior to the election;[96] and a procedure

[89] 29 U.S.C. § 481(e); *see also* 29 CFR § 452.96.

[90] 29 CFR § 452.55.

[91] 29 CFR § 452.56.

[92] *Id.*

[93] 29 CFR § 452.57.

[94] Wirtz v. Nat'l Maritime Union of America, 399 F.2d 544, 58 CCH Lab. Cas. 12857, 68 LRRM 3017 (2d Cir. 1968).

[95] 29 CFR § 452.52.

[96] Wirtz v. Local Union 406, 406-A, 406-B and 406-C, Int'l Union of Operating Engineers, 254 F. Supp. 962, 53 CCH Lab. Cas. 11297, 62 LRRM 2309 (E.D. La. 1966).

by which only self-nomination is permitted[97] (although self-nomination is permissible if alternative means are also available).

Other determinations of reasonable procedures are also found in the regulations. A requirement that nominees be present at nomination meetings in order to be nominated may be reasonable under certain circumstances.[98] An individual who is otherwise eligible to be a candidate cannot be disqualified because of the failure of a union officer to perform his or her duties, which are beyond the candidate's control.[99]

Whenever the officers of a national or international labor organization or of an intermediate body are to be elected by secret ballot (see Section 401(a) and (d) of the Act), a nomination procedure whereby each local nominates only one candidate for each office may be reasonable: "The reasonableness of the number of local union nominations or endorsements required depends upon the size and dispersion of the organization."[100] Bodies above the local level are not required to conduct secret ballot elections, nor are they necessarily required to conform to all of the specifics of the Act.[101] But whenever "nominations are made by the locals or other subordinate organizations fundamental safeguards must be observed including the right of members to vote for and support the candidates of their choice without improper interference."[102] Finally, an ample opportunity to nominate must be provided to delegates chosen by secret ballot whenever the elections are at conventions and nominations are also made.[103]

Therefore, the local organizations are more strictly controlled by the specific provisions of the Act and by the regulations of the Secretary. The requirement is basically that a reasonable opportunity must be provided for the nomination of candidates: a timely notice containing pertinent nomination information and the use of reasonable procedures for nomination. However,

---

97 29 CFR § 452.58.
98 29 CFR § 452.59.
99 29 CFR § 452.62.
100 29 CFR § 452.60(a).
101 29 CFR § 452.96; *see* 29 U.S.C. § 481(a), (d).
102 29 CFR § 452.60(b).
103 29 CFR § 452.63.

nominations for candidates for offices at levels superior to the local may be governed by a lesser standard.

[6] Campaign Safeguards

Given that the "basic objective of Title IV of the LMRDA is to guarantee 'free and democratic' union elections modeled on 'political elections in this country' where 'the assumption is that voters will exercise common sense and judgment in casting their ballots,' "[104] it follows that certain campaigning safeguards are necessary so that members can make an informed choice at the polls.[105] In this respect, Title IV has several provisions relating to the distribution of campaign literature, the use of union membership lists, and the use of union funds and employer funds.[106] These provisions are applicable to candidates for both officer positions and delegate posts if the delegates are to nominate or elect officials.[107]

It is implicit that a right to campaign must be accompanied by a reasonable opportunity to campaign. Although the Act does not specify a time interval between nomination and election—in fact, both may be held at the same time—the regulations require that a reasonable period must be provided to ensure a sufficient opportunity to campaign.[108] What a reasonable period would be depends on, among other things, the method of nomination and the size of the labor organization in terms of operating area and number of members.[109]

To be entitled to the protection of the campaign provisions, one need not be a formally nominated candidate. It is sufficient to be "actively seeking both nomination and election."[110] Thus, a union may not prevent an otherwise qualified candidate from

---

[104] Steelworkers, *supra* note 4, at 309.

[105] 29 CFR § 452.66.

[106] 29 U.S.C. § 481(c), (g).

[107] 29 CFR § 452.66; *see also* 29 CFR § 452.81.

[108] 29 CFR § 452.65.

[109] 29 CFR § 452.79.

[110] Yablonski v. United Mine Workers of America, 60 CCH Lab. Cas. 10204, 77 LRRM 2606 (D.D.C. 1969); *see* 29 CFR § 452.80; *but see* Schonfeld v. Rarback, 49 CCH Lab. Cas. 19039 (S.D. N.Y. 1967).

taking advantage of the campaign safeguards. Note, also, that the definition of campaigning activities is important as to the extent of protection afforded by the Act. In almost all situations, a candidate's right depends on what is considered campaigning by the incumbents.

With regard to the distribution of campaign literature, Section 401(c) provides that a labor organization

> shall be under a duty, enforceable at the suit of any bona fide candidate . . . to comply with all reasonable requests of any candidate to distribute by mail or otherwise at the candidate's expense campaign literature in aid of such person's candidacy. . . .

This is clearly an affirmative duty, legally enforceable, imposed upon the union.[111] It requires compliance, regardless of the content of the material, even if it may constitute libel for which the union may be sued. Thus, a labor organization may not exercise any pre-distribution censorship.[112]

The key to a request for distribution is that it must be at the candidate's request. This may or may not be an onerous burden, for the candidate has some control over the method of distribution (mail or otherwise) and the candidate may request distribution to less than the full membership.[113] The union is required to comply with the request even if it must employ additional staff to do so. In this situation, it would not be unreasonable for the union to require an advance payment.[114]

In addition to advance payment, a union may also adopt "reasonable rules" concerning its responsibility to distribute campaign literature. For example, it may determine to have just one distribution of campaign literature during a campaign. It may also decree that all requests to distribute campaign literature be made by a certain date following nomination. It is very important for a candidate and his or her attorney carefully to scrutinize the union's constitution and bylaws and to be aware of such rules. In addition, some unions, such as the Machinists, issue occasional

---

111 Wirtz v. American Guild of Variety Artists, 267 F. Supp. 527, 54 CCH Lab. Cas. 11680, 64 LRRM 2406 (S.D. N.Y. 1967).

112 29 CFR § 452.70.

113 29 CFR § 452.68.

114 29 CFR § 452.69.

interpretations of their constitutional provisions. The careful candidate would do well to obtain them from union officials or the election committee.

Thus, the union must comply with a candidate's request to distribute campaign literature. However, the candidate will not always be required to foot the bill. Whenever a labor organization authorizes distribution of

> campaign literature on behalf of any candidate or of the labor organization itself with reference to such an election, similar distribution at the request of any other bona fide candidate shall be made by such labor organization and its officers, with equal treatment as to the expense of such distribution.[115]

Thus, if a union distributes any campaign literature without charge, all other candidates shall receive the same treatment.

In addition to the right to distribute campaign literature, a candidate has

> the right, once within 30 days prior to an election . . . in which he is a candidate, to inspect a list containing the names and last known addresses of all members . . . who are subject to a collective bargaining agreement requiring membership therein as a condition of employment, which list shall be maintained and kept at the principal office of such labor organization . . . .[116]

The statute provides only for inspection, not for copying, but the Act also prohibits discrimination in the use of the list. Consequently, if the labor organization permits any candidate to copy, all candidates must have the same opportunity.[117]

The form or organization of the list is not specified; however, the regulations indicate that an index system organized alphabetically or geographically, or by local in a national or international labor organization, is permissible.[118] But a thirty-day period of inspection is specified. This period is designated by the Secretary to be thirty days prior to the casting of ballots. Thus,

---

[115] 29 U.S.C. § 481(c); *see* 29 CFR § 452.69, 73.

[116] 29 U.S.C. § 481(c).

[117] Wirtz v. American Guild, *supra* note 111; 29 CFR § 452.71(b).

[118] 29 CFR § 452.71(a).

in a mail ballot system requiring ballots to be returned as soon as received, the period is the thirty days prior to the mailing of the ballots themselves.[119] The particular time for inspection, to be exercised only once, is at the candidate's option.[120]

Finally, the list need not be continuously maintained and may be compiled prior to the election; however, the list must be kept at the principal office of the labor organization.[121] This duty cannot be circumvented by delegation of election responsibilities to an independent agency. Thus, even though an independent agency is handling all aspects of the election, including the use of membership lists, the labor organization must maintain a list at its principal office.[122] Therefore, a candidate has the right to inspect a membership list kept at the principal office of a labor organization. He or she may exercise the right once within a thirty-day period prior to the casting of ballots. Furthermore, he or she must be afforded treatment similar to that given to any other candidate with respect to the list.

To ensure fair elections, the Act not only provides the right to distribute campaign literature and inspect membership lists but also prohibits expenditures of monies by labor organizations and employers toward the candidacy of any person in an election: "No moneys received by any labor organization by way of dues, assessments, or similar levy, and no moneys of an employer shall be contributed or applied to promote the candidacy of any person in an election. . . ."[123] This "reflects the principle of union democracy that individual members are free to support persons of their own choosing in an election and cannot be forced directly or indirectly by dues diversion to lend support to others whom they oppose.[124]

The prohibition against the union applies "either to direct contributions from union treasury or to contributions made through the use of union facilities. . . . The fact that an expendi-

---

119 29 CFR § 452.72.

120 29 CFR § 452.71(a).

121 *Id.*

122 Wirtz v. American Guild, *supra* note 111.

123 29 U.S.C. § 481(g).

124 Retail Clerks Union, Local 638 v. Retail Clerks Int'l Ass'n, 299 F. Supp. 1012, 1023, 60 CCH Lab. Cas. 10031, 70 LRRM 3366 (D.D.C. 1969).

ture is 'de minimis' does not make it any less a violation."[125] Thus, the use of a union financial journal as a campaign instrument is prohibited;[126] also prohibited is expenditure of union funds for ". . . the printing and distributing of campaign literature, the renting of campaign office, and the paying of campaign personnel . . . ," at least when applied in a discriminatory manner.[127] Use of union office personnel to prepare or distribute campaign information is impermissible if the individual is being paid with union funds, rather than on his or her own time.[128] These restrictions apply to any labor organization, not just to the particular one involved in an election.[129]

Even though a labor organization is prohibited from making direct contributions toward the promotion of a candidacy, such an organization is not prevented from assuming the cost of distributing to the membership on an equal basis campaign literature submitted to the union by the candidates pursuant to the rights granted by Section 401(c), nor is it prevented from expending monies "for notices, factual statement of issues not involving candidates, and other expenses necessary for the holding of the election."[130] Thus, any direct expenditures of union funds by any union toward the promotion of a candidacy is prohibited. Similarly, an employer is also prohibited from making such expenditures.[131] This applies to any employer, not just the one that employs the members of the particular labor organization.[132] Both direct and indirect expenditures are prohibited. For example, campaigning by union stewards on company time with the approval of the company is prohibited, unless such activities are

---

[125] Brennan v. Sindicato Empleados de Equipo Pesado, Construccion y Ramas Anexas de P.R., [hereinafter cited as Sindicato], 370 F. Supp. 872, 879, 73 CCH Lab. Cas. 14486, 85 LRRM 2551 (D. P.R.).

[126] Yablonski v. United Mine Workers of America, 305 F. Supp. 868, 61 CCH Lab. Cas. 10355, 72 LRRM 2172 (D.D.C. 1969).

[127] Retail Clerks, *supra* note 124, at 1024.

[128] Sindicato, *supra* note 125.

[129] 29 CFR § 452.73.

[130] 29 U.S.C. § 481 (g).

[131] *Id.*

[132] 29 CFR § 452.78(b).

only incidental to the performance of work assignments.[133] By prohibiting certain expenditures, the Act prevents improper depletion of union treasuries, prevents incumbent officers from abusing their trust in order to become more entrenched, and prevents a showing of preference for any one candidate.[134]

In applying these provisions of the Act, the determination of what constitutes campaign literature and what constitutes promotion of a candidacy is important because it affects the action a member may take in response to a union's promotion of a candidacy. For example, a union using its membership newspaper to extoll the virtues of the incumbents entitles the other candidate or candidates to take several actions: (1) The individual may request similar coverage without the burden of the cost. The Act provides that a labor organization refrain from discrimination for or against any candidate in the use of its membership list and requires similar treatment when a labor organization authorizes distribution of campaign literature.[135] (2) The candidate has a pre-election course of action to force the union to comply with a request for similar treatment.[136] (3) The candidate has a post-election course of action to set aside the election on the basis of the union's failure to comply with his or her request, upon a charge of discrimination in the use of membership lists, or upon a charge of expending union funds for the promotion of a candidacy.[137]

Of course the problem is in determining when an activity, such as using the union-financed newspaper, becomes impermissible: "A line must be drawn between the use of the Journal to report the activities of union officers, which is permissible, and the use of the Journal, in such a way in reporting such activities, as to promote an individual's candidacy."[138] To draw this line, the

---

133 29 CFR § 452.78(a).

134 Hodgson v. Liquor Salesmen's Union, Local 2, State of N.Y., 334 F. Supp. 1369, 65 CCH Lab. Cas. 11899, 78 LRRM 2020 (S.D. N.Y. 1971), *aff'd*, 444 F.2d 1344, 65 CCH Lab. Cas. 11909, 78 LRRM 2030 (2d Cir. 1971).

135 Yablonski, *supra* note 126; Wirtz v. American Guild, *supra* note 111.

136 Yablonski, *supra* note 126.

137 Hodgson v. Liquor Salesmen, *supra* note 134; Yablonski, *supra* note 126; Wirtz v. American Guild, *supra* note 111.

138 Yablonski, *supra* note 126, at 871.

courts analyze the tone and content of the material.[139] They may look to see if excessive coverage (written or pictorial) is given to an incumbent as compared to other matters reported.[140] But a labor organization may "institute a system for airing of the candidates' views, even a presentation prepared by the candidates themselves, so long as this presentation is conducted on a nondiscriminatory basis."[141]

Another frequent, and even more difficult, problem occurs when union employees actively support the candidacies of incumbent officials. For example, a union business agent, who has access to union members, may often engage in campaign activities while at the job site to investigate or discuss grievances. Unfortunately, neither the Secretary nor the courts have been sympathetic to the argument that such campaigning is illegal. After all, they reason, the union business agent has the right of free speech, and since the hours of many such union employees are not firmly fixed (many insist that they are on call twenty-four hours each day), who can dispute the contention that such job site campaigning is not being done on the business agent's own time? This argument does not address the objection that few rank and file candidates have access to their fellow members while on the job.

Therefore, with regard to ensuring fair elections, Title IV has several specific campaign safeguards: a right to distribute campaign literature; a right not to be discriminated against in the use of membership lists; a right to inspect membership lists; and a right not to have a union's or employer's monies spent to give an advantage to other candidates. In one instance, the candidate has an absolute right to have his or her campaign literature distributed without censorship, although at his or her expense. In other instances, once the union has used funds from its treasury in the support of a candidate or has discriminated against or in favor of some candidate, the complaining candidate has several options: he or she can request similar treatment, bring a pre-election suit, or file a post-election action.

---

[139] Sindicato, *supra* note 125.

[140] Yablonski, *supra* note 126.

[141] Yablonski v. United Mine Workers of America, 305 F. Supp. 876, 61 CCH Lab. Cas. 10477, 72 LRRM 2636 (D.D.C. 1969).

[7] Right to Vote

Free and democratic unions are a reflection of a vital public interest. The Act protects this interest by protecting "the rights of rank-and-file members to participate fully in the operation of their union through processes of democratic self-government, and, through the election process, to keep the union leadership responsive to the membership."[142] An essential means by which the member participates is to cast his or her vote: "[E]very member in good standing . . . shall have the right to vote for or otherwise support the candidate or candidates of his choice. . . . each member in good standing shall be entitled to one vote."[143]

Although the right to vote is fundamental, it is still subject to some qualifications: . . . a member must be in good standing, and a labor organization may impose reasonable rules and regulations. Membership in good standing is a basic qualification for all the rights or safeguards in Section 401. The Act defines "member" or "member in good standing" as

> any person who has fulfilled the requirements for membership in such organization, and who neither has voluntarily withdrawn from membership nor has been expelled or suspended from membership after appropriate proceedings consistent with lawful provisions of the constitution and bylaws of such organization.[144]

To ensure that a union will not arbitrarily deny "good standing" status, the regulations require that any rule or regulation that qualifies the right to vote must be reasonable and must be published in the union's constitution and bylaws.[145]

The regulations promulgated by the Secretary provide guidelines as to reasonableness. It is permissible for a labor organization to condition the right to vote on the payment of dues. The condition must be uniformly applied, with reasonable opportunity to pay dues, including a grace period; an unemployed member must be permitted to maintain his or her membership by continu-

---

142 Steelworkers, *supra* note 4, at 309.

143 29 U.S.C. § 481(e); *see also* 29 CFR § 452.96.

144 29 U.S.C. § 402(o).

145 29 CFR § 452.85.

ing to pay dues.[146] Furthermore, the Act provides protection for a member if there is a delay or default in payment of dues under a dues checkoff system:

> No member whose dues have been withheld by his employer for payment to such organization pursuant to his voluntary authorization provided for in a collective bargaining agreement shall be declared ineligible to vote or be a candidate for office in such organization by reason of alleged delay or default in the payment of dues.[147]

A labor organization may deny voting rights to members suspended or disciplined in accordance with Section 101(a)(5) (Safeguards Against Improper Disciplinary Action). But once the member re-establishes his or her "good standing" status, it is improper for the labor organization to deny voting rights for a period longer than that required for a new member. Thus, a new member and a suspended member may be required to wait a reasonable period of time before being permitted to vote. A period of six months is not necessarily unreasonable.[148]

There are several other reasonable qualifications relating to membership status. It is reasonable to require an apprentice to complete a bona fide training program before being permitted the right to vote. Since a member is usually considered a member only in the local to which he or she pays dues, a labor organization may deny a visiting member the right to vote. A union is free within the constraints of its constitution and bylaws to deny or allow voting rights to employers, supervisors, and retired members.[149] Note, however, that a union is bound to adhere to its constitution and bylaws; reasonableness is not a justification for union conduct contrary to the provisions of its constitution and bylaws.[150]

Although a right to vote is a specific guarantee, the right is meaningless unless there is a reasonable opportunity to exercise

---

[146] 29 CFR § 452.86.

[147] 29 U.S.C. § 481(e); *see* 29 CFR § 452.87.

[148] 29 CFR § 452.88.

[149] 29 CFR § 452.89-.93; *see also* 29 CFR 452.27.

[150] Wirtz v. Laborers Local 125, 270 F. Supp. 12, 53 CCH Lab. Cas. 11213, 62 LRRM 2141 (N.D. Ohio 1966)

that right. Therefore, a labor organization is required to conduct its elections "in such a way as to afford all its members a reasonable opportunity to cast ballots."[151] The regulations do not provide situational guidelines, but they do provide some factors, although not inclusive, to guide a union in meeting its obligation: "the distance between members' work site or homes and the polling place, the means of transportation available, the nature of the members' occupations, and their hours of work."[152]

However, what is reasonable is left for a case-by-case determination. One court has stated what may be a basic test: whether the actual arrangements (no absentee balloting) are so lacking in democratic principles and so unfair as to deny a reasonable opportunity to a significant number of members.[153] In this regard, courts have upheld a union requirement of physical presence, instead of absentee voting, where several members were on the road during the election period[154] and where members were required to travel long distances to vote.[155] However, absentee ballots are required when access to the polls is impracticable.[156] The remoteness of a polling place is not necessarily an unreasonable denial of the right to vote if it is not wholly impracticable for members to travel to vote only once every three years.[157]

In sum, the franchise is subject to reasonable qualifications consistent with the provisions of Title IV. Moreover, the union cannot deprive an individual of this right by failing to provide a reasonable opportunity to exercise the franchise. Finally, neither the union nor any member thereof may chill this right to vote or otherwise support a particular candidate by subjecting the elector to penalty, discipline, or improper interference or reprisal of any

---

[151] 29 CFR § 452.94.

[152] *Id.*

[153] Hodgson v. Local Union 582, 350 F. Supp. 16, 69 CCH Lab. Cas. 13093, 81 LRRM 2458 (C.D. Cal. 1972).

[154] Hodgson v. Teamsters, Local 920, 327 F. Supp. 1284, 66 CCH Lab. Cas. 12079, 78 LRRM 2156 (E.D. Tex. 1971).

[155] Wirtz v. Hod Carriers, *supra* note 45.

[156] Goldberg v. Marine Cooks and Stewards Union, 204 F. Supp. 844, 45 CCH Lab. Cas. 17797, 51 LRRM 2129 (N.D. Cal. 1962); 29 CFR § 452.95.

[157] Hodgson v. Local Union 582, *supra* note 153.

kind.[158]

§ 9.02 Enforcement

Title IV of the Act has two sections. One enumerates the minimum rights of union members necessary to guarantee their participation in the electoral process by which knowledgeable and dedicated leaders can be elected.[159] The second section, with one exception, provides the exclusive mechanism for enforcing those minimum rights.[160]

Unfortunately, there is a great contradiction in practice between the Act's promise of election rights and the mechanism established for their enforcement. Under Title IV, enforcement depends first upon the union itself, second upon the Secretary, and third upon the federal courts. The obstacles placed by each of these institutions in the path of a rank and file union member challenging incumbent union officers are formidable.

A few preliminary suggestions to the union member undertaking, or even contemplating, a campaign for office are in order:

First, obtain, study, and understand the provisions of your union constitution and bylaws pertaining to internal union elections. Many battles have been lost simply because a time limitation was not understood or followed.

Second, start a notebook. Keep track of what happens at nomination and election meetings. Record the time, place, names of witnesses, and content of all conversations between yourself and union officials pertaining to the election. Documentation will be very important if the election results in legal proceedings.

Third, put things in writing. In communicating with your union, it is better to write a letter than to make a phone call. Follow up oral conversations with confirming letters. Of course, keep a copy of your letter and mail it certified, return receipt request. This will avoid arguments over whether or when a letter was sent or received.

Fourth, if possible consult with a knowledgeable and sympa-

---

158 29 U.S.C. § 481(e).

159 Steelworkers, *supra* note 4.

160 Calhoon, *supra* note 12.

thetic attorney. It is sad, but true, that your union officials rarely make a move without consulting their attorney. Don't be overpowered from the beginning if you can help it.

In all enforcement actions, it is the member in good standing who must initiate the process. In one situation, the member may file a civil action in federal court; in all other Title IV situations, the member files a complaint with the Secretary.

[1] Pre-election

Section 401(c) provides that a suit may be brought by a bona fide candidate in the federal district court in which the labor organization maintains its principal office. It may be brought against any labor organization subject to Section 401; i.e., any local, intermediate body, or national or international labor organization, except a federation of national or international labor organizations.[161] The purpose for which a cause of action may be filed is limited: to enforce the union's duty to comply with all reasonable requests to distribute campaign literature and to prevent discrimination in favor of or against any candidate respecting the use of membership lists. A private action under Section 401(c) is available only for pre-election relief. Once the election has been held (ballots cast), only the Secretary may file a civil action.[162] The relief sought is injunctive.

In a private action, it is the injured party who brings suit. As discussed previously, a bona fide candidate need not necessarily be an individual who has been formally nominated, but need only be one who is actively seeking both nomination and election.[163] The complaint need not include the union as a party if suit has been filed against its officers.[164] Note, also, that attorney

---

[161] 29 C.F.R. § 452.81.

[162] Calhoon, *supra* note 12, at 140; *see* Steelworkers, *supra* note 4, at 313; Wirtz v. Glass Bottle Blowers, *supra* note 6; Wirtz v. Local Union 125, Laborers Int'l Union of North America, 389 U.S. 477, 482, 19 L. Ed. 2d 716, 88 S. Ct. 639 (1968); Wirtz v. Hotel, *supra* note 5. *But see,* Kupau v. Yamamoto, 622 F.2d 449 (9th Cir. 1980).

[163] Yablonski v. United Mine Workers, *supra* note 110; 29 CFR § 452.80.

[164] Morrissey v. Curran, 356 F. Supp. 312, 70 CCH Lab. Cas. 13535, 82 LRRM 2983 (S.D. N.Y. 1973).

fees and costs are recoverable by a successful litigant.[165]

The union's duty to comply with reasonable requests to distribute campaign material is relatively straightforward and requires, at a minimum, the establishment of some machinery for use by all candidates.[166] This duty cannot be delegated; thus, even though it is proper for a labor organization to use an independent agency to conduct its election and to handle candidates' distributions, the union cannot escape its responsibility if the agency fails to meet the statutory requirements.[167]

Pre-election suits based upon failure of the union to comply with a candidate's request arise out of two basic situations. One is when the union fails to meet a candidate's request for distribution of campaign literature (a right mandated by Section 401(c)). The second is when the union has used its membership list to distribute campaign material for one candidate and another candidate requests similar treatment. This may arise where a union newspaper extolling the virtues of the incumbents is mailed to the membership.[168]

The relief is injunctive: The court will issue an order directing the union to do or not to do something. Generally, before an injunction will issue, the plaintiff must be able to establish the likelihood that (1) he or she will ultimately succeed when the case is tried on its merits; (2) the plaintiff will be irreparably injured and has no adequate remedy at law; (3) the issuance of injunctive relief will not be harmful to others; and (4) the public interest in fair union elections is clearly on the side of injunctive relief.[169]

Pre-election relief has consisted of a court order directing a labor organization to make mailing lists available to candidates because the union distributed campaign material via union news-

---

165 Yablonski v. United Mine Workers of America, 466 F.2d 424, 69 CCH Lab. Cas. 12921, 80 LRRM 3297 (D.D.C. 1972), *cert. denied,* 412 U.S. 918 (1973); Brennan v. United Steelworkers of America, 554 F.2d 586, 81 CCH Lab. Cas. 13182, 95 LRRM 2178 (3d Cir. 1977), *cert. denied,* 435 U.S. 977 (1978); Usery v. Teamsters, *supra* note 11.

166 Wirtz v. American Guild, *supra* note 111.

167 *Id.*

168 Yablonski v. United Mine Workers, *supra* note 126.

169 Yablonski v. United Mine Workers of America, 305 F. Supp. 868, 62 CCH Lab. Cas. 10657 (D.D.C. 1969).

letter.[170] A court order has been issued to the union to refrain from discrimination in use of its membership lists,[171] and a temporary restraining order has been issued to enjoin an election.[172] However, injunctions, relating to editorial decisions as to matters of form, style, and content may be impermissible because of First Amendment considerations.[173] Thus a court order, enforceable by a contempt citation, directing nondiscriminatory use of membership lists with respect to campaign distribution (union journal used as a propaganda organ) is proper; but a mandatory order requiring equal space to be devoted to a discriminated-against candidate may be improper.

Even though a pre-election private action is available, relief may not be forthcoming because injunctive relief is discretionary, granted only upon a clear showing of probable success and irreparable injury. Most federal judges are both inexperienced in trying cases under the Act and reluctant to interfere in internal union affairs. This reluctance is increased by the knowledge that the violation(s) alleged in a pre-election suit may also be brought to the Secretary's attention after the election. The Secretary may file suit if it is determined that the violation was significant and probably affected the outcome of the election. Thus, although a pre-election suit is possible, it should not be seen as an easy solution to campaign literature distribution problems.

[2] Post-election

[a] Special Role of the Secretary

With the exception of the private pre-election suit to enforce campaign distribution requests permitted by Section 401(c), all other enforcement actions are brought by the Secretary after the

---

170 Sheldon v. O'Callaghan, 335 F. Supp. 325, 66 CCH Lab. Cas. 12135, 78 LRRM 2732 (S.D. N.Y. 1971).

171 Yablonski, *supra* note 126.

172 Backo v. Local 281, United Bhd. of Carpenters and Joiners of America, 308 F. Supp. 172, 61 CCH Lab. Cas. 10592, 73 LRRM 2052 (N.D. N.Y. 1969), *aff'd,* 438 F.2d 176, 64 CCH Lab. Cas. 11397, 76 LRRM 2184 (2d Cir. 1970), *cert. denied,* 404 U.S. 858 (1971).

173 Yablonski v. United Mine Workers, *supra* note 141.

election. Thus, once the election has been held, the Secretary has the exclusive authority to file a civil action in federal district court. The result is that relief is remedial rather than preventive. That the Secretary has this special role is based upon statutory interpretation by the U.S. Supreme Court. The basic rationale for this exclusive role is twofold: a policy of governmental noninterference in internal union affairs and the Secretary of Labor's presumed expertise in this area.[174]

However, the Secretary's exclusivity is only one part of the total enforcement process. Enforcement of Title IV is essentially divided into three stages, with one stage being the prerequisite for the next. Basically, enforcement procedures, as outlined in Section 402 of LMRDA, require that a member of the labor organization first seek resolution of a possible violation from the organization itself and, second, file a complaint with the Secretary only if the union fails to resolve the violation. At this point, the Secretary is required to investigate the member's complaint. If he or she finds that an unremedied violation exists, the Secretary may seek settlement with the union or may bring a civil action in federal court. Third, if the Secretary files a complaint, the court, after finding that a violation has affected the outcome of the election, shall void the election, if any, and direct a new election under the supervision of the Secretary.

[b] Prerequisites

As outlined above, the primary role for enforcement is given to the labor organization.[175] To this end, a basic requirement is that the member must exhaust all internal union remedies available under the constitution and bylaws of the union. This reflects a congressional intent "to foster a situation in which the unions

---

[174] Dunlop v. Bachowski, 421 U.S. 560, 569, 44 L. Ed. 2d 377, 95 S. Ct. 1851 (1975); Trbovich v. United Mine Workers of America, 404 U.S. 528, 532, 30 L. Ed. 2d 686, 92 S. Ct. 630 (1972); Wirtz v. Glass Bottle Blowers, *supra* note 6, at 498; Wirtz v. Laborers Int'l, *supra* note 162, at 482; Calhoon, *supra* note 12, at 140; *see* Steelworkers, *supra* note 4, at 313. *But see,* Kupau, *supra* note 162.

[175] Wirtz v. Hotel, *supra* note 5, at 498; Wirtz v. Glass Bottle Blowers, *supra* note 6, at 472; Calhoon, *supra* note 12, at 140.

themselves could remedy as many election violations as possible without the Government's ever becoming involved."[176] This stage is extremely important, for failure to exhaust all remedies or failure to allege all possible violations may result in an unremedied violation. It is important to understand this requirement. Many members will feel that internal union procedures are stacked against them and that chances for success are almost nonexistent. Nevertheless, it is vital to exhaust those procedures thoroughly in order to preserve further legal remedies.

The "exhaustion" requirement has two essential elements: invocation of internal union procedures and allegation of possible violations of Section 401. The procedures to be followed are those found in the constitution and bylaws of the local organization and its parent body.[177] This places upon a member the duty to inquire what remedies, if any, are available.[178] Failure to follow the procedures may result in dismissal of the complaint.[179]

The content of the member's complaint to the union should be sufficient to give the union fair opportunity to redress the violation.[180] It must, at a minimum, contain all allegations as to all possible violations known to the complaining party.[181] However, in exhausting the internal remedies, a member is not held to procedural niceties or to precision in framing the protest:[182] "Union democracy is far too important to permit these deficiencies to foreclose relief from election violations."[183] Thus, interpretation of the exhaustion requirement must reflect the needs of rank and file union members—those people the requirement is designed ultimately to serve."[184] Moreover, "exhaustion is not required when internal union remedies are unnecessarily com-

---

176 Hodgson v. Local 6799, United Steelworkers of America, 403 U.S. 333, 339, 29 L. Ed. 2d 510, 91 S. Ct. 1841 (1971).

177 20 U.S.C. § 482(a)(1).

178 Wirtz v. Great Lakes District Local 47, Int'l Organization of Masters, Mates and Pilots, 240 F. Supp. 859, 51 CCH Lab. Cas. 19651, 59 LRRM 2085 (N.D. Ohio 1965).

179 Hodgson v. Liquor Salesmen, *supra* note 134.

180 Hodgson v. United Steelworkers, *supra* note 176, at 340-341.

181 *Id.*, at 340.

182 *Id.*, at 341 n.6.

183 *Id.*, at 340-41.

184 *Id.*, at 340.

plex or otherwise operate to confuse or inhibit union protestors."[185] In fact, there may be circumstances where complaining members would not be required to exhaust the available remedies.[186]

In order to file a complaint with the Secretary, a member must have exhausted all available remedies or must wait for three calendar months (ninety days) after beginning to invoke the remedies, provided a final decision has not been rendered.[187] Note that these two options are essentially mutually exclusive. One can wait until a final decision has been made by the union; then, once the decision is rendered, the member may file his or her complaint with the Secretary. But if no final decision is rendered within three calendar months after initiation of the protest, the member may file at that time. Thus an individual need not wait until the final decision in order to file a complaint with the Secretary. As a practical matter, three months will pass before the union makes a final determination.

The importance of this period, three months or final decision, is that within one calendar month thereafter the complaint must be filed with the Secretary.[188] This one calendar month period is mandatory. Failure to meet this provision will result in a dismissal in the district court.[189] Therefore, timely filing with the Secretary is critical.

What is timely depends on the proper utilization of union procedures for protests and on determination of when the complaint was filed. As to the former, a few courts have held that invocation of pre-election remedies does not start the statutory time period. Since the remedy is post-election, the period does not start until then.[190] However, it would appear that the key

[185] *Id.*, at 341 n.6.

[186] *See* Wirtz v. American Guild, *supra* note 111, at 533 n.9; McDonald v. Oliver, 400 F. Supp. 660, 664 (S.D. Miss. 1974); *aff'd in part,* 525 F. 2d 1217, 78 CCH Lab. Cas. 11264, 91 LRRM 2215 (5th Cir. 1976), *cert. denied,* 429 U.S. 817 (1976).

[187] 29 U.S.C. § 482(a)(1)-(2).

[188] 29 U.S.C. § 482(a)(2); Wirtz v. American Guild, *supra* note 111.

[189] Hodgson v. United Steelworkers of America, 459 F.2d 348, 68 CCH Lab. Cas. 12602, 80 LRRM 2252 (3d Cir. 1972).

[190] *See* Wirtz v. H.H. Guy Lodge No. 873, Railroad Trainmen, 279 F. Supp. 873, 874, 57 CCH Lab. Cas. 12369, 67 LRRM 2477 (W.D. Pa. 1967); Wirtz v.

factor is the constitution and bylaws of the union. Thus, where a constitution provided for pre-election protest procedures for pre-election violations, the date of the denial of the pre-election protest was the date when remedies were deemed exhausted.[191] However, where the constitution provided only post-election relief for election violations, a pre-election protest under a union constitution provision relating to unfair treatment did not start the period.[192] Moreover, timeliness of appeals procedures within the union cannot be upheld where union conduct prevented the timeliness.[193] Finally, it has been held that the date of final exhaustion is the date of formal notification.[194]

The timeliness of the complaint filed with the Secretary also depends on the date filed. The date filed is the date the Secretary receives the complaint. It is considered received by the Secretary when received in the mailroom of the Department of Labor.[195] Note, however, that faulty advice from the Secretary does not necessarily extend the time of filing.[196]

Consequently, in order for a complaining member to obtain redress for possible violations of Section 401 of the LMRDA, the member must file a complaint with the Secretary within one calendar month after exhausting the remedies available under the union's constitution and bylaws or after three calendar months from the invocation of such remedies without obtaining a final decision. The member filing the complaint need not necessarily be one in good standing as defined by the union's constitution and bylaws; it is the statutory definition that controls.[197] Nor

---

Local 30, Operating Engineers, 242 F. Supp. 631, 51 CCH Lab. Cas. 19757, 59 LRRM 2654 (S.D. N.Y. 1965), *vacated as moot,* 366 F.2d 438, 54 CCH Lab. Cas. 11382, 62 LRRM 2777 (2d Cir. 1966).

[191] Hodgson v. United Steelworkers, *supra* note 189.

[192] Usery v. Amalgamated Transit Union, Local Division 1205, 545 F.2d 1300, 79 CCH Lab. Cas. 11740, 93 LRRM 2870 (1st Cir. 1976).

[193] Hodgson v. Liquor Salesmen, *supra* note 134.

[194] Usery v. Int'l Organization of Masters, Mates and Pilots, Int'l Maritime Division, ILA, 422 F. Supp. 1221, 1224, 79 CCH Lab. Cas. 11516, 92 LRRM 2274 (S.D. N.Y. 1976).

[195] Wirtz v. Hod Carriers, *supra* note 45.

[196] Hodgson v. United Steelworkers, *supra* note 189; *see* Usery v. Amalgamated Transit, *supra* note 192.

[197] Wirtz v. Independent Petroleum Workers of America, Inc., Independent Oil Workers Union, 307 F. Supp. 462, 62 CCH Lab. Cas. 10776, 74 LRRM 2090 (N.D. Ind. 1969).

must the complainant be one who was wronged: Any member in good standing may challenge a violation of the Act.[198]

[c] Investigation and Filing a Cause of Action

Once the complaint is received by the Secretary, he or she is required to investigate.[199] At this point, the scope of the investigation is not necessarily limited by the member's complaint. The Secretary has the authority to make an independent investigation, which includes compelling attendance of witnesses and issuing subpoenas duces tecum.[200]

In order to file a civil action in federal district court, the investigation must reveal that there is probable cause to believe that a violation has occurred, that the violation is unremedied, and that the violation may have affected the outcome of the challenged election.[201] The last requirement is not literally dictated by the statute to the Secretary, but the Supreme Court has construed the statute "as conferring upon the Secretary discretion to determine both the probable violation and the probable effect.[202] Thus,

> [T]he Secretary is not required to sue . . . whenever the proofs before him suggest the suit might be successful. There remains in him a degree of discretion to select cases, and it is his subjective judgment as to the probable outcome of the litigation that must control.[203]

Indeed, "the Secretary may attempt to settle the matter without any lawsuit. . . ."[204] However, this exercise of discretion is not conclusive. Judicial review is available to test the Secretary's rea-

---

198 Wirtz v. Local Union 57, 57-A, 57-B and 57-C, Int'l Union of Operating Eng'rs, 293 F. Supp. 89, 59 CCH Lab. Cas. 13070, 69 LRRM 2705 (D. R.I. 1968).

199 29 U.S.C. § 482(b).

200 29 U.S.C. § 521; Wirtz v. Laborers, *supra* note 162, at 482 n.5; Local 57, Int'l Union of Operating Eng'rs v. Wirtz, 346 F.2d 552, 51 CCH Lab. Cas. 19730, 59 LRRM 2310 (1st Cir. 1965).

201 29 U.S.C. § 482(b).

202 Dunlop v. Bachowski, *supra* note 174, at 570.

203 *Id.*, at 572.

204 Wirtz v. Glass Bottle Blowers, *supra* note 6, at 472.

sons for making the particular decision.[205] The scope and availability of judicial review is discussed below.

Assuming, for the moment, that the Secretary has found the necessary probable violation and probable effect, then a civil action must be filed in district court in the jurisdiction where the labor organization maintains its principal office.[206] The statute requires this filing to occur within sixty days of the filing of the member's complaint with the Secretary. This sixty-day period is computed according to Rule 6 of the Federal Rules of Civil Procedure.[207] Also, this period has been held not to be jurisdictional;[208] it has been tolled by a labor organization's waiver (at the Secretary's request) of the period;[209] and it has been tolled when the union caused a delay.[210]

The purpose of the civil action is to challenge the election already held or to challenge the union's failure to hold an election within the prescribed time limits.[211] Even though an election is being challenged, the presumption is that the election is valid. The officers elected hold their positions until, or unless, the election is set aside.[212]

The basis of the suit is the member's complaint. Therefore, ordinarily, the Secretary cannot include in the cause of action other violations which his or her investigations have discovered. But the Secretary may include those violations "which the union had a fair opportunity to consider and redress in connection with a member's complaint."[213] Furthermore,

> [C]ourts should impose a heavy burden on the union to show that it could not in any way discern that a member was complaining

---

205 Dunlop v. Bachowski, *supra* note 174.

206 29 U.S.C. § 482(b).

207 Wirtz v. Hod Carriers, *supra* note 45.

208 Marshall v. Local Union 1374, Int'l Ass'n of Machinists and Aerospace Workers, 558 F.2d 1354, 82 CCH Lab. Cas. 10024, 95 LRRM 3066 (9th Cir. 1977).

209 Hodgson v. Int'l Printing Pressmen and Assistants' Union, 440 F.2d 113, 65 CCH Lab. Cas. 11564, 76 LRRM 2706 (6th Cir. 1971), *cert. denied,* 404 U.S. 828 (1971).

210 Wirtz v. Masters, Mates, and Pilots, *supra* note 178.

211 29 U.S.C. § 482(b)-(c); 29 U.S.C. § 481(a)-(b), (d).

212 29 U.S.C. § 482(a)(2).

213 Wirtz v. Laborers, *supra* note 162, at 484.

> of the violation in question. But when a union member is aware of the facts supporting an alleged violation, the member must, in some discernible fashion, indicate to his union his dissatisfaction with those facts. . . .[214]

Thus, a member's unskillful complaint need not necessarily fail when the union is made aware of sufficient facts to discern a possible violation. But when a member is aware of the facts underlying an alleged violation, he or she must protest the violation to the union; otherwise, the member will he held not to have met the exhaustion of remedies requirement.[215]

[d] Adjudication

With the cause of action filed, the role of the court is to determine whether an election has been held within the prescribed time limits or whether a violation of Section 401 may have affected the outcome of an election. In both situations the determination is to be made upon a preponderance of the evidence after a trial on the merits. And, in either case, the remedy is to issue an order requiring that an election be held under the supervision of the Secretary.[216]

Even though the action is filed, the Secretary can agree with the union to settle or to hold the case in abeyance.[217] However, the Secretary may not have the administrative authority to terminate an action without judicial approval. Thus, a settlement that in no significant way corrects or restrains the abuse alleged in the Secretary's complaint may not be permitted.[218]

Also, contrary to the literal meaning of Section 402(c), requiring a "trial on the merits," summary judgment procedures are

---

214 Hodgson v. Steelworkers, *supra* note 176, at 341.

215 *Id.* at 340-41.

216 29 U.S.C. § 482(c).

217 See Brennan v. Conn. State UAW Community Action Program Council, 373 F. Supp. 286, 74 CCH Lab. Cas. 10181, 86 LRRM 3049 (D. Conn. 1974) re settlement; Stein v. Wirtz, 366 F.2d 188, 54 CCH Lab. Cas. 11450, 63 LRRM 2145 (10th Cir. 1966), *cert. denied,* 386 U.S. 996 (1967).

218 See Brennan v. Conn. State Community Action Program, *supra* note 217.

applicable.[219] Therefore, Rule 56 of the Federal Rules of Civil Procedure governs the application of summary judgment. Moreover, a "trial" does not necessarily imply jury trial. Because the relief sought is injunctive, there is ordinarily no right to a jury trial.[220]

The determination of whether an election has been held within the prescribed time limits is relatively straightforward, for the Act specifies the frequency at which the elections should be held.[221] As to whether an election outcome may have been affected, the Supreme Court has held that a prima facie case may be established by a proven violation of Section 401 of the Act. Once the prima facie case is established, the defendant (labor organization and/or its officers) must produce evidence "which supports a finding that the violation did not affect the result."[222] Thus, even "if there is only a single violation and a minimal one at that, it may be more easily rebutted, but it must be met by evidence which supports a finding that the violation did not affect the result.[223]

Note, however, that the Secretary, before filing a civil action, is required to find that the violation may have affected the election. This requires a reasonable possibility that the outcome was affected, i.e., a meaningful relationship between the violation of the Act and the results of the election.[224] In this regard, it is unnecessary, and in many cases impossible, to submit tangible evidence in order to demonstrate the effect of a violation. For example, where a violation of Section 401 has kept a candidate off the ballot, it would be difficult, at best, to show that but for the improper disqualification, the election would have been diff-

---

219 Usery v. Masters, Mates and Pilots, *supra* note 194; Usery v. Teamsters, *supra* note 11.

220 Wirtz v. District Council 21, Bhd. of Painters, Decorators, and Paperhangers of America, 211 F. Supp. 253, 46 CCH Lab. Cas. 17949, 51 LRRM 2591 (E.D. Pa. 1962).

221 29 U.S.C. § 481(a)-(b), (d); 29 CFR § 452.14-15, .23-.31.

222 Wirtz v. Hotel, *supra* note 5, at 506-07.

223 Usery v. Stove, Furnace and Allied Appliance Workers, Int'l of North America, 547 F.2d 1043, 1046, 80 CCH Lab. Cas. 11832, 94 LRRM 2249 (8th Cir. 1977).

224 Wirtz v. Hotel, *supra* note 5, at 507.

erent.[225] As noted above, when a prima facie case is established, the burden shifts to the defendant to produce sufficient evidence to overcome the reasonable possibility that the election outcome was not affected.[226] This burden is particularly heavy where a violation results in a substantial exclusion of candidates from the ballot. In meeting this burden, tangible evidence must be submitted.[227]

It would appear that in certain situations a proven violation is essentially one as a matter of law, for no tangible evidence can be available. One situation was an eligibility qualification that excluded 93 percent of the membership from considering candidacy.[228] Another possible situation is a violation that conceivably might influence every vote cast in a way not susceptible of precise measurement.[229] But in other circumstances tangible evidence was available; e.g., an election margin of 8-1 sufficiently overcame a violation in which 20 percent of the votes had been tampered with.[230] In like manner, a failure to comply with the duty to permit an inspection of a membership list, a violation of Section 401(c), did not affect the election where no candidate in the challenged election had sought inspection.[231]

If the court, after a trial on the merits, finds that a proven violation affected the outcome of an election it "shall declare the election . . . to be void and direct the conduct of a new election under the supervision of the Secretary. . . ."[232] This is mandatory even if an unsupervised election intervenes before final adjudication.[233] At this point, with the election set aside, the Secretary's special role in applying his or her expertise is clearly subordinate to the court's role in fashioning relief.[234] Thus, the court has the primary responsibility for the formulation of a remedial order

---

225 *See id.,* at 507-08.

226 *See id.*

227 *See id.*

228 *Id.*

229 Sindicato, *supra* note 125.

230 Wirtz v. Hotel, *supra* note 5, at 507.

231 *See* Wirtz v. American Guild, *supra* note 111, at 845.

232 29 U.S.C. § 482(c)(2).

233 Wirtz v. Glass Bottle Blowers, *supra* note 6.

234 Trbovich v. United Mine Workers, *supra* note 174; Usery v. Teamsters, *supra* note 11.

with respect to ground rules for a new election, and the Secretary's role is to aid the court in fulfilling that responsibility.[235]

Once the order for a new election is issued, the Secretary is required to supervise the election and promptly to certify the results to the court. The court is then required to enter a decree declaring the validity of that election.[236] Although the Secretary's supervision of the election is entitled to a presumption of fairness and regularity, the court will "attach its imprimatur to the Secretary's certification only if it is satisfied that the supervised election has been conducted in conformance with legal requirements."[237]

[e] Challenging the Secretary's Decisions

In interpretation and enforcement of Title IV, the Secretary has the major role. That role becomes secondary at the remedial stage, i.e., when the election is set aside and the court exercises its responsibility in fashioning a remedial order. However, this does not compel the conclusion that the Secretary's discretionary actions can go unchallenged or that the complaining member's participation ceases once the complaint is filed.

The Secretary's action may be challenged in two basic ways: appeal as a matter of right, and judicial review at the district court level. An appeal as a matter of right against an order directing an election or dismissing a complaint is granted in Section 402(d) of the Act. However, an order directing a new election will not be stayed pending the appeal.

Judicial review of the Secretary's discretionary decision is based upon 5 U.S.C., Section 702 and 704 (Administrative Procedure Act), and upon 29 U.S.C., Section 1337. Also, ". . . since the status relies upon the special knowledge and discretion of the Secretary for the determination of both the probable violation and the probable effect, . . . the reviewing court is not authorized to substitute its judgment for the decision of the Secretary.

[235] Trbovich v. United Mine Workers, *supra* note 174, at 537 n.8; Usery v. Teamsters, *supra* note 11, at 377.

[236] 29 U.S.C. § 482(c)(2).

[237] Usery v. Teamsters, *supra* note 11, at 375-76.

. . ."[238] Thus, the reviewing court is limited to determining whether the Secretary's action "is so irrational as to constitute the decision arbitrary and capricious." Furthermore, in this review an adversarial hearing is not permitted.[239] Needless to say, the chances of successfully challenging the Secretary's decision not to file suit to overturn an election are very slim.

To effectuate judicial review, "the Secretary must provide the court and the complaining witness with copies of a statement of reasons supporting his determination."[240] The statement of reasons must be such that a reviewing court can determine whether or not the Secretary's discretion has been properly exercised. Therefore, it "is necessary for him to delineate and make explicit the basis upon which discretionary action is taken. . . ."[241] The court's review will be confined to an examination of the statement of reasons: if it is inadequate, "the Secretary may be afforded the opportunity to supplement his statement."[242]

Judicial review is invoked by the complaining member who has exhausted his or her remedies. A challenge may be made to the Secretary's decision to file or not file a complaint and to the Secretary's determination of the validity of a supervised election.[243] Thus, it would appear that any discretionary action taken by the Secretary which affects the disposition of the member's complaint is subject to judical review; in any event, such discretionary action requires the issuance of a statement to the complaining member and to the court for the purpose of judicial review.[244] Note, however, that the question of whether the district court can order the Secretary to bring an action against a labor organization to set aside an election has not been deter-

---

238 Dunlop v. Bachowski, *supra* note 174, at 571.

239 *Id.*, at 573.

240 *Id.*, at 571.

241 *Id.*

242 *Id.*, at 574. For a sample of a reasons statement, see *id.*, at 577-89. For a summary of attacks on this reasons statement in the lower court on remand, see 10 Ga. L. Rev. 819 (1976).

243 *Id.*, re decision to file; Usery v. Teamsters, *supra* note 11, re validity of supervised election.

244 See Dunlop v. Bachowski, *supra* note 174; *see* Usery v. Teamsters, *supra* note 11.

mined by the Supreme Court.[245]

[f] Intervention

A member whose complaint has resulted in the Secretary's filing suit, may participate in a significant way at the district court level: "[I]n a post-election enforcement suit, Title IV imposes no bar to intervention by a union member, so long as that intervention is limited to the claims of illegality presented by the Secretary's complaint."[246]

This right to intervene is governed by Rule 24(a) of the Federal Rules of Civil Procedure. An individual can intervene when he or she claims a sufficient interest in the proceedings and that interest is inadequately represented by the parties to the action. A complaining member meets these two requirements: In the first place, there can be no doubt as to his or her interest in the proceedings. Secondly, since the Secretary is serving two distinct interests, the union member's and the public's, the member's interest may not always be adequately represented because the Secretary has a primary obligation to protect the public's interest over that of the member.[247]

Thus, the complaining member may intervene to support the Secretary's complaint but may not add substantive claims.[248] The intervenor's role is one of providing material assistance to the Secretary and the court.[249] This role is especially important once the election is set aside. At this point, the "(i)ntervenors may assist the court in fashioning a suitable remedial order, going beyond the remedies proposed by the Secretary. . . ."[250] But a member is not necessarily entitled to intervene to continue an action that the union and the Secretary have agreed to hold in abeyance.[251] Nor, it has been held, may an intervenor object to

---

[245] Dunlop v. Bachowski, *supra* note 174 at 575.

[246] Trbovich, *supra* note 174, at 537.

[247] *Id.*, at 537-39.

[248] *Id.*, at 537; Brennan v. United Steelworkers, *supra* note 165.

[249] *See* Usery v. Teamsters, *supra* note 11, at 377.

[250] *Id.*

[251] Stein v. Wirtz, *supra* note 217.

the terms of a proposed settlement between the Secretary and the union, although the wisdom of this assertion might be challenged.[252] However, the court will review objections to the terms of the settlement with respect to the reasonableness of the terms.[253] Finally, attorney fees and costs of the intervenor may be recovered.[254]

§ 9.03. Additional Considerations

The text above is an attempt to provide a basic understanding of what is available within the framework of Title IV of the LMRDA with respect to the procedural safeguards pertinent to union elections and to the enforcement of those safeguards. However, as to the enforcement of the procedural safeguards, there are two additional topics for discussion: Practice Tips and Private Enforcement Outside Title IV.

[1] Practice Tips

There is no fixed or specific role for the private attorney in actions brought to challenge an internal union election that has already been completed. However, experience indicates that a complaining union member will fare much better at all stages of the proceedings if he or she is represented by knowledgeable counsel.

[a] Exhaustion of Internal Union Remedies

As noted above, a complaining member must exhaust internal union remedies for three months before making a complaint to the Secretary of Labor. It is crucial that the complaining member

---

[252] *See* Conn. State Community Action Program, *supra* note 217, at 287.

[253] *Id.*

[254] Usery v. Teamsters, *supra* note 11; Brennan v. Steelworkers, 554 F.2d 586 (3d Cir. 1977). *But see* Marshall v. Teamsters Local 20, 509 F. Supp. 926 (N.D. Ohio 1981); dissent in Usery.

and his or her attorney become familiar with the internal union procedures. Generally speaking, these are found in the constitution of the international union and the bylaws of the local union involved. However, many unions also have intermediate bodies between the local and the international structure. The International Association of Machinists, for example has "district lodges" in many areas. The Teamsters Union has two sets of intermediate bodies, the "joint councils" above the local level and the "conferences" above the joint councils. These bodies have their own bylaws, which must be studied. Typically, a complaint concerning an election must be processed from lower to higher bodies, subject, of course, to the three-month period, after which the member may file with the Secretary.

In exhausting internal union procedures, all communications should be in writing, sent certified or registered mail with return receipt requested. Most union procedures require that the member, not the attorney, sign the charges. Time limits for challenging union actions, as set forth in the governing documents, should be followed.

[b] Proceedings before the Secretary

The assistance of counsel can be vital during the investigation of the member's complaint by the Secretary of Labor. Before the Secretary will file suit to overturn an election, an investigation must be completed and the decision to sue reviewed at the local, regional, and national levels. The process can continue interminably, despite the Act's purportedly stringent time requirements.

The member's complaint will be assigned to an investigator working out of an area office. The complaining member and his or her attorney should attempt to establish a cooperative working relationship with the investigator and should make sure that the investigator receives appropriate documentation and that witnesses are actually interviewed. The investigator's report will be reviewed by the area administrator. It is important to maintain contact with the area administrator, to discuss any possible problems with the case, and to urge speedy completion of the investigative report and the administrator's recommendation. When the report has been forwarded to a regional office for approval, counsel should ascertain the name of the person in the regional office who will be handling the case at that level and contact that person.

Finally, the report will be forwarded with recommendations to the Branch of Elections and Trusteeships at the Office of Labor-Management Standards Enforcement at the Department of Labor in Washington. Once again, telephone calls, letters, and even a personal visit, can be very helpful in ensuring that the case receives prompt attention and that a decision to sue is made.

It may well be said that the administrative processing of an election complaint by the Department of Labor is the most important part of the entire case. Experience indicates that little is to be expected of internal union procedures. On the other hand, because of the courts' deference to the Secretary in these matters, you will stand an excellent chance if your case does get to court. The problem is to make sure that it does. The complainant and his attorney can do nothing more important than to remain in constant touch with the Labor Department officials who are handling the case. Patient but persistent prodding and assistance in providing witnesses and documents (even legal citations) will all be of great assistance in both speeding up the process and making sure that the union's Washington attorneys are not successful in torpedoing the complaint. When problems arise, do not neglect the possibility of a letter from a friendly congressperson or senator to the Department of Labor.

[c] Intervention in District Court

The union member who files the complaint with the Secretary of Labor has an all but absolute right to intervene in the litigation brought by the Secretary on the basis of that complaint. The only reasonable obstacle to such intervention in the U.S. District Court would be the court's finding that the member's application to intervene was untimely.

It is suggested that intervention be accomplished if at all possible. The Secretary is represented in Title IV cases by either the Solicitor of Labor or the U.S. attorney, depending upon the location at which the suit is filed. Experience with assistant attorneys involved in such litigation indicates that they often are not knowledgeable in this area of law and uninterested in pursuing the litigation in an aggressive manner. The result is that cases can be so delayed as to become all but moot or that settlements unfavorable to the complaining member are made. Private counsel can undertake needed investigation and pursue a vigorous litigation strategy, with the goal of resolving the case by motion for summary judgment. While restricted to the Secretary's legal theory of the case, private counsel can both utilize whatever proof is available to prove the violations alleged by the Secretary and play an independent role in terms of proposing a remedy to the court or a settlement to the other parties. In many instances both the court and the government counsel will welcome the aggressive role played by knowledgeable private counsel representing the complaining union member.

[2] Private Enforcement Outside Title IV

The private cause of action under Title IV is limited to that provided by Section 401(c): a pre-election civil action with regard to distribution of campaign literature and use of union membership lists.[255] Furthermore, Section 403 precludes any private post-election cause of action; any post-election action is exclusive with the Secretary of Labor.[256] But there may be other pre-election alternatives: a cause of action under Title I or V of LMRDA and a cause of action under state law. However, the purpose of the following discussion is not to provide an exhaustive study of all available alternatives, but only to instill an awareness that other possibilities may exist.

Title I contains two sections particularly relevant to elections: Equal Rights, and Freedom of Speech and Assembly.[257] The Equal Rights section guarantees that "(e)very member of a labor organization shall have equal rights and privileges within such organization to nominate candidates, to vote in elections or

---

[255] 29 U.S.C. § 481(c).

[256] 29 U.S.C. § 483. *But see* Kupau, *supra,* note 162.

[257] 29 U.S.C. § 411(a)(1)-(2).

referendums . . ., subject to reasonable rules and regulations in such organization's constitution and bylaws." However, under this section caution is directed in the characterization of an alleged violation, for jurisdiction under Title I may be denied where an allegation in substance charges a breach of Title IV.[258]

The Freedom of Speech and Assembly section guarantees that "(e)very member of any labor organization shall have the right to meet and assemble freely with other members; and to express any views, arguments, or opinions; and to express at meetings of the labor organization his views, upon candidates in an election. . . ." Thus, allegations based upon the violation of the right to free speech during a campaign may be remedied under Title I. Also, it appears that the caution as to characterization of an alleged violation is not appropriate under this section, i.e., relief may be forthcoming even though the right is recognized by both Title I and Title IV.

Title V, which establishes the fiduciary duty of union officers, may be another approach to pre-election relief.[259] Thus, it has been suggested that a broad reading of this title results in imposition of a duty to conduct fair elections.[260] However, this seems to be a weak argument, since Title IV provides protection of election rights without a broad reading.

An additional possible cause of action may be found under Section 301 of LMRA if there has been a violation of the union constitution or bylaws. The Supreme Court in 1981 held that Section 301 provides jurisdiction in federal court to enforce a union constitution or bylaws.[261] The Court reserved the question of whether such jurisdiction exists in suits between individual union members and the union, but logic suggests that such jurisdiction would be found. The relationship between the

---

[258] Calhoon v. Harvey, 379 U.S. 134, 138, 13 L. Ed. 2d 190, 85 S. Ct. 292 (1964). *See* Bunz v. Moving Picture Machine Operators' Protective Union, Local 224, 567 F.2d 1117, 82 CCH Lab. Cas. 10210 (D.C. Cir. 1977), for some pertinent pre-election examples, as well as an indication that the basic policy rationale of *Calhoon* is being eroded.

[259] 29 U.S.C. § 501.

[260] Note, Union Elections and the LMRDA. Thirteen Years of Use and Abuse, 81 Yale L.J. 407, 553 (1972).

[261] United Assoc. of Journeymen & Apprentices v. Local 334, 101 S.Ct. 2546, 107 LRRM 2715 (1981).

so-called exclusive remedies of Title IV, weakened by the *Kupau* case, is yet to be addressed.

In addition to alternatives provided by actions filed in federal court, one may consider filing a pre-election cause of action in state court to enforce appropriate provisions found in the union's constitution and bylaws.[262] In this situation, state jurisdiction could be based upon breach of contract, since the union's constitution and bylaws are regarded as a contract between the union and its members in most states.[263]

Therefore, even though post-election relief is exclusive to the Secretary of Labor, pre-election relief is not. The union member can seek relief outside Title IV. e.g., a breach of contract action under state law to enforce a union's constitution and bylaws.

---

[262] 29 U.S.C. § 483.

[263] Cecil B. DeMille v. American Federation of Radio Artists, Los Angeles Local, 31 Cal. 2d 139, 187 P.2d 769 (1947), *cert. denied,* 333 U.S. 876 (1948).

CHAPTER 10

Protecting the Right to a Pension

§ 10.01. Historical Background and Statutory Basis

The private pension system has its origin in the worker associations and brotherhoods of the early 1800's which began collecting dues from their members to pay for disability and death benefits for their members. Soon employers recognized that even such rudimentory programs as these were powerful organizing tools for unions, especially in the skilled trades where employment was relatively stable. Both to counteract this organizing tool and to reward company loyalty, private employers began providing their own pension plans. However, in almost all cases the benefits under these plans were small, the payments were irregular and the employer could terminate them at will. No claim for them could be made in the courts because they were considered gratuities and not entitlements.

Although collectively bargained pension plans came into existence during the 1930s, the real impetus for them did not occur until the 1940s. The exemption of contributions to pension funds from the wage freeze imposed during the labor-short years of World War II triggered the tremendous expansion of collectively bargained plans. Additional encouragement was provided in 1948 by the Seventh Circuit holding that employer contributions into a pension fund are considered compensation and are therefore a mandatory subject of collective bargaining within the meaning of the Labor-Management Relations Act (LMRA).[1] The growth of the private pension system was assured by the bountiful tax benefits which have been conferred on qualified plans since the era of the New Deal.

The regulation of these collectively bargained plans began with the passage of the Taft-Hartley Act (29 USC Section 302) in 1947. Ostensibly passed to protect plan participants, one of the principle reasons for the pension regulations was to limit pensions as an organizing tool of the unions. John L. Lewis of the United Mine Workers had been quick to recognize the power of the accumulating capital of the UMW Health and Welfare Fund in organizing the unorganized, not simply in the coal fields but in other basic industries as well. Taft-Hartley's requirement that pension plans be jointly managed equally by union and management appointed trustees for the "sole and exclusive benefit" of the plan participants severely restricted the organizing effect of these collectively bargained plans.

Private employers then began offering pension plans to their workers with what seemed to be liberal benefits. However, for the most part, these benefits were illusory. The plans remained seriously underfunded or unfunded, and the eligibility rules disqualified the majority of the workers from receiving any benefits at all.

On September 2, 1974, the Employee Retirement Income

---

[1] Inland Steel Co. v. NLRB, 170 F.2d 247 (7th Cir. 1948), *cert. denied,* 336 U.S. 960 (1949).

Security Act (ERISA) was enacted into law.[2] This incredibly complex law was enacted in order to eradicate the many employer and trustee abuses of the private pension system. Although ERISA has many shortcomings, it is nevertheless a tremendous improvement over the prior law, under which employees had few, if any, rights. ERISA is divided into four titles. Title I, entitled "Protection of Employee Benefit Rights," is within the jurisdiction of the Department of Labor (DOL). Title II provides amendments to the Internal Revenue Code (IRC) relating to retirement plans. Title III is concerned with internal administrative procedures and coordination between the Internal Revenue Service (IRS) and the DOL, and it establishes a Joint Pension Task Force to make a full study and review of ERISA. Title IV establishes within DOL the Pension Benefit Guaranty Corporation (PBGC), whose main function is to provide and administer a plan termination insurance program. The purpose of this chapter is to provide an overview of ERISA from the perspective of rank-and-file workers.

Section 10.02 is designed to familiarize lawyers and legal workers with some of the major components of a pension plan and enable them to apply that knowledge to the negotiation of a pension plan. Since Section 10.02 is mainly concerned with requirements for qualification under Title II, over which the IRS has jurisdiction, all citations therein will refer to the sections of the Internal Revenue Code as amended by ERISA (mainly IRC Sections 401-415).

In Section 10.03 the focus switches from negotiation of the plans themselves to rights of plan participants. It is in these areas, Title I of ERISA, that the major litigation battles are being fought. The qualification phase of ERISA is ending. Nearly all plans have been amended in order to comply with ERISA. The litigation phase of ERISA is still in its early stages. The remaining sections of this chapter provide a fuller understanding of the private pension system.

---

[2] P.L. 94-406.

§ 10.02. Deferred Compensation Plans

[1] Types of Qualified Plans

A qualified plan is one of deferred compensation that meets the requirements of IRC Section 401(a). A total deferred compensation plan includes individual pension, profit-sharing, stock bonus, and annuity plans under which employer contributions are held in trust for future distribution to employee participants.

All qualified plans must be either defined benefit plans or defined contribution plans. In a defined benefit plan, employee benefits are fixed, while employer contributions are determined actuarially in order to ensure the availability of sufficient funds. In a defined contribution plan, however, contributions are fixed with benefits to be determined. Thus, in a defined contribution plan, the earnings of the trust are directly reflected in the employees' ultimate benefit; in a defined benefit plan, since benefits are fixed, the earnings of the trust concern the employer only.

The following fundamental requisites apply to all qualified plans: A qualified plan must be written, must be intended to be permanent, must be communicated to the employees, and must prohibit the diversion of funds for purposes other than the exclusive benefit of the employees or their beneficiaries.

(*Text continued on page 10-5*)

[a] Defined Contribution Plans

The term "defined contribution plan" is defined to mean "a plan which provides for an individual account for each participant and for benefits based solely on the amount contributed to the participant's account, and any income, expenses, gains and losses and any forfeitures of accounts of other participants which may be allocated to such participant's account."[3]

There are three types of defined contribution plans: profit-sharing, stock bonus, and money purchase pension plans.

[i] Profit-Sharing Plans

The purpose of a profit-sharing plan is to provide for employee participation in the employer's profits. Contributions under the plan must be made out of profits (current or accumulated earnings). The plan must include a profit-sharing contribution formula. Usually, the contribution formula provides that the employer will make an annual contribution, expressed as a percentage of the annual net income. Net income for purposes of the contribution formula can be defined under the plan in any way the employer chooses. Although it is not necessary that the employer contribute every year, to be a profit-sharing plan there must be recurring and substantial contributions out of profits. Generally, the corporation's board of directors, near the end of the year, will set the percentage of profits to be contributed for that year.

The plan must also provide for a definite, predetermined formula for allocating the contributions among the participants. Although contributions are generally allocated in proportion to compensation, any method of allocation can be used as long as prohibited discrimination does not result. Prohibited discrimination occurs when the contributions (or benefits) under the plan favor officers, shareholders, or highly compensated employees. The phrase "highly compensated employees" is a relative term dependent upon each particular set of facts and circumstances. It

[3] IRC § 414(i).

is permissible, however, to discriminate (i.e., provide a disproportionate benefit) in favor of low-paid employees.

The profit-sharing plan must provide a definite formula for distribution after (1) a fixed number of years, (2) upon the attainment of a stated age, or (3) upon the occurrence of some event, such as layoff, illness, disability, retirement, death, or severance of employment. The term "fixed number of years" is considered to mean at least two years. Since amounts contributed to a profit-sharing plan may be distributed to participants after two years (if the plan so provides), it is not generally considered a retirement plan.

Under a pure profit-sharing plan, only the employer makes contributions. However, a plan may permit, or even require, employee contributions. Such a plan is generally referred to as a contributory profit-sharing plan or a thrift or savings plan.

[ii] Stock Bonus Plans

Stock bonus plans are similar to profit-sharing plans except that the contributions by the employer do not depend upon profits and benefits are distributed in stock in the employer company.

[iii] Money Purchase Pension Plans

Money purchase pension plans are also similar to profit-sharing plans except that (1) contributions by the employer cannot be geared to profits and (2) forfeitures (money resulting from employees who terminate prior to being 100 percent vested) *must* be used to reduce required employer contributions to the plan. In a profit-sharing plan forfeitures may be reallocated among the remaining participants.

In a money purchase pension plan, employer contributions must be made in accordance with a stipulated formula that is not subject to the discretion of the employer. Generally, the plan will provide for a stipulated annual contribution by the employer, such as 5 percent of annual compensation of each covered employee. It should be noted that a contribution formula stating that an employer will match each employee's once-a-year election to contribute 2, 3, 4, or 5 percent of his/her compensation is permissible because the formula is not within the discretion of the employer.

As in a profit-sharing plan, a money purchase pension plan must have a definite, nondiscriminatory, predetermined formula for allocating the contributions made among the participants. Each employee will receive whatever benefit the total compensation, plus increment, will purchase at retirement. The benefits of each employee will vary substantially depending upon age, compensation, and years of service under the plan.

A target benefit is a relatively new concept and is considered to be a money purchase pension plan. It contains a defined benefit formula, but the benefit stated in the formula is merely an assumed one. The amount of annual contribution is determined actuarially. Once the amount of the contribution is established, the stated benefit is ignored. Thereafter, the plan is operated much like a money purchase pension plan. When a participant retires, the benefit equals the balance then in the account. The actual benefit will vary upward or downward according to whether or not the earnings of the fund's investments are above or below the assumed earnings rate.

[b] Defined Benefit Plans

Surprisingly, the term "defined benefit plan" is defined to mean any plan that is not a defined contribution plan.[4] Basically, a defined benefit plan is any type of pension plan except a money purchase pension plan.

The key concept is that benefits are definitely determinable. The ultimate pension benefit each employee will receive upon retirement must be definitely determinable from either the benefit formula specified in the plan or actuarial computation. If forfeitures are used to provide increased benefits for the remaining participants, benefits will not be definitely determinable. Consequently, forfeitures must be used to reduce the amount of

[4] IRC § 414(j).

contributions by the employer. Similarly, benefits are not definitely determinable if contributions are dependent on profits.

The plan must provide for payment of benefits over a period of years, usually for life, after retirement. However, plans may include various modes of settlement if, under each mode of settlement, the distribution has the same value as a distribution determined under any other mode of settlement.

The common types of defined benefit plans include fixed benefit, unit benefit, and variable. In a fixed benefit plan, an employee receives a definite percentage of compensation, usually averaged compensation during a stated number of years before retirement. Compensation, not the number of years of service, is used for computing benefits. Once eligibility is established, a participant with twelve years of service would receive the same pension as would an employee with forty years of service. Because of the shorter funding period, this can result in severe cost problems when older employees are hired.

In a unit benefit plan, a participant receives a unit of pension for each year of credited service. The funding problem with older employees is substantially alleviated since the ultimate benefit is dependent upon years of service as well as compensation.

In a variable plan, pension benefits are either related to market value of trust assets or adjusted periodically by reference to a cost-of-living index. This variation does not make benefits indefinitely determinable.

An annuity plan is one qualified under IRC Section 403(a). The only difference between an annuity plan and a pension plan is the funding medium. In an annuity plan, an employer contributes, under an annuity contract, directly to an insurance company. Pension benefits are ultimately paid directly by the insurer. In a pension plan the funding medium is a trust.

[c] Choosing the Best Plan for Rank-and-File Employees

There is, of course, no ideal plan. The provisions within the plan are infinitely more important than the type of plan. Nevertheless, a pension plan is usually preferable to a profit-sharing plan.

The main disadvantages of a profit-sharing plan are the uncertain nature of profits and the effects on employees' vested interests. Employer contributions to a profit-sharing plan occur only when profits, as defined in the plan, exist. Even when profits do exist, the percentage to be contributed is determined annually by the employer, with no guarantee that yearly employer contributions will be made. It must further be considered whether the institution of a profit-sharing plan will undermine the union. Obviously, a profit-sharing plan is counterproductive if employees become hesitant in vigorously pursuing grievances for fear their demands might reduce production, reducing in turn profits and contributions to the plan. This effect on employees is generally more problematic when an employee stock ownership plan is instituted. Conversely, the main advantages of pension plans are that retirement benefits are definitely determinable and that a good pension plan strengthens the union.

The main advantages to a profit-sharing plan are (1) more incidental benefits may be provided, (2) early distributions are permissible, (3) forfeitures may be redistributed among the remaining participants and the problems of unfunded liabilities are avoided. None of these advantages of a profit-sharing plans are, however, detrimental to a pension plan. Although a pension plan is limited in the incidental benefits it can provide, a health and welfare fund can be established to provide for benefits outside its scope. (For further discussion of incidental benefits, see Section 10.02[8]).

The fact that a profit-sharing plan may permit early withdrawals of funds (e.g., after two years of plan participation) is a mixed blessing. If an employee continually depletes his/her account balance with early withdrawals, little will remain at retirement, while in a pension plan an employee is entitled to a fixed, guaranteed benefit.

Since benefits are fixed in a pension plan, it should be of little concern to employees that forfeitures always revert to the employer. Each employee will still receive the same benefit whether or not forfeitures occur.

Until the passage of ERISA, the problem of unfunded liabilities was a severe one for employees who participated in a pension plan. Prior to ERISA, there was no guarantee of adequate funding. Employees had the sole risk for any mishap. In comparison, "benefits" in a profit-sharing plan are never unfunded. At retirement, an employee simply receives his/her account balance. ERISA, however, has to a great extent transferred the risk in a pension plan from employees to employers and shareholders. Consequently, the main disadvantage of a defined benefit pension plan has been greatly alleviated. (For a thorough discussion on unfunded liability, see Section 10.02[7]).

[2] Qualification and Disqualification of a Plan

A plan is qualified if it meets the requirements of IRC Section 401(a). Generally, a plan is submitted to the IRS to receive a determination letter stating that the plan as submitted (and amended) is qualified. However, it is unnecessary to submit the plan initially. A plan that does not apply for and receive a favorable determination letter takes the risk that upon audit, the IRS might find the plan unqualified. As explained below, the disqualification of a plan has disasterous effects on employees and often has little or no effect on the employer. Thus, in negotiating a pension plan for a union, a provision should be inserted stating that the plan does not become operational until a favorable determination is received from the IRS. In practice, union-negotiated plans are invariably submitted to the IRS for qualification.

A qualified plan provides tax benefits for both employer and employees. Employer contributions to a qualified plan are deductible (within certain limits) for federal income tax purposes. Further, all income earned on these contributions accumulates tax free. Meanwhile, employees are not taxed on the contributions made on their behalf until such money and/or property is distributed or made available to them. Since an employee will generally be in a lower tax bracket after retirement, the amount of taxes ultimately paid by the employee on his/her retirement benefits should be substantially reduced.

If a plan is disqualified (or intended in the first place to be nonqualified), then the employer obtains a deduction only to the extent that the employees are vested. Correspondingly, employees are immediately taxed on all vested contributions, regardless of whether they have a right to receive such contributions. Consequently, disqualification of a plan by the IRS is a totally ineffective and counterproductive method for monitoring plans. If a plan is disqualified—and, without exception, disqualification occurs only as a result of actions or omissions by the employer or trustees—the employer is able to keep its complete tax deductions by simply vesting the employees 100 percent in their retirement benefits. The employees, however, are immediately taxed on such benefits, but generally must still wait many years before distribution of the benefits.

The inadequacy of disqualification as an effective sanction to prevent employer or trustee abuse is illustrated by the Teamsters Central States Pension Fund. Because of suspected misuse of the trust assets by the trustees, the Chicago district office of the IRS disqualified the pension plan. Ironically, such disqualification, which was not upheld, would have had disasterous financial consequences on countless rank-and-file employees involved. Our main concern is whether a smaller, less influential union would be granted the same treatment. The end result to be emphasized here is that, under current law and IRS procedures, it is usually not in the best interests of rank-and-file employees to have a plan disqualified.

It should be noted, however, that disqualification can be an effective remedy for small, closely held businesses. Generally, the employer in such businesses is the main employee and the person for whose benefit the plan was designed. Therefore, the employer's wrongdoing harms mainly the employer. Unfortunately, however, even in this situation, the other employees are inadvertently harmed.

[3] The Exclusive Benefit Rule

Under IRS Section 401(a)(2), a qualified plan must be for the exclusive benefit of the employees or their beneficiaries.

This exclusive benefit rule is the central, underlying philosophy governing qualified plan under ERISA. Theoretically, all other requirements for qualification were designed to implement this guiding principle. However, as will be seen in later sections, some qualification requirements (such as vesting) or options (such as integration) often hinder and sabotage the exclusive benefit rule instead of embodying it.

In order to understand more fully the exclusive benefit rule, the terms "employee," "beneficiaries," and "exclusive" will be defined and briefly discussed.

The term "employee" is not defined in IRC Sections 401-15 (that portion of the IRC amended by ERISA), except for IRC Section 401(c), which relates to self-employed individuals. Generally, if an individual is an employee for the purposes of Social Security taxes s/he is also an employee for purposes of a qualified plan.

Any persons, except the employer, may be designated by the employee to be his/her beneficiaries. Although most plans allow the employees to choose their beneficiaries, a plan may provide that the trustee, pension committee, or employer has the exclusive right to designate the employee's beneficiaries. In such case, however, the plan must limit the designation of an employee's beneficiaries to the "objects of his/her natural bounty."

In general, the term "exclusive" (benefit of employees) means that the coverage or eligibility requirements and the contributions or benefits must not discriminate in favor of officers, shareholders, or highly compensated employees, such as supervisors. This group is known as the prohibited group. Those members of the prohibited group who are employees can still benefit from the plan.

Notwithstanding the exclusive benefit rule, it should be noted that qualified plans still, of course, benefit employers. It is unlikely that an employer would install a plan if it did not receive a deduction for contributions. Furthermore, the investment of trust assets in employer securities does not, by itself, violate the exclusive benefit rule; the employer may also participate in the administration and operation of the plan.

[4] Coverage Requirements

The minimum participation standards of IRC Section 410 apply to all qualified plans except (1) governmental plans, (2) church plans, (3) plans not providing for employer contributions after the date of enactment of ERISA, and (4) plans maintained by certain societies, orders, or associations.

Under the minimum participation standards the plan must (with two exceptions noted below) provide for the participation of all employees who have completed one year of service and have attained age 25. A year of service means any twelve-month period in which the employee has at least 1000 hours of service. It should be noted that these standards are minimum; a plan may, of course, provide for more liberal provisions.

There are two exceptions to the age 25, one-year-of-service rule. If a participant will be 100 percent vested after three years of service, then such a plan does not have to cover employees until they have three years of service. Also, in some instances, an educational institution may defer coverage of employees until they attain age 30.

[a] Determination of Coverage

There are two permissible methods of determining whether a plan satisfies the coverage requirements: a mathematical test and a more amorphous nondiscrimination test.

If a plan can meet either one of the two permissible mathematical tests, then coverage is always considered sufficient. Even if the plan cannot meet the mathematical tests, coverage is still considered sufficient if the classification set up by the employer is not discriminatory in favor of employees who are officers, shareholders, or highly compensated. This test will always depend upon the facts and circumstances of each case.

[i] Mathematical Tests

The plan must meet the tests on at least one day of each quarter of the plan's taxable year.

Definition of terms: The terms used in the application of these tests are defined as follows:

(1) "Total employed" means all active employees.

(2) "All employees" means the total number employed reduced by the number of employees excluded by statute. Employees excluded by statute are (a) employees who have not satisfied the minimum age and service requirements, (b) employees covered by a collective bargaining agreement (as long as the retirement benefits were subject to good faith bargaining), (c) air pilots, (d) nonresident aliens, and, (e) in a defined benefit plan or target benefit plan, employees who began employment within five years before the normal retirement age under the plan.[5]

(3) "Eligible employees" means the number of "all employees" reduced by the number of employees excluded by the terms of the plan.

(4) "Covered employees" means the number of employees actually participating in the plan.

The 70 percent test: A plan meets the 70 percent test, if the number of "covered employees" is at least 70 percent of the number of "all employees."

Example:

Total employed		525
Excluded by statute		
(a) part-time (i.e., employees with less than 1000 hours of service)	25	
(b) minimum age	25	
(c) less than one year of service	25	
(d) employees in collective bargaining unit	50	
	125	−125
All employees		400
Excluded by terms of the plan		
(a) ineligible on account of hourly paid	75	− 75
Eligible employees		325
Employees electing not to participate	50	− 50
Covered employees		275

[5] A statutory exclusion for maximum age for a defined or target benefit plan was enacted in ERISA because the cost of funding new employees who are close to retirement age would be astronomical. It should be noted that if a plan provides that normal retirement age is age 65 or after ten years of participation, whichever is later, then the plan cannot have a maximum age requirement

Seventy percent of 400 (all employees) = 280. Since only 275 employees are covered, the plan does not meet the 70 percent test. If participation in the above example were mandatory, then 325 employees would be covered and the plan would meet the 70 percent test.

The 70-80 percent test: This two-step test is unnecessary if the 70 percent test is met.

Step 1. 70 percent or more of all employees must be eligible to participate under the plan.

Step 2. If so, then 80 percent or more of the eligible employees must be covered.

> **Example:** (same facts as above)
>
> Step 1. 70 percent of 400 (all employees) = 280. Since 325 employees are eligible (and only 280 are required), Step 1 is met.
>
> Step 2. 80 percent of 325 (eligible employees) = 260. Since 275 employees are covered (and only 260 are required), Step 2 is also met.

Thus, in the example provided, even though the plan cannot meet the 70 percent test, the 70-80 percent test is met and therefore coverage is considered acceptable.

[ii] The Nondiscrimination Test

As previously stated, coverage is considered acceptable if the classification set up by an employer does not discriminate in favor of employees who are officers, shareholders or highly compensated. The determination as to whether an employee is highly compensated is a facts and circumstances test dependent upon comparing compensation of that employee to other employees. This discrimination is the *only* type that is prohibited. Although many discriminatory classifications may exist within the plan under the general meaning of the term, coverage is entirely satisfactory as long as the prohibited discrimination does not exist.

---

because no employee would ever be within five years of normal retirement when first employed. A maximum age requirement can only exist where the normal retirement age is a specified age.

For example, even if only 500 of 1000 employees are covered because the plan is written for salaried employees only, prohibited discrimination does not necessarily exist. It is possible for coverage to be satisfactory even though limited to employees who have reached a designated age, who have been employed for a designated number of years, who are employed in certain designated departments—or simply to employees with green eyes.[5.1]

[b] Implications of Coverage Requirements for Union-Negotiated Plans

Usually the problem of coverage adequacy is not present in union-negotiated plans. Nevertheless, in negotiating a union pension plan there is an important point to learn from the preceding coverage requirements.

Employers may exclude employees covered by a bona fide "collective bargaining agreement," provided that it was subject to good faith bargaining. If not, then it is unlikely that a plan excluding hourly paid (and unionized) employees could comply with either the mathematical tests or the nondiscrimination coverage one. Consequently, it is extremely important to determine whether a pension plan established by an employer for employees covered by a collective bargaining unit was subject to good faith bargaining. Since employers generally establish generous plans for salaried, highly compensated, non-unionized employees, the possibility that the coverage, and thus the qualification of the salaried plan, will be jeopardized without good faith bargaining is a strong and powerful negotiating tactic for the union.

One final note concerning the mathematical test. Do not assume that just because this test is met and coverage on paper is satisfactory, the plan could thereby exclude say, 29 percent of the lowest-paid employees. Under IRC Section 401(a)(4), a qualified plan in operation still cannot discriminate in favor of the prohib-

---

5.1 See Federal Land Bank Ass'n of Ashville v. Commissioner, 2 EBC 2385, — T.C. — (1982), on remand from 573 F.2d 179 (4th Cir. 1978), in which the Tax Court found that the fair cross section test is not the only valid test in determining whether the plan discriminates in favor of the prohibited group.

ited group. Such a plan would violate the rule requiring that it operate for the exclusive benefit of employees in general.

[5] Vesting

In negotiating a pension plan, the vesting provisions are some of the most important to the employees. Vesting refers to the period of time in which a participant's benefit becomes nonforfeitable. Employer contributions made on behalf of the employees do not necessarily mean that the employees have a right to retirement benefits. Employees are entitled to the amounts contributed only to the extent that they are vested.

Until the enactment of ERISA, there was no provision in the IRC requiring participants' interests to be vested prior to normal retirement age or plan termination. Thus, under the old law, an employee could conceivably work thirty years, be fired before retirement, and not be entitled to a pension.

ERISA established minimum standards for vesting for the first time. IRC Section 411 provides three alternative minimum vesting schedules: ten-year vesting, five- to fifteen-year vesting, and the rule of forty-five. It should be emphasized that these are minimum schedules; a plan may always provide for more liberal vesting provisions.

[a] Ten-Year Vesting

Ten-year vesting means that an employee with at least ten years of service has a nonforfeitable right to 100 percent of his/her accrued benefit derived from employer contributions. No vesting is required prior to the completion of ten years of employment. This vesting schedule is probably the most common and is called cliff vesting.

[b] Five- to Fifteen-Year Vesting

Five- to fifteen-year vesting means that at the completion of five years of service an employee must be at least 25 percent vested, with an additional 5 percent for each of the next five years of service and 10 percent for each of the following five years of service. After fifteen years, an employee's accrued benefit derived from employer contributions must be 100 percent vested. Five- to fifteen-year vesting may be determined from the following table:

Years of Service	Nonforfeitable Percentage
5	25
6	30
7	35
8	40
9	45
10	50
11	60
12	70
13	80
14	90
15 or more	100

[c] Rule of Forty-Five

Under the rule of forty-five, at the completion of five years of service, an employee must be at least 50 percent vested if the sum of his/her age and years of service equals or exceeds forty-five. Additional minimum vesting occurs at the rate determined from the following table:

If Years of Service Equal or Exceed	And Sum of Age and Service Equals or Exceeds	Then the Non-forfeitable Percentage Is
5	45	50
6	47	60

7	49	70
8	51	80
9	52	90
10	55	100

Notwithstanding the above table, any employee who has completed at least ten years of service must have a nonforfeitable right to (1) not less than 50 percent of his/her accrued benefit derived from employer contributions and (2) not less than an additional 10 percent for each additional year of service thereafter.

This straight service test was added to the rule of forty-five (age-service test) so that employees who began employment prior to age 35 would be at least 50 percent vested after ten years of service. It should be noted that of the three minimum vesting schedules, the rule of forty-five provides for the most liberal vesting for employees hired at age 40 or older, but at the same time provides for minimal vesting for employees hired at age 25 or younger.

[d] Examples of Improper Vesting Schedules

(1) A plan provides that employees become vested at the following rate:

Years of Service	Nonforfeitable Percentage
0-9	0
10	50
11	60
12	70
13	80
14	90
15	100

The schedule is defective because (1) it does not satisfy the requirements of the ten-year vesting schedule after the ninth year of service and (2) it does not satisfy the requirements of the five-to fifteen-year vesting schedule or the rule of forty-five for years prior to the 10th year of service.

(2) A plan provides for participation after the completion of one year of service. The plan's vesting schedule provides that employees are 100 percent vested after ten years of participation instead of ten years of service. The vesting schedule is defective because no employee becomes vested until the completion of eleven years of service. Cliff vesting requires 100 percent vesting after ten years of service.

[e] Class Year Plans

Class year plans are not subject to the above minimum vesting schedules. A class year plan is a defined contribution plan (i.e., a profit-sharing, stock bonus, or money purchase pension plan) that provides for separate nonforfeitability of employees' rights to employer contributions for each plan year. A class year plan satisfies the minimum vesting requirements if each employee is 100 percent vested for a plan year not later than the end of the fifth plan year following the plan year for which such contributions were made. For example, if an employee becomes a participant in a plan in 1975, in 1980 the employee becomes 100 percent vested in the amounts contributed on his/her behalf in 1975. In 1981 the employee becomes 100 percent vested in the amounts contributed in 1976, and so on. Defined benefit plans can never be class year plans.

[f] Accelerated Vesting

As already stated, a plan may not discriminate in favor of the prohibited group, i.e., officers, shareholders, and highly compensated employees. If there is a high turnover among rank-and-file employees, whether caused by resignations or dismissals, and a low turnover among the prohibited group, then with respect to vested benefits prohibited discrimination may occur. Consequently, in order to prevent such discrimination, the IRS can require vesting to occur at a more rapid rate than the minimum vesting schedules. Presently, the IRS can require a vesting schedule not more stringent than 40 percent vesting after four years of employment with 5 percent additional vesting for each of the next two years and 10 percent additional vesting for each of the following five years. Accelerated vesting is not required if the rate of turnover for the prohibited group is comparable to that for rank-and-file employees.

Regardless of which type of vesting schedule is chosen, Section 203(a) of ERISA requires that participants be 100 percent vested at normal retirement age. Section 3(24) of ERISA defines normal retirement ages as age 65 or 10 years of participation, whichever occurs later. A plan may, of course, provide for a more liberal definition of normal retirement age.

[g] Miscellaneous Rules

[i] Year of Service

A year of service for purposes of vesting (except for seasonal and maritime industries) is the same as for coverage requirements, i.e., 1000 hours of service. A plan may provide that a participant be employed on the first and last day of the plan year in order for such year to count as a year of service. Although coverage is not required until age 25, years of service for vesting purposes begin at age 22. If the rule of forty-five is used, then years of service before age 22 must be counted for vesting purposes as long as the employee is a participant in the plan at any time during such years. Years of service preceding the period for which an employer did not maintain the plan or predecessor plan may be excluded for vesting purposes. Unless the plan provides for past service credits these years are lost. Years of service during a period for which the employee declined to contribute to a plan requiring employee contributions may be excluded.

[ii] Breaks in Service

A one-year break in service means any twelve-month period as defined in the plan (usually plan year or calendar year) during which the participant has not completed more than 500 hours of service. Since a participant must have 1000 hours of service a year in order to receive credit for a year of service for vesting purposes, a break in service does not affect vesting for the current year. If an employee has less than 1000 hours of service in a year, that year need not count for vesting regardless of whether a break in service also occurred. Therefore, the significance of a break in service is its affects on prior years of service.

Three rules concern breaks in service:

(1) If an employee has any one-year break in service, years of service before that break are not required to be taken into account until the employee has completed a year of service after his/her return.

(2) If an employee has no nonforfeitable right to an accrued benefit derived from employer contributions, i.e., 0 percent vested, then any years of service prior to a one-year break in service are not required to be taken into account if the number of consecutive one-year breaks in service equals or exceeds the aggregate number of such years of service prior to such break. This rule is called the rule of parity. Example: A nonvested participant terminated employment December 31, 1970, after six years of service, and was reemployed January 1, 1974. Since the number of consecutive one-year breaks is less than the employee's prior years of service, the prior years must be counted for vesting purposes. Assume the same employee left service again on December 31, 1975 (after another two years of service) and was reemployed on January 1, 1979. In this example, none of the prior service need be recognized because the number of consecutive one-year breaks (three years) exceeds the aggregate years of service prior to the break (two years). The earlier six years of service are ignored because they are part of a prior break in service.

(3) In a defined contribution plan, years of service after a break in service are not required to be taken into account for purposes of determining an employee's vested percentage which accrued before such break.

[iii] Forfeitures

The general rule is that vested rights can never be forfeited. The main exception to this rule (and for practical purposes the only exception) is that a plan may provide that employees who die prior to early retirement age forfeit all benefits. Vested benefits may not be forfeited between early retirement age and normal retirement age so long as the plan has a joint and survivor annuity option (or the employee has not declined such option). Under no circumstances can an employee's rights to the accrued benefit derived from his/her own contributions be forfeited. Employees are, at all times, 100 percent vested in their own contributions.

There are other exceptions to the general rule on forfeitures. Section 412(c)(8) of the IRC provides that if a plan is in financial trouble, it may obtain government approval for a reduction of benefits. Section 203(a)(3)(B) of ERISA states that if a retiree is reemployed by the same company or, in some cases, in the same industry in the same geographical area, his/her benefits may be temporarily suspended.

In a plan that requires mandatory employee contributions, if an employee withdraws any amount attributable to his/her contribution and is less than 50 percent vested, then such employee "forfeits" all accrued benefits derived from employer contributions. However, if an employee repays the amount withdrawn (plus interest in a defined benefit plan), then the amount "forfeited" is revested. ERISA markedly improved the law by abolishing forfeiture for "cause."

Forfeitures of nonvested interest are allocated in the following manner. In a defined benefit plan or money purchase pension plan, forfeitures must be used to reduce the amount of subsequent contributions by the employer. In a profit-sharing or stock bonus plan, forfeitures are usually allocated among the remaining participants, but may be used to reduce employer contributions. The provisions of the plan will specify which is to occur. Upon termination or partial termination of a plan all participants must be 100 percent vested.

[h] Impact of Vesting Requirements

One of the major reforms of ERISA is its tremendous improvement of the vesting rules. Prior to ERISA, employees were often not vested until retirement; if they were dismissed at any time prior to retirement, they lost all benefits regardless of the number of years employed. One ramification of the minimum vesting standards under ERISA, however, is increased cost of maintaining a pension plan because the adoption of more liberal vesting provisions reduces the amount of forfeitures used to reduce employer contributions.

Although the minimum vesting standards under ERISA are a dramatic improvement over pre-ERISA law, these standards are still designed mainly to benefit long-term employees. Since ten years of service are usually required for vesting, "short-term" employees are generally never entitled to a private pension.

In negotiating a pension plan, it is important to remember that ERISA only prescribes minimum vesting standards. However, without some leverage it will often be difficult to persuade an employer to adopt a more liberal vesting provision because it will increase the costs of maintaining the plan. In a union-negotiated plan, accelerated vesting will generally be unavailable because of the absence of members of the prohibited group.

[6] Integration

One of ERISA's most significant shortcomings is its failure to prohibit integrated plans, which is an egregious loophole in the rule that a qualified plan may not discriminate in favor of the prohibited group, i.e., officers, shareholders, and highly compensated employees. To be nondiscriminatory, employer contributions or benefits must bear a uniform relationship to compensation. However, in an integrated plan, public plans, such as Social Security, are taken into consideration in determining whether contributions or benefits are nondiscriminatory. Thus, by statute an integrated plan is not considered discriminatory even though the proportionate benefits under the plan favor the highly compensated because any "discriminatory" difference is considered to be offset by old-age, survivor, and disability insurance benefits attributable to employer contributions under FICA.

In an integrated excess defined contribution plan, an employer may exclude employee compensation subject to Social Security and make contributions to employees based only upon compensation above the integration level. The maximum integration level is the taxable wage limit under which both employer and employees base their maximum contributions to FICA, which currently (1982) is $32,400. Thus, all employees who receive less than that amount may properly receive no benefits from the plan.

This section will not attempt to delve into the detailed array of rules concerning how a plan is integrated.[5.2] It is sufficient to know that integrated plans may be either excess plans or offset plans. In an excess plan an employee will only receive benefits if his/her compensation exceeds the applicable integration level. In an offset plan an employee's benefit otherwise computed under the plan formula is offset by a stated percentage of the employee's social security benefit. However, there is never any reason for a union to negotiate an integrated plan, which, by being contrary to the interests of rank-and-file employees, violates the guiding principle of ERISA—the exclusive benefit rule. If pension plans were truly for the exclusive benefit of employees, integrated plans would not be permitted to exist.

[7] Minimum Funding Standards

By establishing a pension plan (and nearly all union-negotiated plans are pension plans), an employer is obligated to provide certain retirement benefits. Prior to ERISA, there were no minimum funding standards for an employer. Many employers proceeded on a "promise now, fund later" basis. As a result, the unfunded pension liabilities of many employers are now gigantic.

The minimum funding standards in ERISA[6] were designed to eradicate this problem. This section will not attempt to explain how minimum funding is determined numerically. An actuary is necessary for such calculations. Instead this section will analyze

---

[5.2] See Rev. Rul. 71-446, 1971-2 C.B. 187.

[6] IRC § 412.

the ramifications of the assumptions involved in making such calculations. Small variations in the actuarial assumptions can result in large monetary differences. Through the "liberal" use of actuarial assumptions, a plan may be properly funded on paper, i.e., meet the minimum funding requirements, yet in reality be grossly underfunded. Notwithstanding the PBGC, such underfunding jeopardizes employees' retirement benefits.

The minimum funding standards in ERISA do not apply to profit-sharing plans, stock bonus plans, governmental plans, church plans, certain insurance contract plans, plans that did not provide for employer contributions after September 2, 1974, and plans maintained by certain societies, orders, or associations. The minimum funding standards do apply to nearly all pension plans, i.e., defined benefit plans and money purchase pension plans. However, since money purchase pension plans are defined contributions plans, the problems discussed below concerning minimum funding are not applicable to them because in a defined contribution plan an employee's retirement benefit is simply his/her account balance at time of retirement. No level of benefits is guaranteed. (For a more detailed discussion, see Section 10.02[1]).

Two crucial assumptions must be made in order to determine the current, minimum costs to an employer of funding a future benefit to the employees: (1) the rate of return on the investments of the pension fund assets (interest assumption) and (2) the rate at which wages will grow (wage assumption).

The average interest rate used by employers is approximately 6 to 6.5 percent. The average wage assumption is approximately 3.5 to 4 percent.[7] One pension specialist has calculated that a difference of 1 percent in the interest assumption will affect, on the average, an employer's pension liability by 25 percent. A difference of 1 percent on the wage assumption will affect, on the average, the liability by 13 percent.[8]

The wage and interest assumptions are used to offset each other. For example, in order to arrive at the present cost of providing future benefits, the 3.5 percent increase in future wages is offset by the 6 percent rate of interest earned on investments. It

---

[7] A.F. Ehrbar, *Those Pension Plans Are Even Weaker Than You Think,* Fortune Magazine, November 1977, at 104.

[8] *Id.* at 107, citing Professor Howard E. Winklevoss of Wharton School.

should be noted that the question of what constitutes a proper wage and interest assumption is complex, controversial, and beyond the scope of this chapter.

With an adjustment in its assumptions, a company can reduce past unfunded liability or can pay for a benefit increase by postponing the costs or by simply decreasing the amount of contribution that is necessary to meet minimum funding. By doing so, current profits are maintained. Prior to ERISA, if an employer went bankrupt or terminated its pension plan, an employee had the sole risk for any unfunded vested liabilities. Under ERISA, pension benefits up to a specified limit are guaranteed; currently (1982), the guarantee is $1,380.68 a month.

A company is liable for its unfunded vested benefits up to 30 percent of its net worth. Any remaining guaranteed benefit is provided by a plan termination insurance program administered by the PBGC. Theoretically, since an employee's benefit is 100 percent guaranteed (up to the specified limit), only the shareholders, not the employees, should be concerned with the interest and wage assumptions. However, in negotiating a union pension plan or an increase in benefits, it is strongly recommended that the negotiator not allow the employer to postpone paying for the benefits with unrealistic actuarial assumptions. Most employers, however, will strenuously resist the disclosure of actuarial assumptions.

It is obviously not in the best interests of employees to bankrupt an employer. The "guarantee" of pension benefits, which are often small, does not offset the loss of employment. Therefore, it is counterproductive to allow an employer to underfund a pension plan with improper assumptions. Further, the threat of potential bankruptcy created by a large unfunded vested liability may encourage the company to close down and reopen elsewhere. This is especially true if the unfunded vested benefits exceed 30 percent of the company's net worth. By closing, the company can relieve itself of a large liability and, in some cases, such as a service business with little property or machinery, incur only a small liability. Of course, with regard to runaway shops, the converse may be true. The 30 percent liability may prevent an employer, especially a capital-intensive company, from closing down and reopening elsewhere.

At the present time PBGC's resources are pitifully inadequate to pay for the liabilities resulting from plan terminations. It remains to be seen what will happen if a large retirement fund goes under.

[8] Union-Negotiated Plans

The purpose of this section is to specify the types of union-negotiated plans and briefly discuss special problems that relate to them. There are three types of union-negotiated plans: (1) those negotiated with a single employer, (2) those negotiated on an industry-wide basis, and (3) those negotiated on an area-wide basis. Union-negotiated plans with a single employer have been previously discussed and need no further elaboration.

Industry-wide plans are those adopted by employers in the same industry, but not necessarily in the same area. Generally, these plans will provide for reciprocity of pension credit as long as an employee is employed by any employer in the industry. Although the plan is usually a single plan adopted by participating employers, each employer must still comply with the requirements of Section 401(a) of the IRC. In industry-wide plans that have already been adopted by other employers, the only negotiable issue is whether the employer will accept the plan.

An area-wide plan is usually a single plan adopted by employers in the same area, but not necessarily engaged in the same industry. The rules mentioned above for industry-wide plans are applicable to area-wide plans.

Industry-wide and area-wide plans are generally preferable to plans negotiated with a single employer because they provide for interchange of pension credits and allow mobility for employees within an industry or particular area. The main advantage of a plan negotiated with a single employer is that the plan can be tailored to the particular needs of the employer and its employees.

ERISA has added two sections to the IRC concerning union-negotiated plans: Sections 413 and 414(f). Section 413 provides, in general, for purposes of coverage, discrimination, vesting, funding, and deduction requirements, that all employers who participate in a single collective bargaining agreement and a single trust pursuant to that agreement are to be treated as a single employer. All employees covered by the plan are treated as employees of a single employer.

Section 414(f) defines the term "multiemployer plans" as a plan maintained pursuant to a collective bargaining agreement to

(*Text continued on page 10-29*)

which more than one employer is required to contribute and to which no one employer provides 50 percent of the contributions. After a plan has once qualified as a multiemployer plan, however, up to 75 percent of the contributions may be made by a single employer without affecting its status. Thus, in order to receive its initial qualification, a multiemployer plan must have at least three participating employers.

A qualified plan must be adopted with the intention of being permanent. This raises the question of whether a union-negotiated plan adopted under a contract whose duration is limited is considered permanent. Revenue Ruling 69-159[9] states that a plan meets the permanency requirements if (1) the plan established under the contract does not provide for its termination, (2) all documents indicate that it is intended to be a permanent program, and (3) all funds upon liquidation will be applied to meet its liabilities. If, for example, the plan is to terminate at the end of a specified period or permits reversion of funds to the employer after providing for benefits to employees who become eligible to retire during its existence, then only those employees who can become eligible to retire during the specified period of the plan are considered covered. Consequently, in order to cover all eligible employees during the existence of a contract, the plan must meet the permanency requirements outlined in Revenue Ruling 69-159.

Some collectively bargained pension plans specify the benefits to be received and the rate of employer contributions. This predetermination of annual contributions and fixed final benefits poses a special problem. The general rule is that in a defined benefit plan, benefits are fixed and annual employer contributions vary depending upon actuarial calculations. In a defined contribution plan, such as a money purchase pension plan, the annual contribution rate is fixed and the ultimate benefit is not predetermined. The benefit is simply the employee's account balance at the time of retirement. Revenue Ruling 70-257[10] provides that a union-negotiated plan that provides for fixed benefits and a stated rate of contribution may still qualify so long as the actuarial computa-

---

[9] 1969-1 C.B. 133.
[10] 1970-1 C.B. 90.

tions indicate that the expected contributions will not be less than the full costs of prospective benefits.

If a union negotiates a pension plan and a health and welfare plan, it is important that the funds for these plans not be comingled. The pension plan will not be a qualified plan within the meaning of Section 401(a) of the IRC if a combination welfare and pension plan is funded through the same plan or trust; each plan must be funded separately.

A qualified pension plan may only provide retirement benefits, incidental insurance benefits, and disability benefits. A health and welfare plan provides benefits not customarily included in a pension plan, such as layoff benefits and benefits for sickness, accident, hospitalization, or medical expenses. It should be noted that a qualified profit-sharing plan may provide for benefits normally found in a health and welfare plan so long as the purpose is not to provide primarily for those benefits.

[9] Keogh Plans

A Keogh plan is simply a qualified plan available to self-employed individuals. Since the focus of this chapter is on plans affecting rank-and-file workers, only a brief synopsis of the rules governing Keogh plans will be presented.

A Keogh plan may be established by a noncorporate entity, such as a sole proprietorship or a partnership. Prior to ERISA, a Keogh plan had to be a defined contribution plan. It is now permissible to establish a defined benefit Keogh plan. In order to qualify, a Keogh plan, like a corporate plan, must meet the qualification requirements of Section 401(a) of the IRC. A Keogh plan, however, is subject to many additional rules. Most of these additional rules apply only to Keogh plans covering owner-employees. The term "owner-employee" means a sole proprietor or a partner who owns either more than 10 percent of the capital interest or more than 10 percent of the profits interest in a partnership.

To participate in a Keogh plan, an individual must have earned income resulting from personal services actually rendered. The net income of a silent partner received from the partnership is not considered earned income for purposes of a Keogh plan.

A plan that covers an owner-employee must also cover each employee who has completed three or more years of service. At the time of coverage, each employee must also be 100 percent vested. This more stringent vesting requirement is the main advantage of a Keogh plan to any common-law employee who works for a self-employed individual or partnership.

In order to be qualified, a Keogh plan must expressly limit the contributions made on behalf of any self-employed individual or owner-employee to the lesser of $15,000 or 15 percent. This limitation on contributions is the main reason why doctors, lawyers, and many small businesses incorporate. The contribution limitations in a corporate plan far exceed those in a Keogh plan.[11]

Any distribution to a self-employed individual or owner-employee prior to age 59 1/2 (except on account of disability) is considered a premature distribution and subject to a penalty. Of course, a Keogh plan may provide for distributions to common-law employees upon separation from employment regardless of age.

[10] Individual Retirement Plans

An individual retirement account (IRA) is *not* a qualified plan. In fact to be eligible to establish such a plan and to deduct the contributions to it, an individual must have compensation (or earned income).

The Tax Reform Act of 1976 allows IRAs for nonemployed spouses for tax years beginning after December 31, 1976. A separate spousal IRA or a single IRA with separate subaccounts for each spouse may be established.

For a standard IRA, the deduction limitation is the lesser of $2,000 or 100 percent of includable compensation. For a spousal IRA the maximum contribution is $2,250. This contribution can be divided between the two spouse's IRAs in any manner so long as the amount contributed to either IRA is not more than $2,000.

IRA participants may generally direct the investments in their

[11] IRC § 415.

account. However, IRA investments in collectibles, such as art works, antiques, gems, stamps and coins, are prohibited.

Distributions from an IRA before age 59 1/2 are considered premature distributions and are subject to a 10 percent penalty (unless the distribution is made on account of disability). Excess contributions are subject to a nondeductible 6 percent penalty tax for the year in which the excess contribution is made and for each year thereafter until there is no excess. Distributions from an IRA must begin no later than the close of the taxable year in which the individual attains age 70 1/2. Such distributions may be spread out over the individual's lifetime expectancy. Distributions are taxed as ordinary income when received.

[11] Employee Stock Ownership Plans

The term "employee stock ownership plan" (ESOP) is defined in Section 4975(e)(7) of the IRC as a qualified plan subject to the rules governing qualified plans. The ESOP, unlike other qualified plans, is designed to invest primarily in employer stock.

Of major interest to union-negotiated plans is who controls voting rights on the stock contributed to the ESOP. Prior to the enactment of the Revenue Act of 1978, only a Tax Reduction Stock Ownership Plan (TRASOP) was required to provide voting rights for employees on employer stock held by the plan. The Revenue Act significantly changed the law. For all closely held employer stock acquired after December 31, 1979, by a qualified defined contribution plan that invests more than 10 percent of its assets in such stock, employees must be entitled to direct the trustee as to the voting of the stock on all corporate issues that require more than a majority vote. For publicly traded employer stock, employees must be entitled to direct the trustee as to the voting of the stock so long as the publicly traded stock was acquired by a leveraged ESOP for taxable years beginning after December 31, 1979.

Another area of major interest to union-negotiated plans is the use of dividends on employer stock. Dividends paid on ESOP stock may be used in three ways: (1) allocated to each participant's account on the basis of the number of shares held in the account, (2) if the stock was acquired with indebtedness, used to amortize that indebtedness, and (3) "passed through" the plan and paid to participants on the basis of the number of shares of stock in their accounts.

All qualified plans provide tax benefits to employers and participating employees. An ESOP, however, unlike other qualified plans, is also a vehicle for corporate financing. An ESOP is the only type of qualified plan that is exempt from the general prohibited-transaction rules under Section 406 of ERISA (and Section 4975 of the IRC). As a result, the ESOP may use the credit of the employer to debt finance its acquisitions of employer stock. By doing so, the employer is financing its capital growth with pre-tax dollars.

The promissory note is in effect being repaid by the employer by a tax-deductible payment to the ESOP.

It is our belief that other types of plan are preferable to the ESOP. If the company goes bankrupt, the value of the employer's stock may be worthless. In addition, it is doubtful that participants in the ESOP could exercise any significant control through voting their stock. More important, minority ownership interest in the company may dilute the strength of the union without compensation advantages and cause significant internal dissension within the union.

[12] Distributions from Qualified Plans

The provisions of the plan will provide for the method(s) of distribution. Consequently, in negotiating a plan, it is advantageous to the employees that the plan provide as many options as possible. For example, a pension plan can provide that at retirement a participant may elect to receive a lump sum distribution instead of a joint-and-survivor annuity. Considerations in the taxation of distributions are as follows:

[a] General Rule

The amount distributed or made available to an employee (or beneficiary) is taxable as ordinary income in the year in which it is distributed or made available. An employee is entitled to special tax treatment for a lump sum distribution (see Section 10.02 [12][b]).

If an employee receives an annuity or installment payments from the trust, the employee is taxed only on the installments in the year when they are received. However, this simple rule becomes quite complex if the employee has made contributions (either voluntary or mandatory) to the plan. Since the employee has already paid taxes on his/her own contributions, such employee has a basis in that amount. The employee's cost (basis) is apportioned (amortized) over his/her life expectancy (or joint-and-survivor expectancy). If the aggregate amounts received by an employee during the first three years of an annuity (or direct installment payments from the trust) equal or exceed the employee's basis, then, instead of amortizing the basis over the life expectancy of the employee, no amount of the annuity is included as income until the employee's basis is recovered.[11.1]

[b] Lump Sum Distributions

Distributions from qualified plans are entitled to special tax treatment if such distributions are lump sum distributions within the meaning of Section 402(e)(4)(A) of the IRC. The phrase has a technical and specific definition. In order to be a lump sum distribution, the distribution must be—

(1) paid from a qualified plan (actually the trust related to it);
(2) paid within one taxable year;
(3) paid from the balance to the credit of the employee; and
(4) paid for one of the following reasons: the employee's death, the employee's attainment of age 59 1/2, the employee's separation from service (not applicable to self-

11.1 See IRC Section 72.

employed individuals), or the employee's becoming disabled (only applicable to self-employed individuals).

In addition, the employee must be a participant in the plan for five full taxable years before the taxable year of distribution, except for distributions made because of the employee's death. The five-year rule does not apply to capital gains treatment.

If a distribution is not a lump sum distribution, then the entire distribution is taxable as ordinary income.

Examples of lump sum distributions include the following:

1. An employee who separates from service receives a total distribution from the qualified plan in two payments: $20,000 in October and $15,000 in December. Such distribution is a lump sum distribution. However, if the employee receives $20,000 in October and $15,000 in January, there is no lump sum distribution because the total was not received within one taxable year.

2. Same facts as in Example 1, except that the employee received $20,000 in October and $500 in January. If the additional distribution was attributable to actuarial errors[12] or, in the case of a profit-sharing plan, contributions resulting from the last year in the plan,[13] the lump sum characterization is not lost. The $20,000 is considered the lump sum and the $500 is taxable as ordinary income.

3. Company M merges with Company X. All employees of Company M become employees of Company X. All the assets of Company M's plan are distributed. In such situations, there has been no separation from service. Consequently, only those employees who have attained age 59 1/2 receive a lump sum distribution.

4. An employee, age 60, who receives a total distribution within one taxable year from a qualified pension plan while still employed (and with plan maintained) does *not* receive a lump sum distribution. Although the facts meet the definition of a lump sum distribution the IRS has taken a contrary position. According to the IRS, since the purpose of a pension plan is to provide benefits after retirement, an employee may not receive a lump

---

12 *See* Rev. Rul. 69-190.

13 *See* Rev. Rul. 62-190.

sum distribution from a pension plan while still employed (and with plan maintained) prior to normal retirement age.

[c] Tax Treatment of Lump Sum Distributions

[i] Rollover to an IRA

An employee who has received a lump sum distribution (and participated in the plan for five years) may roll over that distribution tax-free to an IRA or to another qualified plan within sixty days. Self-employed individuals (i.e., participants in Keogh plans), however, may roll over to an IRA only if they have attained age 59 1/2 and never may roll over to another qualified plan.

If an employee rolls over to an IRA, any distribution subsequently received from the IRA is taxed as ordinary income in the year received. Distributions from an IRA must begin in the year the individual attains age 70 1/2. The distribution may be spread out over the life expectancy of the individual or over the life expectancy of the individual and his/her spouse.

If a distribution received upon plan termination does not qualify as a lump sum distribution, the employee may roll it over to an IRA tax-free. In a rollover based upon plan termination, it is not necessary for the employee to have participated in the plan for five years.

The main advantages of a rollover to an IRA are that taxation of the distribution is deferred and that subsequent earnings on the distribution accrue tax-free. The main disadvantage of a rollover to an IRA is that the special tax treatment of a lump sum distribution is lost. Distributions from IRAs are taxed as ordinary income in the year received. Since a distribution from an IRA may be spread out over the individual's life expectancy, the total paid will generally be substantially reduced and often comparable to the tax resulting from the special tax treatment of a lump sum distribution.

[ii] Computation of Tax

The purpose of this section is not to provide detailed mathematical examples of the computation of the tax. For that information see IRS Form 4972.

An employee receiving a lump sum distribution is entitled to utilize the special ten year-averaging method and in some cases entitled to capital gains treatment. In essence, the ten-year-averaging method means that the distribution is treated as if it were spread out over ten years and the tax, which is paid in just one year, is adjusted correspondingly. Unless an employee receives an extremely large distribution, in excess of $200,000, for example, the ten-year-averaging method is generally more advantageous than capital gains treatment. The tax resulting from the ten-year-averaging method is determined without regard to any other income of the employee.

Any portion of a lump sum distribution that is attributable to an employee's years of participation after December 31, 1973, is entitled to the ten-year-averaging method. The portion attributed to years of participation before January 1, 1974, is entitled to capital gains treatment. An individual may elect, however, to have his/her portion of the distribution subject to capital gains treatment taxed instead under the ten-year-averaging method.

It is important to realize that an employee may elect ten-year-averaging only once after age 59 1/2. Consequently, if an employee expects to receive two lump sum distributions after age 59 1/2, he or she must carefully choose the distribution for which s/he will elect the ten-year-averaging method.

§ 10.03. Rights of Participants: Disclosure Requirements

To protect the rights of pension plan participants, learn the plan's structure, operation, and assets. ERISA provides more disclosure rights than did its precursor, the Welfare and Pension Plans Disclosure Act. The former law established certain elementary rights of access but imposed few obligations to keep participants informed. Many participants were denied pensions or retirement when, upon application, they learned, for the first time, of an obscure rule making them ineligible.

To correct this problem, ERISA expanded the standards for information participants must receive and information participants may request. A plan must furnish each participant a summary plan description and summary annual report, the former within 90 days of initial participation[14] and the latter within 210 days of the end of the plan year.[15] A summary of plan changes adopted in any year must also be provided by that year's summary annual report deadline.[16] Annual reports and updated plan descriptions are key sources. The summary plan description must be written in a manner "understood by the average plan participant" and still be "sufficiently accurate and comprehensive to reasonably apprise participants of their rights and obligations under the plan."[17] However, reliance on the explanations found in the summary plan descriptions may be misplaced. While Section 410(a)(1) of ERISA prohibits the use of "any provision in an agreement or instrument which purports to relieve a fiduciary from responsibility or liability for any responsibility, obligation, or duty . . .,"[18] the courts have not seen fit to interpret this provision to include summary plan descriptions.[19] Therefore, plan administrators have come to include broad disclaimers as to the accuracy and sufficiency of the information presented in the summary plan description.[20] The second document automatically provided to each plan participant is the summary of the annual report. It should provide, among other things, accurate information concerning the assets and liabilities of the plan and the receipts and disbursements made by the plan during the reporting year.[21]

While these summary documents are given to the participant

---

[14] 29 U.S.C. § 1024(b)(1)(A).

[15] 29 U.S.C. § 1024(b)(3).

[16] 29 U.S.C. § 1024(b)(1)(B).

[17] 29 U.S.C. § 1022(a)(1).

[18] 29 U.S.C. § 1110(a)(1).

[19] O'Brien v. Sperry Univac, 458 F. Supp. 1179 (D.D.C. 1978). Such practice has been deplored by the Seventh Circuit.

[20] Daniel v. Int'l Bhd. of Teamsters, 561 F.2d 1223, N.56 (7th Cir. 1977), *rev'd on other grounds,* 439 U.S. 551, 590 (1979).

[21] 29 U.S.C. § 1024(b)(3).

automatically, the participant also has a right to inspect a copy of the plan and the entire annual report as submitted to the DOL.[22] The plan is required to make these documents available and may charge a reasonable amount for duplication.[23] They are also available through a Freedom of Information request to the DOL. These two basic documents may be relied upon by the participant.

One additional item that the law expressly allows to be disclosed to a participant upon written request is a statement of the total benefits accrued to him or her and that amount which is nonforfeitable.[24] The participant may ask for this information only once in any one twelve-month period.[25] However, where a plan participant suffers a one-year break in service or terminates employment, the plan must furnish this benefit statement automatically within 180 days after the end of the plan year in which the break or termination occurred.[26]

This requirement is especially significant to employees in industries that are seasonally affected or otherwise suffer slack periods in employment. This benefit statement may provide the first notice to a plan participant that he or she is about to suffer a disqualification that would make her or him ineligible for a pension or otherwise reduce the amount of future benefits.

While these disclosures and reporting requirements of ERISA attempt to eliminate a significant number of the abuses found to have occurred prior to the enactment of ERISA, problems still exist over enforcement of these rights and the remedies available in the event of nondisclosure.

ERISA provides that failure to comply with a legitimate request for information within thirty days may make the administrator of the plan personally liable to the participant or beneficiary in the amount of up to $100 a day in penalties.[27] Imposition of this fine is discretionary, and, as yet, no recovery

---

22 29 U.S.C. § 1024(b)(2).

23 29 U.S.C. § 1024(b)(4).

24 29 U.S.C. § 1025(a).

25 29 U.S.C. § 1025(b).

26 29 U.S.C. § 1059, 29 CFR § 2520.

27 29 U.S.C. § 1132(c).

has been effected through court action.[28] The more serious problems of enforcement concern the availability of remedies where a participant is disqualified from receiving benefits as a result of the plan's failure properly to disclose information. This question has yet to be addressed by the courts.

Even though ERISA expressly provides for disclosure of specific items, this should not be viewed as a limitation on disclosure of additional material. Other statutes or common law, notwithstanding the Supreme Court decision in the *Daniels* case,[29] may provide other justification for requiring disclosure. One example of material not expressly mentioned in ERISA that should be available for inspection is the minutes of the meetings of the plan's board of trustees. It may be argued that disclosure of these meeting minutes should be allowed under ERISA as "other instruments under which a plan is . . . operated"[30] or, alternatively, under accepted common law.[31]

§ 10.04. Terminations

One of the principal worries of pension plan participants prior to ERISA was that the employer would close the plant, leaving no money to cover their expected pension benefits, the money instead having been used as working capital by the employer. ERISA addressed this abuse in several ways: it required the plan to establish a vesting schedule to ensure the participants' entitlement to a pension; it prohibited certain investment transactions;

---

[28] King v. Wagner Elec. Co., 274 BPR D-2 (Jan. 21, 1980); Pollock v. Castrovinci, 476 F. Supp. 606, 618 (S.D. N.Y. 1979).

[29] *Supra,* N. 20.

[30] 29 U.S.C. § 1024(b)(4).

[31] Courts have unanimously recognized the role accorded to them in developing ERISA common law. *See* Wayne Chem., Inc. v. Columbus Agency Serv. Corp., 426 F. Supp. 318 (N.D. Ind. 1977), *aff'd on other grounds,* 567 F.2d 692 (7th Cir. 1977); Cowan v. Keystone Employee Profit Sharing Fund, 586 F.2d 888, 893 (1st Cir. 1978); Reiherzer v. Shannon, 581 F.2d 1266, 1270-72 (7th Cir. 1978); Riley v. Meba Pension Trust, No. 77-7320 (2d Cir., Dec. 15, 1977)(Friendly, J.); Taylor v. Bakery & Confectionary Union, 455 F. Supp. 816 (E.D.N.C. 1978); Hastings v. Merrill Lynch, Pierce, Fenner & Smith, Inc., No. 7-70025 (E.D. Mich. Dec. 22, 1977); In re C.D. Moyer Co. Trust Fund, 441 F. Supp. 1128, 1129 (E.D. Pa. 1977)("the source of this law must be the policies underlying ERISA").

and it set minimum funding standards to avoid deficiencies in the plan's assets. However, two of the most significant developments of ERISA were its regulation of plan terminations and the creation of the PBGC to ensure pension funds.[32]

The PBGC was established to encourage continuation and maintenance of pension plans, to ensure that plan benefits were paid to beneficiaries in a timely fashion, and to maintain pension benefit guaranty funds so that benefits would definitely be available to vested participants of most regulated pension plans.[33] The PBGC covers all qualified plans maintained by an employer engaged in commerce, in industry, or in any activity affecting commerce. It also covers annuity plans of certain educational or tax-exempt organizations and some professional corporation and Keogh plans. Not covered are government pensions, plans maintained by fraternal societies, qualified plans that provide benefits exclusively to "substantial owners," church plans, and plans that do not provide for any employer contributions, and all defined contribution plans.[34]

The PBGC has established four revolving trusts funded by employer premiums to provide insurance coverage for various types of pension plans: one for the basic benefits of single-employer plans, one for the basic benefits of multiemployer plans,[35] and one each for the non-basic benefits of these plans. The 1980 amendments to ERISA created two additional funds to further protect participants in multiemployer plans.[35.1] These funds are expected to enable the PBGC to continue paying benefits to participants of a terminated plan that was grossly underfunded. At the present time, however, these funds are themselves underfunded and could not survive any significant number of plan terminations.

Recognizing this, several barriers, or disincentives to termination have been created. ERISA allows the PBGC to reach a portion of the employer's assets to reimburse the fund for its

---

[32] The constitutionality of the PBGC was upheld in Nachman Corp. v. PBGC & VAN, 592 F.2d 947 (7th Cir. 1979), *cert. not granted on this issue.*

[33] 29 U.S.C. § 1302.

[34] 29 U.S.C. § 1321. See this provision for a precise definition of coverage.

[35] 29 U.S.C. § 1306.

[35.1] 29 U.S.C. § 1305(d), (e).

payment of plan obligations.[36] The employer is required to purchase insurance against termination from either the PBGC or a qualified insurance carrier. However, this insurance does not enable the employer to avoid liability altogether. The employer must have paid its contingent liability insurance for at least five years before it can be freed from liability for plan termination.[37] Furthermore, a substantial employer may not withdraw from a multiemployer plan without depositing in escrow its potential liability for five years by posting a bond of 150 percent to secure liability.[38]

Plans may be terminated either by the plan administrator or by the PBGC when it determines the plan's solvency is in serious question.[39] For proper notice, any plan must file a notice of termination at least ten days in advance of the proposed termination; for a period of ninety days after the proposed termination day, it shall not pay out any money pursuant to the termination procedure of the plan. During this time, the PBGC reviews the assets of the plan to determine if it is sufficiently solvent to meet its obligations. If so, the termination may take place. If, however, the plan is unable to meet its obligations, then the PBGC moves to place the plan under trusteeship as if the PBGC had instituted the termination itself.[40]

When the PBGC determines that a plan will not be able to meet its obligations, it initiates involuntary termination proceedings by applying to the U.S. district court for the appointment of a trustee. The trustee acts to consolidate and conserve the assets of the plan while moving to terminate it under the procedures required by ERISA. A set order of priority has been mandated by law for the allocation of assets of a terminated plan.[41] This was done to prevent a distribution plan that discriminated in favor of officers, shareholders, or highly compensated employees.[42] During involuntary termination proceedings when the plan adminis-

---

[36] 29 U.S.C. § 1363.
[37] 29 U.S.C. § 1323.
[38] 29 U.S.C. § 1363.
[39] 29 U.S.C. § 1342.
[40] 29 U.S.C. § 1341.
[41] 29 U.S.C. § 1344.
[42] Conference Report P.L. 93-406 at 277.

trator, who is usually the employer, and the PBGC are unable to agree to a termination date, the court resolves the issue and sets the date.[42.1] The termination date is important because it establishes the entitlements and obligations of not only the PBGC and the administrator/employer, but also of the plan participants. In setting the termination date, a court must: (1) identify all of the interests of the plan participants and the PBGC, (2) establish the date which most protects each of those interests and (3) balance the interests and set the termination date.[42.2] Quite often a later termination date is better for plan participants since the longer employment period allows more employees to become vested and increases vested employees' rights to benefits.

The creation of the PBGC does not mean that a participant in a plan to be terminated is fully protected. Several problems arise in this regard, the principal one being that the PBGC will be relying primarily on the records supplied to it by the plan administrator. These records may appear sufficient but still not provide all the relevant information concerning particular contributing employer(s) or the unique problems of the industry. It is therefore important for participants to review the records submitted to the PBGC by the plan administrator and the reasons given for termination and to attempt to provide other evidence or at least areas of inquiry for the PBGC during the ninety-day period of review of the termination notice.

As the PBGC does not fully guarantee benefit levels in effect for at least five years, it may attempt to recoup payments made to retirees in excess of the guaranteed amount. This recovery may be accomplished by either acceptance of a lump sum return of the overpayment or a reduction in future benefits until the recovery is accomplished. Such action may create a substantial hardship for the retiree.

Finally, the distribution of residual assets of the plan should be examined. The PBGC regulations issued under 29 U.S.C. Section 4044(d) concerning residual distributions in single employer

---

42.1 29 U.S.C § 1348(3).

42.2 PBGC v. Heppenstall Co., 633 F.2d 293 (3d Cir. 1980); PBGC v. Dickens, 535 F. Supp. 922 (W.D. Mich. 1982); PBGC v. Broadway Maintenance Corp., 547 F. Supp. 629 (S.D.N.Y. 1982); Braniff Int'l Corp. v. Interfirst Bank, Dallas, N.A., 3 EBC 2328 (N.D. Tex. Nov. 9, 1982).

plans provide that residual assets may be distributed to the employer if, as of the termination date, the plan provides for such a distribution and the distribution does not violate any provision of law.[42.3] Otherwise, the residual assets will be distributed to the plan participants.[42.4] Plan amendments allowing residual distribution generally may be made any time prior to the plan's termination date.[42.5] Amendments after the termination date violate the intent of ERISA and are invalid.[43]

§ 10.05. Procedural Issues in ERISA Litigation

[1] Exhaustion of Plan Remedies

As under most entitlement laws, the courts have required plan participants under ERISA to exhaust their internal plan remedies before filing suit. This requirement is predicated on the dictate of ERISA that each plan establish a claims procedure.[44] A participant whose claim for benefits has been denied is entitled to written notice stating the specific reasons for the denial, as well as an opportunity for a "full and fair review" by the named fiduciary of the decision denying the claim.[45] It is extremely important that participants who have been denied benefits avail themselves of these plan remedies; otherwise, their opportunity to obtain judicial relief may be jeopardized.

As a general rule, if participants have failed to exhaust internal plan remedies, the courts either have remanded the matter to the board of trustees of the plan for further review while retaining jurisdiction[46] or have dismissed the case without prejudice.[47] The

[42.3] 29 CFR § 2618.30.

[42.4] 29 CFR § 2618.32.

[42.5] Washington-Baltimore Newspaper Guild v. Washington Star Company, 3 EBC 2609 (D.D.C. Jan. 17, 1983).

[43] Audio Fidelity Corp. v. PBGC, 624 F.2d 513 (4th Cir. 1980).

[44] 29 U.S.C. § 1133.

[45] 29 CFR § 2560.503-1.

[46] Picket v. United Mine Workers of America Health and Retirement Funds, 467 F. Supp. 2 (E.D. Tenn. 1978).

[47] Scheider v. U.S. Steel Co., 486 F. Supp. 212 (W.D. Pa. 1980); Lucas v. Warner & Swasey Co., 475 F. Supp. 1071 (E.D. Pa. 1978); Taylor v. Bakery

courts have followed the case law interpreting the exhaustion requirements found in Section 301 of the LMRA[48] in adhering to the ERISA exhaustion requirement.[49] Possible exceptions to this general rule exist if plaintiffs bring suit to clarify their rights to future plan benefits under ERISA Section 502[49.1] or Section 510.[49.2]

There are several reasons for requiring exhaustion of administrative remedies: (1) to help reduce the number of frivolous lawsuits under ERISA, (2) to promote the consistent treatment of claims for benefits, and (3) to minimize the cost of claims settlement to all concerned.[50] To assist in the development of meaningful administrative remedies, ERISA permits the Secretary of Labor to prescribe regulations governing such remedies;[51] the Secretary has done so.[52] These regulations do not require adversarial hearings, but do allow the review proceedings to make use of grievance and arbitration procedures.[53] Although at least one court has raised the issue, the courts have not yet resolved the question of whether a review of a benefit denial should be based solely upon the record adduced at the fund's administrative proceedings or whether further evidence may be introduced at trial.[54]

The exhaustion of remedies requirement is waived if resort to intrafund procedures would be "futile" or if the claimant is wrongfully denied meaningful access to the established adminis-

Confectionary Union Indus. Int'l Welfare Fund, 455 F. Supp. 816 (E.D. N.C. 1978).

48 29 U.S.C. § 185.

49 Taylor, *supra. See, e.g.,* Buzzard v. Local Lodge 1040 Int'l Ass'n of Mach. & Aero. Workers, 480 F.2d 35 (9th Cir. 1973).

49.1 29 U.S.C. § 1132. Janowski v. Local 710 Pension Fund, Int'l Brotherhood of Teamsters, 673 F.2d 931 (7th Cir. 1982).

49.2 29 U.S.C. § 1140. Gavalik v. Continental Can Co., 3 EBC 1311 (W.D. Pa. 1982); *but see also* Kross v. Western Electric Co., 701 F.2d 1238 (7th Cir. 1983) (exhaustion required if it were unclear whether plan benefit committee could effect relief).

50 Amato v. Bernard, 618 F.2d 599, 567 (9th Cir. 1980); Taylor, *supra,* at 820.

51 29 U.S.C. § 1135.

52 29 CFR § 2560.503-1.

53 29 CFR § 2560.503-1(b)(2).

54 Toland v. McCarthy, 499 F. Supp. 1183 (E.D. Mass. 1980)(issue was mooted when matter was settled out of court).

trative procedures.[55] The frequent result, even in these situations, is for the court to remand the matter to the fund for adjudication while retaining jurisdiction over the matter.[56]

[2] Venue

Section 502(e)(2) of ERISA[57] provides that venue resides in "the district where the plan is administered, where the breach took place, or where a defendant resides or is found."

Venue has not posed a serious problem for plan participants. The courts have been willing to read the venue provision of ERISA broadly.[58] While most courts have relied on the "minimum contacts" test established in *Int'l Shoe Co. v. State of Washington,*[59] one court rejected it, finding no proper venue existed if the only contact were that plaintiff lived and received benefits in the district.[60]

[3] Jury Trials

ERISA does not explicitly address the right of a party to jury trial. Generally, an act that is equitable in nature is not entitled to a jury trial, while a claim characterized as legal is entitled to a jury upon demand. This division between equitable and legal action stems from the Seventh Amendment, which guarantees trial by jury only in those actions that would have been triable by jury under common law at the time the Seventh Amendment

---

55 Amato, *supra,* at 567; Taylor, *supra,* at 820.

56 *See* Picket, *supra.*

57 29 U.S.C. § 1132 (e)(2).

58 Davidson Transfer and Storage Co. v. Teamsters Joint Council No. 83 Pension Fund, 2 EBC 2093 (D. Md. 1981); Bostic v. Ohio River Company Pension Plan, 517 F. Supp. 627 (S.D.W.V. 1981).

59 326 U.S. 310 (1945).

60 Higman v. Anstead Industries, Inc., 2 EBC 1948 (E.D. Pa. 1981).

61 [Reserved.]

62 [Reserved.]

63 [Reserved.]

64 [Reserved.]

was adopted.[65]

Most ERISA cases have held that suits by participants claiming pension benefits are equitable in nature and therefore not entitled to a jury trial.[66] However, some district courts have followed the holding in *Stamps v. Michigan Teamsters Joint Council No. 43*[67] that Section 502 of ERISA allows both legal and equitable claims, which may be distinguished by utilizing the rule of statutory construction that statutes should be construed in a manner that renders none of the subsections superfluous. The *Stamps* court found that Section 502(a)(3) of ERISA specifically creates a civil action for equitable relief, while Section 502(a)(1)(B) of ERISA creates a different civil action for legal relief.[68] At present, only the Fifth and Seventh Circuits have expressly rejected this distinction.[69]

[4] Attorneys' Fees

Section 502(g) of ERISA[70] provides that in a suit by a participant, beneficiary, or fiduciary, the court may allow reasonable attorneys' fees and costs of action to either party.

There is no set standard used by the courts in determining the amount of attorneys' fees under ERISA. Generally, some relief must be obtained before attorneys' fees will be awarded. However, in *Fase v. Seafarers Welfare and Pension Plan,*[71] although the plaintiff won, attorneys' fees were denied because the relief was not obtained under ERISA. In this case, the plaintiff prevailed under

---

65 Klein v. Shell Oil Co., 386 F.2d 659 (8th Cir. 1967).

66 *See, e.g.,* Calamia v. Spivey, 632 F.2d 1236 (5th Cir. 1980); Wardle v. Cent. States S.E. & S.W. Areas Pension Fund, 627 F.2d 820 (7th Cir. 1980), *cert. denied,* 449 U.S. 1112 (1981).

67 431 F. Supp. 745 (E.D. Mich. 1977).

68 *Accord,* Bouton v. Cent. States, S.E. & S.W. Areas Pension Fund, — F. Supp. — (E.D. Tenn. 1978); Oil Chem. and Atomic Workers Int'l Union Local 4-23 v. Texaco, 315 BNA Pens. Rep. A-9 (E.D. Tex. 1978).

69 Calamia Wardle, *supra,* note 66.

70 29 U.S.C. § 1132(g).

71 589 F.2d 112 (2d Cir. 1978).

Section 302(c)(5) of the LMRA,[72] and the court did not reach the merits of the alternate ERISA claim.

Factors considered by the courts in awarding attorneys' fees in pension cases include the amount recovered[73] and the complexity of the case.[74] While relatively few ERISA cases have concerned the amount of attorneys' fees, it can be expected that the courts will generally consider the same factors as in Title VII[75] cases. One of the principal cases in this area, *Johnson v. Georgia Highway Express, Inc.,*[76] set forth twelve factors to be considered in determining the amount of attorneys' fees.[77] Presumably, these factors will apply equally to ERISA cases.

One additional consideration of the courts in determining the award of attorneys' fee to counsel for plan participants is from whom the award will be paid. In *Marshall v. Penn,*[78] the court addressed the issue of whether attorneys' fees may be paid to counsel for plan participants from the assets recovered on behalf of the plan. The court suggested that the following five factors be considered in determining whether to award attorneys' fees from the plan or assess the offending parties personally: (1) the degree of the offending parties' culpability or bad faith; (2) the degree of the ability of the offending parties personally to satisfy an award of attorneys' fees; (3) whether an award of attorneys' fees against the offending parties would deter other persons acting under similar circumstances; (4) the amount of benefit conferred on members of the pension plan as a whole; and (5) the

[72] 29 U.S.C. § 401 et seq.

[73] Busher v. Geightner, 315 BNA Pens. Rep., A-10 (S.D. Ind. 1980).

[74] Pineman v. Oechslin, 312 BNA Pens. Rep. A-21 (D.C. Conn. 1980).

[75] 42 U.S.C. § 200e et seq.

[76] 488 F.2d 714 (5th Cir. 1974).

[77] The twelve factors set forth in *Johnson* are (1) the time and labor required; (2) the novelty and difficulty of the questions; (3) the requisite skill to perform the legal services properly; (4) the preclusion of other employment by the attorney by the acceptance of this case; (5) the customary fee; (6) whether the fee is fixed or contingent; (7) time limitations imposed by the client or the circumstances; (8) the amount involved and the results obtained; (9) the undesirability of the case; (11) the nature and length of the professional relationship with the client; and (12) awards in similar cases.

[78] 585 F.2d 453, 464 (10th Cir. 1978).

relative merits of the parties' position.[79] On remand, the district court upheld its prior determination that attorneys' fees could be paid in this case from assets recovered.[80]

Situations where attorneys' fees and costs have been assessed against trustees or administrators of plans deserve additional comment. The DOL, in an Advisory Opinion,[81] cautioned that reimbursement of legal fees by a pension fund to trustees may conflict with fiduciary responsibility provisions of ERISA. Nevertheless, one court has upheld a contract that provided for reimbursement of the fiduciary by the pension fund of reasonable litigation expenses: In *Central States Southeast and Southwest Areas Pension Fund v. American National Bank and Trust,*[82] the court found that reimbursement is permitted under Section 408(c)(2) of ERISA[83] (an exception to the prohibited-transactions provisions of Section 406). Reimbursement does not shield the fiduciary from liability; it simply covers the fiduciary's legal fee and litigation expenses.

It is extremely important to note that ERISA states that the award of attorneys' fees is discretionary and that either party may be awarded attorneys' fees. On at least one occasion, an unsuccessful participant was charged attorneys' fees. In *Hurn v. Retirement Fund Trust,*[84] early retirement benefits were suspended when the participant accepted other union employment in the same trade. The court assessed the participant $500 in attorneys' fees plus costs because the participant knew of the plan provision suspending benefits. In *Central States Southeast and Southwest Areas Pension Fund v. Hitchings Trucking, Inc.,*[85] an employer who successfully defended a suit for delinquent contributions was awarded attorneys' fees.

Case law under Title VII is much more developed in this area and may be looked to for guidance. In *Christiansburg Garment Co. v.*

---

[79] *Id.* at 465.

[80] Eaves v. Penn, 587 F.2d 453 (10th Cir. 1978).

[81] AO 78-29, 231 BNA Pens. Rep. R-10.

[82] 276 BNA Pens. Rep. D-1 (N.D. Ill. 1980).

[83] 29 U.S.C. § 1108(c)(2).

[84] 460 F. Supp. 112 (C.D. Cal. 1978).

[85] 490 F. Supp. 906 (E.D. Mich. 1980).

EEOC,[86] the Supreme Court found that a defendant in a Title VII case may be awarded attorneys' fees only where plaintiff's action was frivolous, unreasonable, or without foundation. The court noted that two equitable factors favoring an award to prevailing Title VII plaintiffs are absent in considering an award to Title VII defendants. The plaintiff is "the chosen instrument of Congress to vindicate a policy that Congress considered of the highest priority," and when plaintiff is awarded fees, such fees are awarded against a violator of federal law.[87] These two equitable considerations should also apply in ERISA cases.

Generally, courts will be reluctant to impose attorneys' fees on participants in suits that are not patently frivolous. ERISA is a broad remedial statute and should be construed liberally in favor of those it was intended to protect. Thus, a prevailing participant should ordinarily be allowed to recover reasonable attorneys' fees without the necessity of showing bad faith.[88]

§ 10.06. Fiduciary Responsibility

One of the principal concerns addressed by ERISA is the conduct of the administration and operation of pension plans. For the first time, a law specifically addressed questions as to who has a fiduciary responsibility to a pension plan, what standards such fiduciaries must meet, what constitutes a violation of those standards, and what remedies are available to rectify a breach of fiduciary duties.

[1] Who Is a Fiduciary?

Under ERISA, a "fiduciary" is defined as follows:

> [A] person is a fiduciary with respect to a plan to the extent (i) he exercises any discretionary authority or discretionary control respecting management of such plan or exercises any authority or

[86] 434 U.S. 412 (1978).
[87] *Id.* at 418.
[88] Landro v. Glendenning Motorways, Inc., 299 BNA Pens. Rep. A-12.

> control respecting management or disposition of its assets, (ii) he renders investment advice for a fee or other compensation, direct or indirect, with respect to any money or other property of such plan, or has any authority or responsibility to do so, or (iii) he has any discretionary responsibility in the administration of such plan.[89]

This expansive definition does not limit classification as a fiduciary to those persons holding identifiable positions, such as the plan administrator or trustee; rather, it approaches the question from an examination of the actual relationship of the individual to the plan's finances and administration. Thus, if a person is charged with responsibility for some aspect of the maintenance or administration of the pension fund, then that person is probably a fiduciary. In addition to plan officials, other fiduciaries include (1) the individual who exercises control over administration of finances even though the named fiduciary is a corporation,[90] (2) arbitrators who are appointed to resolve disputes concerning a participant's rights to receive a pension,[91] and (3) union officials or other persons who assist in the collection of employee contributions.[92] Plan consultants, such as actuaries, lawyers or other service providers who become involved in business decisions of the pension plan and/or trust, may also be required to meet ERISA's fiduciary standards.[93]

Merely resigning from the position of responsibility does not in and of itself terminate fiduciary duty; the fiduciary remains charged to see that a suitable replacement has been found. Any action that may be considered a breach of fiduciary duty attributable to the resignation itself may return the liability to the re-

---

[89] 29 U.S.C. § 1002(21)(A).

[90] *See, e.g.,* Freund v. Marshall & Ilsley Bank, 485 F. Supp. 629 (W.D. Wisc. 1979); Eaves v. Penn, 587 F.2d 453, 458 (10th Cir. 1978).

[91] Dept. of Labor Letter to the Bd. of Trustees of the Constr. Laborers Pension Trust for S. Cal. (Sept. 14, 1979), 262 BNA Pens. Rep. R-9. It should be noted, however, that it is not a prohibited transaction to pay the arbitrator for these services. *See* Section 408(c)(2) of ERISA.

[92] Nedd v. U.M.W.A., 556 F.2d 190 (3d Cir. 1977), *cert. denied,* 434 U.S. 1013 (1977). *See also* Cent. States, S.E. & S.W. Areas Pension Fund v. Hitchings Trucking, Inc., No. 7-71951 (E.D. Mich. July 20, 1979).

[93] 29 CFR § 2509.75.

signed fiduciary.[94] Conversely, a new trustee is not insulated from the errors of a previous trustee, if s/he does not take steps to rectify those errors.[95]

[2] Fiduciary Standards

The fiduciaries, those persons exerting some control over the pension fund's assets, are expected to follow certain standards of conduct in making any decision that affects the accumulation, investment, or disbursement of the fund's assets. Under Section 404(a)(1) of ERISA,[96] standards of fiduciary responsibility have been established for all plans covered by ERISA. These standards require that a fiduciary must act solely in the interest of plan participants and beneficiaries and do so "with the care, skill, prudence, and diligence" expected of a "prudent man" acting in this capacity.[97] By law, the fiduciary must diversify the investments of the plan to "minimize the risk of large losses,"[98] and act within the confines of the documents governing the plan as long as they are consistent with the law.[99]

Essentially this means that persons charged with maintaining and administering the pension fund are always to act in the best interest of the fund and its participants. They may not take unacceptable risks when investing the funds, but are required to see that the fund's assets provide a reasonable rate of return. To give guidance to plan fiduciaries in the matter of investment, ERISA proscribes certain transactions to prevent self-dealing and to minimize risks (see Section 10.06[3]).

Of more immediate interest to plan participants is that the fiduciary standards also govern decisions about plan participation and eligibility.[100] Changes in eligibility requirements may not be made without careful consideration of the financial viability of

---

[94] Freund v. Marshall & Ilsley Bank, *supra,* at 641.

[95] Marshall v. Kraft, 463 F. Supp. 493 (D.C. Ga. 1978).

[96] 29 U.S.C. § 1104(a)(1).

[97] 29 U.S.C. § 1104(a)(1)(B).

[98] 29 U.S.C. § 1104(a)(1)(C).

[99] 29 U.S.C. § 1104(a)(1)(D).

[100] Winpisinger v. Aurora Corp. of Ill., Precision Castings Div., 456 F. Supp. 559 (D.C. Ohio 1978).

the fund, and these requirements must be applied fairly and evenhandedly.[101] This essentially means that the plan may not operate in an arbitrary or capricious manner.[102] While this standard gives the trustees wide latitude to interpret ambiguous plan language in operating the fund,[103] they must do so in light of the fiduciary duty to preserve the financial security of the fund and yet effectively apply its assets to benefit as many of the participants and intended beneficiaries as is economically possible.[104]

The guidance provided by ERISA to trustees and fiduciaries is embodied in its "prudent man" rule. This rule goes beyond the common law concept that the fund trustees should use the same standard of care as a person of ordinary prudence would exercise in dealing with her or his own property. Rather, under ERISA, trustees should exercise the prudence of a person presumed to have the knowledge or expertise necessary to manage the fund's assets.[105] The larger the fund, the higher the level of expertise that should be expected from the manager.

[3] Prohibited Transactions

In addition to the stricture requiring pension fund fiduciaries to diversify investments, fiduciaries are forbidden to conduct certain transactions that on their face represent a conflict, or potential conflict of interest or that may otherwise jeopardize the financial viability of the fund. Because these prohibitions are more specific, it is easier to prove a violation of a fiduciary's

101 This does not mean that some participants may be not be adversely affected by a decision of the trustees. *See* Rueda v. Seafarers Int'l Union of N.A., 576 F.2d 939 (1st Cir. 1978).

102 Boyles v. Cent. States, S.E. & S.W. Pension Fund, 602 F.2d 97 (5th Cir. 1979).

103 Phillips v. Unity Welfare Ass'n, Inc., 395 F. Supp. 1147 (D.C. Mo. 1973).

104 Mosley v. Nat'l Maritime Union Pension & Welfare Plan, 438 F. Supp. 413 (D.C. N.Y. 1977).

105 *See generally* Scott, The Law of Trusts §§ 174-227 (3d ed.). A helpful article on this subject is M. Klevan, *Fiduciary Responsibility under ERISA's Prudent Man Rule: What Are the Guideposts?,* J. of Tax. (March 1976).

responsibility under these sections of ERISA[106] than under the provision outlining the general fiduciary standards.[107]

Section 406(a)(1) prohibits transactions between a plan and a party-in-interest (broadly defined in Section 3(14) of ERISA),[108] while Section 406(b) proscribes self-dealing by the fiduciary. These prohibitions are absolute and the question of harm or good faith is irrelevant.[109] It has been held that a violation of Section 406 existed even if the court found "no taint of scandal, no hint of self-dealing, no trace of bad-faith . . . [and] the terms of the [prohibited] transaction were fair and reasonable to both plans."[110]

One of the principal problems in the area of prohibited transactions is determining whether the person involved in a transaction is a party-in-interest; beneficial owners may be hidden behind corporate entities. Nevertheless, according to ERISA's legislative history, the burden is on the fiduciary to investigate thoroughly any "significant transaction" to determine whether the borrower is a party-in-interest.[111]

Section 407 of ERISA[112] places specific limitations on the acquisition and holding of employer securities and property by most plans covered by ERISA, the significant exception being ESOP's. Certain types of securities, such as stocks or marketable obligations and property, are excepted from this prohibition; however, their acquisition by a plan would still be governed by the general diversity rule[113] and would be carefully scrutinized because of the increased potential risk to the viability of the pension fund.

This brings us to the question of exemptions from the prohibited-transactions category. Congress recognized that a certain

---

[106] 29 U.S.C. §§ 1106, 1107.

[107] 29 U.S.C. § 1104.

[108] 29 U.S.C. § 1002 (14).

[109] *See* Cutaiar v. Marshall, 590 F.2d 523 (3d Cir. 1979); M & R Co., Inc. v. Fitzsimmons, 484 F. Supp. 1041 (D. Nev. 1980); Freund v. Marshall & Ilsley Bank, 485 F. Supp. 629 (W.D. Wis. 1979); Marshall v. Kelly, 465 F. Supp. 341 (D. Okla. 1978).

[110] Cutaiar, *supra,* at 528.

[111] Conf. Rep. P.L. 93-406 at 307, 308.

[112] 29 U.S.C. § 1107.

[113] 29 U.S.C. § 1104(a)(1)(C).

level of interaction among a pension plan, employers, and parties-in-interest would have to take place. For this reason, the law allows the Secretary of Labor to exempt some transactions that would otherwise be prohibited under a strict interpretation of ERISA.[114] In addition, this same section enumerates specific exemptions from the general prohibitions against self-dealing, acquisition of "qualifying" employer securities or real property.

[4] Remedies for Breach of Fiduciary Duty

Of course, all these standards and prohibitions mean little, unless the relief for a breach of fiduciary duty is adequate. The law provides that a fiduciary is personally liable for any breach and must make good any losses suffered by the plan as a result of the breach.[115] A fiduciary may be removed if she or he has been convicted of a felony.[116] In addition, the courts may effect any equitable relief that is deemed appropriate to rectify a breach of duty.[117]

In one of the first cases decided under ERISA, the court recognized it has "the power and the duty to afford that remedy which is most advantageous to the participants and most conducive to effectuating the purposes of the trust."[118] In this case, the appropriate relief included removal of the trustee who breached his fiduciary duty. The courts have also allowed for the appointment of a receiver.[119]

Punitive damages have not been allowed as a remedy for an arbitrary and capricious breach of fiduciary duty under ERISA.[120] However, some courts have indicated that punitive damages may be appropriate if the breach is malicious, flagrant, or out-

114 29 U.S.C. § 1108.

115 29 U.S.C. § 1109.

116 29 U.S.C. § 1111.

117 29 U.S.C. §§ 1109, 1132(a)(3).

118 Eaves v. Penn, 587 F.2d 462 (10th Cir. 1978).

119 Marshall v. Snyder, 572 F.2d 894 (2d Cir. 1978).

120 Calhoun v. Falstaff Brewing Corp., 478 F. Supp. 357 (D.C. Mo. 1979), *punitive damages awarded under a common law tort theory of malicious breach of contract,* 491 F. Supp. 1188 (D.C. Mo. 1980); Hurn v. Retirement Fund Trust of Plumbing, etc., 424 F. Supp. 80 (C.D. Cal. 1976).

rageous.[121] Other courts are of the opinion that Congress expressed a preference for criminal sanctions rather than punitive damages.[121.1]

[5] Social Investments

In an effort to protect and insure future employment of plan participants and to promote certain desirable social goals, i.e., increased unionization, low-cost housing, opposition to apartheid, etc., unions are making demands on plan fiduciaries to direct the investment of plan assets in a direction to support these social aims. Contrary to popular myth, there are no specific prohibitions in ERISA against social investment. Like all pension investments, they are subject to ERISA's prudence and prohibited transaction provisions.

Though opposition may be expected from non-unionized corporations, their business associations and to some extent the banking industry, social investment will be difficult to challenge as long as there is no self-interest or self-dealing by the fiduciaries. While certain other investment criteria must also be met, such as diversification and adequate rate of return, it is this self-interest aspect of a social investment that will be given the closest scrutiny.

There are no cases prohibiting social investments. In *Blackenship v. Boyle,*[122] the case usually cited by opponents of social investing, the court did not reject *per se* investments that collaterally benefited the union. The trustees in that case disregarded the interests of the beneficiaries and acted in their own self-interest. For a critique of *Blackenship,* see *Culinary Workers and Bartender Union No. 596 Health & Welfare Trust v. Gateway Cafe, Inc.*[123] *In Withers v. Teachers*

---

121 *See* Free v. Gilbert-Hodgman, 3 EBC 1010 (N.D. Ill. 1982); Eaton v. D'Amato, 3 EBC 1003 (D.D.C. 1980); Bittner v. Sandoff & Rudoy Indus., 490 F. Supp. 534 (E.D. Wisc. 1980)(question of retaliatory firing in violation of Section 510 of ERISA, 29 U.S.C. § 1140).

121.1 *See* Whitaker v. Texaco, Inc., 4 EBC 1763 (N.D. Ga. 1983).

122 329 F.Supp. 1089 (D.D.C. 1971).

123 588 P.2d 1334 (Wash. Sup. Ct. 1979).

Retirement System of the City of New York,[124] the court found no evidence of self-dealing and upheld the prudence of a nontraditional investment (investment in municipal securities at a time when city faced severe financial crisis). Department of Labor Regulations concerning prudence are in accord with this viewpoint.[125]

Section 404(a)(1)(D) of ERISA[126] requires that fiduciaries exercise their duties "in accordance with the documents and instruments governing the plan . . . ." This section can be used to enhance social investing. A trust document could specify the areas for investments to be placed. Thus, not only would a fiduciary be bound to follow such mandate, but the failure to do so would violate the prudent person rule.

§ 10.07. Minimum Standards Litigation

Although the enactment of ERISA has greatly encouraged the establishment of pension plans and participation in those plans, plan eligibility provisions and their interpretation by plan trustees continue to come between many workers and their expected pensions. This has led to considerable litigation.

As explained in this section, the courts have generally given great deference to the interpretation of the plan by the trustees. For this reason it is important that the worker read and understand the plan and keep abreast of any changes in the eligibility provisions. Denial of benefits will be reviewed by the courts only to the extent that the action of the plan is arbitrary and capricious[127] or not in compliance with the provisions of ERISA.[128]

---

[124] 447 F. Supp. 1248 (S.D.N.Y. 1978), *aff'd,* 595 F.2d 1210 (2d Cir. 1979).

[125] *See* 29 C.F.R. § 2550.404a-1.

[126] 29 U.S.C. § 1104(a)(1)(D).

[127] The arbitrary and capricious standard for review of actions by the board of trustees was enunciated in Danti v. Lewis, 114 U.S. App. D.C. 105, 312 F.2d 345 (1962) and made applicable in ERISA cases. *See generally* Bayles v. Central States, Southeast and Southwest Areas Pension Fund, 572 F.2d 1208 (5th Cir. 1978).

[128] Winer v. Edison Bros., 593 F.2d 307 (8th Cir. 1979); Riley v. MEBA Pension Trust, 570 F.2d 406 (2d Cir. 1977).

[1] Coverage, Participation and the Break-in-Service Rule

ERISA does not establish a right to a pension and the employer is not required to institute a pension plan. However, if the employer does have a pension or benefit plan, the law sets certain requirements for coverage and vesting. (See Section 10.02[4].) Coverage tends not to be a problem in collectively bargained plans, but close examination should be given to provisions affecting part-time and seasonal employees. These workers often find themselves suffering disqualifying breaks-in-service or other bars to eligibility.

An employee must become a participant in the plan when s/he has completed a year of service or reached the age of 25, whichever is later.[129] However, if the employee ceases work before vesting, s/he is no longer considered a participant in the plan and is not entitled to benefits.[130]

The concept of vesting does not give rise to a legitimate expectation for continued employment.[131] Absent a just cause provision in the collective bargaining contract, the employer is not required to justify any termination or layoff, even one that may cause the employee to lose his/her pension service credits prior to vesting. However, if the reason for termination is to prevent the employee from accruing vested pension benefits, then the employer has violated Section 510 of ERISA.[132] Courts recognize this cause of action, but the burden of proof rests solely on the employee.[133] To date, no court has upheld such a claim.

Separation is not the only way to cancel pension eligibility, as many employees find out. The break-in-service rule remains the

---

[129] 29 U.S.C. § 1052(a)(1)(A).

[130] Nugent v. Jesuit High School of New Orleans, 625 F.2d 1285 (5th Cir. 1980). Plaintiff, a non-vested former employee, could not recover penalties against the plan administrator for his failure to promptly reply to her request for information.

[131] Craig v. Bemis Company, Inc., 517 F.2d 677 (5th Cir. 1975).

[132] 29 U.S.C. § 1140.

[133] Kross v. Western Electric Co., 701 F.2d 1238 (7th Cir. 1983); Moore v. Home Ins. Co., 601 F.2d 1072 (9th Cir. 1979); Calhoun v. Falstaff Brewing Corp., 478 F. Supp. 357 (E.D. Mo. 1979), 491 F. Supp. 1188 (captioned Dependahl v. Falstaff Brewing Co.).

chief stumbling block to achieving pension eligibility. One of the most positive impacts of ERISA has been the reformation of the break-in-service rules. Prior to ERISA it was common for a break-in-service of any length before retirement to cause loss of a pension. Still, litigation abounds over the interpretation of break-in-service rules.

A pension plan may limit the ERISA break-in-service provisions to work performed *after* the effective date of ERISA.[134] A plan may continue to enforce its pre-ERISA rule for benefits accrued prior to that date as long as there is no structural violation. If, however, a pension plan does not have express provisions differentiating between pre-ERISA and post-ERISA breaks-in-service, then ERISA standards should apply.[135]

Most litigation in this area revolves around the dates of specific events, e.g., the date of the break-in-service, the date the participant ceased work covered by the plan, the date s/he was eligible to apply for a pension and the date the application was made.

The decision to grant or deny a pension rests with the trustees of the plan and the decision is to be made only after an application for benefits has been made.[136] The general rule is that the plan in effect at the time the application is submitted governs the trustees' decision.[137] However, if the participant has delayed her or his application until sometime after s/he retired, the plan in effect at the time s/he ceased employment controls.[138] This is to discourage otherwise ineligible retired workers from delaying the determination of their pension eligibility indefinitely in hopes that the provision of the plan barring their qualification for a pension will be amended.

If participants continue to work past the time they would otherwise be eligible for a pension, their applications are still considered under the rules in effect at the time they leave covered

134 29 U.S.C. § 1061(c); Honeycutt v. Board of Trustees, 468 F. Supp. 1213 (C.D. Cal. 1979).

135 Snyder v. Titus, 513 F. Supp. 926 (E.D. Va. 1981).

136 Winer v. Edison Bros. Stores Pension Plan, 593 F.2d 307 (8th Cir. 1979).

137 Reiherzer v. Shannon, 581 F.2d 1266 (7th Cir. 1978); Morgan v. Laborers Pension Trust, 433 F. Supp. 518 (D.C. Cal. 1977).

138 Fremont v. McGraw-Edison, 606 F.2d 752 (7th Cir. 1979), *cert denied,* 11 445 US 951, 100 S.Ct. 1599 (1980); Van Fossan v. Teamsters Local 710 Pension Fund, 649 F.2d 1243, 2 EBC 1457 (7th Cir. 1981).

employment. This may work to the employee's detriment if the plan is subsequently amended to bar eligibility. To protect workers who may be in that situation, the courts have required the plan to demonstrate that proper notice was given to plan participants to enable them to elect to retire or to continue working.[139]

Even if the pension plan's break-in-service rule has been deemed to be acceptable under the law, its application may be successfully challenged as being unreasonable. In determining the reasonableness of the application of the rule the courts have examined what caused the disqualifying break-in-service. In the following cases the particular facts were decisive. In *Krauss v. Gorman,*[140] the participant was laid off and for three and a half years could not find work in covered employment. The court held that in this situation if the rule deprived the otherwise eligible employee of all benefits derived from contributions made on his behalf, the plan was required to justify that the rule fulfills legitimate goals of the fund and is not in violation of the sole and exclusive benefit requirement of Section 302(c)(5) of the Taft-Hartly Act.[141] In a similar case,[142] the participant, a plumber, was encouraged by union officials to work for the city schools, which were not covered by the retirement plan, during a temporary crisis. Afterward the plan was amended to require fifteen years of continuous service which thereby disqualified him from receiving any benefits. The court determined such an application of the rule was arbitrary and unreasonable. In these situations the court gave considerable weight to the voluntariness of the break-in-service.[143]

Finally, as with any plan amendment, the participant must be notified of changes in the break-in-service rule of the plan if it is to have any applicability to her or him.[144] Whether proper notice has been given is usually obvious under the stringent

---

[139] Norton v. I.A.M. Pension Fund, 533 F.2d 1352 (D.C. Cir. 1977); Mosley v. Maritime Union Pension and Welfare Plan, 451 F.Supp. 226 (D.C.N.Y. 1978).

[140] 583 F.2d 82 (3d Cir. 1978).

[141] 29 U.S.C. § 186.

[142] Kraft v. Elder, 452 F. Supp. 933 (D.C.N.Y. 1978).

[143] *See also* Lee v. Nesbit, 453 F.2d 1309 (9th Cir. 1972) (unavailability of work could be considered in determining if pension eligibility could be maintained).

[144] Burroughs v. Board of Trustees, 398 F. Supp. 168 (N.D. Cal. 1975), *aff'd.,* 542 F.2d 1128 (9th Cir. 1976).

disclosure requirements of ERISA, but reasonableness of the notice of plan amendments made prior to ERISA's enactment has been the subject of frequent litigation. The courts have considered posting of the plan amendment at union halls to be sufficient notice in one instance,[145] while in another case relying on union meetings to provide such information has been considered inadequate.[146]

[2] Forfeitures and Suspension of Benefits[146.1]

Prior to the enactment of ERISA, pension plans frequently contained forfeiture provisions, referred to as "bad boy" clauses, under which participants would be denied benefits if they were terminated by their employer for dishonesty or other misconduct such as insubordination, excessive tardiness or absenteeism, or if they engaged in competition with their former employer after termination. Section 233 of ERISA,[147] as its legislative history makes clear, was designed to prevent further enforcement of these provisions for participants who have reached normal retirement age.[148]

One problem that remains regarding "bad boy" forfeiture clauses relates to the effective date of ERISA. The courts have held that only if all events have occurred prior to the effective date of ERISA are forfeitures not proscribed. Thus, if the termination of employment or the action of the plan in denying benefits occurred after December 31, 1975, the forfeiture generally

---

145 Davis v. Central States, Southeast and Southwest Areas Pension Plan, 460 F.Supp. 926 (D.C. Tenn. 1978).

146 Harris v. Joint Plumbing Industry Board, 474 F.Supp. 1284 (S.D.N.Y. 1979).

146.1 See § 10.02(5)(g)(iii), *supra.*

147 29 U.S.C. § 1053.

148 U.S. Code & Admin. News 1974, pp. 4639, 4725. Note, however, that "bad boy" clauses seem to be alive and well for profit-sharing plans. *See* Nedrow v. Macfarlane & Hays Co. Employees Profit-Sharing Plan, 474 F.Supp 934 (E.D. Mich. 1979); Hepple v. Roberts & Dybdahl, Inc. Restated Employees Profit Sharing Plan, 622 F.2d 752 (8th Cir. 1980).

will not be upheld.[149] However, a participant may still be affected by a bad boy clause if the plan contains a more liberal or generous vesting schedule than that required by ERISA. In such a case, a bad boy forfeiture of an interest in benefits is permitted, provided that the forfeiture does not reduce pension rights below the ERISA minimum vesting requirements.[149.1]

Benefit rights deemed by the courts to be ancillary may also be forfeited. Both payments made to induce early retirement and modifications to a plan limiting early retirement have been categorized as ancillary.[149.2] On the other hand, a plan amendment which phased out a cost-of-living adjustment was not ancillary.[149.3]

While most forfeitures have been disallowed, there are still circumstances under which the trustees of a plan may suspend a retiree's benefits. These circumstances generally arise if a retiree returns to work.

As many retirees have discovered, pension benefits, even if supplemented by Social Security, are not adequate to provide a relatively comfortable life. Most pension benefits are frozen at the level in effect at the time of retirement[150] and inflation reduces the value of the pension each year. Often a retiree is forced by circumstances to return to work or to develop addition-

---

[149] Keller v. Graphic Systems of Akron, Inc., 422 F. Supp. 1005 (N.D. Ohio 1976) (forfeiture upheld); Fremont v. McGraw-Edison Co., 460 F. Supp 599 (N.D. Ill. 1978). Forfeiture denied where employment continued after effective date of ERISA even though wrongful acts occurred before that date: Winer v. Edison Bros. Stores, 447 F. Supp. 836 (E.D. Mo. 1978), *aff'd.*, 593 F.2d 307 (8th Cir. 1979). Forfeiture denied where employment continued after effective date of ERISA: Baeten v. VanEss, 474 F. Supp 1324 (E.D. Wisc. 1979) (forfeiture denied where action of the plan occurred after effective date of ERISA even though employees were terminated prior to that date).

[149.1] Montgomery v. Lowe, 507 F. Supp. 618 (S.D. Tex. 1981).

[149.2] Petrella v. N. L. Industries, 529 F. Supp. 1357 (D.N.J. 1982); Sutton v. Weirton Steel Division, 4 EBC 1714 (N.D.W.V. 1983).

[149.3] Shaw v. IAM Pension Plan, 4 EBC 1737 (C.D. Ca. 1983).

[150] There is even an opportunity for a pension plan in financial trouble to reduce the benefits by a retroactive plan amendment. *See* 29 U.S.C. § 1082(c)(8). Though ostensibly stringent standards must be met before such an amendment would be approved by the Internal Revenue Service, the oversight protection has been less than adequate.

al sources of income. Such employment[151] may penalize the retiree under certain circumstances.

ERISA allows benefits to be suspended if the retiree returns to work for the employer maintaining the pension plan or, in the case of multi-employer plan, "in the same industry, in the same trade or craft, and the same geographic area covered by the plan, as when such benefits commenced."[152] If the participant is receiving early retirement benefits and has not yet reached the normal retirement age for the plan, usually age 65, she or he may find even broader restrictions in the plan. In addition to upholding broader restrictions on work after early retirement, the courts have allowed plans to suspend all benefits up to the time the participant reaches normal retirement age.[153] The most notable cases involving suspension of benefits for work after retirement are *Riley v. MEBA*[154] and *Capocci v. General Motors.*[155]

In the *Riley* case, the plaintiff retired under the early retirement provisions of the plan. He then went to work for the United States Maritime Administration and the trustees denied him benefits under the provisions allowing them to suspend benefits to a retired participant who is working in the "American Flag or Foreign Flag Maritime Industry." The trustees declared that, even though the union did not have jurisdiction over this work, it was considered to be working in the maritime industry. The court allowed suspension of the entire amount of the plaintiff's early retirement benefits on the grounds that ERISA did not protect against forfeitures prior to normal retirement age.[156] The court construed the concept of "accrued" benefits to mean only those benefits calculable from normal retirement age.

In *Capocci,* the plaintiff retired under a "twenty-five year and

---

151 Income from investments is not proscribed. A retired capitalist may still be a capitalist, but a retired factory worker must remain retired or suffer possible suspension of benefits.

152 29 U.S.C. § 1053(a)(3)(B).

153 After reaching normal retirement age, the suspension may only last for the period of time the participant has actually worked in prohibited employment. 29 U.S.C. § 1053(a)(3)(B).

154 570 F.2d 406 (2d Cir. 1977), *on remand,* 452 F. Supp 117 (S.D.N.Y. 1978), *aff'd.,* 586 F.2d 968 (2d Cir. 1979).

155 444 F. Supp. 1306 (D.C. Haw. 1978).

156 452 F. Supp at 120; 586 F.2d at 972.

out" provision which was considered an early retirement. However, to discourage early retirements, the plan prohibited participants from earning additional income in excess of the amount allowed by Social Security during the years before reaching the normal retirement age. It did not limit the prohibition to the trade, jurisdiction or geographical area of the plan. When Capocci earned in excess of the allowable amount, he was assessed a penalty against the early retirement supplements equaling twice the excess earned and all his early retirement supplements were suspended until the penalty was recovered. In addition, any supplements paid prior to the discovery of the excess earnings were to be recaptured in an undoubled amount. The court held that ERISA's anti-forfeiture provisions did not govern early retirement benefits and allowed the suspension and recapture of the early retirement supplements. The court did allow consideration of the defense of estoppel and a claim that the penalty of twice the excess earnings was unenforceable as liquidated damages.

[3] Discrimination

Discrimination occurs if there is a disparity in the benefits accorded to participants in the same pension plan. ERISA expressly prohibits only those forms of discrimination which tend to favor officers, shareholders or other highly compensated employees.[157] Other forms of discrimination have not been proscribed.

The most frequent form of discrimination is the integration of pension benefits with Social Security payments.

The courts have specifically sanctioned other forms of discrimination, such as offsetting workers compensation benefits,[158] decreasing benefit levels for future retirees[159] and differentiating

[157] 29 U.S.C. § 411(d)(1).

[158] Alessi v. Raybestos-Manhattan, Inc. and Buczynski v. General Motors Corp, 451 U.S. 504, 68 L.E.2d 402, 101 S.Ct. 1895 (1981).

[159] Adams v. Western Conference of Teamsters Pension Plan, 484 F. Supp 933 (N.D. Utah 1979).

between full-time and part-time workers.[160]

---

[160] Mosley v. National Maritime Union Pension and Welfare Plan, 451 F. Supp. 226 (E.D.N.Y. 1978).

Table of Cases

References are to sections and footnotes

References are to sections and footnotes

References are to sections and footnotes

B

References are to sections and footnotes

References are to sections and footnotes

References are to sections and footnotes

References are to sections and footnotes

References are to sections and footnotes

D

References are to sections and footnotes

References are to sections and footnotes

References are to sections and footnotes

References are to sections and footnotes

References are to sections and footnotes

H

References are to sections and footnotes

References are to sections and footnotes

I

References are to sections and footnotes

References are to sections and footnotes

References are to sections and footnotes

L

References are to sections and footnotes

M

References are to sections and footnotes

References are to sections and footnotes

N

References are to sections and footnotes

References are to sections and footnotes

References are to sections and footnotes

References are to sections and footnotes

O

References are to sections and footnotes

P

References are to sections and footnotes

Q

R

References are to sections and footnotes

References are to sections and footnotes

References are to sections and footnotes

References are to sections and footnotes

References are to sections and footnotes

T

References are to sections and footnotes

U

References are to sections and footnotes

References are to sections and footnotes

References are to sections and footnotes

References are to sections and footnotes

Y

References are to sections and footnotes

Index

References are to sections and subsections

References are to sections and subsections

References are to sections and subsections

References are to sections and subsections

B

References are to sections and subsections

References are to sections and subsections

References are to sections and subsections

References are to sections and subsections

References are to sections and subsections

References are to sections and subsections

References are to sections and subsections

References are to sections and subsections

References are to sections and subsections

References are to sections and subsections

References are to sections and subsections

References are to sections and subsections

References are to sections and subsections

References are to sections and subsections

References are to sections and subsections

References are to sections and subsections

References are to sections and subsections

References are to sections and subsections

References are to sections and subsections

References are to sections and subsections

References are to sections and subsections

References are to sections and subsections

References are to sections and subsections

References are to sections and subsections

References are to sections and subsections

References are to sections and subsections

O

References are to sections and subsections

References are to sections and subsections

References are to sections and subsections

References are to sections and subsections

References are to sections and subsections

References are to sections and subsections

References are to sections and subsections

References are to sections and subsections

References are to sections and subsections

References are to sections and subsections

References are to sections and subsections

References are to sections and subsections

References are to sections and subsections

References are to sections and subsections

References are to sections and subsections

References are to sections and subsections

References are to sections and subsections

References are to sections and subsections

References are to sections and subsections

References are to sections and subsections

References are to sections and subsections

References are to sections and subsections

References are to sections and subsections